Mastering Windows 2022

Fourth Edition

Comprehensive administration of your Windows Server environment

Jordan Krause

BIRMINGHAM—MUMBAI

Mastering Windows Server 2022
Fourth Edition

Senior Publishing Product Manager: Aaron Tanna
Acquisition Editor – Peer Reviews: Gaurav Gavas
Project Editor: Rianna Rodrigues
Content Development Editor: Liam Draper
Copy Editor: Safis Editing
Technical Editor: Srishty Bhardwaj
Proofreader: Safis Editing
Indexer: Subalakshmi Govindhan
Presentation Designer: Ganesh Bhadwalkar
Developer Relations Marketing Executive: Meghal Patel

First published: October 2017
Second edition: June 2020
Third edition: September 2022
Fourth edition: May 2023

Production reference: 1250523
Published by Packt Publishing Ltd.
Livery Place
35 Livery Street
Birmingham
B3 2PB, UK.

ISBN 978-1-83763-450-7

www.packt.com

Contributors

About the author

Jordan Krause is an IT professional of more than 20 years and has received 10 Microsoft MVP awards for his work with Microsoft server and networking technologies. As one of the world's first experts on Microsoft DirectAccess, his authorship journey began with a book on remote access technology and has evolved into numerous writings on more extensive topics such as Windows Server, security, and Group Policy. Jordan lives in beautiful West Michigan (USA) and manages a team of IT engineers spread across the country

About the reviewer

Premnath Sambasivam is a server engineer with 10 years of experience in Windows, Azure, VMware, and SCCM administration. He is an MCSE Cloud Platform and Infrastructure professional and a Microsoft-certified Azure architect. He has developed and deployed Microsoft System Center Configuration Manager solutions to manage over 6,000 assets in his clients' environments and various VMware solutions. Premnath is a technology enthusiast who loves learning and exploring new technologies. He is currently a senior cloud engineer for one of the major retail brands in the USA. He has also reviewed Packt Publishing's books like **Mastering Windows Server 2019** and **Mastering Windows Security and Hardening**.

Join our community on Discord

Join our community's Discord space for discussions with the author and other readers:

`https://packt.link/SecNet`

Table of Contents

Chapter 12: Redundancy in Windows Server 2022   461

Chapter 16: Troubleshooting   609

Preface

The world of servers has always been an interesting place. For more than 20 years, Microsoft has been separated from the pack and has distinguished itself as the leader of serving power in corporate datacenters across the globe. Indeed, there is not much for competition in the server operating system space. During my career I have had the privilege of working within the walls of many hundreds of different networks and environments, and without a single exception they have all been in some way powered by Windows Server. You may think I have blinders on; a lifer in Microsoft technology would naturally seek out work within Microsoft environments, right? But rest assured, I'm no stranger to the sudo command. I fully recognize the uses and benefits that Linux servers offer in certain circumstances, especially in web hosting. Containers bring to light another engaging topic in the Microsoft vs Linux conversation, but as you will find within the pages of this book, we are now seeing ways that these two technologies interact and coexist like they never have before, rather than try to outdo one another.

As many businesses and IT administrators shift attention to cloud resources, the Microsoft trend continues. There are many options for hosting compute resources in the cloud, and serving up data from those resources. Over the last few years, Microsoft has been taking significant steps to outpace competition and build unique ways to tie on-premise datacenters together with Azure. Technology like Azure Stack HCI, the ability to essentially host your own instance of Azure inside datacenter walls, is one of these entities that provides an incredibly unique spin on cloud technology.

Why would I dare to talk about cloud technology in a book that is clearly pointed at administering Windows Servers? Because knowledge of local Windows Server administration is still completely relevant in a cloudy world. When companies started moving resources into the cloud, I heard a lot of speakers and presentations state things like "Moving to the cloud won't negate the need for IT staff, your people will just need different skillsets." These speakers were clearly implying that IT would still be necessary, but they would now be administering cloud-based resources rather than on-premise infrastructure. Cloud transitions are happening every day, but what has proven surprising to some is that this transition is much less about replacing one set of skills with another, but rather maintaining all existing skillsets and tacking on new learning to handle the existence of cloud platforms.

Whether you are running Azure, AWS, or any of the other cloud hosting platforms, it is very likely that within your cloud tenant you have virtual machines that are still running some version of the Windows Server operating system. Windows Server is not magically different simply because it is now running on a VM inside Azure instead of running on a VM inside Hyper-V. It is still Windows Server, and it still needs to be administered, maintained, and troubleshot in the same ways that you have always done with your servers.

Maintaining a skillset to administer Windows Server and its roles is still essential to our IT departments, which loops us back to answering my question about Azure. Even in an infrastructure fully transitioned into the cloud, it is still very likely that you need to maintain the ability to administer Windows Server, which I believe surprised a lot of IT resource coordinators, following cloud migration projects.

A lot of fresh IT engineers are coming into the workforce prepared with some knowledge of SaaS resource administration, like Microsoft 365 and SharePoint, and this is wonderful! One of my primary motivations in writing this book is to provide a resource for new and growing admins to be successful in their careers. You may have learned through school or certification exams how to begin working in these new cloud platforms, but perhaps lack the foundational knowledge of the Microsoft technology that underpins a lot of Azure, Windows Servers. So many of the roles that exist inside Windows Server are foreign to engineers, but this is critical information to know as you continue your IT career journey and grow into more advanced positions. To pinpoint just one example, I often ask questions during interviews about DNS. It is entirely surprising to me how often answers to these questions come up short. DNS has been one of the staple roles in any Windows Server environment for as far back as I can remember, but until you have worked with it and gone through some of the learning hardships firsthand, it seems this is a common area that is somehow missed during standard IT learning.

I use DNS as an example because it's true, but also because it is very meme-worthy. "It's always DNS". You may have heard some of your tenured administrators say these words, but until you experience it for yourself, may not quite appreciate their significance. The answer to so many questions lie within this one little role, incorrect configuration of DNS can cause multitudes of problems. I found the following graphic on the internet and take no credit for it, but also find it completely true, and hilarious.

Technical books are supposed to be a little mundane, that is why they are called technical books. It's the nature of the industry, I suppose. I tried to resist this stereotype wherever possible, you may even find a dad joke or two scattered throughout these pages. I genuinely hope that you find this book to be a helpful resource, and that information learned here can be directly applied to your work in Information Technology.

Who this book is for

Anyone interested in Windows Server 2022 or in learning more in general about a Microsoft-centric datacenter will benefit from this book. An important deciding factor when choosing which content was appropriate for such a volume was making sure that anyone who had a baseline in working with computers could pick this up and start making use of it within their own networks. If you are already proficient in Microsoft infrastructure technologies and have worked with prior versions of Windows Server, then there are some focused topics on the aspects and parts that are brand new and only available in Server 2022. On the other hand, if you are currently in a desktop support role, or if you are coming fresh into the IT workforce, care was taken in the pages of this book to ensure that you will receive a rounded understanding, not only of what is brand new in Server 2022, but also what core capabilities it includes as carryovers from previous versions of the operating system, and that are still crucial to be aware of when working in a Microsoft-driven datacenter.

What this book covers

Chapter 1, Getting Started with Windows Server 2022, gives us an introduction to the latest Server operating system and an overview of the new technologies and capabilities that it can provide. We will also spend a little bit of time exploring the updated interface for those who may not be comfortable with it yet.

Chapter 2, Installing and Managing Windows Server 2022, dives right into the very first thing we will have to do when working with Server 2022: install it! While this seems like a simple task, there are a number of versioning and licensing variables that need to be understood before you proceed with your own installation. From there, we will start to expand upon Microsoft's centralized management mentality, exploring how we can now manage and interact with our servers without ever having to log into them.

Chapter 3, Active Directory, leads us into the most core and essential role that exists in a Windows Server environment. AD is the central repository for many different types of data inside most corporate infrastructures, and without understanding the tools that exist to interface with this directory you will not be able to do much work with those fancy new servers.

Chapter 4, DNS and DHCP, segues into two other important roles that exist in almost every network. DNS and DHCP are both necessary technologies and concepts to understand for any IT administrator, and both happen to be roles that can be serviced from Windows Server 2022. We'll dig into both.

Chapter 5, Group Policy, showcases a fantastic policy engine that can be used inside any Active Directory environment to create a centralized management location for your users and workstations. Whether you are interested in setting up password policies, configuring lockdowns on your systems, automatically mapping network drives, or even distributing software, Group Policy is a powerful tool that is often underutilized.

Chapter 6, Certificates, jumps into one of the pieces of Windows Server that has existed for many years, and yet most server administrators that I meet are unfamiliar with it. We'll take a closer look at certificates as they become more and more commonly required for new technologies that we roll out. By the end of this chapter, you should be able to spin up your own PKI and start issuing certificates for free!

Chapter 7, Networking with Windows Server 2022, begins with an introduction to that big, scary IPv6, and continues from there into building a toolbox of items that are baked into Windows Server 2022 and can be used in your daily networking tasks. We will also discuss the parts and pieces that make up Software-Defined Networking.

Chapter 8, Remote Access, takes a look at the different remote access technologies that are built into Windows Server 2022. Follow along as we explore the capabilities provided by VPN, DirectAccess, Web Application Proxy, and Always On VPN.

Chapter 9, Hardening and Security, gives some insight into security and encryption functions that are built into Windows Server 2022. Security is the primary focus of CIOs everywhere, so we'll explore what protection mechanisms are available to us out of the box.

Chapter 10, Server Core, throws us into the shrinking world of headless servers. Server Core has flown under the radar for many years but is critical to understand as we bring our infrastructures into a more security-conscious mindset. We'll make sure you have the information necessary to make your environment more secure and more efficient, all while lowering the amount of space and resources that are consumed by those servers.

Chapter 11, PowerShell, gets us into the newer, bluer (or black or yellow or purple, or whatever color you desire!) command-line interface so that we can become comfortable using it and also learn why it is so much more powerful than Command Prompt. PowerShell is quickly becoming an indispensable tool for administering servers, especially in cases where you are adopting a centralized management and administration mindset. We will also take a look at the latest Microsoft command-line interface, Windows Terminal.

Chapter 12, Redundancy in Windows Server 2022, looks at some platforms in Server 2022 that provide powerful data and computing redundancy. Follow along as we discuss Network Load Balancing, Failover Clustering, Storage Spaces Direct, and build our own instance of Storage Replica.

Chapter 13, Containers, incorporates the terms open source and Linux into a Microsoft book! Application containers are quickly becoming the new standard for hosting modern, scalable applications. Learn how to start enhancing your DevOps story using tools such as Windows Server containers, Hyper-V containers, Docker, and Kubernetes.

Chapter 14, Hyper-V, covers a topic that every server administrator should be very familiar with. Organizations have been moving their servers over to virtual machines en masse for many years. We'll use this chapter to make sure you understand how that hypervisor works and give you the resources required to build and manage one if and when you have the need.

Chapter 15, Remote Desktop Services, showcases an enormous functionality set built into Windows Server 2022, indeed the administration of RDS servers is a skillset unto its own. Providing users with virtual desktop sessions on a farm (collection) of Windows Servers can literally change your entire ideology about how users access their information.

Chapter 16, *Troubleshooting*, provides information about tools and software included with Windows Server that can be used to troubleshoot common problems. Server 2022 seems to be Microsoft's most stable and reliable server operating system to date, yet as you all know nothing is perfect, and issues are bound to present themselves. Here we discover tools like Resource Manager, Performance Monitor, and System Insights that help to keep our servers tuned and running well.

To get the most out of this book

Each technology that we discuss within the pages of this book is included in, or relates directly to, Windows Server 2022. If you can get your hands on a piece of server hardware and the Server 2022 installer files, you will be equipped to follow along and try these things out for yourself. We will talk about and reference some enterprise-class technologies that come with stiffer infrastructure requirements to make them work fully, and so you may have to put the actual testing of those items on hold until you are working in a more comprehensive test lab or environment, but the concepts are all still included in this book.

We will also discuss some items that are not included in Server 2022 itself, but that are used to extend its capabilities and features. Some of these items help tie us into an Azure cloud environment, and some are provided by third parties, such as using Docker and Kubernetes on your Server 2022 to interact with application containers. Ultimately, you do not need to use these tools to manage your new Windows Server 2022 environment, but they do facilitate some pretty cool things that I think you will want to explore.

As I have done with my own test lab used throughout the pages of this book, if you have one server or high-powered computer available and download the Windows Server 2022 installer to use on top of it, you can easily enable yourself the ability to create many virtual machines and different instances of Server 2022. In this case, you may want to skip ahead to certain sections of Chapter 2 and Chapter 14, so that you are equipped to install a host operating system and configure Hyper-V upon it, then loop back to the beginning of the book so you have the same platform available as I did when building out these pages and the servers I used to populate them.

Download the color images

We also provide a PDF file that has color images of the screenshots/diagrams used in this book. You can download it here: `https://packt.link/4zrrF`.

Conventions used

There are a number of text conventions used throughout this book.

`CodeInText`: Indicates code words in text, database table names, folder names, filenames, file extensions, pathnames, dummy URLs, user input, and Twitter handles. For example: "Inside DNS, I am going to create an alias record that redirects `intranet` to `web1`."

Any command-line input or output is written as follows:

```
Uninstall-WindowsFeature -Name Windows-Defender
```

Bold: Indicates a new term, an important word, or words that you see on the screen. For instance, words in menus or dialog boxes appear in the text like this. For example: "Select **System info** from the **Administration** panel."

 Warnings or important notes appear like this.

 Tips and tricks appear like this.

Get in touch

Feedback from our readers is always welcome.

General feedback: Email feedback@packtpub.com and mention the book's title in the subject of your message. If you have questions about any aspect of this book, please email us at questions@packtpub.com.

Errata: Although we have taken every care to ensure the accuracy of our content, mistakes do happen. If you have found a mistake in this book, we would be grateful if you reported this to us. Please visit http://www.packtpub.com/submit-errata, click **Submit Errata**, and fill in the form.

Piracy: If you come across any illegal copies of our works in any form on the internet, we would be grateful if you would provide us with the location address or website name. Please contact us at copyright@packtpub.com with a link to the material.

If you are interested in becoming an author: If there is a topic that you have expertise in and you are interested in either writing or contributing to a book, please visit http://authors.packtpub.com.

Share your thoughts

Once you've read *Mastering Windows Server 2022, Fourth Edition*, we'd love to hear your thoughts! Scan the QR code below to go straight to the Amazon review page for this book and share your feedback.

https://packt.link/r/1837634505

Your review is important to us and the tech community and will help us make sure we're delivering excellent quality content.

Download a free PDF copy of this book

Thanks for purchasing this book!

Do you like to read on the go but are unable to carry your print books everywhere?

Is your eBook purchase not compatible with the device of your choice?

Don't worry, now with every Packt book you get a DRM-free PDF version of that book at no cost.

Read anywhere, any place, on any device. Search, copy, and paste code from your favorite technical books directly into your application.

The perks don't stop there, you can get exclusive access to discounts, newsletters, and great free content in your inbox daily

Follow these simple steps to get the benefits:

1. Scan the QR code or visit the link below

https://packt.link/free-ebook/9781837634507

2. Submit your proof of purchase
3. That's it! We'll send your free PDF and other benefits to your email directly

1

Getting Started with Windows Server 2022

Many years ago, Microsoft adjusted its operating system release ideology so that the latest Windows Server operating system maintained a similar graphical structure, and very similar release date, to whatever the latest and greatest Windows client operating system was going to have. This has been the trend for some time now, with Server 2008 R2 closely reflecting Windows 7, Server 2012 feeling a lot like Windows 8, and many of the same usability features that came with the Windows 8.1 update also included with Server 2012 R2. This, of course, carried over to Server 2016 as well—giving it the same look and feel as if you were logged into a Windows 10 workstation.

As of the Server 2016 release, we were all familiar and comfortable with the Windows 10 interface, and it felt quite natural to jump right into Server 2016 and start giving it a test drive. Windows Server 2019 diverted from this standard path a little bit, by having a look and feel that was very similar to its predecessor, Server 2016. Why did Server 2019 not come with a fancy new graphical interface to match the new version of a Windows client Operating System (OS)? Because Microsoft changed the game with Windows 10. Now, instead of releasing new versions of Windows (11, 12, 13, and so on), we were, for the time being, simply sticking with Windows 10 and giving it sub-version numbers, indicative of the dates when each operating system version was released. For example, Windows 10 version 1703 was released around March 2017. Windows 10 version 1709 was released in September 2017.

Then came 1803 and 1809—although 1809 was delayed a little and didn't release until somewhere closer to November, which wasn't the original plan. Follow that up with 1903 and 1909, and you start to see a pattern emerge. Then we moved into the year 2020, and suddenly our spring release of Windows 10 was called 2004. Hmm... 2004 sounds fine when you pronounce it twenty-oh-four, indicating the year 2020 and the month of April, but when seeing 2004 on paper, most folks started calling it two-thousand-four, which sounds quite old and outdated, don't you think? I can't say for sure, but perhaps this is part of the reason that the next release version of Windows 10 went by the name 20H2. This nomenclature seems to have stuck around, and we are continuing the trend with bi-annual client OS releases that reflect this pattern. All in all, you can see that Microsoft's current plan is to continue releasing a new feature release version of the Windows operating system every 6 months or so.

However, expecting IT departments to lift and shift all of their servers just for the purposes of moving to an OS that is 6 months newer is crazy; sometimes it takes longer than that just to plan a migration.

Anyway, I'm getting ahead of myself a little, as we will discuss the versioning of Windows Server later in this chapter, in our *Windows Server versions and licensing* section. The point here is that Windows Server 2019 looks and feels like the latest version of the Windows client operating system that was released at about the same time—that OS being Windows 10 1809.

So what about Windows Server 2022? Since the release of Server 2019, Microsoft has unveiled Windows 11! It certainly comes with a new and updated look and feel, being different in many ways from Windows 10. Since Windows 11 was released right around the same time as Windows Server 2022, wouldn't it make sense for Server 2022 will be super futuristic and look just like Windows 11? While that might make a lot of sense, it is not at all what happened.

Figure 1.1: The Server 2022 lock screen

Does that look familiar to anybody? You're right, it looks exactly the same as Server 2019, or Windows 10. This is because Server 2022 is based on Windows 10 code, NOT Windows 11. For the time being, I am going to consider that a smart move. Windows 11 seems to be playing well in the consumer market, but in my experience so far it is working through some struggles within a business environment. The safe play for this new release of the Server operating system was to base it on reliable, tried, and true coding that we know works well with the roles and applications that companies are going to need to install on it. That being said, Server 2022 does certainly come with some enhancements and benefits.

Before we get started talking about the features of Windows Server, it is important to establish a baseline for usability and familiarity with the operating system itself before diving deeper into the technologies running under the hood.

Let's spend a few minutes exploring the new graphical interface and options that are available for finding your way around this latest release of Windows Server, with a view to covering the following topics in this chapter:

- The purpose of Windows Server
- It's getting cloudy out there
- Windows Server versions and licensing
- Overview of new and updated features
- Features deprecated in Server 2022
- Navigating the interface
- Using the newer *Settings* screen
- Task Manager
- Task View

The purpose of Windows Server

What is a server? Is that a silly question? I don't think so. It's a good question to ponder, especially now that the definition of servers and server workloads is changing on a regular basis. The answer to this question for Windows clients is simpler. A Windows client machine is a requester, consumer, and contributor of data.

From where is this data being pushed and pulled? What enables the mechanisms and applications running on the client operating systems to interface with this data? What secures these users and their data? The answers to these questions reveal the purpose of servers in general. Servers house, protect, and serve up data to be consumed by clients.

Everything revolves around data in business today. Our email, documents, databases, customer lists—everything that we need to do business—is data. That data is critical to us. Servers are what we use to build the fabric upon which we trust our data to reside.

We traditionally think about servers using a client-server interface mentality. A user opens a program on their client computer, this program reaches out to a server in order to retrieve something, and the server responds as needed. This idea can be correctly applied to just about every transaction you may have with a server. When your domain-joined computer needs to authenticate you as a user, it reaches out to Active Directory on the server to validate your credentials and get an authentication token. When you need to contact a resource by name, your computer asks a DNS server how to get there. If you need to open a file, you ask the file server to send it your way.

Servers are designed to be the brains of our operation, and often by doing so transparently. In recent years, large strides have been taken to ensure resources are always available and accessible in ways that don't require training or a large effort on the part of our employees. It used to be true that the general user population knew the name of your server and how to contact it because that was generally required for them to be able to get the information they needed.

If their mapped drives disappeared, it wasn't uncommon that everyone would know how to throw \\ server\share into File Explorer to get there via plan B.

It also used to be the case that your average business only ran one single server, enabling this to be true. Today our server landscape is vastly different, with even small businesses running a virtualization host that typically contains a dozen or more virtual servers, and much effort is made so that your workforce doesn't know or care anything about that server infrastructure; they simply expect it to work 100% of the time.

In most organizations, many different servers are needed to provide your workforce with the capabilities they require. Each service inside Windows Server is provided as, or as part of, a **role**. When you talk about needing new servers or configuring a new server for any particular task, what you are really referring to is the individual role or roles that are going to be configured on that server to get the work done. A server without any roles installed is useless, though depending on the chassis can make an excellent paperweight. A 3U SAN device could weigh upward of 100 pounds and keep your desk orderly even in the middle of a hurricane!

If you think of roles as the meat and potatoes of a server, then the next bit we will discuss is sort of like adding salt and pepper. Beyond the overhead roles you will install and configure on your servers, Windows also contains many **features** that can be installed, which sometimes stand alone but, more often, complement specific roles in the operating system. Features may complement and add functionality to the base operating system, such as is the case with **Telnet Client**. Or a feature may be added to a server in order to enhance an existing role, such as adding the **Network Load Balancing** feature to an already equipped remote access or IIS server. The combination of roles and features inside Windows Server is what equips that piece of metal to do work.

This book will, quite obviously, focus on a Microsoft-centric infrastructure. In these environments, the Windows Server operating system is king and is prevalent across all facets of technology. There are alternatives to Windows Server and different products that can provide some of the same functions to an organization, but it is quite rare to find a business environment anywhere that is running without some semblance of a Microsoft infrastructure.

Windows Server contains an incredible amount of technology, all wrapped up in one small installation disk. With Windows Server 2022, Microsoft has got us thinking out of the box about what it means to be a server in the first place, and it comes with some exciting new capabilities, which we will spend some time covering in these pages. Things such as PowerShell, **Windows Admin Center** (**WAC**), software-defined storage, and software-defined networking are changing the way that we manage and size our computing environments; these are exciting times to be or to become a server administrator!

It's getting cloudy out there

There's a new term out there; you may have even heard of it... *the cloud*. I say this tongue in cheek of course, and if smiley faces were appropriate within published works, I would insert one here. While the word "cloud" has certainly turned into a buzzword that is often misused and spoken of inappropriately, the idea of cloud infrastructure is an incredibly powerful one.

A cloud fabric is one that revolves around virtual resources—**virtual machines** (**VMs**), virtual disks, and even virtual networks. Being plugged into the cloud typically enables things like the ability to spin up new servers on a whim, or even the ability for particular services themselves to increase or decrease their needed resources automatically, based on utilization.

Think of a simple e-commerce website where a consumer can go to order goods. Perhaps 75% of the year, the company can operate this website on a single web server with limited resources, resulting in a fairly low cost of service. But, the other 25% of the year, maybe around the holiday seasons, utilization ramps way up, requiring much more computing power. Prior to the cloud mentality, this would mean that the company would need to size its environment to fit the maximum requirements all the time, in case it was ever needed. They would be paying for more servers and much more computing power than was needed for the majority of the year. With a cloud fabric, which gives the website the ability to increase or decrease the number of servers it has at its disposal as needed, the total cost of such a website or service can be drastically decreased. This is a major driving factor of the cloud in business today.

Public cloud

Most of the time, when your neighbor Suzzi Knowitall talks to you about the cloud, she is simply talking about the internet. Well, more accurately, she is talking about some service that she uses, which she connects to by using the internet. For example, Office 365, Google Drive, OneDrive, and Dropbox—these are all public cloud resources, as they store your data *in the cloud*. In reality, your data is just sitting on servers that you access via the internet, but you can't see those servers and you don't have to administer and maintain those servers, which is why it feels like magic and is then referred to as the cloud.

To IT departments, the term *cloud* more often means one of the big three cloud hosting providers. Since this is a Microsoft-driven book, and since I truly feel this way anyway, Microsoft Azure is top-notch in this category. Azure itself is another topic for another book (or many other books) but is a centralized cloud computing architecture that can host your data, your services, or even your entire network of servers.

Moving your datacenter to Azure enables you to stop worrying or caring about server hardware, replacing hard drives, and much more. Rather than purchasing servers, unboxing them, racking them, installing Windows on them, and then setting up the roles you want configured, you simply click a few buttons to spin up new virtual servers that can be resized at any time for growth. You then pay ongoing op-ex costs for these servers—monthly or annual fees for running systems in the cloud—rather than the big cap-ex costs for server hardware in the first place.

Other cloud providers with similar capabilities are numerous, but the big three are Azure, Amazon (AWS), and Google. As far as enterprise is concerned, Azure simply takes the cake and eats it too. I'm not sure that the others will ever be able to catch up with all of the changes and updates that Microsoft constantly makes to the Azure infrastructure.

Private cloud

While most people working in the IT sector these days have a pretty good understanding of what it means to be part of a cloud service, and many are indeed doing so today, a term that is being pushed into enterprises everywhere and is still many times misunderstood is **private cloud**. At first, I took this to be a silly marketing ploy, a gross misuse of the term "cloud" to try and appeal to those hooked by buzzwords. Boy, was I wrong. In the early days of private clouds, the technology wasn't quite ready to stand up to what was being advertised.

Today, however, that story has changed. It is now entirely possible to take the same fabric that is running up in the true, public cloud and install it right inside your datacenter. This enables you to provide your company with cloud benefits such as the ability to spin resources up and down, run everything virtualized, and implement all of the neat tips and tricks of cloud environments, with all of the serving power and data storage remaining locally owned and secured by you. Trusting cloud storage companies to keep data safe and secure is absolutely one of the biggest blockers to implementation on the true public cloud, but by installing your own private cloud, you get the best of both worlds, specifically stretchable compute environments with the security of knowing you still control and own all of your data.

This is not a book about clouds, public or private. I mention this to give a baseline for some of the items we will discuss in later chapters, and also to get your mouth watering a little bit to dig in and do a little reading yourself on cloud technology. You will find that Windows Server 2022 interacts in many ways with the cloud and will notice that so many of the underlying systems available in Server 2022 are similar to, if not the same as, those becoming available in Microsoft Azure.

In these pages, we will not focus on the capabilities of Azure, but rather a more traditional sense of Windows Server as would be utilized on-premises. With the big push toward cloud technologies, it's easy to get caught with blinders on and think that everything and everyone is quickly running to the cloud for all of their technology needs, but it simply isn't true. Most companies will have the need for many on-premise servers for many years to come; in fact, many may never put full trust in the cloud and will forever maintain their own datacenters. These datacenters will have local servers, which will require server administrators to manage them. That's where you come in.

Windows Server versions and licensing

Anyone who has worked with the design or installation of Windows Server in recent years is probably wondering which direction we are taking in this book. You see, there are different capability editions, different technical versions, plus different licensing models of Windows Server. Let's take a few minutes to cover those differences so that you can have a well-rounded knowledge of the different options, and so that we can define which portions we plan to discuss over the course of this book.

Standard versus Datacenter

When installing the Windows Server 2022 operating system onto a piece of hardware, as you will experience in *Chapter 2, Installing and Managing Windows Server 2022*, you will have two different choices of server capability.

The first is Server 2022 Standard, which is the default option and one that includes most of your traditional Windows Server roles. While I cannot give you firm details on pricing because that could potentially be different for every company, depending on your agreements with Microsoft, Standard is the cheaper option and is most commonly used for installations of Windows Server 2022.

Datacenter, on the other hand, is the luxury model. There are some roles and features within Windows Server 2022 that only work with the Datacenter version of the operating system, and they are not available in Standard. If ever you are looking for a new piece of Microsoft technology to serve a purpose in your environment, make sure to check the requirements to find out whether you will have to build a Datacenter server. Keep in mind that Datacenter can cost significantly more money than Standard, so you generally only use it in places where it is actually required. For example, if you are interested in hosting a **Storage Spaces Direct** (**S2D**) environment, you will be required to run the Server 2022 Datacenter edition.

One of the biggest differences between Standard and Datacenter that even small businesses may need to consider is the number of **VMs** that they can legally host. Out-of-the-box Server 2022 Standard can only run two VMs on it at any given time, which is a pretty limiting factor if you are looking to build out a Hyper-V server. Datacenter allows you to run unlimited numbers of VMs, which makes it a no-brainer when building your virtualization host servers. For running Hyper-V, the Datacenter edition is often the way to go.

There is more information on this topic that makes the previous paragraph complicated. Both Server 2022 Standard and Server 2022 Datacenter have the technical ability to run many VMs. Whether or not you are allowed to do so comes down to licensing. We will discuss more on this topic when we discuss Windows Server licensing structures later in this chapter.

Running a container infrastructure will also impact your decision making on Windows Server licensing. While your host container server can run an unlimited number of traditional containers, whether that host server is Windows Server Standard or Datacenter, if you want to move into the enhanced world of Hyper-V-isolated containers, the same restrictions apply. A container host server running Windows Server Standard is limited to running two Hyper-V containers, but bumping up your host to Windows Server Datacenter will bring you back into the unlimited category. An easy way to remember this is that each Hyper-V container is essentially its own VM, and so the limit of two applies in the Standard OS, whether talking about regular VMs or Hyper-V container VMs. Again, remember that this is a licensing limitation, not a technical one.

Windows Server 2022 Essentials

Some of you may remember the "Small Business Server" editions of Windows Server, which were sort of an all-in-one variant of the Windows Server operating system, intended to be the one and only server inside a small business environment. While SBS fell by the wayside many years ago, Microsoft has offered an Essentials edition of each Windows Server release since that time, to fill the small business gap. If your organization has fewer than 25 users and fewer than 50 devices, and if you do not intend to grow beyond that point, purchasing and installing Windows Server 2022 Essentials can be a coupon clipper to getting your data infrastructure up and running in a cost-friendly way. Keep in mind that it comes with limitations and as soon as you want to grow your business to over 25 users, you'll have to bite the bullet and purchase Server Standard.

Windows Server 2022 Datacenter: Azure Edition

Hold up, what is this thing? Brand new for this go-around of Windows Server, 2022 brings a new special edition that obviously ties into Azure. But what does this mean for you? Whether or not you will ever touch the new Azure Edition depends on what kinds of things you are doing in the Azure world. If you host virtual machines in Azure, you now have the option of selecting your new VM to run this special Azure Edition, and it then enables some cool new features that are unique to this edition—things like Hot Patch and SMB via QUIC, both of which we will discuss shortly. These features are not available to a traditional Server Standard or Datacenter, only on Azure Edition.

The big catch with Azure Edition is just that – it can only run in an Azure environment. So if you have Azure cloud-hosted VMs, you can now get those VMs to run Azure Edition. Without making this too complicated, since we are talking mostly about on-premise resources in this book, there is another special scenario where you might be able to run Windows Server 2022 Azure Edition from within the physical walls of your building. That is for those of you running something called Azure Stack HCI. The scope of this book does not include Azure Stack HCI, but the easiest way to think about it is along the lines of running a private cloud, which we already discussed. It is possible to build your own implementation of Azure, right inside your own datacenter, using Azure Stack HCI. If you are running a private cloud such as this, you will then be able to run VMs within that environment that use Windows Server 2022 Datacenter: Azure Edition.

Three different user interfaces

Now let's discuss the different footprints and user interfaces that you can run on your Windows Server 2022 machines. There are three variants of Windows Server that can be used, and the correct one for you depends on what capabilities and security you are looking for.

Desktop Experience

This is the most common choice among Windows Servers everywhere. Whether you are building Windows Server 2022 Standard or Datacenter, you have a choice of running Windows Server with or without a graphical user interface. The point-and-click interface with a traditional look and feel is called **Desktop Experience**. This allows things such as RDPing into your servers, having a traditional desktop, and being able to use the graphical Server Manager right from your logged-in server, and all in all, it is the best way to go if you are new to server administration.

If you are familiar with navigating around inside Windows 10, then you should be able to at least make your way around Windows Server 2022 running Desktop Experience. This is the version of Windows Server 2022 that we will focus on for the majority of this book, and almost all of the screenshots will be taken from within a Desktop Experience environment.

Server Core

As you will see when we install Windows Server 2022 together, the default option for installation is *not* Desktop Experience. What this means is that choosing the default install path would instead place a headless version of Windows Server onto your machine, most commonly referred to as Server Core.

The nature of being headless makes Server Core faster and more efficient than the Desktop version, which makes sense because it doesn't have to run all of that extra code and consume all of those extra resources for launching and displaying a huge graphical interface.

Almost anything that you want to do within Windows Server is possible to do on either Server Core or Desktop Experience, the main differences being the interface and security. To be able to use Server Core, you definitely have to be comfortable with a command-line interface (namely PowerShell), and you also have to consider remote server management to be a reliable way of interacting with your servers. We will talk much more about Server Core in *Chapter 10*, *Server Core*.

The largest benefit that Server Core brings to the table, other than performance, is security. Most malware that attempts to attack Windows Servers is reliant upon items that exist inside the GUI of Desktop Experience. Since those things aren't even running inside Server Core—alas, you couldn't get to a *desktop* even if you wanted to—attacks against Server Core machines are much, much less successful.

Nano Server — now only for containers

A third platform for Windows Server 2022 does exist, known as **Nano Server**. This is a tiny version of Windows Server, headless like Server Core but running an even smaller footprint. The last time I booted up Nano Server, it consumed less than 500 MB of data for the complete operating system, which is incredible.

It seemed like Nano Server was discussed much more surrounding the release of Server 2016, because at that time, Microsoft was pressing forward with plans to include a whole bunch of roles inside Nano Server so that we could start replacing some of our bloated, oversized everyday servers with Nano. It used to be the case that you could use the Windows Server installation media (I suppose you could still make it happen with Server 2016 installation media) to spin out a VHDX file that allowed you to boot into Nano Server and check it out, but that mentality of *Nano Server as an actual server* has since gone by the wayside.

As of Windows Server version 1803 (we'll discuss what *Server 1803* means in the next section of this chapter), Nano Server is married to the use of containers. In fact, the only way to spin up a Nano Server is to download it as a **container base OS image**, and then boot that image on an existing container host server. We will discuss both in more detail in *Chapter 13*, *Containers*. If you know what containers and modern applications are, and are interested in using them, then you will benefit from learning all there is to know about Nano Server. If you are not in a position to work with containers, you will probably never run into Nano Server in your environment.

Licensing models — what happened to SAC?

Up until the release of Windows Server 2022, you had a decision to make on which licensing model and release cadence you wanted to follow. Microsoft releases some versions of Windows Server on a 2–3 year basis, and other versions on a biannual cadence. As of August 2022, there has been a significant change to these rules, which we will discuss next.

Long-Term Servicing Channel (LTSC)

Some of you probably think that LTSC is a typo, as in previous years this model was called **Long-Term Servicing Branch** (**LTSB**). While you can go with either and people will generally know what you are talking about, LTSC is now the proper term.

Windows Server 2022 is an LTSC release. Essentially, LTSC releases are what we have always thought of as our traditional Windows Server operating system releases. Server 2008, Server 2008 R2, Server 2012, Server 2012 R2, Server 2016, Server 2019, and now Server 2022 are all LTSC releases. It is Microsoft's expectation that LTSC versions of Windows Server will continue to be released every 2–3 years, and will include both headless as well as full graphical interface flavors of the operating system.

LTSC versions of Windows Server have always been the most common; indeed, many IT administrators have never even heard of **Semi-Annual Channel** (**SAC**) releases. Anytime that you are building a server with the intention of utilizing Desktop Experience for a fully graphical interface, your only option is LTSC anyway. It has always made the most sense for any servers running with the purpose of a domain controller, certificate server, file server, or similar to run within the context of LTSC.

With LTSC versions of Windows Server, you continue to get the same support we are used to seeing from Microsoft operating systems: five years of mainstream support followed by five years of available extended support.

Throughout this book, we will work and gain experience with Windows Server 2022 – the LTSC release.

Semi-Annual Channel (SAC) (now retiring)

While this is partially irrelevant now, it is still good to understand the history of SAC, and indeed you may well encounter SAC releases of Windows Server in your IT escapades. The first thing you will notice when stumbling upon an SAC release of Windows Server is the strange naming convention for operating system versions. Rather than calling it *Server 2019*, you were really running Windows Server 1803, 1809, 1903, 1909, and so on. It followed the same mentality and release cadence that Windows 10 did. What that implies is that these new versions of Windows Server SAC were released at much shorter intervals than LTSC. The SAC channel received two major releases every year—generally in the spring and the fall. Because of this fast release cadence, support for SAC versions of Windows Server lasted for a short 18 months. If you use SAC, you had better get used to always jumping on the latest version shortly after it releases.

If swapping out your server operating systems twice a year sounds daunting, you're not alone. Thankfully, Microsoft recognizes this and realizes that the general server administrator population is not going to use this model for their regular, everyday servers. Rather, SAC versions of Windows Server are only going to be used to run containers and containerized applications. In this new world of flexible application hosting, where applications are being written in ways that the infrastructure resources behind those applications can be spun up or spun down as needed, containers are a very important piece of that DevOps puzzle. If you host or build these kinds of applications, you will almost certainly be using containers—now or in the future. When you find yourself in the position of researching and figuring out containers, you may then stumble on information and documentation that leads you to those older SAC server releases.

It is important to note that SAC versions of Windows Server only come in the Server Core flavor – you'll find no graphical desktop interface here!

While Microsoft has officially retired SAC licensing and operating systems as of August 2022, customers heavy into containerization may still find some similar benefits by moving to Azure Stack HCI.

License purchase and packs

When defining differences between the Standard and Datacenter versions of Windows Server 2022, we referenced the fact that "out of the box" Server 2022 Standard allows for the running of two virtual machines (VMs), but that it wasn't a technical limitation and that more VMs were possible. This idea segues into a bit of a confusing topic – the way that Windows Server is licensed. When you purchase "a Windows Server 2022 Standard License," you are purchasing the rights to install Server 2022 Standard onto one physical piece of hardware, and to run two virtual machines on top of that host operating system. In effect, you can run three instances of Windows Server 2022 Standard. As soon as you make your move to spin up a third VM, you are required to repurchase the same amount of licensing all over again. Doing so actually gives you the ability to then run a total of four VMs. So if you only need three, well... too bad, you pay for four. Effectively, you repurchase your Windows Server 2022 Standard licensing for every two additional VMs that you need to run.

In addition to considering the number of VMs, the amount of licensing you purchase in the first place depends upon the size of your hardware. More specifically, it depends upon the processors you have installed.

Core Packs

Here is where things get a little dicey. You must license each physical server based on the amount of processor cores that exist inside it. Most physical servers contain one or two CPUs. The number of cores that those CPUs contain could be vastly different. What you are required to license is the number of cores.

Hyperthreading doesn't count. If you have one CPU with one core and it can do hyperthreading (logical cores), this counts as one core. If you have dual CPUs each with 8 cores, now we're talking about 16 cores total. This is the number to license.

At this point we can think of these as "core licenses." That makes sense, right? Except now for another twist—one "core license" actually covers two CPU cores. Holy moly. Thus, we don't refer to them as core licenses, but rather **Core Packs**. One Core Pack covers two CPU cores. At least we're still working with even numbers here, right? If my servers has two CPUs, each with four cores, that is a total of eight cores. If a core pack covers two cores, then I require four core packs to be compliant.

Except...(this is the moment when you realize why large companies employ full-time staff just to deal with licensing)... there are also some rules of minimum. You cannot cover a server with four core packs, because Microsoft says you can't. Here are the rules of a minimum license purchase:

- Any physical server requires a minimum of 8 core packs. In other words, any physical server that you license must be licensed for at least 16 cores.

- Even if your server has fewer than 16 cores, you must adhere to the prior rule and license for at least 16 cores.
- Every physical CPU requires at least four core packs. Again, other words show us that every physical CPU requires licensing for at least eight cores, whether or not that CPU has eight cores. But again, even if your server has only 1 CPU with 8 cores, you must still license the server for 16 cores based on the server-level minimum.

Wow, that is a lot of rules. Ultimately, many physical servers will fall into the category of requiring a minimum of 16 cores to be licensed. Easy math—you need 8 core packs, which cover a total of 16 cores. When you grow your hardware to contain more than 16 CPU cores, then you pull out the calculator.

One more layer of confusion, and then I promise I'm finished. So far we have only talked about individual core packs, each of which cover two CPUs. So 8 core packs equal 16 cores of coverage. A better way to say this is that "8 double-core licenses" equals 16 cores of coverage. There is another option to purchasing core packs, in the flavor of 16. When you purchase a "16-core license," it is a real thing, and as the name implies, it covers 16 cores.

At what point do I turn to Datacenter?

The Server 2022 Standard licensing strategy is scalable up to a certain point. Technically, you could forever increase the licensing that you purchase and the VMs that you run with that licensing, but wait a minute – didn't we say that Server 2022 Datacenter permits you to run unlimited VMs? Indeed we did. While Server 2022 Datacenter costs a lot more than Server 2022 Standard, if you are facing a requirement to run many virtual machines, it may be more cost-effective to simply purchase Datacenter and not have to deal with all of the intricacies of Standard licensing.

The breaking point is usually around 12 VMs. If you run 12 or fewer VMs on a single server, you could save some money by running the numbers on Standard licensing, but it depends on what physical CPUs you have. If you need to run more than 12 VMs, it is most likely true that purchasing a single (16 core) Datacenter license will be your cheaper option.

Client Access Licenses (CALs)

So far all we have talked about is Windows Server licensing, just for the server side. Microsoft also requires businesses to purchase and own **Client Access Licenses (CALs)**, to cover any user who needs to connect to resources on that server. This one is more straightforward to calculate—add up the numbers of users that you are going to point to resources on your server, and make sure you purchase that number or more of CALs. Oftentimes when you purchase Windows Server licensing, you will find options that combine server and CAL licensing, such as "Server 2022 16 core licenses + 25 CALs."

Overview of new and updated features

The newest version of the Windows Server operating system is always an evolution of its predecessor. There are certainly pieces of technology contained inside that are brand-new, but there are even more places where existing technologies have been updated to include new features and functionality. In the case of Windows Server 2022, there are even some functions and features that are specifically called out by Microsoft as being deprecated and leaving us for good. Let's spend a few minutes providing an overview of some of the changes that exist in Windows Server 2022.

Hardware security

Attacks on our servers seem to be the way of life these days, with information security teams on high alert 24 hours a day. These attacks are no longer limited to operating system code. Rather, many forms of malware now attempt to worm their way into hardware components. With Server 2022, Microsoft has introduced improvements to TPM interoperability, which can provide you with the assurance that your server has been started with legitimate code. UEFI secure boot and virtualization-based security are two additional layers of protection that have been improved, protecting servers from rootkits and crypto mining attacks. Even our firmware is now at risk, as attackers have realized that firmware often has high levels of execution permissions on a system and is typically invisible to protection software.

Some of these improvements come by way of something called a **Secured-core server**. This is a certified server purchased from a Microsoft OEM partner that integrates many hardware-level protections that are not available in an off-the-shelf server or one that you build yourself.

Network security

Security, security, security. We must now worry about protecting hardware, software, virtualization fabrics, and firmware. One thing that has always been on the protection radar is data. This includes both data at rest, like with drive encryption, as well as data on the move. Windows Server 2022 includes updates and upgrades to multiple network protocols to help propel the protections that Windows Server offers.

Protocol updates

TCP and UDP packets are the core entity of network traffic. These technologies have been around for a very long time, and any technology that hangs around for a long time becomes a target for attackers. Thankfully, Server 2022 introduces security enhancements to both TCP and UDP.

SMB is another common target of attack and, as such, has been improved numerous times. We still commonly talk about SMBv1 and SMBv2, though the latter is sometimes referred to as SMBv3, but until Server 2022, the highest level of encryption available for SMB traffic was AES-128. With this latest release of the operating system, SMB now works with AES-256, providing us with the most secure ciphers ever available when moving files over a network.

SMB technology used within Storage Spaces Direct (S2D) has also been improved. It is now possible to encrypt inner-cluster communications in your S2D environment, and SMB Direct encryption is now able to be turned on without severe performance degradation, as was the case in previous versions.

SMB over QUIC is yet another place where SMB has been improved, and significantly so. We will expand on this further in the next section of this chapter.

TLS continues to be improved, because attackers continue to find ways to break into current versions. Windows Server 2022 now comes with TLS 1.3 enabled by default, though is still backward-compatible with TLS 1.2 and beyond.

DNS-over-HTTPS

Okay, the more official name for this is actually **Secure DNS**, but I like **DNS-over-HTTPS** better, because the story is all in the name. DNS lookups within your environment have never been protected in this way before, but updates in Server 2022 enable DNS lookups to be encrypted using HTTPS. This can help to prevent eavesdropping and man-in-the-middle attacks.

Azure integrations

There are many different ways that Windows Server 2022 helps companies interact with and migrate to the Azure platform.

An Azure-specific version of the OS

We already discussed Windows Server 2022 Datacenter: Azure Edition, but just the fact that this exists shows how serious Microsoft is about bringing businesses into Azure.

Azure Stack HCI

By building your own private cloud using Azure Stack HCI, you can utilize Azure-specific capabilities and capacities within your physical building.

Hotpatching

Once you find yourself in a position to take advantage of Server 2022 Azure Edition, you will discover that you can now patch these servers on the fly, without requiring operating system restarts. If this functionality rolls into all versions of Windows Server in the future, this is a major game-changer for maintenance windows and NOCs around the world.

SMB over QUIC

I have to admit that I am extremely excited about this. Now that so much of the world is a remote workforce, previously simple tasks like mapping network drives to get documents into users' hands are suddenly challenging on a daily basis. SharePoint and Azure Files have taken some steps to fill this gap, but not in a way that end users really enjoy. SMB over QUIC could flip this entire situation on its head. This new way to carry SMB traffic utilizes TLS 1.3, thereby making it safe and secure to flow across the internet. Think about that—SMB over QUIC means that we are going to be able to map network drives natively, over the internet, without any form of a VPN or synchronization agent to get in the way!

Windows Admin Center

WAC is one of the coolest things I've seen yet, and came to us around the same time as the Server 2019 release. This is a free tool, available to anyone, that you can use to start centrally managing your server infrastructure. While not fully capable of replacing all of the traditional PowerShell, **Remote Desktop Protocol (RDP)**, and **Microsoft Management Console (MMC)** administration tools, it enables you to do a lot of normal, everyday tasks with your servers, all from a single interface.

WAC has been continually updated and improved since its release, and can now be used to manage servers, to build out clusters and HCI environments, and as a centralized administration tool, not only for your on-premise servers but also for those residing inside Azure as well. Prior to its official release and naming, WAC was formerly known as Project Honolulu, if you ever encounter a text that still includes that title.

We will take a closer look at Windows Admin Center in *Chapter 2, Installing and Managing Windows Server 2022*.

Storage

There are numerous improvements to the storage subsystem in Server 2022. Both Storage Spaces and Storage Spaces Direct come with some new arrows in their quivers, and snapshotting with the ReFS filesystem has been given a boost. This is important for virtual machine snapshots and backup jobs.

While the big news in the SMB world is about QUIC, which we already mentioned, SMB compression is also now possible within the protocol. This could mean that zipping files becomes a thing of the past, as the SMB protocol being used to transfer those files over the network can now self-compress on the fly. For anyone who has worked in IT or with computers for many years, it's difficult to even imagine a world without ZIP files, but perhaps that world is now upon us.

Containerization

Microsoft added even more capabilities to run Windows containers in Server 2022. As with every release, the size of container images shrunk and image startup time decreased. Microsoft has further integrated with Kubernetes, the most common orchestration program for handling containers. Containers are even now compatible with IPv6!

The Windows 10 experience continued

Historically, a new release of any Microsoft operating system has meant learning about a slightly new and changed user interface, or sometimes a drastically new and changed interface like that of Windows 8. Server 2019 and Server 2022 have been exceptions to this rule. Anyone who has never seen Server 2022 may expect it to look and feel just like Windows 11, since they were released right around the same time, but it isn't true. The code platform for Server 2022 is closer to Windows 10, and as such it looks, feels, and drives like Windows 10. Logging in and using Windows Server 2022 is, in a lot of ways, the same experience that you have had inside Windows Server 2019. Even so, some reading this book have never experienced logging in to a server of any kind before, and so we will certainly be looking over that interface and learning some tips and tricks to navigate around smoothly and efficiently within Server 2022.

Hyper-Converged Infrastructure

When you see the phrase **Hyper-Converged Infrastructure** (HCI), it is important to understand that we are not talking about a specific technology that exists within your server environment. Rather, HCI is a culmination of a number of different technologies that can work together and be managed together, all for the purpose of creating the mentality of a **Software-Defined Datacenter** (**SDDC** as it is sometimes referred to).

Specifically, HCI in the Microsoft world is most often referred to as the combination of Hyper-V and S2D on the same cluster of servers. Clustering these services together enables some big speed and reliability benefits over hosting these roles separately, and on their own systems.

Another component that is part of, or related to, a software-defined datacenter is **Software-Defined Networking (SDN)**. Similar to how compute virtualization platforms (like Hyper-V) completely changed the landscape of what server computing looked like 12 or more years ago, we are now finding ourselves capable of lifting the network layer away from physical hardware and shifting the design and administration of our networks to be virtual and managed by the Windows Server platform.

Where the idea of HCI really takes a leap as it relates directly to the Windows Server 2022 release is through integration with Azure Stack HCI. Now that we can run private clouds within our datacenter walls, Microsoft has provided us with true cloud capabilities through the use of Windows Server 2022 Datacenter: Azure Edition within that Azure Stack HCI environment.

Microsoft Edge

Even though my brain knew that Internet Explorer was on its way out of the door for workstations, when I first saw the news that even Windows Server was replacing Internet Explorer with Microsoft Edge, I had a hard time believing it actually happened. So I spun up a Server 2022 instance and verified for myself, and sure enough, the default browser has indeed changed. The so familiar, small blue letter "e" signifying Internet Explorer has gone, replaced with the now-familiar blue and green swirls of Microsoft Edge.

While this probably is not a surprise to you, what you may not be aware of is that Internet Explorer 11 is still installed and working in Server 2022. The icon is just hidden away. Clicking inside the search bar and typing `iexplore.exe` will launch the older, now officially unsupported, browser. I am not at all surprised by this, as Internet Explorer security options and functions are very well intermeshed with other parts of the operating system. Due to the way that Internet Explorer is ingrained with Windows, it could be that certain components of IE will continue to exist far into the future.

Windows Defender Advanced Threat Protection

If you haven't done any reading on **Advanced Threat Protection (ATP)**, you may see the words **Windows Defender** and assume I am simply talking about the antivirus/anti-malware capabilities that are now built into both Windows client operating systems, as well as Windows Server, starting with 2016. While it is true that Windows Server 2022 does come out of the box with built-in antivirus, the ATP service and Windows Defender as a whole are becoming much, much more.

We'll discuss it in more depth in *Chapter 9, Hardening and Security*, but the short summary is that Windows Defender ATP is a cloud-based service that you tap your machines into. The power of ATP is that many thousands, or perhaps even millions, of devices submit data, creating an enormous information store that can then be used with some AI and machine learning to generate comprehensive data about new threats, viruses, and intrusions in real time. ATP customers then receive the benefits of protection as those new threats arise. It's almost like crowd-sourced anti-threat capabilities, with Azure handling all of the backend processing.

Integration with Linux

Heresy! Under whose authority did I type the word *Linux* inside a book about Windows Server?! Historically, corporate computing environments have run Windows, or they have run Linux, or maybe they have run both but with a very clear separation between the two. Windows Server 2022 blurs that line of separation. We now have the ability to run Linux VMs within our Microsoft Hyper-V and to even interface with them properly. Did you know some Linux operating systems actually know how to interact with a mouse? Before now, you didn't have much chance of that when trying to run a Linux-based VM on top of Windows Server, but we now have some compatibility implemented in Hyper-V.

Starting with Windows Server 2019 and continuing into 2022, Linux-based containers can also be run on top of your Windows Server, which is a big deal for anyone looking to implement scaling applications via containers.

System Insights

System Insights is not brand new with Windows Server 2022, but it is a technology that I very rarely see any IT administrators utilizing, and so I felt it was still worth a mention as a new-ish technology. As a Windows Server administrator, you may often receive rather ambiguous requests such as *please figure out what is wrong with the server* (when you actually run a shop of 100+ servers) or *server22 puked again this morning; can you fix it?*

These are the types of questions and requests that often show up first thing on a Monday morning, before your coffee has had a chance to do its magic. While *reboot the server!* is still a valid option and oftentimes quells strange issues temporarily, it would be nice to track down the issue further and perhaps have some fair warning in the future of when this behavior might happen next.

To create trends surrounding issues on servers, it makes sense that the storage and analysis of historical data would be necessary. We have event logs, sure, which can sometimes tell a story after a lot of manual searching through them, but with event logs, it is up to the admin to put the puzzle pieces together. Event logs also have a tendency to fill up quickly when an issue is present and will start rolling away the oldest logs in order to keep a certain amount of free space—logs that might be essential to your troubleshooting venture.

New in Windows Server 2019, **System Insights** is a predictive analytics engine that runs locally on our servers, capturing information about the server itself and keeping historical data for up to a year, which can then be translated and manipulated with Windows Admin Center, or PowerShell, to find patterns and trends. We will take a firsthand look at System Insights in *Chapter 15, Troubleshooting*.

Features deprecated in Server 2022

It is quite rare that Microsoft removes technology from their operating systems, but there is a list of features and functions that are being officially deprecated in Server 2022. This does not mean that Microsoft will no longer support customers who utilize these things, but that they have no plans to make future improvements to these technologies.

Semi-Annual Channel (SAC) releases

As we have already discussed, the SAC releases of Windows Server will no longer be built and released. The future of on-premise Windows Server is through the standard LTSC release channel.

Windows Internet Name Service (WINS)

I almost never see WINS in use in a production environment, because DNS took its place many years ago, and WINS has been largely unnecessary for a long time. However, it is important to note that as of Windows Server 2022, Microsoft is officially considering it deprecated and recommending it no longer be used.

Internet Storage Name Service (iSNS) servers

iSNS is a service that has been around in Windows for a long time, used for the automatic discovery of iSCSI devices on your network. While Windows Server 2022 still retains the ability to make connections to iSCSI devices, the iSNS service has been removed and will no longer be utilized for that automatic discovery.

Guarded fabric and Shielded VMs

These were big news in Server 2016, and Microsoft will continue to support customers who use guarded hypervisor fabrics and shielded VMs, but there are no plans for future development on this technology.

Windows Deployment Services (WDS) partial deprecation

While WDS is not being completely removed, workflows that utilize boot.wim files will now be blocked. Microsoft recommends that companies move away from WDS to one of their newer deployment platforms, **Microsoft Endpoint Configuration Manager** or the **Microsoft Deployment Toolkit (MDT)**.

Navigating the interface

Unfortunately, Microsoft turned a lot of people off with the introduction of Windows 8 and Server 2012, not because functionality or reliability was lacking, but because the interface was so vastly different from what it had been before. It was almost like running two separate operating systems at the same time. You had the normal desktop experience, in which all of us spent 99.9% of our time, but then there were also those few moments where you found yourself needing to visit the full-page **Start** menu. More likely, you stumbled into it without wanting to. However, you ended up there, inside that fullscreen tablet-like interface, for the remaining 0.01% of your Server 2012 experience, and you were left confused, disturbed, and wishing you were back in the traditional desktop. I am, of course, speaking purely from experience here. There may be variations in your personal percentages of time spent, but based on the conversations I have been involved in, I am not alone in these views. And I haven't even mentioned the magical self-appearing **Charms bar**. Some bad memories are better left in the recesses of the brain.

The major update of Windows 8.1 and Server 2012 R2 came with welcome relief of these symptoms. There was an actual **Start** button in the corner again, and you could choose to boot primarily into the normal desktop mode. However, should you ever have the need to click on that **Start** button, you found yourself right back on the full-page **Start** screen, which I still find almost all server admins trying their best to avoid at all costs.

Well, it turns out that Microsoft listened and brought some much-needed relief in Windows 10 and Windows Server 2016, and they have not deviated again. While not quite back to the traditional **Start** menu that existed back in 2008, we have a good mix of both old ways and new ways of launching the tools that we need to access on our server platforms.

As far as the graphical interface goes, Windows Server 2022 is mostly unchanged from Server 2019, because we have not seen a major interface update on the Windows 10 client operating system. If you are comfortable navigating around in Windows 10, you will be well suited to Windows Server 2022.

For anyone new to working within Windows or just looking for some tips and tricks to get them rolling, this section is for you.

The updated Start menu

As sub-versions of Windows 10 have been released, there have been small ongoing changes to the **Start** menu. All in all, I consider many of the changes to be backpedaling from the Windows 8 fiasco. We are now back to a real **Start** button that launches a real **Start** menu, one that doesn't take over the entire desktop. To be honest, personally I almost never open the **Start** menu at all, other than to search for the application or feature that I want. We will cover more on that very soon. However, when I do open up the **Start** menu and look at it, there are a few nice things that stand out:

- All of the applications installed on the server are listed here, in alphabetical order. This is very useful for launching an application, or for doing a quick check to find out whether or not a particular app or feature is installed on your server.
- The left side of the **Start** menu includes a few buttons for quick access to items. Probably the most useful buttons here are power controls for shutting down or restarting the server, and the **Settings** gear, which launches system settings.
- By default, the right side of the **Start** menu shows some bigger buttons, sometimes called **live tiles**. Pinning items to be shown here gives you an easy-access location for items that you commonly launch on your server, and having the larger buttons is useful when you are controlling your server from a touchscreen laptop or something similar.

You can see all three of these functions in *Figure 1.2*:

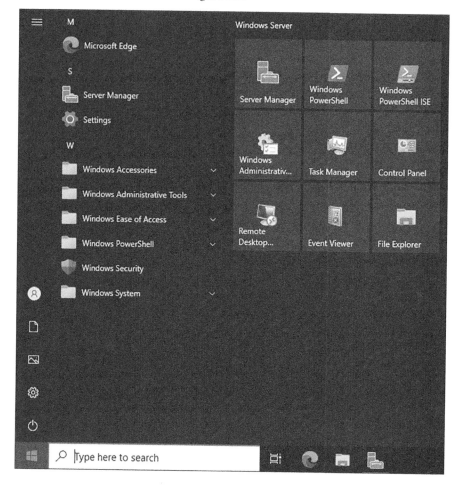

Figure 1.2: The new Start menu

Now that is a breath of fresh air. A simple but useful **Start** menu, and more importantly, one that loads quickly over remote connections such as RDP or Hyper-V consoles.

The Quick Admin Tasks menu

As nice as it is to have a functional **Start** menu, as a server administrator, I still very rarely find myself needing to access the traditional menu for my day-to-day functions. This is because many items that I need to access are quickly available to me inside the **Quick Admin Tasks** menu, which opens by simply right-clicking on the **Start** button. This menu has been available to us since the release of Windows 8, but many IT professionals are still unaware of this functionality.

This menu has become an important part of my interaction with Windows Server operating systems, and hopefully, it will be for you as well. Right-clicking on the **Start** button shows us immediate quick links to do things like open **Event Viewer**, view the **System** properties, check **Device Manager**, and even **Shut down** or **Restart** the server.

The two most common functions that I call for in this context menu are the **Run** function and using it to quickly launch a PowerShell prompt. Even better is the ability from this menu to open either a regular user context PowerShell prompt or an elevated/administrative PowerShell prompt. Using this menu properly saves many mouse clicks and shortens troubleshooting time:

 Alternatively, this menu can be invoked using the *WinKey + X* keyboard shortcut!

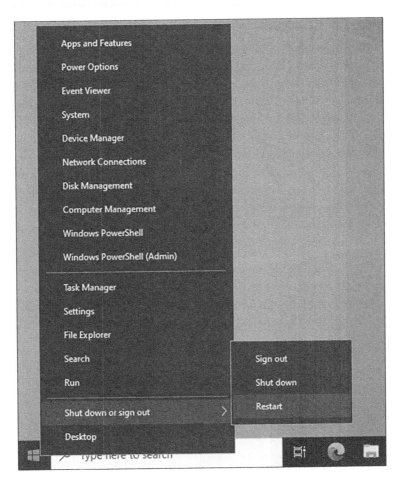

Figure 1.3: The Quick Admin Tasks menu

While I find it extremely beneficial to have PowerShell options listed here in the **Quick Admin Tasks** menu, you may still prefer using Command Prompt over PowerShell. There is an easy way to swap out the PowerShell options in the **Quick Admin Tasks** menu with Command Prompt options – both in a regular user context as well as an admin context. To make that change, take the following steps:

1. Right-click on the taskbar and select **Taskbar settings**.

2. Disable the option (it is enabled by default) to **Replace Command Prompt with Windows Pow-erShell in the menu when I right-click the start button or press Windows key+X**:

> **Replace Command Prompt with Windows PowerShell in the menu when I right-click the start button or press Windows key+X**
>
> ◯ On

Figure 1.4: Replace Command Prompt with Windows PowerShell in the menu

Using the Search function

While the **Quick Admin Tasks** menu hidden behind the **Start** button is useful for calling common administrative tasks, using the **Search** function inside the **Start** menu is a powerful tool for interfacing with literally anything on your Windows Server. Depending on who installed applications and roles to your servers, you may or may not have shortcuts available to launch them inside the **Start** menu. You also may or may not have desktop shortcuts or links to open these programs from the taskbar. I find that it is often difficult to find specific settings, which may need to be tweaked in order to make our servers run like we want them to. **Control Panel** is slowly being replaced by the newer **Settings** menu in newer versions of Windows, and sometimes this results in the discovery of particular settings being difficult. All of these troubles are alleviated with the search bar inside the **Start** menu. By simply clicking on the **Start** button or, even easier, by pressing the Windows key (*WinKey*) on your keyboard, you can simply start typing the name of whatever program, setting, or document that you want to open, and you will see search results from across the entire server.

As a most basic example, press *WinKey* on your keyboard, then type notepad, and press the *Enter* key. You will see that good old Notepad opens right up for us. We never had to navigate anywhere in the Programs folder in order to find and open it. In fact, we never even had to touch the mouse, which is music to the ears of someone like me who loves doing everything he possibly can via the keyboard:

Figure 1.5: Windows Search

An even better example is to pick something that would be buried fairly deep inside **Settings** or **Control Panel**. How about changing the amount of time before the screen goes to power-save and turns itself off? The traditional server admin will open **Control Panel** (if they can find it), probably navigate to the **Appearance and Personalization** section because nothing else looks obviously correct, and still not find what they were looking for. After poking around for a few more minutes, they would start to think that Microsoft forgot to add this setting altogether. But alas, these power settings are simply moved to a new container and are no longer accessible through **Control Panel** at all. We will discuss the new **Settings** screen momentarily in this chapter, but ultimately for the purposes of this example, you are currently stuck at the point where you cannot find the setting you want to change. What's the quick solution? Press your *WinKey* to open the **Start** menu, and type monitor (or power, or just about anything else that would relate to the setting you are looking for). You'll see in the list of available options showing in the search menu one called **Choose when to turn off the screen**. Click on that, and you will have found the setting you were looking for all along:

Figure 1.6: Screen-related settings

You will also notice that you have many more options on this **Search** screen than what you were originally searching for. Search has provided me with many different items that I could accomplish, all relating to the word monitor that I typed in. I don't know of a more powerful way to open applications or settings on Windows Server 2022 than using the search bar inside the **Start** menu. Give it a try today!

Pinning programs to the taskbar

While Windows Server 2022 provides great searching capabilities so that launching hard-to-find applications is very easy, sometimes it's easier to have quick shortcuts for commonly used items to be available with a single click, down in the traditional taskbar. Whether you have sought out a particular application by browsing manually through the **Start** menu or have used the **Search** function to pull up the program that you want, you can simply right-click on the program and choose **Pin to taskbar** to stick a permanent shortcut to that application in the taskbar at the bottom of your screen. Once you have done this, during future logins to your session on the server, your favorite and most used applications will be waiting for you with a single click.

As you can see in *Figure 1.7*, you also have the ability to pin programs to the **Start** menu, which of course is another useful place from which to launch them regularly:

Figure 1.7: Pinning programs to the taskbar

Many readers will already be very familiar with the process of pinning programs to the taskbar, so let's take it one step further to portray an additional function you may not be aware is available to you when you have applications pinned.

The power of right-clicking

We are all pretty familiar with right-clicking in any given area of a Windows operating system in order to do some more advanced functions. Small context menus displayed upon a right-click have existed since the two-button mouse rolled off the assembly line.

We often right-click in order to copy text, copy documents, paste these, or get into a deeper set of properties for a particular file or folder. Many day-to-day tasks are accomplished with that mouse button. What I want to take a minute to point out is that software-makers, Microsoft and otherwise, have been adding even more right-click functionality into application launchers themselves, which makes it even more advantageous to have them close at hand, such as inside the taskbar.

The amount of functionality provided to you when right-clicking on an application in the taskbar differs, depending on the application itself. For example, if I were to right-click on Command Prompt, I have options to either open **Command Prompt**, or to **Unpin from taskbar**. Very simple stuff. If I right-click again on the smaller menu option for Command Prompt, I have the ability to perform the same functions, but I could also get further into **Properties**, or **Run as administrator**. So, I get a little more enhanced functionality the deeper I go:

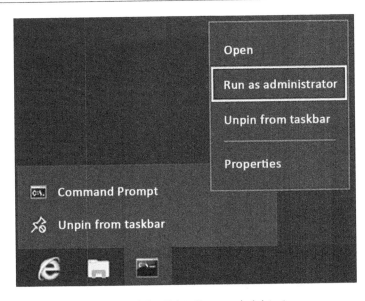

Figure 1.8: Right-click to Run as administrator

With other programs, you may find even more results. And the more you utilize your servers, the more data and options you will start to see in these right-click context menus. Two great examples are Notepad and the Remote Desktop Client. On my server, I have worked on a few text configuration files, and I have used my server to jump into other servers to perform some remote tasks. I have done this using the Remote Desktop Client. Now, when I right-click on Notepad as listed in my taskbar, I have quick links to the most recent documents that I have worked on:

Figure 1.9: Right-clicking reveals recent documents

When right-clicking on my RDP icon, I now have quick links listed right here for the recent servers that I have connected to. I don't know about you, but I RDP into a lot of different servers on a daily basis. Having a link for the Remote Desktop Client in the taskbar, automatically keeping track of the most recent servers I have visited, definitely saves me time and mouse clicks as I work through my daily tasks:

Figure 1.10: Recent RDP connections

These right-click functions have existed for a couple of operating system versions now, so it's not new technology, but it is being expanded upon regularly as new versions of the applications are released. It is also a functionality that I don't witness many server administrators utilizing, but perhaps they should start doing so in order to work more efficiently, which is why we are discussing it here.

Something that is enhanced in the Windows 10 and Server 2022 platforms that is also very useful on a day-to-day basis is the **Quick access** view, which is presented by default when you open File Explorer. We all know and use File Explorer and have for a long time, but typically when you want to get to a particular place on a hard drive or to a specific file, you have many mouse clicks to go through in order to reach your destination. Windows Server 2022's **Quick access** view immediately shows us both recently and frequently opened files and folders that we commonly access from the server. We, as admins, often have to visit the same places on the hard drive and open the same files time and time again. Wouldn't it be great if **File Explorer** lumped all of those common locations and file links in one place? That is exactly what **Quick access** does.

You can see in the following screenshot that opening File Explorer gives you quick links to open both frequently accessed folders as well as links to your recent files. A feature like this can be a real time-saver, and regularly making use of these little bits and pieces available to you, in order to increase your efficiency, demonstrates to colleagues and those around you that you have a real familiarity and comfort level with this latest round of operating systems:

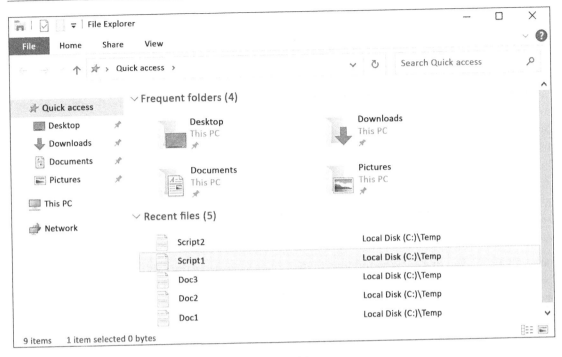

Figure 1.11: Quick access

You'll also notice the small pushpin icons next to some of those **Quick access** locations. You can easily right-click on any folder location via File Explorer and choose **Pin to Quick access**, adding it to your **Quick access** menu, and Windows will maintain that pinned location right here inside the **Quick access** section until you choose to unpin it.

 Yet another way that you can use right-clicking to your advantage is when you want to launch PowerShell into a particular directory on a filesystem. Opening PowerShell in a standard method will land your PowerShell window directly into C:\Users\(username). Depending on what you need to do with PowerShell, you might spend many keystrokes navigating your way to the correct directory on your server from which you need to run a script or make some changes. Alternatively, if you are already inside File Explorer, you can hold down your *Shift* key and then right-click on any directory, and choose the option to **Open PowerShell window here**. This will immediately launch a new instance of PowerShell, with your current directory being the folder you right-clicked on!

Using the newer Settings screen

If you work in IT and have used Windows 10 on a client machine for any period of time, it's a sure bet that you have stumbled across the new **Settings** interface—perhaps accidentally, as was the case for me the first time I saw it. I have watched a number of people now bump into the **Settings** interface for the first time when trying to view or configure Windows Update. You see, **Settings** in Windows Server 2022 is just what the name implies, an interface from which you configure various settings within the operating system.

What's so hard or confusing about that? Well, we already have a landing platform for all of the settings contained inside Windows that has been around for a zillion years. It's called **Control Panel**.

The **Settings** menu inside Windows isn't a brand-new idea but looks and feels quite new when compared to **Control Panel**. Windows Server 2012 and 2012 R2 had a quasi-presence of settings that, as far as I know, went largely unused by systems administrators. I believe that to be the effect of poor execution, as the **Settings** menu in 2012 was accessed and hidden behind the **Charms bar**, which most folks have decided was a terrible idea. We will not spend too much time on technology of the past, but the **Charms bar** in Server 2012 was a menu that presented itself when you swiped your finger in from the right edge of the screen. Yes, you are correct; servers don't usually have touchscreens. Not any that I have ever worked on, anyway. So, the **Charms bar** was also presented when you hovered the mouse up near the top right of the screen. It was quite difficult to access, yet seemed to show up whenever you didn't want it to, like when you were trying to click on something on the right side of the screen and instead you clicked on something inside the **Charms bar** that suddenly appeared out of nowhere.

I am only giving you this background information in order to segue into this next idea. Much of the user interface in Windows 10, and therefore Windows Server 2016+, can be considered a small step backward from the realm of finger swipes and touchscreens. Windows 8 and Server 2012 were so focused on big app buttons and finger swipes that a lot of people got lost in the shuffle. It was so different from what we had ever seen before and difficult to use at an administrative level. Because of feedback received from that release, the graphical interface and user controls, including both the **Start** menu and the **Settings** menu in Windows Server 2022, are sort of smack-dab in the middle between Server 2008 and Server 2012. This backward step was the right one to take, and I have heard nothing but praise so far for the new user interface.

So, getting back to the **Settings** menu, if you click on your **Start** button, then click on that little gear button just above the power controls, you will see this new interface:

Figure 1.12: Windows Settings

There are many settings and pieces of the operating system that you can configure in this new **Settings** menu. Some settings in Windows now only exist in this interface, but many can still be accessed either here or through the traditional **Control Panel**. The goal seems to be a shift toward all configurations being done through the new menu in future releases, but, for now, we can still administer most setting changes through our traditional methods if we so choose. I mentioned Windows Update earlier, and that is a good example to look over. Traditionally, we would configure our Windows Update settings via **Control Panel**, but they have now been completely migrated over to the new **Settings** menu in Windows Server 2022. Search **Control Panel** for Windows Update, and the only result is that you can view currently installed updates. But, if you search the new **Settings** menu for Windows Update, you'll find it right away.

Remember, you can always use the Windows search feature to look for any setting! Hit your *WinKey* and type Windows Update, and you'll be given quick links that take you straight into the appropriate **Settings** menus.

For the moment, you will have to use a combination of **Control Panel** and the **Settings** menu in order to do your work. It gets confusing occasionally. Sometimes, you will even click on something inside the **Settings** menu, and it will launch a **Control Panel** window! Try it out. Open up the **Settings** menu and click on **Network & Internet**. Click on **Ethernet** in the left column. Here, you can see the status of your network cards, but you can't change anything, such as changing an IP address. Then, you notice the link for **Change adapter options**. Oh yeah, that sounds like what I want to do. Click on **Change adapter options**, and you are taken right into the traditional **Network Connections** screen with the **Control Panel** look and feel:

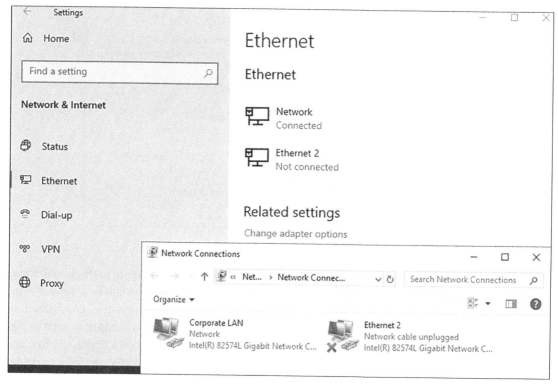

Figure 1.13: Network Connections

Two ways to do the same thing

Potentially confusing as well, until you get used to navigating around in here, is that you can sometimes accomplish the same task in either **Control Panel** or the **Settings** menu, but the process that you take in each interface can have a vastly different look and feel. Let's take a look at that firsthand by trying to create a new user account on our server, once via **Control Panel**, and again via **Settings**.

Creating a new user through Control Panel

You are probably pretty familiar with this. Open **Control Panel** and click on **User Accounts**. Then, click on the **User Accounts** heading. Now, click on the link to **Manage another account**. Inside this screen is your option to **Add a user account**. Click on that and you get the dialog box where you enter a username and password for your new user:

Add a user

Choose a password that will be easy for you to remember but hard for others to guess. If you forget, we'll show the hint.

User name

Password

Reenter password

Password hint

Figure 1.14: Adding a user account via Control Panel

Creating a new user through the Settings menu

Let's take this newer **Settings** interface for a test drive. Open the **Settings** menu and click on **Accounts**. Now, click on **Other users** in the left column. There is an option here to **Add someone else to this PC**; go ahead and click on that:

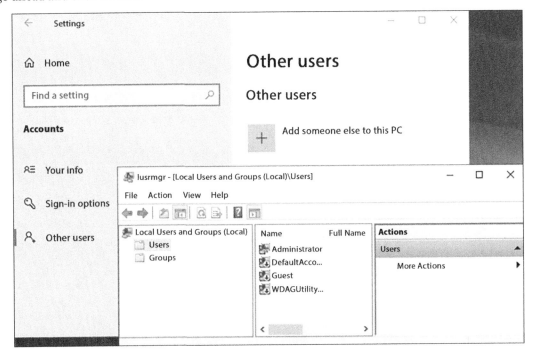

Figure 1.15: Adding a user account via Settings

What in the world is that? Not what I expected, unfortunately. To my surprise, the old **Control Panel** user account launches a nice, fresh-looking interface from which I can create new user accounts. Accessing user accounts via the newer **Settings** console launches me into the old **Local Users and Groups** manager. Technically, from here I could definitely go ahead and create new user accounts, but it seems like there is some sort of a disconnect here. You would naturally think that the new **Settings** would initiate the newer, nicer screen to add new user accounts, but we found the opposite to be true.

We walked through this simple example of attempting to perform the same function through two different interfaces to showcase that there are some items that can, and must, be performed within the new **Settings** menu context, but there are many functions within Windows that still need to be accomplished through our traditional interfaces. While **Control Panel** continues to exist, and probably will for a very long time, you should start navigating your way around the **Settings** menu and figure out what is available inside, so that you can start to shape your ideas for the best combination of both worlds in order to manage your servers effectively.

Just one last thing to point out as we start getting comfortable with the way that the new **Settings** menu looks: many of the settings that we configure in our servers are on/off types of settings. By that I mean we are setting something to either one option or another. Historically, these kinds of configurations were handled by either drop-down menus or radio buttons. That is normal; that is expected; that is Windows. Now, you will start to see little swipe bars, or sliders, that allow you to switch settings on or off, like a light switch. Anyone who has used the settings interface of any smartphone knows exactly what I am talking about. This user interface behavior has now made its way into the full Windows operating systems and is probably here to stay. Just to give you an idea of what it looks like inside the context of the new **Settings** menu, here is a screenshot of the current **Windows Update** settings page inside the **Update & Security** settings.

This is a good example of those on/off slider buttons:

Figure 1.16: Update Settings | Advanced options

Task Manager

Task Manager is a tool that has existed in all Windows operating systems since the first days of the graphical interface, but it has evolved quite a bit over the years. One of the goals for Windows Server 2022 is to be even more useful and reliable than any previous version of Windows Server has been. So, it only makes sense that we finally remove Task Manager altogether, since it simply won't be needed anymore, right?

I'm kidding, of course! While Server 2022 will hopefully prove itself to indeed be the most stable and least needy operating system we have ever seen from Microsoft, Task Manager still exists and will still be needed by server administrators everywhere. If you haven't taken a close look at Task Manager in a while, it has changed significantly over the past few releases.

Task Manager is still typically invoked by either hitting *Ctrl + Alt + Del* on your keyboard and then clicking on **Task Manager,** or by right-clicking on the taskbar and then choosing **Task Manager.** You can also launch Task Manager with the key combination *Ctrl + Shift + Esc* or by typing taskmgr inside the **Run** or **Search** dialog boxes. The first thing you'll notice is that very little information exists in this default view, only a simple list of applications that are currently running. This is a useful interface for forcing an application to close that may be hung up, but not for much else. Go ahead and click on the **More details** link, and you will start to see the real information provided in this powerful interface.

We immediately notice that the displayed information is more user-friendly than in previous years, with both **Apps** and **Background processes** being categorized in a more intuitive way and multiple instances of the same application being condensed down for easy viewing. This gives a faster overhead view of what is going on with our system, while still giving us the ability to expand each application or process to see what individual components or windows are running within the application, such as in *Figure 1.17:*

Figure 1.17: Task Manager: Processes

Make sure to check out the other tabs available inside **Task Manager** as well. **Users** will show us a list of currently logged-in users and the amount of hardware resources that their user sessions are consuming. This is a nice way to identify on Remote Desktop Session Host server, for example, an individual who might be causing a slowdown on the server. The **Details** tab is a little bit more of a traditional view of the **Processes** tab, splitting out much of the same information but in the older style that we were used to seeing in versions of the operating system long ago. Then, the **Services** tab is pretty self-explanatory; it shows you the Windows services currently installed on the server, their statuses, and offers the ability to start or stop these services as needed, without having to open the **Services** console separately.

The tab that I skipped over so that I could mention it more specifically here is the **Performance** tab. This is a pretty powerful one. Inside, you can quickly monitor CPU, memory, and Ethernet utilization. As you can see in the following screenshot, I haven't done a very good job of planning resources on this particular virtual machine, as my CPU is hardly being touched, but I am almost out of system memory:

Figure 1.18: Task Manager: Performance

Another useful piece of information available inside this screen is server uptime. Finding this information can be critical when troubleshooting an issue, and I watch admins time and time again calculating system uptime based on log timestamps. Using **Task Manager** is a much easier way to find that information!

If you are interested in viewing more in-depth data about server performance, there is a link at the bottom of this **Task Manager** window where you can **Open Resource Monitor**. Two technologies provided inside Server 2022 for monitoring system status, particularly for hardware performance, are **Resource Monitor** and **Performance Monitor**. Definitely open up these tools and start testing them out, as they can provide both troubleshooting information and essential baseline data when you spin up a new server. This baseline can then be compared against future testing data so that you can monitor how new applications or services installed on a particular server have affected their resource consumption. We will discuss these additional monitoring tools in *Chapter 15, Troubleshooting Windows Server 2022*.

Moving back to **Task Manager**, there is just one other little neat trick I would like to test. Still inside the **Performance** tab, go ahead and right-click on any particular piece of data that you are interested in. I will right-click on the **CPU** information near the left side of the window. This opens up a dialog box with a few options, of which I am going to click on **Summary view**. This condenses the data that was previously taking up about half of my screen real estate into a tiny little window, which I can move to the corner of my screen. This is a nice way to keep hardware utilization data on the screen at all times as you navigate through and work on your server, so that you can watch for any spikes or increases in resource consumption when making changes to the system:

Figure 1.19: Task Manager: Resources

Task View

Task View is a new feature as of Windows 10 and Windows Server 2016, which carries over to Server 2022. It is a similar idea to that of holding down the *Alt* key and then pressing *Tab* in order to cycle through the applications that you currently have running. For anyone who has never tried that, go ahead and hold down those two keys on your keyboard right now. Depending on what version of Windows you are running, your screen might look slightly different from this, but, in effect, it's the same information. You can see all of the programs you currently have open, and you can cycle through them from left to right using additional presses of the *Tab* button. Alternatively, use *Alt* + *Shift* + *Tab* in order to cycle through them in reverse order. When you have many windows open, it is perhaps easier to simply use the mouse to jump to any specific window:

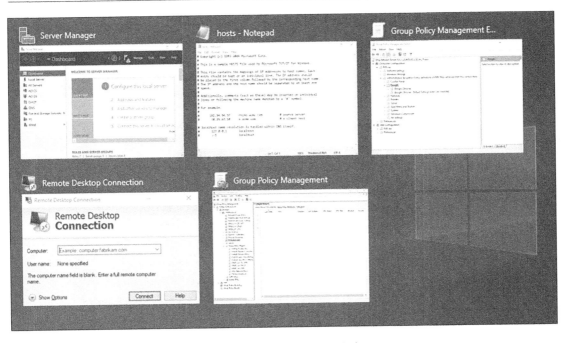

Figure 1.20: Viewing all open windows

Task View is quite a bit more powerful than this, because it adds the capability of managing multiple full desktops' worth of windows and applications. For example, if you were working on two different projects on the same server, and each project required you to have many different windows open at the same time, you would start to burn a lot of time switching back and forth between all of your different apps and windows in order to find what you were looking for. Using **Task View**, you could leave all of your open windows for the first project on your first desktop, and open all of the windows dealing with the second project on a second desktop. Then, with two clicks, you could easily switch back and forth between the different desktops, using the **Task View** button. By default, **Task View** is the little button down in the taskbar, immediately to the right of the search bar. Go ahead and click on it now – it looks like this:

Figure 1.21: The Task View button

You now see a listing of your currently open windows; this looks very similar to the *Alt + Tab* functionality we looked at earlier. The difference is the little button near the top-left corner that says **+ New desktop.** Go ahead and click on that now:

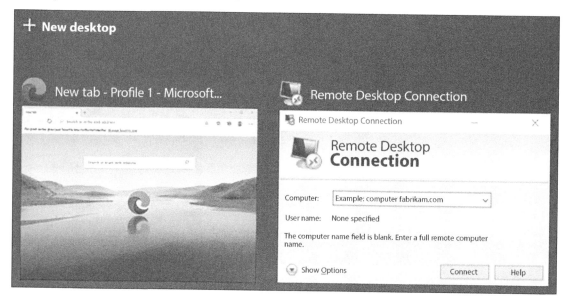

Figure 1.22: Creating a second desktop

Now, you will see **Desktop 1** and **Desktop 2** available for you to use. You can click on **Desktop 2** and open some new programs, or you can even drag and drop existing windows between different desktops, right on this Task View screen:

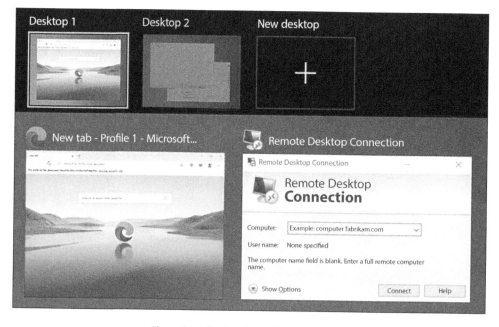

Figure 1.23: Navigating multiple desktops

Task View is a great way to stay organized and efficient by utilizing multiple desktops on the same server. I suppose it is kind of like running dual monitors, or three, four, or more, all from a single physical monitor screen.

If you want to avoid having to click on the icon for Task View, pressing *WinKey* + *Tab* on your keyboard does the same thing!

Summary

This first chapter on Windows Server 2022 was all about getting familiar and comfortable with navigating around the interface. There are various ways to interact with Server 2022, and we will discuss many of them throughout this book, but the majority of server administrators will interface with this new operating system through the full graphical interface, using both the mouse and keyboard to perform their tasks. If you have worked with previous versions of the Windows Server operating system, then a lot of the tools that you will use to drive this new platform will be the same, or at least similar, to the ones that you have used in the past. New operating systems should always be an evolution of their predecessors, and never entirely new. I think this was a lesson learned with the release of Windows 8 and Server 2012.

With Server 2022, we find a great compromise between the traditional familiarity of the prior versions of Windows and the new benefits that come with rounded edges and touch-friendly screens, which will be used more and more often as we move toward the future of Windows-based devices. In the next chapter, we will look into installing and managing Windows Server 2022.

Questions

1. In Windows Server 2022, how can you launch an elevated PowerShell prompt with two mouse clicks?

2. What is the keyboard combination to open the **Quick Admin Tasks** menu?

3. What is the name of Microsoft's cloud service offering?

4. Which Windows Server release model has disappeared with the advent of Windows Server 2022?

5. How many virtual machines can run on top of a Windows Server 2022 Standard host, with default licensing?

6. What installation option for Windows Server 2022 does not have a graphical user interface?

7. Which is the correct verbiage for the latest release of Windows Server 2022, **Long-Term Servicing Branch (LTSB)** or **Long-Term Servicing Channel (LTSC)**?

8. What is the correct tool from which to change configurations on Windows Server 2022, **Windows Settings** or **Control Panel?**

Join our community on Discord

Join our community's Discord space for discussions with the author and other readers:

```
https://packt.link/SecNet
```

2

Installing and Managing Windows Server 2022

Now that we have taken a look at some of the features inside the graphical interface of Windows Server 2022, I realize that some of you may be sitting back thinking, *that's great to read about, but how do I really get started playing around with this for myself?* Reading about technology is never as good as experiencing it for yourself, so we want some rubber to meet the road in this chapter. One of the biggest goals of this book is to make sure we enable you to *use* the product. Rattling off facts about new features and efficiency is fine and dandy but ultimately worthless if you aren't able to make it work in real life. So, let's make this chunk of raw server metal do some work for us.

In this chapter, we will be covering the following:

- Requirements for installation
- Installing Windows Server 2022
- Installing roles and features
- Centralized management and monitoring
- **Windows Admin Center (WAC)**
- Enabling quick server rollouts with Sysprep
- In-place upgrading to Windows Server 2022

Technical requirements

When planning the build of a new server, many of the decisions that you need to make are licensing-type decisions. *What roles do you intend to install on this server? Do they require a special edition? Can the more common Server 2022 Standard edition handle it, or do we need the Datacenter edition for our purposes? Is Server Core going to be beneficial from a security perspective, or do we need the full Desktop Experience?* In these days of Hyper-V Servers having the ability to spin up virtual machines on a whim, we oftentimes proceed without much consideration of the hardware of a server, but there are certainly still instances where physical equipment will host the Windows Server 2022 operating system.

In these cases, you need to be aware of the requirements for this new platform, so let us take a minute to list those specifics. This information is available in longer form on the Microsoft Docs website if you need to double-check any specifics, but here are your summarized minimum system requirements (`https://learn.microsoft.com/en-us/windows-server/get-started/hardware-requirements`):

- **CPU**: 1.4 GHz 64-bit that supports a number of things—NX, DEP, CMPXCHG16b, LAHF/SAHF, PrefetchW, and SLAT.

- **RAM**: 512 MB ECC memory minimum for Server Core, or a recommended 2 GB minimum for a server running Desktop Experience. I can tell you that it is possible to install and run Desktop Experience with far fewer than 2 GB (such as inside a test lab), but the performance of that server will suffer. Interestingly, the Server 2022 installer will not even work unless your Virtual Machine (VM) server has at least 800 MB of RAM, so you'll need to start there. Following OS installation, you could back it down lower if needed.

- **Disk**: Server 2022 requires a **PCI Express** (**PCIe**) storage adapter. ATA/PATA/IDE are not allowed for boot drives. The minimum storage space requirement is 32 GB, but Desktop Experience consumes about 4 GB more space than Server Core, so take that into consideration.

Keep in mind, these are the *bare minimum* specs that your server is going to require. Any real server in a production environment will need far more memory and disk space, and there is no magic number for what you will need. It depends on what workload you are going to expect out of your server.

In fact, there is some cool news about just how far you can go with assigning resources in this new version. Windows Server 2022 now supports 48 TB of memory and 2,048 logical cores across 64 physical sockets! Administrators with an actual need to run 48 TB of memory in a single server are probably using it as a big-time hypervisor, but can you imagine a SQL server with 48 TB of memory? It is a common thing with SQL servers to chew up however much RAM you throw at the server, causing us to impose limits within SQL itself about how much memory it can grab. Perhaps with 48 TB at its disposal, SQL would actually leave some unallocated for the operating system. Nah, probably not...

There are additional components that it would be good to look for when building a new system, which are required for particular roles and features as well. Things such as UEFI and a TPM chip are quickly becoming mainstream and used by more and more services with every operating system update. In particular, if you are interested in security and protection via BitLocker or working with strong certificates, you will want to make sure that your systems include TPM 2.0 chips. This is fairly industry-standard now, so I would be surprised if you have ordered hardware that does not include one.

Installing Windows Server 2022

In general, the installation process for Microsoft operating systems has improved dramatically over the past 15 years. I assume that a lot of you, as IT professionals, are also the de facto *neighborhood computer guru*, constantly asked by friends and family to fix or rebuild their computers. If you're anything like me, this means you are still occasionally rebuilding operating systems such as Windows 7, maybe even XP. Looking at the bright blue setup screens and finding a keyboard with the *F8* key are imperative to this process. To spend two hours simply installing the base operating system and bringing it up to the highest service pack level is pretty normal. Compared to that timeline, installing a modern operating system (OS) such as Windows Server 2022 is almost unbelievably fast and simple.

It is very likely that the majority of readers have completed this process numerous times already, and if that is the case, feel free to skip ahead a couple of pages. But for anyone new to the Microsoft world, or new to IT in general, I'd like to take just a couple of quick pages to make sure you have a baseline to get started with. Without earning your **Installing an OS 101** badge on your tool belt, that shiny server will make for an interesting piece of wall art.

Burning that ISO

The first thing you must do is acquire some installation media. The most simple and straightforward way to implement a single new server is to download a `.ISO` file from Microsoft, burn that `.ISO` to a DVD (don't worry, we will cover USB media next), and slide that DVD in to be used for installation. If you are testing out Server 2022 for personal reasons and do not own any licensing for it, open a search engine like Bing and search for something like `Download Windows Server 2022 Evaluation`. Make sure to click the link that is an actual Microsoft.com entity, and you will find options for either evaluating Windows Server 2022 inside Azure, or downloading a `.ISO` file and saving it onto the hard drive of your computer.

If you do happen to own licensing for Server 2022, or if for any reason you have a Microsoft Visual Studio license, then there is an even better way to acquire your installation media. Simply log in to your Visual Studio portal, and use the **Downloads** section to search for Windows Server 2022. In the past, Microsoft software portals were quite confusing, and it was easy to download some subversion of a product that you didn't actually want. The Visual Studio portal has been recently updated and is by far the most friendly interface for grabbing software and license keys that I have ever seen from Microsoft.

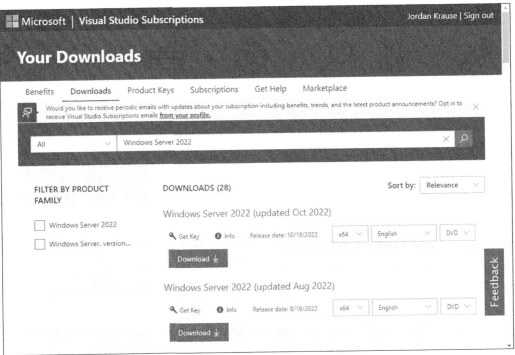

Figure 2.1: Downloading the Windows Server 2022 installer

In the past, the trickiest part of getting a .ISO file to be a workable DVD was the need to download some kind of third-party tool in order to burn it to a disc while making it bootable. If you are running an older client operating system on your computer, this may still be the case for you. I have watched many who are new to this process take the .ISO file, drag it over to their disc drive, and start burning the disc. This creates a DVD with the .ISO file sitting on it, but that .ISO is still packaged up and not bootable in any way, so the disc would be worthless to your new piece of server hardware. Luckily, the newer versions of the Windows client operating systems have built-in functions for dealing with .ISO files, which makes the correct burning process very simple.

Once you have your .ISO file for the Windows Server 2022 installation downloaded onto your computer, insert a fresh DVD into your disc drive and browse to the new file. Simply right-click on the .ISO file, and then choose your menu option for **Burn disc image**. This launches a simple wizard that will extract and burn your new .ISO file the correct way onto the DVD, making it a bootable installation media for your new server, as shown in *Figure 2.2*:

Figure 2.2: Burning your .ISO file onto DVD

It is probable when you attempt to download Windows Server 2022 and use this Windows Disc Image Burner utility with a DVD that you grabbed off your stack of standard blank DVDs that you will receive the following error message: **The disc image file is too large and will not fit on the recordable disc.**

This should come as no surprise because our operating system installer files have been getting larger and larger over the years. We have now reached the critical tipping point where the standard Server 2022 ISO installer is larger than a standard 4.7 GB DVD. To burn this ISO onto a DVD, you will need to hit the store and find some dual-layer discs that can handle more data.

Creating a bootable USB stick

DVDs can be cumbersome and annoying, and now they are also too small for our purposes. Therefore, when installing newer, larger operating systems, it is becoming commonplace to prep a USB stick to use for the installation of the operating system rather than relying on a DVD.

To do this, all you need is a Windows computer, a USB stick that is at least 8 GB, and access to the internet. You will need to download the same ISO that we discussed earlier, as that contains all of the installation files for Server 2022. Then you will also need to download and install some kind of bootable USB creation tool.

There are various free ones available (Rufus is pretty popular), but the one straight from Microsoft is called the **Windows 7 USB/DVD Download Tool**. Why does it still to this day have this crazy name that includes the words *Windows 7* right in it? Don't ask me.

But it works nonetheless and is a quick, easy, and free way to prep your bootable USB sticks for fresh operating system installations. I should point out that this tool has nothing to do with Windows 7. It will take any .ISO file and turn it into a bootable USB stick. That ISO can be a Windows 10 or Server 2022 ISO file, and it still works just fine. You can also install and run the Windows 7 USB/DVD Download Tool on a Windows 10 workstation without any trouble.

Once the USB DVD Download Tool is installed, launch the application and simply walk through the four-step wizard.

This process will erase and format your USB stick. Make sure nothing important is stored there!

You will need to identify the ISO that you want the tool to grab information from, then choose your USB stick from a drop-down list. After that, simply click the **Begin copying** button, and this tool will turn your USB stick into a bootable stick capable of installing the entire Windows Server 2022 OS, as shown in *Figure 2.3*:

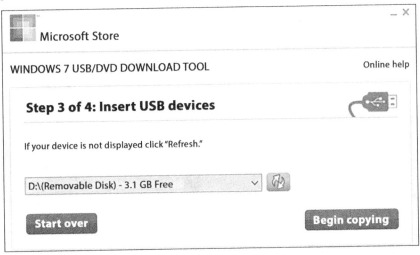

Figure 2.3: Creating a bootable USB stick

Running the installer

Now go ahead and plug your newly created DVD or bootable USB into the new server hardware. Boot to it, and you will finally see the installation wizard for Windows Server 2022. Now, there really are not that many options for you to choose from within these wizards, so we won't spend a lot of time here. For the most part, you are simply clicking on the **Next** button in order to progress through the screens, but there are a few specific places where you will need to make decisions along the way.

After choosing your installation language, the next screen seems pretty easy. There's just a single button that says **Install now**. Yes, that is what you want to click on, but I want you to notice the text in the lower-left corner of your screen. If you are ever in a position where you have a server that cannot boot and you are trying to run some recovery or diagnostic functions in order to resolve that issue, you can click on **Repair your computer** to launch into the recovery console. But for our fresh server installation, go ahead and click on **Install now**, as shown in *Figure 2.4*:

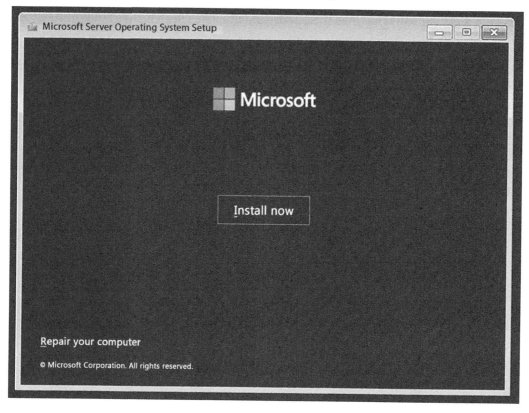

Figure 2.4: Installing Windows Server 2022

Depending on the type of installer you are using, you may now be asked to input a product key to activate Windows. If you have your keys already available, go ahead and enter one now. Otherwise, if you are simply installing this to test Server 2022 and want to run in trial mode for a while, you can click on the link that says **I don't have a product key** in order to bypass this screen.

The next screen is an interesting one and the first place that you really need to start paying attention. You will see four different installation options for Windows Server 2022. There are what seem to be the "regular" installers for Windows Server 2022 Standard or Datacenter, and then other options that include the words (**Desktop Experience**) **for each**. Typically, in the Microsoft installer world, clicking on **Next** through every option gives you the most typical and common installation path for whatever it is that you are installing. *Not so with this wizard.* If you simply glide by this screen by clicking on **Next**, you will find yourself with an installation of **Server Core** in the end.

We will talk more about Server Core in a later chapter of the book, but for now, I will just say that if you are expecting to have a server that looks and feels like what we talked about in *Chapter 1, Getting Started with Windows Server 2022*, this default option is not going to be the one that gets you there. This "Desktop Experience" that the wizard is talking about is the full Windows Server graphical interface, which you are more than likely expecting to see once we are done with our installation. So, for the purposes of our installation here, where we want to interact with the server using full color and a mouse, go ahead and choose the option that includes **Desktop Experience** before clicking on the **Next** button, as shown in *Figure 2.5*:

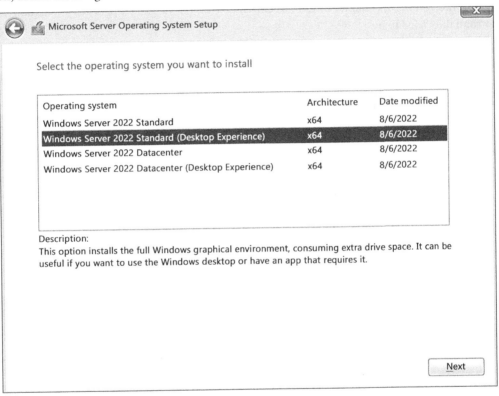

Figure 2.5: Windows Server 2022 installation options

In some previous versions of Windows Server, we had the ability to migrate back and forth from a full Desktop Experience to Server Core and back again, even after the operating system was installed. This does not work in Windows Server 2022! The ability to transition between the two modes has disappeared, so it is even more important that you plan your servers properly from the beginning.

The next screen details the licensing terms to which you need to agree, and then we come to another screen where the top option is most likely *not* the one that you intend to click on. I do understand why the **Upgrade** function is listed first for a consumer-class Windows 10 machine, but it has historically been a pretty rare occurrence that administrators accomplish in-place upgrades to Windows Server. In a perfect world where everything always works flawlessly following upgrades, this would be a great way to go.

You could have many servers all doing their jobs, and every time a new operating system is released, you simply run the installer and upgrade them. Voila—magic! Unfortunately, it doesn't always work like that, and I almost never see server administrators willing to take risks in doing an in-place upgrade to an existing production server. It is much more common that we always build brand-new servers alongside the currently running production servers. Once the new server is configured and ready to accept its responsibilities, then, and only then, does the actual workload migrate over to the new server from the old one. In a planned, carefully sculpted migration process, once the migration of duties is finished, then the old server is shut down and taken away. We will discuss this a little bit more near the end of this chapter and try to convince you that in-place upgrades are actually much better than they used to be.

Now back to the topic at hand. In the Windows Server world, we rarely touch the **Upgrade** option. So go ahead and choose the **Custom: Install Microsoft Server Operating System only (advanced)** option, which is where we will get into our options for installing this copy of Windows Server 2022 fresh into a new location on the hard drive, as shown in *Figure 2.6*:

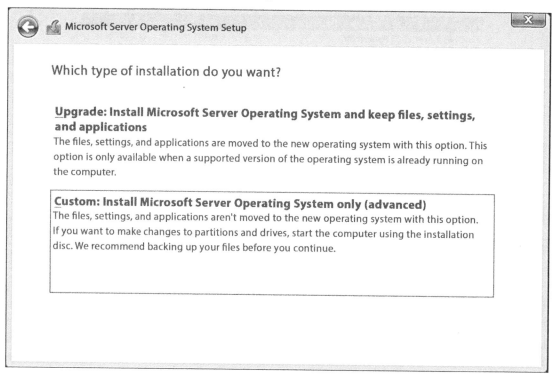

Figure 2.6: In-place upgrade or Custom installation

Now we decide *where* we want to install our new copy of Windows Server 2022. In many cases, you will simply click on **Next** here because your server will have just a single hard disk drive, or maybe a single RAID array of disks, and, in either case, you will see a single pool of free space onto which you can install the operating system. If you have multiple hard drives installed on your server and they have not been tied together in any way yet, then you will have multiple choices here of where to install Windows Server.

We have just a single hard disk attached here, which has never been used, so I can simply click on **Next** to continue. Note here that if your drives had existing or old data on them, you would have the opportunity here, with some built-in disk management tools, to format the disk or delete individual partitions. If you are using some specialized disks that take specific drivers, there is also a **Load driver** button, which you can use to inject these special drivers into the installation wizard in order to view these kinds of disks.

Also, it is important to note on this screen that while there is a button to create a **New** disk partition, you do *not* have to do this in order to continue. Many new admins assume that you must manually create the partition, so Windows knows where to install its files. On the contrary, if you have unallocated space selected as I do in *Figure 2.7* and then simply click **Next**, the installer will take care of creating the necessary partitions for you:

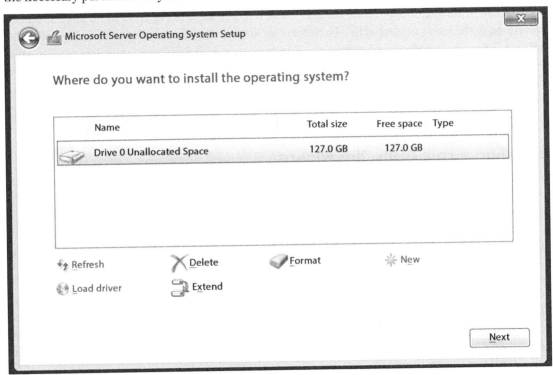

Figure 2.7: Windows installation destination

That's it! You will see the server installer start going to town, copying files, installing features, and getting everything ready on the hard drive. This part of the installer runs on its own for a few minutes, and the next time you need to interact with the server, it will be within the graphical interface where you get to define the administrator password. Once you have specified a password, you will find yourself on the Windows desktop. Now you are really ready to start making use of your new Windows Server 2022.

Installing roles and features

Installing the operating system gets your foot in the door, so to speak, using your server as a server. However, you can't actually do anything useful with your server at this point. On a client desktop system, the base operating system is generally all that is needed to start working and consuming data. The server's job is to serve up that data in the first place, and until you tell the server what its purpose is in life, there really isn't anything useful happening in that base operating system. This is where we need to utilize **roles** and **features**. Windows Server 2022 contains many different options for roles. A role is just what the name implies: the installation of a particular role onto a server defines that server's role in the network. In other words, a role gives a server some purpose in life. A feature, on the other hand, is more of a subset of functions that you can install onto a server. Features can complement particular roles or stand on their own. There are pieces of technology available in Windows Server 2022 that are not installed or turned on by default because these features wouldn't be used in all circumstances. Everything in the later chapters of this book revolves around the functionality provided by roles and features. They are the bread and butter of a Windows server, and, without their installation, your servers make good paperweights, but not much else. As we will not take the time in each chapter to cover the installation of every particular role or feature that will be used within the chapter, let's take some time right now to cover the most common paths that admins can take in order to get these roles and features installed onto their own servers.

Installing a role using the wizard

Without a doubt, the most common place that roles and features get installed is right inside the graphical wizards available as soon as your operating system has been installed. By default, a tool called **Server Manager** launches automatically every time you log in to Windows Server 2022. We will take a closer look at Server Manager itself later in this chapter, but for our purposes here, we will simply use it as a launching platform to get to our wizard, which will guide us through the installation of our first role on this new server we are putting together.

Since you have just logged into this new server, you should be staring at the **Server Manager** dashboard. Right in the middle of the dashboard, you will see some links available to click on, a quick-start list of action items numbered one through five. If you haven't already done so, put into place any local server configuration that you may need on this machine through the first link, which is called **Configure this local server**.

Items that you will likely want in place are things such as a permanent hostname for the server, IP addressing, and, if you are joining this server to an existing domain (we will discuss domains in *Chapter 3, Active Directory*), you typically handle that process prior to implementing any new roles on the server. But, in our case, we are more specifically interested in the role installation itself, so we will assume that you have already configured these little bits and pieces to have your server identified and routing on your network.

Go ahead and click on step 2, **Add roles and features**. Another way you can launch the same wizard is by clicking on the **Manage** menu from the top bar inside Server Manager and then choosing **Add Roles and Features** from the drop-down list. Selecting either link will bring you into our wizard for installation of the roles, as shown in *Figure 2.8*:

Figure 2.8: Adding roles

You are first taken to a summary screen about installing roles. Go ahead and click on **Next** to bypass this screen. Now we get into our first option, which is an interesting one. We are first asked if we want to continue with a **role-based or feature-based installation**, which is exactly what we have been talking about doing. But the second option here, **Remote Desktop Services installation**, is important to note. Most of us consider the **Remote Desktop Services (RDS)** components of Windows Server to be just another role that we can choose when setting up our server, similar to the installation of any other role. While that is basically true, it is important to note that RDS is so functionally different from the other kinds of roles that the entry path into the installation of any of the RDS components invokes its own wizard by choosing the second option here. So, if you ever find yourself looking for the option to install RDS, and you have glossed over this screen because you are so used to clicking **Next** through it like I am, remember that you need to head back there to tell the wizard that you want to deal with an RDS component, and the remainder of the screens will adjust accordingly.

At the moment, I am working on building out a new test lab full of Windows Server 2022 boxes, and I am still in need of a **Domain Controller (DC)** to manage Active Directory in my environment. Before installing Active Directory on a server, it is critical that I have a few prerequisites in place, so I have already accomplished those items on my new server. The items that I need to have in place prior to the AD DS role installation are: having a static IP address assigned and making sure that the DNS server setting in my NIC properties points somewhere, even if only to this server's own IP address. I also need to make sure that the hostname of my server is set to its final name because once you turn it into a Domain Controller, it is not supported to change the hostname. I have already accomplished these items on my server, so I will continue through my role installation wizard here by leaving the option set to **Role-based or feature-based installation** and clicking on **Next**, as shown in *Figure 2.9*:

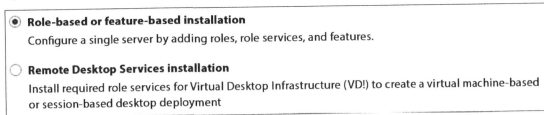

Figure 2.9: Select Role-based or feature-based installation

Our **Server Selection** screen is a very powerful one. If you've been through this process before, you have likely glossed over this screen, simply clicking on the **Next** button in order to progress through it. But, essentially, what this screen is doing is asking you where you would like to install this new role or feature. By default, each server will only have itself listed on this screen, so clicking on **Next** to continue is more than likely what you will be doing. But there are a couple of neat options here. First of all, if your Server Manager is aware of other servers in your network and has been configured to monitor them, you will have the option here to install a role or feature remotely onto one of the other servers. We will dig a little deeper into this capability shortly. Another feature on this page, which I haven't seen many people utilize, is the ability to specify that you want to install a role or feature onto a virtual hard disk. Many of us work with a majority of virtual servers in this day and age, and you don't even need your virtual server to be running in order to install a role or feature to it! If you have access to the .VHDX file, the hard disk file, from where you are running Server Manager, you can choose this option, which will allow you to inject the new role or feature directly into that hard drive. But, as is the case 99% of the times that you will wander through this screen, we are logged directly into the server where we intend to install the role, and so we simply click on **Next**, as shown in *Figure 2.10*:

Figure 2.10: Selecting the destination server

Now we have our list of roles that are available to be installed. Clicking on each role will give you a short description of the purpose of that role if you have any questions, and we will also talk more about the core infrastructural pieces in our next few chapters to give you even more information about what the roles do. All we need to do here in order to install a role onto our new server is check the box and click on **Next**. Since this is going to be a domain controller, I will choose the **Active Directory Domain Services** role, and I will multipurpose this server to also be a **DNS server** and a **DHCP server**. With these roles, there is no need to rerun through this wizard three separate times to install all of these roles; I can simply check them all here and let the wizard run the installers together. Whoops, when I clicked on my first checkbox, I got a pop-up message that the **Active Directory Domain Services** role requires some additional features in order to work properly. This is normal behavior, and you will notice that many of the roles that you install will require some additional components or features to be installed. All you need to do is click on the **Add Features** button, and it will automatically add these extra pieces for you during the installation process. An example of this is shown in *Figure 2.11*:

Figure 2.11: Additional features

Now that we have all three of our roles checked, it's time to click on **Next**. And, just to make it clear to all of you readers, I was not *required* to install all of these roles at the same time; they are not all dependent on each other. It is very common to see these roles all installed onto the same server, but I could split them up onto their own servers if I so desired. In a larger environment, you may have AD DS and DNS installed together, but you might choose to put the DHCP role onto its own server, and that is just fine.

I am configuring this server to support a small lab environment, so for me, it makes sense to put these core infrastructure services together in the same box, as shown in *Figure 2.12*:

Roles

☐ Active Directory Certificate Services
☑ Active Directory Domain Services
☐ Active Directory Federation Services
☐ Active Directory Lightweight Directory Services
☐ Active Directory Rights Management Services
☐ Device Health Attestation
☑ DHCP Server
☑ DNS Server
☐ Fax Server
▷ ■ File and Storage Services (1 of 12 installed)
☐ Host Guardian Service
☐ Hyper-V
☐ Network Policy and Access Services
☐ Print and Document Services
☐ Remote Access
☐ Remote Desktop Services
☐ Volume Activation Services
☐ Web Server (IIS)
☐ Windows Deployment Services
☐ Windows Server Update Services

Figure 2.12: Role selection

After clicking on **Next**, we have now landed on the page where we can install additional features to Windows Server 2022. In some cases, you may have originally intended only to add a particular feature, and in these cases, you would have bypassed the **Server Roles** screen altogether and gone immediately to the **Features installation** screen. Just like with the role installation screen, go ahead and check off any features that you would like to install, and click on **Next** again. For our new domain controller, we do not currently require any additional features to be specifically added, so I will just finish out the wizard, which starts the installation of our new roles.

After the installation process has been completed, you may or may not be prompted to restart the server, depending on which roles or features you installed and whether or not they require a restart. Once you have landed back inside Server Manager, you will notice that you are now being prompted near the top with a yellow exclamation mark. Clicking here displays messages about further configurations that may be required in order to complete the setup of your new roles and finalize their use on the server.

The roles for AD DS, DNS, and DHCP are now successfully installed, but there is some additional configuration that is now required for those roles to do their work. For example, to finish turning my server into a domain controller, I need to run through a promotion process to define my domain or to specify an existing domain that I want to join. There are also some loose ends that I need to tie up before putting DHCP into action:

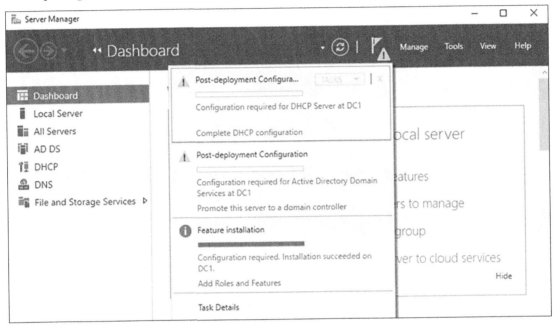

Figure 2.13: Post-deployment Configuration

Installing a feature using PowerShell

Now that you have seen the graphical wizards for installing roles and features, you could certainly always use them to put these components into place on your servers. But Microsoft has put much effort into creating a Windows Server environment where almost anything within the operating system can be manipulated using PowerShell, and the addition of roles and features is included in those capabilities. Let's take a look at the appropriate commands we can use to manipulate roles and features on our server right from a PowerShell prompt. We will view the available list of roles and features, and we will also issue a command to install a quick feature onto our server.

Open up an elevated PowerShell prompt, most easily accomplished via the Quick Admin tasks menu, accessed by right-clicking on the **Start** button. Then use the following command to view all of the available roles and features that we can install onto our server. It will also show you which ones are currently installed:

```
Get-WindowsFeature
```

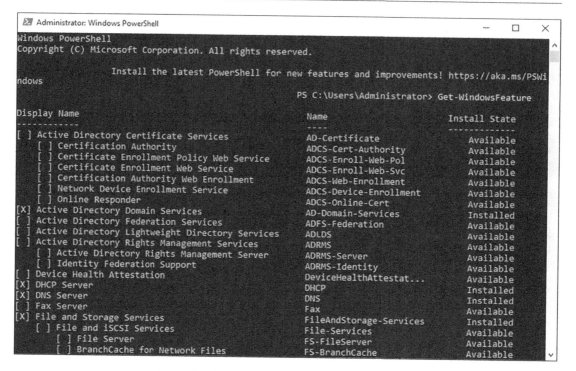

Figure 2.14: A list of all the roles and features available and installed

What I would like to do on this server is install the Telnet Client feature. I use Telnet Client pretty regularly for testing network connections, so it is helpful to have it on this machine. Unfortunately, my PowerShell window currently has pages and pages of different roles and features in it, and I'm not sure what the exact name of the Telnet Client feature is in order to install it. So, let's run `Get-WindowsFeature` again, but this time let's use some additional syntax in the command to pare down the amount of information being displayed. I want to see only the features that begin with the letters TEL, as shown in the following examples:

```
Get-WindowsFeature -Name TEL*
```

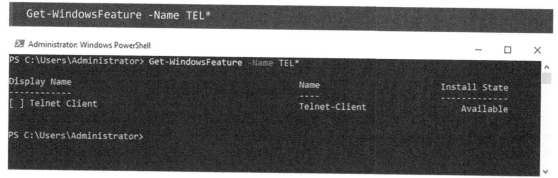

Figure 2.15: A list of features beginning with the letters TEL

There it is! Okay, so now that I know the correct name of the feature, let's run the command to install it, as shown in the following example:

```
Add-WindowsFeature Telnet-Client
```

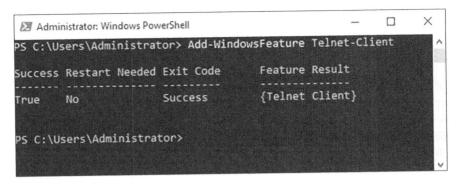

Figure 2.16: Installing Telnet Client via PowerShell

One last thing to show you here—there is also a way to manipulate the Get-WindowsFeature cmdlet in order to quickly show only the roles and features currently installed on a server. Typing Get-WindowsFeature | Where Installed presents us with a list of the currently installed components. If I run that on my domain controller, you can see all the parts and pieces of my roles for AD DS, DNS, and DHCP, as well as my newly installed Telnet Client feature, as shown in *Figure 2.17*:

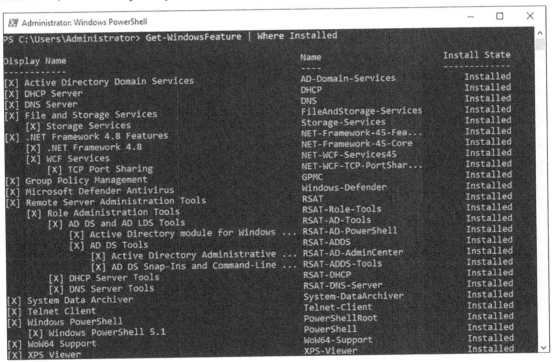

Figure 2.17: A list of currently installed components

Centralized management and monitoring

Whether you are installing new roles, running backups and maintenance programs, or troubleshooting and repairing a server, it is common sense that the first thing you would do is log directly into the server that you need to work on. Long ago, this meant walking up to the server and logging on with the keyboard and mouse that were plugged right into that hardware. Then, quite a number of years ago, this became cumbersome and technology advanced to the point where we had the **Remote Desktop Protocol** (**RDP**) available to us. We quickly transitioned over to logging into our servers remotely using RDP. Even though it's been around for many years, RDP is still an incredibly powerful and secure protocol, giving us the ability to quickly connect to servers from the comfort of our desks. And, as long as you have proper network topology and routing in place, you can work on a server halfway around the world just as quickly as one sitting in the cubicle next to you. In fact, I recently read that mining rights were being granted in outer space. Talk about a co-location for your data center! Maybe someday, we will use RDP to connect to servers in outer space. While this might be a stretch in our lifetimes, and while there are some other tools available for remotely managing your server infrastructure, RDP is the platform of choice for 99% of us out there.

Why talk about RDP? Because you probably all use it on a daily basis, and I needed to let you know that Windows Server 2022 includes some tools that make it much less necessary to our day-to-day workflow. The idea of centralized management in the server world has grown through the last few Windows Server operating system rollouts. Most of us have so many servers running that checking in with them all daily would consume way too much time. We need some tools that we can utilize to make our management and monitoring, and even configuration processes, more efficient in order to free up time for more important projects.

Server Manager

If you have worked on Windows Server recently, you are familiar with the idea that logging in to any of your servers automatically invokes a large window on top of the desktop. This auto-launching program is **Server Manager**. As the name implies, it's here to help you manage your server. However, in my experience, the majority of server administrators do not utilize Server Manager. Instead, they close it as fast as they can and curse at it under their breath because it's been popping up and annoying them during every server login for the past 10 years.

Stop doing that! It's here to help, I promise. *Figure 2.18* shows the default view of Server Manager on my new domain controller:

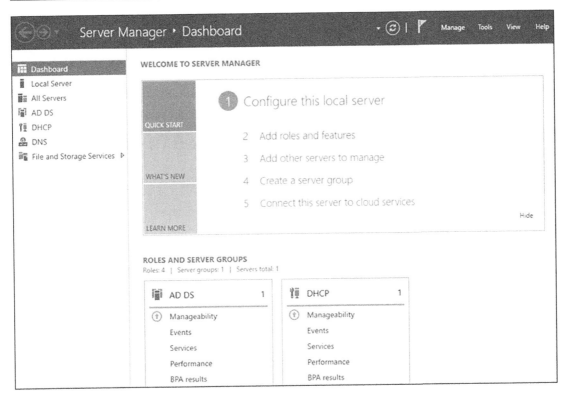

Figure 2.18: Server Manager on my domain controller

What I like about this opening automatically is that it gives me a quick look into what is currently installed on the server. Looking at the column on the left side shows you the list of roles installed and available for management. Clicking on each of these roles brings you to some more particular configuration and options for the role itself. I often find myself hopping back and forth between many different servers while working on a project, and leaving Server Manager open gives me a quick way of double-checking that I am working on the correct server. The **ROLES AND SERVER GROUPS** section at the bottom is also very interesting. You might not be able to see the colors in the picture if you are reading a printed copy of this book, but this gives you a very quick view of whether or not the services running on this server are functioning properly. Right now, both my **AD DS** and **DHCP** functions are running normally, so I have a nice green bar running through them. But, if anything was amiss with either of these roles, it would be flagged bright red, and I could click on any of the links listed under those role headings in order to track down what the trouble is.

Up near the top-right corner, you can see a few menus, the most useful of which, to me, is the **Tools** menu. Click on that, and you will see a list of all the available **Administrative Tools** to launch on this server. Yes, this is essentially the same **Administrative Tools** folder that has existed in each of the previous versions of Windows Server, now stored in a different location. Based on my experience, Server Manager is now the easiest way to access this myriad of tools all from a single location:

Figure 2.19: The Tools menu in Server Manager

So far, the functions inside Server Manager that we have discussed are available on any installation of Windows Server 2022, whether it is standalone or part of a domain. Everything we have done only deals with the local server that we are logged in to. Now, let's explore what options are available to us in Server Manager for the centralization of management across multiple servers. The new mentality of managing many servers from a single server is often referred to as *managing from a single pane of glass*. We will use Server Manager on one of our servers in the network to make connections to additional servers, and after doing that, we should have much more information inside Server Manager that we can use to keep tabs on all of those servers.

Front and center inside the **Server Manager** console is the section entitled **Welcome to Server Manager**. Under that, we have a series of steps or links that can be clicked on. The first one lets you configure settings that are specific only to this local server. We already did some work with the second step when we added a new role to our server. Now we will test out the third step, **Add other servers to manage**.

By the way, this same function can also be called by clicking on the **Manage** menu at the top and then choosing **Add Servers**, as shown in *Figure 2.20*:

Figure 2.20: Adding servers to Server Manager

Most of you will be working within a domain environment where the servers are all domain-joined, which makes this next part really easy. Simply click on the **Find Now** button, and the machines available within your network will be displayed. From here, you can choose the servers that you want to manage and move them over to the **Selected** column on the right, as shown in *Figure 2.21*:

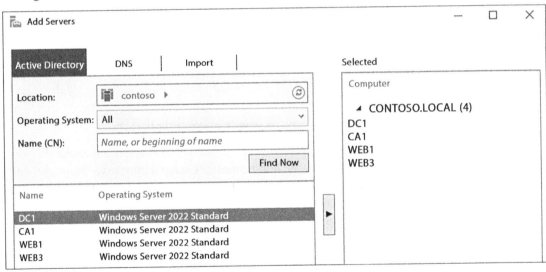

Figure 2.21: Select the servers you want to manage

After clicking **OK**, you will see that Server Manager has transformed in order to give you more information about all of these servers and the roles that are installed on them. Now when you log in to this single server, you immediately see critical maintenance information about **all** of the systems that you have chosen to add here. You could even use one dedicated server to handle the management of your whole arsenal of servers. For example, I am currently logged into a brand new server called CA1. I do not have any roles installed on this server, so, by default, Server Manager looks pretty basic. As soon as I add other servers (my domain controllers) to be managed, my Server Manager on the CA1 server now contains all of the details about CA1 and my domain controllers, so I can view all facets of my infrastructure from this single pane. As you can see in *Figure 2.22*, I even have some flags here indicating that some services are not running properly within my infrastructure:

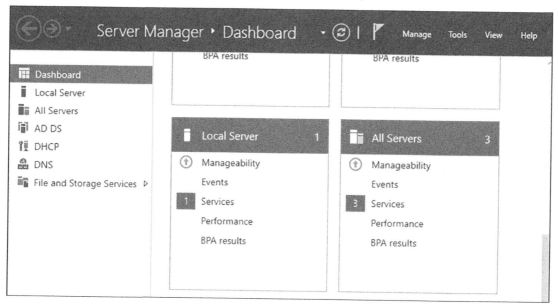

Figure 2.22: Managing servers on Server Manager Dashboard

Clicking on the **All Servers** link or into one of the specific roles gives you even more comprehensive information collected from these remote servers. Adding multiple servers into Server Manager is not only useful for monitoring but for future configurations as well. Do you remember a few pages ago when we added a new role using the wizard? That process has now evolved to become more comprehensive since we have now *tapped* this server into our other servers in the network.

If I now choose to add a new role from inside Server Manager that is aware of multiple servers in the network, when I get to the screen asking me where I want to install that role, I see that I can choose to install a new role or feature onto one of my other servers, even though I am not working from the console of those servers, as shown in *Figure 2.23*:

Figure 2.23: Selecting a server to install a new role or feature on

If I wanted to install the web server role onto WEB1, a new server that I am prepping to be a web server, I would *not* have to log into the WEB1 server. Right here, from Server Manager running on CA1, I could run through the **Add Roles** wizard, define WEB1 as the server that I want to manipulate, and install the role directly from here.

Remote Server Administration Tools (RSAT)

Using Server Manager on a single server to manage and monitor all of your servers is pretty handy, but what if we could take one more step out of that process? What if I told you that you didn't have to log in to *any* of your servers, but could perform all of these tasks from the computer sitting on your desk?

This is possible by installing a toolset from Microsoft called the **Remote Server Administration Tools** (**RSAT**). I have a regular Windows 10 client computer online and running in our network, also domain-joined. I am now going to add an optional feature to this Windows 10 computer to give it the **RSAT toolset**.

Open up **Settings** on the client computer and type the word optional into the search bar. One of the options presented will be **Manage optional features**. Go ahead and click that. Once inside **Optional features**, click the button to **Add a feature**. This will open a list of many optional features to choose from, including a lot of language options, but if you scroll down in the list, you will eventually come to a number of different entries that start with **RSAT:**. If there were only a select number of the tools that you wanted to use from this Windows 10 client, you could be selective here and only install the admin consoles that you actually needed. Since this is a test lab and I want as many options as possible, I am simply going to check the box next to every item that begins with **RSAT:**, as you can see in *Figure 2.24*:

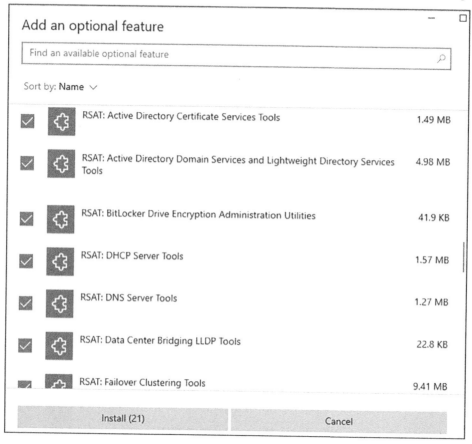

Figure 2.24: Installing RSAT features

If your computer is running a version of Windows 10 that is older than 1809, you won't find these options on your **Settings** screen. Instead, you can download and install the whole RSAT package from the following link: https://www.microsoft.com/en-us/download/details.aspx?id=45520.

After walking through the process to get these tools on my Windows 10 client computer, I can't seem to find any program that is called **Remote Server Administration Tool**. That would be correct. Even though the names of these features we are installing all begin with RSAT, the components that are getting installed onto your system are the actual Windows Server system tools.

If you peruse your **Start** menu, you will now find **Server Manager**, just like on a server, along with a folder full of Windows Administrative tools! This makes sense, except that if you don't realize the name discrepancy, it can take you a few minutes to figure out why you cannot find what you just installed.

So, go ahead and launch Server Manager by finding it in the **Start** menu, by using the search bar, or even by saying *Hey, Cortana, open Server Manager*. Sorry, I couldn't resist. But whatever your method, open up Server Manager on your desktop computer, and you will see that it looks and feels just like Server Manager in Windows Server 2022. And, in the same way that you work with and manipulate it within the server operating system, you can take the same steps here in order to add your servers for remote management.

In *Figure 2.25*, you can see that I have walked through the step to **Add other servers to manage** and selected some of the servers that are within my test network. I now have access, right here from my Windows 10 client computer, to manage and monitor all of the servers in my lab without even having to log in to them:

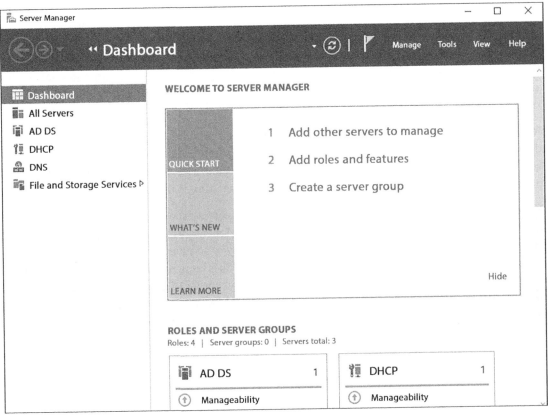

Figure 2.25: Centralized management via Server Manager

Does this mean RDP is dead?

With these new and improved ways to manage the underlying components of your servers without having to log in to them directly, does this mean that our age-old friend RDP is going away? Certainly not! We will still have the need to access our servers directly sometimes, even if we go all-in with using the newer management tools. And I also expect that many administrators out there will continue using RDP and full desktop-based access for all management and monitoring of their servers simply because that is what they are more comfortable with, even if newer, more efficient ways now exist to accomplish the same tasks.

Remote Desktop Connection Manager

Since most of us do still utilize RDP occasionally (or often) when bouncing around between our servers, let's take a quick look at a tool that can at least make this task more manageable and centralized. I won't spend a lot of time looking over individual features or capabilities of this tool since it is a client-side tool and not something that is specific to Windows Server 2022. You can use this to handle RDP connections for any and all of your servers or even all of the client computers in your network. **Remote Desktop Connection Manager** is an incredibly useful platform for storing all of the different RDP connections that you make within your environment. You can save connections so that you don't have to spend time trying to remember server names, sort servers into categories, and even store credentials so that you don't have to type passwords when connecting to servers. Though a disclaimer should come with that one—your security folks may not be happy if you choose to employ the password-storing feature.

Remote Desktop Connection Manager (RDCM) has led a tumultuous life. It was available as a direct download from Microsoft for years and through many versions, until a vulnerability identified in the software caused Microsoft to shut it down and stop offering it to us. Thankfully, the Sysinternals team at Microsoft grabbed it, fixed it up, and resurrected it for continued use.

You can download RDCM from the following link: `https://learn.microsoft.com/en-us/sysinternals/downloads/rdcman`. Once downloaded and extracted, this tool is a standalone executable that can be run on almost any Windows operating system. The beauty of so many Sysinternals tools is that they are self-explanatory. To make use of RDCM all you need to do is launch it, create a new group (saved as an RDG file), and start adding servers to it. After saving your server RDP connections into RDCM, this tool provides you with a centralized and fast way to RDP into any of the servers that you administer. No need to remember their names or IP addresses from this point forward!

Figure 2.26: The RDCM tool

Windows Admin Center (WAC)

Now forget everything I just told you about remote server management and focus on this instead. I'm kidding... sort of. All of the tools we have already discussed are still stable, relevant, and great ways to interact with and manage Windows Server. However, there's a new kid in town, and Microsoft expects them to be very popular.

WAC is a server and client management platform that is designed to help you administer your machines in a more efficient manner. This is a browser-based tool, meaning that, once installed, you access WAC from a web browser, which is great. No need to install a management tool or application onto your workstation—simply sit down and tap into it with a URL.

WAC can manage your servers (all the way back to Server 2008 R2) and your server clusters and even has some special functionality for managing hyper-converged infrastructure clusters. You have the ability to manage servers hosted on-premises as well as inside Azure, and you can even manage client machines in the Windows 10 flavor.

What's the cost of such an amazing, powerful tool? FREE!

WAC even has support for third-party vendors creating extensions for the WAC interface, so this tool is going to continue growing. If you have followed along with the test lab configuration in the book so far, you will recognize the words "Windows Admin Center" from a pop-up window that displays itself every time that Server Manager is opened. Microsoft wants administrators to know about WAC so badly that they are reminding you that you should start using it every time you log into a Server 2022 box, as shown in *Figure 2.27*:

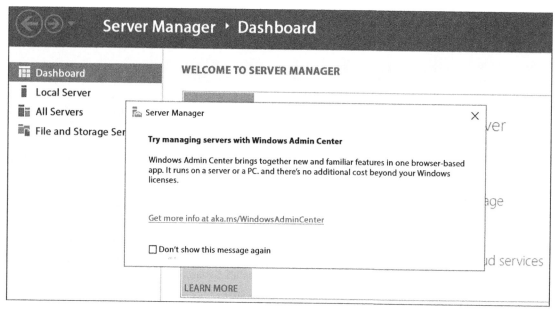

Figure 2.27: Even Server Manager recommends using WAC

Installing Windows Admin Center

Enough talk, let's try it out! First, we need to choose a location to install the components of WAC. True, I did say that one of the benefits was that we didn't need to install a client software component, but what I meant was that once WAC is implemented, then tapping into it is as easy as opening up a browser. That website needs to be installed and running somewhere, right? While you could throw the whole WAC system onto a Windows 10 client, let's take the approach that will be more commonly utilized in the field and install it onto a server in our network. I have a system running called WEB3 that is not yet hosting any roles or websites; it's just an empty server at this point. Sounds like a good place for something like this.

Download WAC here: `https://aka.ms/WACDownload`.

Once downloaded, simply run the installer on the host machine. There are a few simple decisions you need to make during the wizard; the most notable is the screen where you define the port and certificate settings. In a production environment, it would be best to run port 443 and provide a valid SSL certificate here so that traffic to and from this website is properly protected via HTTPS, but for my little test lab, I am going to run 443 with a self-signed certificate, just for testing purposes. Don't use self-signed certificates in production!

Figure 2.28: Installing WAC

Once the installer is finished, you will now be hosting the WAC website on this server. For my particular installation, that new web address is `https://WEB3.contoso.local`.

Launching Windows Admin Center

Now for the fun part, checking this thing out. To tap into WAC, you simply open up a supported browser from any machine in your network and browse to the WAC URL. Once again, mine is `https://WEB3.contoso.local`. Microsoft recommends using Edge, but it also works with Chrome. I am logged into my Windows 10 workstation and will simply open up the Edge browser and try to hit my new site, as shown in *Figure 2.29*:

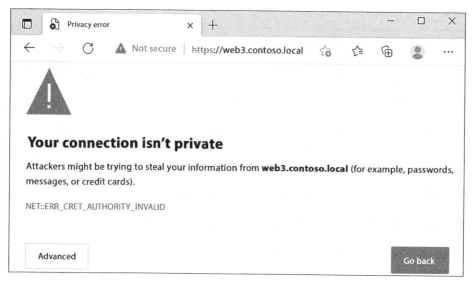

Figure 2.29: Opening a WAC URL in Microsoft Edge

As you can see, I am dealing with a certificate warning. This is to be expected because I am using a self-signed certificate, which, once again, is a bad idea. I only justify it because I'm running in a test lab. If you want to remove the certificate warning, make sure to skip ahead to *Chapter 6, Certificates*, where we will cover all the necessary information to make that possible. Since I am expecting this within my lab and am okay with the risk for our purposes today, I can click the **Advanced** button and then click the **Continue to web3.contoso.local** link to proceed. Interestingly, I am now presented with a credentials prompt:

Figure 2.30: Sign in to use WAC

Even though I am logged into a Windows 10 computer that is domain-joined, and I am logged in with domain credentials, the WAC website does not automatically try to inject those credentials for its own use but rather pauses to ask who you are. If I simply input my domain credentials here, I am now presented with the **WAC** interface, as shown in *Figure 2.31*:

Figure 2.31: WAC interface

Adding more servers to WAC

Logging in to WAC is great but not very useful until you add a bunch of machines that you want to manage. To do that, simply click the + **Add** button that is shown onscreen. You will be presented with choices to add a new server, a new PC, a Windows Server failover cluster, Azure Stack HCI, or even an Azure VM. Make your selection and input the required information. I don't have any clusters in my test lab, not yet anyway, so I am going to add connections to the standard servers that I have been running in the environment. If I select the option to add a Windows Server, I can type out the individual server names, import a list of server names, or even select the option to **Search Active Directory**. I'll go ahead and try that search function to test how well this works.

I have already set up a number of different servers in my lab and joined them to my domain (we'll talk more about domains in the next chapter)—but how do I make WAC search for them here? When I click **Search Active Directory**, I still get a field asking me to type in a server name, but there is a note about wildcards being allowed. Aha! If you simply type an asterisk (*) into the search field and click the **Search** button, WAC polls your domain and presents a full list of machines that can be added to the console:

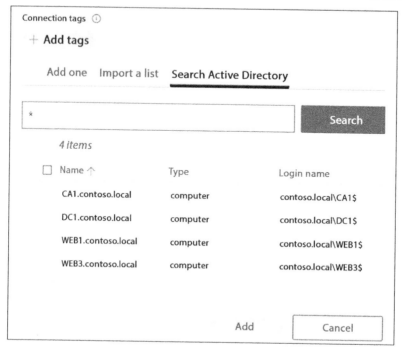

*Figure 2.32: Search using ***

Now simply select the checkboxes next to each server that you would like to administer via Windows Admin Center and click the **Add** button. You can see in *Figure 2.33* that WAC now contains information about all of the servers in my environment:

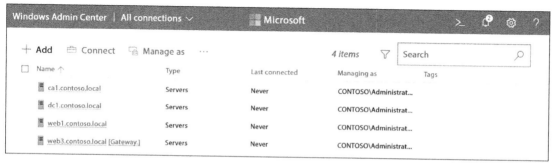

Figure 2.33: Server information in WAC

Managing a server with WAC

Beginning the management of a server from within WAC is as simple as clicking on the server name. As you can see in *Figure 2.34*, I have selected my DC1 server, as it is currently the only machine with some real roles installed and running:

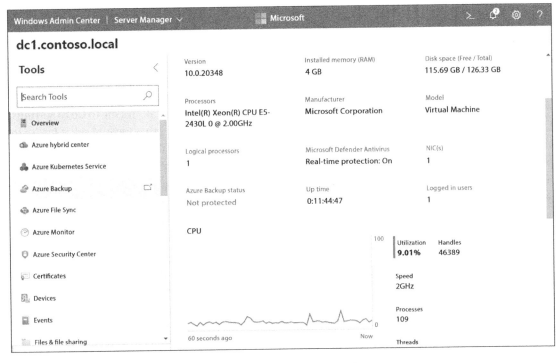

Figure 2.34: DC1 server information

From this interface, I can manage many different aspects of my DC1 server's operating system. There are power control functions, and the ability to run backups on my server, and I can even view and install certificates from here! You can monitor the performance of the server, view its event logs, manipulate the local Windows Firewall, and launch a remote PowerShell connection to the server. The goal with WAC is for it to be your one-stop shop for remotely managing your servers, and I would say it is well on its way to accomplishing that goal.

I don't yet have any Server Core instances running in my lab but rest assured that WAC can be used to manage Server Core instances just as well as servers running Desktop Experience. This makes WAC even more potent and intriguing to server administrators. When we get to *Chapter 10, Server Core*, we'll make sure to wrap back to this idea and in some way manipulate a Server Core instance through this WAC console.

Changes are easy as pie

Monitoring information about your servers from a single place like WAC is great and powerful, but the coolest part about WAC is that you have some serious capabilities to manipulate your servers as well, straight from this web interface.

This is yet another place where you can add roles or features to your servers, create scheduled tasks, start or stop services, or even do things like edit the registry and add Windows Firewall rules. Let's make a quick change to our DC1 server to prove this. All of my VMs are inside a test lab that is running within Hyper-V, and so interaction with my servers to this point has been directly from Hyper-V console sessions. It is basically like I am walking up to these servers and logging in to them from the console every single time I need to interact with them. At this point, RDP has never been enabled on DC1, but I wonder if there is a way to enable that easily right from inside WAC?

Scrolling down through my list of tools on the left side of WAC, I suddenly spot one called **Remote Desktop**. Sounds like the right place to be! Clicking on **Remote Desktop** spins for a second as WAC reaches out and queries information from DC1. Then I am presented with a summary that states, "*Remote desktop connections are not allowed to this computer*" with a button that allows me to **Go to settings**. Inside the **Remote Desktop settings** screen, I have here the same options that I would see if I were to log directly into DC1 and edit the Remote Desktop settings from inside the classic advanced **System properties** screens. You can see in *Figure 2.35* that I have now selected the option **Allow remote connections to this computer**—previously, this was not enabled:

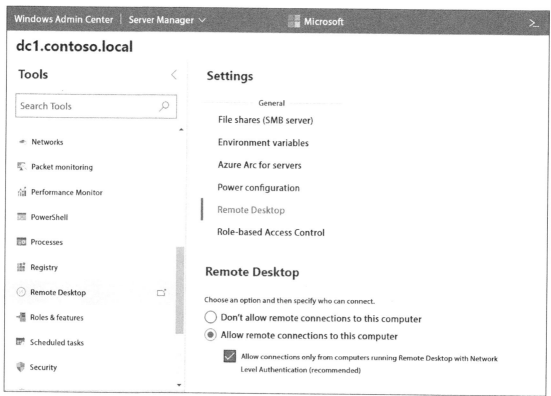

Figure 2.35: Remote Desktop settings

Simply changing the setting here and clicking the **Save** button causes Window Admin Center to reach out to DC1 and enable this Remote Desktop setting, after which I can immediately connect to it using RDP from my Windows 10 computer. I never needed to log into DC1 to enable remote logins to DC1!

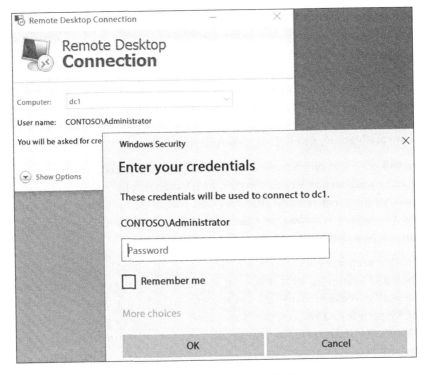

Figure 2.36: RDP is now enabled

Azure integrations

You'll notice inside WAC that there are numerous tools related to Azure. If you have an Azure environment or are thinking about getting started with one, your on-premises WAC can be used to administer both on-premises servers as well as Azure servers. WAC can also be used to bind your on-premises environment together with your Azure environment through things like Azure File Sync and Azure Backup. These tools can be a powerful way of creating a hybrid cloud configuration, where you maintain servers in both environments, and can also be used to help ease a transition from a traditional datacenter into a cloud-only mentality.

Enabling quick server rollouts with Sysprep

At the beginning of this chapter, we walked through the process of installing the Windows Server 2022 operating system onto your new server. Whether this was a physical piece of hardware or a virtual machine that we were working with, the installation process was essentially the same. Plugging in the DVD or USB stick, booting to it, and letting the installer run its course is an easy enough thing to do, but what if you need to build out ten new servers instead of just one? This process would soon start to get tedious, and it would seem like you were wasting a lot of time having to do the exact same thing over and over again. You would be correct—this does waste a lot of time, and there is an easier and faster way to roll out new servers as long as you are building them all from a relatively similar hardware platform. If you are building out your servers as virtual machines, which is so often the case these days, then this process works great and can save you quite a bit of time on new server builds.

Now, before I go too far down this road of describing the Sysprep process, I will also note that there are more involved technologies available within the Windows infrastructure that allow automated operating system and server rollouts, which can make the new server rollout process even easier than what I am describing here. The problem with some of the automated technologies is that the infrastructure required to make them work properly is more advanced than many folks will have access to if they are just learning the ropes with Windows Server. In other words, having a fully automated server rollout mechanism isn't very feasible for small environments or test labs, which is where a lot of us live while we are learning about these new technologies.

So, anyway, we will not focus on an automated approach to server rollouts, but rather we will do a few minutes of extra work on our very first server, which then results in saving numerous minutes of setup work on every server that we build afterward. The core of this process is the **Sysprep** tool, which is baked into all versions of Windows, so you can take this same process on any current Windows machine, whether it be a client or a server.

Sysprep is a tool that prepares your system for duplication. Its official name is the **Microsoft System Preparation Tool**, and to sum up what it does in one line, it allows you to create a master *image* of your server that you can reuse as many times as you want in order to roll out additional servers. A key benefit to using Sysprep is that you can put customized settings onto your master server and install things such as Windows Update prior to Sysprep, and all of these settings and patches will then exist inside your master image.

Using Sysprep saves you time by not having to walk through the operating system installation process, but it saves you even more time by not having to wait for Windows Update to roll all of the current patches down onto every new system that you create.

Now, some of you might be wondering why Sysprep is even necessary. If you wanted to clone your master server, you could simply use a hard disk imaging tool, or if you were dealing with virtual machines, you could simply copy and paste the .VHDX file itself in order to make a copy of your new server, right? The answer is yes, but the big problem is that the new image or hard drive that you just created would be an exact replica of the original one. The hostname would be the same, and, more importantly, some core identification information inside Windows, such as the operating system's **Security Identifier (SID)** number, would be exactly the same. If you were to power on both the original master server and a new server based on this exact replica, you would cause conflicts and collisions on the network as these two servers fought for their right to be the only server with that unique name and SID. This problem exacerbates itself in domain environments, where it is even more important that each system within your network has a unique SID/GUID—their identifier within Active Directory. If you create exact copies of servers and bring them both online, let's just say neither one is going to be happy about it. If you do this inside a production environment, you can wreak havoc on your network. I know from personal experience what it looks like to help someone recover their domain after a domain controller's hard drive was simply copied, pasted, and turned on as a second server. It's the definition of a bad day.

Sysprep fixes all of these inherent problems with the system duplication process by randomizing the unique identifiers in the operating system. To prepare ourselves to roll out many servers using a master image we create with Sysprep, here is a quick-reference summary of the steps we will take:

1. Install Windows Server 2022 onto a new server
2. Configure customizations and updates onto your new server
3. Run Sysprep to prepare and shut down your master server
4. Create your master image of the drive
5. Build new servers using copies of the master image

And now, let's cover these steps in a little more detail.

Installing Windows Server 2022 onto a new server

First, just like you have already done, we need to prepare our first server by getting the Windows Server 2022 operating system installed. Refrain from installing any full roles onto the server because, depending on the role and its unique configuration, the Sysprep process that we run shortly could cause problems for individual role configurations. Install the operating system and make sure device drivers are all squared away and you're ready for the next step.

Configuring customizations and updates onto your new server

Next, you want to configure customizations and install operating system updates onto your new server. Each setting or installation that you can do now that is universal to your batch of servers will save you from having to take that step on your servers in the future. This portion may be slightly confusing because I just told you a minute ago not to install roles onto the master server. This is because a role installation makes numerous changes to the operating system and some of the roles that you can install lock themselves down to a particular hostname running on the system. If you were to do something like that to a master server, that role would more than likely break when brought up on a new server. Customizations that you can put into place on the master server are things such as plugging in files and folders that you might want on all of your servers, such as an `Admin Tools` folder or something like that. You could also start or stop services that you may or may not want running on each of your servers and change settings in the registry if that is part of your normal server prep or hardening process. Whatever changes or customizations you put into place, it's not a bad idea to run a full slew of tests against the first new server that you build from this master image, just to make sure all of your changes made it through the Sysprep process.

Now is also the time to let Windows Update install and to put any patches on this new server that you want to have installed on all of your new servers in the future. There is nothing more frustrating than installing a new operating system in five minutes, only to have to sit around and wait four hours for all of the current updates and patches to be installed before you can use the new server. By including these updates and patches in the master image, you save all of that download and installation time for each new server that you spin up.

 Continue to save yourself time and effort by creating new copies of your master images every few months. This way, the newest patches are always included in your master image, and it continues to save you more and more time throughout the life of Windows Server 2022.

Running Sysprep to prepare and shut down your master server

Now that our master server is prepped how we want, it is time to run the Sysprep tool itself. To do that, open up an administrative Command Prompt and browse to `C:\Windows\System32\Sysprep`. Now you can make use of the `Sysprep.exe` utility inside that folder to launch Sysprep itself.

As with many executables that you run from Command Prompt, there are a variety of optional switches that you can tag onto the end of your command to make it do specific tasks. From your Command Prompt window, if you simply run the `sysprep.exe` command, you will see a graphical interface for Sysprep, where you can choose between the available options, as shown in *Figure 2.37*:

Figure 2.37: Sysprep options

Since I always use the same set of options for Sysprep, I find it easier to simply include all of my optional switches right from the command-line input, therefore bypassing the graphical screen altogether. Here is some information on the different switches that are available to use with `sysprep.exe`:

- `/quiet`: This tells Sysprep to run without status messages on the screen.
- `/generalize`: This specifies that Sysprep is to remove all of the unique system information (SID) from the Windows installation, making the final image usable on multiple machines in your network because each new one spun up from the image will get a new, unique SID.
- `/audit`: This restarts the machine into a special audit mode, where you have the option of adding additional drivers into Windows before the final image gets taken.
- `/oobe`: This tells the machine to launch the mini-setup wizard when Windows next boots.
- `/reboot`: This restarts when Sysprep is finished.
- `/shutdown`: This shuts down the system (not a restart) when Sysprep is finished. This is an important one and is one that I typically use.
- `/quit`: This closes Sysprep after it finishes.

- /unattend: There is a special answerfile that you can create that, when specified, will be used in conjunction with the Sysprep process to further configure your new servers as they come online. For example, you can specify in this answerfile that a particular installer or batch file is to be launched upon the first Windows boot following Sysprep. This can be useful for any kind of cleanup task that you might want to perform, for example, if you had a batch file on your system that you used to flush out the log files following the first boot of new servers.

The two that are most important for our purpose of wanting to create a master image file that we can use for quick server rollouts in the future are the /generalize switch and the /shutdown switch. /generalize is very important because it replaces all of the unique identification information, the SID info, in the new copies of Windows that come online. This allows your new servers to co-exist on the network with your original server and with other new servers that you bring online. The /shutdown switch is also very important because we want this master server to become sysprepped and then immediately shut down so that we can create our master image from it.

 Make sure that your server does NOT boot into Windows again until after you have created your master image or taken your master copy of the .VHDX file. The first time that Windows boots, it will inject the new SID information, and you want that only to happen on new servers that you have created based on your new image.

So, rather than simply throwing all of the switches at you and letting you decide, let's take a look at the ones that I typically use. I will make use of /generalize so that I make my new servers unique, and I also like to use /oobe so that the mini-setup wizard launches during the first boot of Windows on any of my new systems. Then, I will, of course, also use /shutdown because I need this server to be offline immediately following Sysprep so that I can take a copy of the hard drive to be used as my master image. So, my fully groomed sysprep command is shown in the following code:

```
sysprep.exe /generalize /oobe /shutdown
```

After launching this command, you will see Sysprep moving through some processes within Windows, and after a couple of minutes, your server will shut itself down, as shown in *Figure 2.38*:

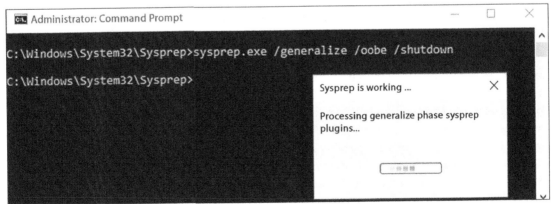

Figure 2.38: Sysprep and shutting down

You are now ready to create your master image from this hard disk.

Creating your master image of the drive

Our master server is now shut down, and we are ready to create our master image from this server. If it is a physical server, you can use any hard disk imaging utility in order to create an image file from the drive. An imaging utility like those from the company Acronis will create a single file from your drive. This file contains an image of the entire disk that you can use to restore onto fresh hard drives in new servers in the future. On the other hand, most of you are probably dealing with virtual servers most often in your day-to-day work lives, and prepping new servers in the virtual world is even easier.

Once our master server has been sysprepped and shut down, you simply create a copy of the `.VHDX` file. Log in to your Hyper-V Server, copy and paste the hard disk file, and you're done. This new file can be renamed `WS2022_Master_withUpdates.VHDX`, or whatever you would like it to be named, in order to help you keep track of the current status of this image file. Save this image file or copy of the `.VHDX` file somewhere safe on your network, where you will be able to quickly grab copies of it whenever you need to spin up a new Windows Server 2022.

Building new servers using copies of the master image

Now we get to the easy part. When you want to create new servers in the future, you simply copy and paste your master file into a new location for the new server, rename the drive file to something appropriate for the server you are creating, and boot your new virtual machine from it. Here is where you see the real benefit from the time that Sysprep saves, as you can now spin up many new servers all at the same time by doing a quick copy and paste of the master image file and booting all of your new servers from these new files. No need to install Windows or pull out that dusty installation DVD!

As the new servers turn on for the first time and boot into Windows, they will run through the out-of-box experience, mini-setup wizard. Also, in the background, the operating system gives itself a new random and unique hostname and SID information so that you can be sure you do not have conflicts on your network with these new servers.

New servers created from a sysprepped image file always receive a new hostname when they boot. This often confuses admins who might have named their master server something such as `MASTER`. After booting your new servers, you can expect to see randomized names on your new servers, and you will have to rename them according to their new duties in life.

For example, before running Sysprep and creating my master image, the server that I was working on was named `DC2` because I had originally intended to use it as a domain controller in my network. However, because I had not installed the role or configured anything domain-related on it, this server was a perfect candidate for displaying the Sysprep process, and so I used it in our text today. I sysprepped it, shut it down, made a copy of its `.VHDX` file (to be my master image file), and then I started `DC2` back up. You can now see inside the system properties that I am back to having a randomized hostname, and so if I still want to use this server as `DC2`, I will have to rename it again now that it has finished booting through the mini setup, as shown in *Figure 2.39*:

Figure 2.39: Randomized hostname following Sysprep

Hopefully, this process is helpful information that can save you time when building new servers in your own environments. Get out there and give it a try the next time you have a new server to build! You can further benefit from the Sysprep tool by keeping many different master image files. Perhaps you have a handful of different kinds of servers that you prep regularly—there is nothing stopping you from creating a number of different master servers and creating multiple master images from these servers.

In-place upgrading to Windows Server 2022

Before wrapping up this chapter, let's enter into this taboo topic. As technology consumers, we are very much used to the idea of in-place upgrades. In fact, we expect them to work flawlessly, and we whine and complain when they don't. iPhone operating systems, Android version updates, Windows feature pack installations, and even something like a Windows 7 to Windows 10 upgrade are all expected to work seamlessly after a couple of simple pushes of a button. Those of us who have worked in Windows Server administration for more than a few years do NOT have this same mindset about server upgrades. For so many years, it was normal that in-place Windows Server upgrades were almost guaranteed to tank your server, causing it to be useless in the end. Due to this, server upgrades almost always meant replacing the server rather than upgrading it. You would leave the production server running, spin up a new one in parallel, configure all of the roles and specs needed on that server, then plan an after-hours migration of data and apps to the new server so that the next morning, hopefully, everything was up and working on the new server. Then, you shut the old server down. This is normal; this is Windows Server upgrades.

Things have changed...

Starting with in-place upgrades from Server 2012R2 to Server 2016, it was suddenly possible to be successful with an in-place Windows Server upgrade. Not all the time, but sometimes. Since it was still sporadic, it was not commonly attempted, and we continued to stick to old methods of replacing servers. Then, Server 2019 came out, and in-place upgrades from 2016 to 2019 were actually quite stable, and you could even get away with upgrading 2012R2 straight to 2019 most of the time. Now that we are three years beyond the release of Server 2019, enough of us have accomplished numerous 2016 > 2019 upgrades that I now consider it to be comfortable territory.

Windows Server 2022 continues that trend. Windows Server operating system in-place upgrades are stable and introduce us to a much more efficient way to upgrade servers than the old rip-and-replace methods. Let's take a minute a prove this. On my Hyper-V host, where I run test labs, I have numerous Server 2022 VMs, but I still have many Server 2019 VMs sitting offline from previous projects.

I just finished joining one of those to my new lab network, and I will now attempt an in-place upgrade from Server 2019 to Server 2022.

Download and run the installer

Running the installer is pretty much all you need to do. Download or copy the .ISO installer files for Windows Server 2022 that you already have from earlier in this chapter to this older Server 2019, and double-click on the file to mount it. If you're using a virtual machine, all you need to do is visit the VM's settings and attach the .ISO to the VM, and it now appears as if the Server 2022 installation DVD is connected to this server. Double-click on that virtual disc and the Windows Server 2022 installation wizard will launch.

Figure 2.40: Starting an in-place upgrade to Server 2022

Very similar to upgrading client-side operating systems, you will encounter a couple of simple questions about whether or not you want to allow the installation wizard to automatically download updates during installation and whether you intend to keep the files that are already on this server or wipe them clean during the upgrade process. In addition to those normal options, you will also be asked whether you want to upgrade to Windows Server 2022 Standard or the (Desktop Experience) version. It is interesting that you could potentially take a 2019 Desktop Experience server and bring it straight to 2022 Server Core. I expect this option will be rarely utilized, and so most likely, you want to continue forward with a match to whatever your server is currently running. I am using the full GUI in a Server 2019 Desktop Experience configuration of Windows, so I will proceed with installing 2022 Desktop Experience.

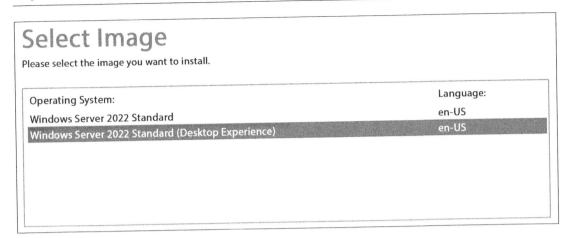

Figure 2.41: Operating system selection

That's it! Once those options have been decided upon, the installation process kicks off, and after a little bit of time and a few automated restarts of the server, you should find yourself back at a login screen of the same server with the same roles and files present, but now running the Windows Server 2022 operating system.

Summary

Anyone interested in being a Windows Server administrator needs to be comfortable with installing and managing their servers, and covering those topics establishes an important baseline for moving forward. It is quite common in today's IT world for new operating system releases to be thoroughly tested by companies before deploying them, both because server hardware resources are so easily available to us through virtualization technologies and because most business systems are now being designed for 100% uptime. This kind of reliability requires very thorough testing of any platform changes, and in order to accomplish such testing of the Windows Server 2022 operating system in your environment, you will burn quite a bit of time spinning through the basic installation processes numerous times. I hope that you can put the suggestions provided in this chapter to good use in saving you precious extra minutes when dealing with these tasks in your Windows Server world.

Years ago, quite a bit of effort was regularly put into figuring out which roles and services could co-exist because the number of servers available to us was limited. With the new virtualization and cloud paradigm shift, many companies have a virtually unlimited number of servers that can be running, and this means we are running much larger quantities of servers to perform the same jobs and functions. The management and administration of these servers then become an IT burden, and adopting the centralized administration tools and ideas available within Windows Server 2022 will also save you considerable time and effort in your daily workload. In the next chapter, we will start to dive into some of the most commonly used roles and tools in a Windows Server environment and the core infrastructure technologies surrounding Active Directory.

Questions

1. What is the name of the new web-based, centralized server management tool from Microsoft (fun fact, this toolset was formerly known as **Project Honolulu**)?

2. True or false—Windows Server 2022 needs to be installed onto rack-mount server hardware.

3. True or false—By choosing the default installation option for Windows Server 2022, you will end up with a user interface that looks quite like Windows 10.

4. What is the PowerShell cmdlet that displays currently installed roles and features in Windows Server 2022?

5. True or false—Server Manager can be used to manage many different servers at the same time.

6. What is the name of the toolset that can be installed onto a Windows 10 computer in order to run Server Manager on that client workstation?

7. Which built-in tool is used to prepare the Windows operating systems for imaging or replication?

Join our community on Discord

Join our community's Discord space for discussions with the author and other readers:

https://packt.link/SecNet

3

Active Directory

Each of you reading this book will have a different acquired skillset and level of experience with the Windows Server environment. As I mentioned previously, being able to make servers run the operating system is great and a very important first step for doing real work in your environment. But until you know and understand what the purposes behind the main roles available to run on Windows Server 2022 are, the only thing your new server does is consume electricity.

A server is intended to serve data. The kind of data that it serves and to what purpose depends entirely on what roles you determine the server must ... well ... serve. Appropriately, you must install roles within Windows Server 2022 to make it *do* something. We already know how to get roles installed onto our server but have not talked about any of the purposes behind these roles. Over the next few chapters, we will start looking into what I commonly refer to as the core infrastructural roles available within Windows Server. This involves discussing the role's general purpose, as well as plugging in some particular tasks dealing with those roles that you will be responsible for doing in your daily tasks as a server administrator.

We begin with the single most important role in all of the on-premise Microsoft world, **Active Directory**. **AD**, as it is commonly referred to, is a directory service that serves as a kind of database, storing and centralizing various types of information about your organization. User accounts, computer accounts, certificates, policies, DNS, and even file replication are all things that you can find hooked into AD.

As we look over the parts and pieces of AD, it will become clearer what information is stored within and why it is so important. If you are new to IT and do not yet have a good grasp of AD, make sure to learn this technology! AD is the hinge upon which almost everything in a Windows Server world revolves. Is it possible to utilize Windows servers without them being connected and joined to Active Directory? Yes. Is it likely you will ever find this scenario at play in the real world? No. In this chapter, we will learn the following:

- What is a domain controller?
- Creating your first domain
- Multiple domain controllers for redundancy
- Active Directory Users and Computers

- Active Directory Domains and Trusts
- Active Directory Sites and Services
- Active Directory Administrative Center
- Active Directory Recycle Bin
- Read-only domain controllers
- FSMO Roles
- Demote an old domain controller
- Group Policy

What is a domain controller?

If we are going to discuss the core infrastructure services that you need to piece together your Microsoft-driven network, there is no better place to start than with the domain controller. A **Domain Controller**, commonly referred to as a **DC**, is simply a server that is hosting Active Directory. It is a central point of contact, a central "hub" so to speak, that is accessed prior to almost any communication that takes place between a client and server in your network. Perhaps the easiest way to describe it is as a storage container for all *identification* that happens on the network. Usernames, passwords, computer accounts, groups of computers, servers, groups and collections of servers, security policies, file replication services, and many more things are stored within and managed by DCs. If you are not planning to have a DC be one of the first servers in your Microsoft-centric network, you might as well not even start building that network. DCs are essential to the way that our computers and devices communicate with each other and with the server infrastructure inside our companies.

Active Directory Domain Services

If you've stopped reading at this point to install the *Domain Controller* role onto your server, welcome back! There is no role called **Domain Controller**. The role that provides all of these capabilities is called **Active Directory Domain Services**, or **AD DS**. This is the role that you need to install on a server. By installing that role, you will have turned your server into a domain controller. The purpose of running a DC really is to create a directory, or database, of objects in your network. This database is known as **Active Directory**, and is a platform inside which you build a hierarchical structure to store objects, such as usernames, passwords, and computer accounts. You might be thinking, "didn't we just say these same words in a slightly different way?" and you're not wrong. AD is important, and I want to make sure you know it. A career in IT guarantees that you will in some way interface with AD in your work.

Most of the time when you hear anyone talking about "Active Directory" it is likely that what they really mean is a single **domain** within the directory. There is a whole hierarchy within an Active Directory schema, comprising forests, trees, domains, and organizational units. We will discuss each of these organizational levels of Active Directory as we navigate through the tools that you will be utilizing to interact with AD further along in this chapter.

Once you have created a domain in which you can store accounts, objects, and devices, you can then create user accounts and passwords for your employees to utilize for authentication. You can then also join your other servers and computers to this domain so that they can accept and benefit from those user credentials. Having and joining a domain is the secret sauce that allows you to walk from computer to computer within your company and log on to each of them with your own username and password, even when you have never logged in to that computer before. Even more powerful is the fact that it enables directory-capable applications to authenticate directly against Active Directory when they need authentication information. For example, when I, as a domain user, log in to my computer at work with my username and password, the Windows operating system running on my computer reaches out to a domain controller server and verifies that my password is correct.

Once it confirms that I really am who I say I am, it issues an authentication token back to my computer and I am able to log in. Then, once I am on my desktop and open an application – let's say I open my Outlook to access my email – that email program is designed to reach out to my email server, called an **Exchange Server**, and authenticate against it to make sure that my own mailbox is displayed and not somebody else's. Does this mean I need to re-enter my username and password for Outlook, or for any other application that I open from my computer? Generally not. And the reason I do not have to re-enter my credentials over and over again is that my username, my computer, and the application servers are all part of the same domain.

When this is true, and it is for most business networks, my authentication token can be shared among my programs. So, once I log in to the computer itself, my applications can launch and open, and pass my credentials through to the application server, without any further input from me as a user. It would be quite a frustrating experience indeed if we required our users to enter passwords all day, every day as they opened up the programs that they need in order to do their work.

Active Directory itself is a broad enough topic to warrant its own book, and indeed there have been many written on the topic. Now that we have a basic understanding of what it is and why it's critical to have in our Windows Server environment, let's get our hands dirty using some of the tools that get installed onto your domain controller during the AD DS role installation process.

Creating your first domain

I must admit that I have cheated a little bit and have already been working from within a domain for the purpose of taking screenshots for the book up to this point. My test lab already has a DC1 server up and running, and on it I have configured a domain called contoso.local. However, saying "domains are important" and not showing you how to create one would not be helpful to you, the reader, and so we are going to build a brand-new domain now, on a brand-new server.

You probably recognize "Contoso" if you've ever read over Microsoft tutorials or example configuration documentation, because it is one of several fake business names Microsoft uses often in documentation or for the purpose of showing example scenarios. I am using it here as well, but you could name your domain anything you want to. For setting up our second domain, I am going to pull another company name from the Microsoft hat, Fabrikam.

One of the first things that needs to be decided before you can build a domain is the name of the domain. We don't want to discuss DNS in depth here because there's another whole chapter for that, but everyone uses DNS every day whether they realize it or not. Every time that you type any website name – `microsoft.com`, `google.com`, `bing.com`, and so on – you are inputting a name, which DNS is then going to turn into an IP address. You also know that the ending of website names can take on many forms. Most common is `.com`, but you may visit websites that also end with `.org`, `.biz`, `.info`, `.tech`, `.edu`, `.mil`, and many more.

Let's take `microsoft.com` as an example. If you simply visit `microsoft.com`, you'll see the main website for the company. If you visit `learn.microsoft.com`, you will land on their documentation and learning platform page. Visiting `portal.microsoft.com` takes you to an Office 365 sign-in page, and if you have an Office 365 account you can sign in here and perform many functions. The different addresses you are typing into the web browser are taking you to vastly different web pages and systems, yet the domain names being called for in the browser all end with the same `microsoft.com`. This means that `microsoft.com` is the primary domain name for all of these things, also known as a **domain suffix** or a top-level domain.

Why am I running down this rabbit hole? Because this is important information to understand when you decide on your internal domain name. Just like a domain suffix on the internet, when you build your internal domain and then later join computers and servers to that domain, each of those devices is going to have a true, full name of *computername.domainname.something*. In my current domain, `contoso.local`, a full server name that exists right now is `DC1.contoso.local`.

Most internal domains that I have encountered in the world end with `.local`. Is it possible to name your internal domain something that ends in one of these internet-based suffixes, like `Contoso.com`? Yes! You can name your internal domain whatever you want, and in fact if you have plans to host email in Office 365, using an internal domain that matches your public domain name used for email carries some advantages. Some of you may be thinking at this point, "I already own contoso.com (insert your own business website name here), so wouldn't it be less confusing overall if I also name my internal domain the same thing? contoso.com?" The answer is yes and no. For certain scenarios that involve cloud resources, like Office 365 and Azure, yes, using a `.com` internal domain can make a more seamless transition to the cloud. However, prior to these cloud technologies it was always Microsoft's recommendation to end your internal domain with `.local`. We will talk more about why this is the case *in Chapter 4, DNS and DHCP*, when we discuss something called **split-brain DNS**.

Prep your domain controller

Okay, I have decided to use `fabrikam.local` as my internal domain name. Now, how do I make that a reality? We only need one server to build a domain, the server that you want to be your domain controller. I have a new Windows Server 2022 VM running and plugged into a network, but so far I have not configured anything at all on the server. There are three simple things that need to happen on any server that you plan to turn into a domain controller:

1. **Set a static IP address** – Head into your NIC properties and define a static IP address for this server. Even if you already have a DHCP server running in your network to hand out IP addresses, you do not want domain controller servers to ever change IPs. It is possible to do so, but quite challenging. So best practice dictates that whatever IP address you define for your DC, plan on that being its IP address forever.

2. **Set a good hostname** – Similar to IP addressing on a domain controller, it is not recommended to ever change the name of a DC server. In fact, this is quite a bit more complicated than IP addressing, and you should definitely plan that whatever name you give your server today will forever be its name on your network until the day you decommission this server entirely.

3. **Set the DNS server address** – Head back into your NIC properties and configure the DNS server address that your domain controller is looking for, to be itself. What? Itself? It's not a DNS server! Not yet, but other than pretty rare circumstances, almost every domain controller will also become a DNS server. DNS integrates with Active Directory and there is a lot of benefit to hosting these services together, so most Microsoft environments you encounter will have AD DS and DNS installed together on domain controller servers. Generally, when setting up your first DC, you will always start by pointing the NIC's DNS settings to the server's own IP address.

You can see in *Figure 3.1* that I have now named my new server FAB-DC1, configured a static IP, and pointed DNS to itself:

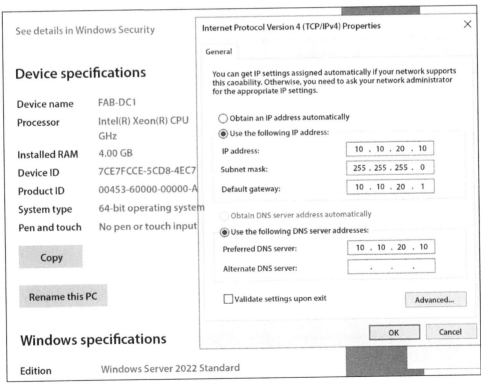

Figure 3.1: Prepping a server to become a DC

Install the AD DS role

Now that the server is prepped to be a domain controller, we install the role! Since you are already familiar with the process of adding roles to servers, we won't step through the whole thing again. Simply utilize Server Manager or PowerShell to install the following components onto your new server:

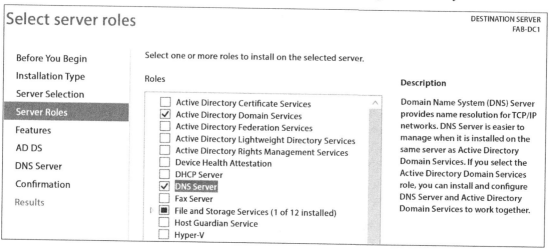

Figure 3.2: Installing AD DS and DNS Server roles

As mentioned, I am going to install **AD DS** for Active Directory, and **DNS Server** so that this domain controller can also serve as a true DNS server for our new business. As you progress through the role installation wizard, you will encounter some informational text that is useful to read over, but there should be no further options that you need to select in order to get both of these roles installed onto your server.

Configure the domain

Following the installation of the roles, you will notice a yellow exclamation mark near the top of Server Manager. Clicking on that icon, you can see text indicating that some configuration is required for the Active Directory Domain Services role:

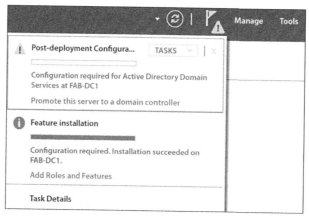

Figure 3.3: Additional configuration is required for the Active Directory Domain Services role

Click on the link that says **Promote this server to a domain controller**. This link will invoke the configuration wizard that is going to walk us through turning the server into a true DC.

Trees, forests, and...domains?

Wait a minute, the first screen we encounter in this promotion wizard where we need to make a decision is talking about shrubbery. What gives? You already know that a domain is like a database, containing information about many kinds of objects, but primarily user accounts and computer accounts that are part of that domain. What we have not really discussed yet is that a domain is not the top tier of its existence, rather a *domain resides within a forest*. These are the two technical terms you will run across when working within Active Directory, domain and forest, and references to a tree are more metaphorical, related to the layout of a forest with domains underneath the forest, with possible child domains listed beneath the domains. The whole schema when mapped out on paper may resemble the many branches of a tree, thus the term tree.

A forest is the top tier in Active Directory, and you could potentially have many different domains inside the same forest. Why would you want to do that? Most companies don't, and most of the time you will find that any given company has one internal domain, residing within one forest, and that's it.

One reason you may find multiple domains inside the same forest would be if the company had different divisions or business units that needed their authentication and systems to be separated from each other. In a single domain, remember that oftentimes any domain user can authenticate and log in to any domain computer, and perhaps you wanted to ensure that nobody in DivisionA was able to log in to computers that were owned by DivisionB. Creating multiple domains would be one way to accomplish that scenario.

As you walk through the domain configuration wizard that we have just launched on our new server, you will see many different options for what kind of domain controller this server may become. You may be adding a DC to an existing domain, adding a new domain to an existing forest, or creating a new forest altogether. Selecting each of these options in the wizard will present you with different sub-options related to that selection. If you click on **Add a new domain to an existing forest**, you will find that you then have options for creating a new child domain, or a tree domain. A child domain would be a new domain that exists under an existing domain in the hierarchical AD tree, while a tree domain would be a new domain that resides directly under the forest itself and would sit alongside any existing domains. Under the same forest but separated from any existing domains.

Today, we have nothing in this Fabrikam network. No forest, no domains, no child domains. So we are going to choose the third option, **Add a new forest**. All that needs to be decided on this screen is the **Root domain name**, which is where I will enter `fabrikam.local`, which we decided on earlier:

Deployment Configuration

TARGET SERVER
FAB-DC1

Deployment Configuration
Domain Controller Options
Additional Options
Paths
Review Options
Prerequisites Check
Instllation
Results

Select the deployment operation

◯ Add a domain controller to an existing domain
◯ Add a new domain to an existing forest
⦿ Add a new forest

Specify the domain information for this operation

Root domain name: fabrikam.local

Figure 3.4: Adding a new forest

The remaining screens in this configuration wizard contain a number of options, but not many of them need to be populated if you are unsure of the answers. Especially if you are building out a test lab, the default options are generally sufficient. We'll do a quick summary here of each screen to point out options and what they mean.

Domain controller options

Now that you understand that there are at least two tiers to every Active Directory, at minimum one forest and one domain, it is important to understand that each of those things has its own **functional level**. Forest and domain functional levels are classified by different versions of Windows Server operating system releases. Windows Server 2016 functional level has more features and accessories baked into it than Server 2012 R2 does, for example, and on and on. Something interesting to note is that Windows Server 2019 and 2022 do not have a new functional level, the newest you can select is Server 2016, even when establishing a brand new forest with a brand new Windows Server 2022 Domain Controller.

Why does the wizard even ask? Wouldn't it make sense that you would always want to select the newest from this list? In almost all cases, the answer is yes. One reason you may need to select an older functional level for either your forest or domain is if some technology you are planning to implement or some version of device you plan to join to that domain requires an older functional level version. This brings to light another valid scenario that might require a company to build a secondary domain under an existing forest, if a technology that you wanted to implement for the business carried some specific requirements that locked you into a certain version of functional level, but your primary production domain could not meet those requirements for whatever reason.

For our purposes today, we simply leave both forest and domain functional levels selected on the default Windows Server 2016.

On this screen of the wizard, you also have options to choose whether or not this domain controller will also be a DNS server (usually yes), whether it will be a Global Catalog server (also usually yes), or a read-only domain controller, which we will discuss later in this chapter.

The third option, and the only one that absolutely requires your attention, is to define a Directory Services Restore Mode password. I sincerely hope that you never have to enter Active Directory recovery mode in order to restore information or your directory, but if you do – this password is going to be very important to that process:

Figure 3.5: Domain Controller Options

DNS Options

If you were creating a new domain controller/DNS Server that was going to live inside an existing tree and particularly if your new server is going to play a child role, then you typically want to ensure that the parent's DNS zones have a delegation for this new DNS server you are creating, to ensure that names in your domain can be successfully resolved in the parent domain as well. The creation of that DNS delegation is the only option on this screen, and in cases where we are creating a brand-new forest and domain, there is no existing authoritative parent zone so there is an expected warning message on-screen:

Figure 3.6: Expected warning message regarding no authoritative parent zone

Since we are building a new forest, there is nothing we need to do with this warning message and we simply click **Next** to proceed.

Additional Options

The NetBIOS domain name should self-populate in the wizard and will be the first portion of your domain name. In my example, it has inserted the word FABRIKAM into this field. Many people seem to think that NetBIOS is obsolete, but it is still used by applications to pass traffic around in many cases, so the options for configuring it here are still important. You don't need to do anything on this screen other than to ensure a NetBIOS name populates in the wizard and continue on.

Paths

Active Directory stores quite a bit of very important information on your domain controller server. If desired, here you can specify paths for storing this data if you wanted it to reside in a special location, such as on a dedicated hard drive. The default options are all within the C:\Windows folder, which is generally where everyone leaves it.

Review Options, Prerequisites Check, Installation

That's it! You have now populated all the available options, and you are presented with a screen that allows you to review the selections you have made. Once satisfied that everything looks good on this screen, the wizard will run through a prerequisites check on your server to ensure it is ready to become a domain controller. This is the point where, if you forgot to assign a static IP or to set a DNS server in the NIC properties, the wizard will fail the prereq check and flag you with some warnings. In fact, you will likely see at least one or two warnings even if you have done everything perfectly: one regarding that DNS delegation that we already talked about and another warning about cryptography algorithms. This is normal behavior for configuring a brand new forest/domain on Windows Server 2022.

Assuming you have everything in order, the wizard will continue on to installation, at the end of which your server will reboot, and is now officially a domain controller for your network.

During the first login to your server, which is now a domain controller, you will notice at the login screen that you are now signing in with a domain account, no longer a local account on this server. Domain controllers don't actually have local user accounts anymore; if you were using the built-in administrator account to sign in to your server before, like I was, that account and password have now been converted into the domain administrator account. This account can now be used to log in to any computer or server that is later joined to your domain and will automatically receive administrative rights on that device. Make sure you're using a good domain administrator password, and don't share it with anybody!

Multiple domain controllers for redundancy

Now having configured our first domain controller, we should jump in and start setting up objects inside Active Directory, right? Not yet! I'm being a little dramatic here, of course you can jump ahead and start using the tools that interface with AD, which we will discuss immediately following this section of our chapter. But if you are setting up a real environment and not just monkeying around in a test lab, it is going to be super critical that you establish redundancy in your domain.

Adding a second domain controller is even easier than spinning up the first one. Simply take the same steps that you did last time, with one exception to the way that the NIC is configured:

1. Spin up a new server.
2. Set a static IP.
3. Configure a good permanent hostname.
4. Deviation from before: Instead of configuring your NIC's DNS server settings to point at the new server itself, point your primary DNS to the existing domain controller's IP address.

Now when you add the AD DS and DNS server roles and walk through the same configuration wizard that we just witnessed a few minutes ago, this time you are going to choose the option **Add a domain controller to an existing domain**. Then all you have to do is select or type the name of the domain and provide administrative credentials on that domain:

Figure 3.7: Adding a DC to an existing domain

The rest of the wizard is pretty straightforward, but you'll notice that you have a new drop-down menu on the **Domain Controller Options** screen that allows you to select a site name. If you had multiple AD sites, you would select here which site this new DC is being installed into. We will discuss more about Active Directory sites and services in a later section of this chapter. You will also notice that you have to once again create a password for Directory Services Restore Mode. This password is configured per domain controller, so it could potentially be different for each of your DC servers.

If you remember everything we have done so far, you will realize that right now both of our domain controller servers are pointing to FAB-DC1 as their primary DNS server, as defined inside the NIC properties. As long as each DC can contact a DNS server, your domain is going to function properly, but now that we have two DCs created for the purpose of redundancy, your overall solution will be made even better if you ensure that both domain controllers are aware of each other from a DNS perspective.

There are two different ways to go about this, both are considered to be good practice:

- Configure each domain controller to have a primary DNS server address of itself, and the secondary DNS server address to be the other DC. This causes DNS lookups on those servers to happen slightly faster but has the potential drawback that you might have to wait on Active Directory replication to happen between the two servers before newly created DNS records are available on both servers.

- Configure both (or all) of your domain controllers to use a single DNS server as the primary DNS server on your network, with themselves as the secondary DNS server. If all of your DCs are looking to a centralized DNS server, then any updates or additions you make to that DNS server are immediately available on all DCs. However, if that central DNS server goes offline, it will cause all other DCs some grief and delays as they have to realize that they now need to fail over to themselves for name resolution.

Whoops, I said there were two ways to do this, and generally you'll find that either option #1 or option #2 above are the way that DNS is configured in most environments. But there is a third possibility here that is sort of a mix between the two. You could configure each domain controller's NIC settings so that the primary DNS server is a different DNS server in your environment, and then make the secondary DNS server point back at itself. This causes DNS lookups to always be happening across the network, which generates more traffic than the other options but also ensures that each DC can stand on its own accord if the other one fails. In this third scenario, if there were two DCs in the network, you are basically just pointing them at each other, while using themselves as a backup.

I can't tell you what is best for your own environment, but what I do most of the time is configure each DC to have itself as the primary DNS server, and just realize that whenever I create new DNS records it might take a few minutes for them to replicate between the DCs.

When you configure a domain controller to point at itself for primary DNS, it is generally recommended to utilize the localhost IP address 127.0.0.1, rather than the DC's actual IPv4 address.

One more important note on the topic of populating DNS server information into the NIC properties of your domain controller servers. NEVER CONFIGURE DCs TO POINT AT PUBLIC DNS SERVERS. Plugging 8.8.8.8 or something similar into a NIC's DNS settings is a common thing to do for internet-connected **home computers**. Not for servers. Do not carry this mentality into your business. Your domain controllers must register special records within Active Directory, and pointing a DC's NIC at a public DNS server will cause that process to fail.

I have actually had to clean up this mess, caused by that exact scenario – a company was having some internet connectivity troubles, and as part of troubleshooting, an IT person decided to replace the actual DNS server information inside the NIC properties of every server in the network with 8.8.8.8. Let's just say that didn't work out very well.

Active Directory Users and Computers

There is not a single tool that is used to manage all facets of Active Directory. Since it is such an expansive technology, our configuration of the directory is spread across a number of different management consoles. Let's take a look at each of them, and a couple of the most common tasks that you will be performing inside these tools. Any of these management consoles can be launched from any of your domain controller servers, and just as we saw in a previous chapter, the easiest way to launch these consoles is right from the **Tools** menu in the upper-right corner of Server Manager.

I'll start with the tool that is alphabetically last in the list of our Active Directory tools, because this is by far the one that the everyday server administrator will use most often. AD Users and Computers is the console from which all of the user accounts and computer accounts are created and managed. Open it up, and you will see the name of your domain listed in the left-hand column. Expand your domain name, and you will see a number of folders listed here. If you are opening this on an existing domain controller in a well-grown network, you may have pages and pages of folders listed here. If this is a new environment, there are only a handful. The most important pieces to point out here are **Computers** and **Users**. As common sense would dictate, these are the default containers in which new computer accounts and user accounts that join the domain will be located.

While this window looks quite a bit like File Explorer with a tree of folders, these *folders* really aren't folders at all. Most of the manila-colored folder icons that you see here are known as **Organizational Units (OUs)**. I say *most of* because there are a few containers that exist out of the box that are legitimate storage containers for holding objects, but they are not official OUs. The ones we pointed out earlier, **Users** and **Computers**, are actually these generic storage containers and are not traditional organizational units. However, any new folders that you create for yourself inside AD are going to be OUs. The difference is depicted in the manila folder icon. You can see in the upcoming screenshots that some of the manila folders have an extra little graphic on top of the folder itself. Only those folders that have the extra little yellow thing are real OUs.

OUs are the structural containers that we use inside Active Directory in order to organize our objects and keep them all in useful places. Just like with folders on a file server, you can create your own hierarchy of organizational units here, in order to sort and manipulate the location inside Active Directory of all your domain-joined network objects and devices. In the following screenshot, you can see that instead of having just a plain **Users** and **Computers** folder, I have created some new OUs including subcategories (more officially known as **nested OUs**) so that as I grow my environment, I will have a more structured and organized directory:

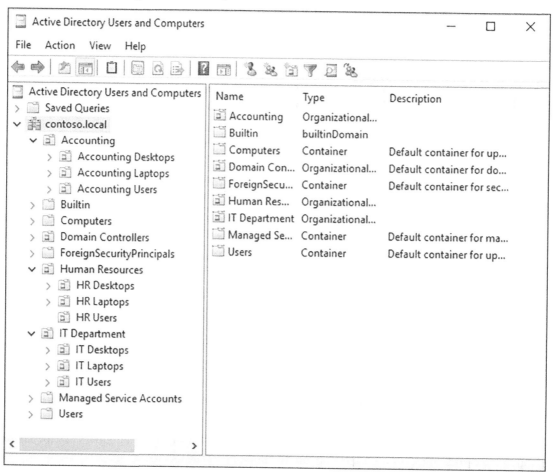

Figure 3.8: Active Directory structure

User accounts

Now that we have some OUs ready to contain our objects, let's create a new user. Say we have a new server administrator coming onboard, and we need to get him an Active Directory login so that he can start his job. Simply find the appropriate OU for his account to reside within, right-click on the OU, and navigate to **New | User**. We are then presented with an information-gathering screen about all the things that AD needs in order to create this new account. Most of the information here is self-explanatory, but if you are new to Active Directory, the one field I will point out is **User logon name**. Whatever information is put in this field is the user's official **username** on the network. Whenever they log in to a computer or server, this is the name they will input as their login.

When finished, our new admin can utilize the new username and password to log in to computers and servers on the network, within the security boundaries we have established on those machines, of course. But that is another topic for another chapter:

Figure 3.9: Creating a new Active Directory user

Security groups

Another useful unit of organization inside Active Directory is **security groups**. We can do quite a bit to distinguish between different types and kinds of users and computer accounts using organizational units, but what about when we need a little cross-contamination in this structure? Perhaps we have an employee that handles some HR and some accounting responsibilities. File and folder permissions on our file servers are typically managed by individualized or group-based access to read and write into particular folders. Susie from HR needs to have access to the payroll folder, but Jim from HR does not.

Both Susie and Jim reside inside the same OU, so at that level, they will have the same permissions and capabilities, but we clearly need a different way to distinguish between them so that only Susie gets access to payroll information. By creating security groups inside Active Directory, we grant ourselves the ability to add and remove specific user accounts, computer accounts, or even other groups so that we can granularly define access to our resources. You create new groups in the same way that you create user accounts, by choosing the OU where you want the new group to reside, and then right-clicking on that OU and navigating to **New | Group**. Once your group has been created, right-click on it and head into **Properties**. You can then click on the **Members** tab; this is where you add in all of the users that you want to be a part of this new group:

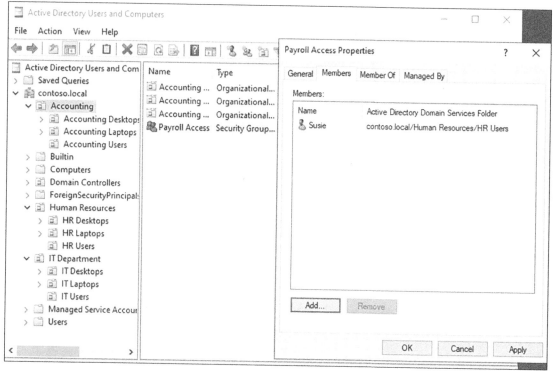

Figure 3.10: Creating a new group

Prestaging computer accounts

It is very common to utilize Active Directory Users and Computers for creating new user accounts because without the manual creation of a user account, that new person is going to be completely unable to log in on your network. It is far less common, however, to think about opening this tool when joining new computers to your domain. This is because most domains are configured so that new computers are allowed to join the domain by actions performed on the computer itself, without any work being done inside Active Directory beforehand. In other words, as long as someone knows a username and password that has administrative rights within the domain, they can sit down at any computer connected to the network and walk through the domain-join process on that local computer. In fact, in many domains you don't even need administrative rights to join a machine to a domain.

By taking a few steps on the computer, you can easily join it to the domain, and Active Directory will create a new computer object for it automatically. These autogenerating computer objects place themselves inside the default **Computers** container, so in many networks, if you click on that `Computers` folder, you will see a number of different machines listed, and they might even be a mix of both desktop computers and servers that were recently joined to the domain and haven't been moved to an appropriate, more specific OU yet. In my growing lab environment, I recently joined several machines to the domain. I did this without ever opening **Active Directory Users and Computers**, and you can see that my new computer objects are still sitting inside that default **Computers** container:

Figure 3.11: Active Directory's default Computers container

Allowing new computer accounts to place themselves inside the default **Computers** container is generally not a big problem for client systems, but if you allow servers to be autogenerated in that folder, it can cause you big issues. Many companies have security policies in place across the network, and these policies are often created in a way that they will be automatically applied to any computer account residing in one of the generalized OUs. Using security policies can be a great way to lock down parts of client machines that the user doesn't need to access or utilize, but if you inadvertently cause these **lockdown** policies to apply to your new servers as soon as they join the domain, you can effectively break the server before you even start configuring it. Trust me, I've done it. And unfortunately, your new server objects that get added to Active Directory will be identified and categorized the same as any client workstation that is added to the domain, so you cannot specify a different default container for servers simply because they are a server and not a regular workstation.

So, what can be done to alleviate this potential problem? The answer is to **prestage** the domain accounts for your new servers. You can even prestage all new computer accounts as a matter of principle, but I typically only see that requirement in large enterprises. Prestaging a computer account is very much like creating a new user account. Prior to joining the computer to the domain, you create the object for it inside Active Directory. By accomplishing the creation of the object before the domain-join process, you get to choose which OU the computer will reside in when it joins the domain. You can then ensure that this is an OU that will or will not receive the security settings and policies that you intend to have in place on this new computer or server. I highly recommend prestaging all computer accounts in Active Directory for any new servers that you bring online. If you make it a practice, even if it's not absolutely required all the time, you will create a good habit that may someday save you from having to rebuild a server that you broke simply by joining it to your domain.

Prestaging a computer object is extremely fast and simple; let's do one together. In the future, I plan to build a Windows Server that hosts the Remote Access role to connect my roaming users into the network from their homes, coffee shops, and so on. Some components in the Remote Access role are finicky when it comes to network security policies, and so I would rather ensure that my new RA1 server will not receive a whole bunch of lockdown settings as soon as I join it to the domain. I have created an OU called **Remote Access Servers**, and I will now prestage a computer object inside that OU for my RA1 server.

Right-click on the **Remote Access Servers** OU and choose **New | Computer**. Then simply populate the **Computer name** field with the name of your server. Even though I have not built this server yet, I plan to name it RA1, so I simply type that into the field:

Figure 3.12: Prestaging a computer inside an OU

That's it! With a couple of simple mouse clicks and typing in one server name, I have now prestaged (pre-created) my computer object for the RA1 server. If you look closely at the previous screenshot, you will notice that you could also adjust which users or groups are allowed to join this particular computer to the domain. If you plan to build a new server and want to make sure that you are the only person allowed to join it to the domain, this field is easily updated to accommodate that requirement.

Once I actually get around to building that server, and I go ahead and walk through the steps of joining it to my domain, Active Directory will realize that the name of my new server matches an object already in Active Directory, and will associate my new server with this prestaged RA1 object instead of creating a brand new object inside the generic **Computers** container:

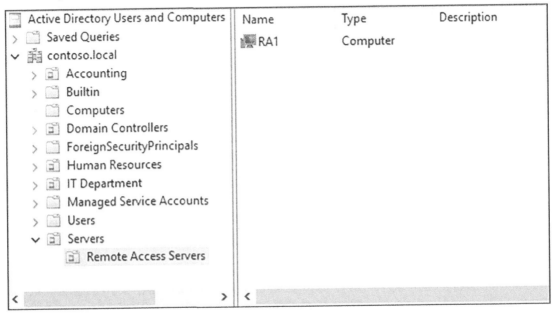

Figure 3.13: RA1's AD object is now prestaged

Active Directory Domains and Trusts

This tool is generally only used in larger environments that have more than one domain within the same network. As we discussed earlier, a company may utilize multiple domain names to segregate resources or services, or for the better organizational structure of their servers and namespaces within the company. You already know the differences between a domain and a forest and how the domain resides within the forest. Another way to think of the forest is as the boundary of your AD structure. If you have multiple domains beneath a single forest, it does not necessarily mean that those domains trust each other. So, users from one domain may or may not have permission to access resources on one of the other domains, based on the level of trust that exists between those domains. When you have a domain and are adding child domains under it, there are trusts placed automatically between those domains, but if you need to merge some domains together in a way other than the default permissions, **Active Directory Domains and Trusts** is the management tool you use to establish and modify those trust relationships.

Growing organizations often find themselves in a position where they need to regularly manage domain trusts as a result of business acquisitions. If Contoso acquires Fabrikam, and both companies have fully functional domain environments, it is often advantageous to work through an extended migration process to bring the Fabrikam employees over to Contoso's Active Directory, rather than suffer all the loss associated with simply turning off Fabrikam's network. So, for a certain period of time, you would want to run both domains simultaneously, and could establish a trust relationship between those domains in order to make that possible.

If you find yourself in a position where a domain migration of any sort is necessary, there is a tool available that you may want to try out. It is called the **Active Directory Migration Tool** (**ADMT**) and can be very useful in situations like the one described earlier. If you are interested in taking a closer look at this tool, you can download it from the following link: `https://www.microsoft.com/en-us/download/details.aspx?id=19188`.

Building a trust

Earlier I mentioned that I already had domain controllers and a whole test lab network built out for `contoso.local`, and in this chapter we built out a new `fabrikam.local` domain. These domains are not associated with each other in any way, they are completely separated forests. As such, a user account in one domain would absolutely not be able to log in to any machine that is joined to the other domain.

Let's change that. We are going to use Active Directory Domains and Trusts to establish a two-way trust relationship between these domains, which will enable exactly that scenario – users from `contoso.local` will be able to log in to computers joined to `fabrikam.local`, and vice versa. It is possible to establish either one-way or two-way trusts. Most commonly in the wild I see two-way trusts because it enables more information to flow between the two domains, and in the case of an acquisition, that is most often what we are looking to accomplish. If there was a need for this trust to only flow in one direction, for example allowing `contoso.local` accounts to log in to `fabrikam.local` machines but not allow Fabrikam employees to sign in to Contoso equipment, that would be possible with a one-way trust.

There are three components to building a successful trust relationship:

- Network connectivity
- Conditional DNS forwarding
- Configuring the trust

Network connectivity

The first one is common sense, those domains need to be able to talk to each other! If you have acquired a company and their servers are in a different physical location, you will likely need to build out some form of site-to-site VPN connectivity between the two physical sites.

In my test lab, I do have Contoso and Fabrikam servers IP addressed into separate subnets, but they are all part of one test lab network, so they already can communicate with each other at a TCP/IP level.

Make sure that you can get packets back and forth between the domain controllers, in both directions, before proceeding with the remaining steps of the trust build.

Conditional DNS forwarding

We haven't done anything in the DNS management console to this point, but it is installed on all of our DCs. Our next chapter is going to cover many more items related to the management of DNS itself, but for now we will need to utilize DNS management and make a change inside each domain. Currently, if I were to log in to a Contoso workstation and ping `fabrikam.local`, or if I signed in to a Fabrikam computer and tried ping `contoso.local` – either of these functions would fail completely, because the two domains have no idea that those DNS namespaces are supposed to resolve to DNS servers in those domains.

To bring name resolution full circle between the two domains, I need to set up conditional forwarding inside each domain.

I log in to DC1, one of my domain controllers for `contoso.local`, and launch the **DNS Manager** tool from Server Manager's **Tools** menu. Once you're inside, beneath my server name there is a folder called **Conditional Forwarders**. If I right-click on that folder, I can then select the option to create a **New Conditional Forwarder...**:

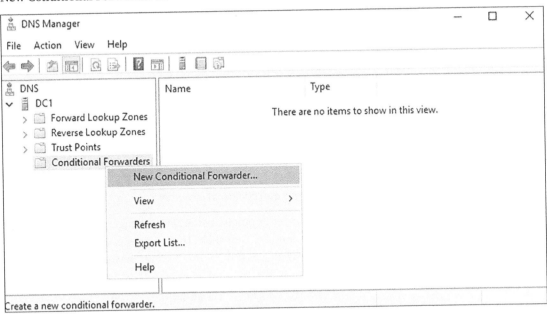

Figure 3.14: Creating a new conditional forwarder

Next, enter the remote domain name that you are trying to contact into the **DNS Domain** field. Then populate the IP addresses of the DNS servers within that other domain. The screen should be able to take your IP address and query the remote server to discover the server FQDN of that server. I also generally select the checkbox to **Store this conditional forwarder in Active Directory**, so that all of my AD-enabled DNS servers can perform this forwarding. Here are the selections I have made within my contoso.local DNS server, which then tells it how to reach out and talk to fabrikam.local:

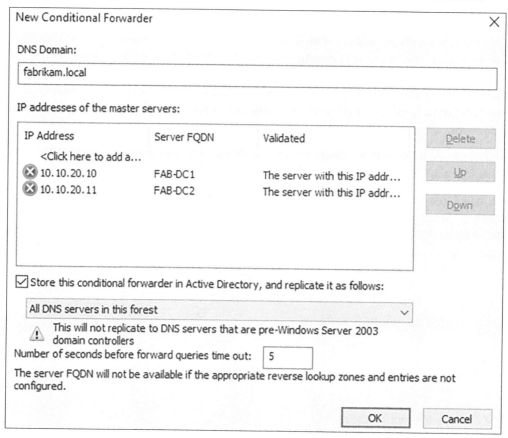

Figure 3.15: Configuring the conditional forwarder

You should now see the new conditional forwarder populate inside DNS Manager, and if you pull up Command Prompt and try to ping the remote domain, fabrikam.local in my case, you can see that name resolution for that remote domain is now successful, where it would have failed prior to our conditional forwarder being created:

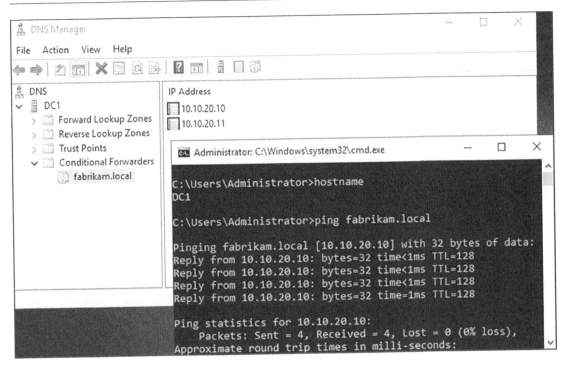

Figure 3.16: Successfully pinging fabrikam.local from a contoso.local server

Do it again!

We have now created a conditional forwarder from contoso.local toward fabrikam.local, but remember that we want to establish a two-way trust, and so we now must configure the same type of forwarder inside the fabrikam.local domain, pointing back at contoso.local's domain controllers. Follow the same steps above to create the second conditional forwarder. Once I complete that step, name resolution is successfully working cross-domain, and I am now ready to configure the trust.

Configuring the trust

VPN or other forms of connectivity between the two domains: Check

Conditional forwarding set up between the two domains: Check

Time to create a trust!

Log in to one of your domain controllers, I am going to use DC1.contoso.local, and launch **Active Directory Domains and Trusts**. Once inside, you should see the name of your domain listed in the left window pane. Right-click on the name of your domain and select **Properties**. Inside **Properties** for your domain, you will see the second tab is called **Trusts**. Go ahead and choose this tab, and at the bottom there is a button to create a **New Trust…**. You can see this screen and button in *Figure 3.17*.

There are a few options for naming your trust, but when creating a trust between two forests, as we are today, you want to specify the full DNS name of the remote forest to which you are connecting. In my example, I am creating this trust from inside the contoso.local domain, so I am going to specify fabrikam.local on this screen, as seen here:

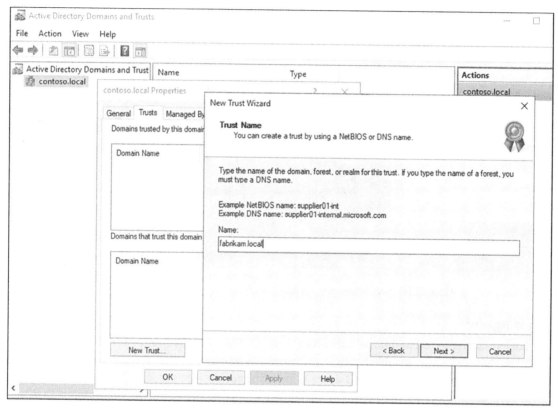

Figure 3.17: Creating a new trust

Now you will encounter a few screens that present various options about how this new trust is to be established. You can create a trust based on domains or forests (**External trust** or **Forest trust**), you can create this as a two-way trust or a one-way trust in either direction, and you can decide to allow authentication to happen forest-wide or to be more selective. There are good descriptions of what each of these options means right inside the wizard interface as you progress, but what I am interested in establishing today is a total two-way transitive trust between contoso.local and fabrikam.local, so I am selecting the following options:

- **Forest trust**
- **Two-way**
- **This domain only**
- **Forest-wide authentication**

A trust password – you can specify anything you want as the trust password, the important part is that you remember it because you will have to enter the same trust password again when you move over to your second forest or domain, and walk through these steps again to create the other side of the trust.

Figure 3.18 summarizes the selected settings:

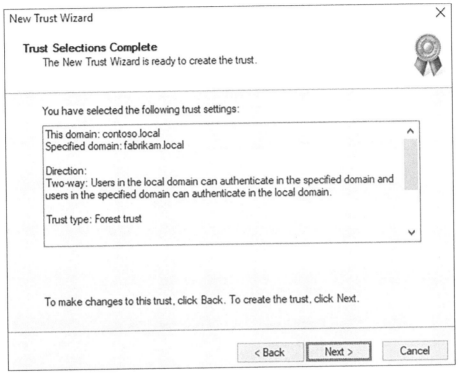

Figure 3.18: Summary of trust settings

The last step of the wizard is whether or not you want to confirm the outgoing trust. Since at this point we have only created one side of the trust, remember we still need to visit `fabrikam.local`'s domain controller and set up the other side of the trust; at this point we do not want to confirm the outgoing trust because the trust setup is not yet complete.

Now that one side of the trust is established in contoso.local, log in to a domain controller in fabrikam.local and walk through the same setup process. Once complete, you now have a complete, two-way transitive trust configured between your two forests:

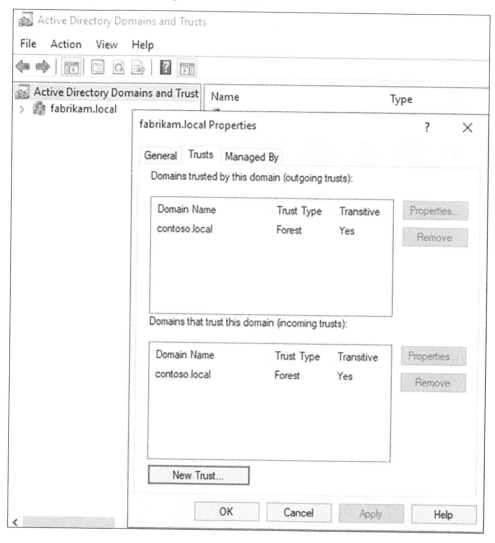

Figure 3.19: Two-way trust completed

Test it out!

We have a trust. Great! Now, what can we do with it? Remember that trusts are all about allowing cross-authentication to happen between domains. You should now be able to hop onto a computer in either domain and log in to it with a user account from the other domain (assuming there is nothing in your network that is restricting logins such as this). Another quick and easy test is to try setting up a file share, which is a very common thing to share back and forth across multiple domains. Set up a folder on any server in one domain and share it as you would with any folder. Now visit the **Security** tab to set some NTFS permissions on this folder.

When you click the **Add...** button to include more permissions on this screen, it of course defaults to the domain that this server is joined to. However, if you click on the **Locations...** button you now have the ability, **only because the trust exists,** to specify your remote domain as the location you are searching, and you are then able to add user accounts or groups to your folder share permissions from that remote domain, granting those users access to your shared folder. You can see in *Figure 3.20* that my Share1 folder is now allowing permissions for groups in both the CONTOSO domain and the FABRIKAM domain:

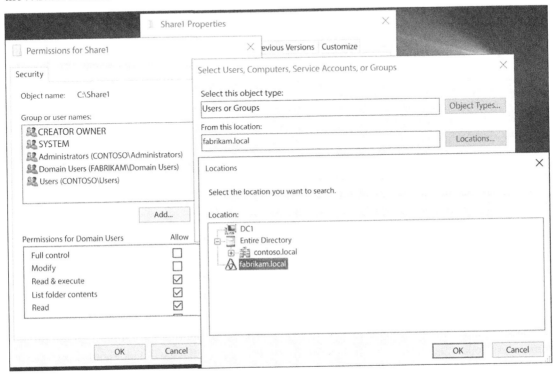

Figure 3.20: Share1 folder permissions reflect both domains

Active Directory Sites and Services

Sites and Services is another tool that is generally only employed by companies with larger Active Directory infrastructures. As is the case with any server, if having one domain controller is good, then having two domain controllers is even better. As your company grows larger, so does your Active Directory infrastructure. Before you know it, you will be looking into setting up servers in a second location, then a third, and so on. In a domain-centric network, having domain controller servers in each significant site is a general practice, and you could soon be looking at dozens of domain controller servers running in your network.

Turning on new domain controllers and joining them to your existing domain so that they start servicing users and computers is pretty easy. The harder part is keeping all of the traffic organized and flowing where you want it to. If you have a primary datacenter where the majority of your servers are located, you probably have multiple DCs onsite in that datacenter. In fact, to make your AD highly available, it is essential that you have at least two domain controllers. But let's pretend you then build a new office that is quite large, where it makes sense to install a local DC server in that office so that the computers in that office aren't reaching over the **Wide Area Network (WAN)** to authenticate all the time. If you were to spin up a server in the new office and turn it into a domain controller for your network, it would immediately start working. The problem is that the client computers aren't always smart enough to know which DC they need to talk to. You may now have computers in the remote office that are still authenticating back to the main datacenter's DCs. Even worse, you probably also have computers in the main office that are now reaching over the WAN to authenticate with the new DC that is in the remote office, even though there are DCs right on the local network with them!

This is the situation where Active Directory Sites and Services become essential. In here, you build out your different physical sites and assign the domain controllers to these sites. Domain-joined users and computers within this network now follow the rules that you have put into place via Sites and Services, so that they are always talking to and authenticating from their local domain controller servers. This saves time, as the connections are faster and more efficient, and it also saves unnecessary bandwidth and data consumption on the WAN, which often saves you dollars.

Here's a look into Active Directory Sites and Services. As you can see, there are multiple sites listed here, and they correspond to network subnet information. This is the way that AD Sites and Services tracks which site is which. When a client computer comes online, it obviously knows what subnet it is part of, based on the IP address it is using. AD Sites and Services then knows, based on that IP address, which site the client now resides in.

That site identification then helps Active Directory to steer authentication requests to the proper domain controllers, and also helps things like Group Policy (which we will talk about shortly) to be able to process site-specific information. There is a good chance you will have to make use of this tool someday if you are part of a growing organization. Adding new objects into AD Sites and Services is about as easy as it gets. Configure all of your sites by simply right-clicking on the **Sites** folder and then choosing **New Site**. You can name your sites anything you like.

Once all sites are placed inside AD Sites and Services, you add your subnets in a similar fashion, by right-clicking on the **Subnets** folder and choosing **New Subnet**. When you create a new subnet, you plug in the identifying network information about that subnet, and the bottom of the screen allows you to select which site the subnet resides within. You can see that process in *Figure 3.21*, as well as a look into my sample AD Sites and Services that is now populated with multiple sites and multiple subnets:

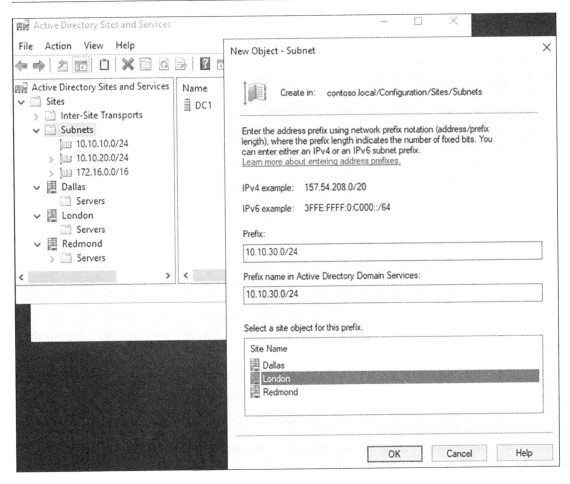

Figure 3.21: Defining subnets in AD Sites and Services

Active Directory Administrative Center

While it is critical to understand and be familiar with the tools we have looked at so far that help us manage Active Directory, you can tell that their aesthetics are a bit dated. The **Active Directory Administrative Center** (**ADAC**), on the other hand, has a much more streamlined interface that looks and feels like the newer Server Manager that we are all becoming more and more comfortable with. Many of the functions available within the ADAC accomplish the same things that we can do through the other tools already, but it pulls these functions into a more structured interface that brings some of the most commonly utilized functions up to the surface and makes them easier to run.

One great example is right on the landing page of ADAC. A common helpdesk task in any network is the resetting of passwords for user accounts. Whether the user forgot their password, changed it recently and mistyped it, or you are resetting a password during some other sort of troubleshooting, resetting a password for a user account typically involves numerous mouse clicks inside AD Users and Computers to get the job done. Now, there is a quick link called **RESET PASSWORD**, shown right there on the main page of the ADAC. Also useful is the **GLOBAL SEARCH** feature right next to it, where you can type anything into the search field, and it will scour your entire directory for results relating to your search. This is another common task in AD that previously required multiple clicks to accomplish:

Figure 3.22: Useful tools inside ADAC

If you click on the name of your domain in the left navigational tree, you will dive a little deeper into the capabilities of ADAC. As you can see, the information listed here is being pulled from Active Directory and looks like the same information you would see in AD Users and Computers. That is correct, except instead of having to right-click for every function, such as new user creations or searches, you now have some quick **Tasks** available on the right that can quickly launch you into accomplishing these functions. Also interesting are the links for raising the forest or domain functional level on this screen.

In order to do this using the classic tools, I see that most admins accomplish this by launching AD Domains and Trusts. So, one of the big benefits of the newer ADAC tool is that it is capable of giving you a centralized management window from which you can accomplish tasks that would normally have taken multiple windows and management consoles. Do you sense a common theme throughout Windows Server 2022 with the centralized management of everything?

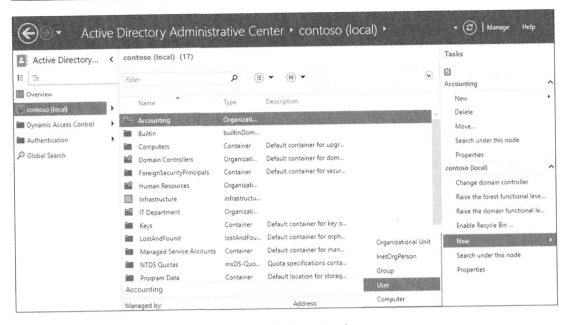

Figure 3.23: ADAC user interface

Dynamic Access Control

In addition to teaching old dogs new tricks, ADAC also brings some new functionality to the table that is not available anywhere in the classic tools. If you once again take a look at the tree to the left, you will see that the next section in the list is **Dynamic Access Control (DAC)**. This is a technology that is all about the security and governance of your files and the company data that you need to hold onto tightly, making sure it doesn't fall into the wrong hands. DAC gives you the ability to tag files, thereby classifying them for particular groups or uses. Then you can create access control policies that define who has access to these particular tagged files. Another powerful feature of DAC is the reporting functionality. Once DAC is established and running in your environment, you can do reporting and forensics on your files, such as finding a list of the people who have recently accessed a classified document.

DAC can also be used to modify users' permissions based on what kind of device they are currently using. If our user Susie logs in with her company desktop on the network, she should have access to those sensitive HR files. On the other hand, if she brings her personal laptop into the office and connects it to the network, we might not want to allow access to these same files, even when providing her domain user credentials, simply because we do not control the security on that laptop. These kinds of distinctions can be made using the Dynamic Access Control policies.

Fine-Grained Password Policy

Just about anyone who has ever had to use a Windows computer as part of employment at a business is familiar with the requirement to "reset your password every x number of days." In a Microsoft Active Directory environment, there are a few different ways that you can enforce password policies that require a certain password length, set complexity requirements on that password, and defining maximum ages for passwords, which result in users needing to reset their passwords every so often. Many times passwords need to be updated every 30 days or so.

The most common and certainly easiest place to define a password policy is by using Group Policy. We will cover this in more detail as we talk about the Default Domain Policy in *Chapter 5, Group Policy*, but that policy is going to apply one set of password requirements settings to *all* of the users in your domain, bar none. What if your needs are slightly more complex? For example, maybe you require a complex password that needs to be changed every 30 days for all of your office staff, but you manage IT for a manufacturing company that also has some shared computers out on the shop floor. These computers log in with domain accounts so that you can effectively push policies to them and grant permissions at the domain level, but you don't need these shop floor logins to have the same complexity on their passwords, nor do you care about those passwords changing since they are only ever used inside the network.

Enter the **Fine-Grained Password Policy**. Such a policy meets those expanded needs to a "T" by allowing you to configure differing password policies for different groups of people inside Active Directory. We are actually going to build a fine-grained password policy in *Chapter 9, Hardening and Security*, so we'll have to wait on the details until then. The reason I mention it here is that the creation of a fine-grained password policy requires the use of Active Directory Administrative Center, so we will be working within this newer console to create the policy.

Active Directory Recycle Bin

Speaking of technologies that are configured from inside Active Directory Administrative Center, and in this case one that can save you a lot of heartburn, let's discuss the Active Directory Recycle Bin. As the name implies, this is a container into which objects that are deleted from Active Directory move before they are permanently deleted. Anyone who has worked on a helpdesk knows about user termination tickets, those often mundane tasks that need to be accomplished on a semi-regular basis. In many cases, those former employee user accounts are deleted from Active Directory to keep things clean. However, many of you who have worked on a helpdesk for a considerable amount of time also know that companies tend to hire the same people back, sometimes within mere days of their departure. Depending on the infrastructure of the business you are supporting, perhaps re-creating the user account from scratch is no big deal, but it is becoming more and more problematic with things like Azure Active Directory synchronization and immutable IDs. In these cases, boy would it be nice if we had an "oops" button we could click to bring the formerly deleted user account back to life.

Enter the AD Recycle Bin. That is exactly the capability provided by this tool. The only trouble? It's not enabled by default. Let's go ahead and enable it together, and test it out.

Open ADAC and click on the name of your domain in the left-hand list. Then glance over at the right side of your screen, and sitting right there is a button to **Enable Recycle Bin....**

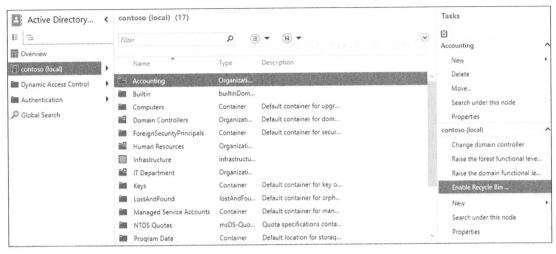

Figure 3.24: Enabling the AD Recycle Bin

Click this task, and you are presented with a simple selection. You should encounter a dialog box that states "Are you sure you want to perform this action? Once Recycle Bin has been enabled, it cannot be disabled." Seems pretty straightforward, if you are ready to make this move in your environment, go ahead and click on the OK button. When you do this, Active Directory is updated to reflect the change, and it may take a few minutes for this to activate on all of your Domain Controller servers. After letting it sit and bake for a while, close and re-launch your ADAC window, and click on the name of your domain again. If you look closely, you will now find a new folder listed in the middle pane called **Deleted Objects.**

This did not exist before you enabled the AD Recycle Bin. My **Deleted Objects** folder is currently empty, but I will go ahead and delete our test account for Susie, and then check inside. After deleting Susie's account, and then double-clicking on that folder called **Deleted Objects**, I can easily find my deleted account for Susie, and from here simply right-click on it and choose to **Restore.**

Figure 3.25: Restoring a user account from AD Recycle Bin

By taking this simple action, my user account for Susie is restored directly into the same HR Users OU that she was part of before, with preexisting user account configuration intact. This is so much faster than re-creating a new account and trying to make sure it has all of the original configuration!

Read-only domain controllers

The first domain controller you set up in your network will be a fully writable one, able to accept data from the domain-joined users and computers working within your network. In fact, most DCs in your network will likely be fully functional and writeable. However, it's worth taking a quick minute to point out a limited-scope DC that can be installed called a **Read-Only Domain Controller (RODC)**. Just like the name implies, an RODC can only have its directory data read from it. Writes that might try to be accomplished to the domain from a user's computer, such as a password change or new user account creation, are impossible with an RODC. Instead, RODCs receive their directory data from other more traditional domain controllers and then utilize that data to verify authentication requests from users and computers. Where would a limited-access domain controller like this be beneficial? Many companies are installing them in smaller branch offices or less secure sites so that the local computers onsite in those smaller offices have quick and easy access to read from and authenticate to the domain without the potential security risk of an unauthorized user gaining access to the physical server and manipulating the entire domain in bad ways. Another valid use-case for an RODC is within a DMZ, a protected network where you would typically never dream of installing a full domain controller because a DMZ network is all about access restriction and keeping internal network information safe.

Configuration of a read-only domain controller is not a totally disparate process, consisting of yet another role or feature, but simply a different option to select when running through the standard installation process of the AD DS role, which we have already worked with a number of times throughout this chapter. In fact, let's set one up right now. I just created a new VM in my environment and have given it an IP address and hostname. After installing the AD DS role as I have done with other domain controllers in my environment already, I am now going to the configuration wizard that helps me promote this server to be a domain controller.

Since I am adding another DC to an existing domain, the first selection is pretty straightforward. It is when we come to the **Domain Controller Options** screen where we make a deviation from the way we have run through this wizard in the past. You see that little checkbox that says **Read only domain controller (RODC)**? Go ahead and check that box:

Domain Controller Options

Deployment Configuration

Domain Controller Options

RODC Options

Additional Options

Paths

Review Options

Prerequisites Check

Installation

Results

Specify domain controller capabilities and site information

☐ Domain Name System (DNS) server
☐ Global Catalog (GC)
☑ Read only domain controller (RODC)

Site name: Redmond ▾

Type the Directory Services Restore Mode (DSRM) password

Password: ●●●●●●●●

Confirm password: ●●●●●●●●

Figure 3.26: Defining a new DC as an RODC

After clicking **Next** on this screen, you are now presented with new options, which we have never seen before, on a screen entitled **RODC Options**. Most interestingly here is that fields exist from which we can define which user accounts, or groups of user accounts, are allowed or denied permission to replicate their passwords to RODCs. There are objects pre-defined in these fields. Take particular note of two Active Directory groups called **Allowed RODC Password Replication Group** and **Denied RODC Password Replication Group**. Are these brand new groups that are going to be added into AD when I finish this wizard? No! While there is a good chance you have never taken notice of these groups before, they already exist inside Active Directory, but are simply unused if you never roll out an RODC in your environment:

Figure 3.27: Built-in groups related to RODC

The choice is yours on whether to utilize these built-in groups or specify your own groups that are either allowed to replicate passwords to this RODC or denied from being able to do so. RODCs are all about keeping security as tight as possible, so you generally don't want any passwords getting cached on an RODC that won't actually be needed for that local office's authentication. Physical security is yet another advantage of using an RODC instead of a full domain controller. What if someone breaks into your branch office and steals the physical server? If bad guys were to get their hands on a full DC, all usernames and passwords in your domain would be stored on that hard drive. With an RODC, only the accounts that have been allowed to cache are contained on the stolen server.

Each RODC has its own definition of allowances and denials. By default, every RODC that you add into your domain will follow through these same wizard steps, and if you leave all default options in place then all RODCs in your environment will treat those built-in allowed and denied RODC groups as their definitions, meaning that all RODCs in your environment will be caching the same passwords because they all pay attention to the same groups. However, each RODC maintains its own set of users and groups that are allowed or denied caching. This RODC Options screen can be configured differently for every RODC that you establish.

What if you want to make changes to these definitions in the future? Easy enough, you simply need to know where to look for this information to be able to change it. The list of accounts that are allowed or denied caching is generally called the **Password Replication Policy** (**PRP**) for each RODC. To find an RODC's PRP, simply open up AD Users and Computers and find the object for your read-only domain controller, right-click on that computer object, and visit **Properties**. Inside the properties of your RODC, navigate to the tab called **Password Replication Policy**. Here, you can view and manipulate the password caching policy for each RODC individually:

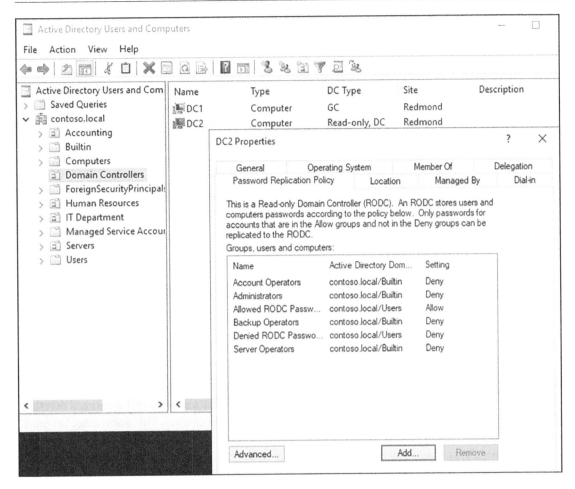

Figure 3.28: Password Replication Policy settings

Denials always win! In the Microsoft world, a permission denial always takes priority over a permission allowance. The same is true for RODC caching. If a user account is a member of groups that fall inside both the allow RODC caching and deny RODC caching categories, it will be denied caching for that account.

FSMO Roles

Active Directory is like a database, a potentially huge database, sync'd across a potentially huge number of different Domain Controller servers in your environment. In an environment with lots of DCs spread across numerous sites, the potential for change conflict is huge. What if DC1 in Redmond receives a change and needs to sync it around the entire domain, and at the same time DC22 in London receives instruction to sync a change that is in conflict with the change of DC1. What now? Who wins? In the early days of Active Directory, there was one single master domain controller server, known as the **Primary Domain Controller** (**PDC**), that was responsible for making all changes like this. Technically, the PDC role no longer exists, but some of the same protections are still in place under the hood by the use of **Flexible Single Master Operation** (**FSMO**) roles. Every instance of Active Directory has FSMO roles, and FSMO role holders. In a lot of cases, the same Domain Controller holds all five of the FSMO roles, but they could technically be managed by different domain controller servers. Here are the five FSMO roles:

- Schema master
- Domain naming master
- RID master
- PDC emulator
- Infrastructure master

We aren't going to discuss each of these in-depth for the purposes of our chapter, because the typical IT admin doesn't need to know that level of detail. What you do need to understand, however, is that they exist and that at least one of your domain controllers is hosting these roles. This knowledge becomes critically important if you remove or replace a domain controller that was hosting one of these roles, or that server dies, and you now have chaos inside your directory. Thankfully, it is quite easy to find out what server or servers are hosting these roles, and also now easy to transfer the FSMO roles to a different domain controller in your environment, should the need arise. The key things to remember are that you have FSMO roles, they are extremely important to the workability and health of Active Directory, and that if their server disappears, you need to move them to another server.

Viewing current FSMO role holders

To find FSMO role holders via graphical interface, you're going to have to check three different administrative tools. This is because some FSMO roles are forest-wide, and some are domain-wide. Therefore, it is possible to have many more than five FSMO roles within a forest, and their technical homes are in different places. Let's first list out where you could find this information via the GUI.

RID, PDC, and Infrastructure master

Open Active Directory Users and Computers, right-click on the name of your domain, and click **Operations Masters...**. The three tabs here will indicate which DC is hosting the corresponding roles.

Schema master

Right-click the **Start** button, and click **Run**. Then type `regsvr32 schmmgmt.dll` and click **OK**. This process enables something called Active Directory Schema to be available from inside the MMC console, which you can then open by...

Right-click the **Start** button, click **Run**, type **MMC** and click **OK**. Now navigate to **File > Add/Remove Snap-in...** and add the Active Directory Schema to your MMC console. Once added, right-click **Active Directory Schema** and look inside **Operations Master** to find the schema master server.

Domain naming master

Open Active Directory Domains and Trusts, right-click on the words **Active Directory Domains and Trusts**, and click on **Operations Master...** to view the Domain naming master server.

View them all in one place

While the graphical interfaces are good to know about and useful for finding individual FSMO role holders, most of the time you would rather just see them all listed out together, right? Thankfully we have some very old tools still hanging around even in Windows Server 2022 that can do exactly this.

Open an administrative Command Prompt on one of your Domain Controller servers, and simply run the following command: `netdom query fsmo`

This single command lists out all five FSMO roles and their current master servers, as seen in the following screenshot.

Figure 3.29: Viewing FSMO role holders with command prompt

FSMO role visibility through PowerShell

And of course we can also see these through PowerShell, though surprisingly it requires two separate commands to do so. Given this, I prefer good ole **netdom** via Command Prompt if I am manually looking for FSMO role ownership information, but there are certainly use cases where pulling this information from PowerShell would be beneficial for scripting or other purposes, so here are the commands to find the same information using PowerShell.

Find domain-level FSMO roles

```
Get-ADDomain | select InfrastructureMaster, PDCEmulator, RIDMaster
```

Find forest-level FSMO roles

```
Get-ADForest | select DomainNamingMaster, SchemaMaster
```

Transferring FSMO roles

Now for the fun part, transferring these FSMO roles to new servers. If you are individually moving FSMO roles, each of the graphical interface methods for viewing the master also includes a **Change** button that can be used to quickly and easily shift individual FSMO roles from one server to another. The key to doing this is that you must connect to the new server to whom you are planning to transfer your role. As you have seen, all FSMO roles in my test lab are held by DC1, which makes sense because it was my first domain controller. I now want to move only the PDC role to my DC2 server. To accomplish this, I log into DC1, if it's available, or could do this just as well from DC2, my second domain controller. Remember, there are three different places you may need to visit to move FSMO roles, depending on which roles you are working with, but for the PDC role I need to perform the following: **Active Directory Users and Computers > Right-click the domain name > Operations Masters > PDC > Change**. Uh oh, when I clicked that **Change** button, I was presented with the error below. What gives?

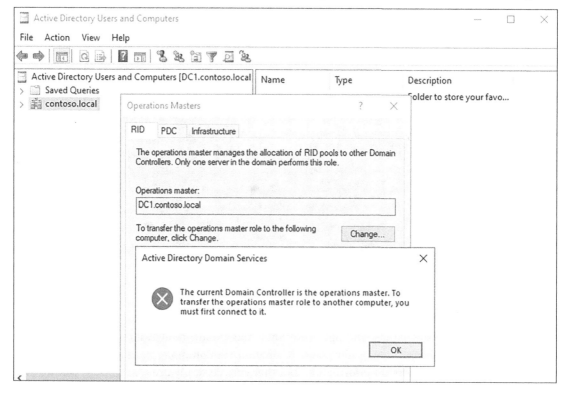

Figure 3.30: Attempting to transfer the PDC role

If you look closely at the previous screenshot, you'll notice that even though I am logged into the DC2 server, my AD Users and Computers has connected to the contoso.local domain through my DC1 server. This is what needs to change to successfully move my role. If I right-click on **Active Directory Users and Computers [DC1.contoso.local]** and choose the option to **Change Domain Controller...** I will be able to connect to the domain through DC2 instead. Once I accomplish that, I can now successfully migrate the PDC role to DC2.

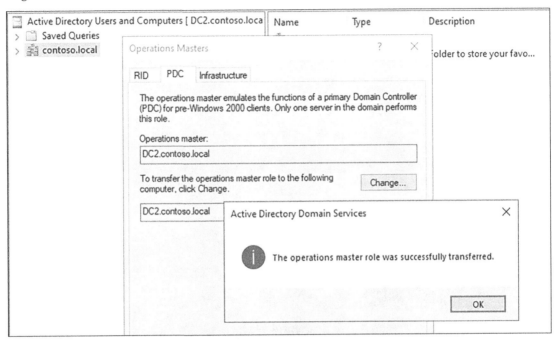

Figure 3.31: PDC role has been moved to DC2

Transferring FSMO roles via PowerShell

As with almost everything inside Windows Server, if you can accomplish it via graphical interface, you can almost certainly find a way to do the same thing with PowerShell. While viewing FSMO role ownership was slightly easier via an old Command Prompt command, transferring the roles between Domain Controllers is definitely easiest to accomplish by using PowerShell. To transfer roles, simply log into the server to whom you are going to transfer the roles, and run as few or as many commands as you need. There is a separate command to run for each FSMO role, and by running all five, we have now quickly and smoothly transferred all FSMO roles onto my DC2 server.

Transfer RID Master

```
Move-ADDirectoryServerOperationMasterRole -Identity "DC2" RIDMaster
```

Transfer PDC Emulator

```
Move-ADDirectoryServerOperationMasterRole -Identity "DC2" PDCEmulator
```

Transfer Infrastructure Master

```
Move-ADDirectoryServerOperationMasterRole -Identity "DC2" InfrastructureMaster
```

Transfer Schema Master

```
Move-ADDirectoryServerOperationMasterRole -Identity "DC2" SchemaMaster
```

Transfer Domain Naming Master

```
Move-ADDirectoryServerOperationMasterRole -Identity "DC2" DomainNamingMaster
```

```
Administrator: Windows PowerShell                                                       —    □    ✕

PS C:\Users\Administrator.CONTOSO> Move-ADDirectoryServerOperationMasterRole -Identity "DC2" RIDMaster

Move Operation Master Role
Do you want to move role 'RIDMaster' to server 'DC2.contoso.local' ?
[Y] Yes  [A] Yes to All  [N] No  [L] No to All  [S] Suspend  [?] Help (default is "Y"): y
PS C:\Users\Administrator.CONTOSO> Move-ADDirectoryServerOperationMasterRole -Identity "DC2" InfrastructureMaster

Move Operation Master Role
Do you want to move role 'InfrastructureMaster' to server 'DC2.contoso.local' ?
[Y] Yes  [A] Yes to All  [N] No  [L] No to All  [S] Suspend  [?] Help (default is "Y"): y
PS C:\Users\Administrator.CONTOSO> Move-ADDirectoryServerOperationMasterRole -Identity "DC2" SchemaMaster

Move Operation Master Role
Do you want to move role 'SchemaMaster' to server 'DC2.contoso.local' ?
[Y] Yes  [A] Yes to All  [N] No  [L] No to All  [S] Suspend  [?] Help (default is "Y"): y
PS C:\Users\Administrator.CONTOSO> Move-ADDirectoryServerOperationMasterRole -Identity "DC2" DomainNamingMaster

Move Operation Master Role
Do you want to move role 'DomainNamingMaster' to server 'DC2.contoso.local' ?
[Y] Yes  [A] Yes to All  [N] No  [L] No to All  [S] Suspend  [?] Help (default is "Y"): y
PS C:\Users\Administrator.CONTOSO>
PS C:\Users\Administrator.CONTOSO>
PS C:\Users\Administrator.CONTOSO> netdom query fsmo
Schema master              DC2.contoso.local
Domain naming master       DC2.contoso.local
PDC                        DC2.contoso.local
RID pool manager           DC2.contoso.local
Infrastructure master      DC2.contoso.local
The command completed successfully.

PS C:\Users\Administrator.CONTOSO>
```

Figure 3.32: All FSMO roles have been transferred to DC2

Demote an old domain controller

Creating new servers and turning them into Domain Controllers is technically known as **promoting** those servers to become Domain Controllers. This process is fairly straightforward, and easy to accomplish in a fresh environment without any history of changes or issues, such as inside a test lab. Now let's cover one of the messier things that you may encounter as a server administrator, removing an old Domain Controller server. The process of removing a DC from your environment is known as **demoting**. Demoting a Domain Controller can be straightforward if the old server is online, or it can be a little convoluted if the old server has died, and you are now trying to remove all traces of it from the domain without being able to take the standard removal steps.

Demoting while the old server is still online

If you are removing an old Domain Controller and it is still online, the process is pretty painless. Log into that server, and accomplish the following steps:

1. Open **Server Manager**

2. **Manage > Remove Roles and Features**

3. Make sure your old server is selected

4. Uncheck **Active Directory Domain Services**

5. If this server is also a DNS server, it is easiest if you remove the DNS Server role before accomplishing the AD DS removal

6. You will receive a pop-up with Validation Results. On this screen, click the link to **Demote this domain controller**

Figure 3.33: Demoting a Domain Controller via Server Manager

You will also be asked if you want to **Force the removal of this domain controller** – it is generally recommended NOT to check this box unless you are removing the very last Domain Controller from your domain.

A few more Next boxes and specifying a new local Administrator password (remember, this server will no longer be a DC, so the wizard will be creating a new local Administrator account), and you're off to the races. The server is demoted and removed from Active Directory, and when it finishes restarting, will be a plain-jane Windows Server sitting on your network.

Clean up AD Sites and Services

The DC demotion process via Server Manager cleans up almost everything, but if you open **Active Directory Sites and Services**, you will still find reference to the old Domain Controller name, listed under the **Servers** folder under whichever site that server resided. Simply right-click on the old server name and delete it, and you're all set.

Demoting when the old server is gone

Here is a scenario that most tenured Active Directory administrators have encountered at least once. The reason we have redundant DCs is in case one of them dies, right? Well...what happens when *that* happens?

Running to Server Manager and attempting to cleanup or remove the old DC will get you nowhere. Without being able to contact the server that is now offline, Server Manager is not going to know what to do in order to remove that server from all of the places it is plugged and referenced inside Active Directory. Instead, you must manually clean up references to the old server, which is surprisingly easier than you might think.

Move FSMO roles

First, as we just finished describing, you'll want to ensure that you get your FSMO roles moved to a working DC in your environment. Thankfully the old server does not need to be online for this to happen.

Delete it

Open Active Directory Users and Computers, and navigate to the OU called **Domain Controllers**. Inside this OU you should find the computer object for every DC in your environment, including the dead one. Simply right-click on this object and **Delete**, and you are presented with a warning message regarding the fact that you are attempting to delete a Domain Controller without performing a proper demotion. If your DC is really gone and not coming back, simply check the box to Delete this Domain Controller anyway and delete it.

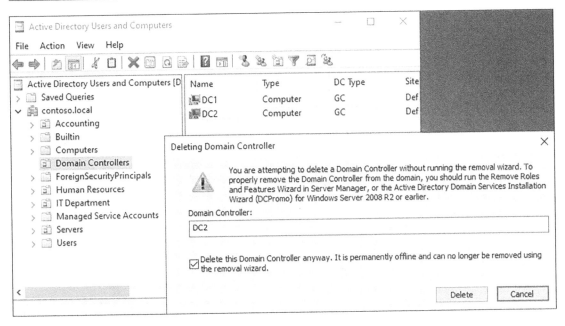

Figure 3.34: Manually removing a Domain Controller for Active Directory

Clean up Sites and Services and DNS

As with the proper removal method, make sure to visit Active Directory Sites and Services to clean up any traces or pointers that still reference the old Domain Controller, DC2 in my case. In addition to Sites and Services, when you forcibly remove a DC from Active Directory, it often leaves behind traces of the old DC inside DNS. We have not talked in-depth about DNS at this point, but if you open the DNS Manager console and expand the available folders, taking a look inside each one, you will almost certainly find traces of the former DC. These records are no longer needed and could cause problems or delays in DNS, so they should all be removed.

Figure 3.35: Cleaning up DNS following a manual DC deletion

Group Policy

In a network that is based upon Windows Server and Active Directory, it is almost always the case that the primary set of client computers is also based upon the Microsoft Windows operating systems, and that these machines are all domain-joined. Setting everything up this way not only makes sense from an organizational perspective inside Active Directory, but also allows centralized authentication across devices and applications, as we have already talked about. I know that a couple of the examples I gave earlier in the book went something like, *What about when a company has a security policy in place that...* or *Make sure your servers don't get those existing security policies because...* So what are these magical **security policies** anyway, and how do I set one up?

This is the power of Group Policy. It enables you to create **Group Policy Objects** (**GPOs**) that contain settings and configurations that you want to apply to either computers or users in your Active Directory domain. Once you have created and built out a GPO with a variety of settings, you then have the option to steer that GPO in whatever direction you choose. If you have a policy that you want to apply to all desktop systems, you can point it at the appropriate OU or security group in Active Directory that houses all of your domain-joined desktop computers. Or maybe you created a GPO that only applies to your Windows 7 computers; you can filter it appropriately so that only those systems are receiving the policy. And the real magic is that the issuance of these settings happens automatically, simply by those computers being joined to your domain. You don't have to touch the client systems at all in order to push settings to them via a GPO. You can tweak or lock down almost anything within the Windows operating system by using Group Policy.

Once again, I'm looking in the list of available roles on my Windows Server 2022, and I am just not seeing one called **Group Policy**. Correct again: there isn't one! In fact, if you have been following along with the lab setup in this book, you already have Group Policy fully functional in your network. Everything that Group Policy needs in order to work is part of Active Directory Domain Services. So, if you have a domain controller in your network, then you also have Group Policy on that same server, because all of the information Group Policy uses is stored inside the directory. Since the installation of the AD DS role is all we need to use Group Policy, and we have already done that on our domain controller, we are already prepared to start using Group Policy to send policies and preferences to our computers and users within the domain.

But wait! Group Policy is a large enough topic that it really needs its own chapter, which is exactly what I have decided to do. If you're interested in centralizing administration and policy with this fascinating tool, which you should be, continue reading and we will dive deeper into all things GPO in *Chapter 5, Group Policy*.

Summary

Anyone who has been around Windows Server before knows that Active Directory is nothing new and certainly not something coming to us new in Windows Server 2022. AD has been the authentication underpinning of any Microsoft-centric environment for a very long time and will continue to be far into the future for anyone who hosts an on-premise datacenter. Knowing and understanding AD is entirely critical for the mastery of Windows Server 2022, because without this knowledge your career in server administration won't even make it off the ground.

Some hints were dropped in this chapter about another core infrastructure technology that is often in place alongside Active Directory on all of your domain controller servers, DNS. To effectively manage a Microsoft infrastructure, in my opinion there are three in-the-box server technologies that any admin must be able to work with fluently: Active Directory, DNS, and DHCP. Follow along to *Chapter 4, DNS and DHCP*, as we cover the latter.

Questions

1. Inside Active Directory, a container (folder) that holds computer and user accounts is called a(n)...?
2. What is the term for creating a computer account inside Active Directory prior to that computer being joined to your domain?
3. Which management tool is used to specify that certain physical locations in your network are bound to particular IP subnets?
4. What is the name of a special domain controller that cannot accept new information, only synchronize from an existing domain controller?
5. What tool is needed to create a fine-grained password policy?
6. What must be configured inside DNS prior to establishing a forest trust?
7. What is the command-line command that shows you all FSMO role holders at once?
8. True or False? It is faster to manually remove a Domain Controller from the domain than it is to follow the Server Manager role removal wizard.

Join our community on Discord

Join our community's Discord space for discussions with the author and other readers:

https://packt.link/SecNet

4

DNS and DHCP

If we consider **Active Directory Domain Services (AD DS)** to be the most common and central role in making our Microsoft-centric networks function, then the DNS and DHCP roles slide in at numbers two and three. I am yet to meet an admin who has chosen to deploy a new domain without deploying DNS at the same time, and every network has a need for DHCP whether or not that service is provided by a Windows server. Either of these roles *could* be served by something other than a traditional server. There are other companies and even dedicated appliances that exist to provide DNS within a corporate network, which have some advantages and some disadvantages. Regarding DHCP, there are plenty of options for providing that service outside of the Windows world, as most firewalls and even switches are capable of also being DHCP "servers" in a network. Although the preceding sentences are true, in reality, the majority of internal DNS and DHCP services for companies around the world are provided by Windows servers, and these two roles are very commonly located alongside AD DS on at least some of the **Domain Controller (DC)** servers in any given network.

In this chapter, we will cover both DNS and DHCP provided by Windows Server 2022, getting to know their purposes and walking through some common terminology and tasks related to these roles. In this chapter, we will be covering the following:

- The purpose of DNS
- Types of DNS records
- Split-brain DNS
- Types of DNS zones
- IP addressing with DHCP
- Creating a DHCP scope
- DHCP reservations
- DHCP failover
- IPAM

The purpose of DNS

Domain Name System (DNS) is similar to Active Directory in that it is a structured database that is often stored on domain controller servers and distributed automatically around your network to other domain controller/DNS servers. Where an AD database contains information about the domain objects themselves, DNS is responsible for storing and resolving all of the *names* on your network. What do I mean by names? Whenever a user or computer tries to contact any resource by calling for a name, DNS is the platform responsible for turning that name into something else in order to get the traffic to the correct destination. You see, the way that traffic gets from the client to the server is via networking, and typically via the TCP/IP stack, using an IP address to get to its destination.

When I open an application on my computer to access some data that resides on a server, I could configure the application so that it communicates directly to my server by using the server's IP address on the network. If an application on my computer needed to communicate with a server called APP01, and that server was using an IP address of 10.10.10.15 on the network, I could plug 10.10.10.15 into my application configuration, and it would open successfully. If I set up hundreds of different computers this way, all pointing to IP addresses, it would work fine for a while. But the day will come when, for whatever reason, that IP address might need to change. Or perhaps I add a second server to share the load and handle my increased user traffic. What to do now? Re-visit every client computer and update the IP address being used? Certainly not.

This is one of the reasons that DNS is critical to the way that we design and manage our infrastructures. By using DNS, we can employ names instead of IP addresses. With DNS, my application can be configured to talk to APP01 or whatever my server name is, and if I need to change the IP address later, I simply change it inside the DNS console to the updated IP address and immediately all of my client computers will start resolving the APP01 name to the new IP address. Or I can even use a more generic name, such as **intranet**, and have it resolve across multiple different servers. We will discuss that a little bit more shortly.

Any time that a computer makes a call to a server, service, or website, it is using DNS to resolve that name to a more useful piece of information to make the network connection happen successfully. The same is true both inside and outside of corporate networks. On my personal laptop right now, if I open Edge and browse to https://www.bing.com/, my internet provider's DNS server is resolving bing.com to an IP address on the internet, which is the address that my laptop communicates with and so that page opens successfully. When we are working inside our own corporate networks, we don't want to rely on or trust a public provider with our internal server name information, and so we build our own DNS servers inside the network. Since DNS records inside a domain network are almost always resolving names to objects that reside inside Active Directory, it makes sense then that DNS and AD DS would be tightly integrated. That rings true in the majority of Microsoft networks, where it is a very common practice to install both the AD DS role, plus the DNS role, on your domain controller servers.

Types of DNS records

Having installed our DNS role on a server in the network, we can start using it to create DNS records, which resolve names to their corresponding IP addresses, or other pieces of information needed in order to route our traffic around the network.

Assuming that you are working in a domain network, you may be pleasantly surprised to see that a number of records already exist inside DNS, even though you haven't created any of them. When you are running Active Directory and DNS together, the domain-join process that you take with your computers and servers self-registers a DNS record during that process, which means creating a DNS record for each new server or computer is not something that you need to remember to accomplish.

I have not yet created any DNS records in my new lab environment, not purposefully anyway, and yet when I open the **DNS Manager** console from inside the **Tools** menu of Server Manager, I can see a handful of records already existing. This is because when I joined each of these machines to the domain, it automatically registered these records for me so that the new servers and clients were immediately resolvable within our domain:

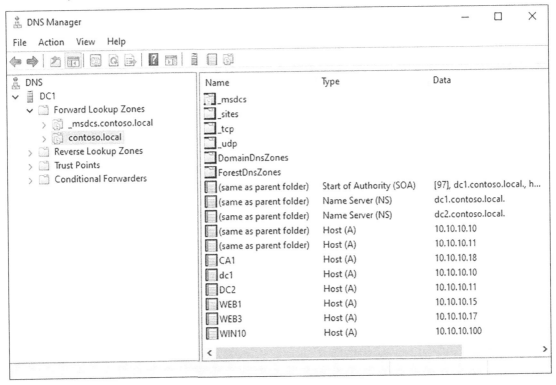

Figure 4.1: DNS Manager

Host record (A or AAAA)

The first kind of DNS record we are looking at is the most common type that you will work with. A **host record** is the one that resolves a particular name to a particular IP address. It's pretty simple, and for most of the devices on your network this will be the only kind of record that exists for them inside DNS. There are two different classes of host records that you should be aware of, even though you will likely only be using one of them for at least a few more years. The two different kinds of host records are called an **A record** and an **AAAA record**, which is pronounced **Quad A**.

The difference between the two? A records are for **IPv4** addresses and will be used in most companies for years to come. AAAA records serve the exact same purpose of resolving a name to an IP address, but are only for **IPv6** addresses, and will only be useful if you use IPv6 in your network.

In *Figure 4.1*, you can see some **Host (A)** records that were self-created when those machines joined our domain. I also have another server running on my network that has not yet been domain joined, and so it has not self-registered into DNS. This server is called RA1, but if I log in to any other system on my network, I fail to contact my RA1 server, since that name is not yet plugged into DNS:

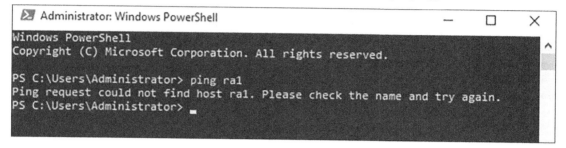

Figure 4.2: RA1 server does not resolve

For now, I am going to choose not to join this server to the domain, so that we can manually create a DNS record for it and make sure that I am able to resolve the name properly after doing that. Back inside DNS Manager on your DNS server, right-click on the name of your domain listed under the **Forward Lookup Zones** folder, and then choose **New Host (A or AAAA)**. Inside the screen to create a new host record, simply enter the name of your server, and the IP address that is configured on its network interface:

New Host   ✕

Name (uses parent domain name if blank):

RA1

Fully qualified domain name (FQDN):

RA1.contoso.local.

IP address:

10.10.10.13

☐ Create associated pointer (PTR) record

☐ Allow any authenticated user to update DNS records with the
   same owner name

                                      Add Host   Cancel

Figure 4.3: Adding a new host record

Now that we have created this new host record, we should immediately be able to start resolving this name inside our domain network. Moving back to the client machine from which I was trying to ping RA1 earlier, I'll try the same command again, and this time it does resolve and reply successfully:

Figure 4.4: Successfully pinging RA1

Alias record — CNAME

Another useful type of DNS record is **CNAME**, which more commonly these days is called an **alias record**. This is a record that you can create that takes a name and points it at another name. It sounds a little silly at first glance, because, in the end, you are still going to have to resolve your final name to an IP address by using a host record in order to get the traffic where it needs to go, but the purposes of an alias record can be vast. A good example to portray the usefulness of an alias record is when you are running a web server that is serving up websites within your network. Rather than force all of your users to remember a URL like http://web1.contoso.local to access a website, we could create an alias record called **intranet**, and point it at WEB1. This way, the more generalized intranet record can always be utilized by the client computers, which is a much friendlier name for your users to remember.

In addition to creating a happier user experience with this new DNS record, you have, at the same time, created some additional administrative flexibility because you can easily change the server components that are running beneath that record, without having to adjust any settings on the client machines or retrain employees on how to access the page. Need to replace a web server? No problem, just prep the new server alongside the old one and then point the alias record at the new server. Need to add another web server? That's easy too, as we can create multiple alias records, all with the same intranet name, and point them at the different web servers that are in play within the environment. This creates a very simple form of load balancing, as DNS will start to round-robin the traffic among the different web servers, based on that intranet CNAME record.

In fact, rather than continue to talk about this, let's give it a try. I have a website running on exactly that URL in my environment, but currently I can only access it by typing in `http://web1.contoso.local`. Inside DNS, I am going to create an alias record that redirects `intranet` to `WEB1`:

Figure 4.5: Creating a new alias record

Now when I ping `intranet`, you can see that it resolves to my `WEB1` server. And when accessing the web page, I can simply type the word `intranet` into my address bar inside a web browser in order to launch my page. The website itself is not aware of the name change being made, so I didn't have to make any modifications to the website, only within DNS:

Figure 4.6: Loading WEB1 using the new alias

Mail Exchanger (MX) record

A third type of DNS record is called a **Mail Exchanger (MX)** record. In your everyday duties, you will not have to encounter or configure MX records nearly as often as A or CNAME records, but they are important to understand nonetheless. An MX record is all about email services and delivery. Whatever domain name follows the @ in your email address, the DNS servers that are handling that domain name must contain an MX record telling the domain where to point for its mail services. MX records are most commonly used within public DNS, for name resolutions happening over the internet. For companies hosting their own email on local Exchange servers, your public DNS servers will contain an MX record that points at your Exchange environment. For companies hosting their email in a cloud service like Office 365, your public DNS records would need to contain an MX record that directs email traffic toward the cloud provider that is hosting your mailboxes.

Whenever an email is sent outbound, the internet needs to determine how to deliver that email. Public internet DNS is checked for whichever domain the email is destined for, and the MX record contained within that DNS configuration defines where the email is sent. If you don't have an MX record, or if it disappears for some reason, you will receive zero emails to your domain. This is important to understand for email delivery troubleshooting purposes. How would an MX record possibly disappear? Usually during website changes. When a business decides to migrate over to a new website, it is typically the website developer making those changes. As part of those changes, they need access to DNS to be able to point your company website name at whatever new IP address is being used to host the website, and if the wrong options are selected during migration, your MX record could become null in the process. If you encounter any email delivery problems following changes in DNS, it is most likely that something is wrong with your MX record.

Microsoft 365 MX records

Now that so many businesses host their email in Microsoft's Office 365 platform, let's take a firsthand look at an MX record that points to this system. Even though millions of mailboxes across thousands of companies now host their email in the same Office 365, every company will have a unique MX record associated with their Office 365 environment. Finding your specific MX record criteria is pretty simple, you just need to know where to look.

Log into your Microsoft 365 admin portal, and navigate to **Settings > Domains**. Here, you will see all of the domain names that you have configured inside the portal. Click on the name of the domain in question, and then click on **DNS records**. Here, you will see all DNS records that need to be present in your company's public DNS provider that are required for Microsoft 365 services to work successfully. The most important for email delivery is the MX record, listed right on top, but all three of the records under the **Microsoft Exchange** heading are very important.

Your MX record will probably resemble something similar to the following:

```
0 contoso-com.mail.protection.outlook.com
```

Once you ensure this MX record is successfully created in your domain's public DNS records, the internet now knows that any email destined for an address ending in @contoso.com needs to be delivered to Microsoft 365 hosting services, and Microsoft takes it and delivers it to your appropriate company and mailbox from there.

TXT record

TXT is simply short for **text** record. TXT records are used within DNS for various purposes, and they can contain just about any kind of information. Sometimes TXT records are placed for actual human reading of some type of info, but more likely you will be asked to create a TXT record at some point as a form of validation.

For example, most websites are protected by SSL certificates, and the process of purchasing an SSL certificate is pretty straightforward. However, you certainly wouldn't want any yahoo with a laptop and internet access to be able to purchase a certificate that can protect a website name that ends in a domain name that your business owns, right? So, **certification authorities (CAs)** (the places where you purchase SSL certificates) will require some sort of validation process before allowing you to purchase a certificate for your domain name.

Sometimes that validation process is simply sending an email to an address associated with that domain name, or sometimes you will be asked to create a TXT record with a very exact set of characters in your public DNS records. The implication and validation, of course, is that if you really do own that domain name, you will have access to create DNS records within that domain. When the CA sees your newly created TXT record that contains the data they asked you to input, they know you really do own that domain, and they will then issue your new certificate. An attacker trying to spoof your website and acquire an SSL certificate maliciously would not have such access into your domain's DNS settings.

SPF record

There are a few special kinds of TXT records, a common one being **Sender Policy Framework (SPF)** records. This record pertains to the delivery of emails, but while an MX record identifies which servers email should flow *toward*, an SPF record identifies which locations email is coming *from*. SPF records are part of spam and spoofing calculations, used to identify the locations on the internet from which email from your domain is expected to be flowing. Let's take a look at a couple of example SPF records, which will help you to understand how they are formatted, and also assist in describing why they are necessary:

```
v=spf1 [IP address 1] [IP address 2] [include:<domain>] -<enforcement rule>
```

The preceding is standard formatting for an SPF TXT record. For simple email systems where all email flows from one public IP address on the internet, or from one hosted email system, your record will be nice and short. A great example is email coming from Office 365. Everyone who hosts email in Office 365 should have an SPF record with the following information inside:

```
v=spf1 include:spf.protection.outlook.com -all
```

SPF record information is used by receiving email servers to validate the mail coming inbound. That mail server will receive the email, discover which domain it came from, and reach back out over the internet to that domain's DNS servers to check for the existence of an SPF record. If it doesn't find such a record, your email has a much higher chance of being flagged as spam. If it does find an SPF record, the mail server then checks the entries in that record, which identifies the safe places that we expect mail to be flowing from, and confirms that the email did, in fact, originate from one of those places. In our preceding Office 365 SPF record, we included the domain spf.protection.outlook.com. All email that flows from Office 365 servers will match this origination, so this simple record is the only thing needed to be in place for safe delivery of email from your Office 365 tenant.

Now pretend that your SPF record is already in place and working with your hosted email, but that you set up an on-premise SMTP relay server so that your copiers on the network have the ability to scan to email. This is a common request by businesses, and something that I find in the wild on a very regular basis. The nature of your SMTP server doesn't really matter; there are various ways to accomplish that. What you'll usually find, though, is that when you send email from your copier, that email may start getting flagged as spam. Sometimes it lands in the recipient's junk mail folder, sometimes it is captured and not delivered to them at all. Why is this? If you have an onsite SMTP relay where the email is coming from, remember the copier just hands email over to the SMTP relay, and that relay is the guy who is shuttling the email over the internet.

That relayed email is not coming from `spf.protection.outlook.com`, but rather email sent from your on-premise SMTP server is coming from your ISP outbound public IP address. Your SPF record needs to be adjusted to include this additional safe sender, so that recipients of your email will know that emails coming from your physical building are legit. Let's build out an SPF record that includes a single IP address:

```
v=spf1 ip4:8.8.8.8 include:spf.protection.outlook.com -all
```

That's it! By simply updating your SPF record to include the public IP address that the copier scans are coming from, your recipient email servers will better trust that incoming mail.

I'm obviously using `8.8.8.8` as an example in the preceding text; don't plug this into your own SPF records! You will want to identify your actual outbound IP address and use that information instead.

It is also easy to add multiple IP addresses, for example, if your business owns multiple buildings, each with their own ISP connections, and want email traffic to be able to flow from devices (such as copiers) in each location:

```
v=spf1 ip4:8.8.8.8 ip4:4.4.2.2 include:spf.protection.outlook.com -all
```

Enforcement rule -all

What is that `-all` at the end of an SPF record, anyway? I'm glad you asked! The declaration at the end of an SPF is telling the receiving mail server how strictly it should enforce these SPF rules. There are three different ways that you could configure that enforcement rule:

```
-all
```

This is generally the way you always want to set up SPF records. `-all` means "hard fail." It sets the SPF rules as firm, so recipient mail servers will follow these rules.

```
~all
```

Use this alternative if you are unsure that you have all IP addresses listed in your SPF record, for a soft fail scenario. I would only use this as a temporary measure, and honestly I don't know that I have ever encountered an SPF record in a production environment that is configured as such.

```
?all
```

The last option here is neutral. Use it only for testing SPF records, as it will not help mail delivery until you later change it over to `-all`.

Name Server (NS) record

Here is another type of DNS record that you don't have to deal with on a day-to-day basis, but you should still know what it's there for. An NS record is an identifier within a DNS zone that tells it which **name servers** (which are your DNS servers) to use as the authorities for that zone. If you look at the NS records listed in your internal DNS right now, you will recognize that it is calling out the names of your DNS servers on the network. When you add a new DC/DNS server to your domain, a new NS record for this server will be automatically added into your DNS zone:

Figure 4.7: Viewing NS records in your zone

Public name server records

NS records are critical to understanding when working with public/internet DNS records. I can't tell you how many times I have assisted admins who were trying to create new DNS records for their zone and struggling because it seemed like no matter what they plugged into the DNS settings, their new records would never show up and work on the internet. After a quick look, we discover that their Name Server record for the domain was pointing at a different server or service altogether, which they didn't even realize was part of the DNS equation. Here's an example scenario that helps explain.

You inherit an already established infrastructure as you take over server administration for a company. The previous admin has all passwords documented; things are looking good so far. The director of marketing for the company has their own company credit card, and comes to you on day two to let you know that rather than navigate the proper IT purchasing channels, they just signed up for xyz marketing service that is going to help send out blasts of emails. This marketing company requires things called CNAME records to be created in your public DNS so that your email and their systems can work together. Now it's up to you to put those CNAME records into place.

No big deal, right? You reference the passwords document and find a record labeled **DNS** that has login credentials for GoDaddy. Sounds like the jackpot, and makes sense as GoDaddy is a pretty common platform on the internet for managing DNS zones. You log in to GoDaddy, edit the DNS zone for your domain, and add your new CNAME records. The CNAME records aren't resolving yet, but you know that DNS propagation takes a while to roll around the internet, so you inform Mr. Marketing that his new service should be up and running within 24 hours. You're a hero!

Except...24 hours roll around, and it's still not working. Mr. M is starting to push back, and you're realizing that that quarterly bonus may not be so sure a bet. Unfortunately, you have forgotten one critical piece of the puzzle. Even though you have a GoDaddy account, *and* it is labeled **DNS**, *and* you were able to create new DNS records within that account, it is entirely possible that the registrar for your domain is actually pointing Name Server records at a different DNS service entirely! A useful tool in this scenario is the DNS Lookup tool from MXToolbox.com.

A quick search for that on the internet will find you the current link, you simply type in your domain name to the DNS Lookup tool, and it will spit back at you which Name Servers are in place, and which service it is that is actually hosting your DNS records on the internet.

Following the previous procedure, you discover that the Name Server records for your domain are actually pointing to Network Solutions, not GoDaddy at all! As it turns out, your IT predecessor wasn't entirely sure how to do a domain transfer, and they got it part-way there but never finished out the process, so while you have GoDaddy available and your domain is even listed inside the GoDaddy console, when any computer on the internet tries to look up DNS info for your domain, the Name Server records are telling that computer to head toward Network Solutions for the domain's DNS servers, not GoDaddy at all. You now have two choices. You can either log in to Network Solutions and add your CNAME records there, and they will work because Network Solutions is currently the service that is doing DNS resolution for your domain, or you can finish out that migration and update your Name Server records so that they point at GoDaddy's DNS servers, instead of Network Solutions.

In summary, this is the flow that happens with a DNS lookup:

1. Client/server makes a call for DNS
2. Name Server records identify which DNS servers are authoritative for the domain your are calling for
3. DNS lookups are steered at those name servers
4. DNS resolution happens

ipconfig /flushdns

Just one final note to finish out this section. I have been saying things like *Now when I do this...* or *Immediately following this change...* and if you are creating some of your own records, you may have noticed that it sometimes takes a while for your client computers to recognize these new DNS records. That is normal behavior, and the time that it takes before your change rolls around to the whole network will depend entirely on how large your network is and how Active Directory replication is configured. When you create a new DNS record on one domain controller, your new record needs to replicate itself around to all of the other DCs in your network. This process alone can take upward of a couple of hours if AD is not configured for faster replication. Typically, it only takes a few minutes. And then, once the new record exists on all of your DC servers, your clients may still take a little bit of time to utilize the new record, because client computers in a domain network hold onto a cache of DNS data. This way, they don't have to reach out to the DNS server for every single name resolution request. They can more quickly refer to their local cache in order to see what the information was from the last time they checked in with the DNS server. If you are trying to immediately test out a new DNS record that you just created and it's not working, you may want to try to run the `ipconfig /flushdns` command on your client computer. This forces the client to dump its locally cached copies of DNS resolver records and go grab new information that is current from the DNS server. After flushing your cache, the new record will more than likely start resolving properly.

Split-brain DNS

In all of our lab configurations, screenshots, and examples you will notice that domains we create on the internal network always end with `.local`. This is purposeful and is generally considered best practice. Public DNS zones, as you well know, can end in a myriad of ways.

Websites or services that live on the internet may end with .com, .org, .edu, .biz, .info, .tech, .construction—the list goes on and on. These are known as top-level domains, and the creative use of such DNS suffixes should remain on the internet and away from our internal DNS zones.

Now, many of you may already work in corporate environments where your internal DNS is configured as something other than a .local, and so you already realize that internal domains can certainly be configured as one of these other suffixes. For example, Microsoft.com is obviously one of the public domains that Microsoft owns, and they could very well also have used Microsoft.com as an internal DNS zone too. In fact, it could even be their primary domain name inside Active Directory right now, and this wouldn't *necessarily* cause any problems, but it certainly increases the *potential* for problems, or at least creates a more complex DNS environment in general.

Whenever a company configures their internal DNS to match their external DNS, this is commonly referred to as **split-brain DNS**. Years ago, there were articles published on the internet by Microsoft warning administrators against doing this, as it caused confusion and problems with some Microsoft roles and technologies that those companies would try to deploy in their environments. As time went on, many people either didn't know or simply ignored this recommendation, and so the world is now awash with networks where split-brain DNS exists. Many of these environments are so populated and complex that they will never be changed at this point, and so Microsoft and the world had no choice but to adapt. Thankfully in today's world, most roles or services that you deploy are written in a way that they accommodate for possible split-brain DNS out of the box, but some still require special considerations.

One example is Microsoft DirectAccess, which we will cover in *Chapter 8, Remote Access*. When deploying DirectAccess, there is a critical piece of client-side technology called the Name Resolution Policy Table that must be populated based on your internal DNS architecture. For companies using a .local domain internally, this configuration is a piece of cake and no special considerations are needed. For anyone with split-brain DNS, this sometimes turns into a convoluted mess and for anyone not well-versed in the intricacies of DirectAccess, simply having split-brain DNS in your environment could very well mean that you are never actually able to get DirectAccess to work in your environment.

At first glance, you would think that administration would be made easier if internal DNS zones matched public DNS zones, but this simply isn't true. The opposite, in fact, is what you will find. Whenever you publish any external service, you will then have to make special considerations with your internal DNS to make that service work as intended from inside the network, because internal DNS zones will typically trump external. Split-brain DNS ends up being more work on a daily basis.

Over the past few years I have seen a couple of Microsoft documents related to Office 365 that recommend administrators setting up new internal domains to do so by intentionally using split-brain DNS, configuring their internal DNS zones to match their public DNS. For example, they might recommend that if your public domain is contoso.com, that your internal domain should also be setup for contoso.com instead of contoso.local. After reading over these articles, and based on my own experiences, I don't agree. Setting up split-brain DNS makes *some* aspects of Office 365 administration and integration easier, but if you step back and look at the whole IT picture, it's still more complicated overall. There is also a new-ish Azure domain service called AADDS (what an acronym!) and configuring your on-prem internal DNS to be split-brain creates extra complexities with AADDS usage in the future.

As the saying goes, you can lead a horse to water but can't make him drink. You have now been informed that utilizing the same DNS zone inside your network as what you use on the internet could cause you some headaches. What you decide to do with this information on future builds, well that's up to you...

Types of DNS zones

You are now familiar with creating different types of DNS records, but that information is only going to enable you to create new records inside of an existing DNS zone. At present in our test lab, we have only one DNS zone available to us, contoso.local, which was created automatically when we built the contoso.local domain. As of right now, computers who are using one of my contoso.local domain controllers as their DNS server are only able to look up DNS records that I have plugged into my DNS zone.

With DNS Server provided by Windows Server 2022, you can certainly build out many different DNS zones, to increase name resolution capabilities in your network. There are plenty of different reasons why you might want to create additional DNS zones, and you should understand what types of zones are available to implement. Let's take a minute and discuss the different types of zones available to us.

Active Directory Integrated Zones

This is not a zone type, per se, but rather an option that can be selected when you create some types of DNS zones. When creating that new zone, you will see a checkbox that states **Store the zone in Active Directory**. When selected, this means that the new zone you are creating is going to be stored inside Active Directory, rather than being stand-alone on the DNS server from which you are creating the zone. Being stored inside AD means that this new zone is capable of being replicated automatically to all domain controller servers in your domain, which means that your DNS zone is highly available and more quickly accessible across your entire network. In general, if the type of zone you are creating allows storage inside Active Directory, do it.

After opening up the DNS Manager tool on your domain controller, you'll notice that any current DNS zones are listed beneath folders entitled **Forward Lookup Zones and Reverse Lookup Zones**. What's the difference?

Forward Lookup Zones

Zones configured inside Forward Lookup Zones are your traditional DNS zones. Their purpose is to take an incoming DNS request, such as from a client computer, and turn that DNS name request into an IP address that is handed back to the client computer. Forward Lookup Zones are almost always where DNS administrators will be working from.

Reverse Lookup Zones

If "reverse" is the opposite of "forward," then the same must be true within a DNS context. Reverse Lookup Zones are responsible for mapping IP addresses backward into names. You may not even realize that these happen in your environment, but you can easily test it out anytime. You likely all know how to use the ping command, which is relying on DNS to turn a name into an IP address. That, of course, is being handled by a Forward Lookup Zone, like we see here:

Figure 4.8: Resolving a name to IP

Did you know you can also use the `ping` command to perform the opposite? What if you want to query DNS to find out what hostname the `10.10.10.11` IP address maps back to?

```
ping -a 10.10.10.11
```

Figure 4.9: Querying DNS to find a hostname from an IP

This reverse lookup, converting IP addresses back to names, has shown us that the IP address `10.10.10.11` has a reverse pointer record mapping back to our DC2 server. This type of lookup is handled by a Reverse Lookup Zone inside DNS.

Now that we understand the difference between Forward and Reverse Lookup Zones, right-clicking on **Forward Lookup Zones** and selecting **New Zone...** lands us with three choices on which type of zone we would like to create:

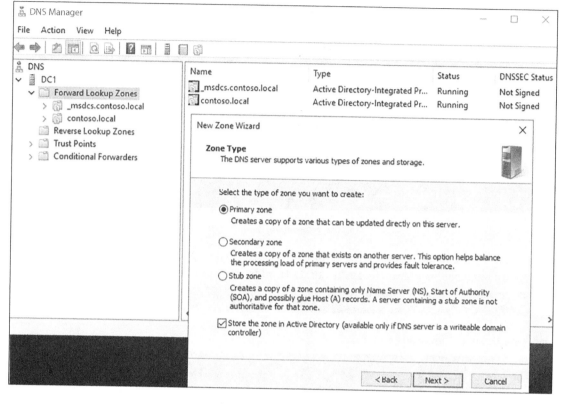

Figure 4.10: DNS zone types

Primary Zone

The majority of DNS zones within internal networks are primary zones. This indicates that it is the "parent," so to speak, the master copy of any particular DNS zone is going to be the primary zone for that domain. When changes and updates are made to DNS records, it always happens within the primary zone. We will create a new primary zone together in just a few minutes. You can choose for primary zones to be stored in Active Directory, or not.

Secondary Zone

Based on their names, it would seem secondary zones might be less important than primary zones, and that is generally true. A secondary zone is simply a read-only copy of a primary zone. Because it is read-only, no updates can be made within a secondary zone, it is always syncing from the primary zone. Secondary zones can be used to spread the DNS computing power among multiple servers, taking the load off of the primary zones, but it is important to know that secondary zones are not Active Directory-integrated. When you try selecting the option to create a new secondary zone, you will notice that the AD checkbox grays out.

Inside most networks I have worked with that are based on Microsoft infrastructure, your primary zones all get set up to be Active Directory-integrated, which means they are syncing around to all of your domain controller-based DNS servers anyway. In this case, secondary zones are less likely to be needed. If you deviate from that mentality and create DNS servers that are not also domain controllers (which you can absolutely do)—then you may want to take care that you understand the use cases of secondary zones because it is more likely in this scenario that you would utilize them.

Stub Zone

The third selection on your new zone screen is Stub Zone. Like secondary zones, stub zones are copies of primary zones but only contain certain pieces of information. Namely, stub zones contain resource records that help clients to identify and more quickly get to the full DNS servers for whatever zone they are calling. Stub zones can be AD-integrated if required.

Stub zones are enabling your DNS servers to know how to direct traffic to resolve records inside another domain. Sounds just like a conditional forwarder that we learned about in the previous chapter, right? Similar, yes, but as you know we pointed our conditional forwarder at a specific IP address, telling DNS that requests for the remote domain should always point at a particular server or servers. Stub zones contain NS records for the remote domain, so even if that remote domain makes some internal adjustments and its DNS servers change or are updated, stub zones can more accurately deal with those scenarios.

AD-integrated DNS zones replicate among domain controllers using domain replication, but non-AD-integrated DNS zones have to sync using their own process, known as **zone transfers**. Stub zones can be used to help make the zone transfer process more efficient and create faster name resolution for client computers.

Creating a new zone

We will finish out this section with a quick walk-through on creating a new DNS zone. The process is straightforward, but there are a few options to consider along the way. In most cases when creating new DNS zones, you will be doing so in order to enable internal client computers to resolve names for a new internal namespace (another .local, for example), so that you can utilize that internal naming scheme for accessing servers and resources inside the network.

For our example, let's create a new primary zone just like we would for any internal namespace, but we are going to configure the DNS zone with a name that conflicts with a well-known internet namespace. This walk-through will not only portray the options available as we configure a DNS zone, but also give a glimpse into what kind of challenges can present in a split-brain DNS scenario. It also portrays the fact that when clients are inside the network, their internal DNS servers have priority over internet DNS servers.

Inside DNS Manager, right-click on **Forward Lookup Zones** and select **New Zone....** Now select the options to create a new **Primary Zone**, and I am going to choose to store mine in Active Directory. Refer to *Figure 4.10* if you need a reference point on these options.

We now encounter a screen titled **Active Directory Zone Replication Scope**. This screen and options only present themselves when the **Store inside AD** option is checked, otherwise the wizard would have bypassed this screen. Here you have options for how extensively you would like this new DNS zone to replicate among your domain controllers. You can replicate to all DCs inside the domain, or even the whole forest.

Next, name the zone. The name that you provide the zone here is the namespace for which the zone is going to contain records. The possibilities here are endless, I could even type in `Jordan.local` as my DNS zone, or `Jordan.com`. This is actually a legitimate website that wraps over to `Nike.com`, which I suppose is fair because Michael Jordan is a little bit more popular than I am.

Now, I typed `Jordan.com` just to be silly, but it will actually portray exactly what I was going to show you, so let's stick with it. This is possibly the silliest thing I've ever done inside DNS Manager.

To prove out what is happening here, first from a client computer in my network I have pulled up a web browser and verified that I can successfully get to `Jordan.com`. If I ping that name, you can see that it resolves to a public IP address, which is expected. This is the public, internet-routable IP address of the web server upon which `Jordan.com` is hosted:

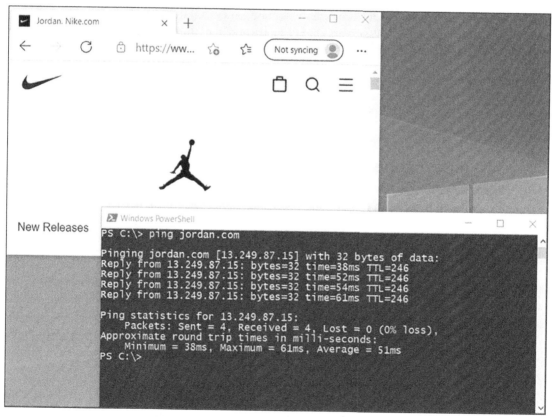

Figure 4.11: Resolving a public DNS zone

This is completely normal behavior, right? Type in a website URL, which is a DNS name; DNS resolves it to the IP address that hosts the website, and your browser takes you there. Next, finish out the creation of our new Jordan.com internal DNS zone, on our internal DNS server.

Walking through the zone creation wizard, I have typed in a zone name of Jordan.com, and the next screen that I have to answer is regarding **Dynamic Update**. Server administrators always have the ability to manually create DNS records inside DNS zones, but if you have hundreds of client computers in your environment, do you really want the creation of DNS records to be a full-time job? Thankfully there is no need to do this, as client computers that are joined to your domain will automatically attempt to register their own hostname and IP address into DNS servers whenever they connect to the network. This process is known as dynamic update, and the settings on this screen show you options regarding these updates. You can allow or disallow dynamic updates for each zone and set some requirements around how secure that updating process needs to be. In most domain environments, configuring the top option is what you will do, only allowing secure updates in your zone. If you have legacy equipment or non-Microsoft products abundant in your network, you may need to select the second option to allow both secure and nonsecure updates:

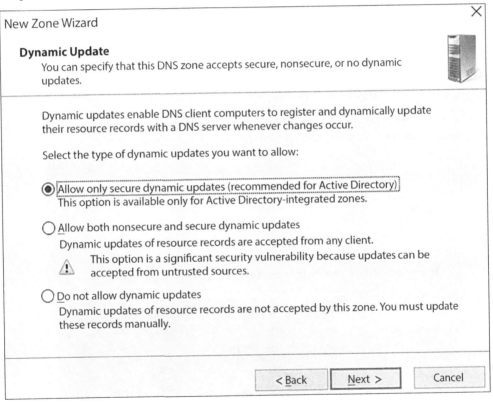

Figure 4.12: Security for DNS updates

That's it! The final screen of the wizard is simply a settings review, and after clicking **Finish**, your new DNS zone is immediately available and working to resolve names in the new Jordan.com namespace, for any client computers who are using this server as their DNS server. As you can see in *Figure 4.13*, the Jordan.com zone is now listed in DNS Manager, and I went ahead and created a couple of A records so that any requests for Jordan.com or www.Jordan.com return an IP address of 10.10.10.23. (See what I did there? Number 23?):

Figure 4.13: Creating an internal Jordan.com DNS zone

Now that our new zone is created inside the network, what has that changed? Let's move back to that client computer in my test network, and try both browsing and pinging Jordan.com again:

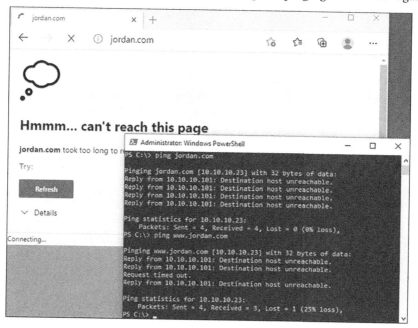

Figure 4.14: Pinging Jordan.com again

Prior to creating this new zone, my client request for Jordan.com was simply forwarded to public internet DNS servers, because my internal DNS servers did not have any of their own definitions for what to do with Jordan.com lookups. After creating an internal DNS zone for Jordan.com, we have now interrupted access to the website, because our own DNS server now has its own ruleset for what to do with these name requests! If I were to build out my own website on a web server and give that server an IP address of 10.10.10.23, my client computer would have successfully loaded my custom website when typing Jordan.com into their browser.

This example had two purposes. First, to walk through the creation of a new DNS zone to review the options available, and to show how easy it is. Second, to make sure you understand that your internal corporate DNS servers have priority over public internet DNS servers. This means you need to take care when creating DNS zones, and when deciding whether or not you want to pursue split-brain DNS by hosting your public namespace inside your network as well, because your internal DNS servers are going to be the primary resolvers for those zones.

IP addressing with DHCP

IP addresses on your network are sort of like home addresses on your street. When you want to send a package to someone, you write their address on the front of the package and set it in the mailbox. In the same way, when your computer wants to send data to a server or another device on a network, each of those devices has an IP address that is used for the delivery of those packets. We know that DNS is responsible for telling the machines which name resolves to which IP address, but how do those IP addresses get put into place on the servers and computers in the first place?

Static addressing is simply the process of configuring IP addresses on your system manually, using your own hands as the configuration tool to plug all of your IP address information into the NIC settings on that device. While this is a quick and easy way to get network traffic flowing between a few endpoints, by giving them each an IP address, it is not scalable. We do often statically address our servers as a way of making sure that those IP addresses are not subject to change, but what about on the client and device side? Even in a small company with 10 employees, each person may have a desktop and a laptop, there are likely going to be printers on the network also needing IP addresses, and you may have a wireless network where employees or even guests can connect phones and other devices in order to gain internet access. Are you going to assign IP addresses by hand to all of these devices? Certainly not.

Our answer to this problem is the **Dynamic Host Configuration Protocol (DHCP)**. This is a protocol that is designed to solve our exact problem by providing the ability for machines and devices to be plugged into your network and automatically obtain IP addressing information. Almost any user on any device in the entire world uses DHCP every day without even realizing it. When you connect your laptop or smartphone to a Wi-Fi router to gain internet access, a DHCP server has given you the ability to route traffic on that Wi-Fi network by assigning you IP addressing information. Often, in the case of public Wi-Fi, your DHCP server is actually running on the router itself, but in our businesses where Windows Server rules the datacenter, our DHCP services are most often hosted on one or more servers across the network.

Creating a DHCP scope

So far in the new Windows Server 2022 lab environment I have been building, I have been statically assigning IP addresses to all of the servers that are being built. This is starting to get old and is hard to keep track of. When the first domain controller was configured, I installed the DHCP role onto it but haven't told it to start doing anything yet. What does a DHCP server need to start handing out IP addresses? It needs to know what IP addresses, subnet mask, default gateway, and DNS server addresses are within your network so that it can package that up and start handing the information out to the computers who request it. This package of information inside the DHCP server is called a **DHCP scope**. Once we define our scope, the DHCP server will start handing out IP addresses from that scope to our new servers and computers that do not already have static addresses defined.

Once again, we need to launch a management tool on our Windows Server 2022, and once again, the easiest way to launch that is by using the **Tools** menu inside Server Manager. Go ahead and launch the **DHCP** console. Inside, you will see the name of your server where the DHCP server is running. Expand that, and you have options for both **IPv4** and **IPv6**. Yes, this means that you can use this DHCP server to hand out both IPv4 addresses as well as IPv6 addresses for those of you who are testing out IPv6, or have plans to in the future. For now, we are sticking with good old IPv4, and so I can right-click on **IPv4** and choose to create a **New Scope**. This launches a **New Scope Wizard** that walks you through the few pieces of information that the DHCP server needs in order to create a scope that is ready to start handing out IP addresses inside your network. I am setting my new scope to hand out IP addresses from 10.10.10.100 through 10.10.10.150:

Figure 4.15: Creating a new DHCP scope

During the course of this DHCP scope setup wizard you will encounter a few additional options. Most have self-explanatory text on the screens, but let's take a moment to review the options you will uncover:

Subnet mask and length: Define the size of the subnet that you are asking DHCP to assign IP addresses within.

Exclusions: If there are any IP addresses within your defined scope which you would like DHCP to refrain from handing out, specify them here. An example of this would be an IP address for a server which is already statically assigned, and falls within the DHCP range that you declared earlier. DHCP will not know about any static IP addresses that fall within its scope, and so DHCP will still hand out that address and create a conflict on the network if you don't specify static addresses as exclusions.

Lease Duration: When a computer or device grabs an IP address from a DHCP server, that address is always "leased" out to the computer, and only for a specific amount of time. When this time expires, the client or device will reach back to DHCP to get another IP address. Perhaps the same one will be issued, perhaps a different IP address. Lease Duration is where you define the amount of time DHCP clients can retain their IP addresses before asking for a new one.

Configure DHCP Options: There are many additional options that you can include with a DHCP issued IP address. This is the place where you would define what information a client receives in addition to their IP address. You can declare your network's Default Gateway, the DNS Servers present within your network, and even specify special options such as provisioning information for VOIP phones. The two most common pieces of information to define here are Default Gateway (router), and DNS Servers.

The last option you encounter is whether or not you want to activate your scope now. Typically, yes you would want to do this. Activating the scope means that the DHCP server is now ready to issue IP addresses based on this scope to any computer who asks for one. However, there is one important thing we have not accomplished yet, as this is the first time that we have touched this new DHCP role.

Authorize the DHCP server

If the DHCP server you are working with has never been authorized within the network, you must do so before it can perform any work. To do this, from inside the DHCP management console, simply right-click on the name of your server and then select the option to **Authorize**.

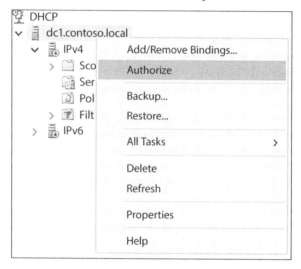

Figure 4.16: Authorizing a DHCP server

As soon as your DHCP server is authorized and your scope is activated, it is immediately active and any computer in your network whose NIC is configured to grab an address automatically from a DHCP server will start doing so against this new DHCP server.

Now that our new scope has been created, you can expand the scope inside the DHCP console and see some additional information about this scope. By clicking on the **Address Leases** folder, you can see all of the DHCP addresses that have been handed out by this DHCP server.

As you can see in *Figure 4.17*, I have a Windows 10 client computer on the network, which does not have a static address, and so it has grabbed a DHCP address from my DHCP server. It has been given the first IP address that I defined in my scope, 10.10.10.100. The next machine that reaches in to grab an IP address from this DHCP server will receive 10.10.10.101, and so on from there:

Figure 4.17: IP addresses assigned by DHCP

Scope Options

DHCP scopes can be configured to hand out a very small set of information, like we have configured so far, or when needed DHCP is capable of handing out a lot more. When a client reaches into DHCP to grab information, we are currently handing out an IP address and a subnet mask, because these two pieces of information are critical to making traffic flow on our networks. Most networks, however, are going to require at least a couple of additional pieces of information to be given to DHCP clients, for those devices to really be usable in a traditional corporate network. We very briefly discussed additional scope options that can be passed to client machines during IP address assignment, now let's take a look at how to get back into those options from within an existing DHCP scope and tweak them to our liking.

Listed under the new scope we just created, you will see a folder titled **Scope Options**. Right-click on **Scope Options**, and then select **Configure Options....**

Here you will find many, many different checkboxes, all of which are available DHCP scope options. By selecting a checkbox and populating the necessary information for that particular scope option, you are then configuring this DHCP scope to give not only simple IP address and subnet mask information to all clients reaching in, but this additional information as well. Two very common ones are 003 **Router** and 006 **DNS Servers**. The 003 **Router** designation is essentially your default gateway setting on the client NIC. Almost all networks will have a default gateway, typically a firewall or a router, and by selecting this option you can define the default gateway address to be assigned to your DHCP clients.

In *Figure 4.18*, you can see that I have selected 006 **DNS Servers**, and configured the IP addresses of the DNS servers in my lab. Now when my client computers pull IP addresses via DHCP, their NICs will also be automatically configured with these two DNS server addresses, which will cause them to be able to resolve DNS names in my environment:

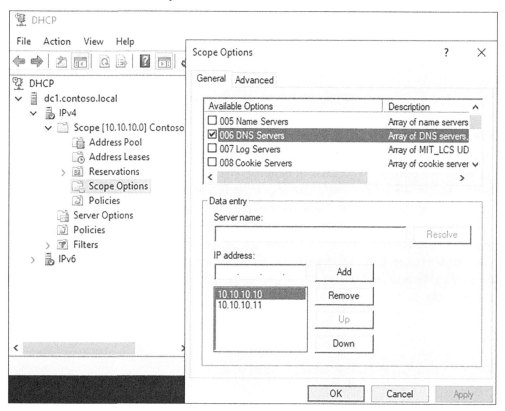

Figure 4.18: Using DHCP options

Another useful DHCP scope option is option 66. If you have a VoIP phone system and want to set up some automatic provisioning of your physical phones, it is easy to create a DHCP scope just for the phones, and use option 66 to point at your phone system's provisioning link. When phones grab an IP address from the DHCP server, they will be automatically provisioned in the phone system as well!

DHCP reservations

Assigning IP addresses from a big pool of available ones is great, but these address leases are subject to expiry and change. This means that a computer that has `10.10.10.100` today might receive `10.10.10.125` tomorrow. Typically, this is fine from a desktop computer perspective, as they don't generally care what IP address they have. Client computers are usually reaching outward on the network, and other devices are rarely trying to find and contact them. What if you have a more permanent fixture in your network, like a Windows server, but you don't want to have to deal with statically addressing this server? Another great example of such a device is a printer that is connected to your network. Some printers don't even have an interface from which you could assign a static IP address, and once your printer gets a DHCP address you typically want that address to remain the same throughout the printer's life, because you'll be configuring computers to send their print jobs to that IP address. This is where **DHCP reservations** come into play. A reservation is the act of taking a single IP address within your DHCP scope, and reserving it to a particular device. This device will receive the same IP address every time it connects through the DHCP server, and this particular IP address will not be handed out to any other device on your network. By using reservations inside DHCP, you can allow the DHCP server to handle the assigning of IP addresses even to your permanent servers, so that you do not have to manually configure the NICs of those servers, yet still maintain permanent IP addresses on those machines.

You can see the folder called **Reservations** in the DHCP console. Currently, there is nothing listed here, but by right-clicking on **Reservations** and choosing **New Reservation…**, we will create one for ourselves. Let's work once again with that `WEB1` server. Right now, I have a static IP address assigned to `WEB1`, but I will instead create a reservation for it on the IP address `10.10.10.150`:

Figure 4.19: Setting up a reservation

Whoa, whoa, whoa ... back the train up. Most of the information on this screen makes sense—a quick description of the server name and the IP address itself—but how did I come up with that MAC address? A **MAC address** is a network card's physical address on the network. When your networking equipment tries to send information to a certain IP address, or, in this case, when the DHCP server needs to hand a certain IP address to a particular NIC on a server, it needs a physical identifier for that network card. So, this MAC address is something that is unique to the NIC on my WEB1 server. Every network card on your network has a unique MAC address. By logging in to my WEB1 server, I can run `ipconfig /all` and see the MAC address listed for my NIC right in that output, that goofy-looking combination of letters and numbers shown as **Physical Address**. That is where I got this information. This is how DHCP decides when to invoke reservations. If a network interface asks it for a DHCP address, and that device's MAC address is listed here in the reservations, then the DHCP server will hand the reserved address back to the device, rather than one from the general pool:

```
Administrator: Windows PowerShell

Ethernet adapter Ethernet:

   Connection-specific DNS Suffix  . :
   Description . . . . . . . . . . . : Microsoft Hyper-V Network Adapter
   Physical Address. . . . . . . . . : 00-15-5D-08-58-08
   DHCP Enabled. . . . . . . . . . . : No
```

Figure 4.20: Finding the MAC address

Now that our DHCP reservation has been created, I will head into the NIC settings on my WEB1 server, and get rid of all the static IP addressing information by choosing the option to **Obtain an IP address automatically**:

Figure 4.21: Removing the static IP address information

After doing that, WEB1 will reach over to the DHCP server and ask for an address, and you can see that I have now been assigned the reserved address of 10.10.10.150:

Figure 4.22: Reserving 10.10.10.150 for WEB1

This will always be the IP address of the WEB1 server from this point forward, unless I change my DHCP reservation or somehow change the MAC address of WEB1. This could possibly happen if I were to install a new NIC into WEB1.

You can also create DHCP reservations for objects other than Windows devices in your network. Since all you need is the MAC address of the device (and every device with a network adapter has a MAC address), it is easy to create reservations for devices such as print servers, copy machines, security alarm systems, cameras, wireless access points, and more.

DHCP failover

Never too much of a good thing? Just like the creation of multiple domain controller servers creates good redundancy for Active Directory, the DHCP servers in your network can be tied together into a failover pair to create their own form of high availability. While it is true that the DHCP server role often happens to co-exist alongside the AD DS and DNS roles, this is not a requirement. You already know that it is easy to store DNS zones right inside Active Directory so there is automatic replication of zone information, but this mentality is not true of DHCP scopes.

DHCP is a useful tool inside domain environments, or outside of domain environments. As such, it is not as tightly integrated a role as DNS. So when we create DHCP failover, we need to take a more manual approach, and whether or not the DHCP role happens to be hosted on top of a domain controller makes no difference.

Two DHCP servers

In a DHCP server failover environment, two DHCP servers can be configured and pointed at each other, and they will then replicate DHCP lease information between themselves, always keeping this information up to date. That way, if one DHCP server goes offline, the other can pick up the slack and continue issuing IPs and renewing the leases of those IPs.

I said "two" DHCP servers above, and this is an important point of clarification. With Windows Server DHCP failover, you can only connect two DHCP servers together. No more. It is also important to note, as we progress into the world of IPv6, that DHCP failover is only intended for use with IPv4 scopes. The failover of DHCP servers would be unnecessary in the IPv6 world anyhow, as most IPv6 implementations are stateless, and the only information that DHCP needs to give to IPv6 clients are the options, which could simply be configured on multiple DHCP servers, and the clients care not from which server they pull that option information.

Hot standby mode

There are two different modes of operation that can be employed by DHCP failover: hot standby mode or load sharing mode. Hot standby, as the name indicates, is more of a primary/failover mentality. One DHCP server is primary and is always responsible for an IPv4 scope, unless it becomes unavailable. In that case, the failover DHCP server starts taking over until the primary can be restored.

Hot standby mode is useful for branch offices that are connected back to the primary network via a WAN of some sort. The local branch offices could have their own local DHCP server that handles DHCP primarily, but if that DHCP server were to go offline, DHCP requests would reach over the WAN link and grab a lease from the standby DHCP server sitting in your main site. In this kind of deployment, you could easily configure one single DHCP server in the main site to be the hot standby for multiple branch offices, as it is easy to configure multiple scopes on a DHCP server.

Load sharing mode

Alternatively, indeed much more common, is load sharing mode. This is the default mode of operation for DHCP failover. In load sharing mode, two DHCP servers are configured with the same scope of information and then both service incoming clients. In doing so, they share the load between servers, both responding and also replicating information between themselves, so both are always aware of which IP addresses have been handed out to clients.

In load sharing mode, you want both DHCP servers to be located in the same physical site. They need to have very fast communication between them to keep replication data straight. I have seen DHCP failover configured across sites before, and can tell you definitively that it can cause IP conflicts and similar issues. Keep them in the same site.

Configuring DHCP failover

Now we know about DHCP failover, how do we set it up? You already know that I have DC1 and DC2 in my test lab environment. Both of these servers are already domain controllers and DC1 is also a DNS server, though those facts have no bearing on DHCP configuration. These could be domain controllers, or simply domain-joined servers, or even non-domain-joined servers, and DHCP would have all of the same options for failover. Since I already have these two servers available to me, I am going to use them to create a DHCP scope that is replicated between both. This is an important point to clarify, that DHCP failover is configured on a per-scope basis. You don't necessarily tie DC1 and DC2 together, but rather inside the DHCP scope properties you establish failover between DC1 and DC2 for a particular scope (or scopes). This implies, then, that you have the ability to create DHCP scopes that are running in failover mode, and additionally create DHCP scopes on those same servers that are not doing any form of failover.

 Make sure the clocks are in sync! If your DHCP servers are domain-joined, their clocks should always be kept in sync automatically by Active Directory. If your DHCP servers are not domain-joined, you will want to ensure that the system clocks on both servers are using the same time source to always retain continuity.

DC1 already has the DHCP role installed, and I already created a quick scope on it way back when I first set up this test lab, so that my Win10 client computer could grab a DHCP address and communicate with the rest of my network. DC2, however, does not yet have the DHCP role installed, so the first step is to go ahead and add that role.

Whenever creating new DHCP servers in a network, the role must be installed of course, but there is a second critical piece of the puzzle to enable them to be recognized as DHCP servers. It is fairly obvious, but after installing the DHCP role onto a server, Server Manager will prompt you to **Complete DHCP configuration**. This pulls up a small wizard with basically just one step to accomplish—**Authorize** your new DHCP server. This mini-wizard can be called via Server Manager, or if you missed the prompt there and opened up right into the DHCP management tool, you can alternatively authorize a DHCP server by right-clicking on the server name inside the DHCP management tool, and then selecting **Authorize**.

OK, we now have two authorized DHCP servers in our environment, and a scope is already present on DC1. This scope is servicing clients already, handing out IP addresses in our network. Creating failover for this scope is quite easy. Open up DHCP management on DC1, and navigate to find your IPv4 scope. Right-click on the scope itself, and select **Configure Failover...**:

Figure 4.23: Configuring DHCP failover

Next, select which scopes you want to configure in failover. As I mentioned before, DHCP failover configuration is individual per DHCP scope. If your DHCP server has multiple scopes already established, you can select to configure failover on all or only some of them. Then on the second screen, we need to define the failover DHCP server. You can type out the name of the server on this screen, but what I like to do is click that **Add Server** button, which then displays any servers in your environment that are recognized as authorized DHCP servers. By using the button and then selecting the second DHCP server from the list, it gives you one more validation that you have properly authorized the second server, DC2 in my case, in your network. You can see this in *Figure 4.24*:

Figure 4.24: Selecting DC2 for DHCP failover

On the following screen of this wizard, we define all of the relationship parameters between the two DHCP servers. As you can see in our next screenshot, this is the screen where you define simple things that don't have too much impact such as **Relationship Name** and creating a **Shared Secret** that the two DHCP servers will use to interact with each other, but this screen is also where you create the definition of which type of failover is happening for this scope. We have already talked about **Load balance** mode and **Hot standby** mode, and here is where you would additionally define, in **Load balance** mode, what weights to assign the two servers for establishing that load balancing.

Unless you have a particular reason to deviate, the default settings are generally what you want. Make sure that **Maximum Client Lead Time** remains configured at one hour or more. You may bump that number down smaller for testing failover in your network, but in a production environment one hour is the general recommendation:

Configure Failover

Create a new failover relationship

Create a new failover relationship with partner dc2.contoso.local

Relationship Name: dc1.contoso.local-dc2.contoso.local

Maximum Client Lead Time: 1 hours   0 minutes

Mode: Load balance

Load Balance Percentage
Local Server: 50 %

Partner Server: 50 %

☐ State Switchover Interval: 60 minutes

☑ Enable Message Authentication

Shared Secret: ········

< Back   Next >   Cancel

Figure 4.25: Configuring failover relationship settings

That's it! Click **Next** a couple more times, and your DHCP failover configuration will be pushed out to the second DHCP server. Now, if one of these servers were to go offline or have some kind of issue, DHCP clients coming in fresh or whose DHCP leases are expiring will be able to acquire a lease from either DHCP server setup for failover.

Now that DHCP failover has been established, you would sort of expect something inside the DHCP management console to have changed to visually indicate to us that there is failover configured on the scope, but that is not really the case. Everything in here looks exactly the same as before failover creation. I point this out to let you know that during future visits to this console, or if you are a new admin to an existing infrastructure and want to quickly identify whether or not DHCP failover is established in your environment, you can find this information by right-clicking on the scope. In the menu list that is displayed with that right-click, you will now find an option called **Deconfigure Failover**, which implies that failover is currently configured for this scope. Additionally, if you head into the properties of that scope, you will find a **Failover** tab that displays all pertinent information about DHCP failover:

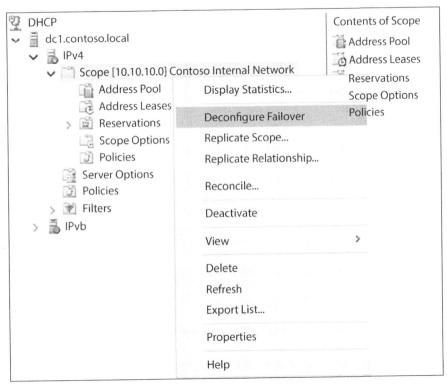

Figure 4.26: Deconfiguring failover

One last verification, let's log into DC2 and see what the DHCP management console looks like now! Remember that previously the only thing I have done on DC2 is to install the DHCP role and to authorize this server. I never even opened up the DHCP management console on that server. If I do so now, you can see that my 10.10.10.0 scope has been replicated over to this server, including the current address lease information!

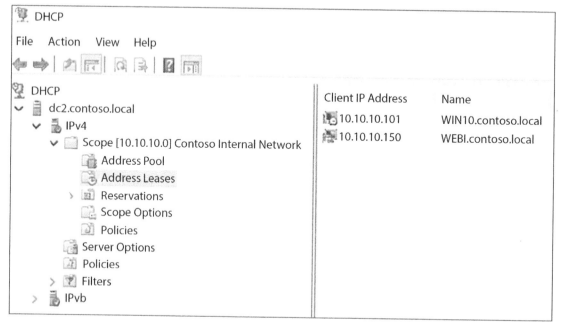

Figure 4.27: The 10.10.10.0 scope is now replicated to DC2

IPAM

The **IP Address Management (IPAM)** feature built into Windows Server 2022 is overlooked by many server administrators because it is a feature and not a full-blown role inside Windows. IPAM is a technology that allows centralized monitoring and management of DHCP and DNS in your environment. If all of your infrastructure is sitting inside one building, it is easy enough to simply use the DNS and DHCP management tools from any server or workstation in your network and have full control over both of those technologies. But how about larger and enterprise-class networks that span many locations, each with its own sets of DNS and DHCP servers? IPAM is useful for gathering up all of those differing namespaces and scopes and providing access to them from one interface.

Let's install the IPAM feature in my lab so you have an idea of where to start, should you choose to employ this feature. Begin by choosing a server upon which you want to install IPAM, and simply walk through the **Add Roles and Features Wizard** to add the feature called **IP Address Management (IPAM) Server**.

It is not recommended to install IPAM onto a domain controller, or onto a DHCP server as that will hinder its ability to acquire information from these systems.

Now that the feature is installed, launching Server Manager will display a new section in the left window pane called **IPAM**. Go ahead and click on **IPAM**, and you are now presented with a set of six tasks that need to be accomplished in order to use IPAM:

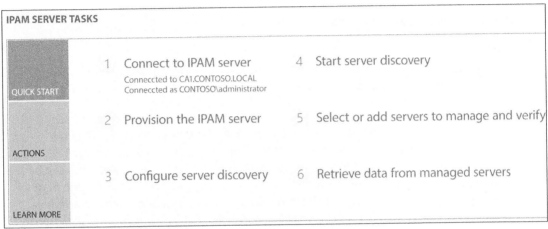

Figure 4.28: IPAM server tasks

The first step is already finished, we are connected to the IPAM server. In my lab, I installed IPAM on my CA1 server, but not for any particular reason. You could dedicate a server to this task or install the feature onto an existing server.

Moving on to s*tep 2,* **Provision the IPAM server,** you will have a chance to read over some good descriptive text about how IPAM plans to interact with your servers. You have the option of manually configuring each server (who's going to do that?) but clearly the way Microsoft expects most of us to roll this out is through the use of Group Policy. We discuss Group Policy in the next chapter of this book, but for the purpose of setting up IPAM we can pretty much just flow through these configuration wizards, selecting the default settings, and understand that under the hood this console is establishing GPOs for us, which will then be pushed down to the servers in our network to configure them for reporting into IPAM.

The only selections that need to be made inside *step 2* are what database for IPAM to utilize, and which provisioning method should be used to send IPAM settings out to your servers. For the database, if you have a SQL server you may certainly use it to store IPAM information, but the default selection is **Windows Internal Database (WID),** which is a built-in database platform used by many of the Windows Server roles and features. We will utilize WID for this new IPAM server, and as we already mentioned, the rolling out of IPAM settings is easily accomplished via Group Policy.

On the screen where you select **Group Policy Based** as the provisioning method, you will also need to define a **GPO name prefix**. When this console creates the GPOs needed for IPAM to work, it will define names for the GPOs and those names cannot be altered, but what Microsoft allows here is for you to assign a prefix to those GPO names, so that when you later look inside the Group Policy management tool, all of the GPO configurations related to IPAM will be listed together, all having the same prefix that you define on this screen:

Managed servers must be configured with settings that allow IPAM to access remote management functions and event information.

Select a provisioning method for managed servers:

○ Manual

The manual provisioning method requires that you configure the required network shares, security groups, and firewall rules manually on each managed server.

◉ Group Policy Based

The Group Policy based provisioning method requires Group Policy Objects (GPO) to be created in each domain that you manage with this IPAM server. IPAM will automatically configure settings on managed servers by adding the server to appropriate GPO. This can be especially useful in a large network with many managed servers. GPOs that you create must follow naming conventions used by IPAM, however you can customize the GPO name with a prefix of your choice. The GPO name prefix you specify should be unique for each IPAM server in the Active Directory forest.

* GPO name prefix: | IPAM_CA1 |

ⓘ You can create GPOs in each IPAM managed domain using the Invoke-IpamGpoProvisiong IPAM Windows PowerShell cmdlet.

Learn more about access provisioning on managed servers

Figure 4.29: Selecting a provisioning method

You'll notice a little informational text in *Figure 4.29*, as well as on the summary screen when you finish *step 2*, regarding a PowerShell cmdlet called `Invoke-IpamGpoProvisioning`. Common sense would tell us that after *step 2* in the IPAM implementation, you would move on to *step 3*, right? Actually not in this case. Configuring server discovery (*step 3*) is a step that we need to take, but at this point the IPAM console is waiting for those GPOs to be created so that they can be used and referenced during the rest of the setup process.

Pause on your work inside the IPAM steps, and open an administrative PowerShell prompt, making sure that you are logged in to your server with a domain admin account. Then simply run `Invoke-IpamGpoProvisioning`. This will ask you to key in the name of your domain, as well as that `GPOPrefixName` you specified during the wizard; be sure to type it in exactly the same!

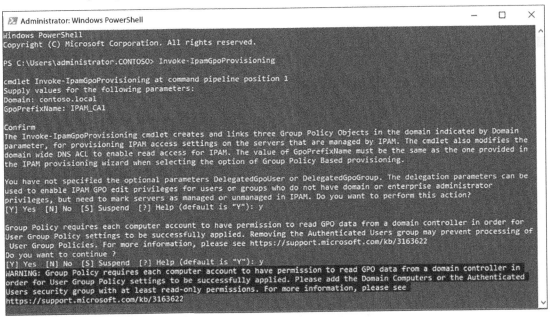

Figure 4.30: Running Invoke-IpamGpoProvisioning

You will be required to enter *Y* and press *Enter* three times to finish through this command. In reading the warning text that is being displayed, the same text three times in a row, this is asking you for confirmation simply because when these GPOs are being created, their security filtering settings are being modified away from default GPO security filtering behavior. We will explain GPO security filtering soon, but for IPAM's purposes, simply type *Y* and continue through these prompts. Now that `Invoke-IpamGpoProvisioning` has done its work, if we sneak a quick peek into Group Policy Management, you can see that there are three new GPOs now that were not there a minute ago:

Figure 4.31: Invoke-IpamGpoProvisioning has added three new GPOs

Now back inside IPAM configuration on `CA1`, we will go ahead and click on *step 3*, **Configure Server Discovery**. Inside, use the **Get forests** and **Add** buttons to query your domain for infrastructure services that can be monitored by IPAM. Your domain should be listed, with checkboxes selected on the components that the wizard was able to discover about your domain. In my case, I have discovered all three—**Domain controller, DHCP server**, and **DNS server**. I will leave all three checked so that IPAM can pull data about all three of these roles and click **OK**:

Select the forest:

contoso.local   ⌄ | Get forests |

Select domains to discover:

⌄ | Add |

Select the server roles to discover:

Domain	Domain controller	DHCP server	DNS server
(root domain) contoso.local	✓	✓	✓

| Remove |

Figure 4.32: Configuring server discovery

Move on to *step 4*, **Start server discovery**. This launches a scheduled task in the background that is reaching out and finding additional information about your infrastructure. Once finished, click on *step 5*, **Select or add servers to manage and verify IPAM access**. Here you should see the servers listed that are hosting your AD DS, DNS, and DHCP roles. Right-click on each server that you want to manage, and then select **Edit Server....** Inside this screen, for each server, change the server's **Manageability status** field to **Managed**:

IPv4

OVERVIEW   IPv4 | 2 total

Add or Edit Server   — ☐ ✕

Provide server details and other custom field mapping details:

	ess Status	Server Name	DNS Suffix
		DC1	contoso.local
		DC2	contoso.local

Basic configurations

	Field	Value	
*	Server name (FQDN)	DC1.contoso.local	Verify
	Server forest name	contoso.local	
*	IP address	10.10.10.10	
*	Server type	✓ DC ✓ DNS server ✓ DHCP server ☐ NPS server	
	Manageability status	Managed ⌄	
	Owner		
	Description		

Figure 4.33: Managing your servers

Finally, click on *step 6*, **Retrieve data from managed servers**, which will set the GPOs into action and start pulling information from those servers into the IPAM database. When finished, you will now have a centralized interface from which you can view information about Active Directory, DNS, and DHCP scopes, as you can see in *Figure 4.34*:

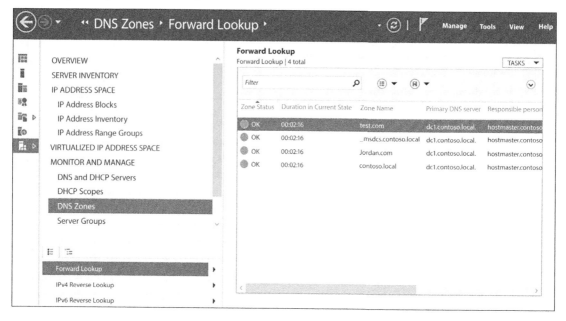

Figure 4.34: IPAM's centralized interface

Management of DHCP from within IPAM is particularly useful, as classic administration of DHCP from within its own management console can get pretty messy in an environment with many different DHCP scopes. IPAM provides an interface from which you can quickly and easily see information about all scopes together, and even run some fun PowerShell cmdlets to quickly gather data that would have otherwise taken manual poking and prodding to discover in the past:

- `Find-IpamFreeSubnet`
- `Add-IpamSubnet`
- `Find-IpamFreeRange` (this one is nice because it helps you to quickly discover a range of available IP addresses)
- `Add-IpamRange`

Summary

The Microsoft core stack of infrastructure technologies generally consists of Active Directory, DNS, and DHCP—and often you will find all three of these housed on the same servers. Understanding these technologies and knowing how to utilize their associated toolsets is an essential part of any server administrator's life. As a manager in an IT company, I will tell you with surety that having a grasp on this will greatly improve your chances of finding that sysadmin role you've been seeking.

I hope these last two chapters have been beneficial to your overall understanding of the ways that companies make use of Windows Server technology and have given you something to help prepare for IT life in a business setting. Next, we turn to another baked-in component of any Active Directory-focused environment, but one that is often underutilized. Group Policy is an amazingly powerful tool that can be used to enhance security and create automation inside any domain.

Questions

1. Which kind of DNS record directs email flow?
2. Which type of DNS record resolves a name to an IPv6 address?
3. Which DNS zone type resolves IP addresses backward into hostnames?
4. Which DHCP option is often used for VoIP phone provisioning?
5. Which mode of DHCP failover is often used between branch offices and a primary site?
6. What is the standard recommendation and default setting for Maximum Client Lead Time when configuring load balanced DHCP failover?
7. Which Windows Server roles can IPAM tap into?

Join our community on Discord

Join our community's Discord space for discussions with the author and other readers:

https://packt.link/SecNet

5

Group Policy

If you find yourself reading this book from front to back, indeed a good and not at all weird way to read a book, you already have a general idea of what Group Policy is and does (because we talked about it for a minute in *Chapter 3, Active Directory*). However, I've been around IT folks long enough to know that reading a book from cover to cover is fairly rare, and attention spans rarely accommodate such a quest. Therefore, any of you hitting up this chapter in a random fashion because the words "Group Policy" drew your attention or you have a specific need that you are hoping to be answered in this chapter, fear not! Let's again summarize the great and glorious power of Group Policy.

It's easy to understand the general use of the word "policy," meaning some kind of ruleset, structure, or standard to which you need something to adhere. In our case, we're talking about Microsoft Windows-based computers (and servers). Applying policies to computers, such as security policies, application policies, or printer policies, sounds like a great idea. If applying policies to a computer is great, applying policies to a group of computers must be even better, hence the term "Group Policy." In a nutshell, Group Policy is a centralized way to issue policies to groups of computers inside your domain network. Here's a quick list of the topics we plan to cover together:

- Group Policy Objects
- Building a GPO
- Scoping a GPO
- Computer settings and user settings
- Policy versus preference
- Default Domain Policy
- Administrative Templates
- The Central Store

Group Policy Objects

This is pretty straightforward. The overlying technology we are talking about here is called Group Policy, and an individual instance of a Group Policy is known as a **Group Policy Object**, commonly referred to as a **GPO**.

A GPO is a single package that contains one or many policy settings and applies to a domain computer, a domain user, or sometimes many computers and users all at the same time.

GPOs are stored inside Active Directory and are replicated among your domain controller servers. Every time a domain user logs into a domain-joined computer that is connected to your network, the computer reaches out to Active Directory and asks, "Hey, got any GPO settings for me?" Then a whole slew of activity commences as a domain controller hands over all of the GPO settings that it contains that apply to the computer and/or user logging in. This is a key piece of information. GPOs are scoped upon creation, giving you the power to define to whom each policy is applied. Extremely powerful stuff. These policy settings then plug themselves into place on your computer, forcing certain things to happen (or not happen) at the discretion of your IT department. You can lock down settings, force settings into place, and configure default settings but still allow users to override them. You can throw certain settings at some computers and completely opposite settings at others. You can even apply conflicting GPOs to the same computers and sit back and watch them fight to see who comes out as the winner in the end. If you don't understand how Group Policy works, it is very easy to cause huge problems in your network, as it is very, very easy to apply settings to every machine in the domain. A single GPO has the potential to bring your entire network to its knees if misused.

So… *that's* reassuring, right? Trust me, while Group Policy comes with a warning label and *"with great power comes great responsibility"* and all that, you will want to use GPOs more than you are now after seeing all that they can do.

Group Policy background refresh cycle

I mentioned that Group Policy processes on your domain-joined computers every time a user logs in, and that is true. What is also true is that Group Policy reprocesses itself at intervals throughout the day, even while the user remains logged in. By default, and almost nobody changes it, something called a background refresh happens every 90 minutes. This means that implementing new GPOs during the day generally works fine because those settings will roll into place even without users needing to log off or restart their computers. There are exceptions to this, though, as some GPO settings are unable to process as background cycles and can only take effect during the login process. Some examples of such GPOs are a login script (which can only run during logon or logoff of a computer) or even something like a mapped network drive. Some GPOs will only push themselves into place during the user login process.

Many times I find myself testing GPO settings as I make changes to them, and it would make for a very inefficient workday if I had to wait 90 minutes or restart my test computer after every little tweak or change to a GPO. Thankfully, we have a quick and easy command-line tool that can be used to force Group Policy to reach out and do its thing, any time of any day!

```
gpupdate /force
```

Running this command inside Command Prompt or PowerShell on a domain-joined client computer will cause it to immediately reach out and grab updated GPO settings. Keep in mind, your computer does need to be able to contact a domain controller for Group Policy to process, so this isn't going to work if your work laptop is sitting in your house and not connected via VPN.

But for any computers inside the office or in some way connected to your corporate network, you can run gpupdate all the live-long day and continually roll new policies and changes into place.

Building a GPO

There's nothing quite as good as jumping in and getting your hands dirty, so let's get down to business and build a new GPO. Don't worry, we will be careful not to apply this GPO to anything yet and save that for the next section. As with most Microsoft technologies, there is a special management console created just for interacting with Group Policy, appropriately named the **Group Policy Management Console (GPMC)**. Logging into any of your domain controller servers, you can launch the GPMC from inside **Administrative Tools**, inside the **Tools** menu of Server Manager, or by launching GPMC.MSC from **Start | Run**, Command Prompt, or PowerShell:

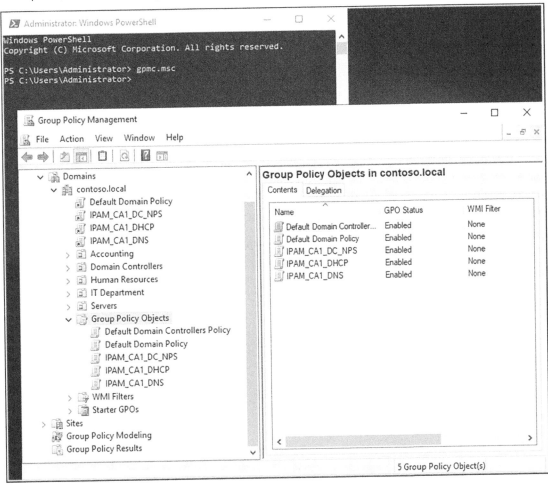

Figure 5.1: GPMC

You'll notice in *Figure 5.1* that there are already some GPOs listed here. They are a combination of default GPOs that always exist when you install Active Directory (we'll talk about the Default Domain Policy a little later in this chapter) and the IPAM GPOs that the IPAM configuration process put into place for us in *Chapter 4, DNS and DHCP*. To create a new GPO in a way that does not yet apply to any workstations or users, right-click on the **Group Policy Objects** folder and select **New**. Create a name for your new GPO, click **OK**, and you have created a Group Policy Object! So far, your new GPO is void of any settings or configurations, and it does not apply to anything or anybody, so it is precisely pointless. We will soon change that...

Adding Trusted Sites

I named my first GPO *Adding Trusted Sites* because I am going to use this new GPO to apply some URLs to be recognized as trusted sites inside Internet Explorer on my Windows 10 client computer. If you run a web application in your network that needs to run JavaScript or ActiveX controls, or something like that, it may be required that the website is part of the trusted sites list inside Internet Explorer for it to run properly. You could print off an instructions page for the helpdesk on how to do this on each computer and ask them to spend the time doing it for every user who calls in because they cannot access the application. Or you could simply create a GPO that makes these changes for you automatically on every workstation and save yourself from dealing with all of those phone calls. This is just one tiny example of the power that Group Policy possesses, but it's a good example because it is useful, and it is a setting that is buried way down in the GPO settings, so you can get a feel for just how deep these capabilities go. Yes, I do realize that Internet Explorer is officially dead, and Edge is the new Microsoft browser of choice. Unfortunately, that is much easier said than done, and there are still many line-of-business or custom-coded apps hanging around in businesses that will force us to continue to see Internet Explorer on some workstations for years to come, and so we proceed onward.

Right-click on the new GPO and choose **Edit...**. Now navigate to **Computer Configuration | Policies | Administrative Templates | Windows Components | Internet Explorer | Internet Control Panel | Security Page**. See, I told you it was buried in there!

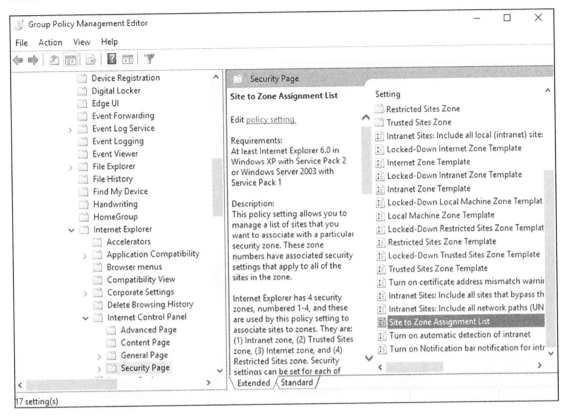

Figure 5.2: Creating a GPO to manage trusted websites

Now double-click on **Site to Zone Assignment List** and set it to **Enabled**. This allows you to click on the **Show...** button, within which you can enter websites and give them zone assignments. Each GPO setting has a nice descriptive text to accompany it, telling you exactly what that particular setting is for and what the options mean. As you can see in the text for this one, in order to set my websites to be trusted sites, I need to give them a zone assignment value of 2. And, just for fun, I also added a site that I do not want to be accessible to my users and gave it a zone value of 4 so that `badsite.contoso.com` is a member of the restricted sites zone on all of my desktop computers.

Here is my completed list:

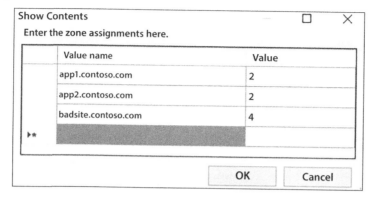

Figure 5.3: Assigning websites to different zones

Are we done? Almost. As soon as I click on the **OK** button, these settings are now stored in my GPO and are ready to be deployed. As you know, we have not assigned this new GPO to apply to anybody yet, so for now the GPO is populated with these settings but still doing nothing. Before we push out these settings, let's build out a few more common GPOs to make sure our examples here are well-rounded.

Mapping network drives

File servers are some of the most common types of servers that exist because all companies across all industries need to create and maintain documentation to run their businesses. This is not a chapter about how to build a file server, set up shares, restrict permissions, or utilize a **Distributed File System (DFS)** to improve the overall flexibility and resiliency of your file server infrastructure, although these are all good things to learn. Today, we are going to assume that you already have file servers in place and that there are already shared folders on those file servers. In my test lab, I have shared folders from a few different servers, as identified here:

- `\\DC1\HR`
- `\\DC2\Accounting`
- `\\WEB3\Installers`

The challenge we are trying to solve is how to automate these shared folder locations being available on all of my user's workstations. I could put together a piece of documentation that shows users how to manually get to these locations by using UNC paths plugged into the address bar of File Explorer. Or maybe even take it a step further and show my folks how to map network drives from inside File Explorer so that they end up with drive letters assigned on their computers for ongoing access to these locations. Doing so would work, but it would put an administrative burden on my users and also lead to the possibility of users having differing drive letters. Grace might use her "R" drive letter to map to the accounting share, while Jackson may decide that "T" is his accounting drive letter of choice.

Obviously, there's a better way to handle this situation. One of the very common chores we task to a GPO is the standardized creation of mapped network drives on client computers. Inside a new GPO, we can define UNC paths for shares and assign drive letters to them. We can then assign that GPO to users and computers, and drive letters will magically map when your users log in to their computers.

Create a new GPO for this purpose, and edit that GPO, as you already know how to do. This time, we are navigating to the following location:

User Configuration | Preferences | Windows Settings | Drive Maps

Right-clicking on **Drive Maps** and choosing **New | Mapped Drive** brings you into the configuration section for a single mapped drive letter. You can see in the screenshot below that I am mapping a drive to \\DC1\HR, and assigning it a drive letter of H:

Figure 5.4: Mapping drives with Group Policy

You'll notice the **Action** dropdown menu has four different options: **Create**, **Replace**, **Update**, and **Delete**.

This is important to understand as many GPO preference configurations have this same drop-down selection. Here is a quick summary of each available option as it relates to our new drive-mapping policy:

- **Create:** Use this action to create the new mapped drive only if it does not already exist. If the H: drive is already in use on a workstation, this new mapping will then be ignored. In our example, if I were to configure this new drive mapping for **Create**, it would only take an action if the H: drive letter was currently open and available.

- **Replace:** Use this action to remove an existing setting and replace it with a new setting. In our case, it will update whatever mapped drive is using H: to our \\DC1\HR. The **Replace** option is redundant because of the **Update** option and is rarely used.

- **Update:** This is the default action for most preference settings and is generally the most useful. If the setting that we are configuring doesn't exist, **Update** will create it. Additionally, if the setting (mapped drive) is already in place on the workstation, it will now be updated to reflect our new definition inside the GPO. Drive mapping policies almost always use the **Update** action to push new drive letters into place.

- **Delete:** This removes the specific setting from the client machine. If you are removing a network share and want to ensure that it is removed from all of the computers in your domain, this would be a useful action to ensure that happens.

Before clicking **OK** on this new drive mapping, go ahead and visit the **Common** tab. This tab and its five options are commonly shown on many preference settings that you plug into a GPO. Most of these are self-explanatory, though we will discuss item-level targeting more in just a few pages. For our drive-mapping GPO, I like to point out the **Run in logged-on user's security context** checkbox. This tells Group Policy to run whatever setting or preference the GPO is putting into place under the logged-in user's account. For mapped drives, this is particularly useful because you typically want users to interface with their mapped drives in their regular user context.

While it is not common to check this box for the majority of GPO settings, for drive-mapping GPOs, I always do:

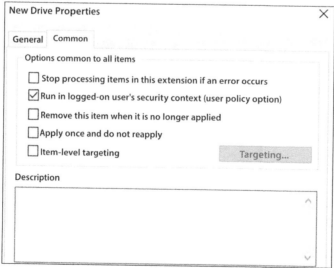

Figure 5.5: Map drives under user's security context

Rinse and repeat for any additional drive letters that you want to include in your new GPO, and you are now well on your way to automating the mapping of all drive letters across your entire network! I set up drive letter mappings for each of my shared folders and also included a GPO setting to delete the Z: drive if it exists.

It doesn't in my lab, but this way, you can also see an example of what that looks like inside the policy:

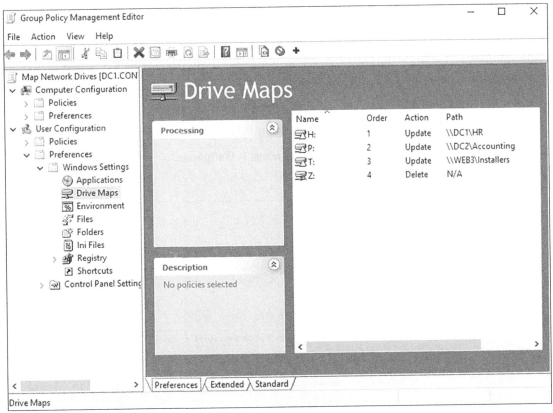

Figure 5.6: Mapped drives via GPO

Once again, this new GPO does not apply to any users yet but never fear – once we finish creating a few more example GPOs, we will move on to scoping GPO settings, which is where we will push the new GPOs into action and verify that settings and mapped drives show up automatically on our client computers.

Installing registry keys

In much the same way that mapped network drives can be pushed to users via GPO, we can implement registry keys and values on computers automatically as well. This is spectacularly powerful because almost anything within a Windows environment can be manipulated by using registry keys. Create yet another new GPO and this time, navigate to the following location:

User Configuration | Preferences | Windows Settings | Registry

Creating, replacing, updating, or deleting registry keys flows in very much the same fashion as it does for mapping network drives. The tricky bit is making sure that the options are specified properly, or they won't work, particularly the **Key Path** and **Value** information. For our example, I am going to push a registry value that prevents users from being able to change their desktop background image and specifies a custom desktop background of my own.

In my experience, the easiest way to ensure the GPO configuration is populated correctly inside the configuration window is to actually place the new registry key and/or value that you are working with on the server or computer from which you are running the GPMC. This way, you can select the ellipsis button and seek out the exact registry setting, rather than trying to remember how it must be formatted for the **Key Path** field.

The registry information that I am putting into place is:

HKCU\Software\Microsoft\Windows\CurrentVersion\Policies\System

Inside the system registry key, the registry value name is **Wallpaper**.

Here is my populated entry inside Group Policy:

Figure 5.7: Adding registry keys via Group Policy

Because I have selected this registry value to be pushed as an **Update** action, every time that Group Policy processes on this computer, it is going to ensure that this registry key is present, thus continually preventing users from being able to adjust their desktop wallpaper.

I chose this example because it is straightforward and because often in Group Policy you will find that there are multiple ways to accomplish the same thing. Instead of using a registry value to lock down wallpaper settings, I could have alternatively created a GPO that utilized the following GPO setting, and it would have accomplished the same thing without having to touch registry settings:

User Configuration | Policies | Administrative Templates | Desktop | Desktop | Desktop Wallpaper

Prevent shut down of system

It is very common to utilize GPOs to push security lockdown parameters to computers or servers. Many corporations use Remote Desktop Servers to provide virtual desktops for users to log in to. When users work inside an RDS session, they are driving from their computers, but everything they work on or click on happens inside a multi-user server environment. If these users were to do something like shut down the server, even accidentally, that would have an enormously negative impact on other users of that server. The same type of logic could apply to common-use kiosk workstations, perhaps shared computers that are often accessed by a myriad of employees. There are many common lockdown restrictions for these types of environments, but one that I often find to be in place is a policy setting that prevents users from being able to shut down the computer they are logged in to.

Creating another GPO, or editing an existing one to implement this restriction alongside settings that already apply to your kiosk machines, navigate to the following location:

Computer Configuration (or User Configuration) | Policies | Administrative Templates | Start Menu and Taskbar

Now seek out the setting called **Remove and prevent access to the Shut Down, Restart, Sleep, and Hibernate commands.**

Figure 5.8: GPO to prevent shut down or restart

Once enabled, this is a simple single-action policy restriction that will prevent select users from being able to shut down computers or servers within your domain environment. If a user were to attempt to shut down a computer, they would no longer see the option to be able to do so. In fact, this policy is not only a graphical update to hide away the button. Even if the user were IT-smart enough to attempt something like pressing *Alt + F4* at the desktop, which would normally invoke system shutdown options, they would be prevented from doing so.

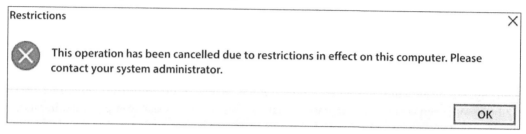

Figure 5.9: User is prevented from shutting down the system

Disable removable USB drives

Have you ever heard of the *Dropped Drive Experiment*? Originally implemented by penetration testers, it is an extremely creative way of testing your workforce to find out how security-savvy they are. You may or may not know that plugging an unknown USB stick into your computer is risky business. There are many viruses and attacks that can be accomplished by simply convincing a user to plug an infected USB drive into their computer. The premise of the Dropped Drive Experiment is simply to load USB sticks with malicious software, drop one or more in a company parking lot, and see what happens. Chances are people are going to find these USB sticks, and plug them into their computers to see what is on them. At that point it is too late, the attacker already has control of your system and your information.

If ever you find a USB stick sitting on the ground, or even if a vendor hands you one as a fancy way of providing marketing materials about their business during a trade show, there is only one appropriate action to take with these USB sticks: throw them in the garbage.

Can you send an email to your staff and inform them of this risk? Sure. Can you ask them to never plug USB drives into their computers? Sure. Will they *actually listen*? I can almost guarantee they won't. Protection against this scenario is what our last example of a GPO setting is all about. Flip one simple switch inside a GPO that applies to all of your domain computers, and you provide immediate protection to your business against this very real vulnerability.

Computer Configuration | Policies | Administrative Templates | System | Removable Storage Access

All removable storage classes: Deny all accesses

Enable this option, and you're good to go.

Scoping a GPO

I briefly mentioned the ability to scope GPOs so that they only apply to machines or users that you desire. This is probably the single most important piece of the Group Policy puzzle to understand. You have already seen a couple of examples of plugging settings into GPOs, and information is abundant on the internet with useful and exact policy settings and how to put those into place. If there is some particular task you are trying to accomplish on a large scale, turn to search engines and look for that item while including the search word *GPO*, and you'll quickly find information about how to set up your new GPO to do that thing.

What those articles, Microsoft documents, and blog posts are *not* going to define for you is to what extent you push those settings into your network, and how to ensure your new GPO is not too far-reaching. That decision is yours alone. In this section, we will discuss the different options available within every GPO that allow you to pinpoint very specific details about who should or should not receive those GPO settings.

Links

A GPO link is arguably the most important tool in your Group Policy toolbox. Links simply take a GPO and bind it to a location in Active Directory. The GPO that you have now linked will start applying its contained settings to users and devices that are within that location.

We have created multiple GPOs inside Group Policy but have not yet applied them to anything. What this means is that we have not yet linked those GPOs to anything, and when we do, that is when they will be set loose and start doing their work. Before we link one of our new GPOs, let's take a look at which GPOs currently apply to my Windows 10 computer. That way, we can check again after creating our link to prove to ourselves that the new GPO is doing something.

Gpresult

So far, we haven't talked at all about how to check machines to discover what policies may or may not apply to them. Let's take a break from configuration and do that now. Logging into my Windows 10 client machine, I can open either Command Prompt or PowerShell and run the following:

```
Gpresult /r
```

This spits out quite a bit of interesting information, but what we are most interested in here is the section called **Applied Group Policy Objects**. In fact, you may notice that there are two sections to this output and find two instances of Applied Group Policy Objects. One will be listed beneath **COMPUTER SETTINGS**, and the other under **USER SETTINGS**. Shortly, we will describe the differences between computer and user settings within a GPO, but for our example now, I want to point out that the output on my test client shows us that no GPOs are being applied at the **User Settings** level, as you can see in *Figure 5.10*:

```
Applied Group Policy Objects
--------------------------------
        N/A
```

Figure 5.10: No GPOs applied to the user

After becoming more familiar with Group Policy, you may often find yourself running gpresult and wanting to narrow down the results to either computer or user settings. You can easily do this by adding a switch to your gpresult command:

```
Gpresult /r /scope computer
Gpresult /r /scope user
```

Continuing with the link

Back inside the GPMC, find the location to which you want to **link** your new GPO. I am going to link my Map Network Drives GPO and prove to you that all of my mapped network drives are created automatically during my next login to a workstation. The user account I am logging in with resides inside an OU called **Accounting Users**. Seeking out the **Accounting Users** OU, I right-click on it and choose the **Link an Existing GPO...** option. On the screen that follows, find your newly created GPO and select it. You have now linked the GPO to this specific OU, and this change is immediately in effect in your network. You can see in *Figure 5.11* that my GPO link is displayed under the **Accounting Users** OU:

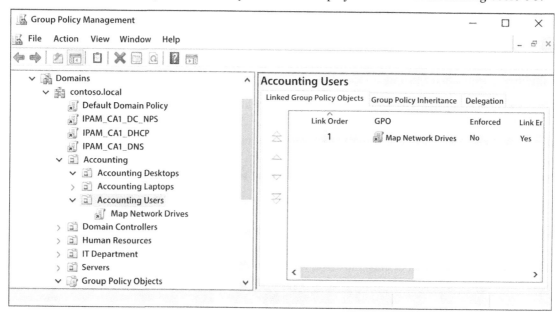

Figure 5.11: Linking a GPO to the Accounting Users OU

The next time users inside this OU log in to a domain-joined computer, their network drives should be mapped for them during the login process.

Logging in to my Windows 10 workstation, I now find that to be true and running `gpresult` again proves that my GPO has successfully been applied!

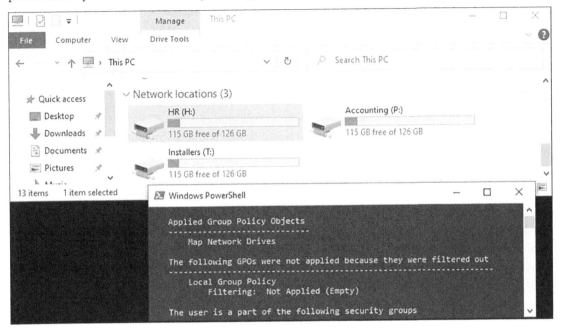

Figure 5.12: GPO has been successfully implemented

You can link a GPO to more than one OU. Just follow the same process again, this time choosing a different OU to make the link, and that GPO will now apply to both OUs that have active links. You can remove links by right-clicking on them and deleting them, or by clicking on the Group Policy Object itself to view and modify its link properties.

Group Policy processing order

In the GPO linking example that was just completed, we linked a GPO to a specific OU. You probably noticed in some of the screenshots that there are GPOs linked at different levels too, like right at the root of my `contoso.local` domain. What's that all about? As it turns out, when logging in to a computer, there are actually four different levels of Group Policy processing that happen. The location of your links can make a big difference to the proper effect your GPO has on your computers and users. Let's discuss these four levels of GPO processing.

Local Policy

Assuming you have worked in IT for a little while, it is very likely that you have followed a blog post or forum that has led you to a modification via `gpedit.msc`. Running `gpedit.msc` on any Windows system brings you into the **Local Group Policy Editor**. This is the set of policy objects and settings that exist on an individual machine. They can be manipulated manually via `gpedit.msc` or they can be manipulated and overwritten by GPOs.

The key point that I want to make is that when your Windows computer boots and logs in, the very first thing that happens is that settings inside the Local Group Policy Editor are processed. Since Local Policy is first to apply, it means that any levels of Active Directory Group Policy, which we are about to discuss, will take priority over Local Policy. In other words, your computer may have Local Policy settings in place, but milliseconds later during the boot process, those local settings could be overwritten by AD policy settings.

Site-level policies

Remember back in *Chapter 3, Active Directory*, when we discussed Active Directory Sites and Services? That comes into play here. If your environment is large enough to contain multiple sites, it is possible to link GPOs at an individual site level, thus enabling Group Policy to issue settings to computers or users based on which site they reside within.

Having GPOs linked to sites is quite a rare occurrence in my experience, but it is something to keep in the back of your mind when troubleshooting GPO applications. Computers and users will only receive site-level policies when they physically reside within those sites, based on the IP addressing scheme and subnets you defined inside AD Sites and Services. If a computer is handed GPO settings based on a site-level link, and these settings contradict what is in Local Group Policy, the site-level policies will override the Local Policy, and these will be the new settings as you continue the login process.

Domain-level policies

Some policies and settings are going to be things that you want to apply to all machines or users in an entire domain, and the appropriate place for those settings is domain-level GPOs. It's important to point out that the GPOs themselves are not different, as we talk about all these different policy levels – a GPO is a GPO. The level at which the GPO is *linked* is what we are discussing in relation to these hierarchical levels.

Links created at the root, or top level, of a domain inside Group Policy Management will by default attempt to apply to any user or computer that is part of the domain. There are many other factors that can filter domain-linked GPOs, but for the most part, if you link a GPO to the domain name, you had better be okay with the settings inside that GPO applying to potentially every workstation, every server, and every user. If you peek back a few pages at some of the screenshots from inside the GPMC, you can see that my IPAM GPOs are all linked directly to contoso.local. These are known as domain-level links.

Pretending that we are still flowing through a computer login process with these examples, domain-level policies apply after site-level policies. So any settings that came down to you via site-level policies have now been added to, or potentially overridden by (if there was a conflict), our domain-level policies.

OU-level policies

We started our login journey with Local Group Policy settings, which were then added to or overwritten by site-level GPOs, and those were then added onto again (or overwritten again in the case of conflicts) by domain-level GPOs. You can guess where this is heading. OU-level policies now apply on top of domain-level GPOs.

OUs, as you know, are containing folders for computer and user accounts that are joined to your domain. Most companies take good advantage of using multiple OUs inside Active Directory to differentiate types of machines and users. Servers are separated from workstations, accounting users are different from HR users, and so on. Nesting OUs is a common practice as well. Just like creating folders inside of other folders by using File Explorer, you can use AD Users and Computers to create OUs inside other OUs. This is important to the organization of your domain objects, and it is also important to Group Policy.

Linking GPOs to particular OUs gives us flexibility in handing different settings to different groups of people or machines. When a GPO is linked to a single OU, only computers or users inside that OU, or downstream from it, will be affected by the GPO. You can even have multiple GPOs linked to the same OU.

Nested OUs provide an additional tier to this GPO workflow. Remember the general rule is that Group Policy processes from the top down, so GPOs that are linked to a nested OU will most likely outweigh GPOs that are linked at a higher-level OU.

Security Filtering

Now that you have created a GPO and linked it to particular OU, you have enough information to start using Group Policy in your environment. Using links to determine what machines or users get what policies is the most common method that I see admins use, but there are many circumstances where you might want to take filtering a step further. What if you had a new GPO and had it linked to an OU that contained all of your desktop computers, but then decided that some of those machines needed the policy and some did not? It would be a headache to have to split those machines up into two separate OUs just for the purpose of this policy that you are building. This is where **GPO Security Filtering** comes into play.

Security Filtering is the ability to filter a GPO down to particular Active Directory objects. On any given GPO in your directory, you can set filters so that the GPO only applies to particular users, particular computers, or even particular groups of users or computers. I find that using groups is especially useful.

For our Map Network Drives GPO, right now I have it linked to my **Accounting Users** OU, but what if I wanted to filter that GPO in a different way? Rather than limit the scope of this GPO to a single OU, I would prefer to make it a little bit further-reaching, and I'm going to link the GPO to my contoso.local domain. Yikes, doesn't that mean it's going to apply to everything? Yes, unless you utilize the **Security Filtering** section to define user accounts or groups of accounts to which it should apply.

 I always make my Security Filtering decisions before creating a link. Links are live as soon as you create them, so building Security Filtering first ensures proper distribution from the start.

Clicking on any GPO inside the GPMC will display information about that GPO, and the **Scope** tab displays any links that exist for this GPO, as well as Security Filtering information. All new GPOs will have **Authenticated Users** defined inside **Security Filtering**, which essentially means "all domain users *and* computers."

Remember that it means both! In the next screenshot, you can see my Map Network Drives GPO, which is linked to the **Accounting Users** OU. It has **Authenticated Users** listed for **Security Filtering**. If I were to simply remove the existing OU link and create a new domain-level link, this GPO would immediately start applying to all user accounts in my whole domain:

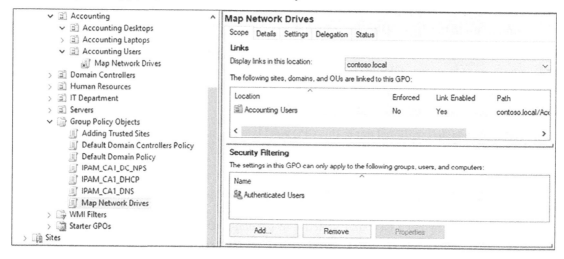

Figure 5.13: Security Filtering settings for GPOs

Instead of doing that, I will adjust my **Security Filtering** settings first. All accounting users are part of a security group called **Acct Group** (I'm so creative!). Adding **Acct Group** to **Security Filtering** for this GPO and **REMOVING Authenticated Users** means that now no matter where I link this GPO, only members of the **Acct Group** group are going to receive the GPO settings. Now that I have added **Acct Group** to my **Security Filtering**, I can safely link the GPO to the top level of my domain and remain confident that only members of **Acct Group** will receive my GPO settings:

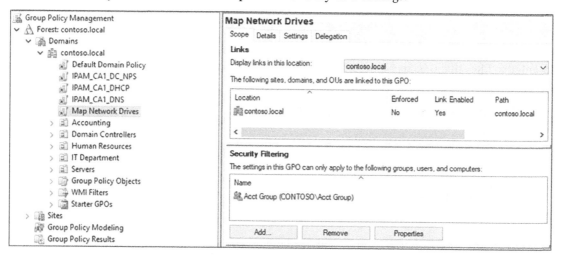

Figure 5.14: Filtering a GPO to Acct Group

Another cool feature that is just a click away is the **Settings** tab on this same screen. Click on that tab, and it will display all of the configurations currently set inside your GPO. This is very useful for checking over GPOs that someone else may have created to see what settings are being modified.

WMI Filtering

Using a combination of well-designed links and Security Filtering to narrow the scope of your GPOs, you will likely be able to perfectly plan and apply policy settings 90% of the time. Our next few sub-headings reflect that remaining 10%, as we cover some of the advanced filtering techniques that are available to get even more granular when filtering GPOs.

WMI Filtering is a genius, although slightly confusing, tool to further define GPO application. WMI filters tap into the WMI information that exists on every Windows computer and use that WMI data to further filter GPO settings. WMI filters can be defined to look for operating system version numbers, types of CPU, quantities of RAM, the amount of available disk space, and sometimes even things like BIOS firmware. Once a WMI filter is defined, you can then select that filter for each GPO, in the section titled **WMI Filtering**, which is immediately below **Security Filtering** inside the GPMC.

WMI filters enable you to do things like "only install this huge piece of software if there is at least 5 GB of available disk space" or "only implement these firewall settings on machines running a Windows Server operating system." Another real-world example uses WMI Filtering to identify whether or not a machine is running mobile hardware, which allows your GPOs to apply only to laptops and tablets, and not desktop computers.

WMI Filtering draws information from other components inside the operating system, and therefore causes Group Policy to take a little bit more time and CPU processing power to function. This can cause an increase in system resources on your endpoint computers and also slows logins, as that processing happens in the background.

Building WMI filters is getting in the weeds with Group Policy, and so for further instruction on that, I will point you toward the *Summary* section at the end of this chapter, where I will reference another publication dedicated entirely to Group Policy.

Item-level targeting

Links, Security Filtering, and WMI Filtering are fantastic ways to determine which GPOs apply to which computers and users. But what if you need to take it a step further? What if you have a single GPO that contains multiple settings, and you only want some of those settings to apply to certain users or computers, and other settings in the same policy to apply to different users and computers?

A prime example of this is a Map Network Drives GPO. It is common to place all network drives in a single GPO in the domain and call it *Mapped Drives* or something similar. It is also common that not all users should get all mapped network drives. What is the best way to handle that? For this scenario, you could break your GPO out into many smaller GPOs, creating a separate GPO for each drive letter and then determining with links and filters which users get which drive letters. But then you have a horde of GPOs to deal with.

Enter **Item-level targeting (ILT)**. You may not remember, but earlier we glanced at a special **Common** tab that exists inside many GPO settings. One of the five settings inside the **Common** tab is **Item-level targeting**, and this is exactly the clarifying setting we need to make our Map Network Drives GPO dreams come true.

Referencing the same Map Network Drives GPO that I have worked with for many pages now, you know that this policy contains multiple drive letters. Currently, my Acct Group users receive all of those mapped drives. Let's pretend for a minute that I only want the Acct Group to receive one of those drive letter mappings and not the others. Editing the GPO, I double-click on my P: drive mapping, and then visit the **Common** tab. Here, I check the box for **Item-level targeting** and click on the **Targeting...** button.

Inside the **Targeting Editor**, choose **New Item** and you will find a large list of criteria that can be utilized for these additional targeting parameters:

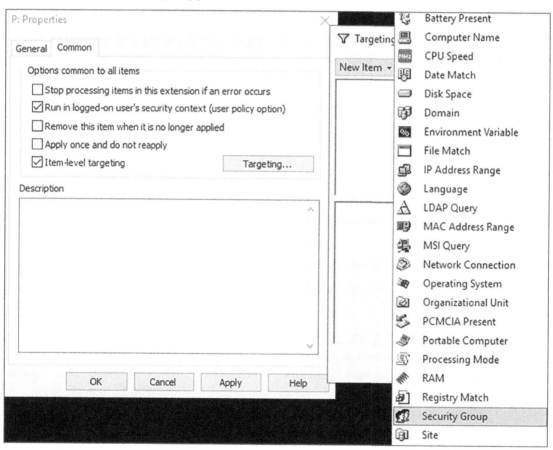

Figure 5.15: Adding a new security group in Targeting Editor

I want to instruct this GPO that the P: drive should only be mapped for users who are part of the Acct Group security group.

Choosing to add a new security group to my ILT, I can define the Acct Group and you can see in *Figure 5.16* that my P: drive ILT settings have now been updated so that only if the user is a member of the CONTOSO\Acct Group security group will that user receive the P: drive mapping when they log in:

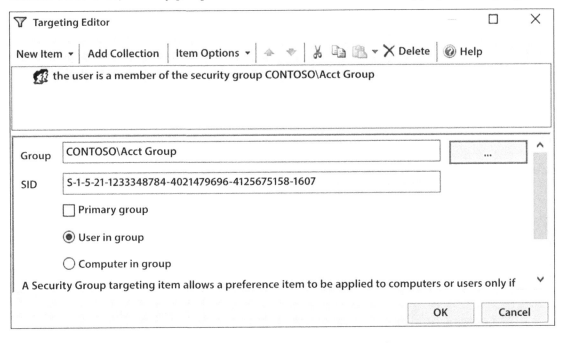

Figure 5.16: Applying the P: drive mapping to CONTOSO\Acct Group

Repeat this process with the rest of the drive letters in your GPO, and you now have a single GPO containing all drive letter mappings for your entire organization. You can link this GPO to the domain, and leave it security-filtered for all authenticated users, as it is by default, and yet based on ILT, only drive letters that correspond to their appropriate groups will now be mapped for each user who logs in. ILT is the bomb! *Wow*, I can't believe I just typed that…

Delegation

Consider this scenario: the executive leadership at your company has asked you to lock down security restrictions on all computers in the domain. That sounds like a job for Group Policy! Except, since they are the leadership and don't want their own systems to hinder their ability to browse Instagram and configure desktop backgrounds of smiling kittens, they have required that these lockdown settings apply to everyone *except* members of the *Leadership* group in Active Directory.

We know plenty of ways to filter GPOs *to* certain users or groups, but how do we filter GPOs for everything *except* a certain user or group? For this, we visit the GPMC click on the GPO in question, and visit the tab called **Delegation**.

If your GPO has custom Security Filtering applied, you'll notice the names of those users or groups inside the **Delegation** screen as well.

When configuring Security Filtering, what the GPMC is really doing is configuring **Delegation** permissions on the GPO in the background. I have navigated to the **Delegation** tab of my Map Network Drives GPO, which is currently still security-filtered for the Acct Group. Inside **Delegation**, clicking on the **Advanced...** button near the bottom left brings me into the nitty-gritty security details behind the delegation and permissions settings on this GPO.

In *Figure 5.17*, you can see that my Acct Group currently has **Read** and **Apply group policy** permissions configured to **Allow**. This is what happened when I added Acct Group to Security Filtering. This is the set of permissions making the magic happen so that whenever someone logs in to a computer in my domain, they are allowed to both read settings in this GPO and to apply settings from this GPO:

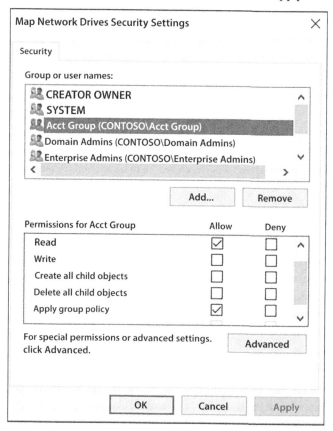

Figure 5.17: Acct Group has read and apply permissions

Circling back to the matter at hand, in the Microsoft world, a denial of permission always trumps a permission allowance. If you need to deny a particular user, computer, or group from receiving GPO settings from a particular GPO, you simply add them to the **Delegation** permissions and check the **Deny** box for **Apply group policy**. Even if they are allowed a Group Policy based on another permission entry in this list, they will now be denied this GPO applying to them. To make this crystal-clear with another screenshot, here you can see that my Jordan user account is now denied from applying the Map Network Drives GPO.

This means that when Jordan logs in, he will NOT receive network drive mappings from this GPO:

Figure 5.18: Denying a user from receiving this GPO

Use with caution! Creating GPO denials inside the **Delegation** tab works great, but it is very easy to forget or overlook these settings in the future. I have assisted admins numerous times with trouble-shooting a GPO that did not seem to be applying properly, only to find out that a denial permission inside **Delegation** was causing all the grief.

Computer settings and user settings

After poking around inside GPOs for a few minutes, you are likely to notice that the Group Policy Management Editor is split up into two different sections. When drilling down inside a GPO to find the particular setting that you are about to roll into place, the first choice you need to make is whether you are working on a **Computer Configuration** or a **User Configuration**. Understanding the differences and always keeping these differences in mind is important not only for finding the setting you are searching for but also for ensuring that your new GPO is linked to the correct place and applies to the proper type of object.

You can see these two sections of any GPO in *Figure 5.19*:

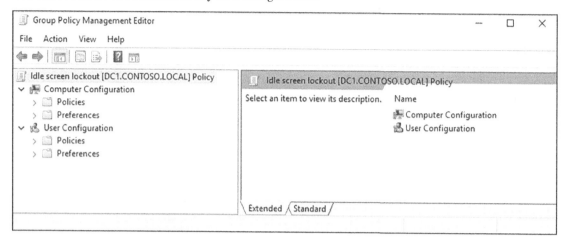

Figure 5.19: Computer Configuration and User Configuration

Computer Configuration

All GPO settings listed beneath **Computer Configuration** are, of course, settings that can apply to your domain-joined computers. Duh! Aren't all GPO settings applied to computers? No, actually they are not. Many GPO settings do apply to the computer object in Active Directory, and all of these types of GPO settings fall beneath **Computer Configuration**. Some GPO settings are even things that you can configure at either a computer level or a user level. And other times you might have similar options inside both computer and user configuration that accomplish the task in slightly different ways.

A good example is an idle screen lockout policy. It is a common requirement for companies to require computer screens to lock themselves after a certain number of minutes of inactivity. This way, if a user walks away from their computer and forgets to manually lock the screen, it will self-lock after, say, 15 minutes.

If you are tasked with creating such a policy, you need to decide whether you want this GPO to apply at the computer level or the user level. This will have to be decided for yourself, based on your normal user activity.

If you determine that the best method for locking the screen is to do so at the computer level, meaning that the screen will lock after 15 minutes no matter who is logged into that computer, then this is the specific configuration that you want to set inside your GPO:

Computer Configuration | Policies | Windows Settings | Security Settings | Local Policies | Security Options

Interactive logon: Machine inactivity limit = Enabled and specified to 900 seconds (15 minutes)

User Configuration

On the other hand, many other GPO settings apply not to the computer account at all, but rather to the domain user who is logging in to that computer. **User Configuration** settings follow the user account around and apply to whichever workstation that user logs into. If you look back at our Map Network Drives GPO, you'll see that the network drive configurations that we created in that GPO all fall under **User Configuration**. This means that those drive mappings will attempt to map themselves anywhere that the user logs in. You cannot create mapped network drives as a native GPO setting from within **Computer Configuration**.

Revisiting our idle screen lockout example, what if you have decided that you want the idle screen to happen for a certain type of user, or perhaps even all users, and that the screen lock would happen for those users no matter which computer they logged in to? In this case, there is not a specific "screen-lock" policy setting that you can configure inside **User Configuration**, but what is generally recommended is to get creative with screen saver settings, which are **User Configuration** settings. If you configure the following four GPO settings, you will effectively create the same behavior as the **Computer Config** machine inactivity limit timeout setting, but now this policy takes effect based on user accounts rather than computer accounts:

User Configuration | Policies | Administrative Templates | Control Panel | Personalization

Enable screen saver = Enabled

Force specific screen saver = Use this to define which screen saver you want to run

Screen saver timeout = Enabled and set to 900 seconds

Password protect the screen saver = Enabled

Linking GPOs accordingly

As you seek out GPO configurations to put into place in your environment, sometimes you will find you have no choice between computer or user configuration, as some options will only exist in one location or the other. Other times, you will find that the settings you are putting into place could be configured from either place, and the decision of how to best set the GPO depends upon which level you want the GPO settings to apply.

This decision ties in directly with the location to which you are going to link this GPO! If your GPO contains **Computer Configuration** settings, those settings can only apply to computer objects and so that GPO would need to be linked to OUs that contain computer objects. Or linked to the domain, of course, which covers all OUs.

Vice versa is also true; if your new GPO contains only **User Configuration** settings, that GPO is only going to apply to user objects, and any links you create for that GPO should be links to OUs that contain the user objects to which you want the GPO to apply.

You may have already figured this out, but it is generally best practice to create GPOs as either computer-based GPOs or user-based GPOs.

A single GPO can contain a lot of different settings, and if that GPO is linked at a high enough tier, it might indeed be able to apply both user and computer configuration settings all from within a single GPO. But this makes for a higher administrative burden on that single GPO, and it is typically considered best practice for any GPO to contain only **Computer Configuration** settings or **User Configuration** settings.

Group Policy loopback processing

There is a special function inside GPOs that essentially blends computer and user configuration together, to be used in special cases: namely, if you have the requirement to push **User Configuration** settings to particular computers but want those computers to treat them as if they were **Computer Configuration** settings, applying the same policy settings to *any* user who was to log in to that computer.

Maybe Laura in HR has a certain set of policies on her everyday workstation, but also occasionally logs into a public kiosk workstation sitting in the lobby. You have a set of lockdown restrictions that are applied to that kiosk, but since it is domain-joined, normally when Laura logs into the kiosk, Group Policy would treat it just like it was her own workstation and apply all of the same user-based GPO settings. If you create a **User Configuration** GPO that has loopback policy processing enabled and link the GPO to this kiosk workstation, it will now apply all of those special configurations to Laura, even though she does not receive these GPO settings on her regular computer. If Laura were to log in to this kiosk and have access to sensitive documents based on her standard login policies, you would probably want to stop that from happening when she logs in to this public access kiosk workstation, just as one example of where this might be useful.

For more detail on loopback processing, I will once again direct you to the *Summary* section at the end of this chapter, where I'll refer you to a great location for learning more on this topic.

Policy versus preference

There is an important distinction that every Group Policy administrator needs to understand about GPO settings. There are two different types of policy settings, and they behave very differently. Now that we understand the differences between Computer Configuration and **User Configuration**, the next tier you'll notice inside Group Policy Management Editor are sub-folders titled **Policies** and **Preferences**.

Policies

Managed policies, the items listed under the **Policies** section of both **computer** and **user configurations**, generally behave like true gentlemen. These are settings that you put into place and expect results, forcing the setting into place, and nothing the user tries to do can change them. When reversing course and removing a GPO from a system, they happily comply. What do I mean by that? When you plug some policy settings into a GPO and then link that GPO to a location, you expect those settings to be put into place on the machines or users to which you have filtered the GPO. And that indeed works for any GPO setting, whether policy or preference, managed or unmanaged. But what about when that GPO no longer applies to a user or machine? What if you delete the GPO link, or adjust security filtering on the GPO so that it no longer applies to a workstation? Do those settings continue to be applied, or are they actively removed?

The answer to that question depends on whether you are working with a policy or a preference. True policy items will actively remove themselves from a computer when a GPO no longer applies. This is true of most built-in configuration settings inside Group Policy. Technically, under the hood, what is really happening is that Group Policy monitors four special sections of the Windows Registry and reprocesses all of them during Group Policy refresh cycles. All GPO settings that affect these certain areas of the registry are capable of self-removal. Unmanaged policy settings, even some of those listed beneath the **Policies** folder, could potentially fail to remove their settings when a GPO is unlinked. It just depends on what setting you are talking about and what it is manipulating on the client machines to make the change.

Technically, there are managed policies and unmanaged policies – and both of these things are outside the scope of Group Policy preferences, which we will discuss next.

Preferences

Policies force things to happen, no matter what the user wants. Preferences, on the other hand, are often reversible by the user. Preferences are a good way to configure settings that will make life easier for the user, but you need to ultimately be OK with the fact that those changes and settings could be changed again manually by your users. Some GPO settings exist inside both policies and preferences, and this is your deciding factor – do you want to allow users to manipulate and change the configuration, or always force it into place?

Preferences are also sticky! While most policy settings will self-remove when a GPO stops applying to a computer, preferences do not. This is very important to understand when deleting GPOs or GPO links. Group Policy preferences do not live in those special sections of the registry that we talked about earlier, and so Windows does not actively rescan those settings to find out whether they should continue to apply. When a GPO puts a preference setting into place, even though the user could adjust that setting if they wanted to, removal of the GPO will NOT revert the computer to its original, default state. The GPO preference setting will hang around and continue to apply to the machine even after the GPO is long gone. To change a preference setting back to defaults, the user will either have to adjust it themselves, or you will need to push out a new GPO that accomplishes that adjustment.

Default Domain Policy

Throughout this chapter, we have bounced in and out of the GPMC a number of times, and now that you know what a GPO looks like and how to identify GPO links, you have probably noticed a GPO linked to the root of the domain called **Default Domain Policy**. This GPO comes built in with Group Policy. Every environment has one unless an admin has taken steps to delete it, which I would not recommend.

The Default Domain Policy applies to every user and computer that is part of your domain directory. Since this GPO is completely enabled right off the bat and applies to everyone, it is commonplace for companies to enforce global password policies or security rules that need to apply to everyone. In fact, many who are unfamiliar with Group Policy and uncomfortable with creating, linking, and filtering their own GPOs will just continually throw more and more settings in the Default Domain Policy.

All of these settings will apply successfully, of course – to ALL users on ALL machines, including servers in your network. Eventually, this mentality is going to come back and bite hard.

My general rule is to never touch the Default Domain Policy except for one reason – creating global password expiry and complexity requirements within your domain. In fact, in some cases, not even a password policy is appropriate for the Default Domain Policy, for example, if you wanted to create a fine-grained password policy that comes with some additional bells and whistles, such as the ability to require different criteria for passwords on some users compared to others. We will cover fine-grained password policies in _Chapter 9, Hardening and Security,_ so for the time being, let's stick with the idea that we want to create one password policy and apply it to everyone. This seems like a good example to walk through, and remember – if you find yourself heading into the Default Domain Policy to do anything other than password management, you're probably doing it wrong. Just create your own GPO, for crying out loud!

With any GPO that you see in the management console, if you right-click on that GPO and then choose **Edit…** you will see a new window open, and this GPO editor contains all of the internals of that policy. This is where you handle any settings or configurations that you want to be a part of that particular GPO. So, go ahead and edit your **Default Domain Policy**, and then navigate to **Computer Configuration | Policies | Windows Settings | Security Settings | Account Policies | Password Policy:**

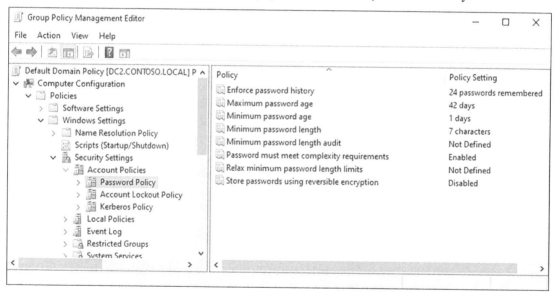

Figure 5.20: Password settings in Default Domain Policy

Here, you can see a list of the different options available to you for configuring the **Password Policy** within your domain. Double-clicking on any of these settings lets you modify them, and that change immediately starts to take effect on all of your domain-joined computers in the network. For example, you can see that the default minimum password length is set to 7 characters. Many companies have already gone through many discussions about their written policy on the standard length of passwords in the network, and in order to set up your new directory infrastructure to accept your decision, you simply modify this field.

Changing the minimum password length to 14 characters here would immediately require the change to be made for all user accounts the next time they reset their passwords.

It's worth repeating: while the Default Domain Policy is a very quick and easy way to get some settings configured and pushed out to everyone, tread carefully when making changes to this default policy. Every time that you make a setting change here, remember that it is going to affect everyone in your domain, including yourself. Many times, you will be creating policies that do not need to apply to everyone. In those cases, it is highly recommended that you stay away from the Default Domain Policy. Instead, set up a new GPO for accomplishing whatever task it is that you are trying to put into place.

Administrative Templates

Go ahead and edit a GPO, any GPO, so that you have the Group Policy Management Editor open in front of you. Expand the **Policies** folder for either **Computer Configuration**, **User Configuration**, or both, and you will notice a folder inside each called **Administrative Templates**. Most of us generally think of Administrative Templates the same as any other GPO configuration setting, simply a collection of items with which you can manipulate users or computers, right? Sort of, but while **Software Settings** and **Windows Settings** are built into Group Policy and are basically the same for any domain environment, **Administrative Templates** are customizable.

Administrative Templates showcase the flexibility of Group Policy. Each setting within Administrative Templates is pulled from template files that reside on your domain controller servers. These template files are ADMX files. All of the information needed to display the setting inside **Group Policy Management Editor** is contained inside these ADMX files. This includes items like which options the setting contains, any drop-down boxes that need to be displayed, and what the description fields will say when an admin double-clicks on the policy setting.

Along with each ADMX file comes an accompanying ADML file. This is a language file that is used to define the language for the settings contained within the ADMX file.

Back on Windows XP (and earlier), these file types did not exist. Settings inside Administrative Templates were based on ADM files instead. Nobody should be running Windows XP anymore, except I know that some of you are, because I still touch Windows XP machines for some of our customers at least once a month. So I figured I would include that info as an FYI. Sidenote: get rid of your Windows XP computers!

Windows 7 and newer know how to work with ADMX/ADML files, so I'm going to assume that your environment is fully up to date, and hopefully doesn't even have too many unsupported Windows 7 machines hanging around.

Implementing ADMX/ADML files

There are two reasons why you might find yourself monkeying around with ADMX files. The first is when moving to a newer version of Windows Server in your environment. Each release of the operating system – 2012, 2012R2, 2016, 2019, 2022 – comes with some new and updated Group Policy settings. When you install your first domain controller in the environment that happens to be running a newer platform, the setup process will generally run through a process called ADPrep. This process prepares the Active Directory schema for the new operating system and also populates the new Group Policy settings. However, there are times when the first new release operating system introduction you are making to the environment is not a domain controller. In this case, Group Policy won't be updated with new settings, but what if you wanted those new settings to be available within Group Policy anyway? Manually copying ADMX/ADML files into place could satisfy that need.

The second and most common reason to be plugging new ADMX/ADML files into place manually is when a software vendor, often Microsoft themselves, releases custom ADMX files. These files, when installed in Active Directory, will provide new settings inside Group Policy that don't exist natively inside Windows Server. Let's try it right now!

Google Chrome (did I just say those words in a Microsoft book???) is one of the most popular web browsers on the planet. The centralized configuration of Chrome is something that many administrators struggle with. What may or may not be news to you is that Google has its own set of ADMX files! You can plug these files into Group Policy and utilize Google-defined settings right from within the GPMC to push Chrome-related settings and configurations out to your workforce.

First, we need to download these files. At the time of writing, this link will do the trick: `https://dl.google.com/dl/edgedl/chrome/policy/policy_templates.zip`.

If you are unable to use that link, simply perform a web search for "`download chrome admx files`" and you should be able to find it.

Copy these files to your domain controller and extract them so that you can find the ADMX and ADML files; they should be inside a folder called **windows**. The ADMX files are located right there inside the **windows** folder, and the ADML files will be grouped into folders by language. This matches what we will find inside Group Policy in just a minute. Now that you have the files in hand, go ahead and open the following folder on the domain controller:

```
%systemroot%\PolicyDefinitions
```

(On most servers this will be `C:\Windows\PolicyDefinitions`.)

In *Figure 5.21,* you can see my Chrome files that have been downloaded, alongside the **PolicyDefinitions** folder. As you can also see, there are already numerous ADMX files inside **PolicyDefinitions**, as to be expected. These ADMX files are the reason that we have any settings currently inside Group Policy, under the **Administrative Templates** folders:

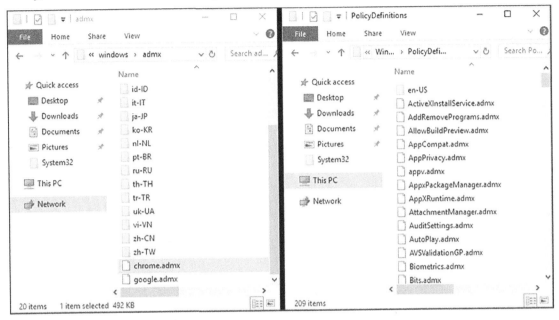

Figure 5.21: Copying new ADMX files to the domain controller

Simply copy your new Chrome ADMX files into **PolicyDefinitions**, and then copy the accompanying language ADML language file from its folder, into the corresponding language folder inside **PolicyDefinitions**. That's it! If you now close and reopen GPMC, looking inside **Administrative Templates**, which displays the new Google Chrome settings.

There are tons of them in here from those two little ADMX files:

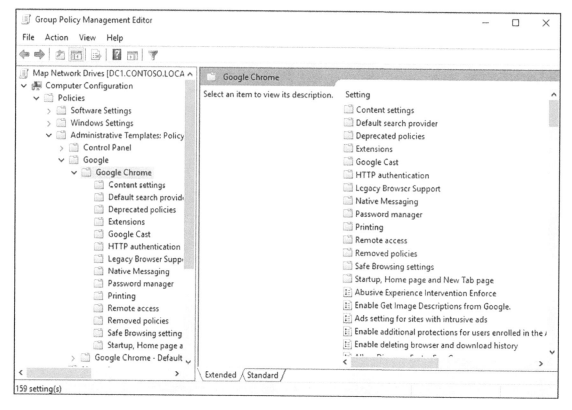

Figure 5.22: Google Chrome GPO settings

For this particular example, I am working with my test lab and making the assumption that you have a single domain controller in your environment. If you have multiple DCs, you will either have to copy these files into %systemroot%\PolicyDefinitions on each of your domain controller servers or continue reading the next section of this chapter to learn more about the Central Store.

The Central Store

When opening up the Group Policy Management Console and creating or editing a GPO, the settings available within your console session are settings pulled from ADMX/ADML files that are on the hard drive of the computer or server from which you are using the GPMC. When implementing new settings via ADMX files, it would be a huge chore to have to copy those new files into place on every one of your domain controllers, in addition to all of the client computers where you might have the RSAT tools installed. Thankfully, there is a solution to automate this for you!

The Central Store is something that can be enabled in Active Directory that allows the replication of ADMX/ADML files. Once you enable the Central Store, all of your Group Policy management machines, such as domain controllers, will look to the store as its repository for these template files.

Enable the Central Store

All that it takes to enable the Central Store in Active Directory is the creation of two folders inside a special folder called **SYSVOL**. Once created, the GPMC will check this location on subsequent launches, and pull in any new ADMX/ADML files that have been added. Log in to a domain controller server, and create the following new folder:

```
%systemroot%\SYSVOL\sysvol\contoso.local\Policies\PolicyDefinitions
```

Create an additional folder within your new **PolicyDefinitions** folder to contain language-specific ADML files. In my case, I need one for English such as the following:

```
%systemroot%\SYSVOL\sysvol\contoso.local\Policies\PolicyDefinitions\en-US
```

Obviously, you'll want to replace contoso.local with your own internal domain name, and you're finished! As soon as you have created these two new folders, utilize this location from this point forward to plug in new ADMX and ADML files, and those new settings will show up from wherever you launch GPMC in the future.

Populate the Central Store

You probably didn't have an immediate reason to check inside one of your GPOs and find out what the **Administrative Templates** folder looks like now that we enabled the Central Store, but let's go ahead and do that now. Open up GPMC and edit any of your existing GPOs. Take a look inside one of the **Administrative Templates** folders, and it's empty! You'll also notice that the name of the **Administrative Templates** folder has now changed to reflect the fact that it is looking to the Central Store for this information: **Administrative Templates: Policy definitions (ADMX files) retrieved from the central store**.

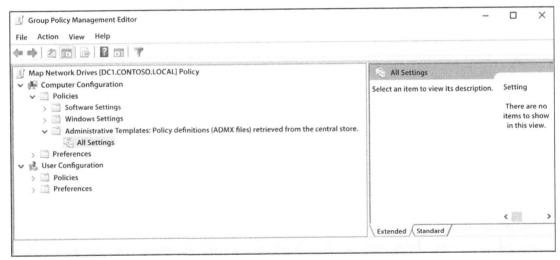

Figure 5.23: The Administrative Templates folder is empty!

Give us our settings back! Thankfully, they are still sitting on the hard drive of your domain controller, in the same location where we added the new Google settings just a few minutes ago. Perform the following file-copy jobs, and you should be back in business with all settings now stored inside the Central Store.

Copy %systemroot%\PolicyDefinitions to %systemroot%\SYSVOL\sysvol\contoso.local\Policies\PolicyDefinitions.

Copy %systemroot%\PolicyDefinitions\en-US to %systemroot%\SYSVOL\sysvol\contoso.local\Policies\PolicyDefinitions\en-US (adjust accordingly for whichever languages you need):

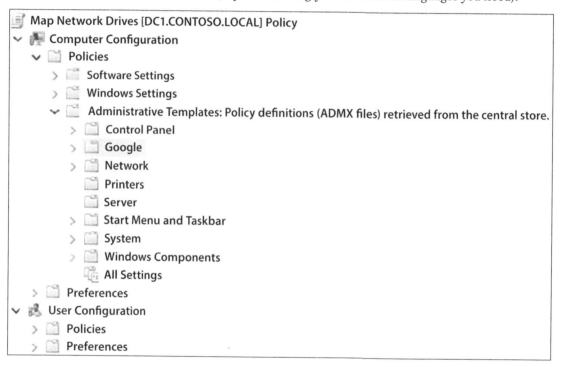

Figure 5.24: The Central Store is now populated with settings

As you can see, the **Administrative Templates** folder is still pulling from the Central Store, but following our file copies, the Central Store is now populated with ADMX files and settings to utilize inside a GPO. The Central Store is now available to all domain controllers in your environment and is being replicated by **SYSVOL**.

Summary

Group Policy is an incredibly powerful tool to have at your disposal when working within a domain environment. Many pre-built configurations and settings exist, and since we can manipulate the registry on client machines, the sky is pretty much the limit on what you can manage on your client computers via GPOs.

As is the case with many topics inside Windows Server, there is so much information related to Group Policy that it warrants a book of its own. Thankfully, I had the opportunity to do exactly that! If you are interested in discovering more about Group Policy and all of the ways that it can be used to secure your infrastructure, check out my title *Mastering Windows Group Policy* (https://www.packtpub.com/networking-and-servers/mastering-windows-group-policy).

Questions

1. Are screensaver settings computer or user configuration?
2. Do domain-level or OU-level links process first?
3. What is the special GPO setting that forces user settings to apply to any user on a given computer?
4. What type of GPO filtering do you configure inside the GPO itself, such as with a mapped network drives policy?
5. True or false – it is possible for a user to override a Group Policy preference.
6. What is the default timer between Group Policy background refresh cycles?
7. What kind of GPO filtering could be utilized to assign settings only to laptop computers?
8. If you find a USB stick on the ground labeled "CEO financials," what should you do with it?

Join our community on Discord

Join our community's Discord space for discussions with the author and other readers:

https://packt.link/SecNet

6

Certificates

"Ugh, we need to use certificates to make this work."

Real-life quote from any admin after discovering their latest software purchase requires the use of certificates

If the quote above, or perhaps a variant more colorful than stated above, sounds familiar, don't scrap that new project just yet! For some reason, the use of certificates seems like a daunting task to many of us, even those who have worked in IT for many years. I think this is probably because there are many different options available on a certificate server, but there is not a lot of common sense or user-friendliness built into the management console for dealing with certificates. This, combined with a general lack of requirements for certificates on servers for so many years, means that, even though this technology has existed for a long time, many server administrators have not had the opportunity to dig in and deploy certificates for themselves. I regularly deploy a couple of technologies that require the broad use of certificates in an organization, often needing to issue them to every workstation or user in the network, and I hear these kinds of concerns all the time. Issuing a certificate to a single business-critical webserver sounds daunting enough if you don't have any experience with the process, let alone issuing hundreds or thousands of certificates across the company.

Another common scenario is one where a company determines certificates to be in their best interests but lacks the on-staff resources to stand it up themselves, and so hires a third party to implement certificates within the network. While this gets certificates rolling, it often leaves a knowledge gap that never gets filled, so you may have a certificate server up and running, but not be at all comfortable with modifying or utilizing it.

The broad term for a certificate environment is **public key infrastructure (PKI)**. I call that out specifically because you will probably see PKI listed in documentation or requirements at some point if you haven't already. Your PKI is provided by servers in your network, and helping you to understand how to configure those servers to issue certificates is the purpose of this chapter.

The servers that you determine to be your certificate servers are known as **certification authority (CA)** servers, and we will refer to them as CA servers throughout this book.

To get you started with using certificates in your network, here are the topics that we will cover in this chapter:

- Common certificate types
- Planning your PKI
- Creating a new certificate template
- Issuing your new certificates
- Creating an auto-enrollment policy
- Obtaining a public authority SSL certificate
- Exporting and importing certificates
- OpenSSL for Linux webservers

Common certificate types

There are a number of different types of certificates that you may find yourself needing to publish. As you will see, when you need a certificate that has a list of particular requirements, you can build a certificate template to whatever specifications you like. So, in a sense, there aren't really certificate *types* at all, but just certificate templates that you scope to contain whatever pieces of information are needed for that certificate to do its job. While this holds true technically, it is generally easier to segment certificates into different groups, making them more distinguishable for the particular job that they are intended to perform.

User certificates

As the name implies, a user certificate is one used for purposes that are specific to the users holding those certificates. One driving force behind higher levels of certificate adoption is the network authentication process. Companies that are looking into stronger authentication in their environments often look at certificates as part of that authentication process. Smart cards are one of the mechanisms that can be used for this purpose, specifically, some sort of physical card to be plugged into a computer in order for the user to gain access to that computer.

Smart cards can also be stored virtually within a special place on modern machines, called the TPM. But that is a discussion for a different day. The reason we mention smart cards here is that, often, the core functionality of smart-card authentication is provided by a user certificate that has been stored on that smart card. If you find yourself in the middle of a project to deploy smart cards or some form of physical key login, you will probably find yourself in need of a PKI.

Another popular strong authentication form is **one-time passwords (OTPs)**. These require the user to enter a randomly generated PIN in addition to their regular login criteria, and in some cases, when the user enters their PIN, they are issued a temporary user certificate to be used as part of the authentication chain.

Additional places where user certificates are commonly found include when companies employ file-encrypting technologies, such as **EFS** (short for **Encrypting File System**), or when building up **virtual private network (VPN)** systems to enable remote users to connect their laptops back to the corporate network. Many companies don't want to rely purely on a username and a password for VPN authentication, so issuing user certificates and requiring that they be present to build that VPN tunnel is commonplace.

Computer certificates

Often referred to as computer certificates or machine certificates, these guys get issued to computers to assist with the interaction between the network and the computer account itself. Technologies, such as SCCM, that interact with and manage the computer systems regardless of which users are logged in to those computers make use of computer certificates. These kinds of certificates are also used for encryption processing between systems on the network, for example, if you were interested in using IPsec to encrypt communications between clients and a highly secure file server. Issuing computer or machine certificates to the endpoints within this communication chain would be essential to make that work properly. I often find myself issuing computer certificates to a business' machines to authenticate DirectAccess tunnels, a form of automated remote access. There are many different reasons and technologies you may be interested in that would require the issuance of certificates to the client workstations in your environment.

SSL certificates

If you find yourself in the middle of the certificate road, where you haven't really managed a CA server but you have at one point issued and installed some kind of certificate, chances are that the certificate you worked with was an SSL certificate. This is by far the most common type of certificate used in today's technology infrastructure, and your company is more than likely using SSL certificates, even if you are not aware of them and do not have a single CA server running inside your network.

SSL certificates are most commonly used to secure website traffic. Any time you visit a website and see HTTPS in the address bar, your browser is using an SSL packet stream to send information back and forth between your computer and the webserver that you are talking to. The webserver has an SSL certificate on it, and your browser has checked over that certificate before allowing you onto the web page, to make sure that the certificate is valid and that the website really is what it says it is. You see, if we did not use SSL certificates on websites, anyone could impersonate our site and gain access to the information being passed to the website.

Let's provide a quick example. Let's say one of your users is at a coffee shop, using public Wi-Fi. An attacker has figured out a way to manipulate DNS on that Wi-Fi network. Your user tries to visit `mail.contoso.com` to access the company's *Outlook Web Access* to check their email, but the attacker has hijacked that traffic and the user is now accessing a website that looks like their company portal but is actually a website hosted by the attacker. Your employee types in their username and password, and *bingo*, the attacker now has that user's credentials and can use them to access your real network.

What prevents this from happening every day in the real world? **SSL certificates.** When you force your externally facing websites, such as that email login page, to be HTTPS sites, it requires the client browsers to check over the SSL certificate that is presented with the website. That SSL certificate contains information that only you as a company have; it cannot be impersonated. This way, when the users access your real login page, the browser checks out the SSL certificate, finds it to be correct, and simply continues on its merry way. The users never even know they are being protected except for the little lock symbol up near their browser's address bar. On the other hand, if their traffic is being intercepted and redirected to a fake website, the SSL certificate check will fail (because the attacker would not have a valid SSL certificate for your company website name), and the user will be stopped in their tracks, at least to read through a certificate warning page before being able to proceed. At this point, the user should back off, realize that something is wrong, and contact IT staff to look into the issue.

SSL certificates used by websites on the internet are almost always provided not by your internal CA server but by a public certification authority. You have probably heard of many of them, such as Verisign, Entrust, DigiCert, and GoDaddy. Companies generally purchase SSL certificates from these public authorities because these authorities are trusted by default on new computers that users might purchase in the field. When you buy a new computer, even straight from a retail store, if you were to open up the local store of certificates that exists out of the box on that system, you would find a list of trusted root authorities. When you visit a website protected by an SSL certificate issued from one of these public authorities, that certificate, and therefore the website, is automatically trusted by this computer. The public CAs are publicly recognized entities, known for their capacity to securely issue SSL certificates.

When a company acquires an SSL certificate from one of these public authorities, there is an in-depth verification process that the authority goes through to make sure that the person requesting the certificate (you) is really someone with the proper company and authorized to issue these certificates. This is the basis of security in using SSL certificates from a public CA. All new computers know by default to trust certificates that have been issued by these authorities, and you don't have to take any special actions to make your websites function on the internet. On the other hand, it is possible to issue SSL certificates from a CA server that you built yourself and have running inside your network, but it requires a couple of things that make it difficult, because your CA server is obviously not trusted by all computers everywhere, nor should it be. First, if you want to issue your own SSL certificate for use on a public website, you need to externalize at least part of your internal PKI, known as the **certificate revocation list (CRL)**, to the internet. Any time you take a component that is internal to your network and publicize it on the internet, you are introducing a security risk, so unless you absolutely have to do this, it is generally not recommended. The second reason it is difficult to utilize your own SSL certificates on public websites is that only your own company's domain-joined computers will know how to trust this SSL certificate. So, if a user brings their company laptop home and uses it to access their email login page, it will probably work fine. But if a user tries to access the same email login page from their home computer, which is not part of your domain or network, they will get a certificate warning message and have to take special steps in order to gain access to the website. What a pain for the users. You should never encourage users to accept risk and proceed through a certificate warning message—this is a recipe for disaster, even if the certificate they are clicking through is one issued by your own CA. It's a matter of principle never to accept that risk.

These issues can be alleviated by purchasing an SSL certificate from one of those public CAs, and so purchasing these kinds of certificates is the normal and recommended way to make use of SSL on your publicly facing websites. Websites that are completely inside the network are a different story, since they are not facing the internet and their security footprint is much smaller. You can use your internal CA server to issue SSL certificates to your internal websites, and not have to incur the cost associated with purchasing certificates for all of those websites.

There are a few different tiers of SSL certificates that you can purchase from a public CA, information for which is listed on the authority's own websites. Essentially, the idea is that the more you pay, the more secure your certificate is. These tiers are related to the way that the authority validates against the certificate requester, since that is really where the security comes into play with SSL certificates. The authority is guaranteeing that when you access the page secured by their certificate, the certificate was issued to the real company that owns that web page.

Other than the validation tier, which you get to choose when purchasing a certificate, there is another option you have to decide on as well, and this one is much more important to the technical aspect of the way that certificates work. There are different naming conventions available to you when you purchase a certificate, and there is no best answer for which one to choose. Every situation that requires a certificate will be unique and will have to be evaluated individually to decide which naming scheme works best. Let's quickly cover three possibilities for an SSL certificate naming convention.

Single-name certificates

This is the cheapest and most common route to take when purchasing a certificate for an individual website or web service. A single-name certificate protects and contains information about a single DNS name. When you are setting up a new website at `portal.contoso.com` and you want this website to protect some traffic by using HTTPS, you would install an SSL certificate onto the website. When you issue the request to your certification authority for this new certificate, you would input the specific name of `portal.contoso.com` into the **Common name** field of the request form. This single DNS name is the only name that can be protected and validated by this certificate.

Multi-domain or subject alternative name certificates

Multi-domain certificates, sometimes called **subject alternative name (SAN)** certificates, generally cost a little bit more than single-name certificates, because they have more capabilities. When you request a SAN certificate, you have the option of defining multiple DNS names that the certificate can protect. Once issued, the SAN certificate will contain a primary DNS name, which is typically the main name of the website, and further, inside the certificate properties, you will find listed the additional DNS names that you specified during your request. This single certificate can be installed on a webserver, or perhaps multiple servers, and used to validate traffic for any of the DNS names that are contained in the certificate. Common use-case examples of a SAN certificate are when setting up a Lync (Skype for Business) server, or an Exchange server. Lync uses many different DNS names, but all names are within the same DNS domain. Here is an example list of the names we might include in a single SAN certificate for the purposes of Lync:

- `Lync.contoso.com` (the primary one)

- Lyncdiscover.contoso.com
- Meet.contoso.com
- Dialin.contoso.com
- Admin.contoso.com

These different websites/services used by Lync are then implemented across one or multiple servers, and you can utilize the same SAN certificate on all of those servers in order to validate traffic that is headed toward any of those DNS names.

It is possible to include multiple names in a SAN certificate that really have nothing to do with each other, and are used by completely different types of systems within your environment. For example, if you have an email portal, RD Gateway, and a VPN solution, you could certainly acquire a SAN certificate with the following names:

- Mail.contoso.com
- Gateway.contoso.com
- VPN.contoso.com

The above certificate would be a little weird, and not a common thing to find in the real world. Instead, when facing the need to use a single certificate across multiple systems, it is much more common to purchase...

Wildcard certificates

Last but certainly not least is the wildcard certificate. This is the luxury model, the one that has the most capabilities, gives you the most flexibility, and at the same time offers the easiest path to implementation on many servers. The name on a wildcard certificate begins with a **star** (*). This star means *any*, as in *anything preceding the DNS domain name* is covered by this certificate. If you own contoso.com and plan to stand up many public DNS records that will flow to many different websites and webservers, you could purchase a single wildcard certificate with the name *.contoso.com, and it may cover all of your certificate needs.

Typically, wildcards can be installed on as many webservers as you need, with no limit on the number of different DNS names that they can validate. I have run across an exception to this once, when a particular customer's agreement with their certification authority specified that they had to report and pay for each instance of their wildcard certificate that was in use. So watch those agreements when you make them with your CA. Most of the time, a wildcard is meant to be a free-for-all within the company so that you can deploy many sites and services across many servers and utilize your wildcard certificate everywhere.

The downside of a wildcard certificate is that it costs more, significantly more. But if you have large certificate needs or big plans for growth, it will make your certificate administration much easier, faster, and more cost-effective in the long run.

Planning your PKI

Since we are revolving all of our discussion in this book around Windows Server 2022, this means that your internal CA server can and should be one provided by this latest and greatest of operating systems. As with most capabilities in Server 2022, the creation of a certification authority server in your network is as simple as installing a Windows role. When you go to add the role to a new server, it is the very first role in the list, **Active Directory Certificate Services (AD CS)**. When installing this role, you will be presented with a couple of important options, and you must understand the meaning behind them before you create a solid PKI environment.

 Your server's hostname and domain status cannot be changed after implementing the CA role. Make sure you have set your final hostname and joined this server to the domain (if applicable), prior to installing the AD CS role. You won't be able to change those settings later!

Role services

The first decision you need to make when installing the AD CS role is which role services you would like to install, as you can see in *Figure 6.1*:

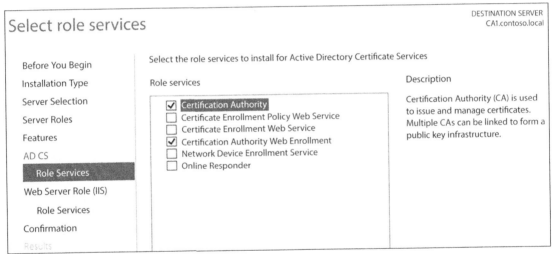

Figure 6.1: Installing the AD CS role

Clicking on each option will give you a description of its capabilities, so you can probably determine which pieces of the role you need by poking around on this screen. Here is a short summary of these options. Note that I am listing them out of order, because of the way that I typically see them configured in the field:

- **Certification Authority:** This is the primary certificate engine that needs to be installed in order for this server to officially become a CA.
- **Certification Authority Web Enrollment:** Often, this one gets installed as well, especially in environments that are small enough to be running a single CA server for the entire environment.

The web enrollment portion will install IIS (webserver) capabilities on this server and launch a small website that is used for the purposes of requesting certificates. We will discuss this further when we walk through issuing certificates from this web interface later in the chapter.

- **Certificate Enrollment Web Service and Certificate Enrollment Policy Web Service:** Most of the time, we are only concerned with issuing certificates to our company-owned, domain-joined systems. In those cases, these two selections are not necessary. If you plan to issue certificates to non-domain-joined computers from this CA server, you want to select these options.

- **Network Device Enrollment Service:** As the name implies, this piece of the CA role provides the capability to issue certificates to routers and other kinds of networking devices.

- **Online Responder:** This is a special function reserved for larger environments. Inside every certificate is a specification for a CRL. When a client computer utilizes a certificate, it reaches out and checks against this CRL in order to make sure that its certificate has not been revoked. The CRL is an important piece of the certificate security puzzle; in an environment with thousands of clients, your CRL may be very, very busy responding to all of these requests. You can deploy additional CA servers that are running Online Responder to help ease that load.

For the purposes of our lab, and to cover the required capabilities of most small-to-medium businesses out there, I am going to select the two options shown in *Figure 6.1*: **Certification Authority** and **Certification Authority Web Enrollment**.

Enterprise versus standalone

Following the installation of your AD CS role, Server Manager will notify you that certificate services need some additional configuration, as is common with many role installations. When configuring your CA role for the first time, you will be presented with a big choice. Do you want this CA server to be an **enterprise CA** or a **standalone CA**?

Let's start with the enterprise CA. As the wizard will tell you, an enterprise CA server must be a member of your domain, and these certificate servers typically stay online so that they can issue certificates to computers and users who need them. Wait a minute! Why in the world would we want to turn a certificate server *off* anyway? We will discuss that in a minute, but if you intend to utilize this CA to issue certificates, it must obviously remain turned on. Most CA servers within a domain environment will be enterprise CAs. When creating an enterprise CA, your templates and some certificate-specific information can store themselves within Active Directory, which makes integration between certificates and the domain tighter and more beneficial. If this is your first interaction with the CA role, I recommend you start with an enterprise CA because this better meets the needs of most organizations.

As you can correctly infer from the preceding text, this means that a standalone CA is less common to see in the wild. Standalones can be members of the domain, or they can remain out of that part of the network and reside in a local workgroup. If you had a security requirement that dictated that your certificate server could not be domain joined, that might be a reason why you would use a standalone CA. Another reason might be because Active Directory simply does not exist in the chosen environment.

In my eyes, it would be extremely rare to find a network where someone was trying to use Windows Server 2022 as their certification authority and at the same time was not running Active Directory Domain Services, but I'm sure there is a corner case somewhere that is doing exactly this. In that case, you would also need to choose standalone. A third example of when you would choose standalone is the event we alluded to already, where you might have a reason to turn off your server. When you employ this scenario, it is typically referred to as having an **offline root authority**. We haven't talked about root CAs yet, but we will in a minute. When you run an offline root, you create the top level of your PKI hierarchy as a standalone root CA, and then you build subordinate CAs underneath it. Your subordinate CAs are the ones doing the grunt work of issuing certificates—which means that the root can be safely shut down since it doesn't have any ongoing duties. Why would you want to do this? Well, most companies don't, but I have worked with some that have very high-level security policies, and this is why this topic might be relevant. If all of a company's CA servers are tied together as enterprise CAs with all of their information being stored inside Active Directory, a compromise to one of the subordinate issuing CAs could spell disaster for your entire PKI. It is possible that the only way to remediate an attack would be to wipe out the whole PKI environment, all of the CA servers, and build them up again. If you had to do this, it would mean not only rebuilding your servers but also re-issuing brand-new copies of all your certificates to every user and device that has them.

On the other hand, if you were running a standalone root CA that was offline, it would not have been affected by the attack. In this case, you could tear down your affected certificate servers, but your core root server would have been safely hidden. You could then bring this root back online, rebuild new subordinates from it, and have an easier path to being 100% operational because your root keys that are stored within the CA would not have to be re-issued, as they never would have been compromised in the attack.

As I said, I do not see this very often in the field, but it is a possibility. If you are interested in learning more about offline root CAs and their uses, I highly recommend checking out the TechNet article at `http://social.technet.microsoft.com/wiki/contents/articles/2900.offline-root-certification-authority-ca.aspx`. If you're thinking about moving forward with an offline root CA only because it seems like it's more secure, but you don't have a specific reason for doing so, I recommend you change gears and go ahead with an online enterprise root CA. While there are some security advantages to the offline root, most companies do not find those advantages to be worth the extra hassle that accompanies using an offline root CA. There are usability trade-offs when going down the offline route. If you find yourself wanting to set up a standalone CA that you are planning to take offline, but that is also domain joined, now you're really asking for trouble. Such a server will quickly fall out of sync with the domain while it is offline, and down the road, when you find the need to turn that root CA back on, you have an enormous headache waiting for you.

In most cases, you'll want to select an **enterprise CA** and proceed from there.

Root versus subordinate (issuing)

This is the second biggest choice you need to make when building a new CA. Is your new server going to be a **root CA** or a **subordinate CA**? In some cases, even in a lot of Microsoft documentation, a subordinate CA is more often called an issuing CA.

Generally, in a multi-tiered PKI, the subordinate/issuing CAs are the ones that do the issuing of certificates to users and devices in your network.

The difference really is just a matter of what you want your CA hierarchy to look like. In a PKI tree, there is a single high-level certificate, self-signed to itself by the root CA, that everything chains up to. A subordinate CA, on the other hand, is one that resides below a root CA in the tree, and it has been issued a certificate of its own from the root above it.

If your plans are to only run a single CA server, it must be a root. If you are creating a tiered approach to issuing certificates, the first CA in your environment needs to be a root, and you can slide subordinates in underneath it. You are allowed to have multiple roots, and therefore multiple trees, within a network. So your particular PKI can be structured however you see fit. In smaller companies, it is very common to see only a single CA server, an enterprise root. For the sake of simplicity in administration, these customers are willing to take the risk that, if something happens to that server, it won't be that big of a deal to build a new one and re-issue certificates.

For larger networks, it is more common to see a single root with a couple of subordinates below it. Typically, in this case, the root is only responsible for being the top dog and the holder of important keys, and the subordinate CAs are the ones doing the real work—issuing certificates to the clients.

Naming your CA server

At this point, now that you have installed the role, the hostname of the server itself is set in stone. You already knew this. But as you progress through the wizards to configure your CA for the first time, you will come across a screen called **Specify the name of the CA**. Huh? I thought we already did that when we set the hostname?

Nope, we do have our final hostname, and that server name is plugged into Active Directory as our server is joined to the domain, but the actual "CA name" is something else altogether. This is the name that will be identified inside the properties of every certificate that this CA issues. This is also a name that will be configured in various places inside Active Directory, since we are building an enterprise CA. The wizard identifies a possible name for you to use, which many administrators simply take and use. If you want to configure your own name, this is where you should do it.

Once you set the name here, this is the name of the CA forever:

Figure 6.2: Setting the name of the CA

Can I install the CA role onto a domain controller?

Since the role is officially called the **Active Directory Certificate Services** role, does that mean I should install this role onto one of my domain controller servers? No! Unfortunately, I have run across many small-to-medium businesses that have done exactly this, and luckily they don't have too many problems. So technically, it does work. However, it is not a Microsoft-recommended installation path, and you should build your CAs on their own servers; try *not* to co-host them with *any* other roles whenever possible.

Creating a new certificate template

Enough talk. It's time to get some work done. Now that our CA role has been installed, let's make it do something! The purpose of a certificate server is to issue certificates, right? So, shall we do that? Not so fast. When you issue a certificate from a CA server to a device or user, you are not choosing which *certificate* you want to deploy; rather, you are choosing which **certificate template** you want to utilize to deploy a certificate based upon the settings configured inside that template. Certificate templates are sort of like recipes for cooking. On the CA server, you build out your templates and include all of the particular ingredients, or settings, that you want to incorporate into your final certificate.

Then, when the users or computers come to request a certificate from the CA server, they are sort of baking a certificate into their system by telling the CA which template recipe to follow when building that certificate. Relating certificates to food? Maybe that's a stretch, but it's getting pretty late at night, and apparently I'm hungry.

When you walk through the steps to configure your first CA server, it comes with some prebuilt certificate templates right in the console. In fact, one of those templates, called **Computer**, is typically preconfigured to the point where, if a client computer were to reach out and request a computer certificate from your new CA, it would be able to successfully issue one. However, where is the fun in using prebuilt templates and certificates? I would rather build my own template so that I can specify particular configurations and settings inside that template. This way, I know exactly what settings are contained within my certificates that will ultimately be issued to my computers in the network.

Once again, we need to launch the proper administrative console in order to do our work. Inside the **Tools** menu of **Server Manager**, click on **Certification Authority**. Once inside, you can expand the name of your certification authority and see some folders, including one at the bottom called **Certificate Templates**. If you click on this folder, you will see a list of the templates that are currently built into our CA server. Since we do not want to utilize one of these pre-existing templates, it is common sense that we would try to right-click here and create a new template, but this is actually not the correct place to build a new template. Knowing the reason why new certificate templates are not built right from this screen must be above my pay grade because it seems silly that they aren't. Alas, in order to get to the proper screen for managing and modifying our templates, we need to right-click on the **Certificate Templates** folder and then choose **Manage**:

Figure 6.3: Managing certificate templates

Now you see a much more comprehensive list of templates, including a number of them you couldn't view on the first screen. To build a new template, what we want to do is find a pre-existing template that functions similarly to the purpose that we want our new certificate template to serve.

Computer templates are becoming commonly issued across many organizations due to more and more technologies requiring these certificates to exist. Yet, we don't want to utilize that baked-in template, which is simply called **Computer,** because we want our template to have a more specific name and we want the flexibility to modify template settings. Perhaps we want the certificate's validity period to be longer than the default settings or some kind of similar specification. Right-click on the built-in **Computer** template and click on **Duplicate Template.** This opens the **Properties** screen for our new template, from which we first want to give our new template a unique name inside the **General** tab.

In an upcoming chapter, we will discuss DirectAccess, the remote access technology that will be used in our environment. A good implementation of DirectAccess includes machine certificates being issued to all mobile client workstations, so we will plan to make use of this new template for those purposes. The **General** tab is also the place where we get to define our validity period for this certificate, which we will set to 2 years:

Figure 6.4: Crafting our certificate template

If the certificates that you want to issue require any additional setting changes, you can flip through the available tabs inside **Properties** and make the necessary adjustments. For our example, another setting I will change is inside the **Subject Name** tab.

I want my new certificates to have a subject name that matches the common name of the computer where it is being issued, so I have chosen **Common name** from the drop-down list:

Figure 6.5: The Subject Name tab

We have one more tab to visit, and this is something you should check for every certificate template that you build: the **Security** tab. We want to check here to make sure that the security permissions for this template are set in a way that allows the certificate to be issued to the users or computers that we desire, and at the same time make sure that the template's security settings are not too loose, creating a situation where someone who doesn't need it might be able to get a certificate. For our example, I plan to issue these DirectAccess certificates to all of the computers in the domain, because the kind of machine certificate I have created could be used for general IPsec authentications as well, which I may someday configure.

So, I am just making sure that I have **Domain Computers** listed in the **Security** tab, and that they are set for **Read** and **Enroll** permissions, so that any computer that is joined to my domain will have the option of requesting a new certificate based on my new template:

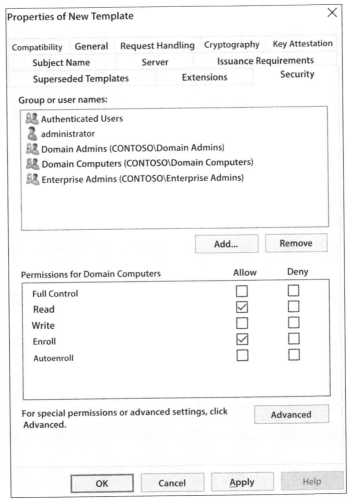

Figure 6.6: Certificate permissions

Since that is everything I need inside my new certificate, I simply click on **OK**, and my new certificate template is now included in the list of templates on my CA server.

Issuing your new certificates

Next comes the part that trips up a lot of people on their first attempt. We now have a brand-new template to issue, and we have verified that the permissions within that certificate template are appropriately configured so that any computer that is a member of our domain should be able to request one of these certificates, right? So our logical next step would be to jump onto a client computer and request a certificate, but there is first one additional task that needs to be accomplished in order to make that possible.

Even though the new template has been **created**, it has not yet been **published**. So at the moment, the CA server will not offer our new template as an option to the clients, even though security permissions are configured for it to do so. The process to publish a certificate template is very quick—only a couple of mouse clicks—but unless you know about the need to do this, it can be a very frustrating experience because nothing in the interface gives you a hint about this requirement.

Publishing the template

If your **Certificate Templates console** is still open (the one where we were managing our templates), close it so you are back at the main certification authority management console. Remember how we noticed that the list of available certificate templates that shows up here is much shorter? This is because only these certificate templates are currently published and available to be issued. In order to add additional templates to the published list, including our new one, we simply right-click on the **Certificate Templates** folder and then navigate to **New | Certificate Template to Issue**:

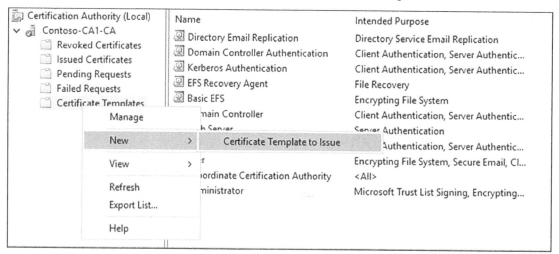

Figure 6.7: Publishing our new template

Now we are presented with a list of the available templates that are not yet issued. All you need to do is choose your new template from the list and click on **OK**. The new template is now included in the list of published certificate templates, and we are ready to request one from a client computer:

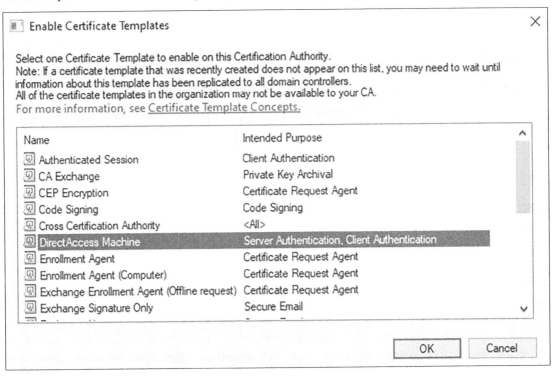

Figure 6.8: Selecting the new certificate template to issue

If you look through this list and do not see your newly created template, you may have to take an additional step. Sometimes simply waiting will resolve this behavior, because occasionally the reason that the new template does not show up in the list is that you are waiting for your domain controllers to finish replicating. At other times, you will find that, even after waiting for a while, your new template is still not on this list. In that case, you probably just need to restart the certification authority service to force it to pull in the new template information. To restart the CA service, you right-click on the CA's name near the top of the **Certification Authority** management console and navigate to **All Tasks | Stop Service**. The stopping of that service typically only takes a second or two, and then you can immediately right-click on the CA name again, and this time navigate to **All Tasks | Start Service**, as seen in *Figure 6.9*.

Now, try to publish your new template again, and you should see it in the list:

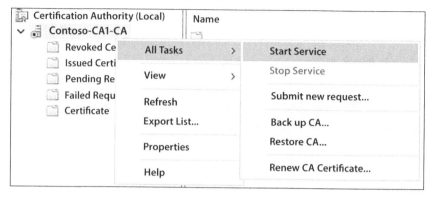

Figure 6.9: Restarting the CA service

Requesting a certificate from MMC

Our new certificate template has been created, and we have successfully published it within the CA console, thereby making it officially ready for issuing. It's time to test that out. Go ahead and log in to a regular client computer on your network in order to do this. There are a couple of standard ways to request a new certificate on a client computer. The first is by using the good old MMC console. On your client computer, launch MMC and add the snap-in for **Certificates**. When you choose **Certificates** from the list of available snap-ins and click on the **Add** button, you are presented with some additional options for which certificate store you want to open. You get to choose between opening certificates for **My user account**, **Service account**, or **Computer account**. Since we are trying to issue a certificate that will be used by the computer itself, I want to choose **Computer account** from this list, and click on **Finish**:

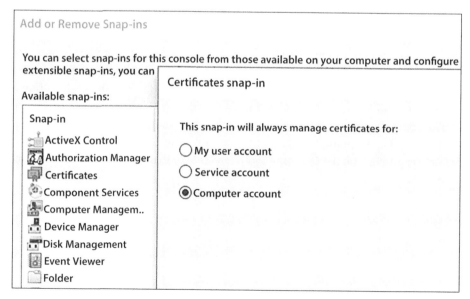

Figure 6.10: Snapping in computer certificates

On the next page, click on the **Finish** button again in order to choose the default option, which is **Local computer**. This will snap in the local machine's computer-based certificate store inside MMC.

On more recent operating systems, such as Windows 8 and 10 and with Windows Server 2012 through 2022, there is an MSC shortcut for opening directly into the local computer's certificate store. Simply type CERTLM.MSC into a **Run** prompt and MMC will automatically launch and create this snap-in for you.

When you are installing certificates onto a computer or server, this is generally the place you want to visit. Inside this certificate store, the specific location where we want to install our certificate is the **Personal** folder. This is true whether you are installing a machine certificate as we are doing here or installing an SSL certificate onto a webserver. The local computer's personal certificate folder is the correct location for both kinds of certificates. If you click on **Personal**, you can see that we do not currently have anything listed there:

Figure 6.11: Personal is empty

To request a new certificate from our CA server, we simply right-click on the **Personal** folder, and then navigate to **All Tasks | Request New Certificate....** Doing so opens a wizard; go ahead and click on the **Next** button once.

Now you encounter the screen shown in *Figure 6.12*, which looks like something needs to be done; but in most cases, because we are requesting a certificate on one of our corporate, domain-joined machines, we actually do not need to do anything on the screen presented in the following screenshot.

Simply click on **Next** again and the wizard will query Active Directory in order to show all of the certificate templates that are available to be issued:

Select Certificate Enrollment Policy

Certificate enrollment policy enables enrollment for certificates based on predefined certificate templates. Certificate enrollment policy may already be configured for you.

Configured by your administrator

  Active Directory Enrollment Policy   ⌄

Configured by you   Add New

                                                                                        Next   Cancel

Figure 6.12: Click Next to query Active Directory

Next, the **Request Certificates** screen is shown, which is the list of templates that are available to us. This list is dynamic; it is based on what computer you are logged in to and what your user account permissions are. Remember when we set up the security tab of our new certificate template? It is there that we defined who and what could pull down new certificates based on that template, and if I had defined a more particular group than domain computers, it is possible that my new **DirectAccess Machine** template would not be displayed in this list. However, since I did open up that template to be issuable to any computer within our domain, I can see and select it here:

Request Certificates

You can request the following types of certificates. Select the certificates you want to request, and then click Enroll.

Active Directory Enrollment Policy

☐ Computer   ⓘ STATUS: Available   Details ⌄

☑ DirectAccess Machine   ⓘ STATUS: Available   Details ⌄

☐ Show all templates

                                                                                        Enroll   Cancel

Figure 6.13: Certificate templates available for issuing

If you do not see your new template in the list, click on the **Show all templates** checkbox. This will give you a full list of all the templates on the CA server, and a description of each one with the reason that it is currently unavailable for issuing.

Put a checkmark next to any certificates that you want and click **Enroll**. Now the console spins for a few seconds while the CA server processes your request and issues a new certificate that is specific to your computer and the criteria that we placed inside the certificate template. Once finished, you can see that your brand-new machine certificate is now inside **Personal | Certificates** in the MMC. If you double-click on the certificate, you can check over its properties to ensure all of the settings you wanted to be pushed into this certificate exist:

Figure 6.14: Certificate properties

Requesting a certificate from the web interface

I typically use the MMC for requesting certificates whenever possible, but in most cases, there is another platform from which you can request and issue certificates. I say *in most cases* because the existence of this option depends upon how the CA server was built in the first place. When I installed my AD CS role, I made sure to choose the options for both **Certification Authority** and **Certification Authority Web Enrollment**.

This second option is important for our next section of text. Without the web enrollment piece of the role, we would not have a web interface running on our CA server, and this part would not be available to us.

If your CA server does not have web enrollment turned on, you can revisit the **role installation** page in **Server Manager** and add it to the existing role:

Roles	Description
▲ ☐ Active Directory Certificate Services (2 of 6 installe ⌃ ☑ Certification Authority (Installed) ☐ Certificate Enrollment Policy Web Service ☐ Certificate Enrollment Web Service ☑ **Certification Authority Web Enrollment (Installe** ☐ Network Device Enrollment Service ☐ Online Responder ☐ Active Directory Domain Services ☐ Active Directory Federation Services ☐ Active Directory Lightweight Directory Services ☐ Active Directory Rights Management Services ☐ DHCP Server	Certification Authority Web Enrollment provides a simple Web interface that allows users to perform tasks such as request and renew certificates, retrieve certificate revocation lists (CRLs), and enroll for smart card certificates.

Figure 6.15: Installing Certification Authority Web Enrollment

Once **Certification Authority Web Enrollment** is installed on your CA, there is a website running on that server that you can access via a browser from inside your network. Having this website is useful if you have the need for users to be able to issue their own certificates for some reason; it would be much easier to give them documentation or train them on the process of requesting a certificate from a website than expect them to navigate the MMC console. Additionally, if you are trying to request certificates from computers that are not within the same network as the CA server, using MMC can be difficult. For example, if you have the need for a user at home to be able to request a new certificate, without a full VPN tunnel, the MMC console is more than likely not going to be able to connect to the CA server in order to pull down that certificate. But since we have this certificate enrollment website running, you could externally publish this website as you do with any other website in your network, using a reverse proxy or firewall to keep that traffic safe and present users with the ability to hit this site and request certificates from wherever they are.

To access this website, let's use our regular client computer again. This time, instead of opening MMC, I will simply launch Edge, or any other browser, and log in to the website running at https://<CASERVER>/ certsrv.

For my specific environment, that exact web address is `https://CA1/certsrv`:

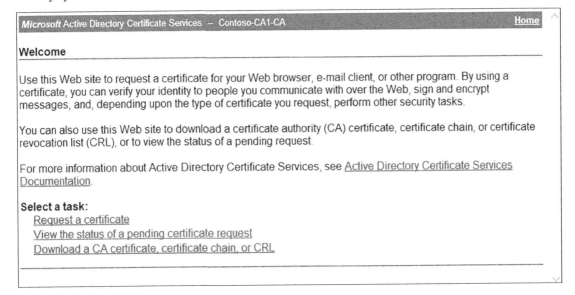

Figure 6.16: Viewing the CA web enrollment site

Our URL starts with HTTPS. This website must be configured to run on HTTPS instead of regular HTTP in order to allow the website to request certificates. It does not allow issuing certificates over HTTP because that information would be traveling in cleartext to the client. Enabling the website on the CA server for HTTPS ensures that the certificate issued will be encrypted while it travels.

Clicking on the **Request a certificate** link brings you into a wizard in which we can request a new certificate from the CA server. When you ask users to navigate their own way through this web interface, it is typically for the purpose of a user-based certificate, since we have some pretty easy ways of automatically distributing computer-level certificates without any user interaction. We will discuss that in a moment. However, for this example, since we are asking our users to log in here and request a new **User Certificate**, on the next page, I will choose that link:

Figure 6.17: Selecting a certificate type

If you were not interested in a user certificate and wanted to use the web interface to request a machine certificate, a webserver certificate, or any other kind of certificate, you could instead choose the link for **advanced certificate request** and follow the prompts to do so.

Next, click the **Submit** button, and once the certificate has been generated, you will see a link that allows you to **Install this certificate**. Click on that link, and the new certificate that was just created for you will be installed onto your computer. You can see in the following screenshot the response that the website gave me, indicating a successful installation, and you can also see I have opened up the current user certificates inside MMC in order to see and validate that the certificate really exists:

Figure 6.18: Certificate being successfully installed

In this section, we have proven that our CA server is working; follow along with the next few pages as we take certificate issuance to the next level.

Creating an auto-enrollment policy

Our certification authority server is configured and running, and we can successfully issue certificates to the client machines. Great! Now let's pretend we have a new project on our plates, and one of the requirements for this project is that all of the computers in our network need to have a copy of this new machine certificate that we have created. Uh oh, that sounds like a lot of work. Even though the process for requesting one of these certificates is very quick—only a handful of seconds on each work-station—if you had to do that individually on a thousand machines, you'd be talking about a serious period of time needing to be spent on this process. Furthermore, in many cases, the certificates that you issue will only be valid for one year. Does this mean we are facing an extreme amount of admin-istrative work every single year to re-issue these certificates as they expire? Certainly not!

Let's figure out how to utilize Group Policy to create a GPO that will auto-enroll our new certificates to all of the machines in the network, and, while we are there, also configure it so that when a certificate's expiration date comes up, the certificate will auto-renew at the appropriate intervals.

Let's pop into the **Certification Authority** management console on our CA server and take a look inside the **Issued Certificates** folder. I only want to look here for a minute in order to see how many certificates we have issued so far in our network. It looks like just a handful of them, so hopefully once we are done configuring our policy, if we have done it correctly and it takes effect automatically, we should see more certificates starting to show up in this list:

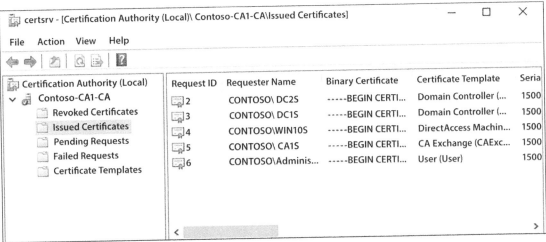

Figure 6.19: Certificates issued by our CA

Log in to a domain controller server, and then open up the **Group Policy Management** console. I have created a new GPO called **Enable Certificate Auto-enrollment,** and am now editing that GPO to find the settings I need to configure to make this GPO do its work:

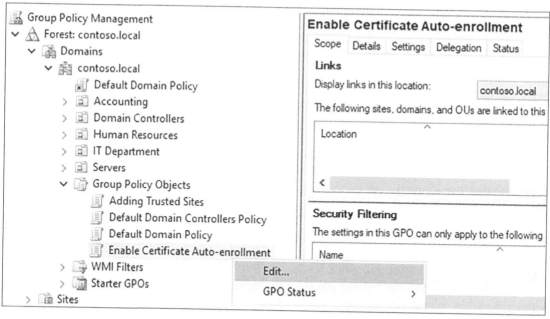

Figure 6.20: Editing the new Auto-enrollment GPO

The settings inside this GPO that we want to configure are located at **Computer Configuration | Policies | Windows Settings | Security Settings | Public Key Policies | Certificate Services Client - Auto-Enrollment.**

Double-click on this setting to view its properties. All we need to do is change **Configuration Model** to **Enabled,** and make sure to check the box that says **Renew expired certificates, update pending certificates, and remove revoked certificates.** Also check the box for **Update certificates that use certificate templates.**

These settings will ensure that auto-renewal happens automatically when the certificates start running into their expiration dates over the next few years:

Figure 6.21: Enabling Auto-Enrollment

What is the last thing we need to do on our GPO in order to make it live? Create a link so that it starts applying! For your own environment, you will probably create a more specific link to a particular OU, as we discussed in the last chapter; but for my lab, I want these certificates to apply to every single machine that is joined to the domain, so I will link my new GPO at the root of the domain so that it applies to all of my clients and servers.

Now that the GPO is created and configured, and we have linked it to the domain, I would think that some new certificates would be issued and there would be more names shown inside my **Issued Certificates** folder inside my certification authority console. But there are not. Wait a minute, in our GPO, we didn't really specify anything particular to my DirectAccess machine certificate template, did we? Could that be the problem? No, there wasn't even an option for specifying which template I wanted to set up for auto-enrollment. So what gives?

When you enable auto-enrollment in **Group Policy**, you are simply flipping an on/off switch and turning it on for *every* certificate template. So now that we have a policy that is configured to enable auto-enrollment and is linked to the domain, thus making it *live*, auto-enrollment has been enabled on every domain-joined computer, for every certificate template that is published on our CA server.

Yet, none of them are issuing themselves to my computers. This is because I need to adjust the security settings on my new **DirectAccess Machine** template. Currently, I have it configured so that all domain computers have **Enroll** permissions, but if you remember that **Security** tab within the certificate template's properties, there was an additional security identifier called **Autoenroll**. Every certificate template has the **Autoenroll** permission identifier, and it is not allowed by default. Now that the light switch has been flipped on for auto-enrollment in our domain, we need to enable the **Autoenroll** permission on any template that we want to start distributing itself. As soon as we enable that permission, these certificates will start flowing around our network.

Head into the **certificate management** section of your CA server and open **Properties** of your new template, then make your way to the **Security** tab and allow **Autoenroll** permissions for the **Domain Computers** group.

This should tell the CA to start distributing these certificates accordingly:

Figure 6.22: Template security for Autoenroll permissions

And sure enough, if I let my environment sit for a little while, giving Active Directory and Group Policy a chance to update on all of my machines, I now see more certificates have been issued from my CA server:

	Request ID	Requester Name	Binary Certificate	Certificate Template
Certification Authority (Local)				
Contoso-CA1-CA	2	CONTOSO\DC2S	-----BEGIN CERTI...	Domain Controller (...
Revoked Certificates	3	CONTOSO\DC1S	-----BEGIN CERTI...	Domain Controller (...
Issued Certificates	4	CONTOSO\WIN10S	-----BEGIN CERTI...	DirectAccess Machin...
Pending Requests	5	CONTOSO\CA1S	-----BEGIN CERTI...	CA Exchange (CAExc...
Failed Requests	6	CONTOSO\Admin...	-----BEGIN CERTI...	User (User)
Certificate Templates	7	CONTOSO\DC2S	-----BEGIN CERTI...	Directory Email Repli...
	8	CONTOSO\DC2S	-----BEGIN CERTI...	Domain Controller A...
	9	CONTOSO\DC2S	-----BEGIN CERTI...	Kerberos Authenticat...
	10	CONTOSO\DC1S	-----BEGIN CERTI...	Directory Email Repli...
	11	CONTOSO\DC1S	-----BEGIN CERTI...	Domain Controller A...
	12	CONTOSO\DC1S	-----BEGIN CERTI...	Kerberos Authenticat...
	13	CONTOSO\BACK1S	-----BEGIN CERTI...	DirectAccess Machin...
	14	CONTOSO\WEB1S	-----BEGIN CERTI...	DirectAccess Machin...

Figure 6.23: Certificates are now being auto-enrolled

To automatically issue certificates from any template you create, simply publish the template and make sure to configure the appropriate auto-enroll permissions on that template. Once the auto-enrollment GPO is in place on those clients, they will reach out to your CA server and ask it for certificates from any template for which they have permission to receive a certificate. In the future, when that certificate is about to expire and the machine needs a new copy, the auto-enrollment policy will issue a new one prior to the expiration date, based on the timestamps you defined inside the GPO.

Certificate auto-enrollment can take what would normally be an enormous administrative burden and turn it into a completely automated process!

Obtaining a public authority SSL certificate

We are now pretty comfortable with grabbing certificates from our own CA server inside our own network, but what about handling those SSL certificates for our webservers that should be acquired from a public certification authority? For many of you, this will be the most common interaction that you have with certificates, and it's very important to understand this side of the coin as well. When you need to acquire an SSL certificate from your public authority of choice, there is a three-step process to do so: create a certificate request, submit the certificate request, and install the resulting certificate.

We are going to use my WEB1 server, on which I have a website running. Currently, the site is only capable of handling HTTP traffic, but when we turn it loose on the internet, we need to enable HTTPS to keep the information that is being submitted to the site encrypted.

To use HTTPS, we need to install an SSL certificate onto the WEB1 server. This webserver is running the Microsoft web services platform, **Internet Information Services (IIS)**.

The three-step process you take is the same if you are running a different webserver, such as Apache, but the particular things that you have to do to accomplish these three steps will be different because Apache or any other webserver will have a different user interface than IIS. Since we are working on a Windows Server 2022 webserver, we are utilizing IIS 10.

Public/private key pair

Before we jump into performing those three steps, let's discuss why any of this even matters. You have probably heard of the term **private key** but may not quite understand what that means. When we send traffic across the internet, from our client computers to an HTTPS website, we understand that the traffic is encrypted. This means that the packets are tied up in a nice little package before leaving my laptop so that nobody can see them while they travel, and are then unwrapped successfully when those packets reach the webserver. My laptop uses a key to encrypt the traffic, and the server uses a key to decrypt that traffic, but how do they know what keys to use? There are two different kinds of encryption methodology that can be used here:

- **Symmetric encryption**: The simpler method of encryption, symmetric, means that there is a single key, and both sides utilize it. Traffic is packaged up using a key, and the same key is used to unwrap that traffic when it reaches its destination. Since this single key is the all-powerful Oz, you wouldn't want it to get into the wrong hands, which means you will not be presenting it out on the internet. Therefore, symmetric encryption is not generally used for protecting internet website traffic. Rather, it is used more commonly in places where you control both sides of the communication stream, such as VPN traffic.

- **Asymmetric encryption**: This is our focus with HTTPS traffic. Asymmetric encryption utilizes two keys: a public key and a private key. The public key is included inside your SSL certificate, and so anyone on the internet can contact your website and get the public key. Your laptop then uses that public key to encrypt the traffic and sends it over to the webserver. Why is this secure if the public key is broadcast to the entire internet? Because the traffic can only be decrypted by using a corresponding private key, which is securely stored on your webserver. It is very important to maintain security over your private key and your webservers, ensuring the key doesn't fall into anyone else's pocket.

Creating a certificate signing request

If you've already jumped ahead and acquired an SSL certificate from your public CA entity by logging in to their website, purchasing a certificate, and immediately downloading it, you've already missed the boat. That certificate obviously would have no way of knowing about a private key that you might have sitting on your webserver, and so that certificate would be effectively useless when installed anywhere.

When you install an SSL certificate onto a webserver, it is very important that the certificate knows about your private key. How do we make sure that happens? This is where the **certificate signing request (CSR)** comes into play. The first step in correctly acquiring an SSL certificate is to generate a CSR from your local webserver. When you create that file, the webserver platform creates the private key that is needed and hides it away on your server.

The CSR is then created in such a way that it knows exactly how to interact with that private key, and you then utilize the CSR when you log in to the CA's website to request the certificate.

The private key is not *inside* the CSR, and your CA vendor never knows what your private key is. This key is ultra-important and is only ever stored on your webserver, inside your organization.

To generate a CSR, open IIS from the **Tools** menu of Server Manager, and then click on the name of the webserver from the navigational tree on the left side of your screen. This will populate a number of different applets into the center of the console. The one we want to work with is called **Server Certificates.** Go ahead and double-click on that:

Figure 6.24: Viewing Server Certificates via IIS

Now, on the **Server Certificates** screen, you can see any existing certificates that reside on the server listed here. This is where we ultimately need to see our new SSL certificate so that we can utilize it inside our website properties when we are ready to turn on HTTPS. The first step to acquiring our new certificate is creating the certificate request to be used with our CA, and, if you take a look on the right side of your screen, you will see an **Actions** section, under which is listed **Create Certificate Request….**

Go ahead and click on that action:

Figure 6.25: Creating a certificate request

In the resulting wizard, you need to populate the information that will be stored within your SSL certificate. The **Common name** field is the most important piece of information here. It needs to be the DNS name that this certificate is going to protect. So basically, you enter the name of your website here, then continue with filling out the rest of your company-specific information. A couple of special notes here that often seem to trip up admins are that the **Organizational unit** can be anything at all; I usually just enter the word Web. Also make sure to spell out the name of your **State**; do not use an abbreviation:

Distinguished Name Properties

Specify the required information for the certificate. State/province and City/locality must be specified as official names and they cannot contain abbreviations.

Common name:	portal.contoso.com
Organization:	Contoso
Organizational unit:	Web
City/locality	Redmond
State/province:	Washington
Country/region:	US

Figure 6.26: Populating information for the certificate

On the **Cryptographic Service Provider Properties** page, you typically want to leave **Cryptographic service provider** set to its default, unless you have a specialized crypto card in your server and are planning to use it for handling encryption processing for this website. On an IIS server, you will almost always have **Microsoft RSA SChannel Cryptographic Provider** listed here. What you **do** want to change, however, is the **Bit length**. The standard bit length for many years was 1024, and that continues to be the default choice in Windows Server 2022. The general industry for SSL encryption has decided that 1024 is too weak, however, and the new standard is 2048. When you head onto your CA's website to request a certificate, you will more than likely find that your request needs to have a minimum of 2048 bits. So go ahead and change that drop-down setting to **2048**:

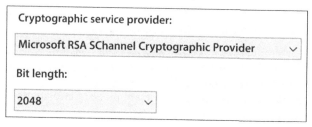

Figure 6.27: Setting the encryption bit length to 2048

The only thing left to do for our CSR is to give it a location and filename. Saving this csr as a text file is the normal way to go and serves our purposes well because all we need to do when we request our certificate is open the file and then copy and paste the contents. We have now created our csr file, and we can utilize this file to request the certificate from our public CA.

Submitting the certificate request

Now, head over to the website for your public certification authority. Again, any of the companies that we mentioned earlier, such as GoDaddy or Verisign, are appropriate for this purpose. Each authority has its own look and feel for its web interface, so I cannot give you the exact steps that need to be taken for this process. Once you have an account and log in to the authority's site, you should be able to find an option for purchasing an SSL certificate. For some CAs, the purchasing process and the certificate acquisition process are two different things. For example, you purchase and pay for your new SSL certificate and then you visit a different section of the interface to use the "certificate credit" you just purchased to create a certificate. On the other hand, some CAs walk you through the entire process from start to finish. In any case, once that certificate has been purchased, there will be a process for requesting and deploying that certificate.

Once you have found the interface used for generating the new certificate, you will generally be asked for four pieces of information:

1. **Validity period** – How long should this SSL certificate last? It used to be common that companies would purchase SSL certificates with one-year, two-year, or even three-year validity periods, meaning that the certificate was "good" for that amount of time. Recently, Apple has flexed its muscles in this space and decided that the Safari web browser will only trust certificates that have a validity period of one year, more or less.

Rather than push back, the industry said "sure, why not?" and so moving forward, SSL certificates will only be valid for one year at a time. For clarity, you can still *purchase* an SSL certificate for multiple years at a time, which can sometimes get you a better deal on the cost per year, but even if you have purchased multiple years' worth of SSL certificate use, you will still need to replace the certificate *every year* with a fresh one from your certificate provider. We will talk more about this shortly, when we discuss re-keying certificates.

2. **Webserver platform** – What type of webserver are you running? The answer to this question impacts what type of file is available to download at the end of this process. When working with Windows Server, your answer will be "IIS," but other possible options include Apache, Tomcat, NGINX, and many more Linux-based webserver selections.

3. **Domain ownership validation** – This one is interesting, and if you haven't been through this process before, you likely haven't thought about why it is necessary. What's to stop hacker Joe sitting in an internet café halfway across the world, or a 12-year-old playing video games in their basement, or even your next-door neighbor from creating their own CA login and purchasing an SSL certificate that has *your* company name and website on it? The validation of domain ownership is a process to prove that you really own contoso.com (or whatever your domain is) so that only you are allowed to purchase valid SSL certificates that protect traffic for your domain name. The most common way to validate domain ownership is to select from a list of pre-defined email addresses inside the CA and have it send some flavor of validation email to that email address. For example, you might have a selection of email addresses like the following:

   - admin@contoso.com
   - administrator@contoso.com
   - webmaster@contoso.com
   - hostmaster@contoso.com

   All you need to do is verify that you can receive an email to one of those email addresses, and by selecting this option, you will receive an email to that address that usually contains a link and a code. Simply copy the code and paste it into the link, and this is an easy way to validate domain ownership because as the owner of that domain, only YOU would have access to those email addresses. A second form of ownership, if email doesn't pan out, is that the CA may give you a special DNS record that can be put into place in your domain's public DNS. You input the record, the CA sees that record show up on the internet, and they validate you are the domain owner. This process takes much longer to accomplish than email verification, so it is rarely used.

4. **CSR** – The last (and most important) thing you will be asked to provide is the text from inside that CSR file we created a few minutes ago. There will be either an upload function or simply an input box, and all you need to do is copy/paste the entire contents of the CSR into that box.

If you open the text file we saved earlier, you will see a big lump of nonsense:

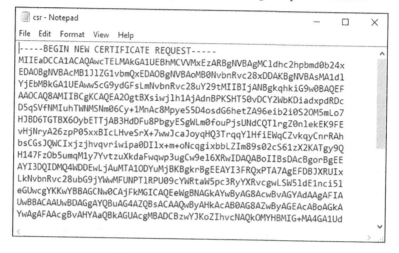

Figure 6.28: The text inside a CSR file

This mess of data contains information about your certificate request and is exactly what the CA needs in order to create your new SSL certificate so that it knows how to interact with your webserver's private key. Only the server that generated the CSR will be able to accept and properly utilize the SSL certificate that is based on this CSR.

Downloading and installing your certificate

Now you sit back and wait. Depending on which authority you are using and on how often your company purchases certificates from this authority, your certificate might be available for download almost immediately, or it could take a few hours before that certificate shows up in the available downloads list. The reason for this is that many CAs utilize human approval for new certificates, and you are literally waiting for someone to take a look at the certificate request and your information to make sure you really work for the company and that you really own this domain name. Remember, the real benefit to a public SSL certificate is that the CA is guaranteeing that the user of this certificate is the real deal, so they want to make sure they aren't, for example, issuing a certificate for portal.contoso. com to someone in the Fabrikam organization by mistake.

Once you are able to download the certificate from the CA's website, go ahead and copy it over to the webserver from which we generated the CSR. It is critically important that you install this new certificate onto the **same server**. If you were to install this new certificate onto a different webserver, one that did not generate the CSR this certificate was built from, that certificate would import successfully, but would not be able to function. Once again, this is because the private key that the certificate is planning to interact with would not be present on a different server.

Back inside the IIS management console, we can now use the next action shown along the right side of *Figure 6.25*, called **Complete Certificate Request….** This launches a short little wizard in which you point at the newly downloaded certificate file, and the wizard then imports it into our server. Now that the certificate resides on the server, it is ready to be used by our website.

There is one additional item that I always check after installing or importing an SSL certificate. You can now see your new certificate listed inside IIS, and if you double-click on your new certificate, you will see the **Properties** page for the certificate. On the **General** tab of these properties, take a look near the bottom. Your certificate should display a little key icon and the **You have a private key that corresponds to this certificate** text. If you can see this message, your import was successful and the new certificate file matched up with the CSR perfectly. The server and certificate now share that critical private key information, and the SSL certificate will be able to work properly to protect our website. If you do not see this message, something went wrong in the process to request and download your certificate. If you do not see the message here, you need to start over by generating a new CSR, because the certificate file that you got back must not have been keyed appropriately against that CSR, or something along those lines. Without the **You have a private key that corresponds to this certificate** text at the bottom of this screen, your certificate will *not* validate traffic properly.

Here is an example of what it should look like when working correctly:

Figure 6.29: This certificate properly matches up with a private key

Re-keying certificates

While poking around in your public CA's interface, you may have noticed a function or button to "re-key" a certificate. What does that mean? When you purchase a certificate such as `portal.contoso.com` from your CA, you are now able to use a CSR to craft a certificate based on that name. You then install that certificate onto your webserver, and it then protects traffic for your website `portal.contoso.com`. Each year, you can re-purchase the certificate, re-create a fresh CSR, and reinstall the certificate as if it were brand new. But what if you need to reinstall this certificate in the middle of the year? Perhaps you paid for a certificate from January through January, but it is now July and your webserver dies? You replace the server, reinstall your website, and now realize that you need to get a new SSL certificate onto this new server to protect traffic for the same `portal.contoso.com` website. Do you need to purchase another SSL certificate and take the hit for the cost of the six months that you didn't use? No, this is where re-keying a certificate can help you out. If you use your new webserver to generate a new CSR, you can then take that new CSR to your CA's website and find the certificate that you already purchased, and simply re-key the certificate against your new CSR. This process will invalidate the old copy of the certificate, and will issue a new certificate based on the new CSR (based, of course, on the new server's private key), which you can then install to your new webserver. This way, you can continue to make use of that SSL certificate you purchased on a new server and finish out the year.

Another possible reason you might find yourself re-keying a certificate is when you have purchased multiple years' worth of an SSL certificate. If you purchased `portal.contoso.com` for three years, remember that you can only issue a certificate for one year at a time. So every year, on or before that certificate's expiration date, you will need to revisit your CA and re-key your certificate to pull down a fresh copy, giving you protection for another year. You won't have to pay for this if you have already purchased the certificate for multiple years, but will still need to perform the certificate re-key and replacement for your webserver to continue working properly.

Exporting and importing certificates

I often find myself needing to use the same SSL certificate on multiple servers. This might happen in the case where I have more than one IIS server serving up the same website and I am using some form of load balancing to split the traffic between them. This need may also arise when working with any form of hardware load balancer, as you sometimes need to import certificates onto not only the webservers themselves but also the load balancer box. Another example is when using wildcard certificates; when you purchase a wildcard, you typically intend to install it onto multiple servers.

Does this mean that you need to generate a new CSR from each server, and request a new copy of the same certificate multiple times? Definitely not, and in fact, doing so could cause you other problems: remember that when a public CA **re-keys** a certificate—in other words, if you have already requested a certificate with a particular name and then come back again later to request another copy of the same certificate—that CA will most likely invalidate the first one as it issues the second copy. This is not always immediately apparent, as there is usually a timer set on the invalidation of the first certificate. If you revisit the CA's web interface and request a new copy of the same certificate using a new CSR for your second webserver, you might discover that everything works fine for a few days, but then suddenly the primary webserver stops validating traffic because its SSL certificate, the original copy, has expired.

When you need to reuse the same SSL certificate on multiple servers, you can simply export it from one and import it on the next. There is no need to contact the CA at all. This process is quite straight-forward, and there are two common places where you can do it: inside either the MMC snap-in for certificates or from within IIS itself. It is important to note, though, that the process is slightly different depending on which avenue you take, and you have to be especially aware of what is happening with the private key as you step through these wizards.

Exporting from MMC

Head back into your **Local Computer** certificate store in MMC and navigate to **Personal | Certificates** so that you can see your SSL certificate listed. Right-click on the certificate, and then navigate to **All Tasks | Export...**. When you walk through this export wizard, the important part that I wanted to mention happens right away in the wizard steps. The first choice you have to make is whether to export the private key. Again, the private key is the secret sauce that allows the certificate to interact properly with the server on which it is installed. If you export without the private key, that certificate will not work on another server. So it is important here that, if you are exporting this certificate with the intention of installing it onto a second webserver and using it for validating SSL traffic, you select the top option for **Yes, export the private key**:

Figure 6.30: Exporting a certificate using MMC

As the wizard sufficiently warns you, when you choose to export a certificate that contains private key information, you are required to supply a password, which will be used to protect the exported PFX file. It is important to choose a good password. If you forget it, your exported file will be completely useless (which isn't terrible, because you can simply export it again). If you input a password that is very simple or easy to guess, anyone who gets their hands on this PFX file may be able to use your certificate and private key on their own webservers, which would not be good.

Exporting from IIS

Alternatively, an exported PFX file can be generated from inside the IIS console. Inside the **Server Certificates** applet for IIS, just right-click on the certificate and choose **Export...**.

This launches a single-page wizard that simply asks you for a location and password:

Figure 6.31: Exporting a certificate using IIS

We had many more options that we could have chosen or denied when we exported using MMC, so why is this so short? IIS makes assumptions for the rest of the settings in order to speed up the export process. When you are exporting an SSL certificate, it is almost a guarantee that you also intend to export the private key. Therefore, IIS simply makes that assumption and bypasses the rest of the choices. You are forced to enter a password because you don't have a choice about the private key; it will be included with the certificate export automatically. So, if you had some reason to export a certificate that did *not* contain the private key info, you could not utilize the IIS console for this task. You would need to open up MMC and walk through the more extensive wizard found there.

Importing into a second server

Whichever direction you take for accomplishing the export, once you have the fully fleshed PFX file available, importing into your second server is very easy. From within either console, MMC or IIS, you can right-click and choose the **Import** action. Walking through the steps, you simply choose the PFX file and then input the password that you used to protect the file. The certificate is then imported, and, if you open **Properties**, you will see that the little key icon and the private key message are displayed properly at the bottom of the **certificate properties** screen. If you do not see the **you have a private key** message, you did something incorrectly during the export process and you'll need to try it again.

Go ahead and try it yourself; find a server with an SSL certificate and test exporting that certificate with and without the private key. When you import into a new server, you will see that importing the certificate file without a private key does not lead to this message being displayed at the bottom of the properties page, but the exported file that does contain the private key results in the proper message being shown here. To take it a step further, try utilizing both certificates on a non-important website and see what happens. You will find that the certificate lacking the private key will fail to validate SSL traffic.

If you attempt to export an SSL certificate and the option to include the private key is grayed out, this means when the original administrator installed this certificate to the webserver, they chose a special option that blocks the ability for the private key to be exported in the future. In this case, you will not be able to export the certificate with the private key.

OpenSSL for Linux webservers

This chapter should give you all the information needed to protect websites with SSL certificates issued from a public CA...on a Windows webserver. While this is obviously a Microsoft-centric book, the majority of webservers out there are not running on Microsoft webserver platforms. Alas, you will likely run into just as many Linux-based webservers as you do instances of IIS, and it will be very helpful to your role as server administrator to be able to install certificates onto these webservers as well.

One significant difference between Windows and Linux webservers is the types of files used for certificates. IIS hides away the private key; you don't really deal with it at all. When downloading certificate files for IIS, those are usually CER or CRT files. A Linux webserver, however, expects something else. On most Linux webservers, the certificate file and the private key are each individual files that are quite visible right on the server. Both of these files generally have the PEM file extension.

Fortunately, the overall three-step process for acquiring and installing a certificate is exactly the same. Generate a CSR, use the CSR to get a certificate from your CA, and install the certificate to your webserver. Within those three steps are some significant differences between a Windows and a Linux platform. Let's discuss them.

Generate a CSR

Shortly, we will install a toolset called OpenSSL and use it for some certificate-related functions. There is a way within the OpenSSL tool to generate a private key file and a corresponding CSR file, but this is not the approach that I find to be the most user-friendly. Instead, when dealing with the requirement to install an SSL certificate onto a Linux-based webserver, I turn right back to the Windows world and generate my CSR from inside IIS. Wait a minute, what?? Didn't I just say that the processes in Windows and Linux are different? Yes, but bear with me for a minute. The CA doesn't care where the CSR file comes from, and so rather than use a CLI-based platform like OpenSSL to monkey around with command syntax and have to resort to Google to come up with the right commands, I simply create a CSR file exactly the same way that I would for a Windows Server, right inside IIS.

If you don't have a server with IIS installed, you can just as easily craft a CSR right from your Windows 10 computer. If you head into Control Panel and find the option to **Turn Windows features on or off**, you will discover an option to install **Internet Information Services**. This installs the same IIS interface and toolset to your Windows 10 computer as it would to a Windows Server. From within this IIS console, you will have the same actions available to generate and complete certificate signing requests, right on your laptop.

Figure 6.32: Installing IIS onto Windows 10

Acquire the certificate

Now that you have a CSR file, follow through the same series of steps we previously discussed to submit your CSR to a CA, validate yourself as the owner of the domain, and download the resulting certificate file.

Install the certificate

Here is where we start to steer the ship differently to deal with a Linux webserver. First of all, you need to install the certificate onto the same IIS server (or workstation) from which you generated the CSR file. Once again, this is critically important so that your new certificate successfully pairs up with the private key that was created when you created your CSR. Once you have the new certificate installed and have validated that it looks good, you can now use the knowledge you have from a few pages ago and export this certificate (including the private key) to a PFX file.

Your newly created PFX file contains both the certificate and the private key. The only remaining step is to pump your PFX file through a couple of OpenSSL commands, which will then convert this PFX file into two separate PEM files, one containing the SSL certificate and another the private key. These two files are exactly what most Linux-based webservers are looking for when they ask you to provide an SSL certificate.

Here are the steps required to accomplish this last piece of the puzzle:

1. Download and install OpenSSL. The available version of this will change occasionally, so I cannot provide a static download link, but you can easily find it by searching the web. A specific version and filename that I know works for this purpose, because it is the one installed on my computer right now, is `Win64OpenSSL-1_1_1n.exe`.

2. Put your PFX file in a location that we will reference in our commands. For the sake of our example, I will assume your PFX file is named `Export.pfx`, and that it is sitting inside a folder called `C:\Cert`.

3. Open Command Prompt and navigate to the folder where OpenSSL is installed. For my version, this is the command to take me to that folder:

```
CD C:\Program Files\OpenSSL-Win64\bin
```

4. Run the following two commands:

```
openssl pkcs12 -in c:\cert\export.pfx -nokeys -out c:\cert\portal.
contoso.com-crt.pem -nodes

openssl pkcs12 -in c:\cert\export.pfx -nocerts -out c:\cert\portal.
contoso.com-key.pem -nodes
```

(You will be asked to enter your PFX password after each of these commands.)

That's it! The two commands above will place two new files inside your `C:\Cert` folder. The first is your certificate, while the second is your private key. These two files will need to be either copied to a particular folder on your Linux webserver or uploaded into a graphical interface of whatever software you have running on that webserver, to specify the SSL certificate that is going to be used by the site.

Figure 6.33: Converting a PFX into Linux-ready certificate files

These steps are kind of a weird combination of using Windows and Linux tools to get an SSL certificate into Apache, Tomcat, NGINX, or other similar webservers. I employ this method because I always have IIS at the ready by having it installed onto my Windows 10 workstation, and this way I can simply have those two OpenSSL commands stored away for quick access to convert certificate files when needed.

Summary

Certificates often get a bad rep, and I believe this is because people think they are a headache to deal with. I see their point. Without knowing how to navigate through the various administrative consoles that deal with your certificate infrastructure, it would be difficult to make even the simplest items function. By walking through the most common certificate-related tasks that any server admin will eventually have to tackle within their own networks, I hope that you have now found some comfort and confidence to progress with those projects that might be currently sitting on hold, waiting for the certificate infrastructure to be built. In the next chapter, we will study networking with Windows Server 2022.

Questions

1. What is the name of the role inside Windows Server 2022 that allows you to issue certificates from your server?
2. What kind of CA server is typically installed first in a domain environment?
3. Should you install the certification authority role onto a domain controller?
4. After creating a new certificate template, what next step needs to be taken before you can issue certificates to your computers or users from that new template?
5. What is the general name of the GPO setting that forces certificates to be issued without manual intervention by an administrator?
6. An SSL certificate will only be able to validate traffic properly if it shares _____ key information with the webserver.
7. What is the primary piece of information that a public certification authority needs in order to issue you a new SSL certificate (hint: you generate this from your webserver)?
8. What kind of file contains both a certificate and a private key?

Join our community on Discord

Join our community's Discord space for discussions with the author and other readers:

https://packt.link/SecNet

7

Networking with Windows Server 2022

As we have discussed so far in this book, servers are the tree trunks of our networks. They are the backbone infrastructure that enables us to get work done. If servers are the trunks, then the networks themselves must be the roots. Your network is the platform that supports the company infrastructure; it makes up the channels that all devices inside your company use to communicate with each other.

Traditionally, there have been *server admins* and *network admins* in the IT industry, separated roles, and in many places that is still the case. An administrator who primarily works on servers does not generally have enough time in the day to also support the network infrastructure in an organization of any size, and the reverse is also true. Network administrators generally stick to their own equipment and management tools and aren't interested in diving too deeply into the Windows Server world. However, many of us work in smaller companies where many hats must be worn. Some days, the server admin and the network admin hats sit on top of each other, so we must understand at least the baseline of networking and the tools that we can use to troubleshoot connections that are not working. In addition, Windows Server 2022 brings a new networking mindset into focus: the virtualization of your networks. There will always be some semblance of a physical network, using physical switches and routers to move the packets around between different rooms and buildings. But now we are also incorporating the idea of **software-defined networking (SDN)** into our Windows servers, which gives us the capability to virtualize some of that configuration. Not only the config itself; we are also actually virtualizing the network traffic and building our networks from within a server console, rather than using command-line interfaces to configure our routers and switches, which was always needed in the past.

Hold the phone; I am getting ahead of myself. First, let's talk about some of the new and useful things inside Windows Server 2022 that do involve working with physical networks (or any networks) because these are going to be important for any administrator in today's networking world to know about. Later, we will take a few moments to further explore this new idea of network virtualization.

The following are the topics we plan to discuss in this chapter:

- Introduction to IPv6
- Your networking toolbox
- Building a routing table
- NIC Teaming
- Software-defined networking

Introduction to IPv6

Welcome to the dark side! Unfortunately, that is how many people think of IPv6 for the time being. While IPv6 is by no means a new thing, in my experience, it is still something that almost no one has deployed in their networks. While working with hundreds of different companies all over the world over the past few years, I came across only two organizations that were running IPv6 over their entire production network, and one wasn't even truly native IPv6. Instead, they were using a tunneling technology, called ISATAP, over their whole network to make all of the servers and clients talk to each other using IPv6 packets, but these packets were still traversing an IPv4 physical network. Don't get me wrong; I found plenty of cases where companies were toying around with IPv6 and had some semblance of it configured in a sectioned-off piece of their networks, but using it for the entire production network? Most of us just aren't ready for that big a change yet. Why is it so difficult to put IPv6 into place? Because we have used IPv4 since basically the beginning of time, it's what we all know and understand, and there really isn't a great need to move to IPv6 inside our networks. Wait a minute; I thought there was some big scare about running out of IPv4 addresses. Yes, that is true for IP addresses on the public internet, but that has nothing to do with our internal networks. You see, even if we run out of public IPv4 addresses tomorrow, the internal networks of our companies are not going to be impacted. We can continue to run IPv4 inside the network for a long time to come, possibly forever and always, as long as we are comfortable using NAT technologies to translate the traffic down into IPv4 as it comes into our network from the internet. We have all used NAT in one form or another for almost as long as IPv4 has existed, so it is obviously something people are very comfortable with.

Let me be clear: I am not trying to convince you that sticking with IPv4 is the way of the future. I am just laying out the fact that, for most organizations over the next few years, this will simply be the truth. The reason I want to discuss IPv6 here is that, eventually, you will have to deal with it. And once you do, you'll actually get excited about it! There are some huge advantages that IPv6 has over IPv4, namely, the enormous number of IP addresses that you can contain within a single network. Network teams in companies around the world struggle every day with the need to build more and more IPv4 networks and tie them together. Think about it: there are many companies now with employee counts in excess of 10,000. Some have many, many times that number. In today's world, everyone needs almost constant access to their data. Data is the new currency. Most users now have at least two physical devices they utilize for work, sometimes more than that: a laptop and a tablet, a laptop and a smartphone, or a desktop and a laptop and a tablet and a smartphone; you get the idea. In the IPv4 world, where you are dealing with comparatively small IP address ranges, you have to get very creative with creating subnets in order to accommodate all of these physical devices. Each needs a unique IP address to communicate on the network.

The biggest advantage of IPv6 is that it resolves all of these problems immediately and by default, by providing the capability to have a *huge* number of IP addresses within a single network. How many more addresses are we talking about? The following is some comparison data to give you a little perspective:

- An IPv4 address is a 32-bit length address that looks like this: `192.168.1.5`
- An IPv6 address is a 128-bit length address that looks like this: `2001:AABB:CCDD:AB00:0123:4567:8901:ABCD`

As you can see, the IPv4 address is much shorter, which obviously means there are fewer possibilities for unique IP addresses. What you don't see is how much longer IPv6 addresses really are. These examples portray IPv4 and IPv6 addresses as we are used to seeing them, in their finished forms. Really though, the IPv4 address is shown in decimal form, and the IPv6 in hexadecimal. IPv6 addresses are shown and used via hex so that the addresses are compressed as much as possible. In reality, if you dig around under the hood, an IPv6 address in its native 128-bit form might look something like this (and indeed, this is how it looks inside the actual packet):

```
00010000001000001000011011001100000000000000000000010000000000000000
00010000000000000000000000001000000000000000000000000000000000000001
```

That's an impressive set of digits, but not something that is very usable or friendly to the human eye. So, rather than show the bits, what about an IPv6 address shown in decimal format in the same way that IPv4 addresses have always been shown? In that case, an IPv6 address might look something like this:

```
192.16.1.2.34.0.0.1.0.0.0.0.0.0.0.1
```

Now we fully understand why IPv6 is always used and shown in hexadecimal; the addresses are long even in that compressed format!

When we set up IPv4 networks, subnetting is extremely important because it is what enables us to have more than one collection of IP addresses within the same network. In the most basic form of networking, where you set up some IP addresses and run a /24 subnet (a subnet mask of `255.255.255.0`), which is very common on small networks such as inside a house or small business office, you are limited to 254 unique IP addresses. Ouch! Some companies have thousands of different servers, without accounting for all of their client computers and devices that also need to connect to the network. Thankfully, we can build out many different subnets within a single IPv4 network in order to increase our usable IP address scope, but this takes careful planning and calculation of those subnets and address spaces and is the reason that we rely on experienced network administrators to manage this part of the network for us. One invalid subnet configuration in a routing table can tank network traffic flow. The administration of subnets in a large IPv4 network is not for the faint of heart.

When we talk about IPv6 addressing, the sky almost seems to be the limit. If you were to calculate all of the unique IPv6 addresses available in the preceding 128-bit space, you would find that there are more than 340 undecillion addresses available to be created. In other words, 340 trillion, trillion, trillion addresses. This is the number being touted out there about how many available addresses there are on the IPv6 internet, but what does that mean for our internal networks?

To discuss the number of addresses we could have inside a typical internal network that runs IPv6, let's first step back and look at the address itself. The address I showed earlier is just something I made up, but we will break down the parts of it here:

`2001:AABB:CCDD:AB00:0123:4567:8901:ABCD`

Compared to `192.168.1.5`, this thing looks like a monstrosity. That is because we are generally not used to dealing with the hexadecimal format; it is just a different way of looking at data. As we mentioned, this is a 128-bit address. It is broken up into 8 different sections, with each section separated by a colon made up of 16 bits. The first 64 bits (the first half) of the address are routing information, and the latter 64 bits are the unique device ID on the network. Within the first part, we have two different components. The first 48 bits (3 groups of hex) are an organizational prefix that will be the same on all of our devices in the network. Then the fourth set of information, the next 16 bits, can be our subnet ID. This gives us the flexibility of still having many different subnets if we so desire in the future by using multiple numbers here as the subnet ID. After dedicating the first half of the address, we now have the latter half to work with, the last 64 bits. These we can leave for device IDs. This part of the address will be different for every device on the network and will define the individual static IPv6 addresses that will be used for communication. Let's lay out our example address into the following parts:

- **Overall IP address:** `2001:AABB:CCDD:AB00:0123:4567:8901:ABCD`
- **Organizational prefix:** `2001:AABB:CCDD`
- **Subnet ID:** `AB00`
- **Device ID:** `0123:4567:8901:ABCD` **is one unique device ID**

How many devices can we have in our network with an IP schema such as this? Well, even in our example, where we only allocated one 16-bit section for subnetting and 64 bits for actual IP addresses, that would provide us with the capability to have more than 65,000 subnets and quintillions of unique device IDs in our IP range. Impressive, isn't it?

If we stick with this and use just a single subnet to contain all of our machines, the first half of our addresses will always be the same, making these long addresses much easier to remember and deal with. It is surprising how quickly you will get used to seeing these large hex numbers in your environment, but even though you will start to recognize them, you still are probably not going to quickly jump into servers or computers in your network anymore by using the static IP addresses. I know a lot of us are still in the habit of saying: "I need to jump into my web server; I'll just RDP into `192.168.1.5`." Just the time that it takes to type out these IPv6 addresses, even if you do remember them, isn't generally worth it. IPv6 will bring with it a larger reliance on DNS to make it more usable.

Now that we understand what sections of the address are going to be used for what purposes, how do we go about assigning the individual device ID numbers for all of the computers, servers, and other devices on our network? You could start with number 1 and go up from there. Another idea is to calculate the old IPv4 addresses into hex and use this as the last 32 bits of the address—open up Windows Calculator on your computer, drop down the menu, and change it into Programmer mode. This is a quick and easy tool that you can use to convert decimal into hexadecimal, and vice versa. Let's take the example of my web server that is running on `192.168.1.5`. I want to implement IPv6 inside my network, and I want my server's IPv6 addresses to reflect the original IPv4 address in the device ID section of the new address. In my calculator, if I type in 192 and then click on **HEX**, it will show me the corresponding hexadecimal for the decimal of 192, as shown in *Figure 7.1*:

Figure 7.1: Using Windows Calculator to convert decimal into hexadecimal

If we do that with each of the octets in our IPv4 address, we will see the following:

```
192 = C0
168 = A8
1 = 01
5 = 05
```

So, my 192.168.1.5 factors out to C0A8:0105. I can now utilize that in combination with my organizational prefix and my subnet ID to create a static IPv6 address for my web server:

2001:AABB:CCDD:0001:0000:0000:C0A8:0105

You'll notice in the preceding IPv6 address that I input the hex for the device ID at the end, but I also made a couple of other changes. Since we are leaving the last 64 bits available for the device ID, but my old IPv4 address only consumes 32 bits, I am left with the 32 bits in the middle. It would be kind of weird to have data in there that didn't mean anything to us, so we will simply make it all zeros to simplify the addressing scheme. In addition to that change, I also adjusted my subnet ID to the number 1, since this is the first subnet in my network.

Our new addressing is starting to look a little cleaner and makes more sense. Now that we see this new address for our web server laid out, I can see that there are some additional clean-up tasks we can perform on the address in order to make it look even better. Right now, the address listed earlier is 100% accurate.

I could plug this IP address into the NIC properties of my web server and it would work. However, there are a whole lot of zeros in my address, and I don't need to keep them all. Any time you have unnecessary zeros within a 16-bit segment that are preceding the actual number, they can simply be removed. For example, our subnet ID and the first 32 bits of our device ID have a lot of unnecessary zeros, so I can consolidate the address down to the following:

```
2001:AABB:CCDD:1:0:0:C0A8:0105
```

Then, to take it even a step further, any time you have full 16-bit sections that are composed entirely of zeros, they can be fully consolidated into a double colon. So, the first 32 bits of my device ID that are all zeros, I can replace with ::. The following is the full address and the consolidated address. These numbers look quite different. My consolidated address is much easier on the eye, but from a technological perspective, they are exactly the same number:

```
2001:AABB:CCDD:0001:0000:0000:C0A8:0105
2001:AABB:CCDD:1::C0A8:0105
```

In fact, if you set up a lab or want to quickly test IPv6, you can use addresses as simple as the following example. The two addresses that I will show you here are precisely the same:

```
2001:0000:0000:0000:0000:0000:0000:0001
2001::1
```

It is important to note that you can only use a double-colon **once** within an IP address. If you had two places where it was applicable within the same address, you could only implement it in one of those places, and you would have to spell out the zeros in the other place. For example, changing `2001:AABB:0000:0000:0001:0000:0000:0123` into `2001:AABB::1::123` would cause your computer grief, as it would not know what to do with that second double-colon.

With the information provided here, you should be able to put together your own semblance of IPv6 and start issuing some IPv6 addresses to computers or servers in your network. There is so much more to be learned on this subject that an entire book could be written, and indeed there are numerous offerings to choose from. Recent Windows computers and servers are well equipped to start using IPv6 right now inside NIC properties but keep in mind that other types of devices on your network, especially older ones, may not have any knowledge of IPv6 nor have a field to even input an IPv6 address. Legacy devices could be a major deciding factor, or roadblock, on your journey toward IPv6.

Your networking toolbox

Whether you are a server administrator, a network administrator, or a combination of the two, there are a number of tools that are useful for testing and monitoring network connections within the Windows Server world. Some of these tools are baked right into the operating system and can be used from Command Prompt or PowerShell, and others are more expansive graphical interfaces that require installation before running. The following are the built-in Windows network tools that we are going to look at:

- ping
- tracert

- pathping
- Test-Connection
- telnet
- Test-NetConnection
- netstat

All of these tools are free and included out of the box, so you have no excuse to delay getting acquainted with these helpful utilities.

ping

Even the newest IT pros are usually familiar with this one. ping is a command that you can utilize from Command Prompt or PowerShell, and it is simply used to query a DNS name and/or IP address to find out whether it responds. ping is, and has always been, our go-to tool for testing network connectivity between two devices on a network. From my Windows 10 client on the LAN, I can open a prompt and use ping <IP_ADDRESS>. Alternatively, because I am using DNS in my environment, which will resolve names to IP addresses, I can also use ping <SERVERNAME>, as shown in *Figure 7.2*. You can see that my server replies to my ping, letting me know that it is online and responding:

```
Administrator: Windows PowerShell                        —    □    ×
PS C:\Users\Administrator> ping web1

Pinging web1.contoso.local [10.10.10.150] with 32 bytes of data:
Reply from 10.10.10.150: bytes=32 time<1ms TTL=128
Reply from 10.10.10.150: bytes=32 time=2ms TTL=128
Reply from 10.10.10.150: bytes=32 time<1ms TTL=128
Reply from 10.10.10.150: bytes=32 time<1ms TTL=128

Ping statistics for 10.10.10.150:
    Packets: Sent = 4, Received = 4, Lost = 0 (0% loss),
Approximate round trip times in milli-seconds:
    Minimum = 0ms, Maximum = 2ms, Average = 0ms
PS C:\Users\Administrator>
```

Figure 7.2: Pinging a server

Ping traffic is technically called **ICMP traffic**. This is important because the ICMP protocol is blocked by default more and more often these days, with firewalls being turned on by default on so many of our systems and devices. Historically, ping was always a tool that we could count on to tell us with a fair degree of certainty whether connectivity was flowing between two devices, but that is no longer the case. If you build a brand new Windows box and plug it into your network, that computer may communicate with the internet and all of the servers on your network just fine, but if you try to ping that new computer from another machine on your network, the ping will probably fail. Why would that happen? Because Windows has some security measures built into it by default, including blocking ICMP traffic in Windows Defender Firewall. In that case, you would need to either turn off the Windows firewall or provide it with an access rule that allows ICMP traffic. Once such a rule is enabled, pings will start replying from this new computer. Keep in mind whenever building new systems or servers in your network that ping is not always the most trustworthy tool to depend upon in today's networking world.

It's easy to allow ICMP responses by plugging a rule into Windows Defender Firewall with Advanced Security, though you still wouldn't want to have to remember to do this manually on every new system you introduce into a network. Thankfully, you already know how to utilize Group Policy to build a GPO and push it out to all machines on your network, and yes, you can absolutely place firewall rules inside that GPO. In fact, we will do exactly this in *Chapter 9, Hardening and Security*. This is a common way to allow or block ICMP throughout an entire organization, by issuing a firewall rule via Group Policy.

tracert

tracert, which is pronounced **Trace Route**, is a tool used to trace a network packet as it traverses your network. What it really does is watch all of the places the packet bumps into before hitting its destination. These bumps in the road that a network packet needs to get through are called **hops**. tracert shows you all of the hops that your traffic takes as it moves toward the destination server or whatever it is trying to contact. My test lab network is very flat and boring, so doing a tracert there wouldn't show us much of anything. However, if I open up a PowerShell prompt from an internet-connected machine and tracert to a web service, such as Bing, we get some interesting results:

```
PS C:\WINDOWS\system32> tracert www.bing.com

Tracing route to any.edge.bing.com [204.79.197.200]
over a maximum of 30 hops:

  1    <1 ms    <1 ms    <1 ms  192.168.8.1
  2     1 ms    <1 ms    <1 ms  192.168.128.1
  3     8 ms     7 ms     5 ms  172.17.224.1
  4    11 ms     9 ms    15 ms  172.19.253.1
  5    10 ms     9 ms    11 ms  172.31.255.1
  6    20 ms     9 ms    13 ms  ht1-max1-1.iserv.net [206.114.55.1]
  7    15 ms    12 ms     8 ms  69.87.144.9
  8    23 ms    18 ms    19 ms  888-2.iserv.net [206.114.40.2]
  9    23 ms    20 ms    15 ms  g5-0-0.core3.grr.iserv.net [206.114.51.20]
 10    19 ms    11 ms    19 ms  g5-0-0.core1.grr.iserv.net [206.114.51.2]
 11    21 ms    28 ms    19 ms  GigabitEthernet4-1.GW5.DET5.ALTER.NET [152.179.10.81]
 12    25 ms    28 ms    28 ms  0.ae1.XL3.CHI13.ALTER.NET [140.222.225.179]
 13    27 ms    37 ms    54 ms  TenGigE0-6-0-1.GW2.CHI13.ALTER.NET [152.63.65.133]
 14    36 ms    34 ms    34 ms  microsoft-gw.customer.alter.net [152.179.105.130]
 15    58 ms    50 ms    46 ms  104.44.81.58
 16    34 ms    33 ms    36 ms  10.201.194.219
 17    26 ms    29 ms    29 ms  a-0001.a-msedge.net [204.79.197.200]

Trace complete.
PS C:\WINDOWS\system32>
```

Figure 7.3: Using tracert

If you utilize tracert but are not interested in seeing all of the DNS information provided in the output, use tracert -d to focus only on the IP addresses.

This information can be extremely useful when trying to diagnose a connection that is not working. If your traffic is moving through multiple hops, such as routers and firewalls, before it gets to the destination, tracert can be essential in figuring out where in the connection stream things are going wrong. Given that the preceding screenshot shows a successful tracert to Bing, now let's see what it looks like when things are broken. I will unplug my internet modem and run the same tracert www.bing.com again, and now we can see that I am still able to communicate with my local router, but not beyond it:

```
Windows PowerShell                                                    —    □    ✕

Windows PowerShell
Copyright (C) 2015 Microsoft Corporation. All rights reserved.

PS C:\Users\jkrause> tracert www.bing.com

Tracing route to any.edge.bing.com [204.79.197.200]
over a maximum of 30 hops:

  1     9 ms      1 ms      1 ms  192.168.8.1
  2      *        192.168.8.1  reports: Destination host unreachable.

Trace complete.
PS C:\Users\jkrause>

<
```

Figure 7.4: Testing tracert to a website when disconnected from the internet

It is important to note that tracert relies on ICMP to receive responses back from the network devices that it contacts. If those network devices don't permit an ICMP response, you won't receive information back from those hops.

pathping

tracert is useful and seems to be the *de facto* standard for tracing packets around your network, but this next command is even more powerful in my opinion. pathping essentially does the same thing as tracert, except that it provides one additional piece of crucial information. Most of the time, with either of these commands, you are only interested in figuring out where in the chain of hops something is broken, but often, when I'm setting up servers for networking purposes, I am working with servers and hardware that have many different network cards. When dealing with multiple NICs in a system, the local routing table is just as important as the external routers and switches, and I often want to check out the path of a network packet in order to see which local NIC it is flowing out of. This is where pathping becomes more powerful than tracert. The first piece of information that tracert shows you is the first hop away from the local server that you are traversing. However, pathping also shows you which local network interface your packets are flowing out of.

Let me give you an example: I often set up remote access servers with multiple NICs, and during this process, create many routes on the local server so that it knows what traffic needs to be sent in which direction, such as what traffic needs to go out the internal NIC, and what traffic needs to go out the external NIC. After completing all of our routing statements for the internal NIC, we test them by pinging a server inside the network. Perhaps that ping fails, and we aren't sure why. I can try a tracert command, but it's not going to provide me with anything helpful because it simply cannot see the first hop; it just times out. However, if I use a pathping command instead, the first hop will still time out, but I can now see that my traffic is attempting to flow out of my *external NIC*. Whoops! We must have set something up incorrectly with our static route on this server. So, then I know that I need to delete that route and recreate it to make this traffic flow through the internal NIC instead.

The following is the same PowerShell prompt from the same computer that I used in my `tracert` screen-shot. You can see that a `pathping` command shows me the local IP address on my laptop where the traffic is attempting to leave the system, whereas the `tracert` command did not show this information:

```
PS C:\Users\jkrause> pathping www.bing.com

Tracing route to any.edge.bing.com [204.79.197.200]
over a maximum of 30 hops:
  0  IVO-PC-328 [192.168.8.113]
  1  192.168.8.1
  2  192.168.128.1
  3      *          192.168.8.1  reports: Destination host unreachable.

Computing statistics for 75 seconds...
                   Source to Here   This Node/Link
Hop  RTT    Lost/Sent = Pct  Lost/Sent = Pct  Address
  0                                            IVO-PC-328 [192.168.8.113]
                                  0/ 100 =  0%   |
  1   1ms    0/ 100 =  0%      0/ 100 =  0%  192.168.8.1
                                100/ 100 =100%   |
  2   ---   100/ 100 =100%      0/ 100 =  0%  192.168.128.1
                                  0/ 100 =  0%   |
  3   ---   100/ 100 =100%      0/ 100 =  0%  IVO-PC-328 [0.0.0.0]

Trace complete.
PS C:\Users\jkrause>
```

Figure 7.5: pathping shows the initial outbound hop

Test-Connection

The commands we have discussed so far can be run from either Command Prompt or PowerShell, but now it's time to dive into a newer one that can only be run from the PowerShell prompt: a cmdlet called `Test-Connection`; it is sort of like `ping` on steroids. If we open up a PowerShell prompt in the lab and run `Test-Connection WEB1`, we see output that is very similar to what we'd get with a regular `ping`, but the information is laid out in a way that I think is a little easier on the eyes. There is also an unexpected column of data here called `Source`:

```
Administrator: Windows PowerShell                        —   □   ✕

PS C:\Users\Administrator> Test-Connection WEB1

Source      Destination    IPV4Address      IPV6Address
------      -----------    -----------      -----------
DC1         WEB1           10.10.10.150
DC1         WEB1           10.10.10.150
DC1         WEB1           10.10.10.150
DC1         WEB1           10.10.10.150


PS C:\Users\Administrator> _
```

Figure 7.6: Using Test-Connection

That is interesting. I was logged into my `DC1` server when I ran this command, so my source computer for this command was `DC1`. But does this mean that I can manipulate the source computer for the `Test-Connection` cmdlet? Yes, this is exactly what it means.

As with everything in Windows Server 2022 management, the need to be logged in to a local server is decoupled. Specific to the `Test-Connection` cmdlet, this means you can open a PowerShell prompt anywhere on your network and test connections between two different endpoints, even if you are not logged in to either of them. Let's test that out.

I am still logged in to my `DC1` server, but I am going to use a `Test-Connection` cmdlet to test connections between a number of my servers in the network. You see, not only can you specify a source computer other than the one you are currently logged in to but you can also take it a step further and specify multiple sources and destinations with this powerful cmdlet. So, if I want to test connections from a couple of different source machines to a couple of different destinations, that is easily done with the following command:

```
Test-Connection -Source DC1, DC2 -ComputerName WEB1, BACK1
```

You can see in *Figure 7.7* that I have ping statistics from both `DC1` and `DC2` to each of the `WEB1` and `BACK1` servers in my network. `Test-Connection` has the potential to be a very powerful monitoring tool:

Figure 7.7: Multiple sources and destinations using Test-Connection

One more useful function to point out is that you can clean up the output of the command pretty easily by using the `-Quiet` switch. By adding `-Quiet` to a `Test-Connection` command, it sanitizes the output and only shows you a simple `True` or `False` for whether the connection was successful instead of showing you each individual ICMP packet that was sent. Unfortunately, you cannot combine both the `-Source` switch and the `-Quiet` switch, but if you use `Test-Connection` from the original source computer that you are logged in to, like most of us will be doing anyway, `-Quiet` works great. Most of the time, all we really care about is yes or no as to whether these connections are working, and don't necessarily want to see all four attempts. By using `-Quiet`, we get exactly that:

```
Test-Connection -Quiet -ComputerName WEB1, BACK1, DC2, CA1
```

If I were to use `Test-Connection` in the standard way to try to contact all of the servers in my network, that would turn into a whole lot of output. But by using the `-Quiet` switch, I get back a simple `True` or `False` on whether each individual server could be contacted:

Figure 7.8: Using the -Quiet switch

Telnet

`telnet` provides quite a bit of remote management capability; it essentially offers the ability to make a connection between two computers to manipulate the remote machine through a virtual terminal connection. Surprisingly, we are not here to discuss any of the actual functionality that `telnet` provides, because with regard to networking, I find it quite useful as a simple connection-testing tool, without knowing anything about what functionality the `telnet` command itself actually provides.

When we discussed `ping`, we talked about the downside of ICMP: it is easily blocked, and it's more common in today's networks for pings not to be successful. This is unfortunate since `ping` has always been the most common form of network connection testing, but the reality is that, if `ping` makes our lives easier, it also makes the lives of hackers easier. If we cannot rely on `ping` to tell us with certainty whether we can contact a remote system, what do we use instead? Another case that I see often is where a server itself might be responding correctly, but a particular service running on that server has a problem and is not responding. A simple `ping` may show the server to be online, but it can't tell us anything about the service specifically. By using the **Telnet Client** commands, we can easily query a server remotely. Even more importantly, we can opt to query an individual service on that server to make sure it is listening as it is designed to do. Let me give you an example that I use all the time.

I often set up new internet-facing web servers. After installing a new web server, it makes sense that I would want to test access to it from the internet to make sure it's responding, right? But maybe the website itself isn't online and functional yet, so I can't browse it with Edge or any other browser. It is quite likely that we disabled pings on this server or at the firewall level because blocking ICMP over the internet is very common for lowering the security vulnerability footprint on the web. So, my new server is running, and we think we have the networking all squared away, but I cannot test pinging my new server because, by design, it fails to reply. What can I use to test this? `telnet`. By issuing a simple `telnet` command, I can tell my computer to query a specific port on my new web server and find out whether it connects to that port. Doing this establishes a TCP socket connection to the port on that server, which is much more akin to real user traffic than a ping would be.

If a telnet command connects successfully, you know your traffic is making its way to the server, and the server service running on the port we queried seems to be responding properly.

The ability to use telnet is not installed by default in Windows Server 2022 or any other Windows operating system, so we first need to head into **Server Manager** and then **Add Roles and Features** to install the feature called **Telnet Client**:

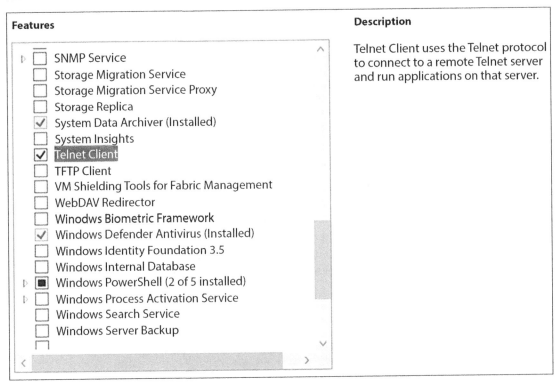

Figure 7.9: Installing Telnet Client

You only need to install **Telnet Client** on the machine from which you want to do command-line testing. You do not have to do anything on the remote server that you are connecting to.

Now that the **Telnet Client** feature has been installed, we can utilize it from Command Prompt or PowerShell to do the work for us by attempting to make socket connections from our computer to the remote service. All we need to do is tell it what server and port to query. Then, telnet will simply connect or time out, and based on that result, we can see whether that particular service on the server is responding. Let's try it with our own web server. For our example, I have turned off the website inside IIS, so we are now in the position where the server is online but the website is dead. If I ping WEB1, I can still see it happily responding. You can see where server-monitoring tools that rely on ICMP would show false positives, indicating that the server is online and running even though our website is inaccessible. Just below the successful ping in *Figure 7.10*, you can see that I also tried querying port 80 on the WEB1 server. The command that I used for that was telnet web1 80. That timed out. This shows us that the website, which is running on port 80, is not responding:

Figure 7.10: Failed connection on port 80

If I turn the website back on, we can try `telnet web1 80` again, and this time, I do not get a timeout message. This time, my PowerShell prompt wipes itself clean and sits waiting on a flashing cursor at the top. While it doesn't tell me *"yay, I'm connected!"* this flashing cursor indicates that a successful socket connection has been made to port 80 on my web server, indicating the website is online and responding:

Figure 7.11: A flashing cursor signals a successful connection

After creating a successful `telnet` socket connection, you may be wondering how to get back to the regular PowerShell interface. Press the *Ctrl +]* keys together (that second one is a closed bracket key, usually next to the backslash key on your keyboard), type the word `quit`, and then press *Enter*. This should return you to a regular prompt. Or simply close the PowerShell prompt and open a fresh one.

Test-NetConnection

If `ping` has an equivalent and improved PowerShell cmdlet called `Test-Connection`, does PowerShell also contain an improved tool that works similarly to `telnet` for testing socket connections to resources? It sure does. `Test-NetConnection` is another way to query particular ports or services on a remote system, and the displayed output is friendlier than that of `telnet`.

Let's walk through the same tests, once again querying port 80 on WEB1. You can see in the following screenshot that I have run the command twice. The first time the website on WEB1 was disabled, and my connection to port 80 failed. The second time, I re-enabled the website, and I now see a successful connection:

```
Test-NetConnection WEB1 -Port 80
```

Figure 7.12: Using Test-NetConnection to test individual port connections

Packet tracing with Wireshark

Eventually, you might need to look a little deeper into your network packets. Now we are entering territory where your network team may also be involved, but if you are familiar with these tools, you may be able to solve the problem before needing to call for assistance. Making use of command-line tools to check on the status of servers and services is very useful, but occasionally, it may not be enough. For example, you have a client application that is not connecting to the application server, but you don't know why. Utilities such as ping and even telnet might be able to connect successfully, indicating that network routing is set up properly, yet the application fails to connect when it opens. If the application's own event logs don't help you troubleshoot what is going on, you might want to take a deeper look inside the network packets that the application is trying to push toward the server.

This is where the **Wireshark** application comes in handy. Microsoft used to supply and support a couple of self-developed tools called NetMon and Message Analyzer that served similar functions, but both have now been officially retired. Probably because Wireshark is great, and it's free! This tool captures network traffic as it leaves from, or arrives at, a system, and captures the information that is *inside* the packets so that you can take a deeper look into what is going on. In our example of an application that cannot connect, you could run Wireshark on the client computer to watch outgoing traffic, and also on the application server to watch for incoming traffic from the client.

There is a whole lot of functionality inside Wireshark, and we don't have the space to cover all of it here, so I will leave you with a link from which to grab this tool so you can start testing it out for yourself: `https://www.wireshark.org/download.html`.

TCPView

The tools that we have discussed so far are great and can be used daily for poking and prodding individual resources that you want to test, but sometimes, there are situations where you need to step back and figure out what it is you are looking for in the first place. Maybe you are working with an application on a computer and are not sure what server it is talking to. Or perhaps you suspect a machine has a virus and is trying to *phone home* somewhere on the internet, and you would like to identify the location that it is trying to talk to or the process that is making the call. In these situations, it would be helpful if there was a tool that you could launch on the local computer that showed you all of the network traffic streams that were active on this computer or server clearly and concisely. That is exactly what **TCPView** does. TCPView is a tool created by Sysinternals; you may have heard of some of their other tools, such as ProcMon and FileMon. Running TCPView on a machine displays all of the active TCP and UDP connections happening on that computer in real time. Also important is the fact that you do not need to install anything to make TCPView work; it is a standalone executable, making it extremely easy to use and clear off a machine when you are finished with it.

You can download TCPView from `https://technet.microsoft.com/en-us/sysinternals/tcpview.aspx`.

Simply copy the file onto the computer or server that you want to monitor and double-click on it. *Figure 7.13* shows the TCPView interface running on my local computer, showing all of the connections that Windows and my applications are currently making. You can pause this output to take a closer look, and you can also set filters to pare down the data and find what you are really looking for. Filters get rid of the *noise*, so to speak, and enable you to look more closely at a particular destination or a specific process ID:

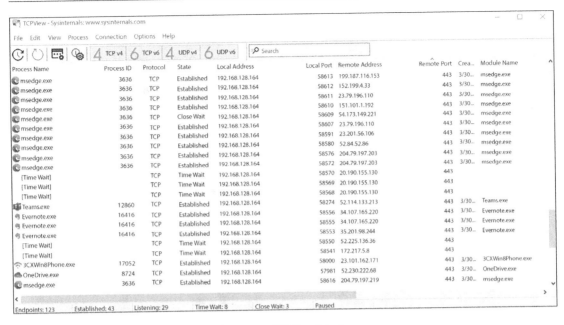

Figure 7.13: TCPView interface

netstat

For anyone who may not be a fan of downloading and running an executable, or just for anyone on the lookout for similar functionality via a built-in Microsoft command, netstat is a command-line tool that has been around for ages and displays similar (if not quite as useful) information to that of TCPView. Netstat will also show you per-port and per-process connection information on what is happening on the machine where you run the command. There are various switches that can be used to manipulate or enhance the netstat command output; if you open Command Prompt and utilize netstat /?, you will be presented with a full list of optional switches and their descriptions.

My go-to method of utilizing netstat is by adding on –ano. Open Command Prompt on any computer or server, and take a look at the output of netstat -ano, as seen in the following screenshot.

```
Administrator: Command Prompt

Microsoft Windows [Version 10.0.20348.887]
(c) Microsoft Corporation. All rights reserved.

C:\Users\administrator.CONTOSO>netstat -ano

Active Connections

  Proto  Local Address          Foreign Address        State           PID
  TCP    0.0.0.0:135            0.0.0.0:0              LISTENING       900
  TCP    0.0.0.0:443            0.0.0.0:0              LISTENING       4
  TCP    0.0.0.0:445            0.0.0.0:0              LISTENING       4
  TCP    0.0.0.0:5985           0.0.0.0:0              LISTENING       4
  TCP    0.0.0.0:47001          0.0.0.0:0              LISTENING       4
  TCP    0.0.0.0:49664          0.0.0.0:0              LISTENING       700
  TCP    0.0.0.0:49665          0.0.0.0:0              LISTENING       604
  TCP    0.0.0.0:49666          0.0.0.0:0              LISTENING       564
  TCP    0.0.0.0:49669          0.0.0.0:0              LISTENING       700
  TCP    0.0.0.0:49698          0.0.0.0:0              LISTENING       1972
  TCP    0.0.0.0:49699          0.0.0.0:0              LISTENING       1040
  TCP    0.0.0.0:49705          0.0.0.0:0              LISTENING       1912
  TCP    0.0.0.0:49712          0.0.0.0:0              LISTENING       688
  TCP    10.10.10.17:139        0.0.0.0:0              LISTENING       4
  TCP    [::]:135               [::]:0                 LISTENING       900
  TCP    [::]:443               [::]:0                 LISTENING       4
  TCP    [::]:445               [::]:0                 LISTENING       4
```

Figure 7.14: netstat displays open connections on my web server

After running your command, scroll back to the top of the output, and take a look at all of those connections showing a Local Address of 0.0.0.0. These are the different ports that your server is currently using to listen for incoming connections. I utilize this output all the time when decommissioning old servers because oftentimes, you can figure out what a server is doing from what ports it is utilizing. In my screenshot above, you can see at a glance that this server is listening on ports 443 and 445, most likely indicating that it is being used as a web server running HTTPS connections and file services over SMB. Over to the right side of the output, visible here due to my use of the -o switch, you can also see which Windows **Process IDs** (**PIDs**) own the ports being used.

Now that we have discovered and tested some tools that are useful for testing connections, let's move on to a new topic where we will begin to manipulate the flow of network traffic from our servers. Follow along as we learn about the Windows routing table.

Building a routing table

When you hear the term **routing table**, it is easy to pass that off as something the network folks need to deal with, something that is configured within the network routers and firewalls. It doesn't apply to server admins, right? Networking servers together has been made pretty easy for us by only requiring an IP address, subnet mask, and default gateway, and we can instantly communicate with everything inside the rest of our network.

While there is indeed a lot of networking magic going on under the hood that has been provided to us by networking equipment and network administrators, it is important to understand how routing inside Windows works because there will be some cases when you need to modify or build out a routing table right on a Windows Server itself.

Multi-homed servers

Running multi-homed servers is a case where you would certainly need to understand and work with a local Windows routing table, so let's start here. If you think this doesn't apply to you because you've never heard of "multi-homed" before, think again. Multi-homed is just a funny-looking word meaning your server has more than one NIC. This could certainly be the case for you, even if you are a small shop that doesn't have a lot of servers. Often, Small Business or Essentials Servers have multiple network interfaces, separating internal LAN traffic from internet traffic. Another instance of a multi-homed server would be a remote access server that provides DirectAccess, VPN, or proxy capabilities at the edge of your network. Yet another reason to be interested and understand multi-homing is Hyper-V servers. It is very common for Hyper-V servers to have multiple NICs because the VMs that run on that server might need to tap into different physical networks within your organization.

Now that we have established what a multi-homed server is, you might still be wondering why we are discussing this. If I have more than one NIC, don't I simply configure each NIC individually inside Windows, giving each one an IP address, just like I would for any NIC on any server? Yes and no. Yes, you configure an IP address on each NIC, because it needs that for the identification and transport of packets on the network. No, you do not set up all of the NICs on your server in the same way. There is one critical item that you need to keep in mind and adhere to in order to make traffic flow properly on your multi-homed server.

Only one default gateway

This is the golden ticket. When you multi-home a server by having multiple NICs, you can only have one default gateway. One for your entire server. This means you will have one NIC with a default gateway, and one or many NICs that do *NOT* have a default gateway inside their TCP/IP settings. This is extremely important. The purpose of a default gateway is to be the *path of last resort*. When Windows wants to send a packet to a destination, it browses over the local routing table—yes, there is a routing table even if you haven't configured it or ever looked at it—and checks to see whether a specific, static route exists for the destination subnet where this packet needs to go. If a route exists, it shoots the packet out of that route and network interface to the destination. If no static route exists in the routing table, it falls back to using the default gateway and sends the traffic to that default gateway address. On all single NIC servers, the default gateway is a router that is designated with all of the routing information for your network, so the server simply hands it to the router, and the router does the rest of the work.

When we have multiple NICs on a Windows Server, we cannot give each one a default gateway because it will confuse the traffic flow from your server. Which default gateway traffic flows toward will be a crapshoot for every network transmission. I have helped many people troubleshoot servers in the field with exactly this problem.

They needed to use their server as a bridge between two networks, or have the server plugged into multiple different networks for whatever reason, and were struggling because sometimes the traffic seemed to work and sometimes it didn't. We start looking through the NIC properties only to discover that every NIC has its own default gateway address in the TCP/IP properties. Bingo, that's our problem. The system is completely confused when it tries to send out traffic because it doesn't know which gateway it needs to use when.

If you have ever tried adding default gateways to more than one NIC on the same server, you are probably familiar with the warning prompt that is displayed when you do this. Let's give it a try. I have added another NIC to one of my servers and have IP settings configured on just one of the NICs. Now, I will add a new IP address, subnet mask, and default gateway onto my second NIC. When I click on the **OK** button to save those changes, I am presented with the following popup:

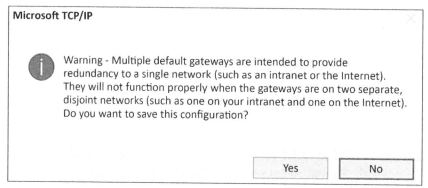

Figure 7.15: Warning message when configuring multiple default gateways

This is one of those warnings that is easy to misread because of its slightly cryptic nature, but you get the essence of it: proceed at your own risk! And then what do most admins do at this point? Simply click through it and save the changes anyway. Then, the routing problems start. Maybe not today, but perhaps the next time you reboot that server, or maybe three weeks down the road, but at some point, your server will start to send packets to the wrong destinations and cause you trouble.

Building a route

So, what is our answer to all of this? Building a static routing table. When you have multiple NICs on a server, thereby making it multi-homed, you must tell Windows which NIC to use for what traffic inside the routing table. This way, when network traffic needs to leave the server for a particular destination, the routing table is aware of the different directions and paths that the traffic will need to take in order to get there and will send it out accordingly. You will still rely on routers to take the traffic the rest of the way, but getting the packets to the correct router by sending them out via the proper physical NIC is key to making sure that traffic flows quickly and appropriately from your multi-homed server.

Now that we understand why the routing table is important and conceptually how we need to use it, let's dig in and add a couple of routes to my dual-NIC server. We will add a route using Command Prompt, and we will also add one using PowerShell since you can accomplish this task from either platform, but the syntax used is different depending on which you prefer.

Adding a route with Command Prompt

Before we can plan our new route, we need to get the lay of the land for the current networking configuration on this server. It has two NICs: one is plugged into my internal network and one is plugged into my demilitarized zone (DMZ) that faces the internet. Since I can only have one default gateway address, it goes onto the DMZ NIC because there is no way that I could add routes for every subnet that might need to be contacted over the internet. By putting the default gateway on my DMZ NIC, the internal NIC does not have a default gateway and is very limited in what it can contact at the moment. The internal subnet that I am physically plugged into is 10.10.10.0/24, so I can currently contact anything in this small network from 10.10.10.1 through 10.10.10.254. This is known as an **on-link** route; since I am plugged directly into this subnet, my server automatically knows how to route traffic inside this subnet. However, I cannot contact anything else at the moment through my internal NIC because the routing table knows nothing about the other subnets that I have inside my internal network. For example, I have an additional subnet, 192.168.16.0/24, and there are some servers running within this subnet that I need to be able to contact from this new server. If I were to try to contact one of those servers right now, the packets would shoot out from my DMZ NIC because the routing table on my server has no idea how to deal with 192.168 traffic, and so it would send it toward the default gateway. The following is the general syntax of the route statement we need to follow in order to make this traffic flow from our server into the new subnet:

```
Route add -p <SUBNET_ID> mask <SUBNET_MASK> <GATEWAY> IF <INTERFACE_ID>
```

Before we can type out our unique route statement for adding the 192.168 network, we need to do a little detective work and figure out what we are going to use in these fields. The following is a breakdown of the parts and pieces that are required to build a route statement:

- -p: This makes the command persistent. If you forget to put -p in the route add statement, this new route will disappear the next time you reboot the server. Not good.
- SUBNET_ID: This is the subnet we are adding; in our case, it is 192.168.16.0.
- SUBNET_MASK: This is the subnet mask number for the new route, 255.255.255.0.
- GATEWAY: This one is a little confusing. It is very common to think it means you need to enter the gateway address for the new subnet, but that would be incorrect. What you are actually defining here is the first hop that the server needs to hit in order to send out this traffic. Or, in other words, if you *had* configured a default gateway address on your internal NIC, what would that address have been? For our network, it is 10.10.10.1. This effectively instructs the server, "for any traffic destined for this route (192.168.16.0/24), shoot those packets at 10.10.10.1 and that guy will figure out what to do."

- **INTERFACE_ID:** Specifying an interface ID number is not entirely necessary to create a route, but if you do not specify it, there is a chance that your route will bind itself to the wrong NIC and send traffic out in the wrong direction. I have seen it happen before, so I always specify a NIC interface ID number. This is typically a one- or two-digit number that is the Windows identifier for the internal NIC itself. We can figure out what the interface ID number is by looking at the route print command:

Figure 7.16: Acquiring the interface ID number

At the top of route print, you see all of the server's NICs. In our case, the internal NIC is the top one on the list. I identified it by running an ipconfig /all command and then comparing my internal NIC's MAC address against the MAC addresses listed here. As you can see, my internal NIC's interface ID number is 5. So in my route add statement, I am going to use IF 5 at the end of my statement to make sure my new route binds itself to that internal physical NIC.

The following is our completed route add statement:

```
route add -p 192.168.16.0 mask 255.255.255.0 10.10.10.1 if 5
```

Figure 7.17: Running the complete route add statement

If you now run a route print command, you can see our new 192.168.16.0 route listed in the Persistent Routes section of the routing table, and we can now send packets into that subnet from this new server. Whenever our server has traffic that needs to go into the 192.168.16.x subnet, it will send that traffic out via the *internal* NIC, toward the router running on 10.10.10.1. The router then picks up the traffic from there and brings it into the 192.168.16.0 subnet:

```
=====================================================================
Persistent Routes:
   Network Address           Netmask   Gateway Address   Metric
             0.0.0.0         0.0.0.0        10.10.10.1   Default
        192.168.16.0   255.255.255.0        10.10.10.1         1
=====================================================================
```

Figure 7.18: Sending traffic to the 192.168.16.0 subnet

Deleting a route

Occasionally, you may key in a route statement incorrectly. The best way to handle this is to simply delete the bad route and then rerun your `route` add statement with the correct syntax. There are possibly other reasons why you might need to delete routes every now and then, so you'll want to be familiar with this command. Deleting routes is much simpler than adding new ones. All you need to know is the subnet ID for the route that you want to remove and then simply use `route delete <SUBNET_ID>`. For example, to get rid of the `192.168.16.0` route that we created while we were working inside Command Prompt, I would simply issue this command:

```
route delete 192.168.16.0
```

Adding a route with PowerShell

Since PowerShell is king when it comes to most command-line-oriented tasks inside Windows Server, we should accomplish the same mission from this interface as well. You can utilize the same `route` add command from inside the PowerShell prompt and that will work just fine, but there is also a specialized cmdlet that we can use. Let's utilize `New-NetRoute` to add yet another subnet to our routing table. This time, we are going to add `192.168.17.0`. The following is a command we can utilize:

```
New-NetRoute -DestinationPrefix "192.168.17.0/24" -InterfaceIndex 5 -NextHop
10.10.10.1
```

```
Administrator: Windows PowerShell                                    —    □    ×

PS C:\> New-NetRoute -DestinationPrefix "192.168.17.0/24" -InterfaceIndex 5 -NextHop 10.10.10.1

ifIndex DestinationPrefix                            NextHop                     RouteMet
                                                                                      ric
------- -----------------                            -------                     --------
5       192.168.17.0/24                              10.10.10.1                       256
5       192.168.17.0/24                              10.10.10.1                       256

PS C:\>
```

Figure 7.19: Adding another subnet to our routing table

 I already knew that my interface number was 5 for this NIC because of my route print output earlier. If you do not know that information and want to stick with PowerShell cmdlets to find it, a quick `Get-NetAdapter` will tell you everything you need to know!

You can see that the structure is similar, but a little bit friendlier. Instead of having to type the word mask and specify the whole subnet mask number, you can use the *slash* method (CIDR) to identify the subnet and mask within the same identifier. Also, where before we were specifying the *gateway*, which is always a little confusing, with the New-NetRoute cmdlet, we instead specify what is called the NextHop. This makes a little bit more sense to me.

Where we previously utilized route print to see our full routing table, the PowerShell cmdlet to display that table for us is simply Get-NetRoute:

```
Administrator: Windows PowerShell

PS C:\> Get-NetRoute

ifIndex DestinationPrefix                                    NextHop
------- -----------------                                    -------
6       255.255.255.255/32                                   0.0.0.0
5       255.255.255.255/32                                   0.0.0.0
1       255.255.255.255/32                                   0.0.0.0
6       224.0.0.0/4                                          0.0.0.0
5       224.0.0.0/4                                          0.0.0.0
1       224.0.0.0/4                                          0.0.0.0
5       192.168.17.0/24                                      10.10.10.1
1       127.255.255.255/32                                   0.0.0.0
1       127.0.0.1/32                                         0.0.0.0
1       127.0.0.0/8                                          0.0.0.0
5       10.10.10.255/32                                      0.0.0.0
5       10.10.10.13/32                                       0.0.0.0
5       10.10.10.0/24                                        0.0.0.0
6       0.0.0.0/0                                            1.1.1.1
6       ff00::/8                                             ::
5       ff00::/8                                             ::
1       ff00::/8                                             ::
6       fe80::1c58:5bf4:8b46:3559/128                        ::
5       fe80::402:a7ae:81ac:e95b/128                         ::
6       fe80::/64                                            ::
5       fe80::/64                                            ::
1       ::1/128                                              ::

PS C:\>
```

Figure 7.20: Displaying our full routing table

Building routing tables is essential knowledge for any server admin who encounters a server with multiple network interfaces that are connected to different networks. Now, let's discuss another use case where you may find multiple network cards on the same server, but this time, connected to the same network.

NIC Teaming

Moving on to another network topic that is becoming more and more popular on server hardware, let's walk through the steps to create NIC Teaming. The ability to team NICs essentially consists of binding two or more physical network interfaces together so that they behave as if they were a single network interface within Windows. This allows you to plug two physical cables into two different switch ports, all using the same settings. That way, if one NIC port, switch port, or patch cable goes bad, the server continues working and communicating without hesitation, because teaming allows the NIC that is still working to handle the network traffic.

NIC Teaming itself is nothing new. It has been around for 10 years or more inside the Windows Server operating system. However, early versions were problematic, and in the field, I find that Server 2016 is the earliest server operating system most IT personnel consider to be stable enough to use NIC Teaming in production. So, based on that, it is still relatively new to the wild.

To begin teaming together your NICs, you need to make sure that you have multiple network cards on your server. I currently have four NIC ports on this machine. I have plans to create two teams: my first and second NICs will be bound together to become an **Internal Network Team**, and my third and fourth NICs will become a **DMZ Network Team**. This way, I have network card redundancy on both sides of my network flow on this server.

The first thing I want to do is clear out any IP addressing settings that might exist on my NICs. You see, once you tie together multiple NICs into a team, you will configure IP addressing settings for the team—you will no longer dive into individual NIC properties to assign IP addresses. So, open up the properties of each NIC and make sure they are clear of static IP information, like so:

Figure 7.21: Clearing the static IP addresses of each NIC

Now open up Server Manager and click on **Local Server**. Looking inside the properties information for your server, you will see listings for each of your NICs, as well as an option called **NIC Teaming**, which is currently set to **Disabled**:

Windows Defender Firewall	Public: On
Remote management	Enabled
Remote Desktop	Disabled
NIC Teaming	Disabled
NIC1	IPv4 address assigned by DHCP, IPv6 enabled
NIC2	Not connected
NIC3	Not connected
NIC4	Not connected

Figure 7.22: NIC Teaming is initially disabled

Go ahead and click on the word **Disabled**, and now look for a section entitled **Teams**. Click on the **Tasks** button and choose to create a **New team**.

Give your new team an appropriate name and select the NICs that you want to be part of this team. Once finished, you can walk through the same steps as many times as you need to create additional teams with your remaining NICs:

Figure 7.23: Creating a new NIC team

Dropping down the **Additional properties** arrow, you will notice some optional settings that require a little bit of explanation. Depending on what type of system you are running (virtual or physical servers), you may not be able to see or use all of these options.

Teaming mode: Switch Independent is the default, and usually the route you want to travel. This selection means your NICs that are about to be teamed together can be plugged into different switches. Alternatively, **Switch Dependent** mode does require all NICs to be connected to the same switch and comes with some additional options that need to pair up with your switch configuration.

Load balancing mode: Three options to choose from here. **Address Hash** is the default, and indicates that packets will be assigned a hash value that is used to direct them toward particular adapters. **Hyper-V Port**, on the other hand, uses VM MAC addresses to distribute traffic. The third option, **Dynamic**, sort of meshes the other two options, with outbound traffic using the address hash and incoming traffic being distributed based on the MAC address.

Standby adapter: Your NIC team will be created so that both NICs are handling traffic unless you visit this option and choose differently. Here, you could specify for one of your NICs in a team to run in standby mode, meaning that it will not process network traffic unless one of the other NICs fails.

Once finished, you will see your teams listed inside Server Manager, and if you open the **Network Connections** screen inside Windows, you can see in *Figure 7.23* that, in addition to the four physical NICs, I now have two new entries listed here, which are the configuration locations for our new teams. From here, I can right-click on each of my network teams and configure IP addressing information just like I would have done for a single NIC. IP information input into the team properties will be in effect on all NICs that are part of the team:

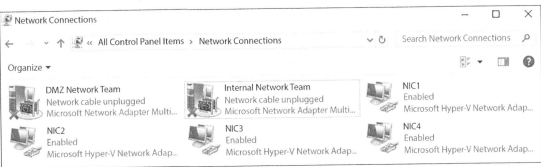

Figure 7.24: Additional NIC Teaming options under Network Connections

The items we have discussed so far in this chapter are useful for any environment utilizing Windows Server 2022, and can also be applied to many previous versions of the Windows Server operating system. Next, we will move on to a topic that some of you may already be living with, but many others may have never even heard of – software-defined networking.

Software-defined networking

The flexibility and elasticity of cloud computing cannot be denied, and most technology executives are currently exploring their options for utilizing cloud technologies. One of the big stumbling blocks with adaptation is trust. Cloud services provide enormous computing power, immediately accessible at the press of a button. For companies to store their data on these systems, the level of trust that your organization has in that cloud provider must be very high. After all, you don't own any of the hardware or networking infrastructure that your data is sitting on when it's in the cloud, and so your control of those resources is limited at best. Seeing this hurdle, Microsoft has made many efforts in recent updates to bring cloud-like technology to the local data center. Introducing server elasticity into our data centers means virtualization. We have virtualized servers for many years now, although the capabilities there are continually being improved. Now that we have the ability to spin up new servers so easily through virtualization technologies, it makes sense that the next hurdle will be our ability to easily move these virtual servers around whenever and wherever we need to.

Do you have a server that you want to move into a data center across the country? Are you thinking of migrating an entire data center into a new colocation across town? Maybe you have recently acquired a new company and need to bring its infrastructure into your network but have overlapping network configuration. Have you bought into some space at a cloud service provider and are now trying to wade through the mess of planning the migration of all your servers to the cloud and onto the cloud provider's infrastructure? These are all questions that require an answer, and that answer is SDN.

SDN is a broad, general term that umbrellas many technologies working together to make this idea possible. Its purpose is to extend your network boundaries whenever and wherever you need. Let's take a look at some of the parts and pieces available in Windows Server 2022 that work in tandem to create a virtual networking environment, the first step in adopting our software-defined networking ideology.

Hyper-V Network Virtualization

The central components that exist right now that bring the ability to pick up your networks and slide them around on a layer of virtualization lie within Hyper-V. This makes sense because this is the same platform that we utilize to virtualize servers. With Hyper-V Network Virtualization, we create a separation between virtual networks and physical networks. You no longer need to accommodate IP scheme limitations on the physical network when you set up new virtual networks because the latter can ride on top of the physical network, even if the configurations of two or more networks would normally be incompatible.

This concept is a little bit difficult to wrap your head around if this is the first time you are hearing about it, so let's discuss some real-world situations that would benefit from this kind of separation.

Private clouds

Private clouds are steamrolling through data centers around the world because they make a tremendous amount of sense. Anyone interested in bringing the big benefits of the cloud into their environments, while at the same time staying away from cloud negatives, can benefit from this.

Building a private cloud gives you the ability to have dynamically expanding and shrinking compute resources and the ability to host multiple tenants or divisions within the same compute infrastructure. It provides management interfaces directly to those divisions so that the nitty-gritty setup and configuration work can be done by the tenant and you don't have to expend time and resources on the infrastructure-provider level, making small, detailed configurations.

Private clouds enable all of these capabilities while staying away from the big scare of your data being hosted in a cloud service provider's data center, which you have no real control over, and all of the privacy concerns surrounding that.

To provide a private cloud inside your infrastructure, particularly one where you want to provide access to multiple tenants, the benefits of network virtualization become apparent, and even a requirement. Let's say you provide computing resources to two divisions of a company, and they each have their own needs for hosting some web servers. No big deal, but these two divisions both have administrative teams who want to use IP schemes that are within 10.0.0.0. They both need to be able to use the same IP addressing subnets on the same physical core network that you are providing, yet you need to keep all of their traffic completely segregated and separated. These requirements would have been impossible on a traditional physical network, but by employing the power of network virtualization, you can easily grant IP subnets and address schemes of whatever caliber each division chooses. They can run servers on whatever subnets and IP addresses they like, and all of the traffic is encapsulated uniquely so that it remains separated, completely unaware of the other traffic running around on the same physical core network that runs beneath the virtualization layer. This scenario also plays out well for corporate acquisitions. Two companies who are joining forces at the IT level often have conflicts with domains and network subnetting. With network virtualization, you can allow the existing infrastructure and servers to continue running with their current network config, but bring them within the same physical network by employing Hyper-V Network Virtualization.

Another simpler example is one where you simply want to move a server within a corporate network. Maybe you have a legacy line-of-business server that many employees still need access to, and their daily workload includes the requirement for that LOB application to be working at all times. The problem with moving the server is that the LOB application on the client computers has a static IPv4 address configured, through which it communicates with the server. When the user opens their app, it does something such as *talk to the server at* 10.10.10.10. Traditionally, that could turn into a deal-breaker for moving the server because moving that server from its current data center into a new location would mean changing the IP address of the server, and that would break everyone's ability to connect to it. With virtual networks, this is not an issue. With the ability to ride network traffic and IP subnets on the virtualization layer, that server can move from New York to San Diego and retain all of its IP address settings because the physical network running underneath doesn't matter at all. All of the traffic is encapsulated before it is sent over the physical network, so the IP address of the legacy server can remain at 10.10.10.10, and it can be picked up and moved anywhere in your environment without interruption.

Hybrid clouds

While adding flexibility to your corporate networks is already a huge benefit, the capabilities provided by virtualizing your networks expand exponentially when you do finally decide to start delving into real cloud resources. If and when you make the decision to move some resources to be hosted by a public cloud service provider, you will likely run a hybrid cloud environment. This means that you will build some services in the cloud, but you will also retain some servers and services on-site. In fact, some companies may remain in a hybrid cloud scenario for the rest of eternity, as a 100% movement to the cloud is simply not possible given the ways that many of our companies do business. So, now that you want to set up a hybrid cloud, we are again looking at all kinds of headaches associated with the movement of resources between our physical and cloud networks. When I want to move a server from on-site into the cloud, I need to adjust everything so that the networking configuration is compatible with the cloud infrastructure, right? Won't I have to reconfigure the NIC on my server to match the subnet that is running in my cloud network? Nope, not if you have your network virtualization infrastructure up and running. Once again, software-defined networking saves the day, giving us the ability to retain the existing IP address information on our servers that are being moved and simply run them with those IP addresses in the cloud. Again, since all of the traffic is encapsulated before being transported, the physical network that is being provided by the cloud does not have to be compatible with, or distinct from, our virtual network, and this gives us the ability to seamlessly shuttle servers back and forth from on-premises to the cloud without having to make special accommodations for networking.

How does it work?

So far, it all sounds like a little bit of magic; how does this actually work and what pieces need to fit together in order to make network virtualization a reality in our organization? Something this comprehensive surely has many moving parts and cannot be turned on by simply flipping a switch. There are various technologies and components running within a network that has been enabled for network virtualization. Let's do a little explaining here so that you have a better understanding of the technologies and terminology that you will be dealing with once you start your work with software-defined networking.

System Center Virtual Machine Manager

Microsoft System Center is a key piece of the puzzle for creating your software-defined networking model, particularly the **Virtual Machine Manager (VMM)** component of System Center. The ability to pick up IP addresses and move them to other locations around the world requires some coordination of your networking devices, and VMM is here to help. This is the component that you interface with as your central management point to define and configure your virtual networks. System Center is an enormous topic with many options and data points that won't fit in this book, so I will leave you with a link as a starting point on VMM learning: https://docs.microsoft.com/en-us/system-center/vmm/?view=sc-vmm-2022.

Network Controller

Microsoft's Network Controller is a role that was initially introduced in Windows Server 2016, and as the name implies, it is used for control over network resources inside your organization. In most cases, it will be working side by side with VMM to make network configurations as centralized and seamless as possible. Network Controller is a standalone role and can be installed onto Server 2016, 2019, or 2022 and then accessed directly, without VMM, but I don't foresee many deployments leaving it at that. Interfacing with Network Controller directly is possible by tapping into its APIs with PowerShell, but is made even better by adding on a graphical interface from which you configure new networks, monitor existing networks and devices, or troubleshoot problems within the virtual networking model. The graphical interface that can be used is System Center VMM.

Network Controller can be used to configure many different aspects of your virtual and physical networks. You can configure IP subnets and addresses, configurations, and VLANs on Hyper-V switches, and you can even use it to configure NICs on your VMs. Network Controller also allows you to create and manage **Access Control List** (ACL)-type rules within the Hyper-V switch so that you can build your own firewalling solution at this level without needing to configure local firewalls on the VMs themselves or have dedicated firewall hardware. Network Controller can even be used to configure load balancing and provide VPN access through **Routing and Remote Access Service** (RRAS) servers.

Keep in mind that Network Controller should not be installed on physical servers; rather, Microsoft recommends installing Network Controller onto multiple, dedicated Hyper-V VMs that are running on Hyper-V hosts for the best experience.

Generic Routing Encapsulation

Generic Routing Encapsulation (GRE) is just a tunneling protocol, but it's imperative in terms of making network virtualization happen successfully. Earlier, when we talked about moving IP subnets around and about how you can sit virtual networks on top of physical networks without regard for making sure that their IP configurations are compatible, we should add that all of that functionality is provided at the core by GRE. When your physical network is running 192.168.0.x but you want to host some VMs on a subnet in that data center, you can create a virtual network of 10.10.10.x without a problem, but that traffic needs to be able to traverse the physical 192.168 network for anything to work. This is where routing encapsulation comes into play. All of the packets from the 10.10.10.x network are encapsulated before being transported across the physical 192.168.0.x network. The 192.168.0.x network sees these packets as 192.168.0.x packets, but they are actually carrying payloads for the 10.10.10.x network.

There are two different specific routing-encapsulation protocols that are supported in our Microsoft Hyper-V Network Virtualization environment. In previous versions of the Windows Server operating system, we could only focus on **Network Virtualization Generic Routing Encapsulation** (NVGRE), since this was the only protocol that was supported by the Windows flavor of network virtualization. However, there is another protocol, called **Virtual Extensible Local Area Network** (VXLAN), that has existed for quite some time, and many of the network switches—particularly Cisco—that you have in your environment are more likely to support VXLAN than they are NVGRE. So, for the newer network virtualization platforms provided within Windows Server 2016+, you are now able to support either NVGRE or VXLAN, whichever best fits the needs of your company.

You don't necessarily have to understand how these GRE protocols work in order to make them work for you since they will be configured for you by the management tools that exist in this Hyper-V Network Virtualization stack. But it is important to understand in the overall concept of this virtual networking environment that GRE exists, and that it is the secret to making all of this work.

Microsoft Azure Virtual Network

Once you have Hyper-V Network Virtualization running inside your corporate network and get comfortable with the mentality of separating the physical and virtual networks, you will more than likely want to explore the possibilities around interacting with cloud service provider networks. When you utilize Microsoft Azure as your cloud service provider, you have the ability to build a hybrid cloud environment that bridges your on-premises physical networks with remote virtual networks hosted in Azure. Azure's virtual network is the component within Azure that allows you to bring your own IP addresses and subnets into the cloud. You can get more info (and even sign up for a free trial for Azure Virtual Network) here: `https://azure.microsoft.com/en-us/services/virtual-network/`.

RAS Gateways/SDN Gateways

When you are working with physical networks, virtual networks, and virtual networks that are stored in cloud environments, you need some component to bridge those gaps, enabling the networks to interact and communicate with each other. This is where a RAS Gateway (also called an **SDN Gateway**) comes into play. This role has enjoyed a few different names over the years; you may also see these servers referenced as a Windows Server Gateway or even the Hyper-V Network Virtualization Gateway in some documentation. A RAS Gateway's purpose is pretty simple: to be the connection between a virtual network and some other network, most often, a gateway between a virtual network and a physical network. These virtual networks can be hosted in your local environment, or in the cloud. In either case, when you want to connect networks, you will need to employ a gateway. When you are creating a bridge between on-premises and the cloud, your cloud service provider will utilize a gateway on their side, which you will tap into from the physical network via a VPN tunnel.

A RAS Gateway can be a virtual machine, or an entire pool of virtual machines, and is integrated with Hyper-V Network Virtualization. A single gateway or pool of gateways can be used to route traffic for many different customers, tenants, or divisions. Even though these different customers have separated networks that need to retain separation from the traffic of the other customers, cloud providers—public or private—can still utilize RAS Gateway to manage this traffic because the gateways retain complete isolation between those traffic streams. You can even run entire pools of gateways on a single public IP address, enabling multiple tenants to connect to the same IP, while still maintaining separation between all of those tenants' traffic streams.

The Windows Server Gateway functionality existed back in Server 2016, but once it was put into practice, some performance limitations that restricted network traffic throughput were discovered. Those overheads have been increased dramatically in Windows Server 2022, meaning that you can flow more traffic and additional tenants through a single gateway than was previously possible.

Virtual network encryption

Security teams are continually concerned with the encryption of data. Whether that data is stored or on the move, making sure that it is properly secured and safe from tampering is essential. Prior to Server 2019, getting inner-network traffic encrypted while it was moving was generally the responsibility of the software application itself, not the network's job. If your software can encrypt traffic while it is flowing between the client and server, or between the application server and the database server, great! If your application does not have native encryption capabilities, it is likely that the communications from that application are flowing in cleartext between the client and server. Even for applications that do encrypt, encryption ciphers and algorithms are often being cracked and compromised. Your application vendors may or may not be on top of the security game as new vulnerabilities are discovered, and even if your applications are protected today, it's possible they will not be tomorrow.

Fortunately, Windows Server 2022 brings us some comfort on this topic, provided within the boundaries of software-defined networking. This capability is called **virtual network encryption**, and it does just what the name implies. In an SDN environment, when traffic moves between virtual machines and between Hyper-V servers (within the same network), entire subnets can be flagged for encryption, which means that all traffic flowing around those subnets is automatically encrypted at the virtual networking level. The VM servers and the applications that are running on those servers don't have to be configured or changed in any way to take advantage of this encryption, as it happens within the network itself, automatically encrypting all traffic that flows on that network.

With Server 2022 SDN, any subnet in a virtual network can be flagged for encryption by specifying a certificate to use for that encryption. If the future happens to bring the scenario where the current encryption standards are out of date or insecure, the SDN fabric can be updated to new encryption standards, and those subnets will continue to be encrypted using the new methods, once again without having to make changes to your VMs or applications. If you are using SDN and virtual networks in your environments, enabling encryption on those subnets is a no-brainer!

Bridging the gap to Azure

Most companies that host servers in Microsoft Azure still have physical, on-premises networks and one of the big questions that always needs to be answered is, *how are we going to connect our physical data center to our Azure data center?* Usually, companies will establish one of two different methods to make this happen.

A VPN gateway

You can deploy gateway servers or firewalls at the edges of your on-site networks and create a connection to Azure with an IPSec site-to-site VPN tunnel. This establishes a continuous tunnel between the two networks, which is managed by you on your own servers or appliances. One benefit to this simple site-to-site VPN tunnel is that it is quick to set up as long as your on-prem equipment is stable and compatible. If your local ISP goes down, then of course your connection to Azure will go down with it. With these types of connections, it is generally expected that the traffic throughput between your datacenter and Azure is going to be fairly low.

Azure ExpressRoute

If you require higher bandwidth between a local datacenter and Azure, or a higher guaranteed percentage of uptime, Microsoft provides a service called **Azure ExpressRoute** that can be used for these more intense networking requirements. ExpressRoute is a dedicated connection between your building and Azure; the edge environments on both your side and the Azure side, as well as the connection itself, are dedicated and provided by a third party. ExpressRoute comes with a 99.99% availability **Service Level Agreement** (**SLA**) across the entire connection, which is pretty impressive. ExpressRoute is, of course, more expensive than setting up your own VPN, and you need to work with a third-party provider to build and maintain your ExpressRoute connection.

Third-party options

Microsoft partners with various vendors and third parties to provide additional connectivity options between your on-premise datacenter and Azure networks. As an example, the company that I work for deploys and maintains a lot of Cisco Meraki gear. Meraki firewalls have a unique SD-WAN capability that very easily ties all of your different sites together with constant site-to-site VPN tunnels. This can extend into the Azure environment as well if you place a Meraki firewall into your Azure network. How in the world would I do that? By deploying a Meraki vMX (virtual firewall) appliance into Azure. Once deployed, the vMX simply shows up as one more firewall to be managed and maintained inside your Meraki portal, and it taps into the rest of your Meraki infrastructure seamlessly.

There are other network vendors that provide similar services, but I have not personally tried them. I can tell you that the Meraki setup works well, and is often our preferred connectivity method to the cloud.

Azure Network Adapter

In the event that you have an on-premises server that you need to quickly connect to your Azure environment, and you don't already have a permanent connection established between your physical and Azure sites, there is a hybrid cloud capability called **Azure Network Adapter** that can be attached to Windows Server. In order to use one of these new network adapters, you must utilize the new Windows Admin Center to manage your servers.

Using Windows Admin Center, you can quickly add Azure Network Adapter to an on-premises server, which connects it straight to your Azure network using a point-to-site VPN connection. Cool! This capability is helpful for small businesses that have cloud resources and want to connect just a single on-premises server to Azure, or even within a branch office scenario at a larger company. Rather than creating site-to-site connections between your primary data center and every branch office, if your primary data center was already permanently connected to Azure, you could then connect branch office servers directly to Azure using Azure Network Adapter.

What Azure Network Adapter really does is configure a **point-to-site** (**P2S**) VPN for you on that server, connecting the server to Azure via a VPN tunnel. As you know, a VPN tunnel requires both client configuration and a VPN concentrator or gateway on the receiving side, which is exactly what Azure Network Adapter does. It configures the P2S client VPN on the server and spins up a virtual network gateway inside Azure to receive that connection.

Even better, this capability has been back-ported so that you can add one of these adapters not only to Server 2022 machines but also to Server 2019, Server 2016, and Server 2012 R2 machines as well.

To make this happen, there are a few requirements that need to be in place. You must have an active Azure subscription, and you need to have at least one Azure virtual network configured.

Next, you need to register your Windows Admin Center with Azure. This is accomplished by opening up **Windows Admin Center** and visiting **Settings**. Once inside, navigate to **Gateway | Register** and walk through the registration process:

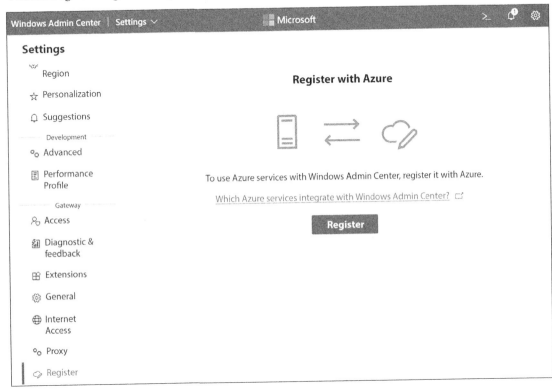

Figure 7.25: Registering WAC with Azure

Now that WAC is registered with Azure, open up the server that you are managing from inside WAC and head over to the **Networks** section. You will see any NICs that are present on your server listed here, and near the top of the window is an ellipsis that can be selected to show additional options. Inside, click on **+ Add Azure Network Adapter (Preview)**:

You'll notice in this text and screenshots that the word **"Preview"** still exists in the title of this feature, but this capability has existed and continues to be titled **"Preview"** ever since it was released a few years ago. Microsoft documentation no longer declares this to be a preview feature; I believe they have simply forgotten to remove the word **"Preview"** from the text inside WAC.

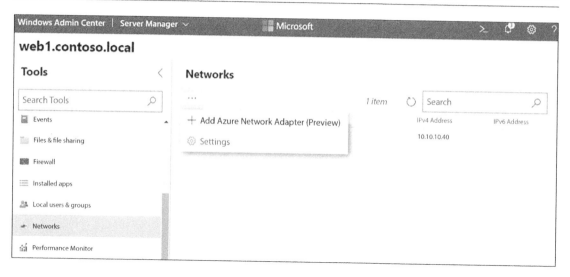

Figure 7.26: Adding Azure Network Adapter

You will find that all of the values that Azure needs in order to make this connection are auto-populated for you, based on your Azure network and subscription. If you don't already have an Azure virtual network, this wizard can even create one for you. You also get the opportunity to specify your own certificate for authenticating this connection, and doing so would be a good practice if you planned for this to be a long-term connection to Azure; otherwise, you can proceed without any input by allowing WAC/Azure to generate a self-signed certificate and simply clicking on the **Create** button. Windows Admin Center will go ahead and create a connection between your on-premises server and the Azure virtual network. That was only a couple of mouse clicks! This is an ingenious way of creating ad hoc connections between your servers and Azure very quickly and without complications.

If you later need to disconnect this server from the Azure network, you can open up **Network Connections** on that on-premises server, just like you would when trying to modify NIC properties on your server, and you will find that what WAC has done under the hood is configure a point-to-site VPN connection, which is listed inside **Network Connections**. You can simply right-click on that Azure VPN connection and disconnect it.

Summary

Server administration and network administration used to be segregated pretty clearly in most organizations, but over time, those lines have blurred. There are numerous networking configurations and tasks that now need to be accomplished by Windows Server administrators without needing to involve a networking team, so it is important that you have a good understanding of how your infrastructure is connected. Familiarity with the tools laid out in this chapter will provide you with the ability to configure, monitor, and troubleshoot the majority of Microsoft-centric networks.

Our introduction to software-defined networking may have been a partially confusing section if you had never encountered this idea before, but hopefully, it will prompt you to dig a little deeper and prepare yourself for dealing with this in the future. Ready or not, the cloud is here to stay. Microsoft on-premises networks now have numerous ways to interact with Microsoft Azure, and it will soon be imperative that IT staff are familiar with these concepts. The idea of SDN will grow in popularity over the coming years. At the moment, it may seem daunting, but in 5 years, we may all look back and wonder how we ever made things work without virtual networks. There is much more information both on Microsoft Learn and in published books about Hyper-V Virtual Networking and System Center VMM if you are interested in setting this up for yourself. For now, continue on to our next chapter, where we will discuss the componentry in Windows Server 2022 that is going to enable our employees to work remotely, which is particularly interesting content in this new working-from-home world we are living in.

Questions

1.   How many bits in length is an IPv6 address?

2.   Re-write the following IPv6 address in condensed form: `2001:ABCD:0001:0002:0000:0000:0000:0001`.

3.   What is the name of the command that is similar to tracert but displays the local NIC that traffic is flowing out of?

4.   True or False—On a server with multiple NICs, you should input a default gateway address onto each of those NICs.

5.   What is the PowerShell cmdlet that can be used to create new routes on Windows Server?

6.   Which Windows Server operating systems can be used with Azure Network Adapter in order to connect them directly to Azure virtual networks?

7.   Which connectivity method between a local datacenter and Azure provides the fastest, most robust, and most reliable connection?

Join our community on Discord

Join our community's Discord space for discussions with the author and other readers:

`https://packt.link/SecNet`

8

Remote Access

Giving employees the ability to remotely access corporate resources used to be a big benefit to most companies, but not necessarily a requirement. That mindset has changed significantly over the past few years, as many of us now work from home full-time following the COVID-19 pandemic. Most companies and employees now expect to get their work done from wherever they happen to be. Cell phones are a big part of this equation but are limited by the scope of what can be done with small screens and restricted operating systems. To grant remote workers the ability to do their jobs from home, coffee shops, or hotels, we have traditionally used **Virtual Private Networks** (**VPNs**).

Most VPNs in today's businesses are provided by products from companies other than Microsoft. The Remote Access role in Windows Server 2022 is here to change that. With many improvements having been made to the VPN components right in Windows Server, it is now a feasible and secure platform for providing access to corporate resources from remote computers. In addition to VPN connectivity, we have a couple of newer technologies baked into Windows Server 2022 that are also designed to provide remote access to corporate resources in a different way than traditional VPN. The topics that we will cover in this chapter are the following:

- Regular ol' VPN
- Always On VPN
- DirectAccess
- Remote Access Management Console
- DA, VPN, or AOVPN? Which is best?
- Web Application Proxy
- Requirements for WAP
- Latest improvements to WAP

Regular ol' VPN

A traditional VPN involves users clicking on a VPN connection that is configured on their local device, and that device then creates a secure virtual private networking connection to another device sitting in your datacenter, most often a firewall.

However, if your firewall doesn't provide VPN endpoint capabilities, or if you simply want to protect your VPN traffic in a different way, you can utilize a Windows Server to be the VPN termination device.

We already mentioned the Remote Access role, and indeed this is a Windows Server role that is ready to be selected and installed on a fresh Windows Server instance. However, before making that leap, you want to formulate a plan for networking with this server. A VPN server can utilize a single NIC that is inside your corporate network, and in this case, you would need to configure your firewall to **Network Address Translation** (NAT) traffic from a public IP address into that internal NIC's private IP address. This is necessary because your VPN clients are going to be creating connections from the internet to this VPN server. For that traffic stream to be successful, the client's traffic must land on the server.

Another option is to provide dual NICs on this server. One can be your internal NIC, connected to the internal network. The second NIC can be your external or DMZ NIC, and connected accordingly. This NIC could have its own public IP address and hang right on the internet, or it could be connected inside a DMZ with some protections around it, and traffic passed through to it there. The reasons you might go dual-NIC are security-related so that this Windows Server and its traffic sit behind some layers of firewall protection. If you choose to employ dual NICs, you may want to reference back to our conversation about proper Windows routing table configuration, as you will be in a position to define a default gateway on your external NIC but not the internal, and will then be required to define static routes to navigate VPN traffic around your internal network.

Routing and Remote Access Service (RRAS)

Once networking has been established on your VPN server, it is time to install the Remote Access role. All of the different connectivity components that we will discuss in this chapter are contained within this same Remote Access role, so you will find that, upon installing the role, you are asked for some further specifics about what role components you are trying to enable. For the purposes of VPN connectivity, as well as **DirectAccess**, which we will discuss shortly, simply check the top box and proceed.

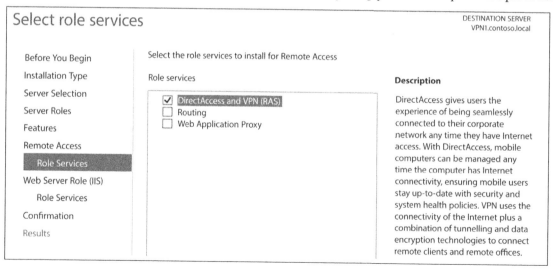

Figure 8.1: Installing the Remote Access role for VPN

After role installation is complete, you will find a couple of new tools available inside Server Manager. We will talk more about the Remote Access Management Console near the end of this chapter as that toolset interacts with both VPN and DirectAccess, but when working on traditional VPN connectivity, we want to utilize the console called **Routing and Remote Access**.

Configuring VPN inside RRAS

Nothing is really happening inside RRAS by default; you can see the name of your server listed with a red arrow next to it, indicating that it is not active. To initiate a configuration wizard that will take us through VPN configuration, simply right-click on the name of your server and select **Configure and Enable Routing and Remote Access**. The first option we encounter is important. There are a few different uses for RRAS, including the routing of both incoming traffic (VPN) and outgoing traffic (proxy/NAT). RRAS can also be used as a site-to-site connectivity platform! For our purposes today, the top option will suffice. We are going to configure **Remote access (dial-up or VPN)**.

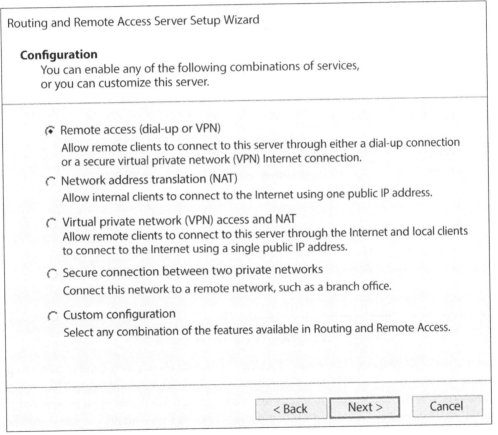

Figure 8.2: RRAS usage options

The following screen is pretty self-explanatory, and kind of funny. Are we setting up a VPN or a dial-up connection? I haven't encountered anybody using dial-up internet in many, many years. This indicates just how long it has been since Microsoft put any work into updating the RRAS interface and wizards.

I suppose "if it ain't broke, don't fix it" applies here, because even though this interface looks like it came straight out of Server 2003, an RRAS VPN is still a stable and secure connection method, if configured properly.

At this point, you will realize that if you only have one NIC installed in your VPN server, you receive a message about RRAS expecting there to be two. It is possible to configure VPN or DirectAccess with a single NIC, but it is not Microsoft's default or recommended method. A proper Microsoft remote access server has dual NICs, separating the traffic coming in from the internet and the traffic that moves onward toward your internal network. That is, after all, the purpose of this role: *Routing* and Remote Access. Assuming you have two NICs on this server, one connected internally and one externally, the next screen will ask you to select the NIC that is facing toward the internet.

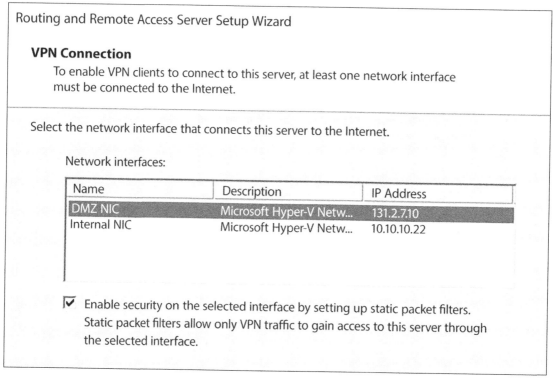

Figure 8.3: Defining internal and external NICs

The assignment of IP addresses to remote VPN client computers is our next configuration step, and the default option is to utilize DHCP for this purpose. You almost never want to use DHCP to provide IP addresses to VPN clients, because your network is then going to think that those remote computers are within your internal network, and routing packets back to those clients becomes problematic. Instead, it is recommended to choose the option to define your own range of IP addresses to assign to VPN client computers, and that this range of IP addresses be from a new subnet that you do not have in use at all inside your network currently. In my case, my internal network is **10.10.10.0/24**, and I am going to define *172.16.1.0/24* as my VPN IP addressing subnet.

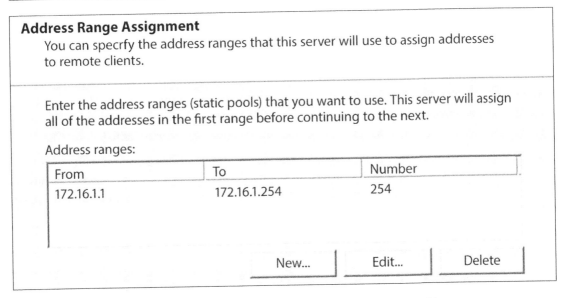

Figure 8.4: Best practice is to define a new subnet for VPN client IP addresses

Now we define authentication for VPN connections. If you employ another Windows Server running the **Network Policy Server (NPS)** role, you can point RRAS at NPS to get very nitty-gritty with the authentication of remote computers. This is definitely a good thing, and it will enable you to only allow users who are part of a certain group to be able to connect to a VPN, or only during certain times. You can even use NPS to further enhance VPN connections by requiring MFA when NPS is tied in with an MFA provider.

RRAS VPN is now configured on your server!

Securing your VPN

Wait a minute, let's wrap back to the fact that this RRAS management console appears to be lacking any updates over the past 20 years. While that is not technically true, there are many items in here that have not been updated with the changing times. Primarily what I'm referring to are the different protocols that RRAS is listening on, which could be used to establish a VPN connection between the client and server. It is important to understand what these protocols are so that you can decide which to allow, as they are all enabled on the server by default. I'll list them here in order of *strongest and most secure*, all the way down to **don't touch this one!**

IKEv2

The newest, strongest, and all-in-all best way to connect your client computers via VPN or AOVPN, IKEv2 is the only way to connect the AOVPN device tunnel, which we will hear about in the next section of this chapter. IKEv2 requires machine certificates to be issued to your client computers in order to authenticate. This generally means that if you want clients to connect via IKEv2, those clients will be domain-joined. It is very important to note that IKEv2 uses UDP ports 500 and 4500 to make its connection, which is sometimes a hindrance and blocked by firewalls.

SSTP

SSTP VPN uses an SSL stream to connect. Because of this, it requires an SSL certificate to be installed on the Remote Access server but does not require machine certificates on the client computers. SSTP uses TCP port 443, so it is able to connect even from inside very restrictive networks where IKEv2 may fail (because of IKEv2's reliance on UDP). I have to say that SSTP is my favorite flavor of Windows RRAS-based VPN connectivity protocol, but it only works from Windows clients. If you have the requirement to connect other devices such as Macs, iPhones, Android, etc, you'll want to jump below to L2TP.

To enable SSTP VPN to be successful on your RRAS server, simply decide on a DNS name to point at your RRAS public IP address, and then acquire a standard SSL certificate for that name. For example, I might choose vpn.contoso.com, and get an SSL certificate for the same name. Install that SSL certificate onto your VPN server, and then inside the RRAS console:

1. Right-click on the name of your server, and head into **Properties**.
2. Visit the **Security** tab.
3. Down near the bottom is a section called **SSL Certificate Binding**. Once your SSL certificate is installed on the server, simply use the drop-down menu here to select your certificate. This enables an SSTP VPN to work properly when clients connect and request SSTP.

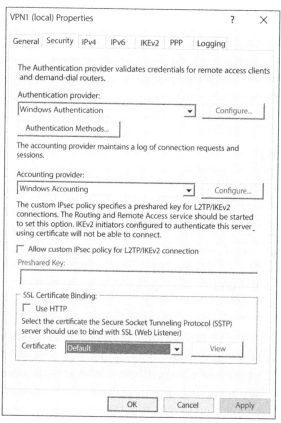

Figure 8.5: Selecting an SSL certificate to be used by SSTP VPN

L2TP

L2TP is able to establish VPN connections by using certificates or a **pre-shared key (PSK)**. If you are only connecting Windows clients to your VPN, stay away from this one and focus on SSTP. If you have a requirement to connect non-Windows devices to your VPN, utilizing L2TP to establish VPN connections through the use of a PSK is generally the approach that is taken.

PPTP

While still a valid configuration option inside RRAS, stay away from this guy! PPTP is no longer a secure method of tunneling, and if you are still running VPN connections based on PPTP, you essentially need to consider those traffic streams to be unencrypted and clear-text over the internet.

After installing RRAS and walking through the wizard to configure a VPN, PPTP is still enabled by default. Thankfully, it is a simple task to disable it on your RRAS server:

1. Inside RRAS, right-click on **Ports** and select **Properties**.
2. Select **WAN Miniport (PPTP)**.
3. Click **Configure...**.
4. Uncheck both boxes, which disables PPTP from being used by incoming VPN clients.

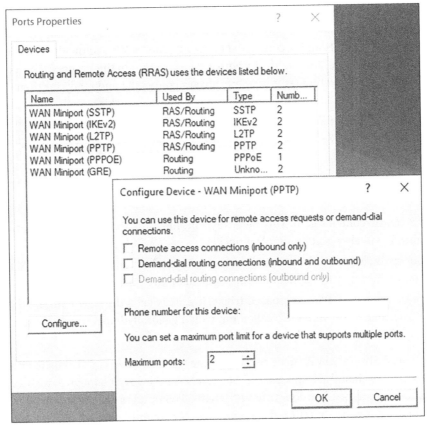

Figure 8.6: Disabling PPTP

Always On VPN

Giving a user access to a VPN connection traditionally means providing them with a special network connection link that they can launch and enter credentials to pass authentication to connect to their work environment's network and then communicate with company resources. This is what we configured inside RRAS. After launching a VPN, users can open their email, find documents, launch their line-of-business applications, or otherwise work in the same ways that they can when physically sitting in their office. Also, when connected via a VPN, management of their laptop is possible, enabling successful communication flow for systems such as Group Policy and **System Center Configuration Manager (SCCM)**. VPN connections offer great connectivity back to your network, but (remember, we are talking about traditional, regular VPN connections here) they only work when the user manually launches them and tells them to work. Anytime that a user has not connected to their VPN, they are navigating the internet with no connectivity back to the company datacenter. This also means that a traditional VPN connection has no form of connectivity on the Windows login screen because, until they get logged in to the computer and find their way to the Windows desktop, users have no way of launching that VPN tunnel. This means that anything that might attempt to happen on the login screen, such as live authentication lookups, or during the login process, such as Group Policy processing or logon scripts, will not function via a traditional VPN.

AOVPN, just as you have probably guessed based on the name, is simply the idea of making a VPN connection continuous and automatically connected. In other words, any time that the user has their laptop outside the office walls and is connected to the internet, a VPN tunnel back to the corporate network is automatically established, ideally with zero user input to the process. This enables users to forget about the VPN altogether, as it is simply always connected and ready for them to use. They can log in to their machines, launch their applications, and start working. It also means that IT management functions such as security policies, updates, and installer packages can push out to client machines a greater percentage of the time, since we no longer wait for the user to decide when they want to connect back to work; it happens automatically and pretty much all the time.

There are actually three different ways in which AOVPN can be triggered on the client machine, and none of them involve the user having to launch a VPN connection:

- AOVPN can be configured to truly be always on, meaning that as soon as internet access is available, it will always attempt to connect.
- Another option is **application triggering**, which means that you can configure AOVPN to launch itself only when specific applications are opened on the workstation.
- The third option is DNS name-based triggering. This calls the VPN connection into action when particular DNS names are called for, which generally happens when users launch specific applications.

Since you don't need Always On VPN to be connected and working when your laptop is sitting *inside* the corporate network, we should also discuss the fact that AOVPN is smart enough to turn itself off when the user walks through those glass doors. AOVPN-enabled computers will automatically decide when they are inside the network, therefore disabling VPN components, and when they are outside the network and need to launch the VPN tunnel connection.

This detection process is known as **Trusted Network Detection**. When configured properly, Always On VPN components know what your company's internal DNS suffix is, and they monitor your NIC and firewall profile settings to establish whether or not that same suffix has been assigned to those components. When it sees a match, it knows you are inside the network and then disables AOVPN.

Types of AOVPN tunnels

Before we get started on the particulars of the client and server components required to make AOVPN happen, there is an important core topic that needs to be understood to make appropriate decisions about how you want to utilize AOVPN in your company. There are two very different kinds of VPN tunnels that can be used with Always On VPN: a **user tunnel** and a **device tunnel**. As you will learn later in this chapter, the ability to have two different kinds of tunnels is something included with AOVPN to bring it closer to feature parity with **DirectAccess**, which also has this dual-tunnel mentality. Let's take a minute and explore the purposes behind the two tunnels.

User tunnels

The most common way of using AOVPN in the wild (so far) involves a user tunnel being authenticated at the user level. User certificates are issued from an internal PKI to your computers, and these certificates are then used as part of the authentication process during connection. User tunnels carry all of the machine and user traffic, but it is very important to note that user tunnels cannot be established while the computer is sitting on the login screen because user authentication has not happened at that point. So, a user tunnel will only launch itself once a user has successfully logged in to the computer. With only a user tunnel at play, the computer will not have connectivity back to the corporate network for management functions until someone has logged in to the computer, and this also means that you will rely on cached credentials in order to pass through the login prompt.

Device tunnels

A device tunnel is intended to fill the gaps left by only running a user tunnel. A device tunnel is authenticated via a machine certificate, also issued from your internal PKI. This means that the device tunnel can establish itself even prior to user authentication. In other words, it works even while sitting on the Windows login screen. This enables management tools such as Group Policy and SCCM to work regardless of user input, and it also enables real-time authentication against domain controllers, enabling users to log into a workstation they have never logged into before. This also enables real-time password expiry resets.

Device tunnel requirements

A user tunnel can work with pretty much any Windows 10 machine, but there are some firm requirements to be able to make use of a device tunnel. In order to roll out a device tunnel, you need to meet the following requirements:

- The client must be domain-joined.
- The client must be issued a machine certificate.
- The client must be running Windows 10 1709 or newer.

- The client must be running Windows 10 Enterprise or Education SKUs.
- A device tunnel can only be IKEv2. This is important to understand because, as you already know, IKEv2 utilizes UDP to make its connection. This means that computers that are sitting behind port-restricting firewalls may be unable to establish that device tunnel connection.

AOVPN client requirements

It is important to understand that the *Always On* part of Always On VPN is really client-side functionality. You can utilize AOVPN on a client computer to connect to many different kinds of VPN infrastructure on the backend. We will talk about that shortly, in the *AOVPN server components* section.

While creating regular, manual VPN connections has been possible on Windows client operating systems for 20+ years, Always On VPN is quite new. Your workforce will need to be running Windows 10 to make this happen. Specifically, they will need to be running at minimum Windows 10 version 1607.

The following are the supported SKUs:

- Windows 10 1607+
- Windows 10 1709+
- Windows 10 1803+

Wait a minute—that doesn't make any sense. Why list those three items separately if they are inclusive of one another? Because, while technically Always On VPN was officially introduced in Windows 10 1607, it has had some improvements along the way. Let's list those again, with a brief summary of what has changed over the years:

- Windows 10 1607: The original capability to auto-launch a VPN connection, thus enabling Always On VPN.
- Windows 10 1709: Updates and changes included the addition of device tunnels. If you intend to run a device tunnel for computer management purposes (and most enterprises will), then consider 1709 to be your minimum OS requirement.
- Windows 10 1803: Includes some major fixes that were discovered in 1709. In reality, what this means is that I never see anyone implementing Always On VPN unless they are running 1803. Thankfully, the Windows 10 update platform is much improved, meaning that many more companies are rolling out newer versions of Win10 on an ongoing basis, and 1803 is now mostly in the dust, having long ago been replaced by even newer versions.

Whether you are running 1607, 1709, 1803, 1809, or whatever the latest and greatest version is, the particular SKU within those platforms does not matter. Well, it hardly matters. Always On VPN works with Windows 10 Home, Pro, Enterprise, and all of the other flavors. That is, the *user tunnel* works with all of those.

It is important enough to point out once again: if you want to utilize a device tunnel with Always On VPN, using domain-joined Windows 10 Enterprise or Education SKUs is a firm requirement.

Domain-joined

As we have already established, when you're interested in using the AOVPN device tunnel, your client computers must be domain-joined. However, if you are okay with only running the user tunnel for AOVPN access, then there are no domain-membership requirements. Clients still need to be running Windows 10 1607 or newer, but they could be any SKU and could even be home computers that are joined to simple workgroups; no domain is required.

This is emphasized specifically in Microsoft documentation in many places because it enables Always On VPN to be utilized (somewhat) by the **Bring Your Own Device (BYOD)** crowd. While this is interesting, I don't foresee it being at all common that companies would allow employees' personal computers to be connected to their VPN. Most organizations are trying to cater in a small way to the BYOD market by providing access to some resources via the cloud, such as Office 365 for email and documents. But connecting those personal computers and devices back to your network with a full-scale layer 3 VPN tunnel? I don't think so. That is the stuff of security administrators' nightmares.

Rolling out the settings

Let's say you have all of the server-side parts and pieces ready to roll for VPN connectivity, and in fact, you have successfully established the fact that you can create ad hoc traditional VPN connections to your infrastructure with no problems. Great! Looks like you are ready from the infrastructural side. Now, what is necessary to get clients to start doing Always On connections?

This is currently a bit of a stiff requirement for some businesses. The configuration itself of the Always On VPN policy settings isn't terribly hard; you just have to be familiar with the different options that are available, decide on which ones are important to your deployment, and put together the configuration file/script. While we don't have space here to cover all of those options in detail, the method for putting those settings together is generally to build a manual-launch VPN connection, tweak it to the security and authentication settings you want for your workforce, and then run a utility that exports that configuration out to some configuration files. These VPN profile settings come in XML and PS1 (PowerShell script) flavors, and you may need one or both of these files in order to roll the settings around to your workforce. The following is a great starting point for working with these configurations: `https://docs.microsoft.com/en-us/windows-server/remote/remote-access/vpn/always-on-vpn/deploy/vpn-deploy-client-vpn-connections`.

Once you have created your configuration files, you then face the task of pushing that configuration out to the clients. You ideally need to have a **mobile device management (MDM)** solution of some kind in order to roll the settings out to your workforce. While many technologies in the wild could be considered MDMs, the two that Microsoft is focused on are SSCM and Microsoft Intune.

If you have SCCM on-premises, great! You can easily configure and roll out PowerShell-based configuration settings to your client computers and enable them for Always On VPN.

Perhaps you don't have SCCM, but you are cloud-focused, and you have all of your computers tapped into Intune. Wonderful! You could alternatively use Intune to roll out those AOVPN settings via XML configuration. One of the benefits of taking the Intune route is that Intune can manage non-domain-joined computers, so you could theoretically include users' home and personal computers in your Intune-managed infrastructure and set them up to connect.

SCCM and Intune are great, but not everybody is running them. There is a third option for rolling out Always On VPN settings via PowerShell scripting. While this is *plan B* from Microsoft (they would really prefer you to roll out AOVPN via an MDM solution), I'm afraid that PowerShell will be the reality for many SMB customers who want to utilize AOVPN. The biggest downside to using PowerShell to put AOVPN settings in place is that PowerShell needs to be run in elevated mode, meaning that it's difficult to automate because the logged-on user (for whom you need to establish the VPN connection) needs to be a local administrator for the script to run properly.

I am hopefully and anxiously waiting for the day that they announce a Group Policy template for rolling out Always On VPN settings, but so far, there is no word on whether or not that will ever be an option. Everyone has Group Policy; not everyone has MDM. You will read in a few moments that the rollout of Microsoft DirectAccess connectivity settings (an alternative to AOVPN) is done via Group Policy, which is incredibly easy to understand and manage. As far as I'm concerned, at the time of writing, DirectAccess holds a major advantage over AOVPN in the way that it handles the client-side rollout of settings. But, make sure you check out Microsoft Docs online to find the latest information on this topic, as AOVPN is being continuously improved and there will likely be some changes coming to this area of the technology.

AOVPN server components

Now that we understand what is needed on the client side to make Always On VPN work, what parts and pieces are necessary on the server/infrastructure side in order to allow these connections to happen? Interestingly, the *Always On* component of AOVPN has nothing to do with server infrastructure; the Always On part is handled completely on the client side. Therefore, all we need to do on the server side is make sure that we can receive incoming VPN connections. If you currently have a workforce that is making successful VPN connections, then there is a good chance that you already have the server infrastructure necessary for bringing AOVPN into your environment.

Remote Access server

Obviously, you need a VPN server to host VPN connections, right? Well, not so obviously. As we have already discussed, the Windows Server role that hosts VPN, AOVPN, and DirectAccess connections is called the **Remote Access** role, but you can actually get Always On VPN working without Windows Server as your Remote Access server. Since the *Always On* part is client-side functionality, this enables VPN server-side infrastructures to be hosted by third-party vendors. Even though that is technically accurate, it's not really what Microsoft expects, nor is it what I find in the field. In reality, those of us interested in using Microsoft Always On VPN will use Microsoft Windows Server to host the Remote Access role, which will be the inbound system that our remote clients connect to.

A lot of people automatically assume that AOVPN is married to Windows Server 2019 or 2022 because it is a fairly new technology, but that is actually not the case at all. You can host your VPN infrastructure (the Remote Access role) on Server 2022, Server 2019, Server 2016, or even Server 2012 R2. It works the same on the backend, giving clients a place to tap into with their VPN connections.

The setup of your Remote Access server to handle AOVPN connections is really the same process that we already took in the last section of this chapter, configuring RRAS VPN for manual client VPN connections. These same VPN protocols are the ones that your AOVPN clients will be tapping into. The two VPN protocols most utilized by AOVPN are going to be IKEv2 and SSTP. IKEv2 is required for a successful device tunnel, but if you don't need those and are focused on more flexible user tunnels for AOVPN, then you can get away with running SSTP as a fallback tunneling method, which connects successfully from almost any internet connection.

Certification Authority (CA)

Machine certificates, user certificates, SSL certificates... Oh, my! Clearly, you need to be familiar with working with and deploying certificates to make use of Always On VPN. This is becoming more and more common with newer, well-secured technologies of any flavor. The major requirement here is that you will need to have PKI inside your environment and at least one Windows CA server to issue the necessary certificates. The following is a list of the places in which certificates could be used by an AOVPN infrastructure:

- **User certificates:** These are the certificates issued to your VPN users from an internal CA, used for authentication of the user tunnel
- **Machine certificates:** These are certificates issued to your workstations (mostly laptops) from an internal CA, used for authentication of the device tunnel
- **SSL certificates:** These are installed on your Remote Access server to validate the incoming traffic for SSTP VPN connections
- **VPN and NPS machine certificates:** Your Remote Access server, as well as your NPS servers, which we will talk about in just a minute, require machine certificates issued from your internal CA

Network Policy Server (NPS)

NPS is basically the authentication method for VPN connections. When a VPN connection request comes in, the Remote Access server hands that authentication request over to an NPS server to validate who that user is and also to verify that the user has permissions to log in via the VPN.

Most commonly when working with Microsoft VPN connections, we configure NPS so that it allows only users who are part of a certain Active Directory Security Group. For example, if you create a group called **VPN Users** and then point NPS to that group, it will only allow users whom you have placed inside that group to make successful VPN connections.

NPS is another Windows Server role that can be hosted on its own system or spread across multiple servers for redundancy. As with the Remote Access role, there is no Server 2022 requirement for NPS. You could easily deploy it on previous versions of Windows Server just as well.

Keep in mind that you should *not* install NPS onto the same server where you are running Remote Access. You need to spin up a second server for the purposes of NPS.

DirectAccess

Throughout our discussion about Always On VPN, I mentioned Microsoft DirectAccess a couple of times. DA is another form of automatic VPN-like connectivity, but it takes a different approach compared to Always On VPN. Where AOVPN simply uses expected, well-known VPN protocols and does some crafty magic to automatically launch those otherwise traditional VPN tunnels, DirectAccess tunnels are quite proprietary. Tunnels are protected by IPsec and are essentially impenetrable and also unable to be impersonated. I find that security teams love the protection and complexity surrounding DirectAccess tunnels because they are a connection platform that attackers have no idea how to tamper with or how to replicate.

In my experience, at this point in the game, Microsoft DirectAccess is the most common reason that administrators deploy the Remote Access role on a Windows Server instance. As stated, the easiest way to think about DA is to think of it as an automatic VPN. Similar to a VPN, its purpose is to connect users' computers to a corporate network when they are outside the office. Different from a VPN, however, is the method that employees use to make this connection possible. DirectAccess is not a piece of software; it is a series of components that are already baked into the Windows operating system, working in tandem to provide completely seamless access to the user. What do I mean by seamless? In the same way that AOVPN connects without user interaction, there is nothing the user needs to do to make DirectAccess connect. It does that all by itself. As soon as a mobile computer receives an internet connection, whether that connection is home Wi-Fi, public internet at a coffee shop, or a cell phone hotspot connection, DirectAccess tunnels automatically build themselves using whatever internet connection is available, without any user input.

Whether using Always On VPN or DirectAccess, when your computer connects automatically, it saves you time and money. Time is saved because the user no longer has to launch a VPN connection. Money is saved because time equals money, but also because having an *always-on* connection means that patching, security policies, and the management of those remote computers always happen, even when the user is working remotely. You no longer have to wait for users to get back into the office or for them to choose to launch their manual VPN connection in order to push new settings and policies down to their computers; it all happens wherever they are, as long as they have internet access. Clearly, with the advent of two different remote access technologies that are both focused on automatic connectivity for remote users, Microsoft is clearing the way for a more productive workforce. The terms user-friendly and VPN have never gone hand-in-hand before, but in the latest versions of the Windows operating systems, that is exactly the goal.

DirectAccess has actually been around since the release of Windows Server 2008 R2, and yet I regularly bump into people who have never heard of it. In the early days, it was quite difficult to deploy and came with a lot of awkward requirements, but much has changed over the past few years and DirectAccess is now easier than ever to deploy, and more beneficial than ever to have running in your environment.

The truth about DirectAccess and IPv6

One of the awkward requirements I mentioned *used* to be the need for IPv6 inside your network. With the first version of DirectAccess, this was an unfortunate requirement. I say unfortunate because, even today, almost nobody runs IPv6 inside their corporate networks, let alone years ago when this technology was released—a lot of admins didn't even understand what IPv6 was. Fortunately, the requirement for IPv6 inside your networks is no more. I repeat, just in case anybody wasn't paying attention or is reading old, outdated TechNet documents—*you do not need IPv6 to use DirectAccess!* I have seen too many cases where DA was considered by a company, but the project was tossed aside because reading something on TechNet made them believe that IPv6 was a requirement, and they discarded DA as something that wouldn't work. You absolutely do not have to be running IPv6 in your network to make DA function, but it is important to understand how DA uses IPv6 because you will start to encounter traces of it once your deployment gets underway.

When I am sitting at home, working on my company laptop, DA connects me to the corporate network. My internal network at work has absolutely no IPv6 running inside of it; we are a completely IPv4 network at the moment. This is true for most companies today. However, when I open Command Prompt and ping one of my servers from my DA laptop, this is what I see—apologies for the sanitized output of the screenshot:

```
Pinging     -vdt-02.   .local [fd63:c3  :4b8:7777::c0a8:  10]
ta:
Reply from fd63:c3   :4b8:7777::c0a8:  10: time=133ms
Reply from fd63:c3   :4b8:7777::c0a8:  10: time=59ms
Reply from fd63:c3   :4b8:7777::c0a8:  10: time=74ms
Reply from fd63:c3   :4b8:7777::c0a8:  10: time=54ms
```

Figure 8.7: Pinging an internal server from a DirectAccess laptop

What in the world is that? Looks like IPv6 to me. This is where IPv6 comes into play with DA. All of the traffic that moves over the internet part of the connection, between my laptop and the DA server that is sitting in my datacenter, is IPv6 traffic. My internal network is IPv4, and my DA server only has IPv4 addresses on it, yet my DA tunnel is carrying my traffic using IPv6. This is the core of how DA works and cannot be changed. Your DA laptop sends IPsec-encrypted IPv6 packets over the internet to the DA server, and when the DA server receives those packets, it has the capability to spin them down into IPv4 in order to send them to the destination server inside the corporate network. For example, when I open Outlook and it tries to connect to my Exchange server, my Outlook packets flow over the DA tunnel as IPv6. Once these packets hit my DA server, that DA server reaches out to internal DNS to figure out whether my Exchange server is IPv4 or IPv6.

If you are actually running IPv6 inside the network and the Exchange server is available via IPv6, the DA server will simply send the IPv6 packets along to the Exchange server. Connection complete! If, on the other hand, you are running IPv4 inside your network, the DA server will only see a single A host record in DNS, meaning that the Exchange server is IPv4-only. The DA server will then manipulate the IPv6 packet, changing it down into IPv4, and then send it on its way to the Exchange server. The two technologies that handle this manipulation of packets are DNS64 and NAT64, which you have probably seen in some of the documentation if you have read anything about DA online.

The purposes of these technologies are to change the incoming IPv6 packet stream into IPv4 for networks where it is required, which is pretty much every network at the moment, and spin the return traffic from IPv4 back up into IPv6 so that it can make its way back to the DA client computer over the IPv6-based IPsec tunnel that is connecting the DA client to the DA server over the internet.

It is important to understand that DA uses IPv6 in this capacity because any security policies that you might have in place that squash IPv6 on the client computers by default will stop DA from working properly in your environment. You will have to reverse these policies to allow the clients to push out IPv6 packets and get their traffic across the internet. However, it is also very important to understand that you do *not* need any semblance of IPv6 running *inside* the corporate network to make this work, as the DA server can spin all of the traffic down into IPv4 before it hits that internal network, and most DA implementations that are active today run in exactly this fashion.

Prerequisites for DirectAccess

DA has a lot of moving parts, and there are many different ways in which you can set it up. However, not all of these ways are good ideas. So, in this section, we are going to discuss some of the big decisions that you will have to make when designing your own DA environment.

Domain-joined

The first big requirement is that the systems involved with DA need to be domain-joined. Your DA server, or servers, all need to be joined to your domain, and all of the client computers that you want to be DA-connected need to be joined to a domain as well. Domain membership is required for authentication purposes, and also because the DA client settings that need to be applied to mobile computers come down to these computers via Group Policy.

I always like to point out this requirement early in the planning process, because it means that users who purchase their own laptops at a retail location are typically not going to be able to utilize DA—unless you are somehow okay with adding home computers to your domain—and so DA is really a technology that is designed for managing and connecting corporate assets that you can join to the domain. It is also important to understand this requirement from a security perspective since your DA server or servers will typically be facing the edge of your network. It is common for the external NIC on a DA server to sit inside a DMZ, but they also have to be domain-joined, which may not be something you are used to doing with systems in a perimeter network.

Supported client operating systems

Not all Windows client operating systems contain the components that are necessary to make a DA connection work. Enterprise does, which covers the majority of larger businesses that own Microsoft operating systems, but that certainly does not include everyone. I still see many small businesses using professional or even home SKUs on their client machines, and these versions do not include DA components. The following is a list of the operating systems that do support DA. During your planning, you will need to make sure that your mobile computers are running one of these:

- Windows 11 Enterprise

- Windows 10 Enterprise
- Windows 10 Education
- Windows 8.0 or 8.1 Enterprise
- Windows 7 Enterprise
- Windows 7 Ultimate

DirectAccess servers — one or two NICs?

One big question that needs to be answered even prior to installing the Remote Access role on your new server is, how many NICs are needed on this server? There are two supported methods for implementing DA.

Single NIC mode

Your DA server can be installed with only a single NIC. In this case, you would typically plug that network connection directly into your internal network so that it had access to all of the internal resources that the client computers are going to need to contact during the user's DA sessions. In order to get traffic from the internet to your DA server, you would need to establish a NAT from a public IP address into whatever internal IP address you have assigned to the DA server.

Many network security administrators do not like this method because it means creating a NAT that brings traffic straight into the corporate network without flowing through any kind of DMZ.

I can also tell you from experience that the single NIC mode does not always work properly. It does a fine job of spinning up a quick test lab or proof of concept, but I have seen too many problems in the field with people trying to run production DA environments on a single NIC. The ability to use only a single network card is something that was added to DA in more recent versions, so it was not originally designed to run like this. Therefore, I strongly recommend that, for your production DA install, you do it the right way and go with...

Dual NICs

Here, we have two network cards in the DA server. The internal NIC typically gets plugged right into the corporate network, and the external NIC's physical placement can vary depending on the organization. We will discuss the pros and cons of where to place the external NIC immediately after this section of the chapter. Edge mode with two NICs is the way that DA works best. As you may recall from earlier in the book, implementing a Windows Server instance with multiple NICs means that you will be multihoming this server, and you will need to set up the network settings accordingly. With a Remote Access server, your external NIC is always the one that receives the default gateway settings, so you need to make sure you follow this rule and *do not configure a default gateway on the internal NIC*. On the other hand, you do want to configure DNS server addresses into the internal NIC properties, but you do *not* want to configure DNS servers for the external NIC. Since this server is multihomed, you will likely need to create some route statements to add your corporate subnets into the Windows routing table of this server before it can successfully send and receive traffic.

The only networks that would not need to accommodate adding static routes would be small networks, where all of your internal devices are on a single subnet. If this is the case, then you do not need to input static routes. But most corporate networks span multiple subnets, and in this case, you should refer back to *Chapter 7, Networking with Windows Server 2022*, where we discussed multihoming and how to build out those route statements.

More than two NICs

Nope, don't go there. If you are familiar with configuring routers or firewalls, you know that you have the potential to install many different NICs on a server and plug them all into different subnets. While there are many reasons why splitting up network access like this on a Remote Access server might be beneficial, it won't work how you want it to. The DA configuration itself is only capable of managing two different network interfaces.

As you can see in *Figure 8.8*, in the course of the setup wizards, you will have to define one NIC as External, and the other as Internal. Any more NICs that exist in that server will not be used by DA, unfortunately. Maybe this is something that will change in future versions!

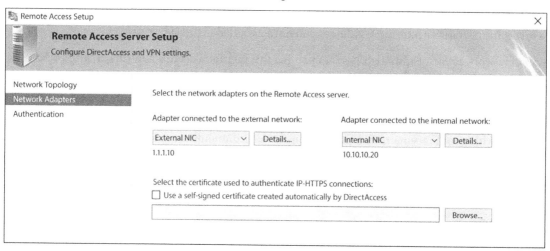

Figure 8.8: Defining NICs during DirectAccess configuration

To NAT or not to NAT?

Now that you have decided to roll with two NICs in your DA server, where do we plug in the external NIC? There are two common places that this external network interface can be connected to, but depending on which you choose, the outcome of your DA environment can be vastly different. Before we talk about the actual placement of the NIC, I would like to define a couple of protocols that are important to understand, because they pertain very much to answering this question about NIC placement. When your DA laptop makes a connection to the DA server, it will do so using one of the three IPv6 transition tunneling protocols. These protocols are 6to4, Teredo, and IP-HTTPS. When the DA client connects its DA tunnels, it will automatically choose which of these protocols is best to use, depending on the user's current internet connection.

All three protocols perform the same function for a DA connection: their job is to take the IPv6 packet stream coming out of the laptop and encapsulate it inside IPv4 so that the traffic can make its way successfully across the IPv4 internet. When the packets get to the DA server, they are decapped so that the DA server can process these IPv6 packets.

6to4

DA clients will only attempt to connect using 6to4 when a remote laptop has a truly public internet IP address. This hardly ever happens these days, with the shortage of available internet IPv4 addresses, and so 6to4 is typically not used by any DA client computers. In fact, it can present its own set of challenges when users are connecting with cell phone cards in their laptops, and so it is common practice to disable the 6to4 adapter on client computers as a DA best-practice setting.

Teredo

When DA clients are connected to the internet using a private IP address, such as behind a home router or a public Wi-Fi router, they will attempt to connect using the Teredo protocol. Teredo uses a UDP stream to encapsulate DA packets, and so, as long as the user's internet connection allows outbound UDP 3544, Teredo will generally connect and is the transition protocol of choice for that DA connection.

IP-HTTPS

If Teredo fails to connect, such as in the case where a user is sitting in a network that blocks outbound UDP, then the DA connection will fall back to using IP-HTTPS, pronounced *IP over HTTPS*. This protocol encapsulates the IPv6 packets inside IPv4 headers, but then wraps them up inside an HTTP header and encrypts them with TLS/SSL, before sending the packet out over the internet. This effectively makes the DA connection an SSL stream, just like when you browse an HTTPS website.

Installing on the true edge — on the internet

When you plug your DirectAccess server's external NIC directly into the internet, you grant yourself the ability to put truly public IP addresses on that NIC. In doing this, you enable all three of the preceding transition tunneling protocols, so that DirectAccess client computers can choose between them for the best form of connectivity. When installing via the true edge method, you would put not only one but two public IP addresses on that external NIC. Make sure that the public IP addresses are consecutive as this is a requirement for Teredo. When your DirectAccess server has two consecutive public IP addresses assigned to the external NIC, it will enable the Teredo protocol to be available for connections.

The NIC does not necessarily have to be plugged directly into the internet for this to work. Depending on your firewall capabilities, you might have the option to establish a *bridged DMZ* where no NATing is taking place. You need to check with your firewall vendor to find out whether or not that is an option for your organization. In this scenario, you are still able to configure truly public IP addresses on the external NIC of the server, but the traffic flows through a firewall first, in order to protect and manage that traffic.

Installing behind a NAT

It is much more common for the networking team to want to place the external NIC of your DA server behind a firewall, inside a DMZ. This typically means creating a NAT to bring this traffic into the server. While this is entirely possible and better protects the DirectAccess server itself from the internet, it does come with a big downside. When you install a DirectAccess server behind a NAT, Teredo no longer works. In fact, the DA configuration wizards will recognize when you have a private IP address listed on the external NIC and will not even turn on Teredo.

When Teredo is not available, all of your DirectAccess clients will connect using IP-HTTPS. So why does it even matter if Teredo is unavailable? Because it is a more efficient protocol than IP-HTTPS. When Teredo tunnels packets, it simply encapsulates IPv6 inside IPv4. The DirectAccess traffic stream is already and always IPsec-encrypted, so there is no need for the Teredo tunnel to do any additional encryption. On the other hand, when IP-HTTPS tunnels packets, it takes the already-encrypted IPsec traffic stream and encrypts it a second time using SSL. This means all of the packets that come and go are subject to double encryption, which increases processing and CPU cycles and makes for a slower connection. It also creates additional hardware load on the DirectAccess server itself, because it is handling twice the amount of encryption processing.

This is a particularly apparent problem when you are running Windows 7 on client computers, as double encryption processing will cause a noticeably slower connection for users. DA still works fine, but if you sit a Teredo-connected laptop next to an IP-HTTPS-connected laptop, you will notice the speed difference between the two.

Thankfully, in Windows 8 and higher, there have been some countermeasures added to help with this speed discrepancy. These newer client operating systems are now smart enough that they can negotiate the SSL part of the IP-HTTPS tunnel by using the NULL encryption algorithm, meaning that IP-HTTPS doesn't do a second encryption and IP-HTTPS performance is now essentially on par with Teredo.

However, this only works for the newer client operating systems (Win7 will always double-encrypt with IP-HTTPS), and it still doesn't work in some cases. For example, when you enable your DirectAccess server to also provide VPN connectivity, or if you choose to employ a **One-Time Password (OTP)** system alongside DA, then the NULL algorithm will be disabled because it is a security risk in these situations, and so even your Windows 8 and Windows 10 computers will perform double encryption when they connect via IP-HTTPS. You can see where it would be beneficial to have Teredo enabled and available so that any computers that can connect via Teredo will do so.

To summarize, you can certainly install your DA server's external NIC behind a NAT, but be aware that all DA client computers will connect using the IP-HTTPS protocol, and it is important to understand the potential side-effect of implementing it in this way.

Network Location Server

This major component in a DA infrastructure is something that does not even exist on the DA server itself, or at least it shouldn't if you are setting things up properly. The **Network Location Server (NLS)** is simply a website that runs inside the corporate network. This website does not need to be available for access over the internet; in fact, it should not be.

The NLS is used as part of the inside/outside detection mechanism on DA client computers, similar to the way that Trusted Network Detection works for Always On VPN. Every time a DA client gets a network connection, it starts looking for the NLS website. If it can see the site, then it knows that you are inside the corporate network, and DA is not required, so it turns itself off. However, if your NLS website cannot be contacted, it means you are outside the corporate network, and DA components will start turning themselves on.

This prerequisite is easily met; all you need to do is spin up a VM and install IIS on it to host this new website, or you can even add a new website to an existing web server in your network. There are only two things to watch out for when setting up your NLS website. The first is that it must be an HTTPS site, and so it requires an SSL certificate. We will discuss the certificates used in DA, including this one, in the next section of this chapter. In addition to making sure that the website is accessible via HTTPS, you must also make sure that the DNS name you are using to contact this website is unique. You want to do this because, whatever name you choose for the NLS website, that name will not be resolvable when client computers are outside the corporate network. This is by design because you obviously don't want your DA clients to be able to successfully contact the NLS website when they are working remotely, as that would then disable their DA connection.

The reason I bring up the unique DNS name is that I often see new DA admins utilizing an existing internal website as their NLS website. For example, if you have `https://intranet` running as a SharePoint site, you could simply use this in the DA config as the NLS server definition. However, once you set it up this way, you will quickly realize that nobody who is working remotely can access the `https://intranet` website. This is by design, because the DA environment now considers your intranet website to be the NLS server, and you cannot resolve it while you are mobile. The solution to this problem? Make sure that you choose a new DNS name to use for this NLS website. Something like `https://nls.contoso.local` is appropriate.

The most important part about the NLS that I want to stress is that you should absolutely implement this website on a server in your network that is *not* the DA server itself. When you are running through the DA config wizards, you will see on the screen where we define NLS that it is recommended to deploy it on a remote web server, but it also gives you the option to self-host the NLS website right on the DA server itself. Don't do it! There are many things that can go wrong when you co-host NLS on the DA server. Running the NLS on your DA server also limits your DA potential in the future, because some of the advanced DA configurations require you to remove the NLS from the DA server anyway, so you might as well do it correctly the first time you set it up. Changing your NLS website after you are running DA in production can be very tricky, and often goes sideways. I have helped numerous companies move their NLS website after realizing that they cannot co-host NLS on the DA server if and when they want to add a second DA server for growth or redundancy. The following is a screenshot of the section in the DA config wizard where you choose the location of NLS. Make sure you stick with the top box!

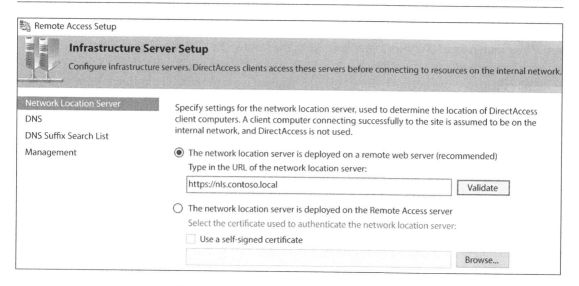

Figure 8.9: Defining the Network Location Server

Certificates used with DirectAccess

Aside from reading and misunderstanding how DA uses IPv6, here is the next biggest "turn-off" for administrators who are interested in giving DA a try. Once you start to read about how DA works, you will quickly come to realize that certificates are required in a few different places. While VPNs generally also require the use of certificates, it is admittedly difficult to distinguish which certificates need to go where when you are wading through Microsoft DirectAccess documentation, so this section clears up any confusion that exists about DA certificates. It really is not very complicated, once you know what does and does not need to be done.

The core prerequisite is that you have a Windows CA server somewhere in your network. The stature of your PKI implementation is not that important to DA. We simply need the ability to issue certificates to our DA server and clients. There are only three places where certificates are used in DA, and two of them are SSL certificates.

SSL certificate on the NLS web server

As mentioned previously, your NLS website needs to be running HTTPS. This means that you will require an SSL certificate to be installed on the server that is hosting your NLS website. Assuming that you have an internal CA server, this certificate can be easily acquired from that internal CA, so there are no costs associated with this certificate. You do not need to purchase one from a public CA, because this certificate is only going to be accessed and verified from your domain-joined machines, the DA clients. Since domain-joined computers automatically trust the CA servers in your network, this certificate can simply be issued from your internal CA, and it will do exactly what we need it to do for the purposes of DA.

SSL certificate on the DirectAccess server

An SSL certificate is also required to be installed on the DA server itself, but this one should be purchased from your public CA. This certificate will be used to validate IP-HTTPS traffic streams coming in from the client computers because that is SSL traffic and so we need an SSL certificate to validate it. Since the IP-HTTPS listener is facing the public internet, it is definitely recommended that you use a certificate from a public CA, rather than trying to use a certificate from your internal PKI.

If your company already has a wildcard SSL certificate, use it here to save costs!

Machine certificates on the DA server and all DA clients

The last and most complicated part of the DA certificate puzzle is machine certificates. Once you know what is required though, it's really not hard at all. We simply require that a computer or machine certificate be installed on the DA server, as well as each of the DA client machines. This machine certificate is used as part of the authentication process for IPsec tunnels. It is a big part of the way in which DA verifies that you really are who you say you are when your computer makes that DA connection happen.

The best way to go about issuing these machine certificates is to log into your CA server and create a new certificate template that is duplicated from the built-in *Computer* template. When setting up your new certificate template, just make sure that it meets the following criteria:

- The **Common Name (subject)** of the certificate should match the FQDN of the computer.
- The **Subject Alternative Name (SAN)** of the certificate should equal the DNS name of the computer.
- The certificate should serve the intended purposes (Enhanced Key Usage) of both Client Authentication and Server Authentication.

I should note here, though I don't really want to, that issuing these certificates is not absolutely necessary to make DA work. If you are running Windows 8 or higher on the client side, then it is possible to get DA working without machine certificates. It is possible for client computers running without machine certificates to instead utilize something called **Kerberos Proxy** for their computer authentication when the IPsec tunnels are being built, but I highly recommend sticking with certificates. Using certificates as part of the authentication process makes the connection more stable and more secure. Additionally, as with the placement of NLS, if you want to perform any advanced functions with DA, such as load balancing or multisite, or even if you simply want to make some Windows 7 computers connect through DA, then you will be required to issue certificates anyway. So, stick with the best practice in the first place and issue these certificates before you even get started with testing DA.

Do not use the Getting Started Wizard (GSW)!

After making the necessary design decisions and implementing the prerequisites we have talked about so far, it is finally time to install the Remote Access role on your new DA server! After you have finished installing the role, similar to many roles in Windows Server 2022, you will be shown a message informing you that additional configuration is required to use this role. If you follow the yellow exclamation mark inside Server Manager, the only option that you are presented with is **Open the Getting Started Wizard**. Ugh! This is *not* what you want to click on:

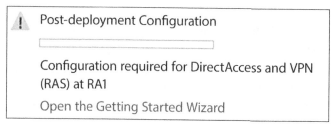

Figure 8.10: Do not click on this!

Don't do it!

Your home for DA configurations is the **Remote Access Management Console**, which is available from inside the **Tools** menu of Server Manager now that our Remote Access role has been installed. Go ahead and launch that, and now we are presented with a choice:

 Configure Remote Access

DirectAccess & VPN settings have not yet been configured. Select one of the wizard options.

→ Run the Getting Started Wizard

Use this wizard to configure DirectAccess and VPN quickly, with default recommended settings.

→ Run the Remote Access Setup Wizard

Use this wizard to configure DirectAccess and VPN with custom settings.

Figure 8.11: Configuring Remote Access

Do *not* click on **Run the Getting Started Wizard**! The GSW is a shortcut method for implementing DA, designed only for getting DA up and running as quickly as possible, perhaps for a quick proof of concept. Under no circumstances should you trust the GSW for your production DA environment, because in an effort to make configuration quick and easy, many configuration decisions are made for you that are not best practices.

You want to make sure you click on **Run the Remote Access Setup Wizard** when you are first prompted in the console; this will invoke the full set of DA configuration screens. DA setup consists of a series of four different steps, each containing a handful of screens that you will navigate through to choose your appropriate configuration options. There is a good amount of detail on these screens as to what each one of them means and what your options are, so don't be afraid to dive in and set this up in the proper way. If you have already configured DA and used the **Getting Started Wizard**, DA may be working for you, but it will not be running as efficiently or securely as it could be. The following is a quick list of the reasons why the Getting Started Wizard is not in your best interests. These are the things that it does that go directly against a best-practice DA install, with accompanying *peanut gallery* commentary from yours truly:

- GSW co-hosts the NLS website on the DA server—*bad*
- GSW applies the DA client GPO settings to all Domain Computers—*this is a terrible idea*
- GSW utilizes self-signed certificates—*a Security 101 level no-no*
- GSW automatically disables Teredo—*inefficient*
- GSW does not walk you through any of the advanced options for DA, probably because the way that it sets everything up invalidates your ability to even use the advanced functions—*lame*

Remote Access Management Console

You are well on your way to giving users remote access capabilities on this new server. As with many networking devices, once you have established all of your configurations on a Remote Access server, it is pretty common for admins to walk away and let it run. There is no need for a lot of ongoing maintenance or changes to that configuration once you have it running well. However, **Remote Access Management Console (RAMC)** in Windows Server 2022 is useful not only for the configuration of remote access parts and pieces but for monitoring and reporting as well.

When working with DA, this is your home for pretty much everything: configuration, management, monitoring, and troubleshooting. On the VPN/AOVPN side of the remote access toolset, you will be making many of the VPN configuration decisions inside RRAS, but the Remote Access Management Console is the place to go when checking over server-side monitoring, client-connection monitoring, and reporting statistics. Whether you use DA, VPN, or a combination of the two, the Remote Access Management Console is a tool you need to be comfortable with.

Let's take a look inside this console so that you are familiar with the different screens you will be interacting with:

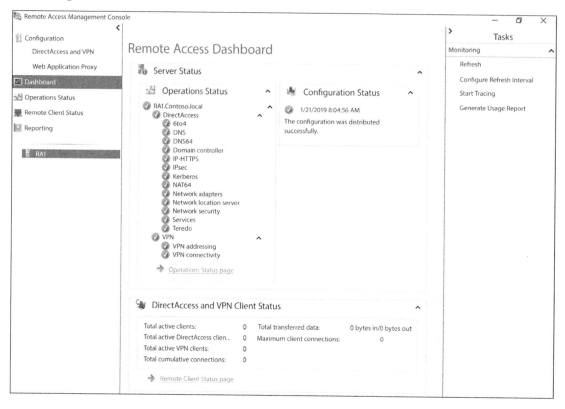

Figure 8.12: Remote Access Dashboard

Configuration

The configuration screen is pretty self-explanatory; this is where you create your initial remote access configuration, and where you update any settings in the future. As you can see in *Figure 8.12*, you can configure **DirectAccess** and **VPN**, and even **Web Application Proxy** (**WAP**), right from this **Remote Access Management Console**.

Do not follow my lead with this screenshot. I have installed the DirectAccess/VPN portion of the Remote Access role alongside the WAP portion of the same role, but it is not recommended to run both DA/VPN and WAP together on the same server. I did it simply for the purpose of creating screenshots in my test lab.

There is not a lot to configure as far as the VPN goes; you really only have one screen of options where you define what kinds of IP addresses are handed down to the VPN clients connecting in, and how to handle VPN authentication. It is not immediately obvious where this screen is, so I wanted to point it out. Inside the **DirectAccess and VPN** configuration section, if you click on **Edit...** under **Step 2**, this will launch the **Step 2** mini-wizard. The last screen in this mini-wizard is called **VPN Configuration**. This is the screen where you can configure these IP addresses and authentication settings for your VPN connections. The remainder of your VPN configuration duties will fall within the traditional VPN configuration console, called RRAS. However, everything about DA connections is configured right from inside **Remote Access Management Console** and those four mini-wizards:

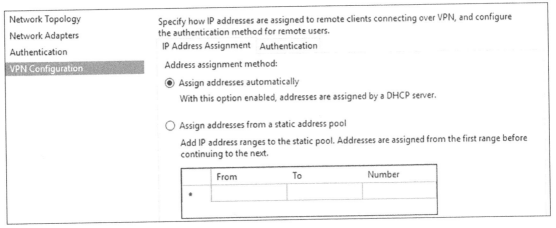

Figure 8.13: VPN Configuration settings inside RAMC

Dashboard

Remote Access Dashboard gives you a 30,000-foot view of the Remote Access server status. You can view a quick status of the components running on the server, whether or not the latest configuration changes have been rolled out, and some summary numbers near the bottom about how many DA and VPN connections are ongoing:

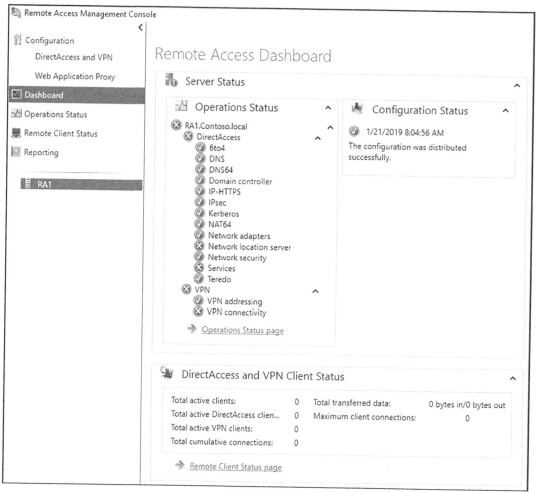

Figure 8.14: Summary stats on Remote Access Dashboard

Operations Status

If you want to drill down further into what is happening on the server side of the connections, that is what the **Operations Status** page is all about. Here, you can see more details on each of the components that are running under the hood to make your DA and VPN connections happen. If any of them have an issue, you can click on the specific component to get a little more information. For example, as a test, I have turned off the NLS web server in my lab network, and I can now see on the **Operations Status** page that the NLS is flagged with an error:

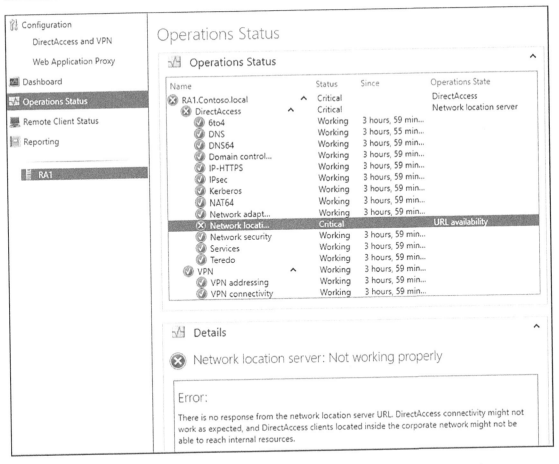

Figure 8.15: The Operations Status page displays information about server components

Remote Client Status

Next up is the **Remote Client Status** screen. As indicated, this is the screen where we can monitor client computers that are connected. It will show us both DA and VPN connections here. We will be able to see computer names, usernames, and even the resources that they are utilizing during their connections. The information on this screen can be filtered by simply putting any criteria into the **Search** bar at the top of the window.

It is important to note that the **Remote Client Status** screen only shows live, active connections. There is no historical information stored here.

Reporting

You guessed it: this is the window you need to visit if you want to see historical remote access information. This screen is almost exactly the same as the **Remote Client Status** screen, except that you have the ability to generate reports for historical data pulled from date ranges of your choosing. Once the data is displayed, you have the same search and filtering capabilities that you had on the **Remote Client Status** screen.

Reporting is disabled by default, but you simply need to navigate to the **Reporting** page and click on **Configure Accounting**. Once that is enabled, you will be presented with options for storing historical information. You can choose to store the data in the local WID or on a remote RADIUS server.

You also have options here for how long to store logging data and a mechanism that can be used to clear out old data:

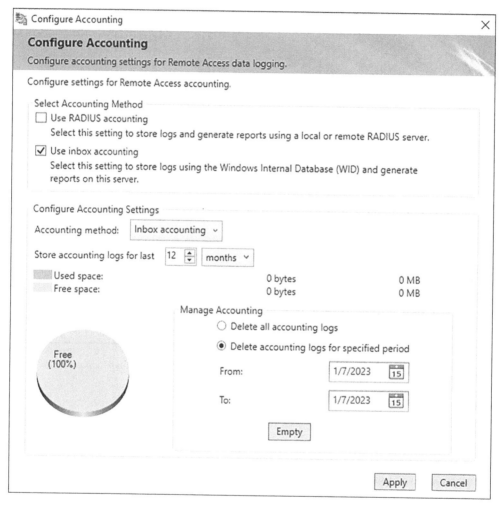

Figure 8.16: Configure Accounting (reporting) settings

Tasks

The last window pane in **Remote Access Management Console** that I want to point out is the **Tasks** bar on the right-hand side of your screen. The actions and options that are displayed in this taskbar change depending on what part of the console you are navigating through. Make sure you keep an eye on this side of your screen to set up some more advanced functions. Some examples of available tasks are creating usage reports, refreshing the screen, enabling or disabling VPNs, and configuring network load balancing or multisite configurations if you are running multiple Remote Access servers.

DA, VPN, or AOVPN? Which is best?

VPNs have been around for a very long time, making them a pretty familiar idea to anyone working in IT. Always On VPN certainly brings its share of new capabilities, but under the hood, what AOVPN is doing is launching a traditionally configured VPN connection, so the connection flow is similar to what we have always known. In this chapter, we have also discussed quite a bit about DA in order to bring you up to speed on this alternative method of automatically connecting your remote clients back to the datacenter. Now that you know there are two great connectivity platforms built into Windows Server 2022 for enabling your mobile workforce, which one is better?

You don't have to choose! You can run both of these technologies side by side, even on the same Remote Access server. Each technology has its pros and cons, and the ways that you use each, or both, will depend upon many variables. Your users, your client computers, and your organization's individual needs will need to be factored into your decision-making process. Let's discuss some of the differences between DA and VPNs so that you can make intelligent decisions on which connectivity platforms fit into your organization.

Domain-joined or not?

One of the biggest requirements for a DA client computer is that it must be domain-joined. While this requirement in and of itself doesn't seem so major, it carries some implications. Trusting a computer enough to be joined to your domain more than likely means that the laptop is owned by the company. It also probably means that this laptop was initially built and prepped by the IT team. Companies that are in the habit of allowing employees to purchase their own computers to be used for work purposes may not find that DA fits well with that model. DA is also not ideal for situations where employees use their existing home computers to connect to work remotely.

In these kinds of situations, such as home and personally owned computers, a VPN may be better suited to the task. You can connect to a VPN (including Always On VPN) from a non-domain-joined Windows machine, and you can even establish VPN connections (manual connections) from many non-Microsoft devices. iOS, Android, Windows phones, and Mac—all these platforms have a VPN client built into them, which can be used to tap into a VPN listener on a Windows Server 2022 Remote Access server. If your only remote access solution was DA, you would not be able to provide non-domain-joined devices with a connectivity platform.

Keep in mind that, while the Always On VPN user tunnel is more flexible than DA in this regard, if you intend to use the AOVPN *device tunnel*, then your machines will still need to be domain-joined.

Auto or manual launch

There are multiple different ways to look at this one. When discussing whether DA or a traditional VPN is better, DA is the clear winner. Nobody wants to make their users open a connection and manually launch it to establish VPN connectivity when an automated platform is available to use.

Always On VPN, however, brings automated and seamless connectivity to the VPN world. AOVPN is almost as seamless as DA in this regard. I say *almost* because, at the time of writing, it's fairly difficult to make a device tunnel work well. This means that most companies rolling out AOVPN only use the user tunnel. In the user tunnel scenario, the VPN does launch automatically, but not until the user has already passed the login screen. That means in these situations, DA still holds an advantage over AOVPN because DA connects seamlessly *at* the login screen. This enables password resets and new domain users to log in to DA-connected machines. I hope that future improvements will enable AOVPN devices and user tunnels to co-exist in a stable way, which will give true always-on connectivity to AOVPN clients.

Software versus built-in

I'm a fan of Ikea. They do a great job of supplying quality products at a low cost, and somehow package up these products inside incredibly small boxes. After you pay for the product, unbox it, put it together, and then test it to make sure it works—it's great. If you can't see where this is going, I'll give you a hint: it's an analogy for traditional, third-party VPNs, as in, you typically pay a vendor for their VPN product, unbox it, implement it at more expense, then test the product. That VPN software then has the potential to break and need reinstallation or reconfiguration, and will certainly come with software updates that need to be accomplished down the road. Maintenance, maintenance, maintenance.

Maybe I have watched too many home improvement shows lately, but I am a fan of houses with built-ins. Built-ins are essentially furniture that is permanent to the house, built right into the walls, corners, or wherever it happens to be. It adds value, and it integrates into the overall house much better than furniture that was pieced together separately and then stuck against the wall in the corner.

DA and Always On VPN are like built-ins. They live inside the operating system. There is no software to install, no software to update, and no software to reinstall when it breaks. Everything that DA and AOVPN need is already in Windows today; you just aren't using it. Oh, and it's free! Well, built into the cost of your Windows license anyway. There are no user CALs, and no ongoing licensing costs related to implementing one of Microsoft's Remote Access solutions.

If your workforce consists of Windows 10 and 11 machines, Microsoft DirectAccess or Microsoft Always On VPN are clear winners when compared to any third-party VPN connectivity solution.

Password and login issues with traditional VPNs

If you have ever worked on the helpdesk for a company that uses a VPN, you know what I'm talking about. There are a series of common troubleshooting calls that happen in the VPN world related to passwords. Sometimes, the user forgets their password. Perhaps their password has expired and needs to be changed—ugh! A VPN doesn't handle this scenario very well either. Or perhaps the employee changed their expired password on their desktop before they left work for the day, but are now trying to log in remotely from their laptop and it isn't working.

What is the solution to password problems with a VPN? Reset the user's password in Active Directory, and then ask the user to come into the office for the laptop to re-sync with the domain and recognize the new password. Yup, this kind of phone call still happens every day. This is unfortunate, but a real potential problem with old-school VPNs.

What's the good news? New Microsoft Remote Access solutions don't have these kinds of problems! Since DA and AOVPN are part of the operating system, they have the capability to be connected anytime that Windows is online. This includes the login screen! Even if I am sitting on the login or lock screen, and the system is waiting for me to input my username and password, as long as I have internet access, I also have a DA tunnel or an Always On VPN device tunnel. This means that I can actively do password management tasks. If my password expires and I need to update it, it works. If I forgot my password and I can't get into my laptop, I can call the helpdesk and simply ask them to reset my password. I can then immediately log in to my DA or AOVPN laptop with the new password, right from my house.

Another cool function that this seamlessness enables is the ability to log in with new user accounts. Have you ever logged into your laptop as a different user account in order to test something? Yup, that works over DA and AOVPN as well. For example, I am sitting at home and I need to help one of the salespeople troubleshoot some sort of file permission problem. I suspect it's got something to do with their user account, so I want to log in to my laptop as them in order to test it. The problem is that their user account has never logged in to my laptop before. With a VPN, not a chance; this would never work. With DA, piece of cake! I simply log off, type in their username and password, and bingo. I'm logged in, while still sitting at home in my pajamas.

It is important to note that you can run both DA and VPN connections on the same Windows Server 2022 Remote Access server. This enables you to host clients who are connected via DA, via AOVPN, and also via traditional VPN connections if you have non-Windows machines that need to connect. If any of these connectivity technologies have capabilities that you could benefit from, use them all!

Port-restricted firewalls

One of the other common VPN-related helpdesk calls has always been *my VPN won't connect from this hotel*. Unfortunately, most protocols that VPNs use to connect are not firewall-friendly. Chances are that your router at home allows all outbound traffic and so, from your home internet connection, everything is fine and dandy when connecting with a VPN protocol. But take that same laptop and connection over to a public coffee shop, a hotel, or an airport, and suddenly the VPN fails to connect, with a strange error. This is usually caused by that public internet connection flowing its traffic through a port-restricting firewall. These firewalls restrict outbound access, oftentimes blocking things such as ICMP and UDP, which can interfere with VPN connections. In the most severe cases, these firewalls may only allow two outbound ports: TCP 80 for HTTP and TCP 443 for HTTPS website traffic. Then they block everything else.

In the event that you are sitting behind a port-restricted firewall, how do these newer remote access technologies handle connectivity?

DA is built to handle this scenario out of the box. Remember those three different protocols that DA can use to connect? The *fallback* option is called IP-HTTPS, and it flows its traffic inside TCP 443. So, even while sitting behind the most severe firewalls, DA will generally connect automatically and without hesitation.

Always On VPN is generally deployed (as it should be) with best practices in mind, which includes prioritizing IKEv2 as the VPN connectivity protocol. In fact, some companies deploy AOVPN with only IKEv2. For these folks, a port-restricting firewall would be detrimental to that user's VPN connection, as IKEv2 uses UDP ports to connect. It wouldn't work. So, hopefully, the main point you take from this is that, when setting up AOVPN, make sure that you take the necessary steps to also enable SSTP VPN connectivity as a fallback method. SSTP flows traffic inside TCP 443, which can connect even through hardcore firewalls.

Super important: The AOVPN device tunnel can only use IKEv2. If you are behind a port-restricting firewall and are relying on a device tunnel for connectivity, it's not going to work. The AOVPN user tunnel is the only one capable of doing SSTP fallback.

In fact, I recently worked on this exact scenario with someone who was trying to decide whether they wanted to set up DA or Always On VPN for their remote machines. This was a company that manages computers for numerous hospitals and doctors' offices, and they did not have WAN links to those offices. The offices did have internet access though, and so we needed the ability to keep those computers automatically connected back to the main datacenter at all times. So far in the scenario, either DA or Always On VPN would fit the bill. Then, during testing, we discovered that many hospital networks restrict outbound internet access. The only way that DA would connect was via IP-HTTPS, and the only way that AOVPN would connect was via SSTP. Not a problem, right? Except that it was. You see, these remote workstations are often treated as kiosks, walk-up machines, where dozens of different employees could walk up at any moment and log into them. Oftentimes, this means that users who have never logged into these machines before are now logging in to them, so they don't have cached credentials on those computers.

If you haven't figured it out already, we had no choice but to go with DA in this scenario. DA is always connected at the login screen, even when using its *fallback* IP-HTTPS method. Always On VPN, however, can only do IKEv2 at the login screen, because the device tunnel requires IKEv2. This uses UDP and was blocked by the firewall, so the only way that AOVPN would connect was by using SSTP, but that wasn't available until the user tunnel could launch, which was only after the user had logged in to the machine. It was an extremely interesting real-world use case that helped shed some light on the decision-making process you may need to take for your own environments.

Manual disconnect

If you aren't already convinced that old-school, traditional VPNs are yesterday's news, let's throw another point at you. When you use VPNs that require the user to manually launch the connection, you are relying on the user themself to keep that machine managed, patched, and up to date. Sure, you may have automated systems that do these things for you, such as WSUS, SCCM, and Group Policy. But when the laptop is out and about, roaming around away from the LAN, those management systems can only do their jobs when the user decides to establish a VPN connection. It's very possible that a laptop could spend weeks completely outside the corporate network, connecting to dozens of insecure hotspots while that employee works their way around the Caribbean on a cruise ship.

After weeks of partying and Netflix, they then connect back into the LAN or via VPN to do some work, and wouldn't you know it, that machine has been offline for so long that it's picked up all kinds of fun and creative new software that you now have to deal with.

Not so with the Microsoft remote access tools! Providing an automatic connectivity option such as Always On VPN or DA means that the laptop would have been connected and receiving all of its security policies and patches during that entire vacation.

In fact, to take it one step further, on a DA connected machine, the user cannot disable their DA tunnels even if they want to. You do have the ability to provide them with a **Disconnect** button, but that basically just fakes out the connection from the user's perspective to make it feel to them like DA is offline. In reality, the IPsec tunnels are still flowing in the background, always allowing management-style tasks to happen.

Native load-balancing capabilities

Long story short, DA is the winner here. The Remote Access Management Console in Windows Server 2022 has built-in capabilities for configuring and managing arrays of DA servers. You can stack multiple DA servers on top of each other, tie them together in load-balanced arrays, and provide redundancy and resiliency right from inside the console, without any extra hardware or traditional load-balancer consideration. You can even configure something called **DirectAccess Multisite**, where you can configure DA servers that reside in different geographical locations together in arrays, giving cross-site resiliency. Almost every company that runs DA configures a redundant environment, providing either inner-site load balancing or multisite, or sometimes both, because these capabilities are built in and easy to configure.

Unfortunately, these capabilities are not (not yet, anyway) ported over into the Microsoft VPN world. Whether you are connecting Windows 7 clients via traditional VPN connectivity or getting Windows 10 clients to connect using Always On VPN, the backend infrastructure of an RRAS VPN is the same and has no built-in accommodation for multiple servers or sites. It is certainly possible to do so, making that VPN system redundant, but that would require you to set it up on your own by using external load balancers and, oftentimes, would require the use of global site/server load balancers to make that traffic flow properly.

Anyone who has set up load-balanced VPNs of any flavor in the past may be well aware of this process and be able to configure that easily, and that is great. But this is definitely a limiting factor for small business customers who have a limited number of servers, network equipment, and IT experience. All in all, the extra capabilities built into the console related to DA put it a step ahead of any VPN solution in terms of building up your remote access infrastructure to be resilient to failure.

Distribution of client configurations

The last primary consideration that you need to take into account when deciding which direction you want to go in for remote access is the method by which client-side settings get pushed down to their respective computers:

- **Third-party VPN**: We have already discussed the downsides of dealing with software applications for third-party VPN vendors. If you can use something baked into the Windows operating system instead, that seems like a no-brainer.

- **Always On VPN**: The recommended way to roll out AOVPN settings to client computers is through the use of an MDM solution, namely either SCCM or Intune. If you have one of these systems, rolling out AOVPN settings to your workforce is a breeze. If you do not have one of those systems, it is still possible, but not a straightforward process.

- **DirectAccess**: I think DA's approach to client settings distribution is the easiest to work with, and the most flexible. You have to keep in mind that DA is only for your domain-joined systems. Given that you can expect all clients to be domain-joined, you have access to rolling DA connectivity settings out via Group Policy, which exists inside any Microsoft-driven infrastructure.

I genuinely hope that we will see a Group Policy distribution option added in the future for Always On VPN configuration rollouts. If such a capability were introduced, I am completely confident that it would immediately become the most popular way to roll out AOVPN settings.

To summarize this whole topic, when comparing DA against traditional, manual-launch VPNs, DA cleanly takes first prize. There really is no comparison. Now that we have Always On VPN at our disposal, the benefits of one over the other (DA or AOVPN) are quite fuzzy. They both accomplish a lot of the same things, but in different ways. The primary deciding factors for most customers so far seem to be client-side rollout capabilities, whether or not they have access to an MDM solution, and how important device tunnel connectivity is to them. Microsoft's goal is for AOVPN to have feature parity with DA, and it's getting close. Always On VPN also has some advanced authentication features that DA does not have, such as integration with Windows Hello for Business or Azure MFA.

Web Application Proxy

DA and VPN are both great remote access technologies, and combining the two of them together can provide a complete remote access solution for your organization, without having to pay for or work with a third-party solution. Better still, in Windows Server 2022, there is yet another component of the Remote Access role available to use. This third piece of the remote access story is **Web Application Proxy**. This is essentially a reverse-proxy mechanism, giving you the ability to take some HTTP and HTTPS applications that are hosted inside your corporate network and publish them securely to the internet. Any of you who have worked with Microsoft technologies in the perimeter networking space over the last decade will probably recognize a product called Forefront **Unified Access Gateway (UAG)**, which accomplished similar functionality. UAG was a comprehensive SSL VPN solution, also designed for publishing internal applications to the internet via SSL. It was considerably more powerful than a simple reverse-proxy, including components such as pre-authentication, SSTP VPN, and RDS gateway; DA itself could even be run through UAG.

If all of your mobile workers have access to launching either DA or VPN, then you probably don't have any use for WAP. However, with the growing cloud mentality, it is quite common for users to expect that they can open up a web browser from any computer, anywhere, and gain access to some of their applications.

Document access is now often provided by web services such as SharePoint. Email access is available remotely, from any computer, by tapping into Outlook Web Access. This is very easy to accomplish when using cloud services such as Azure and Microsoft 365, but many don't realize that this can also be true of on-premises Exchange and SharePoint services.

So many applications and so much data can be accessed through only a web browser, and this enables employees to access this data without needing to establish a full-blown corporate tunnel such as a VPN. So what is the real-world use case for WAP? Home computers that you do not want to be VPN-connected. This way, you don't have to worry as much about the health and status of the home or user-owned computers, since the only interaction they have with your company is through the web browser. This limits the potential for a sinister activity to flow into your network from these computers. As you can see, technology such as WAP does certainly have its place in the remote access market.

I have hopes that, over time, WAP will continue to be improved and evolve into a true replacement for UAG. UAG ran on Windows Server 2008 R2 and has now been officially discontinued as a Microsoft product. The closest solution Microsoft now has to UAG is the WAP role. It is not yet nearly as comprehensive, but they are working on improving it. Currently, WAP is useful for publishing access to simple web applications. You can also publish access to rich clients that use basic HTTP authentication, such as Exchange ActiveSync, although, more recently, basic authentication has been put on the naughty list by security teams and so I don't see this one being utilized very often. Also included is the ability to publish data to clients that use MSOFBA, such as when users try to pull down corporate data from their Word or Excel applications running on the local computer.

WAP can be used to reverse-proxy (publish) remote access to things such as Exchange and SharePoint environments. This is no small thing, as these are technologies that almost everyone uses, so it can certainly be beneficial to your company to implement WAP for publishing secure access to these resources; it's certainly better than NATing directly to your Exchange server.

WAP as AD FS Proxy

Another useful way in which you can utilize a WAP server is when setting up **Active Directory Federation Services (AD FS)** in your network (this is perhaps the most common use for WAP right now). AD FS is a technology designed to enable single sign-on for users and federation with other companies, and so it involves taking traffic coming in from the internet into your internal network. In the past, there was a Windows Server role component that accompanied AD FS, called the **AD FS Proxy**. In the latest versions of AD FS, this separate role no longer exists and has been replaced by the WAP component of the Remote Access role. This better unifies the remote access solution, bringing your inbound AD FS traffic through the official Remote Access server, rather than needing a separate AD FS Proxy server. Anyone implementing outward-facing AD FS in their environments will likely find themselves required to deploy WAP at some point.

Requirements for WAP

Unfortunately, the ability to make use of Web Application Proxy comes with a pretty awkward requirement: you must have AD FS installed in your environment to be able to use it, even to test it, because the WAP configuration is stored inside AD FS.

None of the WAP configuration information is stored on the Remote Access server itself, which makes for a lightweight server that can be easily moved, changed, or added to. The downside to this is that you must have AD FS running in your environment so that WAP can have a place to store that configuration information.

While a tight integration with AD FS does mean that we have better authentication options, and users can take advantage of AD FS single-sign-on to their applications that are published through WAP, so far, this has proven to be a roadblock to implementation for smaller businesses. Many folks are not yet running AD FS, and if the only reason they are looking into implementing AD FS is so that they can use WAP to publish a few web applications to the internet, they may not choose to invest the time and effort just to make that happen.

One thing to keep in mind if you are interested in using WAP and are therefore looking at the requirement for AD FS is that AD FS can certainly be used for other functions. In fact, one of its most common uses at present is integration with Office 365. If you are planning to incorporate, or thinking of incorporating, Office 365 into your environment, AD FS is a great tool that can enhance the authentication capabilities for that traffic.

Latest improvements to WAP

WAP was introduced in Server 2012 R2 and had many improvements when Windows Server 2016 was released. There have been few major modifications since that time, but it is still important to point out the latest benefits that have been rolled into this feature to show that it is still learning to do new things. The following are some of the improvements that have been made if you haven't taken a look at WAP since its first iteration.

Pre-authentication for HTTP Basic

There are two different ways that users can authenticate to applications that are being published by WAP pre-authentication or pass-through authentication. When publishing an application with pre-authentication, this means that users will have to stop by the AD FS interface to authenticate themselves before they are allowed through to the web application itself.

In my eyes, pre-authentication is a critical component of any reverse proxy and I would have to be stuck between a rock and a hard place to externally publish an application that did not require pre-authentication. However, the second option is to do pass-through authentication, and it does exactly that. When you publish access to an application and choose pass-through authentication, all WAP is doing is shuttling the packets from the internet to the application server, in the true reverse proxy form. Users are able to get to the web application without authentication, so in theory, anyone on the internet can hit the web frontend of your application. From there, the application itself will likely require the user to authenticate, but there is no man-in-the-middle protection happening; that web application is available for the public to view. As you can tell, I do not recommend taking this route.

We already know that WAP can pre-authenticate web applications, but the original version could not do any form of pre-authentication on HTTP Basic applications, such as when a company wanted to publish access to Exchange ActiveSync.

This inability leaves ActiveSync a little bit too exposed to the outside world and is a security risk. Thankfully, this changed in Windows Server 2016—you can now pre-authenticate traffic streams that use HTTP Basic.

HTTP to HTTPS redirection

Users don't like going out of their way or wasting time by having to remember that they need to enter HTTPS:// in front of the URL when they access applications. They would rather just remember email.contoso.com. The inability of WAP to do HTTP to HTTPS redirection was an annoyance and a hindrance to adoption, but that has since changed. WAP now includes the capability for WAP itself to handle HTTP to HTTPS redirection, meaning that users do not need to type HTTPS into their browser address bar any longer; they can simply type in the DNS name of the site and let WAP handle the translations.

Wildcard domain publishing

Early versions of WAP didn't play nicely with some SharePoint environments, because of limitations in the way that WAP handled domain names. The external URL utilized for publishing an application through WAP can now include a wildcard identifier, which enables the newer versions of on-premises SharePoint to be successfully published to the internet, via WAP.

Client IP addresses forwarded to applications

In the reverse proxy and SSL VPN world, we occasionally run across applications that require knowing the client's local IP address. While this requirement doesn't happen very often and is typically segregated to what we would call legacy applications, it does still happen. When the backend application needs to know what the client's IP address is, this presents a big challenge with reverse-proxy solutions. When the user's traffic flows through WAP or any other reverse proxy, it is similar to a NAT, where the source IP address information in these packets changes. The backend application server is unable to determine the client's own IP address, and trouble ensues. WAP now has the ability to propagate the client-side IP address through to the backend application server, alleviating this problem.

Publishing Remote Desktop Gateway apps

One of the items that UAG was commonly used for was publishing access to Remote Desktop Services. UAG was essentially its own Remote Desktop Gateway, which gave you the ability to publish access to RDSH servers, individual RDP connections to desktop computers, such as in a VDI implementation, and even access to RemoteApp applications. Unfortunately, WAP cannot do any of this, even in the new version, but the fact that they have added a little bit of functionality here means movement in the right direction is happening.

What has been improved regarding WAP and Remote Desktop is that you can now use WAP to publish access to the Remote Desktop Gateway server itself. Traditionally, a Remote Desktop Gateway sits on the edge of the network and connects external users through to internal Remote Desktop servers or RemoteApps. Placing WAP in front of the Remote Desktop Gateway allows stronger pre-authentication for Remote Desktop services and creates a bigger separation between the internal and external networks.

All of my fingers are crossed that we will continue to see improvements in this area and that WAP can be expanded to handle traffic like Remote Desktop natively, without even needing a Remote Desktop Gateway in the mix.

Improved administrative console

The original version of WAP inside Windows Server 2012 R2 was best served using PowerShell to implement it. You can certainly still use PowerShell to create your publishing rules if you so choose, but the Remote Access Management Console has now been improved in terms of how it relates to WAP. Before you can find WAP in the Remote Access Management Console, you need to make sure that the appropriate box was checked during the Remote Access role installation. If you did not select **Web Application Proxy** when you first installed that role, revisit the **add/remove Roles** function inside Server Manager in order to add WAP to this server:

Select the role services to install for Remote Access	
Role services	**Description**
☐ DirectAccess and VPN (RAS) ☐ Routing ☑ Web Application Proxy	Web Application Proxy enables the publishing of selected HTTP- and HTTPS-based applications from your corporate network to client devices outside of the corporate network. It can use AD FS to ensure that users are authenticated before they gain access to published applications. Web Application Proxy also provides proxy functionality for your AD FS servers.

Figure 8.17: Adding WAP to a server

Note that, while WAP is a component of the same Remote Access role that houses DA and VPN, it is not recommended to run WAP alongside DA and VPN on the same server. As you already know, you can co-host DA and VPN connections together, simultaneously, on a single Remote Access server. But once you make the foray into WAP, this should be a standalone component. Do not run WAP on a DA/VPN server, and do not run DA/VPN on a WAP server.

Now that we have added **Web Application Proxy** to our server, you can open up the **Remote Access Management Console** and see it listed inside the **Configuration** section. From here, you launch the **Web Application Proxy Configuration Wizard** and start walking through the steps to define your AD FS server, the certificates you are planning to use, and other criteria needed for the role:

Figure 8.18: Configuring WAP from the Remote Access Management Console

Summary

The nature of the world today demands that most companies enable their employees to work from wherever they are. Working from home has become normal over the past few years; with a worldwide pandemic, we have seen staggering increases in the percentage of employees who work outside of an office building. Companies need a secure, stable, and efficient way to provide access to corporate data and applications for these mobile workers. The Remote Access role in Windows Server 2022 is designed to do exactly that. With three different ways of providing remote access to corporate resources, IT departments have never had so much remote access technology available at their fingertips, built right into the Windows operating system that they already own. If you are still supporting a third-party or legacy VPN system, you should explore the new capabilities provided here and discover how much they could save your business.

DA and Always On VPN are particularly impressive and compelling connectivity options—a fresh way of looking at remote access. Automatic connectivity means your machines are constantly patched and updated because they are always connected to your management servers. You can improve user productivity and network security at the same time. These two things are usually oxymorons in the IT world, but with the Microsoft remote access stack, they hold hands and sing songs together.

Next, we are going to take a look at some of the security functions built into your Windows Server 2022 operating system, and at some of the ways that your servers can be hardened to provide even better security than what comes out of the box.

Questions

1. What does AOVPN stand for?
2. What are the two primary protocols used for connecting AOVPN clients?
3. In which version of Windows 10 was AOVPN released?
4. In what special instance would an AOVPN client be required to be joined to your domain?
5. Does DirectAccess require your corporate internal network to be running IPv6?
6. What is the name of the internal website that DirectAccess clients check in with to determine when they are inside the corporate network?
7. What ports are used by Teredo and IP-HTTPS?

8. How do you provision DirectAccess configuration settings to the client machines?

9. What role does a Web Application Proxy server hold in a federation environment?

Join our community on Discord

Join our community's Discord space for discussions with the author and other readers:

https://packt.link/SecNet

9

Hardening and Security

9.44 million dollars. For anyone who read that in the voice of Dr. Evil, my hat goes off to you. For anyone who has no idea what I'm talking about, you may have had a sheltered childhood. Joking aside, that number is significant to IT security. Why? Because 9.44 million dollars is the average cost to a US-based business when they are the victim of a data breach. I originally heard this and other scary statistics at a Microsoft conference in Redmond, and the numbers have continued to climb year on year. How about looking at another statistic that can be used to get approval for an increase in your security budget? Depending on which study you read, the average number of days of **dwell time** an attacker has in your network (the time they spend hanging around inside your files and infrastructure before they are detected and eradicated) can be as high as 200. Think about that—200 *days*! That is the better part of a year that they're camping out before you discover them! What are they typically doing during those 200 days? Siphoning all of your data bit by bit out the back door. Another number is 76%—as in, the percentage of network intrusions that happen as a result of compromised user credentials. Furthermore, it is becoming more and more difficult to identify these attacks in the first place because attackers use legitimate IT tools to grab what they want. For instance, an attacker could socially engineer their way into the trust of a single employee and leverage that trust to get a remote access connectivity tool installed on the user's work computer. Why use malware when you can install a valid remote connection tool that is going to fly under the radar of intrusion detection systems? Makes sense to me.

Data security, network security, credential and identity security—these things are all becoming harder to accomplish, but there are always new tools and technologies coming out that can help you fight off the bad guys. Windows Server 2022 is the most secure server OS that Microsoft has produced; in this chapter, let's discuss some of the functionality included that makes that statement true:

- Microsoft Defender Antivirus
- Windows Defender Firewall—no laughing matter
- Encryption technologies
- Azure AD Password Protection
- Fine-grained password policy

- Advanced Threat Analytics—end of support
- General security best practices
- Protocol enhancements

Microsoft Defender Antivirus

The term Windows Defender has been around for many years, but its terminology and capabilities have evolved numerous times with new OS releases. Defender existed even as far back as 2005, at the time providing very simple antimalware protection. The Windows 8 era introduced a fairly staggering change for Windows users, including Windows Defender in the OS, free and out of the box. Although this sounds great on paper, Defender's capabilities were not taken too seriously by the IT population. Fast forward to today, however, and what is now known as Microsoft Defender Antivirus is a much improved antimalware/antivirus that is running on millions of Windows 10 and 11 client computers as well as, you guessed it, current versions of Windows Server. Defender Antivirus exists in the OS and is enabled by default, and as a result has a level of integration and responsiveness that is hard for third-party vendors to match. I can't tell you how many times I have tracked memory leaks and random server reboots back to poorly functioning third-party antivirus software, which is unacceptable in today's server world. Some still consider the antivirus capabilities provided by Defender to be lackluster, perhaps only because it is free, but it does certainly carry some advantages over third-party AV. I have yet to see a Windows Defender product tank a client or server.

You have likely also seen and heard references to Windows Defender **Advanced Threat Protection** (**ATP**), now renamed Microsoft Defender ATP. This is a family of products and systems that work together to protect your Windows machines. Antivirus/antimalware is only one of those capabilities, and built-in antivirus is a relatively new idea when talking about the Windows Server family of OSes.

The first server OS that we found with built-in Defender for antivirus was Server 2016. Many servers running in production for companies around the world are still Server 2012 R2 at this point (I know because I work on them every day), and so the improved existence of the Defender toolset in Server 2022 is yet another reason to start planning your migration today.

We simply do not have enough page space to dive into every aspect of Windows Defender ATP, and it is being continually improved upon. In fact, as I type this another revolution is beginning, with references and articles starting to appear about Microsoft Defender for Cloud. What we will do is explore some of the interfaces, make sure you know how to use the most common components that don't require policy-level manipulation or centralized administration, and expand your knowledge of some of the more advanced features that are available for further learning and digging.

Installing Microsoft Defender Antivirus

You're done! Microsoft Defender Antivirus is installed by default in Windows Server 2022. In fact, unless you have somehow changed it, not only is Defender AV installed but it also automatically protects your system as soon as the OS is installed. But don't take my word for it: if you open up Server Manager, choose **Add roles and features**, and click ahead to the **Select features** page, you should find a checkbox already selected next to **Microsoft Defender Antivirus**:

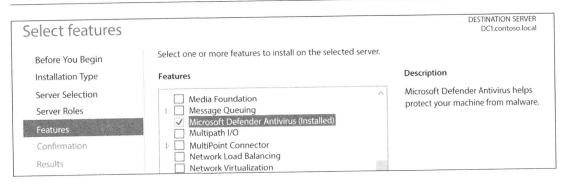

Figure 9.1: Microsoft Defender Antivirus is preinstalled

If it's not already checked for some reason, then this is exactly the place to visit to get it installed and working.

Exploring the user interface

The interface for the Microsoft Defender toolset is the same as within the latest versions of Windows 10, but if you haven't explored that yet, we will take a quick look at it here. Go ahead and launch **Settings** from inside the **Start** menu, then click on **Update & Security**.

Once inside that section, you will see **Windows Security** listed on the left. Here you get an overhead view of the different Defender components that are working together to protect your system.

Remember, you have done nothing to enable any of this functionality; these are all out-of-the-box capabilities:

Figure 9.2: Microsoft Defender capabilities

Clicking further into any of these **Protection areas** will bring you more detailed descriptions of each capability, as well as many options for enabling or disabling particular protections that exist. For example, if you were to click on **Virus & threat protection**, you would see summary information about Defender AV, when its definition files were updated, what it's scanning, and so on. Then clicking further into a link called **Manage settings** will give you options for disabling Defender AV if you ever have the need, as well as numerous other options that can be selected or deselected. *Figure 9.3* shows you a few of the settings available inside Defender AV. I chose to display these three because they are important to another topic we will cover shortly, when we discuss the ATP portion of Defender ATP:

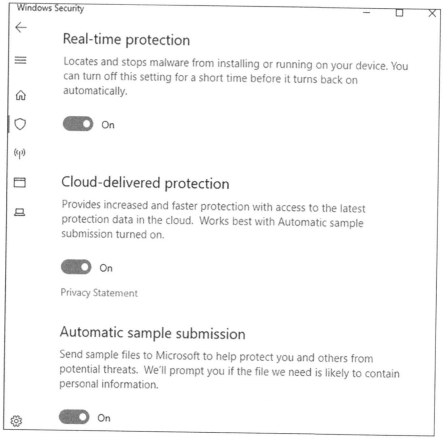

Figure 9.3: Managing virus and threat protection options

Disabling Microsoft Defender Antivirus

You already know that Defender AV is enabled by default, as are many other components that make up the Microsoft Defender family of products. By flipping the **Real-time protection** radio option shown in *Figure 9.3*, you can temporarily disable AV. Taking it a step further, if you are absolutely sure that you do not want to use Defender AV because you have your own AV software that you have already paid for, you have two different avenues that could be taken.

First, Defender AV is designed to automatically step down in the event that another AV is installed. More than likely, all you need to do is install your other third-party AV tool, and after the server finishes restarting, Defender AV will stand down and allow the third-party product to run, so that they don't conflict with each other. This is important because a fact that even many computer technicians don't realize is that multiple AV programs running on a single system is generally a terrible idea. They often cause conflicts with each other, have memory allocation errors, and cause otherwise slow and strange behavior on the system.

By default, Microsoft Defender runs in what is known as **Active mode**, which makes a lot of sense. If you employ an additional capability in the Defender family called **Microsoft Defender for Endpoint**, when a third-party AV product is installed, Defender changes gears and enters **Passive mode**. In this instance, Defender AV is not the primary antivirus. It may still scan some files and detect threats if it sees them, but Defender now takes no action to remediate these potential threats.

If you are planning to utilize your own AV and want to make sure Defender is *completely* removed, it is possible to uninstall the Defender feature from your server. This is most easily done via PowerShell, with the following command:

```
Uninstall-WindowsFeature -Name Windows-Defender
```

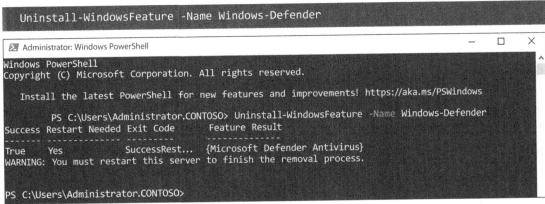

Figure 9.4: Uninstalling Defender

What is ATP anyway?

It's hard to define what exactly **Advanced Threat Protection** means because it is a culmination of Microsoft Defender parts, pieces, and security mechanisms working together in order to protect clients and servers from bad stuff: AV, firewalling capabilities, hardware protections, and even specific resistance against ransomware.

The combination of capabilities inside the *Windows Security* section of Windows 10 and Server 2022 work together to become ATP.

Something that should be incredibly intriguing to all of us is the smart way that Microsoft is now utilizing cloud connectivity and computing to improve Defender AV on a daily basis. Whether we realize it or not, most of the internet-connected Windows machines in the world are now continuously helping each other out by reporting newly discovered vulnerabilities and malicious activity to Microsoft. This information is then parsed and investigated via machine learning, and the resulting information can be immediately used by the rest of the Windows machines around the globe.

While this sounds a little *Big Brother* and full of privacy concerns, I believe we as a community have mostly surpassed that fear and realize that the benefits outweigh the potential fears. Millions of users now flow their email through Office 365; you may not even realize it, but Office 365 does this kind of data handling as well to identify and block exploits. For example, if an email address within a company is suddenly sending emails to a large group of people, and that email contains a macro-enabled Word document, which is something that a user does not typically do, Office 365 can very quickly take that document offline into a secure zone, open it (or launch it if the attachment happened to be an executable), and discover whether or not this file is malware of some kind. If it is, Office 365 will immediately start blocking that file, thereby stopping the spread of this potentially disastrous behavior. All of this happens without input from the user or the company's IT staff. This is not even inner company-specific. If one of my users' emails is the first to receive a new virus and it is identified by Microsoft, that discovery will help to block the new virus for any other customers who also host their email in Microsoft's cloud. This is pretty incredible stuff!

This same idea holds true for Defender AV when you choose to allow it to communicate with and submit information to Microsoft's cloud resources. Earlier, I pasted in a screenshot of some Defender AV capabilities called **cloud-delivered protection and automatic sample submission**—it is these pieces of Defender AV that allow this cloud-based magic to happen and benefit the entire computer population.

Windows Defender ATP Exploit Guard

Once again, we are taking a look at what seems to be a long title for a technology that must have a very specific purpose, right? Nope. Exploit Guard is not *a* capability but rather a whole *set* of capabilities baked into the Windows Defender family. Specifically, these protections are designed to help detect and prevent some of the common behaviors that are used in current malware attacks.

Here are the four primary components of Defender ATP Exploit Guard:

- **Attack Surface Reduction** (ASR): ASR is a series of controls that block certain types of files from being run. This can help mitigate malware being installed by users clicking on email attachments or prevent the opening of certain kinds of Office files. We are quickly learning as a computer society that we should never click on files in an email that appear to be executables, but often a standard computer user won't know the difference between an executable and any other kind of file. ASR can help to block the running of any executable or scripting file from inside an email.

- **Network protection**: This enables Windows Defender SmartScreen, which can block potential malware from phoning home, communicating back to the attacker's servers to siphon or transfer company data outside of your company. Websites on the internet have reputation ratings, deeming sites or IP addresses to be trusted or not trusted, depending on the types of traffic that have headed to that IP address in the past. SmartScreen taps into those reputation databases to block outbound traffic from reaching bad destinations.

- **Controlled folder access**: Ransomware protection! This one is intriguing because ransomware is a top concern for any IT security professional. If you're not familiar with the concept, ransomware is a type of malware that installs an application onto your computer that then encrypts files on your computer. Once encrypted, you can't open or repair those files without the encryption key, which the attackers will (most of the time) happily hand over to you for lots of money. Every year, many companies end up paying that ransom (and therefore engaging in passive criminal behavior themselves) because they do not have good protections or good backups from which to restore their information. Controlled folder access helps to protect against ransomware by blocking untrusted processes from grabbing onto areas of your hard drive that have been deemed protected.

- **Exploit protection**: Generalized protection against many kinds of exploits that might take place on a computer. The exploit protection function of Defender ATP is a rollup of capabilities from something called the **Enhanced Mitigation Experience Toolkit (EMET)**, which was previously available but reached its end of life in mid-2018. Exploit protection watches and protects system processes as well as application executables.

These controls, particularly exploit protection controls, can be managed in many different ways. They can be rolled out in a centralized fashion via Intune, Group Policy, or the Microsoft Endpoint Configuration Manager. Additionally, they can be configured on a per-machine basis by using PowerShell or the Windows Security app, which is built into every current Windows version.

Let's take a peek at the settings on an individual instance of Windows Server 2022. Open up **Windows Settings | Update & Security**. Inside, in the left navigation pane, you will see a shield icon that says **Windows Security**. Go ahead and click on that. Now into **App & browser control**. On this screen, you have options for configuring **Reputation-based protection**, which is the section where the configuration of SmartScreen URL-based protection is accomplished, and also a section for **Exploit protection**. Clicking on **Exploit protection settings**, now we get into the nitty gritty of these protection mechanisms. There are many different pieces of exploit protection that can be globally enabled or disabled (many are enabled by default), and clicking on **Program settings** allows you to get granular, defining to what extent exploit protection handles individual programs, as you can see in *Figure 9.5*:

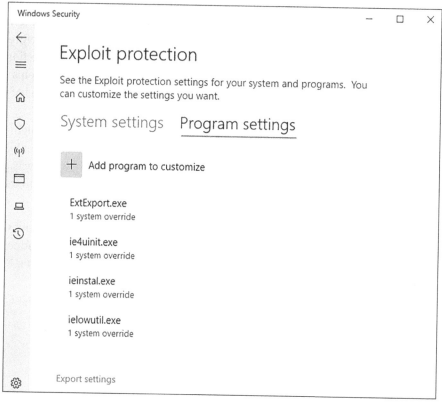

Figure 9.5: Exploit protection settings

Windows Defender Firewall — no laughing matter

Let's play a word association game. I will say something, and you say the first word that comes to mind.

Network security.

Did you say *firewall*? I think I would have. When we think of securing our devices at the network level, we think of perimeters. Those perimeters are defined and protected by firewalls, mostly at the hardware level, with specialized networking devices made to handle that particular task in our networks. Today, we are here to talk about another layer of firewalling that you can and should be utilizing in your environments. Yes, we are talking about Windows Firewall. Stop laughing, it's rude!

It is easy to poke fun at Windows Firewall based on its history. In the days of Windows XP and Server 2003, it was pretty useless and caused way more headaches than it solved. These feelings were so common that I still today find many companies who completely disable Windows Firewall on all of their domain-joined systems as a matter of default policy. If you ask them, there is usually no specific reason they are doing this—*it's always been this way* or *it's in our written security policy* are standard replies. This is a problem because the **Windows Defender Firewall with Advanced Security (WFAS)** that exists in the Windows OSes of today is much more robust and advanced than ever before and can absolutely be used to enhance your security architecture. I would go as far as to say that it is entirely silly to disable WFAS on a current OS, unless you have a very good, very specific reason to do so.

Three Windows Firewall administrative consoles

First, it is important to know that there are three different consoles from which you can configure Windows Firewall settings. Two of these consoles make each other redundant, and the third is much more capable than the others. Let's take a quick look at each one.

Windows Defender Firewall (Control Panel)

When trying to launch any application or setting in Windows Server 2022, it is usually most efficient to simply click on the **Start** button and then type a word relating to the task you are trying to accomplish. In my case, I clicked on **Start** and typed the word `firewall`. One of the top matches that was provided in my search results was **Windows Defender Firewall,** so I went ahead and clicked on that.

Interestingly, this link opens the Windows Defender Firewall configuration console from inside **Control Panel**, the old-school way of doing system settings. This console is still online and fully capable of manipulating basic firewalling functions, such as enabling or disabling the Windows Firewall, but since this tool resides inside **Control Panel**, we have to assume that this is actually not the tool that Microsoft intends for us to utilize. Remember, all new configuration capabilities have been migrated to the **Windows Settings** screens, rather than the old **Control Panel**:

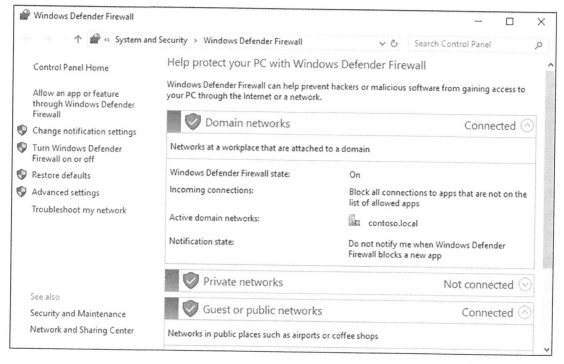

Figure 9.6: Firewall settings inside Control Panel

Firewall & network protection (Windows Security Settings)

While the **Control Panel**-based tools were always the proper place to make these changes in past versions of the OS, we already know that there are many Windows Defender options stored inside **Windows Settings**. Could it be the case that there are also Windows Defender Firewall configuration settings stored inside the **Windows Security** section of **Settings**?

Yes, there definitely are. Open up **Windows Settings** and click on **Update & Security**, then on **Windows Security**. You've been here before—this is the screen that gives a quick summary of the Windows Defender components. Sure enough, there is one here called **Firewall & network protection**.

Click on that button, and you will be taken into a newer configuration platform for the Windows Firewall functions that did not exist in earlier versions of Windows Server:

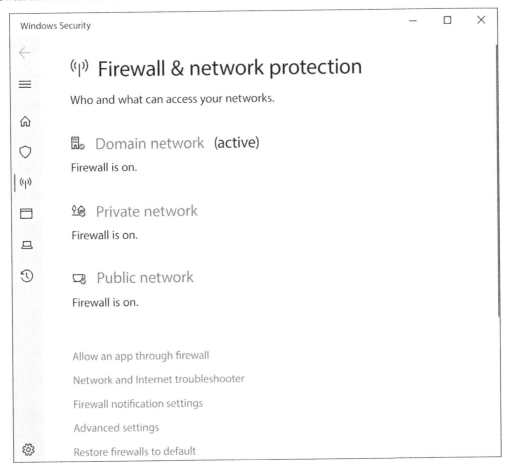

Figure 9.7: Firewall settings inside Windows Settings

Clicking on any of the links provided here will open additional configuration options. For example, if you wanted to quickly enable or disable particular firewall profiles (we will learn about those shortly), you could click on the profile you wanted to configure, such as the **Domain network** profile, and from there easily turn off the firewall for this networking profile. Many companies disable the domain network profile on their machines so that the firewall is not protecting traffic that happens inside a corporate LAN network.

While disabling the firewall is generally a bad idea, sometimes it is required to fit your business model:

Figure 9.8: Disabling the Windows Firewall while on Domain network

The firewall configuration screen available inside **Windows Settings** is a good place to make simple, overhead decisions about Windows Defender Firewall, but this interface is limited in capabilities. For any real utilization of firewall functionality or configuration...

Windows Defender Firewall with Advanced Security (WFAS)

If you are anything like me, you won't be satisfied with the firewall information provided inside **Windows Settings**, and you will want to see what is going on under the hood, and so you will want a little more information than the basic Windows Firewall tools alone can give you. You can either click on one of the **Advanced settings** links shown in previous screenshots or simply open Command Prompt or a **Start | Run** prompt and type wf.msc. Either of these functions will launch the full **WFAS** administration console:

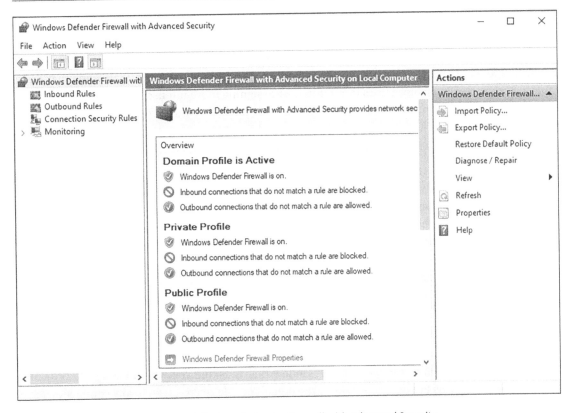

Figure 9.9: Windows Defender Firewall with Advanced Security

Here you can see much more in-depth information about the activity and rules that are at play with Windows Firewall and make more acute adjustments in your allowances and blocks. There is also a **Monitoring** section where you can view actively engaged rules, including **Connection Security Rules**. This is an important section because it highlights the fact that WFAS does much more than block network traffic. It is not only a firewall; it is also a connectivity platform. If you plan to utilize IPsec for the encryption of network traffic, whether it be native IPsec inside your network or through the remote access technology DirectAccess, you will see rules populated in this section that are the definitions of those IPsec tunnels.

Believe it or not, Windows Firewall is actually responsible for making those encrypted connections and tunnels happen. This is way more advanced than the Windows Firewall of yesteryear.

Three different firewall profiles

When any NIC on a computer or server is connected to a network, Windows Firewall will assign that connection one of the three different profiles. You have probably interfaced with this decision-making process before without even realizing it. When you connect your laptop to the Wi-Fi at your local coffee shop, did Windows ask you whether you were connecting to a home, work, or public network? Or in more recent versions of Windows, it asks you a question more along the lines of, "Would you like to allow your computer to be discoverable on this network—yes or no?" This is your Windows Firewall asking you which profile you would like to assign to the new network connection.

The reason that you can assign NICs and network connections to different firewall profiles is that you can assign different access rules and criteria for what is or is not allowed over those different profiles. Effectively, it is asking you, *how much do you trust this network?* For example, when your laptop is connected to the corporate network, you can probably be a little bit more lax than when that same laptop is connected at a hotel across the country. By assigning more intense firewall rules to the profile that is active when you are in the hotel, you build bigger walls for attackers to face when you are out working on that public internet. Let's take a look at the three different types of profiles that are available, with a quick description of each:

- **Domain Profile:** This is the only one that you cannot choose to manually assign. The Domain Profile is only active when you are on a domain-joined computer that is currently connected to a network where a domain controller for your domain is accessible. So, for any corporate machine inside the corporate network, you can expect that the Domain Profile will be active. The detection of this connectivity happens automatically, via a Windows service called **Network Location Awareness (NLA)**.

- **Private Profile:** When connecting to a new network and you are prompted to choose where you are connected, if you choose either **Home** or **Work**, that connection will be assigned the Private Profile.

- **Public Profile:** When prompted, if you choose **Public**, then of course you are assigned the public firewall profile. Also, if you are not prompted for some reason, or if you do not choose an option at all and simply close the window that is asking you what to assign to your new connection, this Public Profile will be the default profile that is given to any connections that do not have a different profile already assigned.

In the more recent versions of Windows (particularly in Win10), you don't usually get the prompt asking what kind of network it is; instead, you get that prompt asking whether or not you want to allow your computer to communicate with other devices on the new network. Effectively, this is still the same prompt, and the decision you make at that prompt will assign your connection to either the public or private firewall profile.

Each network connection gets assigned its own profile definition. You could certainly have more than one firewall profile active at the same time on the same system. For example, my RA1 server that we used in the last chapter is connected to both the corporate network as well as the public internet. Inside WFAS, you can see that both the Domain Profile and Public Profile are active:

Figure 9.10: Multiple NICs can mean multiple active firewall profiles

Alternatively, if you open up **Network and Sharing Center** on this server, we can also see the profiles listed here, and you can easily tell which NIC is using which profile:

Figure 9.11: Firewall profiles assigned to each NIC

Building a new inbound firewall rule

Now that we know that the real meat and potatoes of Windows Firewall is inside the WFAS console, let's use WFAS to build ourselves a new rule. On this RA1 server, I have enabled RDP access so that I can more easily manage this server from my desk. However, by turning on RDP, I have now allowed RDP access from all of the networks on this server. That means I can RDP into RA1 from inside the network, but I can also RDP into RA1 from the internet, since this is a remote access server and happens to be connected straight to the internet. This is a big problem, because now any yahoo on the internet could potentially find my server, find the RDP login prompt, and try to brute-force their way into RA1. This is literally how most ransomware happens.

To alleviate this problem, I want to squash RDP only on my external NIC. I want it to remain active on the inside so that I can continue to access the server from my desk, but is there an easy way inside WFAS to create a firewall rule that blocks RDP access only from the outside? Yes, there certainly is.

Open up wf.msc to launch Windows Defender Firewall with Advanced Security, navigate to the **Inbound Rules** section, and you will see all of the existing inbound firewall rules that exist on this server (there are many rules listed here even if you have never visited this console before; these rules are installed with the OS). Right-click on **Inbound Rules** and choose **New Rule....** This launches a wizard from which we will create our new firewall rule. The first screen is where we identify what kind of a rule we want to create. You can create a rule that modifies traffic for a particular program or port number, or you can look through a list of **Predefined** protocols.

I like knowing exactly what my rule is doing because of the way that *I* defined it, not because of a pre-existing protocol definition, and I know that RDP runs over TCP port 3389. So, I am going to choose **port** on this screen, and after I click on **Next**, I will define 3389 as the specific port that I want to modify:

Steps:	
Rule Type	Does this rule apply to TCP or UDP?
Protocol and Ports	● **TCP**
Action	○ **UDP**
Profile	
Name	Does this rule apply to all local ports or specific local ports?
	○ **All local ports**
	● **Specific local ports:** `3389`
	Example: 80. 443. 5000-5010

Figure 9.12: This firewall rule is going to manipulate port 3389 (RDP) traffic

Our third step is to decide whether we want to allow or block this particular port. There is a third option listed about only allowing the connection if it is authenticated by IPsec, which is a powerful option, but necessitates having IPsec established in our network already. Because of that requirement, this option doesn't apply to most people.

For our example, we already have RDP working, but we want to block it on one of the NICs, so I am going to choose **Block the connection**:

Figure 9.13: Blocking port 3389

We don't want to block RDP for *all* of the NICs, though, so this next screen is very important. Here we need to reference back to our knowledge about those firewall profiles we talked about. Remember that internal NICs connected to our domain network will have the Domain Profile assigned to them. But any NICs that are not connected to an internal network where a domain controller resides will have either Public or Private Profiles active. That is the knowledge we need to employ on this screen. If we want to disable RDP only on the external NIC, we need this rule to be active for only the Private Profile and Public Profile. In fact, in looking back through previous screenshots, we can see that the external NIC is assigned the Public Profile specifically, and so we could check only the **Public** checkbox here and RDP would then be blocked on the external NIC. But in case we add more NICs to this server in the future for which we want to make sure RDP access is not possible, we will leave both **Public** and **Private** checked, to ensure better security for the future.

Make sure that you **uncheck** the **Domain** profile! Otherwise, you will block RDP access completely, and if you are currently using RDP to connect to this server, you will kick yourself out of it and be unable to reconnect:

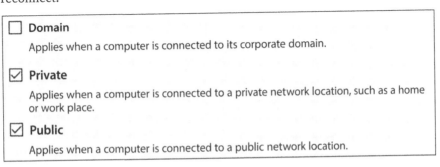

Figure 9.14: Blocking RDP only on our external NIC

And now we simply create a name for our new rule, and we are done! Our ability to RDP into this server from the internet has immediately been disabled, and we can rest much easier tonight.

Creating a rule to allow pings (ICMP)

Very often I find myself needing to create either an allow or a block rule for ICMP. In other words, I often find myself needing to adjust the firewall on servers in order to enable or disable their ability to reply to ping requests. You've probably noticed with newer server OSes that it is pretty normal for the firewall to automatically block pings (ICMP) out of the box.

This is a problem for environments where ping is the standard method for testing whether an IP address is consumed or available. You may be laughing, but trust me, there are still plenty of IT administrators out there that don't keep track of which IP addresses they have used inside their networks, and when faced with the need to set up a new server and decide what IP address to give it, they simply start pinging IP addresses in their network until they find one that times out! I have seen this so many times. While this is obviously not a good way to manage IP addresses, it happens. Unfortunately, this method encounters big problems, because most new Windows installations are designed to block ICMP responses out of the box, which means that you may ping an IP address and receive a timeout, but there could actually be another server or PC running on that IP address.

So, back to the point. You may have a need to enable ICMP on your new server, so that it responds when someone tries to ping it. When we need to create a new rule that allows pings to happen, we set up a rule just like we did for RDP, but there is one big catch. On that very first **Rule Type** screen when creating the new rule, where you have to identify what kind of rule you are creating, there are no options or predefinitions for ICMP. I find this strange because this is a very common type of rule to put into place, but alas, choosing ICMP from the drop-down list would just be too easy. Instead, what you need to do is create a new inbound rule just like we did for RDP, but at the very first screen for **Rule Type**, make sure you select the option that says **Custom**.

Next, leave the option selected to define this rule for **All programs**. Click **Next** again, and now you have a drop-down box called **Protocol type**. This is the menu where you can choose your new rule to manipulate ICMP traffic. As you can see in *Figure 9.15*, you can choose **ICMPv4** or **ICMPv6**, depending on what your network traffic looks like. My test lab is IPv4-only, so I am going to choose **ICMPv4**:

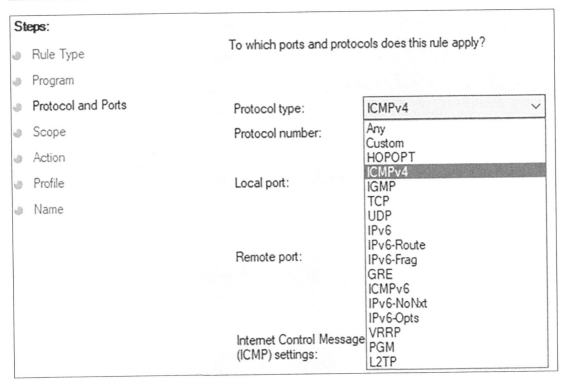

Figure 9.15: Applying the rules to specific protocols

For the rest of the ICMP rule creation, follow the same procedures outlined when we created the RDP rule, choosing to either allow or block this traffic, and for which firewall profiles. Once finished, your new ICMPv4 rule is immediately enacted, and if you have configured an Allow rule, your new server will now successfully respond to ping requests:

```
PS C:\Users\administrator.CONTOSO> ping ra1

Pinging ra1.contoso.local [10.10.10.13] with 32 bytes of data:
Reply from 10.10.10.13: bytes=32 time<1ms TTL=128
Reply from 10.10.10.13: bytes=32 time<1ms TTL=128
Reply from 10.10.10.13: bytes=32 time<1ms TTL=128
Reply from 10.10.10.13: bytes=32 time<1ms TTL=128
```

Figure 9.16: Pinging your server and now receiving an ICMP response

If ever you need to modify a rule or dig into more advanced properties of a firewall rule, back on the **Inbound Rules** screen you can right-click on any individual firewall rule and head into **Properties**. Inside these tabs exists the opportunity to modify any criteria about the rule. For example, you could accommodate additional ports, you could modify which firewall profiles it applies to, or you could even restrict which specific IP addresses this rule applies to through the use of the **Scope** tab.

This enables you to apply your firewall rule only to traffic coming or going from a specific portion of your network, or a certain subset of machines. For example, here I have modified my **Scope** tab to reflect that I only want this firewall rule to apply to traffic that is coming in from the 192.168.0.0/16 subnet:

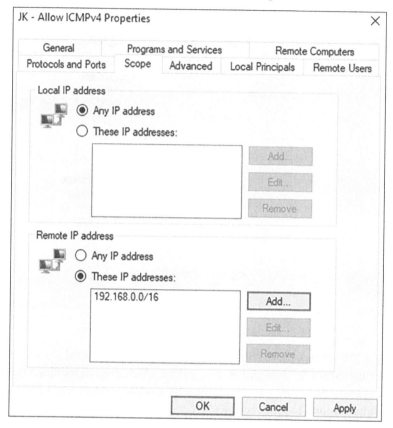

Figure 9.17: Scoping a firewall rule to specific IP addresses or subnets

Managing WFAS with Group Policy

Managing firewall rules on your servers and clients can be a huge step toward a more secure environment for your company. The best part? This technology is enterprise-class and free to use since it's already built into the OSes that you use. The only cost you have associated with firewalling at this level is the time it takes to put all of these rules in place, which would be an administrative nightmare if you had to implement your entire list of allows and blocks on every machine individually.

357

Thank goodness for **Group Policy**. As with most settings and functions inside the Microsoft Windows platform, setting up a firewall policy that applies to everyone is a breeze for your domain-joined machines. You can even break it up into multiple sets of policies, creating one GPO that applies firewall rules to your clients and a separate GPO that applies firewall rules to your servers, however you see fit. The point is that you can group many machines together into categories, create a GPO ruleset for each category, and automatically apply it to every machine by making use of Group Policy's powerful distribution capabilities.

You are already familiar with creating GPOs, so go ahead and make one now that will contain some firewall settings for us to play with. Link and filter the GPO accordingly so that only the machines you want to have the settings will actually get them. Perhaps a good place to start is a testing OU, so that you can make sure all the rules you are about to place inside the GPO work well together and with all of your other existing policies, before rolling the new policy out to your production workforce.

Once your new GPO is created, right-click on it from inside **Group Policy Management Console** and click on **Edit...**:

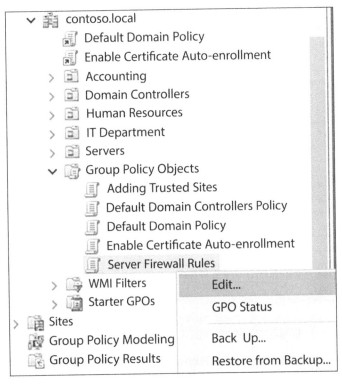

Figure 9.18: Using Group Policy to centrally manage Windows Firewall rules

Now that we are looking at the insides of this new GPO, we just need to figure out where the correct location is for us to create some new firewall rules. When you are looking inside the rules on the local machine itself, everything is listed under a **Windows Defender Firewall with Advanced Security** heading, and that is located at **Computer Configuration | Policies | Windows Settings | Security Settings | Windows Defender Firewall with Advanced Security | Windows Defender Firewall with Advanced Security:**

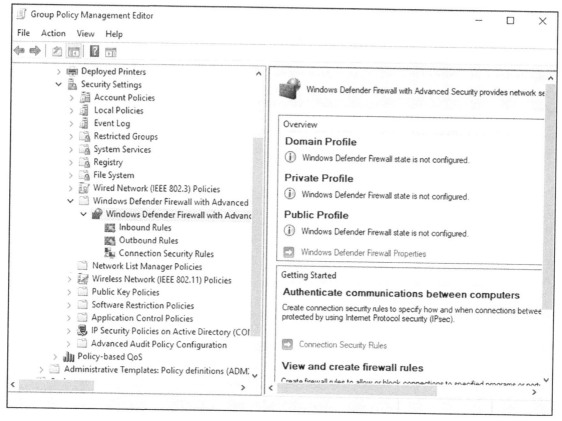

Figure 9.19: Location of firewall rule settings inside a GPO

As you can see, this is also the place to go when you want to make sure that particular firewall profiles, or Windows Firewall as a whole, are specifically turned on or off. So, this is the same place that you would go if you wanted to disable Windows Firewall for everyone.

By clicking on the **Windows Defender Firewall Properties** link shown in *Figure 9.19*, you can determine the status of each firewall profile individually:

Figure 9.20: Separate tabs to modify each firewall profile's behavior

Once you are finished setting your profiles according to your needs, click on **OK**, and you find yourself back at the WFAS part of the GPO. Just like inside the local WFAS console, you have categories for **Inbound Rules** and **Outbound Rules**. Simply right-click on **Inbound Rules** and click on **New Rule...** to get started with building a rule right into this GPO. Walk through the same wizard that you are already familiar with from creating a rule in the local WFAS console, and when you are finished, your new inbound firewall rule is shown inside the GPO:

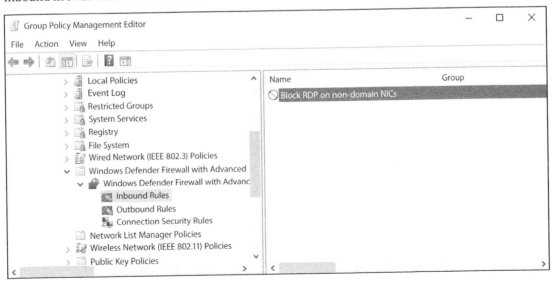

Figure 9.21: A successfully implemented firewall rule, inside the GPO

Faster than you can say Jack Robinson, this new firewall rule is already making its way around Active Directory and installing itself onto those computers and servers that you defined in the policy's links and filtering criteria.

Encryption technologies

An idea that has taken a fast step from *something the big organizations are playing around with* to *everybody needs it* is the use of encryption. Most of us have been encrypting our website traffic for many years by using HTTPS websites, but even in that realm, there are surprising exceptions, with a lot of the cheap web-hosting companies still providing login pages that transmit traffic in clear text. This is terrible, because with anything that you submit over the internet now using regular HTTP or an unencrypted email, you *have to assume* that it is being read by someone else. Chances are you are being paranoid and nobody is actually intercepting and reading your traffic, but you need to know that if you are accessing a website that says HTTP in the address bar, or if you are sending an email from any of the free email services, any data that is being entered on that web page or in that email can easily be stolen by someone halfway around the world. Data encryption is an absolute requirement for corporate information that needs to traverse the internet; though at the same time I say that, the back of my mind is telling me that the vast majority of companies are still not using any kind of encryption technology on their email system, and so that is still a potential disaster waiting to happen for many.

While we are getting better and better at protecting internet browser and web traffic, we traditionally are still not paying a lot of attention to data that is "safe" within the walls of our organization. The bad guys aren't dumb, and they have a very large toolbox of tricks to socially engineer their way into our networks. Once inside, what do they find? In most cases, it's a big free-for-all. Get a hold of one user account or one computer and you've got keys to a large part of the kingdom. Fortunately, there are several technologies built into Windows Server 2022 that are designed to combat these intrusions and protect your data even while it sits within the four walls of your datacenter. Let's look at some information on them so that you can explore the possibility of using these encryption technologies to further protect your data.

BitLocker and the virtual TPM

BitLocker is a technology that has become familiar to see on our client systems within corporate networks. It is a full-drive encryption technology, giving us the advantage of making sure our data is fully protected on laptops or computers that might be stolen. If a thief gets their hands on a company laptop, claws out the hard drive, and plugs it into their computer... sorry, Charlie, no access. The entire volume is encrypted. This makes all kinds of sense for mobile hardware that could be easily lost or stolen. But in the beginning stages of this technology, there was never real consideration of using BitLocker to protect our servers.

With the escalated adoption of cloud computing resources, suddenly it makes much more sense to want BitLocker on our servers. More particularly when talking about the cloud, what we really want is BitLocker on our **Virtual Machines** (**VMs**), whether they be client or server OSes. Whether you are storing your VMs in a true cloud environment provided by a public cloud service provider or you are hosting your own private cloud where tenants reach in to create and manage their own VMs, without the possibility of encrypting those virtual hard drives—the VHD and VHDX files—your data is absolutely **not** secure.

Why not? Because anyone with administrative rights to the virtualization host platform can easily gain access to any data sitting on your server's hard drives, even without any kind of access to your network or user account on your domain. All they have to do is take a copy of your VHDX file (the entire hard drive contents of your server), copy it to a USB stick, bring it home, mount this virtual hard disk on their own system, and bingo—they have access to your server hard drive and your data. This is a big problem for data security compliance.

Why has it historically not been feasible to encrypt VMs? Because BitLocker comes with an interesting requirement. The hard drive is encrypted, which means that it can't boot without the encryption being unlocked. How do we unlock the hard drive so that our machine can boot? One of two ways.

The best method is to store the **unlock keys** inside a **Trusted Platform Module (TPM)**. This is a physical microchip that is built right into most computers that you purchase today. Storing the BitLocker unlock key on this chip means that you do not have to connect anything physically to your computer to make it boot, you simply enter a pin to gain access to the TPM, and then the TPM unlocks BitLocker. On the other hand, if you choose to deploy BitLocker without the presence of a TPM, to unlock a BitLocker volume and make it bootable, you need to plug in a physical USB stick that contains the BitLocker unlock keys. Do you see the problem with either of these installation paths in a VM scenario? VMs cannot have a physical TPM chip, and you also have no easy way of plugging in a USB stick! So, how do we encrypt those VMs so that prying eyes at the cloud hosting company can't see all our stuff?

Enter the **virtual TPM**. This capability came to us brand new in Windows Server 2016; we now have the ability to give our virtual servers a virtual TPM that can be used for storing these keys! This is incredible news and means that we can finally encrypt our servers, whether they are hosted on physical Hyper-V servers in our datacenter or sitting in the Azure cloud.

Shielded VMs

Using BitLocker and virtual TPMs to encrypt and protect virtual hard drive files produces something called **Shielded VMs**. Shielded VMs are a capability first introduced in Windows Server 2016 and were improved quite a bit in Server 2019. With Microsoft's redirected focus on cloud hosting and Azure-supported servers, it is likely that Microsoft won't be adding additional development or capabilities to on-prem Shielded VMs in the future, but they still exist in Server 2022 and are still fully supported.

We will cover more details of Shielded VMs in *Chapter 14, Hyper-V*.

Encrypted virtual networks

Wouldn't it be great if we could configure, control, and govern our networks from a graphical administrative interface, rather than looking at router CLIs all day? Would we not benefit from the networking flexibility to move servers and workloads from one subnet to another, without having to change IP addressing or routing on those servers? Couldn't we find some way to automatically encrypt all of the traffic that is flowing between our servers, without having to configure that encryption on the servers themselves?

Yes, yes, and yes! Through the use of **Software Defined Networking (SDN)** and a new capability called **encrypted virtual networks,** we can accomplish all of these things. This section of text is really just a reference point, a place to steer you back toward *Chapter 7, Networking with Windows Server 2022,* if you skipped over it and landed here instead. We have already discussed SDN and its new capability to create and automatically encrypt virtual networks that flow between Hyper-V VMs and Hyper-V host servers, so if this idea intrigues you, make sure to head back and revisit that chapter.

Encrypting File System

Encrypting File System (EFS) is a component of Microsoft Windows that has existed on both client and server OSes for many years. Whereas BitLocker is responsible for securing an entire volume or disk, EFS is a little more particular. When you want to encrypt only certain documents or folders, this is the place you turn to. When you choose to encrypt files using EFS, it is important to understand that Windows needs to utilize a user certificate as part of the encrypt/decrypt process, and so the availability of an internal PKI is key to a successful deployment. Also important to note is that authentication keys are tied to the user's password, so a fully compromised user account could negate the benefits provided by EFS.

I think that many companies don't employ EFS because you leave the decision on what documents to encrypt up to the user. This also means that you depend on them to remember to do the encryption in the first place, which means they will have to understand the importance of it to make it worthy of their time. I wanted to mention EFS because it is still alive and is still a valid platform for which you can encrypt data, but most administrators land on BitLocker as a better solution. The lack of responsibility on the user's part and a good centralized management platform do put BitLocker a solid step ahead of EFS. The technologies could certainly co-exist, though, keeping data safe at two different tiers instead of relying on only one of the data encryption technologies available to you.

IPsec

A lot of the encryption technology built into OSes revolves around data at rest. But what about our data on the move? We talked about using SSL on HTTPS websites as a way of encrypting web browser data that is on the move across the internet, but what about data that is not flowing through a web browser?

And what if I'm not even concerned about the internet; what if I am interested in protecting traffic that could even be flowing from point to point *inside* my corporate network? Is there anything that can help with these kinds of requirements? Certainly.

IPsec is a protocol suite that can be used for authenticating and encrypting the packets that happen during network communication. IPsec is not a technology that is particular to the Microsoft world, but there are various ways in Windows Server 2022 that IPsec can be utilized in order to secure data that you are shuttling back and forth between machines.

The most common place where IPsec interaction shows up on Windows Server is when using the **Remote Access (RA)** role. When configuring VPN on your RA server, you will have a number of different connection protocols that the VPN clients can use to connect to the VPN server. Included in this list of possible connection platforms are IPsec (IKEv2) tunnels. The second remote access technology that uses IPsec is DirectAccess.

When you establish DirectAccess in your network, every time that a client computer creates a Direct-Access tunnel over the internet to the DirectAccess server, that tunnel is protected by IPsec. Thankfully, the Remote Access Management Console that you use to deploy both VPN and DirectAccess is smart enough to know everything that is needed to make IPsec authentication and encryption work, and you don't need to know a single thing about IPsec in order to make these remote access technologies work for you!

The big missing factor with IPsec provided by the Remote Access role is traffic *inside* your network. When you are talking about VPN or DirectAccess, you are talking about traffic that moves over the internet. But what if you simply want to encrypt traffic that moves between two different servers inside the same network? Or the traffic that is flowing from your client computers inside the office to their local servers, also located in the office? This is where some knowledge of the IPsec policy settings comes in handy because we can specify that we want traffic moving around inside our corporate networks to be encrypted using IPsec. Making that happen is a matter of putting the right policies in place.

Configuring IPsec

There are two different places that IPsec settings can be configured in a Microsoft Windows environment. Both current and very old systems can be supplied with IPsec configurations through the traditional **IPsec Security Policy snap-in**. If you are running all systems that are Windows 7 and Server 2008 or newer (and hopefully you are!), then you can alternatively employ WFAS for setting up your IPsec policies. WFAS is the most flexible solution but isn't always an option depending on the status of legacy systems in your environment.

First, let's take a glance at the older IPsec policy console. We will start here because the different options available will help to build a baseline for us to start wrapping our minds around the way that IPsec interaction works between two endpoints. There are three different classifications of IPsec policy that can be assigned to your machines that we will encounter in this console. Let's take a minute to explain each one, because the policy names can be a little bit misleading. Understanding these options will put you a step ahead in understanding how the settings inside WFAS work as well.

Server policy

Server policy should probably be renamed *Requestor* policy because that is really what this one does. When a computer or server makes a network request outbound to another computer or server, it is requesting to establish a network connection. On these requesting computers—the ones initiating the traffic—this is where we tell the IPsec Server policy to apply. Once applied, the Server policy tells that computer or server to request IPsec encryption for the communication session between the initiating machine and the remote computer. If the remote system supports IPsec, then the IPsec tunnel is created to protect traffic flowing between the two machines. Server policy is pretty lenient, though, and if the remote computer does not support IPsec, then the network connection is still successful but remains unencrypted.

Secure Server policy

The difference here is that the Secure Server policy *requires* IPsec encryption to allow the network communication to happen. The regular Server policy that we talked about earlier will encrypt with IPsec when possible, but if not possible, it will continue to flow the traffic unencrypted. The Secure Server policy, on the other hand, will fail to establish the connection at all if IPsec cannot be negotiated between the two machines.

Client policy

Client policy needs to be renamed *Response* policy, because this one is on the other end of the connection. The Client policy does not care about requesting an IPsec session; it only cares about **receiving** one. When a computer makes a network request to a server, and that computer has the Server or Secure Server policy so it is requesting IPsec, then the server to which that computer is trying to connect would need to have the Client policy assigned to it in order to accept and build that IPsec tunnel. The Client policy responds by allowing the encryption to happen on that session.

IPsec Security Policy snap-in

The original console for manipulating IPsec settings is accessed via MMC. Open that up, and add the **IP Security Policy Management** snap-in. Interestingly, when adding this snap-in, you will notice that you can view either the local IPsec policy of the machine that you are currently logged in to, or you can open the IPsec policy for the domain. If you are interested in configuring a domain-wide IPsec implementation, this would be your landing zone for working on those settings. But for the purposes of just sticking our head in here to poke around a little, you can choose **Local computer** to take a look at the console:

Figure 9.22: Exploring the IPsec configuration for our local server

Once inside, you can see any existing IPsec policies that might be in place, or you can start creating your own by using the **Create IP Security Policy...** action available when right-clicking on **IP Security Policies**. Doing this will invoke a wizard that will walk through the configuration of your own IPsec policy:

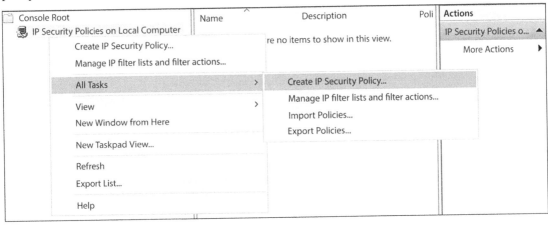

Figure 9.23: Creating an IP security policy

Using WFAS instead

The newer platform used for establishing IPsec connection rules is WFAS. Go ahead and open that up, as you are already familiar with doing. Once inside, navigate to the **Connection Security Rules** section, which is listed immediately below **Inbound Rules** and **Outbound Rules**. **Connection Security Rules** is where you define IPsec connection rules. If you right-click on **Connection Security Rules** and choose **New Rule...**, you will then walk through a wizard similar to the one for creating a firewall rule:

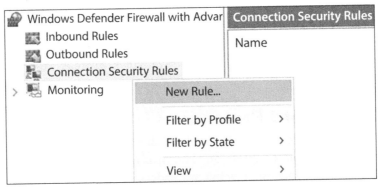

Figure 9.24: WFAS can also be used to create IPsec policy rules

Once inside the wizard to create your new rule, you start to see that the options available to you are quite different from the ones shown when creating a new firewall rule. This is the platform from which you will establish IPsec connection security rules, which define what the IPsec tunnels look like and on which machines or IP addresses they need to be active:

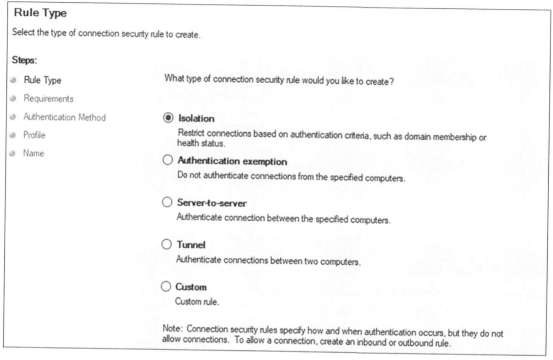

Figure 9.25: Types of connection security rules

We do not have space here to cover all of the available options in this wizard, but I definitely recommend picking up from here and taking it a step further with the following Microsoft Docs article: https://docs.microsoft.com/en-us/previous-versions/windows/it-pro/windows-server-2012-R2-and-2012/hh831807(v=ws.11).

Azure AD Password Protection

If you are an Azure Active Directory customer, you already have access to this new function called **Azure Active Directory Password Protection**, formerly known as **banned passwords**. The idea is this: Microsoft maintains a global ongoing list of commonly bad passwords (such as the word *password*) and automatically blocks all variants of that password, such as *P@ssword*, *Password123*, and so on. Any of these potential passwords would be blocked altogether if a user ever tried to create one as their own password. You also have the ability to add your own custom banned passwords inside the Azure Active Directory interface. Once you have banned passwords up and running in Azure, this capability can then be ported to your on-premises Active Directory environment as well, by implementing the Azure Active Directory Password Protection proxy service (whew, that's a mouthful).

This proxy is an agent that gets installed onto your local Domain Controller servers and pulls down password policies from Azure Active Directory, ensuring all passwords that users attempt to put into place on your local domain controllers fit within the rules defined by Azure's banned password algorithms.

To use this technology, you must of course be utilizing Azure Active Directory, so this isn't for everyone. However, if you do have and sync to Azure Active Directory, then this capability is even backported to older versions of on-premises domain controllers. These servers can be as old as Windows Server 2012.

Here is a link to further information on Azure AD Password Protection for AD DS: `https://docs.microsoft.com/en-us/azure/active-directory/authentication/concept-password-ban-bad-on-premises`.

Fine-grained password policy

As promised way back during our discussion of domain-level password policy, we are here to walk through the building of a fine-grained password policy. Most organizations do require specific password complexity for their users, but almost always by way of the default domain policy GPO, which means that the password complexity and expiration settings are exactly the same for everyone within the domain.

What if you have requirements to enable complexity on some user accounts but not on others? Perhaps you have sales personnel who travel constantly and requiring very strong and complex passwords makes a lot of sense for them. But let's say you also have a machine shop where users have to log in to computers every day, but those computers never leave the office and the users never type in their credentials into any systems other than those physically secure devices.

Is it really necessary for those machine shop users to have the same level of password complexity as the traveling sales personnel? Should they also be required to update their password every 30 days simply because you also ask it of your sales folks?

Starting with Windows Server 2012, log in to any domain controller server and launch Server Manager, and at the very top of your Tools list, you will see something called **Active Directory Administrative Center** (**ADAC**). This ADAC tool can be used to manipulate many things within Active Directory, but most importantly for our purposes today, this new tool is the mechanism that enables you to create a **fine-grained password policy** (**FGPP**). An FGPP enables the scenario we alluded to a paragraph ago, the ability to create multiple password policies and assign those policies to different classes of users and user accounts.

Log in to a domain controller as a domain admin and open ADAC. In the left navigation pane, expand the name of your internal domain, then **System | Password Settings Container**. In my lab environment, I am clicking on **contoso (local) | System | Password Settings Container**. Currently, the Password Settings Container is empty, but using the **New | Password Settings** task will get things rolling:

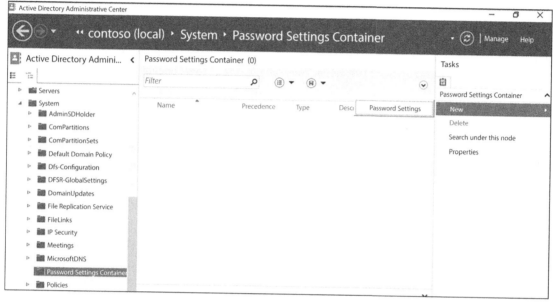

Figure 9.26: Fine-grained password policies are configured inside ADAC

The **Password Settings** screen is fairly self-explanatory. Here you define the same types of password complexity, length, and expiration criteria that you would normally configure inside the default domain policy GPO. You can see in *Figure 9.27* that I have created a Password Settings policy called **Sales Users**, with a number of specific criteria.

I was able to configure password settings as well as account lockout settings (another security setting commonly done globally via a GPO) and filtered this password policy so that it only applies to users that are inside my AD group called **Sales Users**:

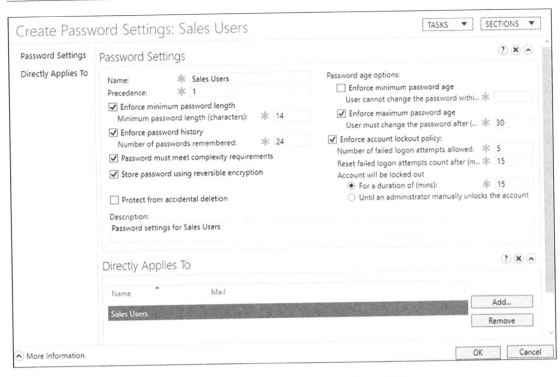

Figure 9.27: Creating new Password Settings policies

Now I'm going to repeat the process a couple more times, after which you can see that I have three separate Password Settings policies inside my ADAC container:

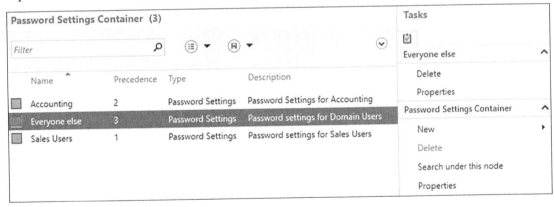

Figure 9.28: Creating more than one Password Settings policy

Something that is important to note here is that each Password Setting policy has a **Precedence** declaration. Since we apply these password settings to groups, it is certainly possible that a particular user could be part of multiple groups, which would give them multiple password policies. The **Precedence** number helps FGPPs to distinguish which settings should apply.

That's it! As soon as you have defined a fine grained password policy inside ADAC, these new password settings will now take priority over settings inside the default domain policy GPO. Rather than pushing password settings via Group Policy, using a fine-grained password policy utilizes its own objects inside Active Directory to do its work. These objects are called **Password Settings Objects (PSOs)**. If you want to see a little bit further under the hood of a PSO, now that you have created an FGPP inside ADAC, head over to **Active Directory Users and Computers** and enable **Advanced Features** under the **View** menu. Once **Advanced Features** is enabled, you can navigate to **Domain | System | Password Settings Container** and see the new PSOs that you created a minute ago.

Double-clicking on any of these objects and then visiting the **Attribute Editor** tab will display details on the password criteria for that object. There is no *need* to visit these objects from inside ADUC, as you can always make tweaks and changes to your FGPP from inside the ADAC console, but seeing these PSOs helps us to understand how Active Directory is storing and processing these policies:

Figure 9.29: Viewing password criteria outside of ADAC

Advanced Threat Analytics — end of support

In my opinion, one of the coolest security features to have ever breathed life at Microsoft is **Advanced Threat Analytics** (**ATA**), and yet I have hardly heard anyone talk about it. Perhaps because they never went so far as to add it as a native feature built into the Windows Server OS. ATA is an on-premises software that rides on top of Windows to produce some amazing functionality. Essentially, what ATA does is monitor all of your Active Directory traffic and warn you of dangerous or unusual behavior in real time, immediately as it is happening.

Unfortunately, ATA reached the end of mainstream support in January 2021. Extended support will continue until 2026, however, and so I am choosing to retain information in this latest book edition because this is still a valid technology and will continue to exist in environments where it is installed for years to come. There is additional information at the end of this section regarding the ATA roadmap.

What is (was) ATA?

The idea of ATA is pretty simple to understand and makes so much sense that we are all going to wonder why it took so many years for someone to come up with this idea. Active Directory has been around for a very long time, and attacks against your environment utilizing user accounts for just as long. Discovering and troubleshooting attacks within the directory is complicated and messy; there is so much information being logged all the time inside AD that it is almost impossible to catch or track bad guys as they do their worst. Following some form of attack, you can certainly pore over log data from multiple domain controllers and piece together some semblance of what happened, but being able to identify that happening *as it is happening* is just a pipe dream. Or is it...?

ATA is an advanced form of Active Directory monitoring that uses machine learning. This is the coolest part of ATA. You configure your network so that all of the traffic flowing in or out of your domain controllers also lands in the ATA system. The most secure way to accomplish this is at the networking level, establishing port mirroring so that all of the domain controller packets also make their way to ATA, but at a level that an attacker would not be able to see.

This way, even if someone nefarious is inside your network and is on the lookout for some kind of protection working against them, ATA remains invisible to their prying eyes. However, port-mirroring that traffic is something that smaller companies may not be able to do or may be too complex for an initial setup, and so a second option exists to install an ATA lightweight agent right onto the domain controllers themselves. This agent then sends the necessary information over to the ATA processing servers.

In either case, those ATA processing servers receive all of this data and start finding patterns. If Betty uses a desktop computer called **BETTY-PC** and a tablet called **BETTY-TABLET**, ATA will see that pattern and associate her user account with those devices. It also watches for her normal traffic patterns. Betty usually logs in around 8 a.m. and her traffic usually stops somewhere around 5 p.m. She typically accesses a few file servers and a SharePoint server. After a week or so of collecting and monitoring data, ATA has a pretty good idea of Betty's standard MO.

Now, one night, something happens. ATA sees a bunch of password failures against Betty's account. That in itself might not be something to get too excited about, but then all of a sudden Betty logs in to a terminal server that she doesn't typically access. From there, her credentials are used to access a domain controller. Uh oh, this clearly sounds like an attack to me. With the tools built into Active Directory that we currently have at our disposal, what do we know? Nothing, really. We might see the password failures if we dig into the event logs, and based on that, we could try poking around other servers' event logs in order to find out what that account was accessing, but we really wouldn't have any reason to suspect anything, nor any prompts or warnings that anything was happening whatsoever. This could be the beginning of a very large breach, and we would never see it. Thankfully, ATA knows better.

The management interface for ATA is like a social media feed, updated almost in real time. During the events I have just laid out, if we had been looking at the ATA media feed, we would have seen all of these items happen, as they happened, and it would be immediately obvious that someone compromised Betty's account and used it to gain access to a domain controller. There has never been a technology that watches Active Directory traffic so intensely, and there has certainly never been anything that learns patterns and behavioral diversions like this. It is truly an amazing technology, and I don't say that only because I happen to know the guys who built it. But since I do, I can tell you that they are brilliant, which is already pretty obvious since Microsoft scooped them up.

Even though this technology is now being morphed into something at the cloud level, let's take a few minutes and review a couple of screenshots from the ATA interface so you have an idea of what this social-media-style feed looks like. This screenshot was taken from a Microsoft demo where they purposefully stole the Kerberos ticket from a user, and then utilized it on another computer in order to access some confidential files that only Demi Albuz should have been able to access. While ATA did not stop this activity, it immediately—and I mean within seconds—alerted inside this feed to show the **Pass-the-Ticket Attack**:

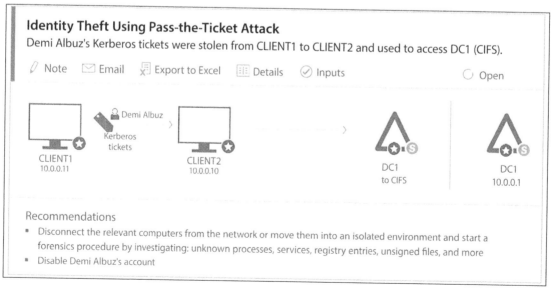

Figure 9.30: ATA identifying a pass-the-ticket-attack

Here's another example where a user named Almeta Whitfield suddenly accessed 16 computers that she does not usually access, another big red flag that something is going on with her user account:

Suspicion of identity theft based on abnormal behavior OPEN

Almeta Whitfield exhibited abnormal behavior when performing activities that were not seen over the last month and are also not in accordance with the activities of other accounts in the organization. The abnormal behavior is based on the following activities:

- Performed interactive login from 16 abnormal workstations.
- Requested access to 5 abnormal resources.

Figure 9.31: ATA alerts on abnormal behavior

Microsoft Defender for Identity

While ATA is an on-premises solution, its replacement lives in the cloud. **Microsoft Defender for Identity** is our new home for this type of technology, hosted of course within Microsoft Azure and M365 environments. Defender for Identity was not always named as such, and you will still find some documentation about this technology labeled as **Azure Advanced Threat Protection**, the name for what was to have been the direct ATA replacement, before Microsoft slid the capabilities under the Defender umbrella.

Documentation is still online for ATA, and further learning materials can be found here: `https://docs.microsoft.com/en-us/advanced-threat-analytics/what-is-ata`.

For more information on the new Microsoft Defender for Identity, the following link is a good starting point: `https://learn.microsoft.com/en-us/defender-for-identity/`.

General security best practices

Sometimes we need only to rely on ourselves, and not necessarily on functionality provided by the OS, to secure our systems. There are many common-sense approaches to administratorship (it's kind of fun being behind this keyboard: I get to make up new words all day long) that are easy to accomplish but are rarely used in the field.

The following are a few tips and tricks that I have learned over the years and have helped companies implement. Hopefully, you as the reader have even more to add to this list as to what works well for you, but if nothing else, this section is intended to jog your thinking into finding creative ways with which you can limit administrative capability and vulnerability within your network.

Getting rid of perpetual administrators

Do all of your IT staff have domain admin rights the day they are hired? Do any of your IT staff have access to the built-in domain administrator account password? Do you have regular users whose logins have administrative privileges on their own computers? You know where I'm going with this—these are all terrible ideas!

Unfortunately, that was all the status quo for many years in almost every network, and the trend continues today. I still regularly watch engineers use the **administrator** domain account for many tasks when setting up new servers. This means they not only have access to potentially the most important account in your network and use it for daily tasks but it also means that anything that is set up with this user account is not accountable. What do I mean by that? When I set up a new server or make changes to an existing server using the general administrator account, and I end up causing some kind of big problem, nobody can prove that I did it. Using generalized user accounts is a sure way to thwart responsibility in the event that something goes wrong. I'm not trying to imply that you are always on the lookout for "who dunnit," but if I mess something up on an application server that I don't normally administer, it would be nice if the guys trying to fix it could easily figure out that it was me and come ask me what I did so that they can reverse it. There are many reasons that using the built-in administrator account should be off-limits for all of us.

To address the client side, do your users really need administrative rights on their computers? *Really?* I think you could probably find ways around it. Bringing regular users down to user or even power user rights on their systems can have a huge impact on the security of those computers. It gives viruses a much harder time installing themselves if the user needs to walk through a prompt asking for admin privileges before they can proceed with the install. It also keeps all of your machines in a much more consistent behavioral pattern, without new and unknown applications and settings being introduced by the user.

Using distinct accounts for administrative access

This idea piggybacks off the last one and is something that I have started employing even on all of the home computers that I install for friends and family members. It really boils down to this: utilize two different user accounts. One with administrative access and one without. When you are logged in for daily tasks and chores, make sure that you are logged in with your regular user account that does not have administrative privileges, either on the local computer or on the domain. That way, if you attempt to install anything, or if something attempts to install itself, you will be prompted by the **User Account Control (UAC)** box, asking you to enter an administrative username and password before the installer is allowed to do anything. I can tell you that this works, as I have stopped a number of viruses and/or bloatware software on my own computer from installing themselves as I browsed around the internet trying to do research for one project or another. If I get a UAC prompt asking me for an admin password and I haven't intentionally clicked on an installer file, I know it's something I don't want. All I have to do is click on **No**, and that installer will not get a hold of my computer. On the other hand, if it is something that I am intending to install, then it is a minor inconvenience to simply enter the password of my administrative account and allow the installer to continue.

Maintaining two separate accounts allows you to work your way through most daily tasks while putting your mind at ease that you do not have the rights to inadvertently do something bad to your system. This mindset also naturally limits the amount of activity or changes performed on any given computer by an administrative account, meaning that the logging and tracking of changes by those accounts becomes easier. This results in greater accountability and better change management processes.

Using a different computer to accomplish administrative tasks

If you want to progress even further with the idea of separate user accounts, you could make your computing experience even more secure by utilizing a separate computer altogether when accomplishing administrative-level tasks: one computer for regular knowledge worker tasks and another computer for administration. This would certainly help to keep your administrative system secure, as well as the remote systems that it has access to. And while it does seem cumbersome to have two physical computers at your desk, remember that with most SKUs in Windows 10, we can run Hyper-V right on our desktop computers.

I do exactly this with my own computer. I have a computer that is running Windows 10, and then inside that computer, I am running a virtual machine via Hyper-V from which I do all administrative tasks on the sensitive servers. This way, a compromise of my day-to-day OS doesn't mean a compromise of the entire environment.

You could also employ this idea in reverse. When needing to test some new software, functionality, or link, you could spin up a VM in Hyper-V on your workstation, keep it fully disconnected from any networks so that it is sandboxed away, and test out whatever new or sketchy thing it is that you need to test. If it bombs your VM, no big deal. Just delete it and create a new one.

Whether you choose to split up administrative access at the user account level or the computer level, remember this simple rule: **never administer Active Directory from the same place that you browse Facebook**. I think that pretty well sums this one up.

Never browse the internet from servers

Seems like a no-brainer, but everyone does it. We spend all day working on servers and very often have to reach out and check something from a web browser. Since Edge and Internet Explorer exist on Windows servers, sometimes it is just quicker and easier to check whatever it is that we need to check from the server console where we are working, rather than walk back over to our desks. Sometimes (perhaps oftentimes) we even go the extra step, consciously installing a different, better browser onto servers just so it's there if ever we need it. Resist the temptation! It is so easy to pick up bad things from the internet, especially on servers because if any machines in our network are running without antivirus protection, it is probably on the server side. The same is true for internet filters. We always make sure that client traffic is flowing through our corporate proxy (if we have one) or other protection mechanisms, but we don't always care whether or not the server traffic is moving outward the same way.

Don't even do it for websites that you trust. A man-in-the-middle attack or a compromise of the website itself can easily corrupt your server, or worse give someone access to it and therefore the rest of your network. It's much easier to rebuild a client computer than it is to a server.

Role-Based Access Control (RBAC)

The phrase **Role-Based Access Control (RBAC)** is not one that is limited to Microsoft environments. It also is not a particular technology that can be utilized inside Windows Server 2022, but rather it is an ideology all about separating job roles and duties.

When we think about separating our employees' job roles from an IT perspective, we traditionally think in terms of Active Directory groups. While adding user accounts to groups does solve many problems about splitting up levels of permissions and access, it can be complicated to grow in this mentality, and ultimately AD groups still empower administrators with full access to the groups themselves. RBAC technologies divide up roles at a different level, caring about more than permissions. RBAC focuses more on employee job descriptions than access restrictions. There are a number of different technologies that take advantage of RBAC tools integrated into them, and there are even third-party RBAC solutions that ride on top of all your existing infrastructure, making it widely accessible across your entire organization and not restricted to working in the confines of a single domain or forest.

Just Enough Administration (JEA)

A great example of an RBAC technology that is included in Windows Server 2022 is **Just Enough Administration (JEA)**, which is part of PowerShell. JEA provides you with a way to grant special privileged access for people, without needing to give them administrative rights, which would have been required to accomplish the same duties in the past. The necessity to add someone to the administrators group on a server so that they can do their job is quite common, but JEA is a first step away from that necessity.

In our old way of thinking, it might be easy to think of JEA as doing something like allowing users to have administrative access within PowerShell even when they don't have administrative access to the OS itself, but it's even more powerful than that. The design of JEA is such that you can permit users to have access only to run particular PowerShell commands and cmdlets at an administrative level, leaving other commands that they do not need access to in the dark.

In fact, if a user is working within a JEA context of PowerShell and they try to invoke a cmdlet that is not part of their **allowed** cmdlets, PowerShell pretends as though it doesn't even recognize that cmdlet. It doesn't say, *sorry, you can't do this*—it just ignores the command! This definitely helps to keep prying fingers out of the cookie jar, unless you want to let them in.

Here's an example scenario that helps portray JEA capability. Maybe you are a DNS administrator, and you might occasionally need to restart DNS services. Since we are adopting the JEA/RBAC mentality, you are not going to have administrative rights on the OS of that DNS server, but you will have JEA-based rights within PowerShell so that you can run the tools that you need in order to do your work.

Restarting the DNS service requires access to use the `Restart-Service` cmdlet, right? But doesn't that mean I would be able to restart any service on that server and could potentially do all sorts of things that I don't need to do? JEA is even powerful enough to deal with this scenario. When setting up the level of access that the user needs to get, you can dive into particular cmdlets and divide up permissions. In our example, you could provide your DNS administrator with access to use the `Restart-Service` cmdlet, but only give permissions to restart particular services, such as those pertaining to DNS. If your admin tried `Restart-Service` on WINrm, they would be denied.

Adjust RDP away from 3389

Any IT engineer is familiar with RDPing into Windows Servers, and very likely this is the approach that *you* most often take when remotely controlling servers in your environment. Any hacker worthy of the title is also familiar with this, and would know that every single Windows machine, be it a client workstation or a server, listens by default on TCP port 3389 for those RDP connections to flow in. What is the point of this statement? If an attacker has gained access to a computer on your network, they have very quick and easy tools to discover the names of servers in your network. They can immediately attempt to start connecting to your servers via RDP, by simply typing the server name and using default port 3389. If they have already gained credentials in your network, they could potentially access all of your critical servers within seconds of entering the environment.

One barrier you can put in the bad guys' way is the use of ambiguous port numbers for RDP connectivity. There are still plenty of bad things they can do without RDPing into servers, and ultimately they will still eventually seek out these random RDP ports if they really want to, but you certainly will have slowed the process way down if each of your servers listens for RDP connections on a different port number.

Won't it become an annoyance and a burden on our IT administration team if they now have to document or remember all of these differing port numbers? You bet it will. But it will also annoy and burden your enemies, which is the point.

Many of you reading this may have had no idea this was even possible, and how would you unless you had done it before? There is no graphical-based setting for changing RDP port numbers, but this capability has existed for many generations of the Windows operating system.

Let's demonstrate. RDP is enabled on my WEB1 server. Currently, I can connect to it easily by opening `MSTSC.EXE`, typing WEB1, and clicking **Connect**. After entering credentials, I am immediately connected to WEB1 and driving its interface. The Remote Desktop Connection tool (MSTSC) is smart enough to know that if I don't specify a port number along with my server name, I intend to use the default port 3389 for connectivity. To change the port number that WEB1 uses to listen for RDP connections, I need to edit the registry and visit the following key:

```
HKEY_LOCAL_MACHINE\SYSTEM\CurrentControlSet\Control\ Terminal Server\
WinStations\RDP-Tcp
```

Inside that key, the registry value we want to change is called **PortNumber**. If you have never modified this before, you will find 3389 specified in decimal form.

Figure 9.32: Updating the RDP port number inside the registry

All you need to do is enter a new port number (make sure it isn't one that your server is already using by reviewing a `netstat` command output), and then reboot the server. Now that my WEB1 server is back up and running, you can see in the following screenshot that I can no longer create an RDP connection to WEB1 by simply using the server name; I now have to manually specify the new port number that I used (4095) to create that connection.

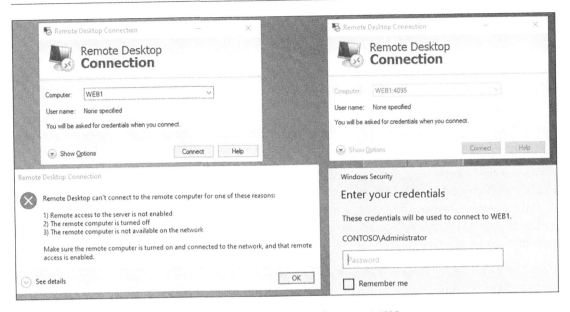

Figure 9.33: WEB1 is now listening on port 4095

Disable external RDP... NOW

We all know how to RDP into servers, and indeed I bet 99% of everyone reading this RDPs into servers most days of the week. Doing so from inside the corporate network is a fast and easy way to interact with servers, and it makes a lot of sense that we employ this technology. Have you ever thought about the possibility of allowing RDP access over the internet? Wouldn't it be nice if you could simply open up MSTSC on your home computer and hop right into your servers without having to first establish a cumbersome VPN? Have you done it? Do you have servers that right now have NAT rules configured in your firewall so that you can hit a certain port using RDP from anywhere in the world and RDP directly into your server?

STOP IT RIGHT NOW!

Shut down the port, delete the NAT rule, do not pass Go, do not collect $200.

This is the absolute worst idea, and yet I discover NAT rules just like this on a very regular basis. I often work with new companies, supporting various parts of their infrastructure, and during the discovery of these client networks, we always check over firewall rules. It is truly amazing how many places in the world have RDP access to servers open to the entire internet.

Now, perhaps you're saying to yourself, "Of course I don't do that! Well, I do, but I am tricky and use ambiguous port numbers for this access. You certainly won't find RDP port 3389 open on my firewall because I set up my NAT rules so that you have to connect to crazy things like port 33343 and 5896; nobody will ever find those. I'm surprised you are even asking us about this, Jordan, since you just showed us two pages ago how to change our RDP ports!"

You. Are. Wrong.

We're talking about the internet here. We're talking about thousands of 12-year-old Minecraft aficionados with absolutely infinite amounts of time on their hands. Oh no, I may have just offended any "professional hacker" reading this. Sorry not sorry.

It makes no difference whether your external ports are 3389 or 12345 or anything else. Attackers have port scanners that can easily seek out any open RDP channels; the port those RDP channels use makes no difference to them.

What's the risk? Everything. Ransomware. Your entire network going down. That is the risk. How do I know? Because I have helped multiple companies through restoring everything from backup, all of their servers, because of one little NAT rule that allowed RDP access into a single server from the internet. Just one little rule to one little server and the entire infrastructure was locked down by ransomware overnight.

If you allow RDP connections to flow into your network from a NAT rule that allows communication from the internet, it is literally only a matter of time before someone bad is inside your network. It will happen. The fact that it has not happened yet is simply luck.

Delete the firewall rules and lock it down immediately, and then look into a better way of providing RDP access remotely. This could mean launching a VPN from your client, or it could mean setting up an RD Gateway server in your environment. RD Gateways are secure, and I am in no way saying that your RD Gateway servers are risks because they allow RDP access to internal machines from the internet. That is their purpose, and they have mechanisms to make that kind of communication secure.

Disable insecure encryption protocols

Those of you who have managed web servers in recent years are likely familiar with disabling certain protocols, ciphers, and encryption algorithms that are old, out of date, and no longer secure by today's security standards. Anyone new to IT or server administration may have never even heard of these things, so let's talk about them now. When information crosses the internet between your user's computers and your servers, *hopefully* there is encryption happening on that traffic. If there is not, then you have bigger worries than what we are talking about right now.

Assuming there is encryption happening, it is quite likely that your traffic is using some flavor of encryption technology that has both old versions and new versions. The kinds of things I am talking about are SSL, TLS, AES, DES, Triple DES, SHA, Diffie-Hellman... the list goes on and on. These funny acronyms are the inner workings of how your traffic transports itself securely between the client and the server. Sometimes, these things fall out of date and out of support. As a couple of good real-world examples, SSL 3.0 and TLS 1.0 are still valid protocols, but they have become bad news over the past few years. These protocols have been replaced with newer versions, and the old ones are no longer being supported or patched in any way, and if you have websites or applications making use of these old protocols, all of that traffic is in real danger of compromise.

It is a fairly common service desk ticket to receive communication from a software vendor, or from your PCI compliance vendor, asking you to review your such-and-such system and make sure that some of these protocols or ciphers are disabled. If they are disabled on your servers, no clients (good or bad) will be able to tap into them. When you receive such a request and need to make sure that the old, bad protocols are disabled, where do we even start with making a change like this?

Windows Registry

On Windows Server, you can enable or disable these protocols and ciphers by modifying the registry. This is fairly straightforward once you have the locations saved and have been through the process a few times, but no matter how many times I do it this way, I am never left feeling 100% confident that I accomplished the change properly. In any case, to round out knowledge on this baseline way to adjust protocols in Windows Server, here is the primary registry location from which you can add or remove registry values to enable or disable specific protocols and cipher suites:

```
HKEY_LOCAL_MACHINE\SYSTEM\CurrentControlSet\Control\SecurityProviders\SCHANNEL\
Protocols
```

It would take many pages to type up all of the different exact registry values that pertain to different protocols and suites, so I am not going to do that. Instead, here is a link to a Microsoft article that outlines many of the possible settings for an AD FS server:

https://learn.microsoft.com/en-us/windows-server/identity/ad-fs/operations/manage-ssl-protocols-in-ad-fs

Take a look over all the possible registry changes here, and I think you'll agree with me that it quickly becomes a muddy mess of confusion. So, while it is absolutely possible to disable old and insecure ciphers using the registry method, I strongly recommend...

IIS Crypto

This free tool created by Nartac Software makes protocol, cipher, hash, and key exchange adjustments *so much easier* than editing the registry. All you need to do is search the web for a quick download and run this program on the server for which you want to make changes. It is a standalone executable, no need to install software to make this happen. As soon as IIS Crypto opens, it will show you all of the different protocols and ciphers that could be used on this server, with checkboxes next to each one.

To enable or disable each protocol, simply check or uncheck the box next to its name. It's that easy! What this tool is really doing is making the registry changes for you, so that you don't have to worry about finding them and inputting the correct syntax. When you check a box, it creates the corresponding registry value and sets it to enabled. When you uncheck a box, it changes the regkey to disabled. You'll notice a lot of gray checks when you first launch IIS Crypto, and that is indicating that there is currently no registry value whatsoever for that particular protocol, which is the default state on any server. When you check or uncheck a box and click the **Apply** button, it then creates the regkey and sets its value accordingly.

You can see in the following screenshot that I have some protocols disabled on this server, including SSL 3.0 and TLS 1.0.

Figure 9.34: IIS Crypto is an easy way to implement protocol security

Any changes that you make, whether they be via IIS Crypto or taking the hard road and modifying the registry yourself, will be active the next time you restart your server. Remember, a restart is necessary before you can consider your security changes to be working!

Summary

The number-one agenda item for many CIOs is security. Security for your client machines, security for your networks, security for your cloud resources, and most importantly security for your data. There is no single solution for securing your infrastructure; it requires many moving parts and many different technologies all working together to provide safety for your resources. The purpose of this chapter was to provide examples of security measures and technologies that can be utilized in anyone's environment, as well as to reprioritize the importance that security has in today's IT world. Concerns about privacy and security need to be discussed for any and every technology solution that we put into place. Too many times do I find new applications being implemented inside organizations without any regard for how secure that application platform is. Applications that transmit or store data unencrypted need to be modified or dumped. Protection of information is essential to the longevity of our businesses.

We cannot complete a discussion about security in Windows Server 2022 without discussing the other OS installation option that we have thus far ignored throughout this book. In the next chapter, we'll dive into Server Core, our headless and less vulnerable version of Windows Server.

Questions

1. What is the name of the antimalware product built into Windows Server 2022?
2. When a domain-joined computer is sitting inside the corporate LAN, which Windows Defender Firewall profile should be active?
3. Other than the Domain Profile, what are the other two possible firewall profiles inside Windows Defender Firewall?
4. When creating a firewall rule to allow IPv4 ping replies, what protocol type must you specify inside your inbound rule?
5. What is the easiest way to push standardized Windows Defender Firewall rules to your entire workforce?
6. A virtual machine whose virtual hard disk file is encrypted is called a...?
7. What is the name of the Microsoft technology that parses domain controller information in order to identify pass-the-hash and pass-the-ticket-attacks?
8. Which inbound RDP port number is considered safe to open on your external firewall?
9. What third-party tool can you use to disable TLS 1.0 on Windows Server?

Join our community on Discord

Join our community's Discord space for discussions with the author and other readers:

`https://packt.link/SecNet`

10

Server Core

Honey, I shrunk the server! Another chapter, another outdated movie reference. Over the past 20 years or so, we have seen nothing but growth from Microsoft operating systems. Growth can be good; new features and enhancements make our lives easier. But growth can also be bad, such as bloated file structures and memory-hogging graphical interfaces. If you were to chronologically graph the Windows and Windows Server operating systems in terms of their footprints, based on factors such as disk space consumption and memory requirements, it would show a steady upward slope. Every new release seems to require just a little more processing power and just a little more hard drive space than the previous version. I always find it intriguing how many critical pieces of the operating system are still hanging around in locations and folders left over from Server 2003 or even earlier. Even on a brand-new Windows Server 2022 instance you will find all kinds of things inside `C:\Windows\System32`. We're not even going to talk about what's in the registry. I suppose that moving, renaming, or changing these core components could prove to be detrimental to many aspects of Windows, and so they may remain the same forevermore. This limits the amount of cleanup and downsizing that could ever happen, unless a fairly drastic approach were to be taken by approaching Windows Server as a whole different type of operating system platform.

Here, we are going to talk about an alternative way to use Windows Server 2022 on a much, much smaller scale. Server Core has been around for quite some time now, but I'm hard-pressed to find people who actually use it. This miniaturized version of Server 2022 has been built to provide you with a smaller, more efficient, and more secure server platform.

We will cover the following topics in this chapter:

- Why use Server Core?
- Interfacing with Server Core
- Windows Admin Center to manage Server Core
- The `Sconfig` utility
- Roles available in Server Core
- Building a Server Core domain controller
- What happened to Nano Server?

Why use Server Core?

Why am I even talking about Server Core? Hasn't it been around since 2008? Yes, that is exactly why I *am* talking about it. The Server Core variant of the Windows Server operating system has been around for quite some time, but it seems like many admins are afraid to use it. I work with many different companies from many different industries. Most of them have one big thing in common: they use a lot of Windows Servers, and all of these Windows Servers run the full GUI (Desktop Experience). Have they heard of Server Core? Sure. Have they tested it out in a lab? Sometimes. Everyone seems to have a slightly different experience level with Core, but it's quite rare to find one in production. Maybe I'm just talking to the wrong people, but I have to assume that there is a majority of us out there, myself included, who need to start using Server Core on a more regular basis.

Why do we need to start using Server Core? Because GUI-less servers are the future, says Microsoft. Would you believe that early in the previews for Windows Server 2016, the Desktop Experience option didn't even exist? You couldn't run a full GUI desktop shell on Server 2016 even if you wanted to (which everyone did), other than a mini-shell that could be plopped on top of Server Core. Microsoft received so much flack about this that the full Desktop Experience was added back during one of the technical preview rollouts. Even so, since that time, you have probably noticed that Server Core is the default option when installing any Windows Server operating system. Remember the beginning of our book, where we did a quick review of the actual Server 2022 installation? The default option for installation is not Desktop Experience; rather, the top option in *Figure 10.1* is the one to install the command-line-driven Server Core:

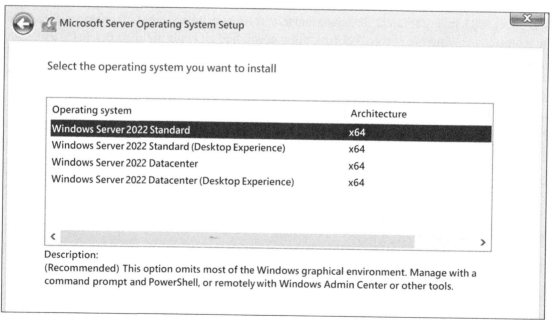

Figure 10.1: The default installation option is Server Core

One of the reasons for a move away from the graphical interface is increased capabilities for automation and scalability. When all of our servers are built similarly, it means that we can do more cloud-like functions with them. Automatic spinning up and down of resources as they are needed, rolling out dozens of servers at the flip of a switch—this kind of automation and sizing is possible in the cloud, but it is only possible because the infrastructure is set up in a way that it is so standardized. Cloud hardware resources need to be so streamlined that the operations and automation tools can make them do what is needed, without worrying about all of the variables that would be present in a user-tweaked graphical interface.

There are other obvious advantages to running all of your servers on this limited, restricted version. Server Core boasts reduced hard drive space, reduced memory consumption, and a reduced attack surface when compared to a traditional, full-blown server experience. Now you can see why I made the hefty statements a minute ago about how we all need to start becoming more comfortable with Server Core! In fact, let's take a look at that reduced footprint. A base Server 2022 Standard running Desktop Experience consumes around 10 GB of hard drive space; I just verified this by taking a look at the properties of my virtual hard disk file being used by my RDS1 server. RDS1 is a standard Windows Server 2022 that runs the full Desktop Experience. Now, I have just finished running through the installation for my first Server Core 2022 operating system, and we can see in *Figure 10.2* that the VHDX file being used by this new VM is only 6.75 GB, a 30% reduction in space:

Figure 10.2: Server Core has a smaller footprint than Standard

No more switching back and forth

There is a very important note that I wanted to make here: those of you who worked with Server Core in Windows Server 2012 R2 know that we had the option of changing a server *on the fly*. What I mean is that if you created a new server as the full Desktop Experience, you could later change it to Server Core. The opposite approach was equally possible; you could take Server Core and flip it over to a full Desktop Experience. While this capability existed, it actually enabled more people to use Server Core because it meant that even if you knew nothing about interfacing with Server Core, you could build a new server in a graphical way as you would with any other server, install roles and get them configured, and when you were finished, switch it to Server Core, effectively disabling the graphical interface.

Not anymore! This capability to move servers back and forth between platforms has been removed. I repeat, *this is no longer possible*. So, plan carefully from here on out when installing these operating systems. If you implement a server as Server Core, that guy is going to remain a Server Core for its lifetime.

Interfacing with Server Core

After running through your first installation of Server Core, you will be presented with the following lock screen:

Figure 10.3: Server Core lock screen

Is that really a Command Prompt window that says **Press Ctrl-Alt-Del to unlock**? Yes, yes it is. This usually gets a few chuckles when an admin sees it for the first time. I know it did for me, anyway. It reminds me a little of when we used to code if/then games on our TI-83 calculators during high school math class. Press *Ctrl + Alt + Del*, and you will be prompted to change your administrator password for the first time, which is the same task that must always be performed first inside GUI versions of Windows Server. Except, of course, that you do it all from within the Command Prompt window using only your keyboard. After configuring your administrator account password, the login process continues, and you'll even notice some familiar things fly past on this Command Prompt window, such as "Preparing Windows" and "Applying settings."

If you are installing Server Core in earlier versions of Windows Server, such as 2019 or 2016, then you will find yourself now looking at a standard blinking Command Prompt cursor, awaiting your input. The operating system is loaded in the background, and it presents you with this simple interface from which you can run any standard commands as you wish.

One of the common things for administrators to run from this Command Prompt window is a configuration utility called Sconfig. We will talk more about what exactly Sconfig is and can do for you later in this chapter, but the primary point to mention here is that, starting with Windows Server 2022, Server Core now launches Sconfig automatically upon login, as you can see in *Figure 10.4*.

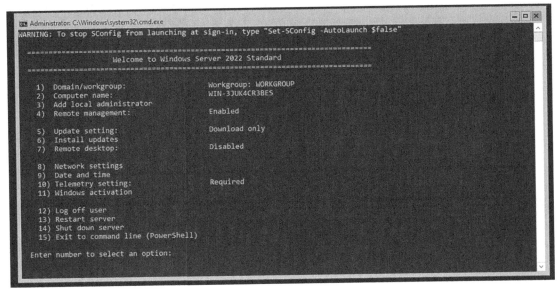

Figure 10.4: Server Core now auto-launches Sconfig

Interestingly, this Command Prompt window doesn't consume our entire screen real estate; it is clear that there is a black background and cmd.exe is riding on top of it. I find this interesting because you can tell that the Core operating system itself is something other than Command Prompt, and that cmd.exe is just an application that auto-launches upon login. You can even utilize the mouse here and resize or move that Command Prompt window around. I do wonder again and again with every new Server iteration if and when this will be replaced with a PowerShell prompt as the default interface.

Even more interesting and good to know is that you can launch some GUI-like applications from this prompt. The easiest way to do this is to exit the Sconfig utility by typing option 15 and pressing *Enter*. This will eject your Sconfig session and bring you back to a standard Command Prompt.

From here, you can do something like open up Notepad and utilize it with both a keyboard and mouse, just like you would from any version of Windows. If you have Notepad open, create a note and then save it; you can see that there is a real file structure and a set of relatively normal-looking system folders.

So, rather than some form of black magic, Server Core is actually the real Windows Server operating system, wrapped up in a smaller and more secure package:

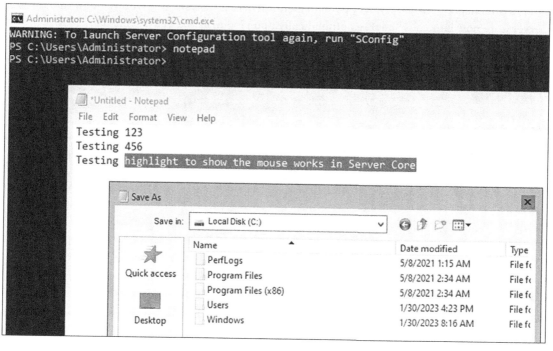

Figure 10.5: Opening Notepad on Server Core

PowerShell

So, as far as managing Server Core, you can obviously work straight from the console and use Command Prompt to accomplish many things on this server. In reality, though, the commands and functions available from inside Command Prompt will be limited. If you are working from the console of a Windows Server Core box, it makes much more sense to use Command Prompt for just one purpose—to invoke PowerShell, and then use it to accomplish whatever tasks you need to do on that server. The quickest way I know to move into PowerShell from the basic Command Prompt is to simply type the word powershell and press *Enter*. This will bring PowerShell capabilities right into your existing Command Prompt window so that you can start interfacing with the PowerShell commands and cmdlets that you need, in order to really manipulate this server:

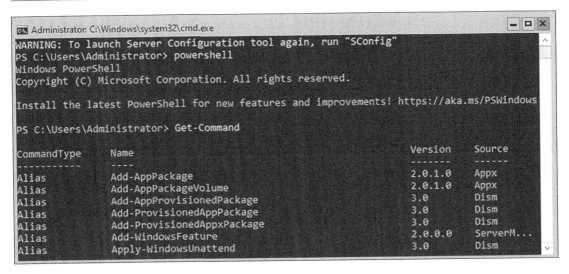

Figure 10.6: Loading PowerShell inside Server Core

What is the first thing we typically do on new servers? Give them IP addresses, of course. Without network connectivity, there isn't much that we can do on this server. You can assign IP address information to NICs using PowerShell on any newer Windows Server, but most of us are not in the habit of doing so. Since we can't just open up **Control Panel** and get into the Network and Sharing Center like we can from inside the Desktop Experience GUI of Windows Server, where do we begin to get network connectivity on this new Server Core?

Using cmdlets to manage IP addresses

There are cmdlets that you can use to view and manipulate IP address settings from within PowerShell. Again, these same cmdlets can be used in the full GUI version of Windows Server or from within Server Core.

As we are currently working from Server Core where we only have command-line interfacing available to us, these cmdlets are essential to get network connectivity flowing on our new server:

- `Get-NetIPConfiguration`: This displays the current networking configuration.
- `Get-NetIPAddress`: This displays the current IP addresses.
- `Get-NetIPInterface`: This shows a list of NICs and their interface ID numbers. This number is going to be important when setting an IP address because we want to make sure we tell PowerShell to configure the right IP on the right NIC.
- `New-NetIPAddress`: This is used to configure a new IP address.
- `Set-DNSClientServerAddress`: This is used to configure DNS server settings in the NIC properties.

Let's quickly walk through the setup of a static IP address on a new Server Core instance to make sure this all makes sense. I want to assign the `10.10.10.12` IP address to this new server, but first, we need to find out which NIC interface ID number it needs to be assigned to. The output of `Get-NetIPInterface` tells us that the `ifIndex` for my Ethernet NIC is number 4:

Figure 10.7: Finding the interface ID number for your NIC

Alternatively, or as a double-check, you could also run `route print` and verify your interface ID number near the top of that output. You can see in *Figure 10.8* that my Hyper-V NIC on this Server Core VM is interface 4 (shown at the left of the output):

Figure 10.8: Confirming the interface ID via route print

Now that we know the interface number, let's build the commands that are going to assign the new IP address settings to the NIC. I am going to use one command to assign the IP address, subnet mask prefix, and default gateway. I will use a second command to assign DNS server addresses:

```
New-NetIPAddress -InterfaceIndex 4 -IPAddress 10.10.10.12 -PrefixLength 24
-DefaultGateway 10.10.10.1
Set-DNSClientServerAddress -InterfaceIndex 4 -ServerAddresses
10.10.10.10,10.10.10.11
```

Figure 10.9 shows us the resulting output:

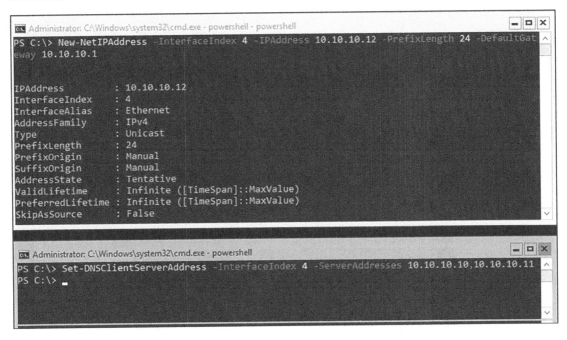

Figure 10.9: Assigning IP and DNS server addresses

 Hold the phone! How did I get *two* PowerShell prompts open at the same time within the Server Core interface? Make sure to read the *Accidentally closing Command Prompt* section later in this chapter to discover how you can launch multiple windows and tools inside the Server Core console.

Now, all of these IP settings should be in place on the NIC. Let's double-check that with a Get-NetIPConfiguration command, seen in *Figure 10.10*. Alternatively, you could use good old ipconfig to check these settings, but where's the fun in that?

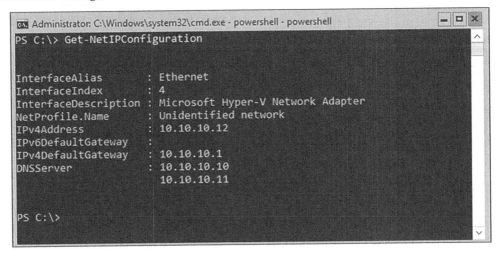

Figure 10.10: Checking IP configuration

Remember, you can always utilize DHCP reservations to make this a little bit easier. If you were to run a simple `ipconfig /all` from your Server Core and jot down the MAC address of your NIC, you could use this address to create a reservation in DHCP and assign a specific IP address to the new server that way.

Setting the server hostname

Now that we have network connectivity, a good next step is setting the hostname of our server and joining it to the domain. First things first, let's see what the current name of the server is, and change it to something that fits our standards. When you freshly install Windows, it self-assigns a random hostname to the server. You can view the current hostname by simply typing `hostname` and pressing *Enter*:

Figure 10.11: Checking the current server hostname

To change the hostname of your server, we need to use PowerShell. Bring yourself into a PowerShell prompt if not already there, and all we need to do is use the `Rename-Computer` cmdlet to set our new hostname. I have decided to name this new server WEB4 because, later, we will install the Web Services role onto it and host a website. Remember, after renaming your computer, just like in the GUI version of Windows Server, a system restart is necessary to put that change into action. So, following your `Rename-Computer` command, you can issue a `Restart-Computer` command to reboot the VM:

```
Rename-Computer WEB4
Restart-Computer
```

```
Administrator: C:\Windows\system32\cmd.exe
PS C:\Users\Administrator> Rename-Computer WEB4
WARNING: The changes will take effect after you restart the computer WIN-3JUK4CR3BES.
PS C:\Users\Administrator> Restart-Computer_
```

Figure 10.12: Changing the hostname and restarting your system

Joining your domain

The next logical step is, of course, joining your domain. These are the standard functions that we would perform on any new server in our environment but done in a way that you may have never encountered before, since we are doing all of this strictly from the Command Prompt and PowerShell interfaces.

To join a Server Core to your domain, head into PowerShell and then use the `Add-Computer` cmdlet. You will be asked to specify both the domain name and your credentials for joining the domain—the same information you would have to specify if you were joining a Windows Server 2022 in Desktop Experience mode to a domain.

First, you must specify the credentials that will be used to accomplish this domain join:

Figure 10.13: Entering credentials authorized to join this system to your domain

Then you tell it what domain you would like to join:

```
PS C:\> Add-Computer

cmdlet Add-Computer at command pipeline position 1
Supply values for the following parameters:
Credential
DomainName: Contoso.local
WARNING: The changes will take effect after you restart the computer
WEB4.
PS C:\> _
```

Figure 10.14: Specifying the domain to join

Alternatively, you could utilize the `-DomainName` parameter in combination with the original `Add-Computer` cmdlet to specify the name of the domain as part of the original command. And of course, after joining the domain, you need to utilize `Restart-Computer` once again to finalize this change.

Remote PowerShell

Once the new server is IP-addressed, named, and domain-joined, we can start doing some real administration on this new Server Core instance. You could certainly continue to log in and interface directly with the console, but as with managing any other server in your environment, there must be ways to handle this remotely, right? One of the ways that you can manipulate Server Core without having to sit in front of it is by using a remote PowerShell connection.

We will cover the process to use remote PowerShell to manipulate servers (both GUI and headless) in more detail in *Chapter 11*, *PowerShell*, but here is a glimpse of the commands necessary and the capabilities present when you can achieve a remote session from a PowerShell prompt, on a workstation inside a domain-joined environment.

Open up PowerShell from another system—this can be a server or even a client operating system. This PowerShell window is obviously open within the context of whatever machine you are currently logged in to, and any commands you issue via PowerShell will elicit a response from the local system. To tap PowerShell into the WEB4 Server Core instance, I will issue the following command. After running this, I am prompted for a password corresponding to the administrator account, and I will then be able to issue remote PowerShell commands against our Server Core:

```
Enter-PSSession -ComputerName WEB4 -Credential administrator
```

Figure 10.15: Using Enter-PSSession to remotely connect to WEB4

Now we are sitting at a PowerShell prompt, remotely connected to the WEB4 Server Core box. You can see this by [WEB4] being listed to the left of our prompt. Perhaps you don't trust that little identifier, and you want to make sure that this PowerShell window now accesses and manipulates the remote WEB4 server?

Let's issue a couple of quick commands, such as hostname and ipconfig, to prove that the information being given to us in this PowerShell session really comes from the new WEB4 server:

```
Administrator: Windows PowerShell                                       —   □   ×
PS C:\> Enter-PSSession -ComputerName WEB4 -Credential administrator
[WEB4]: PS C:\Users\Administrator.CONTOSO\Documents>
[WEB4]: PS C:\Users\Administrator.CONTOSO\Documents> hostname
WEB4
[WEB4]: PS C:\Users\Administrator.CONTOSO\Documents>
[WEB4]: PS C:\Users\Administrator.CONTOSO\Documents> ipconfig

Windows IP Configuration


Ethernet adapter Ethernet:

   Connection-specific DNS Suffix  . :
   Link-local IPv6 Address . . . . . : fe80::e434:239b:762f:6b19%4
   IPv4 Address. . . . . . . . . . . : 10.10.10.12
   Subnet Mask . . . . . . . . . . . : 255.255.255.0
   Default Gateway . . . . . . . . . : 10.10.10.1
```

Figure 10.16: PowerShell now responds as if I was logged in to WEB4

Now that we have a remote PowerShell connection to this new Server Core, we can do pretty much whatever we want to that server, right from this console. Commands and cmdlets issued inside this remote PowerShell session will manipulate WEB4, rather than our local workstation.

Server Manager

While the initial configuration of your server will be handled to a degree from the command-line interfaces available at the console, once your server has been established on the network, it will likely be more advantageous for you to expand your horizons a little. You could probably find PowerShell cmdlets that allow you to manage and manipulate anything in your new server, but that is still a pretty new mentality for most of us—we are generally more accustomed to using graphical tools such as Server Manager. You already know that Server Manager can be used to manage multiple servers, local and remote, and is a piece of the Microsoft *centralized management* puzzle. This remote management capability in Server Manager, which we explored earlier in the book, allows you to tap into not only GUI-based Windows Servers but also Server Core instances.

I want to install a role on my new WEB4 server. I could do that with PowerShell right on the server console, but instead let's try adding WEB4 into Server Manager, which runs on another one of my servers. I am going to log in to WEB3 and use Server Manager from there. Just like we already saw, I can add a new server into Server Manager by using the **Manage** menu and choosing **Add Servers**:

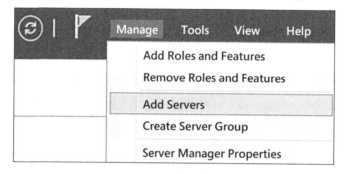

Figure 10.17: Adding new servers to be managed inside Server Manager

Let's add the new WEB4 server to our list of managed machines, and it is now manageable from inside this instance of Server Manager. Getting back to what my original intentions were, I want to install the Web Server (IIS) role on WEB4. If I use the **Add roles and features** function inside Server Manager, I can now choose to manipulate the WEB4 server:

Figure 10.18: Modifying WEB4 from WEB3's Server Manager

Just like with any server running the full Desktop Experience version of Windows Server, we can now finish walking through the role installation wizard, and the Web Server role will be installed on WEB4.

Remote Server Administration Tools

Also true is the fact that you can manage Server Core instances with the **Remote Server Administration Tools (RSAT)** in Windows 10. RSAT is essentially just a copy of Server Manager and accompanying administrative tools that are designed to run on the client operating system. In our case, I already have a Windows 10 machine on which I installed RSAT earlier in the book, so I will test this by logging in to that guy and adding WEB4 to the interface. I just finished installing the IIS role on WEB4 in our previous task, so I should be able to see that listed inside RSAT when I connect it to WEB4.

If you haven't used RSAT before and haven't read over that section of our text, it is important to know that there is no application called **Remote Server Administration Tools**. Instead, after the RSAT installation has been completed, take a look inside your **Start** menu for the application called **Server Manager**. This is how you utilize a Windows 10 client to remotely manage Windows Server 2022 (or other version) instances:

Figure 10.19: Server Manager inside Windows 10, courtesy of RSAT

Precisely as you would do from a Server Manager interface of Windows Server 2022, go ahead and walk through the wizard to add other servers to manage. Once I have added WEB4 as a managed server in my Windows 10's Server Manager, I can see **IIS** listed inside my **Dashboard**. This indicates that the IIS service running on WEB4 is visible, accessible, and configurable right from my Windows 10 desktop computer. For the majority of the tasks that I need to accomplish on WEB4, I will never have to worry about logging in to the console of that server.

If I right-click on the WEB4 server name from within this RSAT console, you can see that I have many features available to me that I can use to manage this remote Server Core instance:

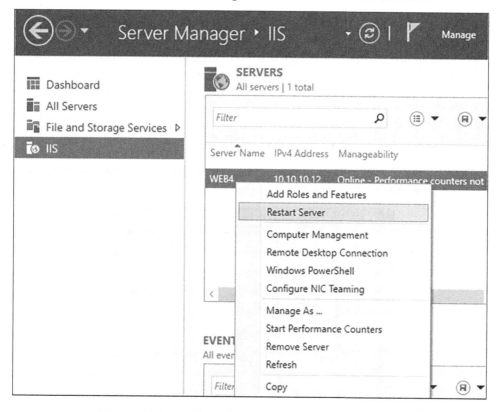

Figure 10.20: Interacting with remote servers via Server Manager

So, you can see that there are ways to use the GUI tools to manage our GUI-less instances of Windows Server. It's just a matter of putting your mind into a place where you think of servers as headless, and that tools such as PowerShell or Server Manager really don't care at all whether the server they are changing is local or remote. The processes and tools are the same either way. You can see in the previous screenshot that I could even click from here to launch a remote PowerShell connection to WEB4. Clicking on this button immediately launches a PowerShell prompt that is remotely tied to the WEB4 server, even though I am currently only logged in to my Windows 10 workstation. This is even easier than issuing the Enter-PSSession cmdlet from inside PowerShell.

Accidentally closing Command Prompt

Let's now take a look at one more thing directly from the Server Core console; this is a common hurdle to overcome if you haven't utilized Server Core much. We tend to close windows and applications that are no longer being used, so you might unconsciously close the Command Prompt window that serves your entire administrative existence within a Server Core console session. Now you're sitting at a large blank screen, with seemingly no interface and nowhere to go from here.

How do you get back to work on this server? Do we have to turn the server off and back on to reset it? That would interrupt any roles or traffic that this server might serve up to users, so obviously isn't the ideal approach.

New in Windows Server 2022 is a feature where, if an administrator accidentally closes the Server Core Command Prompt instance, it will automatically re-launch a new one. This is so nice! And it even works most of the time, but I have had some instances where the auto-re-launch did not happen, and so I was still stuck sitting on a completely empty black screen, just like what happens in any previous versions of Server Core.

In the event that the auto-launch does not happen, or if you administer Server Core on an older version of Windows Server, there is a simple way to get Command Prompt back, and that is by using **Task Manager** to launch a new instance of Command Prompt. After mistakenly closing your current Command Prompt window, when sitting at the empty black screen of a Server Core console, you can press *Ctrl + Alt + Del* and you will be presented with the following options:

Figure 10.21: Ctrl + Alt + Del works inside Server Core

There are a few different functions you can perform here, which is pretty neat. But to get our Command Prompt window back, arrow-down to **Task Manager** and press *Enter*. This will launch the **Task Manager** application that we are all familiar with. Now, click on **More details** to expand Task Manager's screens. Drop down the **File** menu, and then click on **Run new task**:

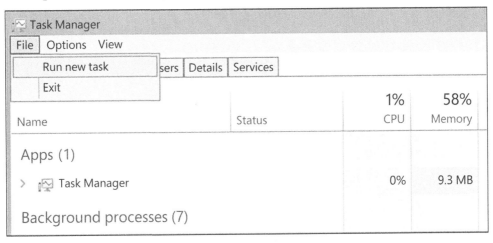

Figure 10.22: Running a new task via Task Manager

In the **Create new task** box, type cmd and then click **OK**:

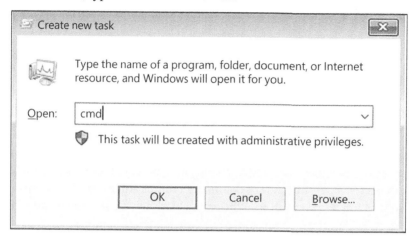

Figure 10.23: Opening Command Prompt

Alternatively, you could specify to launch any application directly from this **Create new task** prompt. If you were interested in moving straight into PowerShell, instead of typing cmd, you could instead simply type powershell into that prompt, and it would open directly:

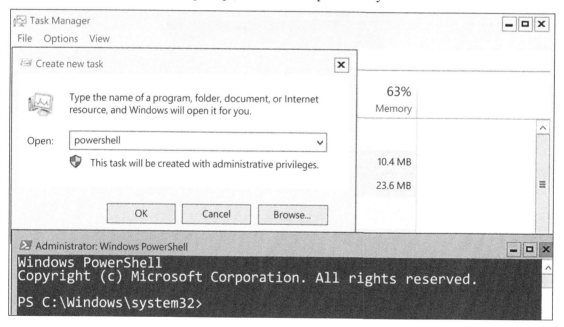

Figure 10.24: Opening PowerShell in Server Core

Windows Admin Center to manage Server Core

While Command Prompt from the console, remote PowerShell connections, remote Server Manager administration, and even the RSAT tools running on a Windows 10 workstation are all valid and powerful tools to administer our Server Core instances, they have all now been upstaged by the release of **Windows Admin Center (WAC)**. You already learned what WAC can do to centrally manage your entire server infrastructure, but what we need to point out here is that WAC can be used for servers both with and without graphical interfaces.

I have spoken with many Windows Server administrators about the topic of Server Core, and one of the biggest blocks to implementing these more efficient and secure server platforms is an apprehension that, once configured, ongoing administration and maintenance of these servers will be more difficult to handle. Admins who are familiar and comfortable working with the Windows Server Desktop Experience know exactly what needs to be done to accomplish their daily tasks, but remove that point-and-click interface and suddenly the workday gets a lot more complicated.

Thankfully, you don't have to memorize the PowerShell handbook to use Server Core! WAC treats Server Core instances in the same way that it does a server running Desktop Experience. It just works!

We already have WAC installed on a server in our test lab, so let's open it up, add the new WEB4 server to be administered, and take a look at what options are available for the ongoing maintenance of this server.

When we first connect to WEB4 via the WAC console, there is nothing in here that even indicates this is a Server Core instance. We have all of the WAC tools and utilities available to click on:

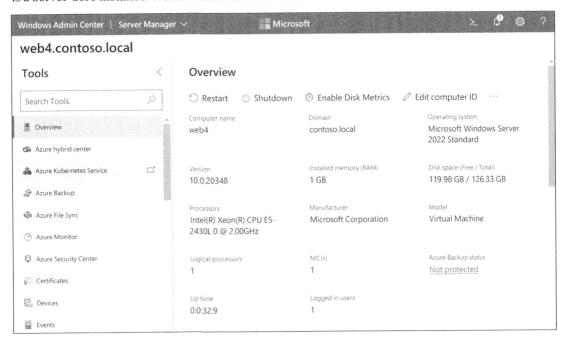

Figure 10.25: WAC overview of WEB4

Let's try a couple of things from WAC. You have power controls right near the top of the screen from which you can easily shut down or restart the server. That is much easier and faster than having to establish a remote PowerShell connection from which you can issue commands to accomplish the same actions. There are also performance metrics on the home screen (if you scroll down), showing your consumed **CPU**, **Memory**, and **Networking** resources. Without WAC, you would need to log in to WEB4 and launch **Task Manager** to see these statistics:

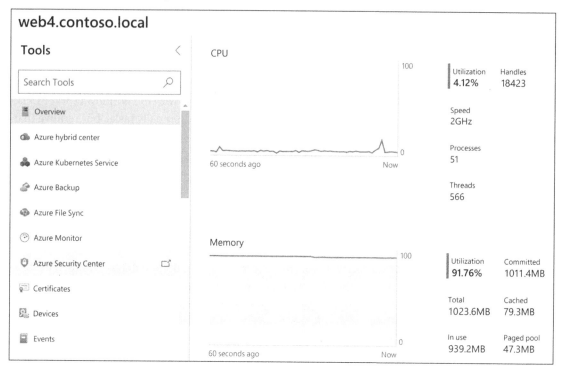

Figure 10.26: Server performance metrics

Moving away from the home screen, as useful as it is, try clicking on one of the tools listed along the left side of the screen, such as **Events**. Without WAC, if you wanted to troubleshoot an issue on a Server Core, it would make sense to look into the Windows event logs on that server, but how would you go about doing that from a command-line interface? I suppose you could have logged on to the Server Core console and used **Task Manager** to launch EventVwr, but opening up WAC and simply clicking on **Events** is much easier:

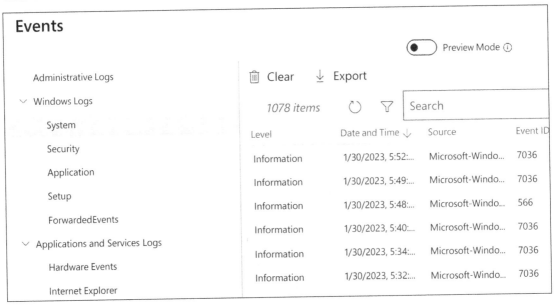

Figure 10.27: System event logs

Other examples of useful functions inside WAC, particularly when working with a Server Core instance, are using **Files & file sharing** to navigate the file and folder structure of the hard drive of WEB4, or using the **Firewall** function here to create or remove Windows firewall rules on WEB4. There is also a **Networks** tool, from which you can manipulate IP addressing configurations.

While many more tools exist inside WAC, the last thing I want to point out is that, once again, we have a **PowerShell** option (similar to what we can launch from inside Server Manager). This **PowerShell** button will invoke and display for us a remote PowerShell connection to the WEB4 Server Core instance, for if ever we can't find a function that is needed inside WAC and need to dive a little further under the hood to accomplish something from a command-line interface. And the best part is that you never actually have to launch PowerShell! This still all happens from within your internet browser window:

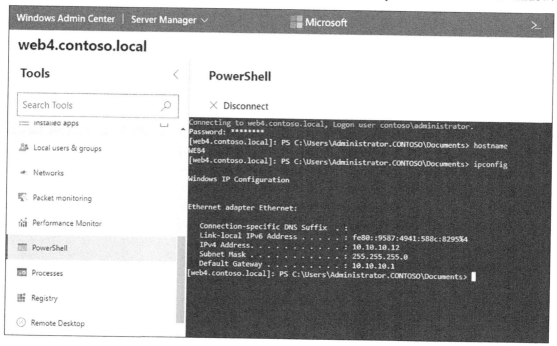

Figure 10.28: Using PowerShell inside WAC

There is so much more that can be accomplished from inside WAC—editing the **Registry**, adding **Roles & Features**, checking the status of your **Services**, and even interfacing with Windows Update. If you aren't already using WAC, you're missing the boat!

The Sconfig utility

Now we will take a step backward and check out a tool that is available inside Server Core, but one that is generally only useful when working on the console of your server. We mentioned Sconfig earlier in the chapter, but breezed right past it at the time so that you could focus on getting to know Server Core a little bit more intimately from Command Prompt and PowerShell. While you can certainly ignore Sconfig completely and make all configurations and adjustments to your Server Core from the traditional command-line interfaces and centralized administration tools, Sconfig is a very nice utility to make initial networking, hostname, and domain membership changes to your new server.

`Sconfig` has existed for most versions of Server Core, but in the past you always had to intentionally launch it to make use of the capabilities within. Windows Server 2022 is the first time we see it with an auto-launch feature when your server boots. If you have built your own Server Core version of Server 2022 while reading through this chapter, you certainly already saw the `Sconfig` interface, as it launches immediately after logging into your Server Core.

```
■ Administrator: C:\Windows\system32\cmd.exe                                      _ □ ✕
WARNING: To stop SConfig from launching at sign-in, type "Set-SConfig -AutoLaunch $false"

        =======================================================================
                        Welcome to Windows Server 2022 Standard
        =======================================================================

        1)  Domain/workgroup:               Domain: contoso.local
        2)  Computer name:                  WEB4
        3)  Add local administrator
        4)  Remote management:              Enabled

        5)  Update setting:                 Download only
        6)  Install updates
        7)  Remote desktop:                 Disabled

        8)  Network settings
        9)  Date and time
        10) Telemetry setting:              Required
        11) Windows activation

        12) Log off user
        13) Restart server
        14) Shut down server
        15) Exit to command line (PowerShell)

Enter number to select an option: _
```

Figure 10.29: Sconfig auto-launches upon server login

The options available inside `Sconfig` are fairly self-explanatory, but we'll cover the common tasks performed here. Again, these are all things that you could instead accomplish via PowerShell cmdlets, but I find it easier to take the Sconfig approach. The most common uses of this interface are to configure initial networking settings by pressing *8,* or to configure the server hostname and domain membership by using options *2* and *1.*

I will go ahead and press *2* on my keyboard and then press *Enter*, and I am immediately presented with a prompt asking me to specify a new computer name. This is an extremely fast way to configure the hostname of new Server Core servers. Since I don't actually want to rename `WEB4`, I will leave the selection blank and press *Enter* to return to the main screen.

Now I want to check out the networking settings. Pressing *8* and then *Enter* brings me into `Network adapter settings`, where I can see that my current IP address on `WEB4`'s NIC is `10.10.10.12`. This is correct, but let's change that address for the sake of walking through a real Sconfig setting change.

I first select my network adapter index, which is number 1. I am now shown additional information about what is already configured on this NIC and have options to change this information. Selecting option 1 again will allow me to set the network adapter address:

```
================================================================
                      Network adapter settings
================================================================

NIC index:     1
Description:   Microsoft Hyper-V Network Adapter
IP address:    10.10.10.12,
               fe80::9587:4941:588c:8295
Subnet mask:   255.255.255.0
DHCP enabled:  False

Default gateway:        10.10.10.1
Preferred DNS server:   10.10.10.10
Alternate DNS server:   10.10.10.11

   1) Set network adapter address
   2) Set DNS servers
   3) Clear DNS server settings

Enter selection (Blank=Cancel):
```

Figure 10.30: Configuring an IP address with Sconfig

Input the letter *S*, which tells Sconfig that you want to enter a static IP address, and then input the new IP address that you want to be configured on this NIC. I will change WEB4 to 10.10.10.30, just to prove that this works.

After inputting the IP address, I must also define a new subnet mask and gateway address:

```
================================================================
                      Network adapter settings
================================================================

NIC index:     1
Description:   Microsoft Hyper-V Network Adapter
IP address:    10.10.10.12,
               fe80::9587:4941:588c:8295
Subnet mask:   255.255.255.0
DHCP enabled:  False

Default gateway:        10.10.10.1
Preferred DNS server:   10.10.10.10
Alternate DNS server:   10.10.10.11

   1) Set network adapter address
   2) Set DNS servers
   3) Clear DNS server settings

Enter selection (Blank=Cancel): 1
Select (D)HCP or (S)tatic IP address (Blank=Cancel): S
Enter static IP address (Blank=Cancel): 10.10.10.30
Enter subnet mask (Blank=255.255.255.0): 255.255.255.0
Enter default gateway (Blank=Cancel): 10.10.10.1
```

Figure 10.31: Setting the subnet mask and default gateway

The NIC of WEB4 has been immediately updated to a new IP address of 10.10.10.30, and we can move on with another configuration if needed. While it may not be a common occurrence to visit the Sconfig tool after the initial configuration of a Server Core instance, this tool can be a real timesaver when used for the initial configuration of the network and naming settings of any new Server Core instance. Once you have moved through assigning an IP address, setting a hostname, and joining this machine to your domain, it is most likely that you will never revisit this interface and will instead work from tools like WAC, Server Manager, or a remote PowerShell session to accomplish day-to-day tasks.

Roles available in Server Core

Server Core is obviously a restricted form of the operating system, and some of the roles inside Windows Server are just not designed to work properly within that limited context. Fortunately for us, most of them are, which enables Server 2022 administrators to deploy most of their critical infrastructure via the more secure Server Core platform. Here is a list of the roles that are currently supported to run on a Windows Server 2022 Server Core instance, and I marked the ones in bold that I see most often used within the businesses I work with:

- Active Directory Certificate Services
- **Active Directory Domain Services**
- Active Directory Federation Services
- Active Directory Lightweight Directory Services
- Active Directory Rights Management Services
- Device Health Attestation
- **DHCP Server**
- **DNS Server**
- **File and Storage Services**
- Host Guardian Service
- **Hyper-V**
- Print and Document Services
- Remote Access
- Remote Desktop Services*
- Volume Activation Services
- **Web Server (IIS)**
- **Windows Server Essentials Experience**
- Windows Server Update Services

You'll notice that I placed a * next to Remote Desktop Services in the preceding list. While you can install the RDS role on a Server Core, you cannot perform *all* the functions of Remote Desktop with a Server Core instance. You can use Server Core to be your RDS Connection Broker or RDS Licensing server, but you cannot use Server Core as a Remote Desktop Session Host. Similar limitations exist for other roles as well.

For an always-updated, comprehensive list of which parts and pieces of which roles and features are supported on Server Core, check out the following Microsoft document: `https://docs.microsoft.com/en-us/windows-server/administration/server-core/server-core-roles-and-services`.

Building a Server Core domain controller

You are now equipped to spin up Server Core instances, configure them with hostnames, IP addresses, and domain memberships, and administer these new servers using various administrative toolsets. One of the most frequent uses of Server Core that I have seen in production environments is as a secondary domain controller. Let's walk through the process of setting one up so that you have the exact steps if ever this situation applies to you.

Begin by prepping the new server. You already know all of this, but here is the basic outline of steps that you want to accomplish before thinking about turning this server into a domain controller:

1. Spin up the new server and install Server Core.
2. Use Sconfig or PowerShell from the console to configure a static IP address and a permanent hostname. Remember, once you turn this server into a domain controller, it no longer supports name changes, and it is not so easy to change the IP – so choose wisely. I have named mine DC3-CORE since I already have a DC1 and a DC2 in my lab, and I want to easily distinguish this one as a Server Core instance.
3. Make sure to specify an existing domain controller as the NIC's DNS server address.
4. Use Sconfig or PowerShell to join this new server to your existing domain.
5. At this point, your server is online and communicable on the network but has no roles installed. You could proceed from here with the installation of any role to serve any purpose.

Install the AD DS role

There are numerous ways in which this step could be accomplished. Using WAC or remotely manipulating the new server via Server Manager on another machine would be valid ways of installing the new role. You should already be familiar with those processes based on what we have covered in this chapter so far.

Instead, let's stick to pure PowerShell to convert this new Server Core into a headless domain controller. From the console of DC3-CORE, make sure that you are logged in to a Domain Admin account. Then, use the powershell command to change a Command Prompt into a PowerShell prompt. Then, run the following command to install the AD DS role onto the new server:

```
Install-WindowsFeature -Name AD-Domain-Services -IncludeManagementTools
```

If you also want this server to respond to DNS lookups (as most domain controllers do), also install the DNS role with the following command:

```
Install-WindowsFeature DNS
```

```
Administrator: C:\Windows\system32\cmd.exe
WARNING: To launch Server Configuration tool again, run "SConfig"
PS C:\Users\Administrator.CONTOSO> powershell
Windows PowerShell
Copyright (C) Microsoft Corporation. All rights reserved.

Install the latest PowerShell for new features and improvements! https://aka.ms/PSWindows

PS C:\Users\Administrator.CONTOSO> Install-WindowsFeature -Name AD-Domain-Services -IncludeManagementTools

Success Restart Needed Exit Code    Feature Result
------- -------------- ---------    --------------
True    No             Success      {Active Directory Domain Services, Group P...

PS C:\Users\Administrator.CONTOSO> Install-WindowsFeature DNS

Success Restart Needed Exit Code    Feature Result
------- -------------- ---------    --------------
True    No             Success      {DNS Server}

PS C:\Users\Administrator.CONTOSO> _
```

Figure 10.32: Installing AD DS and DNS roles onto a Server Core

Promote this server to a domain controller

With roles installed, we are now ready to promote this server to a domain controller. The old `dcpromo` command still exists and could be used to perform this function, or we could, of course, utilize one of the graphical administrative tools to handle this remotely as well. Since we started with PowerShell, though, we'll finish out the process using the same:

```
Install-ADDSDomainController -InstallDns -DomainName "contoso.local"
```

(Replace `contoso.local` with your own domain name, of course.)

As this command runs, you will be asked to input the required information, such as the AD SafeMode password and administrative credentials, with permission to create a new domain controller:

Figure 10.33: Creating your first Server Core DC

Once finished, the server will restart automatically, and your new Server Core is now a headless domain controller in your environment!

Verify that it worked

I know you trust me implicitly, but just for the sake of argument, what if we wanted to verify that those simple PowerShell commands really did what they said they did? Let's verify that DC3-CORE really is a domain controller through a couple of different methods.

All domain controllers in an environment automatically get their computer object moved into the **Domain Controllers** OU inside Active Directory. Logging in to any DC in your network, open Active Directory Users and Computers, and navigate to the **Domain Controllers** OU. You can see in *Figure 10.34* that DC3-CORE is now inside this container, indicating that it is a DC for my domain:

Figure 10.34: Verification that DC3-CORE is a domain controller

To verify the DNS side of things, you can now open up the DNS Management console from inside your network and go into **Properties** of your primary internal DNS zone. In my case, that is contoso. local. Opening up those properties, I can see that my **Name Servers** tab now displays DC3-CORE as a name server for this zone:

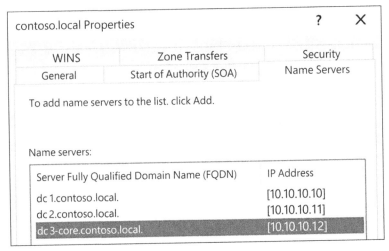

Figure 10.35: DC3-CORE is a confirmed DNS server

There's one final test and verification. Let's use a command that queries and displays the replication status between domain controller servers in our environment. Open Command Prompt or PowerShell on any DC and run the following command:

```
Repadmin /showrepl
```

> Administrator: C:\Windows\system32\cmd.exe

```
==== INBOUND NEIGHBORS ======================================

DC=contoso,DC=local
    Default-First-Site-Name\DC2 via RPC
        DSA object GUID: f2985b11-d5de-4432-8267-198233a7589a
        Last attempt @ 2023-02-04 06:43:01 was successful.
    Default-First-Site-Name\DC3-CORE via RPC
        DSA object GUID: 8020e0c8-9be8-4931-9cec-2f25cafb9ec7
        Last attempt @ 2023-02-04 06:46:42 was successful.
CN=Configuration,DC=contoso,DC=local
    Default-First-Site-Name\DC3-CORE via RPC
        DSA object GUID: 8020e0c8-9be8-4931-9cec-2f25cafb9ec7
        Last attempt @ 2023-02-04 06:46:08 was successful.
    Default-First-Site-Name\DC2 via RPC
        DSA object GUID: f2985b11-d5de-4432-8267-198233a7589a
        Last attempt @ 2023-02-04 06:46:29 was successful.
CN=Schema,CN=Configuration,DC=contoso,DC=local
    Default-First-Site-Name\DC2 via RPC
        DSA object GUID: f2985b11-d5de-4432-8267-198233a7589a
        Last attempt @ 2023-02-04 05:52:10 was successful.
    Default-First-Site-Name\DC3-CORE via RPC
        DSA object GUID: 8020e0c8-9be8-4931-9cec-2f25cafb9ec7
        Last attempt @ 2023-02-04 06:42:20 was successful.
```

Figure 10.36: DC3-CORE is part of domain controller replication

There you go! Proof in three different flavors that our DC3-CORE Server Core instance really is a domain controller and DNS server in our domain. How cool is that?!

What happened to Nano Server?

This story about small-footprint Windows Server platforms didn't used to end with Server Core. Anyone who kept tabs on the new features coming out with Server 2016 is aware that there was another installation option for the Server 2016 operating system, called Nano Server. The premise of Nano Server was an even smaller, more secure, more efficient, and super-tiny operating system that could run a very limited set of roles. Though limited, it could still be installed on a physical or virtual server platform, run as a true server operating system, and still host traditional workloads on it.

Unfortunately for Nano Server enthusiasts, and especially for anyone who already did the work of installing and using it, the story behind Nano Server has flipped around completely over the last few years. To cut a long story short, you can no longer use Nano Server for anything that a traditional server can do. You cannot install it on physical hardware; you cannot even install Nano on a VM. Additionally, management functionalities, such as PowerShell and WinRM, have been removed from Nano Server, and you cannot install any of the Microsoft infrastructural roles onto it.

With all of this functionality ripped out of Nano Server's scope, what is left? Is it dead? Can Nano Server do *ANYTHING*?

The answer is **containers**. If you are interested in utilizing containers to build and host cloud-ready and scalable applications, this is where Nano is now focused. We will cover more information about containers and the fact that Nano Server is completely married to them in *Chapter 13, Containers*, but suffice it to say that downloading container images from Microsoft will now be the *only* place where you will find Nano Server.

Summary

I said it in previous versions of this book, and I'll say it again now—writing this chapter has been exactly the (re)-kick in the pants that I needed to start thinking about shrinking my own servers. I am in the same boat as many of you—I know what Server Core is and have played around with it, have worked through the exercises in this book numerous times, and have even supported a handful of them in customer environments to a limited extent. But I have never attempted to change my default mindset when spinning up new servers within production environments that I support. Now that tools such as Sconfig and the new WAC are available to us, we have officially run out of excuses as to why we shouldn't at least consider using Server Core for new instances of Windows Server in our environments. In fact, as I was building out the new DC3-CORE server, I realized just how much faster it is to get a Server Core instance off the ground compared to the full graphical interface. Reboots are faster, and using Sconfig to set the IP address, hostname, and domain membership all took me about 2 minutes in total.

While it never hurts to learn something new, using Server Core no longer comes with the requirement that you must be fluent in PowerShell. The early days of Server Core came with a requirement to be really good with PowerShell, as this was the only reliable way to configure and interface with your tiny servers, but the tools we have learned about in this chapter allow us to utilize a smaller platform and administer it without memorizing a bunch of new cmdlets.

Security is the primary reason that we should all consider Server Core as our new standard. The Windows graphical interface adds a lot of code and grants a lot of ability to those logged in to the servers, such as the ability to browse the internet. This opens up all kinds of doors to vulnerabilities that simply don't exist in Server Core.

Questions

1. True or false—Server Core is the default installation option for Windows Server 2022.
2. True or false—You can utilize PowerShell to change a Server 2022 from *Server Core* mode to *Desktop Experience* mode.
3. Bonus points: What is the last version of Windows Server that allowed you to change a server on the fly back and forth between Server Core and Desktop Experience?
4. When sitting at the console of a freshly booted Windows Server 2022 Server Core instance, what application do you see on the screen?

5. When sitting at the console of a freshly booted Windows Server 2019 Server Core instance, what application do you see on the screen?

6. What cmdlet can be used to view the current networking configuration on a Server Core?

7. Which PowerShell cmdlet can be used to configure the hostname of a Server Core?

8. Name some of the management tools that can be used to remotely interface with a Server Core.

9. What is the name of the utility built into Server Core that can be launched from a console to provide quick task links to configure IP addresses, hostnames, and domain membership?

10. What movie reference did I make at the beginning of this chapter?

Join our community on Discord

Join our community's Discord space for discussions with the author and other readers:

`https://packt.link/SecNet`

11

PowerShell

If you've had some drive-time with Windows 11, you may be wondering to yourself, "Self, why are we reading about PowerShell when it has been replaced by Windows Terminal?" The "replacement" of PowerShell with Windows Terminal inside Windows 11 is generating a little bit of confusion among the user population, but they are not at all the same thing, nor is Terminal an actual replacement for PowerShell. PowerShell is much more than a console screen from which you run commands. It is integrated into all facets of Windows itself. We will discuss Windows Terminal a little bit more at the end of this chapter, and indeed walk through the steps of installing it inside Windows Server 2022 (because it's not there by default). But for the purposes of PowerShell learning, we can safely leave Terminal out of scope.

So far, we've been talking about PowerShell and Terminal, but let's be honest, many of us are still using Command Prompt on a daily basis. If you have moved over and are using the PowerShell prompt as a total replacement for Command Prompt, I applaud you! I, however, still use a pretty good mix of both, and tend to open cmd.exe as a matter of lazy habit. Adjusting this behavior within myself is in part what I hope to accomplish with this chapter, and we are going to explore some of the reasons why you should do so too. PowerShell is more useful and powerful than Command Prompt could ever dream of being.

In this chapter, we will cover the following topics:

- Why move to PowerShell?
- Working within PowerShell
- Importing a module
- Using a pipeline
- PowerShell Integrated Scripting Environment
- Remotely managing a server
- Desired State Configuration
- Windows Terminal

Why move to PowerShell?

I don't think there is any question in people's minds that PowerShell is indeed the evolution of Command Prompt, but the reason that many of us still default to the old interface is that it still contains all of the functionality required to accomplish what we historically have needed to do on our servers. What Command Prompt really contains is the ability to do the same things that we have always done from Command Prompt, and nothing else. Without realizing it, there are a lot of functions that you use the GUI to accomplish that cannot be done well from within a Command Prompt window.

The limitations within Command Prompt that force you into using your mouse to interface with the GUI do not exist with PowerShell. It is fully comprehensive and capable of modifying almost any aspect of the Windows operating system. How did PowerShell become so much more powerful than Command Prompt? It differs from any classic I/O shell in that it is built on top of .NET and runs much more like a programming language than simple input and output commands.

PowerShell is also built with centralized computing in mind. Running ad hoc commands is great if you are logged directly in to one server, and only need to make changes on that one server. Most server administrators are responsible for maintaining dozens or even hundreds of servers, and PowerShell scripting can be formulated to centrally monitor or manipulate all of them from the same console interface, and all at the same time. This can be an incredible timesaver and tool of efficiency in day-to-day chores.

Cmdlets

Most of the functionality that a traditional server admin will use within PowerShell comes in the form of **cmdlets** (pronounced *command-lets*). These are commands that you run from within the PowerShell prompt, but you can think of them as tools rather than simple commands. Cmdlets can be used to both get information from a server and set information and parameters on a server. Many cmdlets have intuitive names that begin with get or set, and similar to the way that most command-line interfaces work, each cmdlet has various switches or variables that can be configured and flagged at the end of the cmdlet, to make it do special things. It is helpful to understand that cmdlets are always built using a verb-noun syntax. You specify the action you want to accomplish, such as get or set, and then your noun is the piece inside Windows that you are trying to manipulate. Here are a few simple examples of cmdlets in PowerShell to give you an idea of what they look like and how they are named in a fairly simple way:

- Get-NetIPAddress: With this cmdlet, we can see the IP addresses on our system
- Set-NetIPAddress: We can use this guy to modify an existing IP address
- New-NetIPAddress: This cmdlet allows us to create a new IP address on the computer
- Rename-Computer: As we saw earlier in the book, Rename-Computer is a quick and easy way to set the computer hostname of a system

If you're ever struggling to come up with the name or syntax of a particular command, the online Microsoft Learn platform (formerly and sometimes still called either Microsoft Docs or Microsoft TechNet) has a full page of information dedicated to each cmdlet inside PowerShell. That can be incredibly useful, but sometimes you don't want to take the time to pop onto the internet just to find the name of a command that you are simply failing to remember at the moment.

One of the most useful cmdlets in PowerShell shows you a list of all the available cmdlets. Memorizing the names of cmdlets isn't critically important, as long as you commit this one, Get-Command, to permanent memory:

```
Administrator: Windows PowerShell                                          —  □  ×

Windows PowerShell
Copyright (C) Microsoft Corporation. All rights reserved.

Install the latest PowerShell for new features and improvements! https://aka.ms/PSWindows

PS C:\Users\Administrator> Get-Command

CommandType     Name                                        Version     Source
-----------     ----                                        -------     ------
Alias           Add-AppPackage                              2.0.1.0     Appx
Alias           Add-AppPackageVolume                        2.0.1.0     Appx
Alias           Add-AppProvisionedPackage                   3.0         Dism
Alias           Add-ProvisionedAppPackage                   3.0         Dism
Alias           Add-ProvisionedAppxPackage                  3.0         Dism
Alias           Add-WindowsFeature                          2.0.0.0     ServerManager
Alias           Apply-WindowsUnattend                       3.0         Dism
Alias           Disable-PhysicalDiskIndication              2.0.0.0     Storage
Alias           Disable-PhysicalDiskIndication              1.0.0.0     VMDirectStorage
Alias           Disable-StorageDiagnosticLog                2.0.0.0     Storage
Alias           Disable-StorageDiagnosticLog                1.0.0.0     VMDirectStorage
Alias           Dismount-AppPackageVolume                   2.0.1.0     Appx
Alias           Enable-PhysicalDiskIndication               2.0.0.0     Storage
Alias           Enable-PhysicalDiskIndication               1.0.0.0     VMDirectStorage
Alias           Enable-StorageDiagnosticLog                 2.0.0.0     Storage
Alias           Enable-StorageDiagnosticLog                 1.0.0.0     VMDirectStorage
Alias           Expand-IscsiVirtualDisk                     2.0.0.0     IscsiTarget
Alias           Export-DnsServerTrustAnchor                 2.0.0.0     DnsServer
Alias           Flush-Volume                                2.0.0.0     Storage
Alias           Flush-Volume                                1.0.0.0     VMDirectStorage
Alias           Get-AppPackage                              2.0.1.0     Appx
```

Figure 11.1: Results of Get-Command

Whoa, there are pages and pages and pages of cmdlets! Rather than scrolling through the entire list to find the one you are looking for, it is easy to filter this list down based on any criteria that you would like. If we were interested in seeing only the commands that deal with IP addressing, we could give this a try:

```
Get-Command -Name *IPAddress*
```

The Get-Command cmdlet combined with the -Name parameter allows you to selectively search for useful items in PowerShell that relate to any name or portion of a name:

```
Administrator: Windows PowerShell

PS C:\Users\Administrator> Get-Command -Name *IPAddress*

CommandType     Name                                           Version     Source
-----------     ----                                           -------     ------
Function        Get-DhcpServerv4FreeIPAddress                  2.0.0.0     DhcpServer
Function        Get-DhcpServerv6FreeIPAddress                  2.0.0.0     DhcpServer
Function        Get-NetIPAddress                               1.0.0.0     NetTCPIP
Function        New-NetIPAddress                               1.0.0.0     NetTCPIP
Function        Remove-NetIPAddress                            1.0.0.0     NetTCPIP
Function        Remove-NetworkSwitchEthernetPortIPAddress      1.0.0.0     NetworkSwitchManager
Function        Set-NetIPAddress                               1.0.0.0     NetTCPIP
Function        Set-NetworkSwitchEthernetPortIPAddress         1.0.0.0     NetworkSwitchManager

PS C:\Users\Administrator> _
```

Figure 11.2: Searching with Get-Command

As with many toolsets, PowerShell utilizes * as a wildcard indicator. In the search we just accomplished, and in truth for almost any cmdlet search that I ever run, using the * wildcard on both ends of the term I am searching for helps to display any results that contain that term.

PowerShell is the backbone

As you will discover in this chapter, interfacing with PowerShell puts all kinds of power at your fingertips. What we sometimes find, though, is that admins don't fully trust PowerShell because they are used to taking these actions and making these changes from a graphical interface. After running a single PowerShell cmdlet to set a configuration that would have taken you a dozen different mouse clicks to accomplish the same thing, it is easy to think that it must not have actually done anything. That was too easy, and it processed my command way too quickly, right? I'd better go into that graphical interface anyway, just to double-check that PowerShell actually did the job.

When I started using PowerShell, I was tempted to do exactly that all the time. But the more I used it, and the more I started digging into those graphical interfaces themselves, the more I realized that I'm not the only one using PowerShell. A lot of the administrative tool GUIs use PowerShell too! Without even realizing it, you use PowerShell for quite a few graphically driven tasks inside the Windows Server operating system. When you open up that management console for whatever you happen to be changing on the server, make your configurations, and then click on the **Go** or **Finish** button, how does that graphical console put your configuration into place? With PowerShell. Under the hood, in the background, the console is taking the information that you input, plugging that information into PowerShell cmdlets, and running them to do the actual configuration work.

Many of the administrative tools that we run from inside Server Manager take this approach, accepting changes and configurations from you and then formulating those settings into PowerShell commands that run in the background to push the changes into action.

So, if you're hesitant to start using PowerShell because it just feels different, or you don't trust the process to be uniform with the way that it would have worked in the GUI, forget all of that. Because often, when you are using mouse clicks to change settings on your server, you are actually invoking PowerShell cmdlets to do the work.

Scripting

The more you use PowerShell, the more powerful it becomes. In addition to running ad hoc single commands and cmdlets, you can build extensive scripts that can accomplish all sorts of different things. I mentioned that PowerShell has similarities to a regular programming language, and scripting is where we start to navigate into that territory. PowerShell provides the ability to create script files, which we will do for ourselves shortly, saving scripts for easy running time and time again. You can also use variables, like in other forms of coding, so that you can provide variable input and objects that scripts can use to make them more flexible and squeeze even more functionality out of them.

Server Core

If there were any one area where I think we as server admins could do a better job of using the technology at our disposal, it is using PowerShell to fulfill the Microsoft model of centralized management. When we have a task that needs to be accomplished on a server, it is our default tendency to log in to that server (usually via RDP), then use our mouse to start clicking around and doing the work. Logging in to the server is becoming more and more unnecessary, and we could save a lot of time by using the central management tools that are available to us. PowerShell is one of these tools. Rather than RDPing into that server, simply use the PowerShell prompt on your local machine to reach out and change that setting on the remote server.

This kind of remote management becomes not only efficient but also necessary as we start dealing more with headless servers. I hope to see increased utilization of Server Core in our organizations in the coming years, and interacting with these servers is going to require a shift in your administrative mindset. By becoming familiar with accomplishing daily tasks from inside PowerShell now, you will better equip yourself for the future administration of these headless machines, which will require you to interface with them differently than you are comfortable doing today.

Working within PowerShell

The first step to doing real work with PowerShell is getting comfortable interfacing with the platform and becoming familiar with the daily routines of working from this command-line interface, rather than relying on your mouse pointer. Here, we will explore some of the most common ways that I have seen server administrators make use of PowerShell to enhance their daily workflow.

We will be working, throughout this chapter, inside the version of PowerShell that comes out of the box with Windows Server 2022, PowerShell 5.1. You may have heard the news of PowerShell 7's release. If you are familiar with this and already utilizing it, everything that we discuss will work perfectly well on that updated platform. To administer a Windows Server instance, the differences between versions won't have much of a bearing. Installing PowerShell 7 will not update PowerShell 5.1, but rather they will run side by side. This is in part because PowerShell 5.1 is built upon .NET Framework, while PowerShell 7.x runs on .NET Core. Having foundations in the open-source .NET Core means that PowerShell 7 comes with the ability to work cross-platform, with Windows, Linux, and even macOS (gasp!). It also includes some additional support for working with Docker containers. If you would like to seek out and install PowerShell 7, there are a variety of different ways you could do so. The following Microsoft article outlines them all:

```
https://learn.microsoft.com/en-us/powershell/scripting/install/installing-powershell-
on-windows?view=powershell-7.3
```

For those of you following the path toward PowerShell 7 installation, keep in mind that this shell is entirely separate from our "normal" PowerShell, and is launched by a different executable. This may be a helpful quick reference to ensure you are launching the shell that you intend:

- PowerShell 5.1 = `powershell.exe`
- PowerShell 7 = `pwsh.exe`

Launching PowerShell

The first thing we need to do is get PowerShell opened up to start using it. The PowerShell console is installed by default in all recent versions of Windows, so you can run it from the Start menu, pin it to the Desktop, or access it in any way that you normally open any application.

Since I tend to prefer using my keyboard for everything, the way that I normally open PowerShell is to hold down the *Windows key* and press *R* to open a **Run** prompt, type the word powershell, and press *Enter*:

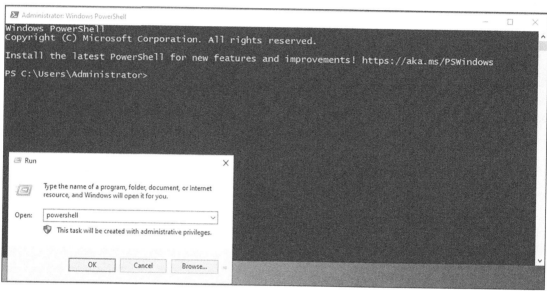

Figure 11.3: Launching PowerShell via keyboard

As you can see, since I am logged in to an administrative account on my server, my PowerShell prompt has been opened with elevated permissions. The word **Administrator** is listed in the top toolbar of the PowerShell window. It is important to note that, just like Command Prompt, you can open a PowerShell prompt with either regular user permissions or elevated administrator privileges. It is generally safer to work from within a regular PowerShell session that does not have elevated rights unless the task that you are trying to accomplish requires those extra permissions.

Another quick and easy way to open PowerShell on any newer Windows platform is by right-clicking on the **Start** button and selecting it right from the quick tasks list that is presented. As you can see in *Figure 11.4*, I have right-clicked on the **Start** button of one of my new Server 2022 machines and can choose from here to open PowerShell or even an elevated (administrative) PowerShell prompt:

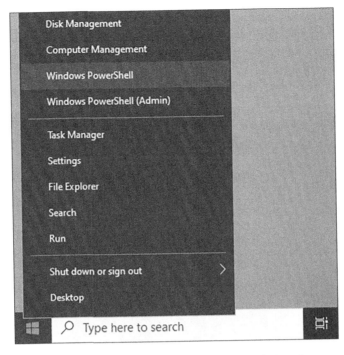

Figure 11.4: Launching PowerShell from the quick admin tasks menu

If you right-click on your **Start** button and do not find options for PowerShell but rather for opening Command Prompt, do not be dismayed. This is a configurable option; you can show either Command Prompt or PowerShell options in the quick admin tasks menu. If you right-click on your taskbar and select **Taskbar settings**, you will find an option that is called **Replace Command Prompt with Windows PowerShell** in the menu when I right-click the **Start** button or press *Windows key + X*. Wow, that is possibly the longest name for a single option in the entire Windows operating system, but toggling this option will swing your quick admin menu back and forth between the two command-line interfaces.

You also have the option of entering into a PowerShell prompt from inside an existing Command Prompt window. Normally, when you are working from Command Prompt, you cannot make use of any PowerShell cmdlets. Let's go ahead and give this a shot. Open an administrative Command Prompt window and try to type in the name of one of the cmdlets we mentioned earlier. Perhaps type Get-NetIPAddress to show us what IP addresses reside on this system. Whoops—that failed because Command Prompt doesn't recognize the Get-NetIPAddress cmdlet.

Now type the word powershell and press *Enter*. Instead of opening a separate PowerShell window, your prompt changes, but the application window itself remains the same. You have now entered the PowerShell shell from inside the traditional Command Prompt window, and you can start utilizing cmdlets as you wish. Running Get-NetIPAddress again now produces some information:

```
Administrator: C:\Windows\system32\cmd.exe - powershell                                      —    □    ×
Microsoft Windows [Version 10.0.20348.887]
(c) Microsoft Corporation. All rights reserved.

C:\Users\Administrator>Get-NetIPAddress
'Get-NetIPAddress' is not recognized as an internal or external command,
operable program or batch file.

C:\Users\Administrator>powershell
Windows PowerShell
Copyright (C) Microsoft Corporation. All rights reserved.

Install the latest PowerShell for new features and improvements! https://aka.ms/PSWindows

PS C:\Users\Administrator> Get-NetIPAddress


IPAddress            : fe80::9048:87d1:e61c:e649%8
InterfaceIndex       : 8
InterfaceAlias       : Ethernet
AddressFamily        : IPv6
Type                 : Unicast
PrefixLength         : 64
PrefixOrigin         : WellKnown
SuffixOrigin         : Link
AddressState         : Preferred
ValidLifetime        : Infinite ([TimeSpan]::MaxValue)
PreferredLifetime    : Infinite ([TimeSpan]::MaxValue)
SkipAsSource         : False
PolicyStore          : ActiveStore
```

Figure 11.5: Invoking PowerShell from within Command Prompt

You can move from PowerShell mode back to regular Command Prompt mode by typing exit.

Default execution policy

When you are working with the PowerShell command-line interface directly, you can simply open up PowerShell, start typing cmdlets, and get work done. However, one of the big advantages of using PowerShell comes when you start playing around with creating, saving, and running scripts. When first creating and running a PowerShell script, you may find that it fails with a big messy error message, such as this one:

```
Administrator: Windows PowerShell                                                           —    □    ×
PS C:\Scripts> .\script1.ps1
.\script1.ps1 : File C:\Scripts\script1.ps1 cannot be loaded because running scripts is disabled on this system. For
more information, see about_Execution_Policies at https:/go.microsoft.com/fwlink/?LinkID=135170.
At line:1 char:1
+ .\script1.ps1
+ ~~~~~~~~~~~~~
    + CategoryInfo          : SecurityError: (:) [], PSSecurityException
    + FullyQualifiedErrorId : UnauthorizedAccess
PS C:\Scripts> _
```

Figure 11.6: A common PowerShell script execution error

This shouldn't happen on a fresh instance of Windows Server 2022 but could if you have any GPOs being applied to your new server or if you are using a different operating system and are trying to run some PowerShell scripts; you might find yourself stuck at one of these error messages right out of the gate. While the nature of some versions of Windows to block the running of scripts by default is a security enhancement, it can be a nuisance to work around when you are trying to get something done. Thankfully, if you do encounter this problem, the resolution is easy: you simply need to adjust the **Default Execution Policy (DEP)** inside PowerShell so that it allows the execution of scripts to happen properly.

This is not a simple on/off switch. There are five different levels within the DEP, and it is important to understand each one so that you can set your DEP accordingly, based on the security that you want in place on your servers. Here are descriptions of each level, in order of most to least secure.

Restricted

The `Restricted` policy allows individual commands and cmdlets to be run but stops the running of scripts altogether.

AllSigned

This requires that any script being run is signed by a trusted publisher. When set to `AllSigned`, even scripts that you write yourself will have to be put through a validation process and signed before they will be allowed to run.

RemoteSigned

`RemoteSigned` is the default policy in Windows Server 2022. For scripts that have been downloaded from the internet, it requires that these scripts are signed with a digital signature from a publisher that you trust. However, if you choose to create your own scripts, it will allow these local scripts to run without requiring that digital signature.

Unrestricted

Scripts are allowed to run, signed or unsigned. You do still receive a warning prompt when running scripts that have been downloaded from the internet.

Bypass mode

In `Bypass` mode, nothing is blocked and no warnings are given when you run scripts. In other words, you're on your own.

Sometimes a single execution policy doesn't meet all of your needs, depending on how you utilize PowerShell scripts. DEPs can be further enhanced by setting an execution policy scope that allows you to set different execution policies for different aspects of the system. For example, the three scopes that you can manipulate are `Process`, `CurrentUser`, and `LocalMachine`. By default, the DEP affects `LocalMachine` so that any scripts running adhere to the DEP. But if you need to modify this behavior so that different DEPs are set for `CurrentUser` or even an individual process, you have the ability to do that.

If you are unsure about the current status of your DEP or suspect that someone may have changed it, you can easily view the currently assigned execution policy with a simple cmdlet called `Get-ExecutionPolicy`. As you can see in *Figure 11.7*, mine is set to `Restricted`, which explains my earlier error message when I tried running a script:

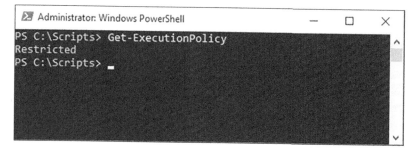

Figure 11.7: ExecutionPolicy is currently set to Restricted

Once you have decided on the level of DEP that you want on your server or workstation, you can set it accordingly with a quick cmdlet. For this particular server, I want it configured back to the default setting of **RemoteSigned**. Here is my command for doing just that:

```
Set-ExecutionPolicy RemoteSigned
```

```
Administrator: Windows PowerShell                                    —    □    ×

PS C:\Scripts> Set-ExecutionPolicy RemoteSigned

Execution Policy Change
The execution policy helps protect you from scripts that you do not trust. Changing the
execution policy might expose you to the security risks described in the
about_Execution_Policies help topic at https:/go.microsoft.com/fwlink/?LinkID=135170. Do
 you want to change the execution policy?
[Y] Yes  [A] Yes to All  [N] No  [L] No to All  [S] Suspend  [?] Help (default is "N"): y

PS C:\Scripts> Get-ExecutionPolicy
RemoteSigned
PS C:\Scripts>
```

Figure 11.8: Setting ExecutionPolicy to RemoteSigned

Remember, right now, we are running PowerShell on this local system (I happen to be logged in to my WEB3 server), so the only execution policy I am setting is the local one for my WEB3 system. If I wanted to change this setting globally or for a group of machines at the same time, I could utilize Group Policy for that change. The location inside Group Policy for configuring PowerShell script execution policy is **Computer Configuration | Policies | Administrative Templates | Windows Components | Windows PowerShell | Turn on script execution**.

Using the Tab key

Before we get started navigating inside PowerShell, there is one important thing I want to point out: get used to pressing the *Tab* key when you are inside the PowerShell prompt! If you type the first few letters of any command or cmdlet or even an added variable to a cmdlet and then press *Tab*, the remainder of the cmdlet name or option will be automatically populated on the screen.

If we type get-co and then press *Tab*, the prompt automatically populates the full Get-Command cmdlet. Since there are multiple cmdlets that start with get-co, if you press *Tab* numerous times, you can see that it cycles through all of the available cmdlets that start with those letters.

Tab also works with file and folder names. For example, say I download a hotfix that needs to be installed onto a server. I want to launch this hotfix using the PowerShell prompt that I already have open, but I don't want to spend an entire minute or more trying to type out the huge filename of this hotfix. I have already navigated to the folder where my hotfix resides, and now if I simply type the first few letters of the filename and press the *Tab* key, PowerShell will populate the remainder of the filename. From there, all I need to do is press *Enter* to launch that installer. In the screenshot below, I navigated to the Hotfixes folder and then typed the letter a and pressed *Tab* to generate the following:

Figure 11.9: The Tab key auto-fills file or command names

Useful cmdlets for daily tasks

When I started incorporating PowerShell into my daily workflow, I found it useful to keep a list of commonly used commands and cmdlets handy. Until you get to the point where they become memorized and second nature, if you don't have a quick and easy way to recall those commands, chances are you aren't going to use them and will revert to the old method of configuring your servers.

Here is a list of some of the items I use regularly when I'm building or troubleshooting servers. Some are traditional commands that would also work from Command Prompt and some are cmdlets, but they are all useful when working inside a PowerShell window:

- Get-Command: This is useful for finding additional commands or cmdlets that you may want to run or research.
- Get-Command -Name *example*: Enhances the usefulness of Get-Command by adding the -Name switch to the end of it, so that you can filter results to whatever types of cmdlets you are searching for.
- GCM: This is simply a short alias for Get-Command. I only wanted to point this one out because many of the PowerShell cmdlets have aliases, such as gcm, that allow you to launch these commonly used cmdlets with fewer keystrokes.

- **Get-Alias**: Since we just mentioned the gcm alias for Get-Command, you may be wondering what other aliases are available inside PowerShell. To see a complete list, simply plug in the Get-Alias cmdlet. Using aliases rather than full cmdlet names can greatly reduce the number of characters you type inside PowerShell.
- **Rename-Computer**: This allows you to set a new hostname for the server.
- **Add-Computer**: Use the Add-Computer cmdlet to join servers or computers to a domain.
- **hostname**: This displays the name of the system you are currently working on. I use hostname all the time to make sure that I really am working on the server that I think I am. Have you ever rebooted the wrong server? I have. By running a quick hostname command prior to issuing your restart command, you can get peace of mind that the function you are about to perform is really happening on the correct system.
- **$env:computername**: This also presents you with the hostname of the system you are working on, but I'm calling it out to show that PowerShell can easily tap into your environment variables in order to pull out information. The simpler hostname command is useful when you are logged in to a local system and are simply trying to verify its name, but the ability to pull information from a variable, such as $env:computername, will be much more useful when creating scripts or trying to perform a function against a remote system.
- **Get-ComputerInfo -Property csname**: The Get-ComputerInfo cmdlet outputs tons of information about your system, and buried in the middle of that output is the name of your computer or server. If you wanted to use a true cmdlet for finding the name of your server rather than a traditional command or environment variable, here's your answer. I included -Property csname in this cmdlet because adding that specification will output only the computer name.
- **Logoff**: The name is self-explanatory; Logoff just logs you out of the system. Rather than trying to find the **Sign out** function by clicking around inside your server's **Start** menu (which carries with it the very real possibility of accidentally clicking **Restart**), you can throw a quick Logoff command into either a Command Prompt or PowerShell window, and you will be immediately logged out of that server. I use this one all the time when closing out RDP connections.
- **Install-WindowsFeature**: Use PowerShell to simplify the addition of new roles or features on your servers.

Both shutdown and Restart-Computer are useful for shutting down or restarting a server. On my own computer, these commands are most commonly preceded by the hostname command. When rebooting a server, you want to take special care that you restart the correct machine, so I find it best to open a PowerShell prompt, do a quick hostname check, and then run a Restart command from that same prompt. This ensures that I am restarting the server that was returned in the hostname output.

```
shutdown /r /t 0
```

If you run a simple shutdown command, the system will shut down in one minute. I'm not sure why this is the default, as I have never found any IT administrator who actually wanted to wait that extra minute before shutting down their system. Instead, it is more efficient to set a time limit before that shutdown commences.

In the preceding command, I have told the shutdown command that I want to restart instead of shutting down; that is what /r does. I have also told it to wait zero seconds before performing this restart. This way, it happens immediately; I don't have to wait for that default 60-second timer.

 Pro tip: Try playing around with shutdown /i. The special /i switch prompts a graphical interface from which you can select various options and impress your IT friends!

Query user or quser

Most useful in RDS environments, the quser command will display all of the users that are currently logged in to a server, including statistics about whether they are logged in locally or remotely, and how long their session has been active. I commonly use quser to discover RDS sessions that have been sitting around idle for a long time, so that I can end those sessions and free up resources on the server:

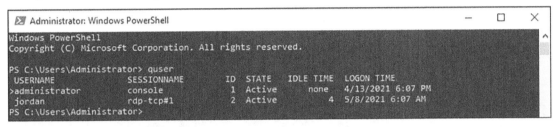

Figure 11.10: The quser command displays logged-in sessions

```
quser /server:WEB1
```

Using quser in combination with the /server switch allows you to see the currently logged-in users on a remote system. This way, you can remain logged in to a single server in your RDS farm but can check on the user sessions for all of your systems without having to log in to them. You could even write a script that runs this command against each of your session host servers and outputs the data to a file. This output could then be run on a schedule and used as a reporting mechanism for keeping track of which users were logged in to which RDS session host servers at any given time.

IP addressing cmdlets

When we built a Server Core instance together earlier in this book, we utilized the Sconfig tool to define IP addressing for that server. While that was a quick and easy way to accomplish such a task, let's define the PowerShell cmdlets that are used for the configuration of IP addressing information on a server NIC:

```
New-NetIPAddress -InterfaceIndex 12 -IPAddress 10.10.10.40 -PrefixLength 24
    -DefaultGateway 10.10.10.1
```

The above is just an example command with some sample numbers; the point here is that we can use New-NetIPAddress to assign IP addresses to NICs on our servers, and the above syntax is the correct way to go about doing it.

Often used in combination with New-NetIPAddress, use the following command to set the DNS server addresses in your NIC properties:

```
Set-DnsClientServerAddress -InterfaceIndex 12 -ServerAddresses
10.10.10.2,10.10.10.3
```

Using Get-Help

How many hundreds of times have you used the /? switch in Command Prompt to pull some extra information about a command that you want to run? The extra information provided by this help function can sometimes mean the difference between a command being useful or completely useless. PowerShell cmdlets have a similar function, but you cannot simply add /? at the end of a PowerShell cmdlet because a space following a cmdlet in PowerShell indicates that you are about to specify a parameter to be used with that cmdlet. For example, if we try to use /? with the Restart-Computer cmdlet to find more information about how to use Restart-Computer, it will fail to recognize the question mark as a valid parameter, and our output will be as follows:

Figure 11.11: PowerShell cmdlets do not work with /?

Instead, there is an even more powerful help function inside PowerShell. Get-Help is a cmdlet itself, and like any cmdlet, we need to use parameters following the cmdlet to specify and pull the information that we are looking for. So instead of using Get-Help at the end of a command, like we used to do with the question mark, we use it as its own entity.

Running Get-Help by itself only gives us more information about the Get-Help command, which may be useful to look over, but right now we are more interested in finding out how we can use Get-Help to give us additional information for a cmdlet we want to run, such as the Restart-Computer function. What we need to do is use Get-Help as a cmdlet, and then specify the other cmdlet as a parameter to pass to Get-Help by placing a space between them:

```
Get-Help Restart-Computer
```

```
Administrator: Windows PowerShell                                    —    □    ✕
PS C:\> Get-Help Restart-Computer

NAME
    Restart-Computer

SYNTAX
    Restart-Computer [[-ComputerName] <string[]>] [[-Credential]
    <pscredential>] [-DcomAuthentication <AuthenticationLevel>
    {Default | None | Connect | Call | Packet | PacketIntegrity |
    PacketPrivacy | Unchanged}] [-Impersonation
    <ImpersonationLevel> {Default | Anonymous | Identify |
    Impersonate | Delegate}] [-WsmanAuthentication <string>
    {Default | Basic | Negotiate | CredSSP | Digest | Kerberos}]
```

Figure 11.12: Displaying help information for any cmdlet

The information provided by Get-Help is very comprehensive; in some cases, it has all of the same information that you can find on Microsoft Learn. Using Get-Help is a quick way of finding example syntax for commands and cmdlets that you may be unfamiliar with, and negates the need for you to launch a web browser to find that information. Make sure to start utilizing Get-Help to further your knowledge of any cmdlet in PowerShell!

> When using PowerShell on a fresh system, or one that you haven't worked on in a while, take a minute to run a command called Update-Help. This will cause PowerShell to reach out to Microsoft and download the latest versions of help files, so that you know you are viewing the most up-to-date information when using Get-Help.

Formatting the output

When searching for information in PowerShell, I often encounter cases where so much information is provided to me that it's difficult to sort through. Are you trying to find useful cmdlets from Get-Command, or maybe track down a particular alias with Get-Alias? The output from these cmdlets can be staggeringly long. While we have discussed some parameters you can use to whittle down this output, such as specifying particular -Name parameters, there are a couple of formatting parameters that can also be appended to cmdlets, in order to modify the data output.

Format-Table

The purpose of Format-Table is pretty simple: it takes the data output from a command and puts it into a table format. This generally makes the information much easier to read and work with. Let's look at an example. We have used Get-NetIPAddress a couple of times, but, let's be honest, its output is a little messy. Running the cmdlet by itself on my virtual server, which only has a single NIC assigned to it, results in four pages of data inside my PowerShell window, with all kinds of informational fields that are either empty or not important for finding the IP addresses assigned to my server:

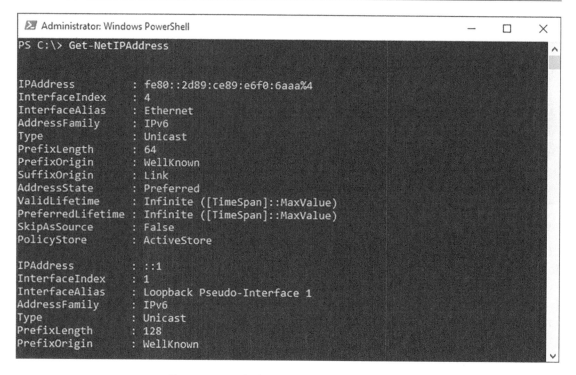

Figure 11.13: Default output from Get-NetIPAddress

If I simply add Format-Table to the end of my Get-NetIPAddress cmdlet, the generated data is much easier on the eyes, while still giving me the important information that I am really looking for, that is, the IP addresses being used on the system:

```
Get-NetIPAddress | Format-Table
```

Figure 11.14: Formatted output of Get-NetIPAddress

Some of you may be familiar with a cmdlet called Select-Object, which can perform the same functions as Format-Table. While Select-Object seems to be the more widely known cmdlet, in my experience, it is actually less powerful than Format-Table, so I suggest you spend some time playing around with the one we have discussed here.

Format-List

Similar to the way that Format-Table works, you can utilize Format-List to display command output as a list of properties. Let's give it a quick try. We already know that Get-Command gives us the available cmdlets within PowerShell, and by default, it gives them to us in a table format.

If we wanted to view that output in a list instead, with more information being provided about each cmdlet, we could tell Get-Command to output its data in list format, with the following command:

```
Get-Command | Format-List
```

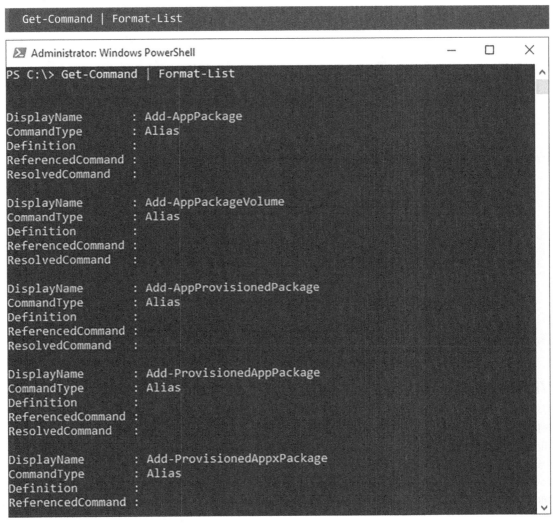

Figure 11.15: Using Format-List to modify cmdlet output

This results in a tremendously long output of information, so long in fact that my PowerShell window had a problem displaying it all. Maybe we need to whittle that info down a little bit by narrowing our focus. Let's search for all of the cmdlets that include the word Restart while displaying them in list format:

```
Get-Command -Name *Restart* | Format-List
```

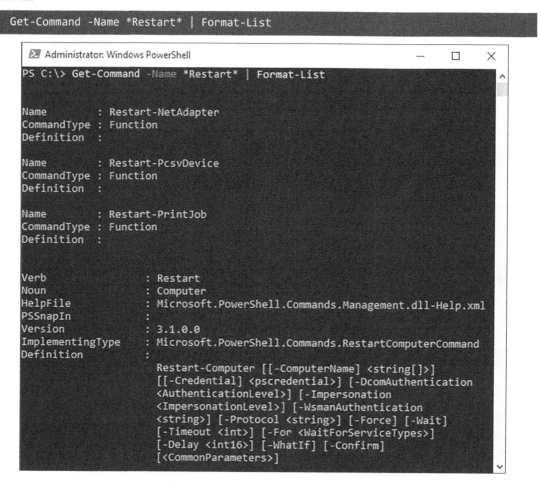

Figure 11.16: List format information about Restart-related cmdlets

Visual customizations

If viewing this chapter in color, you may have noticed that I intentionally have some screenshots with a blue PowerShell window (the classic PowerShell color), and some running a black background. I did not change anything within PowerShell to accomplish these differences; they are showcasing that PowerShell on different operating system versions may appear visually different from each other. Many former Windows Server and client operating systems will default to blue, while the newest display black. Windows Server 2022 is by default a black prompt.

However, you can change the colors in PowerShell to whatever you want! Simply right-click the up-per-left corner of a PowerShell prompt window and navigate into **Properties**. Here you have options to change the font type and size, cursor size, window sizes, and even the color of both **Screen Text** and **Screen Background**. The following screenshot shows an example of a modified PowerShell prompt, along with the options I selected to make it so.

Figure 11.17: Adjust PowerShell to whatever color scheme you choose

Importing a module

A PowerShell module is a grouping of items that are generally all related, and add a set of new func-tionality to your PowerShell session. You see, PowerShell can't have everything in the world installed into it by default, or it would be enormous! So, it operates with a standard set of items, and when you need to work with specific pieces of technology, like Active Directory, remote access, or Office 365, there are modules offered by Microsoft that bring those functions into PowerShell. Importing a module most often gives you access to additional cmdlets, but it could also include aliases, variables, assemblies, or workflows.

Active Directory (AD) is super common, so let's take a look at some AD-related cmdlets and prove that PowerShell doesn't know what to do with them by default. Once we import a module into our PowerShell session, however, we will find more functionality than before. Here are some Active Directory-related cmdlets that are useful for the administration of AD. There are many, many more available:

- `Get-ADDomain` – Queries information about the current AD domain
- `Get-ADForest` – Queries information about the current AD forest
- `Get-ADUser` – Queries and displays information about AD users as specified by parameters. For example, `Get-ADUser -Filter 'Name -like "*admin*"'`
- `Get-ADComputer` – Queries information about AD computers as specified. For example, to see all computers joined to the domain, use `Get-ADComputer -Filter *`
- `Get-ADDefaultDomainPasswordPolicy` – Outputs the currently configured password policy settings from the domain

If you log in to a domain controller, launch PowerShell, and then run these commands, it may seem like I am lying to you because they will work, without importing a module! In this scenario, you are unintentionally cheating because the Active Directory PowerShell module gets installed when you installed the AD DS role onto that server, so the commands already exist.

Logging in to any other server that is not a domain controller, however, and running any of these commands will present you with a whole lot of nothing, except error messages.

Figure 11.18: Prior to the AD module being installed

Let's change that. The process to implement PowerShell modules for Windows Server roles is pretty simple, and exists in the same place where you would go to install a role or feature into the operating system. Open Server Manager, and use the option to **Add Roles and Features.** Navigate all the way to the **Features** screen, and here you will find a Windows feature called **Remote Server Administration Tools.** Drop down the menu on that, and then expand **Role Administration Tools.** At the top of this list is **AD DS and AD LDS Tools,** and finally, listed under that category is **Active Directory module for Windows PowerShell.**

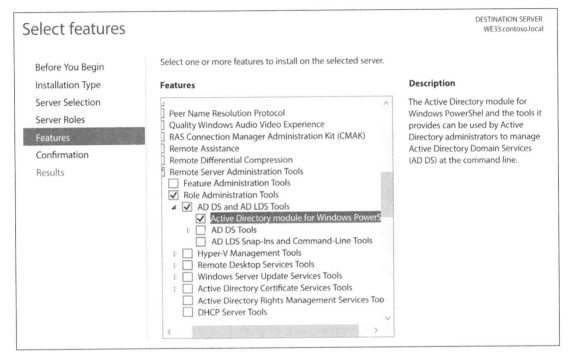

Figure 11.19: Installing AD PowerShell module via RSAT

Once this feature has finished installing, you will find that all of your Active Directory-related Power-Shell cmdlets now come to life on this non-domain controller server!

```
Administrator: Windows PowerShell                                    —    □    ×
PS C:\Users\administrator.CONTOSO> hostname
WEB3
PS C:\Users\administrator.CONTOSO> Get-ADDefaultDomainPasswordPolicy


ComplexityEnabled            : True
DistinguishedName            : DC=contoso,DC=local
LockoutDuration              : 00:30:00
LockoutObservationWindow     : 00:30:00
LockoutThreshold             : 0
MaxPasswordAge               : 42.00:00:00
MinPasswordAge               : 1.00:00:00
MinPasswordLength            : 7
objectClass                  : {domainDNS}
objectGuid                   : 801a7051-9f2a-4305-8f63-066489b28c97
PasswordHistoryCount         : 24
ReversibleEncryptionEnabled  : False


PS C:\Users\administrator.CONTOSO> _
```

Figure 11.20: AD module is now installed on WEB3

Even easier than plugging your way all through that installation wizard, you can accomplish the same thing with the following simple PowerShell command.

```
Install-WindowsFeature -Name "RSAT-AD-PowerShell" -IncludeAllSubFeature
```

Using a pipeline

Following the last couple of example cmdlets that we ran, you may be thinking to yourself, "I see that he is using that vertical line on the key above *Enter* on my keyboard, but why?"

Great question. In Command Prompt, we generally issue one command at a time. The same is often true for PowerShell when we are manually interacting with it, but in PowerShell, we have the potential for so much more power. One of those items of power is the ability to create a pipeline of commands. In other words, you can connect, or chain, commands together. This is commonly referred to as *piping* information from one cmdlet to another cmdlet and is done by using that little |.

Cmdlets often output data. If you then want to utilize that set of data against another cmdlet, this is where the pipe comes in handy. In our last example command, we told PowerShell to gather all of the commands that included the word Restart by performing Get-Command -Name *Restart*.

Then we **piped** that output to `Format-List`. PowerShell took the outputted dataset and threw it at `Format-List` to display a different set of output. The pipe is used very often in PowerShell commands. Keep in mind, when using a pipe, that the parameter defined needs to be something that knows how to accept the data you are piping toward it. If ever you try piping and it doesn't work, you may be attempting syntax that is unacceptable.

Export to CSV

One common way to use a pipe is when grabbing information via PowerShell that you want to retain, document, or send to somebody else. A common method for storing output data is within CSV files, a popular enough request that Microsoft has baked a cmdlet in for just that purpose. Let's work with another cmdlet that is very useful, `Get-EventLog`, and combine it with `Export-CSV` to show off this capability.

Event logs are essential information in a Windows Server environment. Troubleshooting issues on a server almost always involves a step of reviewing the Windows event logs. There is, of course, a graphical interface from which to accomplish this, but filtering and searching within that GUI is not as useful as it should be. Instead, we can turn to PowerShell to output event log information, such as the following:

```
Get-EventLog System
```

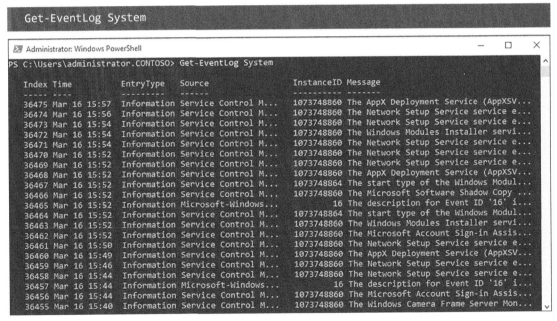

Figure 11.21: Viewing the system event logs in PowerShell

As you can see, the system event logs on this server contain a lot of information, and reading through it all within the PowerShell window could take the next three years. Filtering and searching are key to making this data useful, so let's see what this does instead:

```
Get-EventLog System | Export-CSV C:\Logs\SysLog.csv
```

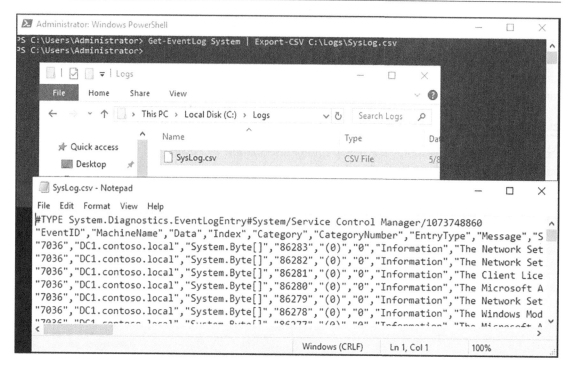

Figure 11.22: Piping output to a CSV file

PowerShell grabbed all of the information from system event logs and spit that info into a CSV file for us. We can now take that CSV file, open it inside a program like Microsoft Excel, and easily sort, filter, or search on these events in a much easier way than we could do from within the default Windows Event Viewer.

You can also export to XML or HTML, or even pipe output directly to a printer!

Pipes can invoke action

So far, we have only seen pipes modify outputted data. This is very useful, but I don't want you to walk away from this thinking that pipes are only useful for generating information. They can also take the output from one command and throw it at another command, but perhaps a command that actually causes a change or action to be performed. A good example is stopping a process or service. Let's pretend that for some reason you want to have a way to immediately stop all of the Hyper-V services on a server. Those services all have a `DisplayName` that begins with the word `Hyper-V`. We can verify that by using the following command to view all of those services:

```
Get-Service -DisplayName hyper*
```

```
Administrator: Windows PowerShell
PS C:\Users\Administrator> Get-Service -DisplayName hyper*

Status   Name                 DisplayName
------   ----                 -----------
Running  vmcompute            Hyper-V Host Compute Service
Stopped  vmicguestinterface   Hyper-V Guest Service Interface
Stopped  vmicheartbeat        Hyper-V Heartbeat Service
Stopped  vmickvpexchange      Hyper-V Data Exchange Service
Stopped  vmicrdv              Hyper-V Remote Desktop Virtualizati...
Stopped  vmicshutdown         Hyper-V Guest Shutdown Service
Stopped  vmictimesync         Hyper-V Time Synchronization Service
Stopped  vmicvmsession        Hyper-V PowerShell Direct Service
Stopped  vmicvss              Hyper-V Volume Shadow Copy Requestor
Running  vmms                 Hyper-V Virtual Machine Management


PS C:\Users\Administrator> _
```

Figure 11.23: Viewing services related to Hyper-V

We can take the output of this Get-Service cmdlet and pipe it to Stop-Service, and the resulting command will immediately stop all services that begin with the word Hyper:

```
Get-Service -DisplayName hyper* | Stop-Service
```

 Obviously, you'll want to be careful with this particular cmdlet piping! It would be easy to bomb an entire server by stopping all of its services with one little command.

PowerShell Integrated Scripting Environment

Most server administrators are familiar with the concept of creating batch files for use in the Command Prompt world. Have a series of commands that you want to run in sequence? Need to run this sequence of commands multiple times across different servers or over and over again in the future? Throwing multiple commands inside a text document and then saving it with the .BAT file extension will result in a batch file that can be run on any Windows computer, issuing those commands in sequence, which saves you the time and effort of having to plunk out these commands over and over inside the command-line interface.

Scripting in PowerShell is the same idea but is much more powerful. Commands in Command Prompt are useful but limited, while PowerShell cmdlets have the ability to manipulate anything within the operating system. With PowerShell, we can reference items from inside environment variables or the registry, we can easily issue commands to remote systems, and we can even utilize variables inside a PowerShell script, just like you would do with any full programming language.

Let's explore a couple of different ways that can be used to start creating your first PowerShell scripts.

PS1 files

Creating a simple .PS1 file (a PowerShell script file) uses almost exactly the same idea as creating a .BAT file. Simply open up a text document using your favorite editor, throw in a series of commands or cmdlets, and then save the file as FILENAME.PS1. As long as your PowerShell environment allows the running of scripts – see earlier in the chapter about the DEP – you now have the ability to double-click on that .PS1 file, or launch it from any PowerShell prompt, to run the series of cmdlets inside that script. Let's give it a try and prove that we can get a simple script up and operational.

Since you are only going to create scripts that serve a purpose, let's think of a real-world example. I work with terminal servers quite a bit – pardon me, RDS servers – and a common request from customers is a log of which users logged in to which servers.

A simple way to gather this information is to create a logon script that records information about the user session to a file as they are logging in. To do this, I need to create a script that I can configure to run during the logon process. To make the script a little bit more interesting and flexible down the road, I am going to utilize some variables for my username and the current date and time and record the name of the RDS server being logged in to. That way, I can look at the collective set of logs down the road, and easily determine which users were on which servers. I am going to use Notepad to create this script. I have opened up a new instance of Notepad and entered the following commands, and am now saving this as C:\Scripts\UserReporting.ps1:

```
$User = $env:username
$RDSH = $env:computername
$Date = Get-Date
echo $User,$Date,$RDSH | Out-File C:\Scripts\UserReporting.txt -append
```

Figure 11.24: Creating a simple PS1 script

You can probably already tell what this script is doing, but let's walk through it anyway. First, we are defining three variables. I am telling the script that $User needs to equal the environment variable username. This will give me the username of the person who is signing in. $RDSH is going to be the name of the server where the user is logging in, also pulled by accessing the server's environment variables. The third variable defined is $Date, which simply pulls the current system date by calling a PowerShell cmdlet named Get-Date.

After pulling all of the information into the PowerShell variables, I am then outputting these three items into a text file that is sitting on my server's hard drive.

If I run this script a few times, I can open my UserReporting.txt file and see that every time the script is run, it successfully logs my specified variables into this report file:

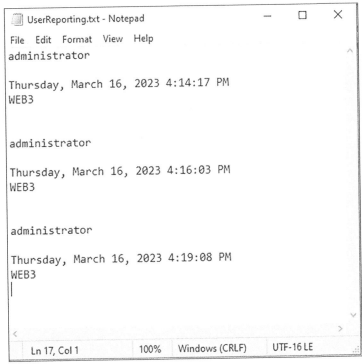

Figure 11.25: Results of our PowerShell script

Working with PowerShell ISE

If I'm being honest, putting together that simple script we just ran took some trial and error. I didn't have a copy of it readily available to work from, and I needed to test a couple of the lines individually in PowerShell before I was confident they would work in my script. I also first tried to pull the username without using the environment variable, and it didn't work. Why did I have so much trouble putting together just a few simple lines of code? Because as I typed those lines in Notepad, I had absolutely no idea whether they were going to work when I saved and attempted to run that script. All of the text is just black with a white background, and I am fully trusting my own knowledge and scripting abilities to put together something that actually works.

Thankfully, we have access to the PowerShell **Integrated Scripting Environment (ISE)**. This is a program that is installed by default in Windows Server 2022; it is a scripting shell that allows you to write PowerShell scripts and provides help along the way. Let's go ahead and open it up. If you have any PS1 PowerShell script files, you can simply right-click on one of them and choose **Edit**. Otherwise, by right-clicking on the PowerShell application icon (from the taskbar, for example), you will find an option to launch **Windows PowerShell ISE** right from that menu:

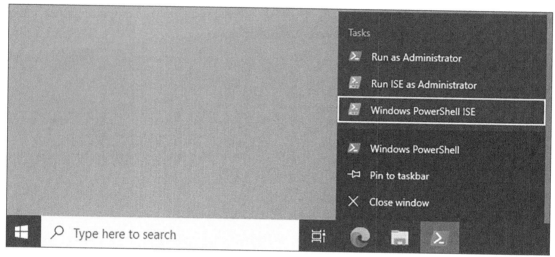

Figure 11.26: Launching PowerShell ISE

Now, if we start typing in the same script information that I used in Notepad a few minutes ago, you can see that even as we type, we get popups and prompts that help us decide which cmdlets or variables we want to utilize. Similar to the way that auto-complete keyboards on our smartphones work, ISE will give suggestions about what you are starting to type, so that you don't necessarily have to remember what the cmdlets or parameters are called; you can take an educated guess on what letter it starts with and then choose one from the list that is presented. There is also a list off to the right of all the commands available, and it is searchable! That is a great feature that really helps to get these scripts rolling:

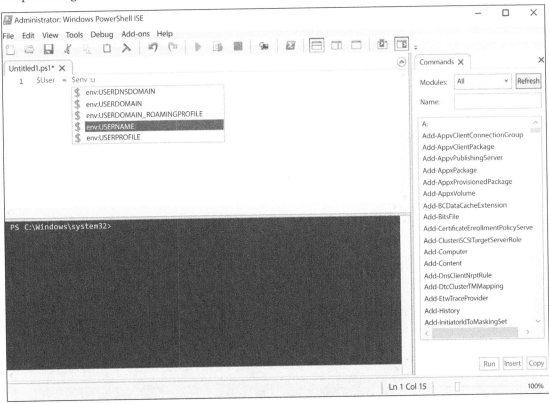

Figure 11.27: ISE provides suggestions for cmdlets and variables

Also useful is the blue PowerShell mini screen that consumes the bottom half of the development window inside ISE. Basically, when you type in some commands, ISE helps to make sure they are all going to work by color-coding the cmdlets and parameters for easy identification, and then you can click on the green arrow button in the taskbar that is labeled **Run Script (F5)**. Even if you haven't saved your script anywhere yet, ISE launches through your commands and presents the output in the following PowerShell prompt window. This allows you to test your script, or test changes that you are making to an existing script, without having to save the file and then launch it separately from a traditional PowerShell window:

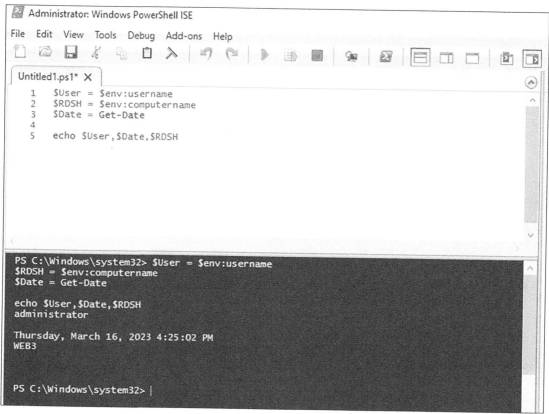

Figure 11.28: Testing the script inside ISE

What's even better is that you can highlight particular sections of your script and choose to run only isolated pieces of the code. This allows you to test certain sections of a script, or do something creative, such as keep one big PS1 script file that is full of common PowerShell commands that you might use on a daily basis. When you need to run just one of them, you can simply highlight the text that you want to run and click on the **Run Selection (F8)** button. By highlighting text before running the script from within ISE, only the selected cmdlet(s) will be put into action. In the following screenshot, you can see that I have numerous cmdlets listed inside my script file, but only the one that is highlighted ran when I pressed *F8*:

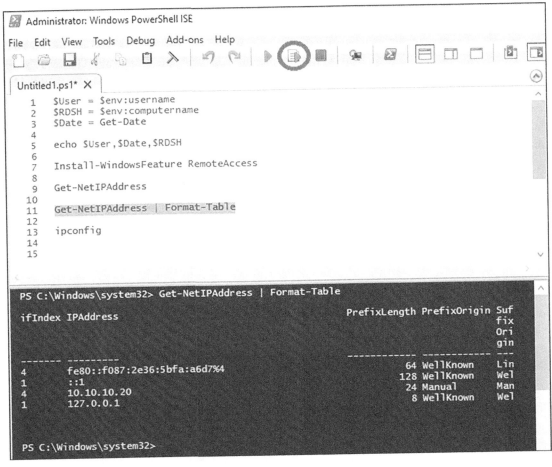

Figure 11.29: Running only highlighted commands in ISE

Remotely managing a server

Now that we have worked a little bit in the local instance of PowerShell and have explored a couple of methods that can be used to start creating scripts, it is time to take a closer look at how PowerShell fits into your centralized administration needs. If you start using PowerShell for server administration but are still RDPing into the servers and then opening PowerShell from there, you're doing it wrong. We already know that you can tap remote servers into Server Manager so that they can be managed centrally. We also know that the tools inside Server Manager are, for the most part, just issuing a series of PowerShell cmdlets when you click on the buttons. Combine those two pieces of information, and you can surmise that PowerShell commands and cmdlets can be easily run against remote systems, including ones that you are not currently logged in to.

Taking this idea and running with it, we are going to look over the criteria necessary to make this happen in our own environment. We are going to make sure that one of our servers is ready to accept remote PowerShell connections, and then use a PowerShell prompt on a different machine to pull information from and make changes to that remote server.

Preparing the remote server

There are just a couple of items that need to be running and enabled on your remote servers for PowerShell to be able to tap into them from a different machine. If all of your servers are Windows Server 2022 (in fact, if they are all Windows Server 2012 or higher), then PowerShell remoting is enabled by default, and you may be able to skip the next couple of sections. However, if you try to use PowerShell remoting and it's not working for you, it is important that you understand how it works under the hood. This way, you can troubleshoot it and manually establish remote capabilities in the event that you run into problems or are running some older operating systems where these steps may be necessary. It is also possible that you have pre-existing security policies that are disabling components used by the remote connection capabilities of PowerShell, so if you find your remote access to be blocked, these are the items to look into on those systems.

The WinRM service

One piece of the remote management puzzle is the WinRM service. Simply make sure that this service is running. If you have stopped it as some sort of hardening or security benefit, you will need to reverse that change and get the service back up and running to use PowerShell remoting.

You can check the status of the WinRM service from `services.msc`, of course, or since we are using PowerShell in this chapter, you could check it with the following command:

```
Get-Service WinRM
```

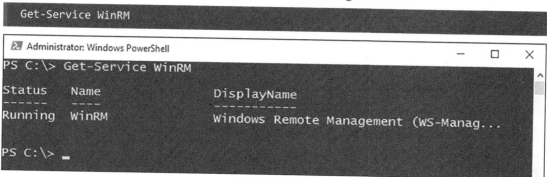

Figure 11.30: Ensuring that the WinRM service is running

Enable-PSRemoting

Typically, the only other thing that needs to be accomplished on your remote server is to run a single, simple cmdlet. Well, the server needs to have network access, of course, or you won't be able to see it on the network at all. But other than making sure network connectivity and flow are working directly from the console of your new server, you are then ready to issue the PowerShell command that enables this server to be able to accept incoming, remote PowerShell connections:

```
Enable-PSRemoting -Force
```

Using -Force at the end of the Enable-PSRemoting command causes the command to roll without asking you for confirmation. There are a few different things that Enable-PSRemoting is doing in the background here. First, it is attempting to start the WinRM service. Why did I already specify that you should check it manually? Because if you have it disabled as part of a lockdown strategy, you will interfere with this process. Checking WinRM before using Enable-PSRemoting increases your chances of success when running the Enable-PSRemoting cmdlet. There are two other things that this command is doing: starting the listener for remote connections and creating a firewall rule on the system to allow this traffic to pass successfully.

If you intend to use PowerShell remoting on a large scale, it is daunting to think about logging in to every single server and running this command. Thankfully, you don't have to! As with most functions in the Windows world, we can use Group Policy to make this change for us automatically. Create a new GPO, link and filter it appropriately so that it only applies to those servers that you want to be centrally managed, and then configure this setting: **Computer Configuration** | **Policies** | **Administrative Templates** | **Windows Components** | **Windows Remote Management (WinRM)** | **WinRM Service**.

Set **Allow remote server management through WinRM** to **Enabled**, as follows:

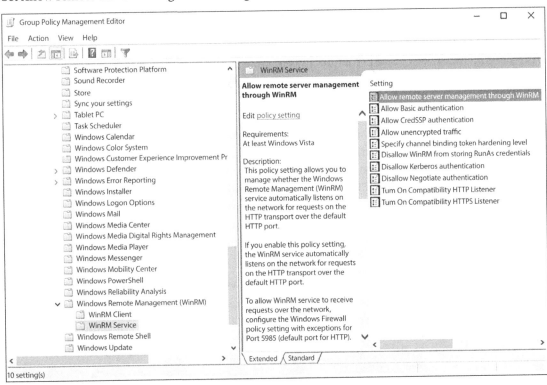

Figure 11.31: Enabling remote management via GPO

Allowing machines from other domains or workgroups

If you are working with servers that are all part of the same corporate domain, which will most often be the case, then authentication between machines is easy to accomplish. They automatically trust each other at this level. However, on the server you are prepping to accept remote connections, if you expect those remote computers will be members of a different domain that is not trusted – or even members of a workgroup – then you will have to issue another command to manually trust the individual computers that are going to be connecting in. For example, if I were planning to manage all of my servers from a client computer called Win10Client that is not trusted by the servers, I would need to run the following command on these servers:

```
Set-Item wsman:\localhost\client\trustedhosts Win10Client
```

If you wanted to allow *any* machine to connect remotely, you could replace the individual computer name with a *, but in general, this wouldn't be a good practice, as you may be inviting trouble by allowing *any* machine to connect to your server in this way.

Connecting to the remote server

I typically see administrators utilize remote PowerShell in two different ways. You can perform some commands against remote systems on an ad hoc basis while your PowerShell prompt is still running in a local context, or you can launch a full-blown remote PowerShell session to make your PowerShell prompt behave as if it is running directly on that remote system. Let's take a look at both options.

Using -ComputerName

Many of the cmdlets available in PowerShell, particularly ones that begin with Get-, can be used with the -ComputerName parameter. This specifies that the command you are about to run needs to execute against the remote system that you specify in the -ComputerName section. For our remote PowerShell examples, I will be using a PowerShell prompt on my Windows 10 client computer to access information on some of my servers in the network. I want to query the WinRM service, to make sure that it is up and running. For the sake of proving to you that I am remotely communicating with WEB3, you will see in the output that I have first queried my local WinRM service, which I happened to disable on my Win10 workstation.

You see in *Figure 11.32* that my local WinRM service shows as Stopped, but when I issue the same command specifying to query -ComputerName of WEB3, it reaches out and reports back to me that the WinRM service is indeed running successfully on the WEB3 server:

```
Hostname
Get-Service WinRM
Get-Service WinRM -ComputerName WEB3
```

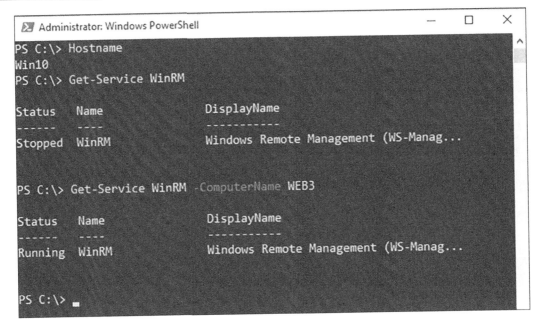

Figure 11.32: Using -ComputerName to query a remote system

Alternatively, perhaps I want to query the new Server Core instance we set up a little while ago and check which roles are currently installed on WEB4:

```
Get-WindowsFeature -ComputerName WEB4 | Where Installed
```

Figure 11.33: Roles and features installed on WEB4

The -ComputerName parameter can even accept multiple server names at the same time. If I wanted to check the status of the WinRM service on a few of my servers, by using a single command, I could do something such as this:

```
Get-Service WinRM -ComputerName WEB1,WEB2,DC1
```

Figure 11.34: Remote PowerShell running against multiple machines

Using Enter-PSSession

On the other hand, sometimes you have many different cmdlets that you want to run against a particular server. In this case, it makes more sense to invoke the fully capable, fully remote PowerShell instance to that remote server. If you open up PowerShell on your local system and utilize the Enter-PSSession cmdlet, your PowerShell prompt will be a full remote representation of PowerShell on that remote server. You are then able to issue commands in that prompt, and they will execute as if you were sitting at a PowerShell prompt from the console of that server. Once again, I am logged in to my Windows 10 client computer and have opened PowerShell. I then use the following command to remotely connect to my WEB4 server:

```
Enter-PSSession -ComputerName WEB4
```

The prompt will change, indicating that I am now working in the context of the WEB4 server.

If your user account does not have access to the server, you can specify alternative credentials to be used when creating this remote connection. Simply append your Enter-PSSession cmdlet with -Credential USERNAME to specify a different user account.

Commands that I issue from this point forward will be executed against WEB4. Let's verify this. If I check a simple $env:computername, you can see that it presents me with the WEB4 hostname:

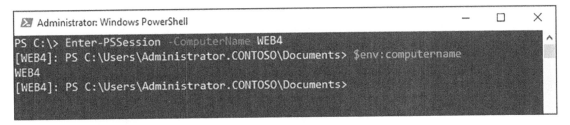

Figure 11.35: PowerShell is remotely connected to WEB4

And to further verify this, if I check the installed Windows roles and features, you can see that I have the Web Server role installed, as we accomplished when we initially configured this Server Core to be a web server. Clearly, I do not have the Web Server role installed on my Windows 10 workstation; PowerShell is pulling this data from the WEB4 server:

```
Get-WindowsFeature | Where Installed
```

```
[WEB4]: PS C:\Users\Administrator.CONTOSO\Documents> Get-WindowsFeature | Where Installed

Display Name                                Name                        Install State
------------                                ----                        -------------
[X] File and Storage Services               FileAndStorage-Services        Installed
    [X] Storage Services                    Storage-Services               Installed
[X] Web Server (IIS)                         Web-Server                     Installed
    [X] Web Server                          Web-WebServer                  Installed
        [X] Common HTTP Features            Web-Common-Http                Installed
            [X] Default Document            Web-Default-Doc                Installed
            [X] Directory Browsing          Web-Dir-Browsing               Installed
            [X] HTTP Errors                 Web-Http-Errors                Installed
            [X] Static Content              Web-Static-Content             Installed
        [X] Health and Diagnostics          Web-Health                     Installed
            [X] HTTP Logging                Web-Http-Logging               Installed
        [X] Performance                     Web-Performance                Installed
            [X] Static Content Compression  Web-Stat-Compression           Installed
        [X] Security                        Web-Security                   Installed
```

Figure 11.36: Roles and features installed on WEB4

This is pretty powerful stuff. We are sitting at our local desktop computer, have a remote PowerShell session running to the WEB4 server, and are now able to pull all kinds of information from WEB4 because it is as if we are working from PowerShell right on that server. Let's take it one step further and try to make a configuration change on WEB4, just to verify that we can. Maybe we can install a new feature on this server. I use Telnet Client quite a bit for network connectivity testing but can see that it is currently not installed on WEB4:

```
Get-WindowsFeature -Name *telnet*
```

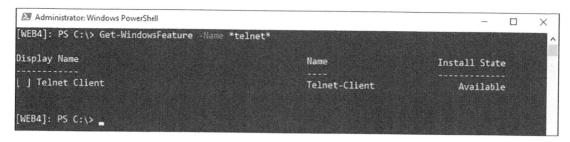

Figure 11.37: Telnet Client is currently not installed on WEB4

By using the Add-WindowsFeature cmdlet, I should be able to make quick work of installing that feature:

```
Add-WindowsFeature Telnet-Client
```

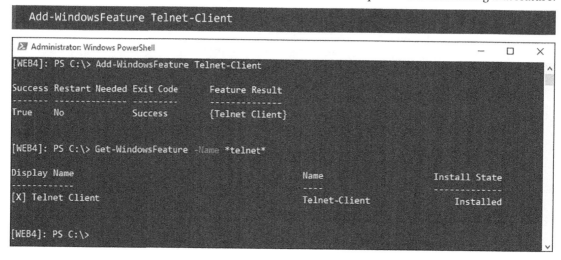

Figure 11.38: Installing Telnet Client on WEB4 via remote PowerShell

There is a ton of potential in utilizing remote PowerShell daily, not only for your servers running the full-blown Desktop Experience graphical interface but also for interacting with your security-focused Server Core deployments. Becoming familiar with working in remote PowerShell sessions will be essential to a successful deployment of Server Core in your infrastructure.

Desired State Configuration

There is some powerful functionality in the more recent versions of PowerShell, provided by something called **Desired State Configuration (DSC)**. DSC is a management platform plugged into PowerShell, which provides some new functions and cmdlets that you can take advantage of in your scripts to enable some really cool features. As the name implies, it allows you to build configurations inside PowerShell that will provide a *desired state*. What do I mean by that? Well, in a basic sense, DSC makes sure that the PowerShell scripts you build will always work the same way across all of the servers where you apply them by making sure the servers themselves are configured in the same way. It is quite easy to build a script in a way that means it will work correctly on the server you are currently working on. But, if you try to roll that same script out to a different server that might reside in a different **organizational unit (OU)**, or have different items installed on it to begin with, then the script could produce different results than what it was originally intended to do. DSC was built to counteract these differences.

In building your DSC configuration, you identify particular roles, settings, functions, accounts, variables, and so on that you want to retain in your specific desired state. Once you identify and configure these variables, DSC will work to ensure they stay where you have them set, and that they remain uniform according to your DSC configuration policy, which means they are uniform against the other servers where you have run this script.

DSC also helps to prevent unwanted changes on servers. If your DSC-enabled script has identified that a particular service should be running all the time on your servers, and that service stops for some reason, DSC can be there to help spin it back up so that you don't experience an outage. Alternatively, perhaps you have a script that configures a server to a particular set of standards, and another person in IT comes along and adjusts a configuration on the server—perhaps they log in and stop a service purposefully for some reason. Normally, this could result in an outage for that server, but DSC will get that service running again to maintain your originally configured *desired state* for this server. DSC is your *scripting nanny*, so to speak. It helps to build configurations that will remain uniform across multiple platforms and will then work to ensure these configurations are always true. You can then be confident that your servers are always running within the context of your specified desired state.

After building a configuration that identifies the items you want to be installed or monitored, an engine called the **Local Configuration Manager (LCM)** works to ensure the resources remain within the configuration specifications. LCM polls the system regularly, watching for irregularities and changes, and takes action when needed to bring your servers back into DSC.

The ultimate goal of DSC is to keep everything constant and consistent across your servers and services. DSC's capabilities and access to reach more and more places in the operating system grows constantly, as roles are rewritten to accept DSC parameters and monitoring. This technology helps to ensure that servers are always working with your defined standards, helping to maintain your 99.999% uptime status.

There is a lot to learn about DSC, and I encourage you to explore this topic more once you are familiar with creating and using PowerShell scripts. Here are some great starting points for learning more about DSC:

- `https://docs.microsoft.com/en-us/powershell/scripting/dsc/getting-started/winge ttingstarted?view=powershell-7.1`
- `https://docs.microsoft.com/en-us/powershell/scripting/dsc/configurations/write-compile-apply-configuration?view=powershell-7.1`
- `https://mva.microsoft.com/en-US/training-courses/getting-started-with-powershell-desired-state-configuration-dsc--8672?l=ZwHuclG1_2504984382`

Windows Terminal

Way back at the beginning of this chapter, we referenced Windows Terminal, and if you are a Windows 11 user you have probably interfaced with this new terminal console already. Windows Terminal is not a replacement for commands or cmdlets that come to us via Command Prompt or PowerShell but is a new console from within which we can utilize any command, cmdlet, script, or other thing to be run that we would classically open one of the other consoles to accomplish. Windows Terminal can run items from Command Prompt, PowerShell, WSL, SSH, and even Azure Cloud Shell Connector.

One of the coolest things about Windows Terminal is that it comes with tabs! Just like a web browser, you can separate out multiple instances of Terminal by creating new tabs and keeping command or script workflows separate from each other. This alone is reason enough for me to fall in love with it, and to use it by default moving forward.

Unfortunately, Windows Terminal is not installed by default in Windows Server 2022. If ever it were appropriate to plug an emoji into a technical book, it would be here. *Insert frowny-face.*

Take heart! With a simple download and package installation command, we are going to add Windows Terminal to a brand-new Windows Server 2022 right now.

First, we need to know exactly what we are downloading. Microsoft releases new versions of Windows Terminal occasionally, and we want to make sure we grab the latest. This URL will bring you straight to the GitHub site for identifying the latest version hash number:

https://github.com/microsoft/terminal/releases

Remember that Server 2022 is built on Windows 10 code, so I am going to focus on the latest Windows 10 version. As of the time of writing, I'm looking at the following filename:

Microsoft.WindowsTerminal_Win10_1.16.10261.0_8wekyb3d8bbwe.msixbundle

Below the asset hash names and info, you will find download links. You can either utilize your browser to download the MSIX bundle that you want, and then bring it over to your server, or you can right-click on one of these bundles and copy the URL. I am going to use PowerShell to download the bundle for me, which will also provide an example of another cool PowerShell cmdlet called `Invoke-WebRequest`. From the Microsoft GitHub page, I simply right-click on the version of bundle that I want and copy the URL, and utilize it as follows:

```
Invoke-WebRequest -Uri https://github.com/microsoft/terminal/releases/download/
v1.16.10261.0/Microsoft.WindowsTerminal_Win10_1.16.10261.0_8wekyb3d8bbwe.
msixbundle -outfile Microsoft.WindowsTerminal_Win10_1.16.10261.0_8wekyb3d8bbwe.
msixbundle
```

Following download, simply run a second command in PowerShell that will install this MSIX bundle. The following are a generic flavor of the command that you can use with whichever version number is current while you are reading this and also the exact command that I am going to run based on the 1.16.10261 version that I just downloaded.

General syntax:

```
Add-AppxPackage -Path <PathToFile>\Microsoft.WindowsTerminal_<VersionNumber>.
msixbundle
```

The exact command used at the time of writing (remember the trick about using the *Tab* key; all I had to do to populate this command was type `Add-AppxPackage -Path` and then press the *Tab* key to populate that big long filename):

```
Add-AppxPackage -Path .\Microsoft.WindowsTerminal_
Win10_1.16.10261.0_8wekyb3d8bbwe.msixbundle
```

Figure 11.39: Downloading and installing the Windows Terminal MSIX bundle

If you happen to receive any error messages about a missing dependency, you will need to download and install the second file from that GitHub page, ending with PreinstallKit.zip. Download this file and extract it into the same directory. Then use the same Add-AppxPackage cmdlet to run whichever APPX file is appropriate for your server. Most often, you are going to be running the one for x64, so your command would be exactly like this, though you may need to perhaps swap out the version number for whichever is currently on the GitHub page:

```
Add-AppxPackage -Path .\Microsoft.VCLibs.140.00.UWPDesktop_14.0.30704.0_
x64__8wekyb3d8bbwe.appx
```

Figure 11.40: Implementing both PreinstallKit and MSIXbundle

Once these dependencies are installed, run the command one more time for installing the Windows Terminal MSIX bundle file, and you should now have Windows Terminal in your Start menu, ready for use!

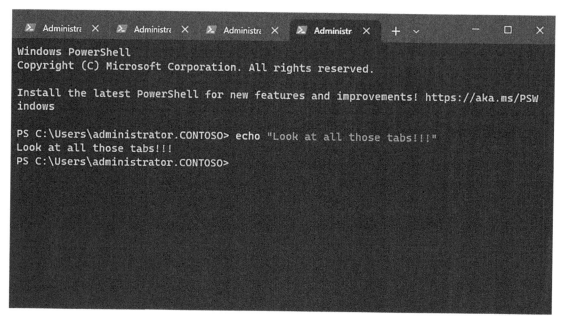

Figure 11.41: Windows Terminal on Server 2022!

Summary

In Windows Server 2022, we see in multiple places that administration via PowerShell is the recommended path for interacting with our servers. Because the management GUIs are now just shells running PowerShell scripts and the default installation option for Windows Server is Server Core, we can assume that headless, command-line-oriented servers are expected to be our servers of the future. Even though PowerShell has been at the core of our operating system functionality since Server 2012, I believe that so far, PowerShell is still viewed by many admins as simply an alternative way of managing servers. "Yeah, I know it exists and that I should start using it, and the scripting looks pretty cool, but I can still do anything I want to with the old Command Prompt or my mouse button." That old mentality is quickly changing. As we just finished installing for ourselves, the new Windows Terminal brings arguably an even better way to run PowerShell scripts and cmdlets than the PowerShell shell itself; the only thing that is stopping you from using it is you!

Now that we are experiencing an onset of new technologies, such as DSC and open-source PowerShell 7, we can see that PowerShell is starting to develop functionality that simply does not exist anywhere else in the operating system. This, combined with the remote management accessibility provided by the standardized PowerShell platform that can be used across all of your current Windows devices (even against servers sitting inside Azure!), means that we will definitely be seeing more and more PowerShell in subsequent Microsoft operating systems and services.

Questions

1. What is the fastest way to get from Command Prompt into PowerShell?
2. What is the cmdlet that will display all available PowerShell cmdlets?
3. What PowerShell cmdlet can be used to connect your PowerShell prompt to a remote computer?
4. What file extension does a PowerShell scripting file have?
5. To which setting is the Default Execution Policy configured on a fresh Windows Server 2022 instance?
6. What key on your keyboard can be used to auto-populate the remainder of a cmdlet or filename when working in a PowerShell prompt?
7. Which service must be running on a system before it can be connected to by a remote PowerShell connection?
8. Why do you think Windows Terminal is not installed in Windows Server 2022 by default?

Join our community on Discord

Join our community's Discord space for discussions with the author and other readers:

https://packt.link/SecNet

12

Redundancy in Windows Server 2022

Multiply that by two. This is a phrase I hear all the time when planning server deployments for work. I'm sure you have as well. Any time you are rolling out new technology, you want to plan that rollout very carefully. Figure out what servers you need, where they need to be placed, and how the networking needs to be configured for those guys. Once the planning is done, order two of everything, in case one breaks. We live in a world of always-on technology. Services going down is unacceptable, particularly if we are hosting cloud or private cloud services. Any application or service that our users depend on to get their work done is mission-critical and needs 100% uptime, or darn close to it. The problem with redundancy is that it's much easier to talk the talk than to walk the walk. Maybe one day we will be blessed with a magic "Press here to make this server redundant" button – but today is not that day. We need to understand the technologies that are available to us that enable us to provide redundancy in our systems. This chapter will introduce us to some of those technologies. This book is focused on Server 2022 used on-premises, so the technologies we cover are ones that you can utilize in your local datacenters on real (physical or virtual) servers that you are responsible for building, configuring, and maintaining. Yes, the cloud can provide us with some magical scalability and redundancy options, but those are easy, and often we don't even need to understand how they work. When we use our servers within our own walls, how can we add some increased reliability to our systems?

We will cover the following topics in this chapter:

- **Network Load Balancing (NLB)**
- Configuring a load-balanced website
- Failover clustering
- Clustering tiers
- Setting up a failover cluster
- Clustering improvements in Windows Server 2022
- **Storage Replica (SR)**
- **Storage Spaces Direct (S2D)**

Network Load Balancing (NLB)

Often, when I hear people discussing redundancy on their servers, the conversation includes many instances of the word *cluster*, such as, "If we set up a cluster to provide redundancy for those servers..." or "Our main website is running on a cluster..." or "This situation is a real cluster..." (oh wait, that is something else entirely). While it is great that there is some form of resiliency being used on the systems to which these conversations pertain, it is often the case that clustering is not actually involved anywhere. When we boil down the particulars of how their systems are configured, we discover that it is NLB doing this work for them. We will discuss real clustering further along in this chapter, but first I wanted to start with the more common approach to making many services redundant. NLB distributes traffic at the TCP/IP level, meaning that the server operating systems themselves are not completely aware of or rely on each other, with redundancy instead being provided at the network layer. This can be particularly confusing—NLB versus clustering—because sometimes Microsoft refers to something as a cluster when, in fact, it is using NLB to make those connections happen. Prime examples are the Microsoft remote access technologies. When you have two or more remote access servers together in an array, there are TechNet documents and even places inside the console where it is referred to as a cluster. But there is no failover clustering going on here; the technology under the hood that is making connections flow to both nodes is actually Windows NLB.

You've probably heard some of the names in the hardware load balancer market—**F5**, **Cisco**, **Kemp**, **Barracuda**, and many more. These companies provide dedicated hardware or virtual appliances that can take traffic headed toward a particular name or destination and split that traffic between two or more application servers. While this is generally the most robust way that you can establish NLB, it is also the most expensive and makes the overall environment more complex. One feature these guys offer that the built-in Windows NLB cannot provide is SSL termination, or SSL offloading, as we often call it.

These specialized appliances are capable of receiving SSL website traffic from user computers and decrypting the packets before sending them on their way to the appropriate web server. This way, the web server itself is doing less work, since it doesn't have to spend CPU cycles encrypting and decrypting packets. It's important for you to know that hardware load balancer solutions exist, but today, we are not going to talk about hardware load balancers at all, but rather the NLB capabilities that are provided right inside Windows Server 2022.

Not the same as round-robin DNS

I have discovered, over the years, that some people's idea of NLB is really round-robin DNS. Let me give an example of that: say you have an intranet website that all of your users access daily. It makes sense that you would want to provide some redundancy to this system, and so you set up two web servers, in case one goes down. However, in the case that one does go down, you don't want to require manual cutover steps to fail over to the extra server; you want it to happen automatically. In DNS, it is possible to create two host A records that have the same name but point to different IP addresses. If `Server01` is running on `10.10.10.5` and `Server02` is running on `10.10.10.6`, you could create two DNS records both called `INTRANET`, pointing one host record at `10.10.10.5` and the other host record at `10.10.10.6`. This would provide round-robin DNS, but not any real load balancing. Essentially, what happens here is that when the client computers reach out to `INTRANET`, DNS will hand them one or the other IP address to connect.

DNS doesn't care whether that website is actually running, it simply responds with an IP address. So even though you might set this up and it appears to be working flawlessly because you can see that clients are connecting to both Server01 and Server02, be forewarned. In the event of a server failure, you will have many clients who still work, and many clients who are suddenly getting **Page cannot be displayed** when DNS decides to send them to the IP address of the server that is now offline.

NLB is much more intelligent than this. When a node in an NLB array goes down, traffic moving to the shared IP address will only be directed to the node that is still online. We'll get to see this for ourselves shortly when we set up NLB on an intranet website of our own.

What roles can use NLB?

NLB is primarily designed for *stateless* applications, in other words, applications that do not require a long-term memory state or connection status. In a stateless application, each request made from the application could be picked up by Server01 for a while, then swing over to Server02 without interrupting the application. Some applications handle this very well (such as websites), and some do not.

Web services (IIS) definitely benefit the most from the redundancy provided by NLB. NLB is pretty easy to configure and provides full redundancy for websites that you have running on your Windows Servers, without incurring any additional cost. NLB can additionally be used to enhance FTP, firewall, and proxy servers.

Another role that commonly interacts with NLB is the remote access role. Specifically, DirectAccess can use the built-in Windows NLB to provide your remote access environment with redundant entry-point servers. When setting up DirectAccess to make use of load balancing, it is not immediately obvious that you are using the NLB feature built into the operating system because you configure the load-balancing settings from inside the Remote Access Management console, rather than the NLB console. When you walk through the Remote Access Management wizards to establish load balancing, that remote access console is actually reaching into the NLB mechanism within the operating system and configuring it, so that its algorithms and transport mechanisms are the pieces being used by DirectAccess in order to split traffic between multiple servers.

One of the best parts about using NLB is that you can make changes to the environment without affecting the existing nodes. *Want to add a new server to an existing NLB array?* No problem. Slide it in without any downtime. *Need to remove a server for maintenance?* No issues here either. NLB can be stopped on a particular node, allowing another node in the array to pick up the slack. In fact, NLB is actually NIC-particular, so you can run different NLB modes on different NICs within the same server. You can tell NLB to stop on a particular NIC, removing that server from the array for the time being. Even better, if you have a little bit of time before you need to take the server offline, you can issue a drainstop command instead of an immediate stop. This allows the existing network sessions that are currently live on that server to finish cleanly. No new sessions will flow to the NIC that you have drain-stopped, and old sessions will evaporate naturally over time. Once all sessions have been dropped from that server, you can then yank it and bring it down for maintenance with zero user interruption.

Virtual and dedicated IP addresses

It is important to understand how NLB utilizes IP addresses on your servers. First of all, any NIC on a server that is going to be part of a load-balanced array must have a static IP address assigned to it. NLB does not work with DHCP addressing. In the NLB world, a static IP address on a NIC is referred to as a **Dedicated IP Address** (**DIP**). These DIPs are unique per NIC, obviously meaning that each server has its own DIP. For example, in my environment, WEB1 is running a DIP address of 10.10.10.40, and my WEB2 server is running a DIP of 10.10.10.41.

Each server is hosting the same website on its own respective DIP addresses. It's important to understand that when establishing NLB between these two servers, I need to retain the individual DIPs on the boxes, but I will also be creating a new IP address that will be shared between the two servers. This shared IP is called the **Virtual IP Address** (**VIP**). When we walk through the NLB setup shortly, I will be using the IP address 10.10.10.42 as my VIP, which is so far unused in my network. Here is a quick layout of the IP addresses that are going to be used when setting up my network load-balanced website:

```
WEB1 DIP = 10.10.10.40
WEB2 DIP = 10.10.10.41
Shared VIP = 10.10.10.42
```

When establishing my DNS record for intranet.contoso.local, which is the name of my website. I will be creating just a single host A record, and it will point to my 10.10.10.42 VIP.

NLB modes

Shortly, we will find ourselves in the actual configuration of our load balancing and will have a few decisions to make inside that interface. One of the big decisions is what NLB mode we want to use. Unicast is chosen by default and is the way that I see most companies set up their NLB, perhaps because it is the default option and they've never thought about changing it. Let's take a minute to discuss each of the available options, to make sure you can choose the one that is most appropriate for your networking needs.

Unicast

Here, we start to get into the heart of how NLB distributes packets among the different hosts. Since we don't have a physical load balancer that is receiving the traffic first and then deciding where to send it, how do the load-balanced servers decide who gets to take which packet streams?

To answer that question, we need to back up a little bit and discuss how traffic flows inside your network. When you open up a web browser on your computer and visit HTTP://WEB1, DNS resolves that IP address to 10.10.10.40, for example. When the traffic hits your switches and needs to be directed somewhere, the switches need to decide where the 10.10.10.40 traffic needs to go. You might be familiar with the idea of MAC addresses.

Each NIC has a MAC address, and when you assign an IP address to a NIC, it registers its own MAC address and IP with the networking equipment. These MAC addresses are stored inside an ARP table, which is a table that resides inside most switches, routers, and firewalls.

When my WEB1 server was assigned the 10.10.10.40 IP address, it registered its MAC address corresponding to 10.10.10.40. When traffic needs to flow to WEB1, the switches realize that traffic destined for 10.10.10.40 needs to go to that specific NIC's MAC address and shoot it off accordingly.

So in the NLB world, when you are sending traffic to a single IP address that is split between multiple NICs, how does that get processed at the MAC level? The answer with unicast NLB is that the physical NIC's MAC address gets replaced with a virtual MAC address, and this MAC is assigned to all of the NICs within the NLB array. This causes packets flowing to that MAC address to be delivered to all of the NICs, and therefore, all of the servers, in that array. If you think that sounds like a lot of unnecessary network traffic is moving around the switches, you would be correct. Unicast NLB means that when packets are destined for the virtual MAC address of an array, that traffic is basically bounced through all ports on the switch (or at least on the VLAN) before finding and landing on their destinations.

The best part about unicast is that it works without having to make any special configurations on the switches or networking equipment in most cases. You set up the NLB configuration from inside the Windows Server tools, and it handles the rest. A downside to unicast is that, because the same MAC address exists on all the nodes, it causes some intra-node communication problems. In other words, the servers that are enabled for NLB will have trouble communicating with each other's IP addresses. Often, this doesn't really matter, because WEB1 would rarely have reason to communicate directly with WEB2. But if you really need those web servers to be able to talk with each other consistently and reliably, the easiest solution is to install a separate NIC on each of those servers and use that NIC for those intra-array communications, while leaving the primary NICs configured for NLB traffic.

The other downside to unicast is that it can create some switch flooding. The switches are unable to learn a permanent route for the virtual MAC address because we need it to be delivered to all of the nodes in our array. Since every packet moving to the virtual MAC is being sent down all avenues of a switch so that it can hit all of the NICs where it needs to be delivered, it has the potential to overwhelm the switches with this flood of network packets. If you are concerned about that or are getting complaints from your networking people about switch flooding, you might want to check out one of the multicast modes for your NLB cluster.

An alternative method for controlling unicast switch flooding is to get creative with VLANs on your switches. If you plan an NLB server array and want to ensure that the switch traffic being generated by this array will not affect other systems in your network, you could certainly create a small VLAN on your switches and plug only your NLB-enabled NICs into that VLAN. This way, when the planned flood happens, it only hits that small number of ports inside your VLAN, rather than segmenting its way across the entire switch.

Multicast

Choosing multicast as your NLB mode comes with some upsides and some headaches. The positive is that it adds an extra MAC address to each NIC. Every NLB member then has two MAC addresses: the original and the one created by the NLB mechanism. This gives the switches and networking equipment an easier job of learning the routes and sending traffic to its correct destinations, without an overwhelming packet flood. To do this, you need to tell the switches which MAC addresses need to receive this NLB traffic; otherwise, you will cause switch flooding, just like with unicast.

Telling the switches which MACs need to be contacted is done by logging into your switches and creating some static ARP entries to accommodate this. For any company with a dedicated networking professional, usually proficient in Cisco equipment, this will be no sweat. If you are not familiar with modifying ARP tables and adding static routes, it can be a bit of a nuisance to get it right. In the end, multicast is generally better than unicast, but it can be more of an administrative headache. My personal preference still tends to be unicast, especially in smaller businesses. I have seen it used in many different networks without any issues, and going with unicast means we can leave the switch programming alone.

Multicast IGMP

Better yet, but not always an option, is multicast with **Internet Group Management Protocol (IGMP)**. Multicast IGMP really helps to mitigate switch flooding, but it only works if your switches support IGMP snooping. This means that the switch has the capability to look inside multicast packets to determine where exactly they should go. So where unicast creates some amount of switch flooding by design, multicast can help to lower that amount, and IGMP can get rid of it completely.

The NLB mode that you choose will depend quite a bit on the capabilities of your networking equipment. If your servers have only a single NIC, try to use multicast or you will have intra-array problems. On the other hand, if your switches and routers don't support multicast, you don't have a choice—unicast will be your only option for configuring Windows NLB.

Configuring a load-balanced website

Enough talk; it's time to set this up for ourselves and give it a try. I have two web servers running on my lab network, WEB1 and WEB2. They both use IIS to host an intranet website. My goal is to provide my users with a single DNS record for them to access, but have all of that traffic split between the two servers with some real load balancing. Follow along as we set up this scenario.

Enabling NLB

First things first, we need to make sure that WEB1 and WEB2 are prepared to do NLB because it is not installed by default. NLB is a feature available in Windows Server 2022, and you add it just like any other role or feature, by running through the **Add roles and features** wizard. Add this feature on all of the servers that you want to be part of the NLB array:

Figure 12.1: Adding NLB to your servers

Enabling MAC address spoofing on VMs

Remember when we talked about unicast NLB and how the physical MAC address of the NIC gets replaced with a virtual MAC address that is used for NLB array communications? Yeah, VMs don't like that. If you are load balancing physical servers with physical NICs, you can skip this section. But many of you will be running web servers that are VMs. Whether they are hosted with Hyper-V, VMware, or some other virtualization technology, there is an extra option in the configuration of the VM that you will have to choose so that your VM will happily comply with this MAC addressing change.

The name of this setting will be something along the lines of **Enable MAC address spoofing**, though the specific name of the function could be different depending on what virtualization technology you use. The setting should be a simple checkbox that you have to enable in order to make MAC spoofing work properly. Make sure to do this for *all* of your virtual NICs upon which you plan to utilize NLB. Keep in mind, this is a per-NIC setting, not a per-VM setting. If you have multiple NICs on a VM, you may have to check the box for each NIC, if you plan to use them all with load balancing.

Depending on how old your hypervisor is, the VM may need to be shut down to make this change. Other than that potential gotcha, all we need to do is find the checkbox and enable it. Since everything that I use is based on Microsoft technology, I am of course using Hyper-V as the platform for my VMs here in the lab. Within Hyper-V, if I right-click on my WEB1 server and head into the VM's settings, I can then click on my network adapter to see the various pieces that are changeable on WEB1's virtual NIC. In the latest versions of Hyper-V, this setting is listed underneath the NIC properties, inside the section titled **Advanced Features**. And there it is, my **Enable MAC address spoofing** checkbox. Simply click on that to enable it, and you're all set:

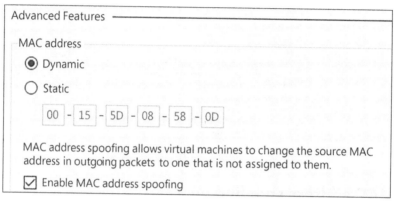

Figure 12.2: Enabling MAC address spoofing

If **Enable MAC address spoofing** is grayed out, remember that the VM may need to be completely shut down before the option appears. Shut it down, then open **Settings** and take another look. The option should now be available to select.

Configuring NLB

Let's summarize where we are at this point. I have two web servers, WEB1 and WEB2, and they each currently have a single IP address. Each server has IIS installed, which is hosting a single website. I have enabled MAC address spoofing on each (because these servers are VMs), and I just finished installing the NLB feature onto each web server. We now have all of the parts and pieces in place to be able to configure NLB and get that web traffic split between both servers.

I will be working from WEB1 for the initial configuration of NLB. Log in to this, and you will see that we have a new tool in the list of tools that are available inside **Server Manager**, called **Network Load Balancing Manager**. Go ahead and open up that console. Once you have NLB Manager open, right-click on **Network Load Balancing Clusters** and choose **New Cluster**, as shown in *Figure 12.3*:

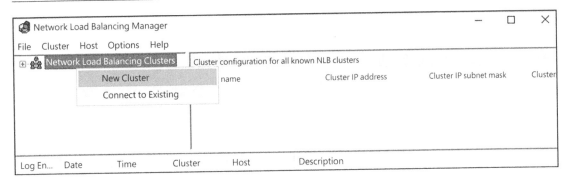

Figure 12.3: Creating a new NLB cluster

When you create a new cluster, it is important to note that, currently, there are zero machines in this cluster. Even the server where we are running this console is not automatically added to the cluster, and we must remember to manually place it into this screen. So first, I am going to type in the name of my WEB1 server and click on **Connect**. After doing that, the NLB Manager will query WEB1 for NICs and will give me a list of available NICs upon which I could potentially set up NLB:

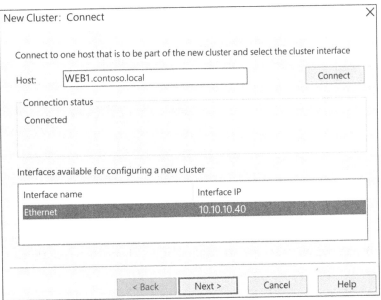

Figure 12.4: Choosing a NIC to establish NLB

Since I only have one NIC on this server, I simply leave it selected and click on **Next**. The following screenshot gives you the opportunity to input additional IP addresses on WEB1, but since we are only running one IP address, I will leave this screen as is, and click on **Next** again.

Now we have moved on to a window asking us to input **Cluster IP Addresses**. These are the VIPs that we intend to use to communicate with this NLB cluster. As stated earlier, my VIP for this website is going to be `10.10.10.42`, so I click on the **Add...** button and input that IPv4 address along with its corresponding subnet mask:

Figure 12.5: Adding a VIP address

One more click of the **Next** button, and we can now see our option for which **Cluster operation mode** we want to run. Depending on your network configuration, choose between **Unicast**, **Multicast**, and **IGMP multicast**:

Figure 12.6: Choosing a cluster operation mode

The following screenshot of our NLB wizard allows you to configure port rules. By default, there is a single rule that tells NLB to load balance any traffic coming in on any port, but you can change this if you want. I don't see a lot of people in the field specifying rules here to distribute specific ports to specific destinations, but one neat feature in this screenshot is the ability to disable certain ranges of ports.

That function could be very useful if you want to block unnecessary traffic at the NLB layer. For example, *Figure 12.7* shows a configuration that would block ports 81 and higher from being passed through the NLB mechanism:

Figure 12.7: Blocking specific traffic

Finish that wizard, and you have now created an NLB cluster! However, at this point, we have only specified information about the VIP, and about the WEB1 server. We have not established anything about WEB2. We are running an NLB array, but currently, that array has just a single node inside of it, so traffic to the array is all landing on WEB1. Right-click on the new cluster and select **Add Host To Cluster**:

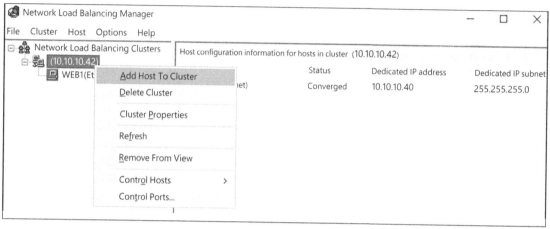

Figure 12.8: Adding a host to the new cluster

Input the name of our WEB2 server, click on **Connect**, and walk through the wizard to add the secondary NLB node of WEB2 into the cluster. Once both nodes are added to the cluster, our NLB array, or cluster, is online and ready to use. (See, I told you that the word cluster is used in a lot of places, even though this is not talking about a failover cluster at all!)

If you take a look inside the NIC properties of our web servers and click on the **Advanced** button inside the TCP/IPv4 properties, you can see that our new cluster IP address of 10.10.10.42 has been added to the NICs. Each NIC will now contain both the DIP address assigned to it, as well as the VIP address shared in the array:

Figure 12.9: Updated IP addresses on the NIC

The traffic that is destined for the 10.10.10.42 IP address is now starting to be split between the two nodes, but right now, the websites that are running on the WEB1 and WEB2 servers are configured to only be running on the dedicated 10.10.10.40 and 10.10.10.41 IP addresses, so we need to make sure to adjust that next.

Configuring IIS and DNS

Just a quick step within IIS on each of our web servers should get the website responding on the appropriate VIP address. Now that the NLB configuration has been established and we confirmed that the new 10.10.10.42 VIP address has been added to the NICs, we can use that IP address as a website binding. Open the IIS management console and expand the **Sites** folder so that you can see the properties of your website. Right-click on the site name, and choose **Edit Bindings...**:

Figure 12.10: Editing website bindings

Once inside **Site Bindings**, choose the binding that you want to manipulate, and click on the **Edit...** button. This intranet website is just a simple HTTP site, so I am going to choose my HTTP binding for this change. The binding is currently set to `10.10.10.40` on `WEB1`, and `10.10.10.41` on `WEB2`. This means that the website is only responding to traffic that comes in on these IP addresses. All I have to do is change that **IP address** drop-down menu to the new VIP, which is `10.10.10.42`. After making this change (on both servers) and clicking **OK**, the website is immediately responding to traffic coming in through the `10.10.10.42` IP address:

Figure 12.11: Updating your binding so the website runs on your new VIP

Now we come to the last piece of the puzzle: DNS. Remember, we want users to have the ability to simply enter `http://intranet` into their web browsers to browse this new NLB website, so we need to configure a DNS host A record accordingly. That process is exactly the same as any other DNS host record; simply create one and point `intranet.contoso.local` to `10.10.10.42`:

Figure 12.12: Configuring the DNS record

Testing it out

NLB configured? Check.

IIS bindings updated? Check.

DNS record created? Check.

We are ready to test this thing out. If I open up an internet browser on a client computer and browse to http://intranet, I can see the website:

Figure 12.13: Site 1 running on the WEB1 server

But how can we determine that load balancing is really working? I could shut down the WEB1 server, simulating an outage, and that would work fine. Alternatively, if I simply continue refreshing the page, or browse from another client, I continue accessing my web page via the same name of http:// intranet, and eventually, the NLB mechanism will decide that a new request should be sent over to WEB2, instead of WEB1. When this happens, I am presented with this page instead:

Figure 12.14: Site 2 running on the WEB2 server

As you can see, I modified the content between WEB1 and WEB2 so that I could distinguish between the different nodes, just for the purposes of this test. If this were a real production intranet website, I would want to make sure that the content of both sites was exactly the same, so that users were completely unaware of the NLB even happening. All they need to know is that the website is going to be available and working, all the time.

Flushing the ARP cache

Earlier, we had a little discussion about how switches keep a cache of ARP information, which lessens the time those switches take when deciding where packets should flow. When you assign a NIC an IP address, the MAC address of that NIC gets associated with the IP address inside the ARP table of certain pieces of networking equipment.

Switches, routers, firewalls – these tools commonly have what we refer to as an ARP table, and they have a set of data in that table that is known as the ARP cache.

When configuring NLB, particularly unicast, the NIC's MAC address gets replaced with a new, virtual MAC address. Sometimes, the switches and networking equipment are very quick to catch on to this change, and they associate the new MAC address with the new IP address, and everything works just fine. However, I find that when configuring NLB, the following is generally true: *The smarter and more expensive your networking equipment is, the dumber it gets when configuring NLB*. What I mean is that your networking equipment might continue to hold onto the old MAC address information that is stored in its ARP table, and doesn't get updated to reflect the new virtual MAC addressing.

What does this look like in real life? Network traffic will stop flowing to or from those NICs. Sometimes when you establish NLB and it turns itself on, all network traffic will suddenly stop cold to or from those network interfaces. *What do you need to do to fix this situation?* Sometimes you can wait it out, and within a few minutes, hours, or even a few days, the switches will drop the old ARP info and allow the new virtual MACs to register themselves in that table. *What can you do to speed up this process?* Flush the ARP cache.

The procedure for doing this will be different depending on what kind of networking equipment you are working on – whether it is a switch or router, what brand it is, what model it is, and so on. But each of these guys should have this capability, and it should be named something along the lines of *flushing the ARP cache*. When you run this function on your equipment, it cleans out that ARP table, getting rid of the old information that is causing you problems and allowing the new MAC addresses to register themselves appropriately in the fresh table.

I only wanted to point this out in the event that you configure NLB, only to see traffic flow cease on your server. More than likely, you are dealing with the ARP cache being stuck on one or more pieces of network equipment that are trying to shuttle the traffic to and from your server.

Failover clustering

We have established that NLB is a great solution for stateless applications, with a prime example being websites that you want to make highly available. *What about other server roles or functions that you want to make redundant?* Well, the opposite of stateless is stateful, so *how about giving high availability to stateful pieces of technology?*

Failover clustering provides this level of capability and can be used in cases where the nodes within the cluster are accessing *shared data*. This is a key factor in the way failover clustering is designed. The storage used by the cluster nodes must be shared and accessible by each node that needs it. There are many different roles and services that can take advantage of failover clustering, but there are four specific technologies that seem to make up the majority of clusters running in datacenters today: Hyper-V, file services, Exchange, and SQL. If you are working with any of these technologies – and chances are that you work with all of them – you need to look into the high-availability capabilities that can be provided for your infrastructure by the use of failover clustering.

While failover clustering provided by Windows Server is Microsoft-built and has the capacity to work very well out of the box with many Microsoft roles and services, it is important to note that you can establish failover clustering for non-Microsoft applications as well.

Third-party applications that run on Windows Server in your environment, or even homegrown applications that have been built in-house, can also take advantage of failover clustering. As long as that application uses shared storage and you can specify the tasks that it needs to be able to perform against those applications for the clustering administration tools – how to start the service, how to stop the service, how to monitor the service health, and so on – you can interface these custom services and applications with failover clustering and provide some major redundancy for just about any type of application.

Clustering Hyper-V hosts

One of the most powerful examples of failover clustering is displayed when combining clustering with Hyper-V. It is possible to build out two or more Hyper-V servers, cluster them together, and give them the capability to each host all of the VMs that are stored in that virtual environment. By giving all of the Hyper-V host servers access to the same shared storage where the virtual hard disks are stored, and configuring failover clustering between the nodes, you can create an incredibly powerful and redundant virtualization solution for your company. When a Hyper-V server goes down, the VMs that were running on that Hyper-V host will fail over to another Hyper-V host server and spin themselves up there instead.

After minimal service interruption while the VMs spin up, everything is back online automatically, without any administrative input. Even better, *how about when you need to patch or otherwise take a Hyper-V host server offline for maintenance?* You can easily force the VMs to run on a different member server in the cluster; they are live-migrated over to that server so there is zero downtime, and then you are free to remove the node for maintenance and finish working on it before reintroducing it to the cluster. We use VMs and servers for all kinds of workloads, so *wouldn't it be great if you could get rid of any single point of failure within that virtualization environment?* That is exactly what failover clustering can provide.

Virtual machine load balancing

In fact, not only does a Hyper-V cluster have the ability to quickly self-recover in the event of a Hyper-V server node going offline, but we now have some smart load-balancing logic working along with these clustered services. If your Hyper-V cluster is becoming overloaded with VMs, it makes sense that you would add another node to that cluster, giving the cluster more capability and computing power. But once the node is added, *how much work is involved in sliding some of the VMs over to this new cluster node?*

None! As long as you have VM load-balancing enabled, the cluster's weights will be evaluated automatically, and VM workloads will be live-migrated, without downtime, on the fly, in order to better distribute the work among all cluster nodes, including the new host server. VM load-balancing can be run and evaluated on demand, whenever you deem fit, or can be configured to run automatically, taking a look at the environment every 30 minutes, automatically deciding whether any workloads should be moved around.

Clustering for file servers

Clustering for file servers has been available for quite a while; this was one of the original intentions behind the release of clustering. Originally, file-server clustering was only useful for document and traditional file utilization; in other words, when knowledge-worker types of users need to access files and folders daily, and you want those files to be highly available. To this day, this general-purpose file-server clustering works in an active-passive scenario. When multiple file servers are clustered together for general-purpose file access, only one of those file-server nodes is active and presented to the users at a time. Only in the event of downtime on that node does the role get flipped over to one of the other cluster members.

Scale-out file server

While general file-server clustering is great for ad hoc access of files and folders, it isn't comprehensive enough to handle files that are continuously open or being changed. A prime example of these files is virtual hard disk files used by Hyper-V VMs.

There is a need for virtual hard disk files to be redundant; losing these files would be detrimental to our businesses. Thankfully, hosting application-data workloads such as this is exactly what **Scale-Out File Server (SOFS)** does. If you plan to host VMs using Hyper-V, you will definitely want to check out the failover clustering capabilities that are available to use with Hyper-V services. Furthermore, if you intend to use clustered Hyper-V hosts, you should check out SOFS as an infrastructure technology to support that highly available Hyper-V environment.

SOFS helps support failover clustering by providing file servers with the capability to have multiple nodes online (active-active) that remain persistent between each other constantly. This way, if one storage server goes down, the others are immediately available to pick up the slack without a cutover process that involves downtime. This is important when looking at the difference between storing static data, such as documents, and storing virtual hard disk files accessed by VMs. The VMs can stay online during a file server outage with SOFS, which is pretty incredible!

Clustering tiers

An overhead concept to failover clustering that is important to understand is the different tiers at which clustering can benefit you. There are two levels upon which you can use clustering: you can take an either/or approach and use just one of these levels of failover clustering, or you can combine both to really impress your high-availability friends.

Application-layer clustering

Clustering at the application level typically involves installing failover clustering onto VMs. Using VMs is not a firm requirement but is the most common installation path. You can mix and match VMs with physical servers in a clustering environment, as long as each server meets the installation criteria. This application mode of clustering is useful when you have a particular service or role running within the operating system that you want to make redundant. Think of this as more of a microclustering capability, where you are really digging in and making one specific component of the operating system redundant with another server node that is capable of picking up the slack in the event that your primary server goes down.

Host-layer clustering

If application clustering is micro, clustering at the host layer is more macro. The best example I can give of this is the one that gets most admins started with failover clustering in the first place: Hyper-V. Let's say you have two physical servers that are both hosting VMs in your environment. You want to cluster these servers together so that all of the VMs being hosted on these Hyper-V servers can be redundant between the two physical servers. If a whole Hyper-V server goes down, the second one can spin up the VMs that had been running on the primary node. And after a minimal interruption of service, your VMs that are hosting the actual workloads in your environment will be back up and running, available for users and their applications to tap into.

A combination of both

These two modes of using failover clustering mentioned earlier can certainly be combined together for an even better and more comprehensive high-availability story. Let's let this example speak for itself: you have two Hyper-V servers, each one prepared to run a series of VMs. You are using host clustering between these servers, so if one physical box goes down, the other picks up the slack. That in itself is great, but you use SQL a lot, and you want to make sure that SQL is also highly available. You can run two VMs, each one a SQL server, and configure application-layer failover clustering between those two VMs for the SQL services specifically. This way, if something happens to a single VM, you don't have to fail over to the backup Hyper-V server; rather, your issue can be resolved by the second SQL node taking over. There was no need for a full-scale Hyper-V takeover by the second physical server, yet you utilized failover clustering to ensure that SQL was always online. This is a prime example of clustering on top of clustering, and by thinking along those lines, you can start to get pretty creative with all of the different ways that you can make use of clustering in your network.

How does failover work?

Once you have configured failover clustering, the multiple nodes remain in constant communication with each other. This way, when one goes down, they are immediately aware and can flip services over to another node to bring them back online. Failover clustering uses the registry to keep track of many per-node settings. These identifiers are kept synced across the nodes, and then when one goes down, those necessary settings are blasted around to the other servers and the next node in the cluster is told to spin up whatever applications, VMs, or workloads were being hosted on the primary box that went offline. There can be a slight delay in services as the components spin up on the new node, but this process is all automated and hands-off, keeping downtime to an absolute minimum.

When you need to cut services from one node to another as a planned event, such as for patching or maintenance, there is an even better story here. Through a process known as **live migration**, you can flip responsibilities over to a secondary node with zero downtime. This way, you can take nodes out of the cluster for maintenance or security patching, or whatever reason, without affecting the users or system uptime in any way. Live migration is particularly useful for Hyper-V clusters, where you will often have the need to manually decide which node your VMs are being hosted on so that you can accomplish work on the other node or nodes.

In many clusters, there is the idea of a **quorum.** This means that if a cluster is split, for example, if a node goes offline or if there are multiple nodes that are suddenly unavailable through a network disconnect of some kind, then quorum logic takes over to determine which segment of the cluster is the one that is still online. If you have a large cluster that spans multiple subnets inside a network, and something happens at the network layer that breaks cluster nodes away from each other, all the two sides of the cluster know is that they can no longer communicate with the other cluster members, and so both sides of the cluster would automatically assume that they should now take responsibility for the cluster workloads.

Quorum settings tell the cluster how many node failures can happen before action is necessary. By the entire cluster knowing the quorum configuration, it can help provide answers to those questions about which section of the cluster is to be primary in the event that the cluster is split. In many cases, clusters provide quorum by relying on a third party, known as a **witness.** As the name implies, this witness watches the status of the cluster and helps to make decisions about when and where failover becomes necessary.

There is a lot more information to be gained and understood if you intend to create clusters large enough for quorum and witness settings. If you're interested in learning more, check out `https://docs.microsoft.com/en-us/windows-server/storage/storage-spaces/understand-quorum`.

Setting up a failover cluster

We are going to take a few minutes to set up a small cluster of servers so that you can see the management tools and the places that have to be visited to accomplish this. I have now backed out all of the NLB config on my `WEB1` and `WEB2` servers that we set up earlier so that they are just simple web servers at the moment, once again, with no redundancy between them. Let's set up our first failover cluster and add both of these servers into that cluster.

Building the servers

We have two servers already running with Windows Server 2022 installed. Nothing special has been configured on these servers, but I have added the **File Server** role to both of them because, eventually, I will utilize these as a cluster of file servers. The key point here is that you should have the servers as identical as possible, with the roles already installed that you intend to make use of within the cluster.

One other note during the building phase: if possible, it is a best practice with clustering that member servers belonging to the same cluster reside within the same **organizational unit (OU)** in **Active Directory (AD).** The reason for this is twofold: first, it ensures that the same GPOs are being applied to the set of servers, in an effort to make their configurations as identical as possible. Second, during cluster creation, some new objects will be auto-generated and created in AD, and when the member servers reside in the same OU, these new objects will be created in that OU as well. It is very common with a running cluster to see all of the relevant objects in AD be part of the same OU, and for that OU to be dedicated to this cluster:

Figure 12.15: Cluster servers should be stored in the same OU

Installing the feature

Now that our servers are online and running, we want to install the clustering capabilities on each of them. **Failover Clustering** is a feature inside Windows Server, so open up the **Add roles and features** wizard and add it to all of your cluster nodes:

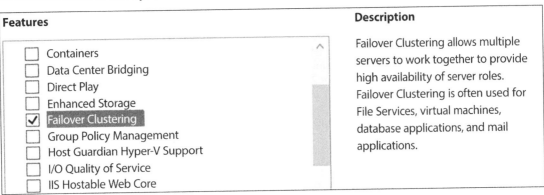

Figure 12.16: Adding Failover Clustering to your cluster nodes

Running Failover Cluster Manager

As is the case with most roles or features that can be installed on Windows Server 2022, once implemented, you will find a management console for it inside the **Tools** menu of Server Manager. If I look inside there on WEB1 now, I can see that a new listing for **Failover Cluster Manager** is available for me to click on. I am going to open that tool, and start working on the configuration of my first cluster from this management interface:

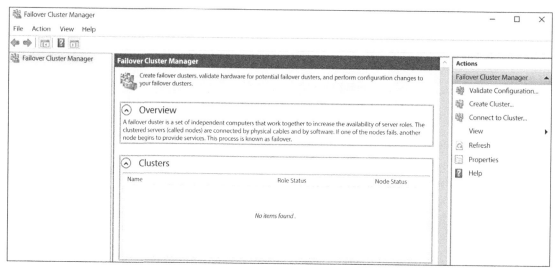

Figure 12.17: Failover Cluster Manager

Running cluster validation

Now that we are inside Failover Cluster Manager, you will notice a list of tasks available to launch under the **Management** section of the console, near the middle of your screen:

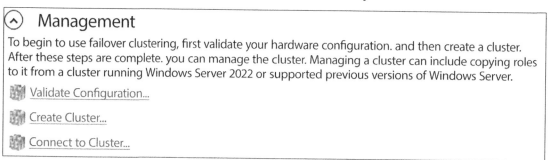

Figure 12.18: Cluster configuration tasks

Before we can configure the cluster itself or add any server nodes to it, we must first validate our hardware configuration. Failover clustering is a pretty complex set of technologies, and there are many places where misconfigurations or inconsistencies could set the whole cluster askew. Your intentions behind setting up a cluster are obviously for reliable redundancy, but even a simple mistake in the configuration of your member servers could cause problems large enough that a node failure would not result in automated recovery, which defeats the purpose of the cluster in the first place. To make sure that all of our *t's* are crossed and *i's* dotted, there are some comprehensive validation checks built into Failover Cluster Manager, sort of like a built-in best practices analyzer. These checks can be run at any time – before the cluster is built or after it has been running in production for years. In fact, if you ever have to open a support case with Microsoft, it is likely that the first thing they will ask you to do is run the **Validate Configuration** tools and allow them to look over the output.

To start the validation process, click on the **Validate Configuration...** link. We are now launched into a wizard that allows us to select which pieces of cluster technology we would like to validate. Once again, we must put on our Microsoft centralized management theology thinking caps and realize that this wizard doesn't know or care that it is running on one of the member servers that we intend to be part of the cluster. We must identify each of the server nodes that we want to scan for validation checks, so in my case, I am going to tell it that I want to validate the WEB1 and WEB2 servers:

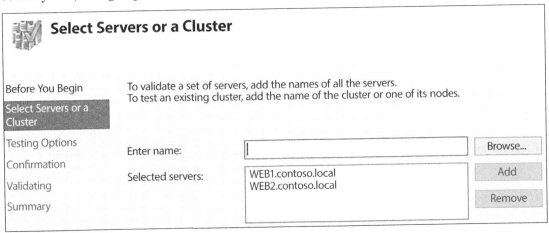

Figure 12.19: Selecting server nodes for cluster validation checks

The **Testing Options** screen allows you to choose the **Run only tests I select** radio button and you will then be able to run only particular validation tests. Generally, when setting up a new cluster, you want to run *all* of the tests so that you can ensure everything measures up correctly. On a production system, however, you may choose to limit the number of tests that run. This is particularly true with respect to tests against **Storage**, as those can actually take the cluster offline temporarily while the tests are being run, and you wouldn't want to interfere with your online production services if you are not working within a planned maintenance window:

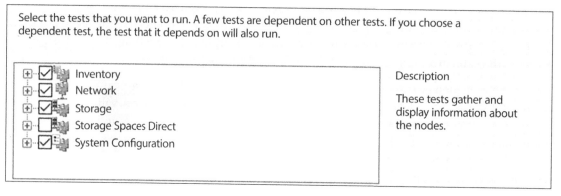

Figure 12.20: You have the option of selecting individual validations

Since I am setting up a new cluster, I am going to let all of the tests run. So I will leave the recommended option selected, **Run all tests (recommended)**, and continue:

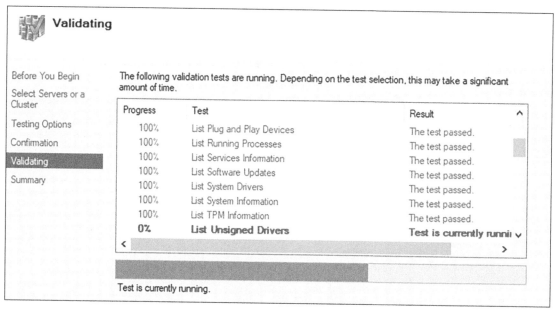

Figure 12.21: Running all tests

Once the tests have completed, you will see a summary output of their results. You can click on the **View Report...** button to see a lot of detail on everything that was run. Keep in mind that there are three tiers of pass/fail. Green is *good* and red is *bad*, but yellow is more like *it'll work but you're not running best practices*. For example, I only have one NIC in each of my servers; the wizard recognizes that, and for my setup to be truly redundant in all aspects, I should have at least two. It'll let this slide and continue to work, but it is warning me that I could make this cluster even better by adding a second NIC to each of my nodes.

If you ever need to reopen this report or grab a copy of it off the server for safekeeping, it is located on the server where you ran the tests, inside **C:\Windows\Cluster\Reports**:

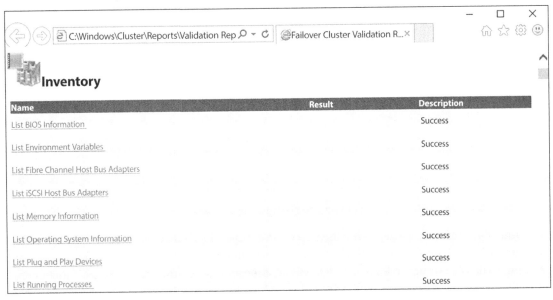

Name	Result	Description
List BIOS Information		Success
List Environment Variables		Success
List Fibre Channel Host Bus Adapters		Success
List iSCSI Host Bus Adapters		Success
List Memory Information		Success
List Operating System Information		Success
List Plug and Play Devices		Success
List Running Processes		Success

Figure 12.22: Cluster validation report

Remember, you can re-run the validation processes at any time to test your configuration using the **Validate Configuration...** task inside Failover Cluster Manager.

Running the Create Cluster wizard

The validation phase might take a while if you have multiple results that need fixing before you can proceed. But once your validation check comes back clean, you are ready to build out the cluster. For this, click on the next action that we have available in our Failover Cluster Manager console: **Create Cluster...**.

Once again, we must first specify which servers we want to be part of this new cluster, so I am going to input my WEB1 and WEB2 servers. After this, we don't have a whole lot of information to input about setting up the cluster, but one very key piece of information is on the **Access Point for Administering the Cluster** screen. This is where you identify the unique name that will be used by the cluster and shared among the member servers. This is known as a **Cluster Name Object (CNO)**, and after completing your cluster configuration, you will see this name show up as an object inside AD:

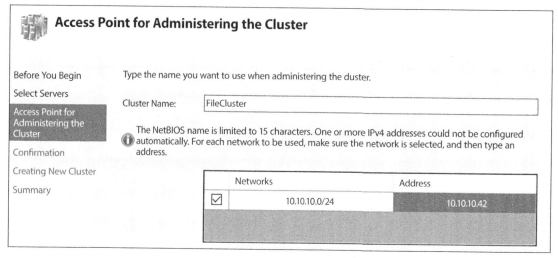

Figure 12.23: Setting a cluster name

After finishing the wizard, you can see the new cluster inside the **Failover Cluster Manager** interface and can drill down into more particular functions within that cluster. There are additional actions for things such as **Configure Role...**, which will be important for setting up the actual function that this cluster is going to perform, and **Add Node...**, which is your spot to include even more member servers in this cluster down the road:

Figure 12.24: Viewing nodes in our first cluster

Clustering improvements in Windows Server 2022

The clustering feature has been around for a while and every new release of Windows Server comes with some improvements and new features, but they often fly under the radar. There were some good changes in 2019, and more followed in 2022. Some of these improvements wrapped into Server 2022 directly from Azure Stack HCI, bringing cloud capability back into our datacenters. Let's review some of those so you can see the ways that Microsoft continues to be committed to improving our datacenter resiliency.

AutoSites

Many administrators don't even pay attention to Active Directory Sites and Services because many only have one site to deal with, but even if you have multiple physical sites that include servers, it is often true that most Windows Server technology will work just fine even if you leave all of your servers plugged into the default AD site. Failover clustering is one of the roles that can now take advantage of properly configured AD sites. If you configure your physical sites and ensure that your failover cluster nodes are assigned to the proper sites in AD, failover clustering will automatically create site fault domains according to the names of your sites, and place failover nodes into the appropriate locations.

Clustering Affinity

Prior to Windows Server 2022, failover clustering had the capability of AntiAffinity rules. AntiAffinity is a way to specify roles (like VMs) within a failover cluster and create rules for these roles to keep them away from each other. For example, if you wanted to ensure that two servers that were part of the same failover cluster remained separated and running on different Hyper-V host servers.

What is new in 2022 is that we can now configure Affinity rules in addition to AntiAffinity rules. Affinity rules work the same way but in reverse. It is a more common sense approach to grouping roles or nodes together, by specifying that you want certain ones to remain within the same host or site, rather than needing to think backward and decide which ones to keep apart from each other.

Improvements to BitLocker protected cluster storage

You know that failover cluster servers must share the same storage for the cluster to be successful, and you are likely aware that BitLocker is a very common way to encrypt and protect any Windows-based data volume. In prior versions of Windows Server, BitLocker-encrypting a shared cluster storage volume would be risky, as the BitLocker key always needed to be pulled live from Active Directory to allow access to that storage and successfully mount the drive. If a Domain Controller was not available, it could result in your cluster resource failing to start. In Server 2022, there is now an additional key protector specific to the cluster itself. During the boot or unlocking of that volume, it will always reach out and *try* to contact Active Directory for the real unlock information. If AD happens to be unavailable, the cluster can still be successful by utilizing a locally-stored unlock key to mount the drive.

Slightly older improvements (but still cool)

It's always difficult to decide whether "new releases" that came with a previous version of Windows Server should remain in an updated book, but I believe that understanding anything requires knowing where it came from. Here are some new-ish components of clustering that came to us by way of Windows Server 2019, and remain as helpful technology to this day.

True two-node clusters with USB witnesses

When configuring quorum for a failover cluster, prior to Server 2019, a two-node cluster required three servers, because the witness for quorum needed to reside on a witness share of some kind, usually a separate file server.

Starting in 2019, that witness can now be a simple USB drive, and it doesn't even have to be plugged into a Windows Server! There are many pieces of networking equipment (switches, routers, and so on) that can accept USB-based file storage media, and a USB stick plugged into such a networking device is now sufficient to meet the requirements for a cluster witness. This is a win for enhanced clustering in small environments.

Higher security for clusters

A number of security improvements have been made to failover clustering in Windows Server 2019. Previous versions relied on **New Technology LAN Manager (NTLM)** for authentication of intra-cluster traffic, but many companies are taking proactive steps to disable the use of NTLM (at least the early versions) within their networks. Failover clustering can now do intra-cluster communication using Kerberos and certificates for validation of that networking traffic, removing the requirement for NTLM.

Another security/stability check that has been implemented when establishing a failover cluster file share witness is the blocking of witnesses stored inside DFS. Creating a witness inside a DFS share has never been supported, but the console previously allowed you to do so, which meant that some companies did exactly this, and paid the price for it as this can cause cluster stability issues. The cluster-management tools have been updated to check for the existence of a DFS namespace when creating a witness and will no longer allow it to happen.

Multi-site clustering

Can I configure failover clustering across subnets? In other words, if I have a primary datacenter and I also rent space from a CoLo down the road, or I have another datacenter across the country, *are there options for me to set up clustering between nodes that are physically separate?* There's a quick, easy answer here: yes, failover clustering doesn't care! Just as easily as if those server nodes were sitting right next to each other, clustering can take advantage of multiple sites that each host their own clustered nodes and move services back and forth across these sites.

Cross-domain or workgroup clustering

Historically, we were only able to establish failover clustering between nodes that were joined to the same domain. Windows Server 2016 brought the ability to move outside of this limitation, and we can even build a cluster without Active Directory being in the mix at all. In Server 2016 and 2019, you can, of course, still create clusters where all nodes are joined to the same domain, and we expect this will be the majority of installations out there. However, if you have servers that are joined to different domains, you can now establish clustering between those nodes. Furthermore, member servers in a cluster can now be members of a workgroup and don't need to be joined to a domain at all.

While this expands the available capabilities of failover clustering, it also comes with a couple of limitations. When using multi-domain or workgroup clusters, you will be limited to PowerShell as your cluster management interface. If you are accustomed to interacting with your clusters from one of the GUI tools, you will need to adjust your thinking cap on this. You will also need to create a local user account that can be used by clustering and provision it to each of the cluster nodes, and this user account needs to have administrative rights on those servers.

Migrating cross-domain clusters

Although establishing clusters across multiple domains has been possible for a few years, migrating clusters from one AD domain to another was not an option. Starting with Server 2019, this changed. We have more flexibility in multi-domain clustering, including the ability to migrate clusters between those domains. This capability will help administrators navigate company acquisitions and domain consolidation projects.

Cluster operating system rolling upgrades

This new capability given to us in 2016 has a strange name but is a really cool feature. It's something designed to help those who have been using failover clustering for a while be able to improve their environment. If you are running a cluster currently, and that cluster is Windows Server 2012 R2, this is definitely something to look into. Cluster Operating System Rolling Upgrade enables you to upgrade the operating systems of your cluster nodes from Server 2012 R2 to Server 2016, then to Server 2019, and again to Server 2022, all *without downtime*. There's no need to stop any of the services on your Hyper-V or SOFS workloads that are using clustering; you simply utilize this rolling upgrade process and all of your cluster nodes will run the newer version of Windows Server. The cluster is still online and active, and nobody knows that it even happened. Except you, of course.

This is vastly different from the previous upgrade process where, in order to bring your cluster up to Server 2012 R2, you needed to take the cluster offline, introduce new server nodes running 2012 R2, and then re-establish the cluster. There was plenty of downtime and plenty of headaches associated with these upgrades.

The trick that makes this seamless upgrade possible is that the cluster itself remains running at the 2012 R2 functional level until you issue a command to flip it over to the Server 2016 functional level. Until you issue that command, clustering runs on the older functional level, even on the new nodes that you introduce, which are running the Server 2016 operating system. As you upgrade your nodes one at a time, the other nodes that are still active in the cluster remain online and continue servicing the users and applications, so all systems are running as normal from a workload perspective. As you introduce new Server 2016 boxes into the cluster, they start servicing workloads like the 2012 R2 servers, doing so at a 2012 R2 functional level. This is referred to as **mixed mode**. This enables you to take down even that very last 2012 R2 box, change it over to 2016, and reintroduce it, all without anybody knowing. Then, once all of the OS upgrades are complete, issue the `Update-ClusterFunctionalLevel` PowerShell command to flip over the functional level, and you have a Windows Server 2016 (or 2019 or whatever) cluster that has been seamlessly upgraded with zero downtime.

Storage Replica (SR)

SR is a modern way to synchronize data between servers. It is a data-replication technology that provides the ability for block-level data replication between servers, even across different physical sites. SR is a type of redundancy that we hadn't seen in a Microsoft platform prior to Windows Server 2016; in the past, we had to rely on third-party tools for this kind of capability. SR is also important to discuss on the heels of failover clustering because SR is the secret sauce that enables multi-site failover clustering to happen.

When you want to host cluster nodes in multiple physical locations, you need a way to make sure that the data used by those cluster nodes is synced continuously, so that a failover is actually possible. This data flow is provided by SR.

One of the neat data points about SR is that it finally allows a single-vendor solution, that vendor being Microsoft of course, to provide the end-to-end technology and software for storage and clustering. It is also hardware-agnostic, giving you the ability to utilize your own preference for storage media.

SR is meant to be tightly integrated and one of the supporting technologies of a solid failover clustering environment. In fact, the graphical management interface for SR is located inside the Failover Cluster Manager software – but is of course also configurable through PowerShell – so make sure that you take a look into failover clustering and SR as a *better together* story for your environment.

Storage Replica is now available inside Server 2019 and 2022 Standard editions! (Previously, it required the Datacenter edition, which was prohibitive to some implementations.) Administration of SR is also now available inside the new **Windows Admin Center** (**WAC**). Let's put together a Storage Replica environment, so you can see how quick and easy it is to create storage redundancy.

Configuring Storage Replica

I have created two new servers in my lab, with the intention of turning them into redundant file servers via SR. These servers are called FS01 and FS02 and are joined to my domain, and there are a few important things I have done with them:

- Attached a new disk to be used for data storage. Windows is running on a normal virtual disk on my server, but I added a second one that will be dedicated to storage. The important part here is that the data disk must be initialized with GPT.
- Created a volume to contain data. This volume in Windows is labeled as the S: drive and, once again, I am just making sure that this data volume resides on a GPT-initialized disk.
- Created a separate volume to contain SR logging data. When creating the SR replication set shortly, we will need to define a location for keeping SR logs, and it is easiest to do so on its own drive letter. I have called mine the L: drive. It also resides on my GPT-initialized data disk. The volume used for logs must be a minimum of 9GB.
- Installed the Storage Replica feature inside Windows, on both servers.

Initializing disks as GPT

If you're not familiar with the process stated above to initialize your new data disk as GPT, let's cover that for a minute. After attaching a new disk to your server, right-click on the **Start** Button and head into **Disk Management**. This tool should automatically recognize the new disk and ask whether you want to initialize it using MBR or GPT. Make sure to select **GPT** here:

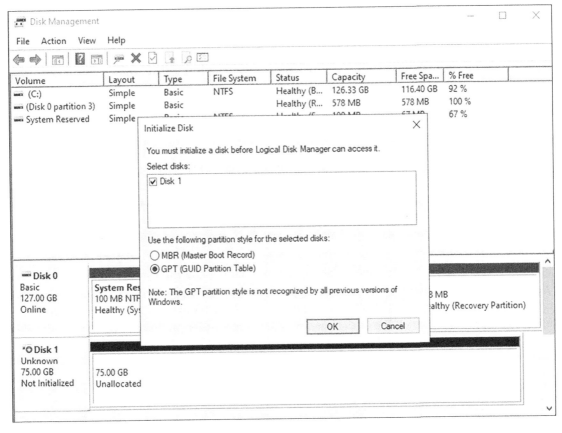

Figure 12.25: Initializing a new disk as GPT

Testing preparedness for Storage Replica

We now have two file servers, each with a new GPT data disk that contains two new volumes. One will be used for SR data storage, and the other for SR logs. Here's a quick look at the volumes I have. They are set up exactly the same on both servers:

Figure 12.26: Volumes created on the servers

At this point, we could plow forward with creating the Storage Replica environment, and since these are brand-new servers with identical configurations, it would most likely work. However, you will often be configuring SR on servers that have already been running in production for a while, or at least the primary file server where your source data is going to be located. Knowing whether or not SR is going to be successful would be comforting knowledge.

Thankfully, there is a testing process that SR can run before putting your configurations into place. Using PowerShell, let's issue a big long command from our primary FS01 server. The following is the command I am running. You will, of course, have to adjust it to accommodate your own server names and volume letters. As you can see at the end of the command, I specify for the output to be placed inside the C:\SR_TEST folder, so make sure that folder exists on your server:

```
Test-SRTopology -SourceComputerName FS01 -SourceVolumeName S:
 -SourceLogVolumeName L: -DestinationComputerName FS02 -DestinationVolumeName S:
 -DestinationLogVolumeName L: -DurationInMinutes 10 -ResultPath C:\SR_TEST\
```

This test will gather information about the servers and volumes and run some sample data transfers in the background for 10 minutes (as specified in the command). After completion, you will find a results file inside C:\SR_TEST that should launch in a web browser to show you all kinds of resulting information. Any issues with the environment that may hinder SR's ability to work will be detailed here so that you can go resolve those issues:

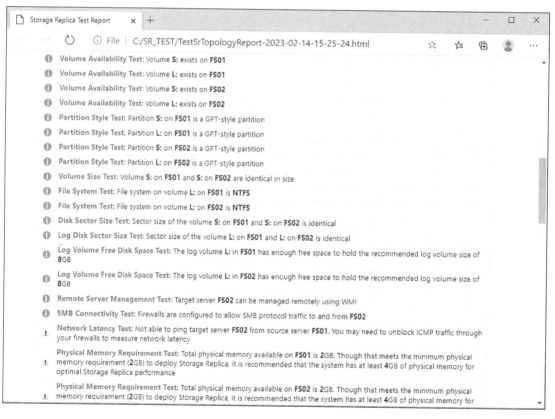

Figure 12.27: Storage Replica test report

You'll notice in *Figure 12.27* that I do have some warnings in my lab, which I did intentionally so that you had a visual of what the warnings look like. I never opened up ICMP traffic between these servers, so I received a warning about not being able to perform the network latency test. Also shown are some physical memory warnings. In a Storage Replica group, each server needs to have 2GB of RAM for SR to work properly, which is what I assigned to my VMs. While 2GB is required, 4GB is recommended, and the warnings are simply letting me know. In a production environment, you would never run a file server with even as little as 4GB of RAM, so you will likely not encounter these warnings during a real implementation.

Configuring Storage Replica

Now that our servers are prepped and tested, it's time to build the real deal! Since we have met all of our prerequisites and built out servers with SR in mind, all it takes is one PowerShell command to get this Storage Replica partnership started. I will list the command below, which is pretty self-explanatory. The only pieces that may be slightly unfamiliar are `SourceRGName` and `DestinationRGName`. The "RG" stands for "Replication Group," which is simply a name you must define for the replication group on each server:

```
New-SRPartnership -SourceComputerName FS01 -SourceRGName RepGroup1
 -SourceVolumeName S: -SourceLogVolumeName L: -DestinationComputerName
 FS02 -DestinationRGName RepGroup2 -DestinationVolumeName S:
 -DestinationLogVolumeName L:
```

Boom! Just like that, Storage Replica is configured with FS01's S: drive being primary storage, automatically and synchronously replicated to FS02's S: drive. Depending on performance and networking specs, the initial sync between volumes can take a bit of time, during which you will see **ReplicationState = InitialBlockCopy** in the results of the Get-SRGroup command. Once the initial sync has completed, that field will instead show **ReplicationState = ContinuouslyReplicating**, as you can see in *Figure 12.28*. Any data that is stored on FS01's S: drive is automatically replicated over to FS02:

```
Administrator: Windows PowerShell                                                    —

PS C:\Users\administrator.CONTOSO> Get-SRGroup


AllowVolumeResize    : False
AsyncRPO             :
ComputerName         : FS01
Description          :
Id                   : bb034862-527d-4398-9b59-416e25de2374
IsAutoFailover       :
IsCluster            : False
IsEncrypted          : False
IsInPartnership      : True
IsMounted            : False
IsPrimary            : True
IsSuspended          : False
IsWriteConsistency   : False
LastInSyncTime       :
LogSizeInBytes       : 8589934592
LogType              : FileBased
LogVolume            : L:\
Name                 : RepGroup1
NumOfReplicas        : 1
Partitions           : {4b77494e-8475-4c89-9b40-37b0df85a7b0}
Replicas             : {MSFT_WvrReplica (PartitionId = "4b77494e-8475-4c89-9b40-37b0df85a7b0")}
ReplicationMode      : Synchronous
ReplicationStatus    : ContinuouslyReplicating
TemporaryPath        :
PSComputerName       :
```

Figure 12.28: Details of our Storage Replica group

Shifting the primary server to FS02

After poking around on the file servers, you'll notice that you can see data on FS01's S: drive, but if you try to browse FS02's S: drive, you are met with an error message – "S:\ is not accessible. The device is not ready." This is by design. You are unable to browse and see data on the destination SR server, until you run another command to make it primary, such as in the event of a disaster recovery scenario. To prove that SR is really working, let's follow that step to make sure data is automatically replicating from FS01 to FS02.

I have created some sample text files on FS01's S: drive, but I am unable to verify that they exist on FS02. Let's pretend that FS01 has gone offline or is having some other kind of issue, and I need to make FS02 my new primary file server. All I need to do is run the following PowerShell command on FS02 to flip roles, turning FS02 into the new primary SR partner:

```
Set-SRPartnership -NewSourceComputerName FS02 -SourceRGName RepGroup2
 -DestinationComputerName FS01 -DestinationRGName RepGroup1
```

Immediately after running this command, I can now see and browse through the data on FS02's S: drive, which means that it is now the primary SR member, and also proves to me that SR was working in the first place:

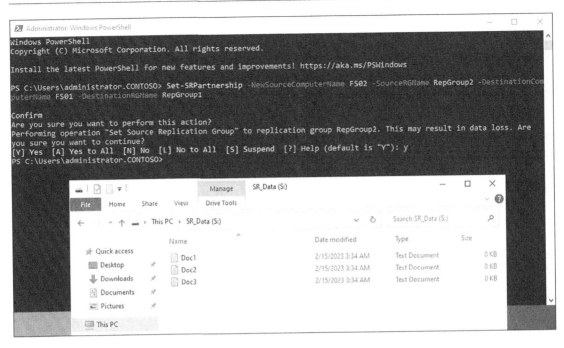

Figure 12.29: We have shifted primary drive access to FS02

And as expected, if I attempt to open and browse the `S:` drive on `FS01`, I now receive the error message on that node instead.

Storage Spaces Direct (S2D)

S2D is a clustering technology, but I list it here separate from general failover clustering because S2D is a core component of the **software-defined data center** (**SDDC**) and has had so much focus on improvements over the past few years that it really is in a category of its own. As a forewarning, I am in no way going to be able to cover the entirety of Storage Spaces Direct in this chapter; it really deserves its own book. There are links at the end of this section that will bring you into the swaths of documentation that accompany S2D.

In a nutshell, S2D is a way to build an extremely efficient and redundant centralized, network-based storage platform entirely from Windows Server. While serving the same general purpose (file storage) as a traditional NAS or SAN device, S2D takes an entirely different approach in that it does not require specialized hardware, nor special cables or connectivity between the nodes of the S2D cluster.

To build S2D, all you need are Windows Servers – the faster, the better – but they could be normal, everyday servers. They do need to be Windows Server Datacenter Edition, but you could run S2D on either Desktop Experience or Server Core nodes. These servers must be connected through networking, and that networking needs to be pretty serious for S2D to work properly. You will need high bandwidth and low latency between servers to make this successful – a minimum of 10Gb is what we're talking about here. Once you have these servers running and connected, you can utilize clustering technologies or WAC to bind these servers together into S2D arrays.

S2D is part of the overall **Hyper-Converged Infrastructure (HCI)** story and is a wonderful way to provide extremely fast and protected storage for anything, especially for workloads such as clusters of Hyper-V servers. As you already know, when building a Hyper-V Server cluster, the nodes of that cluster must have access to shared storage upon which the VM hard disk files will reside. S2D is the best way to provide that centralized storage.

S2D will take the hard drives inside your S2D cluster node servers and combine all of their space together into software-defined pools of storage. These storage pools are configured with caching capabilities and even built-in fault tolerance. You obviously wouldn't want a single S2D node, or even a single hard drive going offline, to cause a hiccup in your S2D solution, and of course, Microsoft doesn't want that to happen either. So when you group servers and all of their hard drives together into these large pools of S2D storage, they are automatically configured with parity among those drives so that particular components going offline does not result in lost data or even a slowdown of the system.

S2D is the best storage platform for both SOFS and Hyper-V clusters.

While early versions of S2D were configured mostly through PowerShell (which unfortunately means that a lot of administrators haven't tried it yet), our current version of Windows Admin Center includes built-in options for configuring an S2D environment:

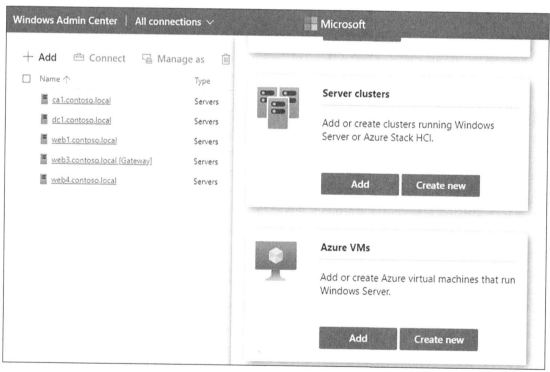

Figure 12.30: Using WAC to add new server clusters

As mentioned, S2D is one of those technologies that warrants its own book, but anyone looking to try out or get started with this amazing storage technology should start at https://learn.microsoft. com/en-us/azure-stack/hci/concepts/storage-spaces-direct-overview.

New in Server 2022 and 2019

Many great changes have come to Storage Spaces Direct over the past few years, through the releases of both Windows Server 2019 and 2022. Moving forward, Microsoft is focusing primarily on S2D changes to hit Azure Stack HCI, as they really expect most companies to utilize that technology stack to support Storage Spaces Direct. As new features are introduced to Azure Stack HCI, some or all of those then get ported down to the latest version of Windows Server as well.

Specifically for Windows Server 2022, I only know of two enhancements made in this space:

- **Adjustable Storage Repair Speed:** S2D's capability to self-repair data copies between servers is not a new thing, but starting with Windows Server 2022, you now have options for controlling how many workload resources are dedicated to this task.

- **Storage Spaces Tiering:** You already know that Storage Spaces Direct is all about taking storage of multiple servers and combining them all together. Stepping back a bit from that idea, you have probably heard of Storage Spaces, which is a similar but different technology that is used on a per-server basis. Storage Spaces uses software to combine combines multiple drives in a single server to create a larger usable storage space, and this new feature is specifically for Storage Spaces. We now have the option of tiering storage, giving us access to utilize SSD drives for caching.

There were more enhancements in S2D during the Windows Server 2019 release, and they are still relevant today:

- **Improved use of Resilient File System (ReFS) volumes:** We now have deduplication and compression functions on ReFS volumes hosted by S2D.

- **USB witness:** We already discussed this one. When using a witness to oversee an S2D cluster that is only two nodes, you can now utilize a USB key plugged into a piece of networking equipment, rather than running a third server for this witnessing purpose.

- **WAC:** WAC now includes tools and functionality for defining and managing S2D clusters. This will make adoption much easier for folks who are not overly familiar with PowerShell.

- **Improved capability:** We can now host four petabytes per cluster, compared to one petabyte in Server 2016. Keep in mind, though, that it is recommended to maintain a maximum of 400TB per server within the cluster.

- **Improved speed:** While S2D has been fast since the very first version, we had some efficiency improvements in Server 2019. At that year's Ignite conference, Microsoft showcased an 8-node S2D cluster that was capable of achieving 13,000,000 IOPS. Holy moly!

Summary

Redundancy is a critical component in the way that we plan infrastructure and build servers in today's world. Windows Server 2022 has some powerful capabilities built right into it that you can utilize in your own environments, starting today! I hope that by gleaning a little more information about both NLB and failover clustering, you will be able to expand the capabilities of your organization by employing these techniques and stretching the limits of your service uptime.

Even for a small-medium business, there are some great replication options in Windows Server, made possible with a limited set of servers. You could use Storage Replica to replace many other third-party options that currently exist in these environments, giving you redundant file servers in a quick-and-easy fashion. For any enterprise-class organization that hasn't tested the waters with S2D yet, what's stopping you? Let's get serious about resiliency for your Hyper-V infrastructure. HCI will change the way that you work and give you peace of mind that you didn't think was possible in a world aiming for 99.999% uptime.

Questions

1. Which technology is more appropriate for making web server traffic redundant – Network Load Balancing or failover clustering?

2. Is website traffic generally stateful or stateless?

3. In Network Load Balancing, what do the acronyms DIP and VIP stand for?

4. What are the three NLB modes?

5. In Windows Server 2022, is Network Load Balancing a role or a feature?

6. What roles are most often used with failover clustering?

7. What type of small device can now be used as a cluster quorum witness (this is brand new as of Server 2019)?

8. True or False? Storage Spaces Direct requires the use of SSD hard drives.

9. What is the difference between Storage Spaces, and Storage Spaces Direct?

Join our community on Discord

Join our community's Discord space for discussions with the author and other readers:

https://packt.link/SecNet

13

Containers

Many of the new technologies included in Windows Server 2022 are designed to reflect the capabilities provided by cloud computing, bringing your private and hybrid clouds to life and granting you the ability to produce the same solutions given to you by public cloud providers within your physical infrastructure. The last few iterations of the Server operating system have also revolved around virtualization, and the idea of application containers is something that taps into both of these mindsets. Application containers will make the deployment of applications more streamlined, more secure, and more efficient. Containers are a relatively new idea in the Microsoft world, and outside of conversations about DevOps, I haven't heard many IT admins talking about them. This is something that has been enhancing Linux computing for a while now, and this newest Windows Server operating system brings it a little bit closer to home for us Microsoft-centric shops.

Application developers will be very interested in application containers provided by Windows Server 2022, and in truth, they probably understand the concepts behind containers much better than a traditional server administrator. While the premise of this book is not focused on development opportunities and clearly not focused on Linux, we will discuss containers because the benefits provided are not only for developers. We, as system operations, will also benefit from using containers, and if nothing else, it is going to be important for us to know and understand how to conceptualize and spin up containers, so that we can provide the infrastructure that our developers are going to require as they begin to build modern applications.

In this chapter, we will cover some topics dealing with application containers; hopefully this will help prepare your administrators to support this technology in your data centers:

- Understanding application containers
- Container base images
- Windows Server containers versus Hyper-V containers
- Docker and Kubernetes
- Working with containers
- Where is Azure in all this?

Understanding application containers

What does it mean to *contain* an application? We have a pretty good concept these days of containing servers through virtualization. Taking physical hardware, turning it into a Hyper-V virtualization host, and then running many **virtual machines** (**VMs**) on top of it is a form of containment for those VMs. We are essentially tricking them into believing that they are their own entity, completely unaware that they are sharing resources and hardware with other VMs running on that host. Although we share hardware resources, we can provide strong layers of isolation between VMs, because we need to make sure that access and permissions cannot bleed across VMs – particularly in a cloud provider scenario, as that would spell disaster.

Application containers are the same idea, at a different level. While VMs are all about virtualizing hardware, containers are more like virtualizing an operating system. Rather than creating VMs to host our applications, we can create containers, which are much smaller. We then run applications inside those containers, and the applications are tricked into thinking that they are running on top of a dedicated instance of the operating system.

A huge advantage of using containers is the unity that they bring to the development and operations teams. We hear the term DevOps all the time these days, which is a combination of development and operation processes working together to make the entire application rollout process more efficient. The utilization of containers is core to creating a successful DevOps mentality since developers can now do their job (developing applications) without needing to accommodate the operations and infrastructure side of things. When the application is built, operations can take the container within which the application resides, and simply spin it up inside their container infrastructure, without any worries that the application is going to break servers or have compatibility problems.

I foresee containers taking the place of many VMs, but this will only happen if admins jump in and try it out for themselves. Let's discuss a few particular benefits that containers bring to the table.

Sharing resources

Just like when we talk about hardware being split up among VMs, application containers mean that we take physical chunks of hardware and divide them up among containers. This allows us to run many containers from the same server, be it a physical or virtual server.

However, in that alone, there is no benefit over VMs, because they simply share hardware as well. Where we really start to see the benefits of using containers rather than separate VMs for all of our applications is that all of our containers can share the same base operating system. Not only are they spun up from the same base set, which makes it extremely fast to bring new containers online, but they also share the same kernel resources. Every instance of an operating system has its own set of user processes. Often, it is a tricky business to run multiple applications together on servers because those applications traditionally have access to the same set of processes and have the potential to be negatively affected by those processes. In other words, it's the reason that we tend to spin up so many servers, keeping each application on its own server so that they can't negatively impact each other. Sometimes apps simply do not like to mix. The kernel in Windows Server 2022 has been enhanced so that it can handle multiple copies of the user-mode processes.

This means you not only have the ability to run instances of the same application over many different servers but can also run many different applications, even if they don't typically like to coexist, on the same server.

Isolation

One of the huge benefits of application containers is that developers can build their applications within a container running on their own workstation! A host machine to host containers can be a Windows Server instance, or it can be a Windows 10 or 11 workstation. When built within this container sandbox, developers will know that their application contains all of the parts, pieces, and dependencies that it needs to run properly and that it runs in a way that doesn't require extra components from the underlying operating system. This means the developer can build the application, make sure it works in their local environment, and then easily slide that application container over to the hosting servers, where it will be spun up and ready for production use. That production server might be an on-premise container server that an IT admin has built, or it could even be a cloud-provided resource – the application doesn't care. The isolation of the container from the operating system helps to keep the application standardized in a way that is easily mobile and movable, saving the developer time and headaches, since they don't have to accommodate differences in underlying operating systems during the development process.

The other aspect of isolation is the security aspect. This is the same story as multiple VMs running on the same host, particularly in a cloud environment. You want security boundaries to exist between those machines; in fact, most of the time you do not want them to be aware of each other in any way. You even want isolation and separation between the VMs and the host operating system because you sure don't want your public cloud service provider snooping around inside your VMs. The same idea applies to application containers.

The processes running inside a container are not visible to the hosting operating system, even though you are consuming resources from that operating system. Containers maintain two different forms of isolation. There is namespace isolation, which means the containers are confined to their own filesystem and registry. Then there is also resource isolation, meaning that we can define what specific hardware resources are available to the different containers, and they are not able to steal from each other. Shortly, we will discuss two different categories of containers, Windows Server containers and Hyper-V containers. These two types of containers handle isolation in different ways, so stay tuned for more info on that topic.

We know that containers share resources and are spun up from the same base image, while still keeping their processes separated so that the underlying operating system can't negatively affect the application, and also so that the application can't tank the host operating system. But how is the isolation handled from a networking aspect? Well, in the Windows Server world, application containers utilize technology from the Hyper-V virtual switch to keep everything straight on the networking side. In fact, as you start to use containers, you will quickly see that each container has a unique IP address assigned to it, helping to maintain network isolation.

Scalability

The combination of spinning up from the same base image and the isolation of the container makes a very compelling scalability and growth story. Think about a web application you host whose use might fluctuate greatly from day to day. Providing enough resources to sustain this application during busy times has traditionally meant overpaying for compute resources when that application is not being heavily used. Cloud technologies provide dynamic scaling for these modern kinds of applications, but they often do so by spinning up or down entire VMs. There are three common struggles with dynamically scaling applications like this. First is the time that it takes to produce additional VMs; even if that process is automated, your application may be overwhelmed for a period of time while additional resources are brought online. Our second challenge is the struggle that the developer needs to go through to make that application so agnostic that it doesn't care if there are inconsistencies between the different machines upon which their application might be running. Creating non-dependent applications should be a requirement from any modern developer, yet in some industries I still regularly find new software releases that are coded in poor ways from many years ago, requiring us as administrators to take great care in making sure the environment matches up with what the application needs.

The third is cost – not only a hardware resource cost, as new VMs coming online will each consume an entire set of kernel resources, but monetary costs as well. Spinning VMs up and down in your cloud environment can quickly get expensive. These are all hurdles that do not exist when you utilize containers as your method to deploy applications.

Since application containers use the same underlying kernel and the same base image, their time to live is extremely fast. New containers can be spun up or down very quickly and in batches, without having to wait for the boot and kernel mode processes to start. Also, since we have provided the developer with this isolated container structure within which to build the application, we know that our application is going to be able to run successfully anywhere that we spin up one of these containers. No more worries about whether or not the new VM that is coming online will be standardized correctly, because containers for a particular application are always the same and contain all of the important dependencies that the application needs, right inside that container.

What's new in Server 2022?

Containers have been included in Windows Server for a few versions, but every release includes some additional or changed features. Here are highlights of new offerings specifically in Windows Server 2022.

Smaller image size for Server Core

When starting a container instance, the container image base layers need to be downloaded and extracted on the host. Many of the containers in use today are based on a Server Core image, and the RTM portion of this image has been reduced by approximately 33% in Windows Server 2022.

Virtualized time zones

New in Windows Server 2022 is the ability for each Windows container instance to maintain its own virtualized time zone, separated from the container host server upon which it is running.

Initial IPv6 support

While there is still development being made for full IPv6 support in Windows container land, improvements in Kubernetes now give us the ability to start making use of this newer networking stack.

HostProcess containers

There are two primary types of containers in the world of Windows Server container hosts, which we will discuss later in this chapter. New in Server 2022, and still being enhanced, is a third container type that is not exactly brand new but rather an extension of Windows Server containers. **HostProcess containers** enable enhanced cluster management scenarios through Kubernetes. When orchestrating many nodes and groupings of containers, administrative tasks within those containers can be made more efficient through the use of HostProcess containers.

Enhanced management through Windows Admin Center

Limited container management was already available via WAC, primarily helpful to containerize web applications. The latest version of WAC now includes integration with Azure Container Registry to upload container images to that registry, as well as the ability to start and stop container instances.

A new base image option

In the very next section of this chapter, we will talk more in depth about container base images and why they matter. Historically with LTSC versions of Windows Server (2016 and 2019), there were only two base images from which containers could be built. New with Windows Server 2022 is a third option, somewhat confusingly called... "Windows Server". We'll discuss this further in a moment.

Container base images

This topic brings us full circle to our discussion about Server Core and Nano Server. If you have worked with Windows Server for many years, you have probably wondered why Microsoft introduced a new installation option called Nano Server, only to remove it during the next LTSC release. This change happened right around the same time that Microsoft started diving into using Windows Servers as container host servers, and this information directly relates to the question, "What happened to Nano Server?"

Nano Server is now only useful for containers. In fact, you cannot install a Nano Server instance outside of a container. This is its purpose. You do not *have* to use Nano inside your containers, but it's one of the options.

Containers are sort of like VMs but at a different level. With VMs you share hardware among multiple full instances of the Windows operating system. Each VM maintains a completely separated kernel from one another, creating strong isolation between VMs, and between the VMs and the host server. Microsoft has some great diagrams to describe these differences, which I am going to use here and show you.

Figure 13.1: Layers of a Windows virtual machine

Windows Server containers, on the other hand, are like multiple individual instances of the Windows operating system running on a host server, except they share not only hardware resources but also the Windows kernel itself. Thanks again to Microsoft Learn documentation, here is a screenshot displaying the makeup of a Windows Server container; you can see here how it differs from a true virtual machine.

Figure 13.2: Layers of a Windows container environment

Each container is comprised of multiple layers that lay on top of each other to make up a fully functioning container. This container will have an operating system, roles and services, and the application for which the container is purposed. When deploying a container, the core layer of that container is the base operating system that will run within the container, and that is always provided by a container base image.

In Windows Server 2016 and 2019, there were only two base images available to use for containers, **Server Core** and **Nano Server**. If you're familiar with SAC versions of Windows Server (also only used for container purposes), you may know that there was a third flavor of container image specific to these versions of the operating system, called **Windows**. We are not going to focus any attention on this one, because SAC versions of Windows Server are a moot point for the future as Microsoft moves away from using them. However, as described when we talked about container improvements in Windows Server 2022, we now have a brand-new option for container base images, somewhat confusingly called **Windows Server**. Let's spend some time discussing these three types of base container images.

Nano Server

While Server Core is a great operating system to build small and efficient servers, it is still a heavyweight compared to Nano Server.

Nano is so incredibly different, and so incredibly tiny, that it really isn't a comparison. You may remember earlier when we installed Server Core and came out with a hard drive size of around 6 GB. While that is much smaller than a Desktop Experience version of Windows Server, think about this – a Nano Server base image can be less than 500 MB!

That is amazingly small. Additionally, updates to Nano Server are expected to be few and far between. This means you won't have to deal with monthly patching and updates on your application containers. In fact, there is technically no patching component inside containers. Since containers include all that they need to run the applications hosted on them, it is generally expected that when you need to update something about a container, you'll just go ahead and build out a new container image that includes your patches or changes, rather than update existing ones. If Nano Server receives an update, just build out a new container, install and test the application on it, and roll out container instances based on the new image. Need to make some changes to the application itself? Rather than figuring out how to update the existing container image, it's quick and easy to build a new one, test it outside of your production environment, and once it is ready, simply start deploying and spinning up the new container image into production, letting the old version fall away.

Nano Server is now only used as a base operating system for containers. This is a major change since the release of Server 2016, when the scope that Nano was expected to provide was much larger. If you utilize Nano Server for workloads outside of container images, you need to start working on moving those workloads into more traditional servers, such as Server Core.

Server Core

You may be wondering, "Why would anybody use Server Core as the base for a container image if Nano Server is available?" The easiest answer to that question is application compatibility. Nano Server is incredibly small, and as such it is obviously lacking much of the code that exists inside Server Core. When you start looking into utilizing containers to host your applications, it's a great idea to utilize the smaller Nano Server as a base *if possible*, but often your applications simply won't be able to run on that platform, and in these cases, you may need to call on Server Core as the base operating system.

.NET applications can help to portray scenarios when one type of container may be used over another. If the app you are building is based on .NET Core, a Nano Server container image likely includes all of the needed dependencies to run that application. This will provide you with the smallest possible footprint for your container and will run most efficiently. However, if you find yourself building an app that requires the full .NET framework, Nano Server won't cut it. You will have to change gears and utilize a Server Core container to bring your application to life.

What may be a decent general rule of thumb is that if anybody builds out a new modern cloud application that you want to be as scalable and efficient as possible, focus that development around containers based on Nano Server. This way you can code around those restrictions in Nano, and end up with an app that can work on these incredibly small and lightweight containers.

If, instead, you find yourself faced with the task of taking existing application code and moving it into containers, it is pretty likely that you will have to shift over to Server Core-based containers to give yourself the extra flexibility to get those applications to work.

Windows Server

There are some tasks that DevOps engineers call on containers to perform that even Server Core cannot handle. Or, in some cases, there are limitations and restrictions even in Server Core that an application may need to overcome in order to work successfully. Up until Server 2022, the answer to this was a third container image type called Windows, which used a more full code base of the Windows operating system. This was, of course, a heavier footprint than Nano Server or Server Core, but it enabled more things to be possible. The Windows container image type was exclusive to SAC versions of Windows Server, which you already know are being deprecated. So, what is there to fill in that gap? Windows Server 2022 comes with a new container base image type called **Windows Server**. This container image is based on essentially a full Windows Server edition; in fact, the code is based on Windows Server 2022 Desktop Experience. Now don't take that the wrong way; no container includes a GUI. This is core to what containers are. But with the code coming from the Desktop Experience version, doors are open in this container type that would normally be closed in a Nano or Server Core container.

Windows Server container base images have fewer restrictions inside IIS than Server Core instances, and they have a broader API support scope. Since they are based on LTSC code, containers based on the Windows Server container image are supported as standard for 5 years, which is considerably different and longer than SAC versions currently are.

Windows Server containers versus Hyper-V containers

When spinning up your containers, it is important to know that there are two categories of containers that you can run in Windows Server 2022. I know this is all a bit confusing, since we just talked about how there are three (or four, depending on how you view SAC) different container base image types. Those are all about what OS runs *within* the container itself. Here we are talking about what different types of containers there are, which is moreso from the perspective of the container *host* operating system, and what functionality your containers as a whole will have. All aspects of application containers that we have been talking about so far apply to either Windows Server containers or Hyper-V containers. Hyper-V containers can run the same code or images as Windows Server containers, while keeping stronger isolation guarantees to make sure the important stuff stays separated. The decision on whether to use Windows Server containers or Hyper-V containers will likely boil down to what level of security you need your containers to maintain. Let's discuss the differences between the two so that you can better understand the choice you are facing.

Windows Server containers

Like Linux containers, Windows Server containers share their host operating system kernel files in order to make the containers efficient. What this means, however, is that while a namespace, filesystem, and network isolation are in place to keep the containers separated from each other, there is some potential for vulnerability between the different Windows Server containers running on a host server. For example, if you were to log into the host operating system on your container server, you would be able to see and manipulate the running processes of each container.

The container cannot see the host or other containers and is still isolated from the host in various ways, but knowing that the host can view the processes within the container shows us that some interaction does exist with this level of sharing. Windows Server containers will be most useful in circumstances where your container host server and the containers themselves are within the same *trust boundary*. In most cases, this means that Windows Server containers are going to be most useful for company-owned servers that only run containers owned and trusted by the company. If you trust both your host server and your containers, and are okay with those entities trusting each other, deploying regular Windows Server containers is the most efficient use of your hardware resources.

HostProcess containers

As previously mentioned, a new container type is coming to town, called HostProcess containers. I'm including this as a sub-heading under Windows Server containers, because HostProcess containers are essentially Windows Server containers that can be centrally managed and orchestrated in better ways. As more and more companies get more involved in working with containers, Microsoft has expectations that containers being used to run modern applications will likely be hosted in Azure or Azure Stack HCI, and that they will be orchestrated by something like Kubernetes. HostProcess containers come with advantages over classic Windows Server containers when used in this way.

Hyper-V containers

If you're looking for an increased amount of isolation and stronger boundaries, it's worth foraying into Hyper-V containers. Hyper-V containers are more like a super-optimized version of a VM. While kernel resources are still shared by Hyper-V containers, making them still much more performant than full VMs, each Hyper-V container gets its own dedicated Windows shell within which a single container can run. This means you have isolation between Hyper-V containers that is more on par with isolation between VMs, and yet you are still able to spin up new containers at will and very quickly because the container infrastructure is still in place underneath. Hyper-V containers are more useful in multi-tenant infrastructures, where you want to make sure no code or activity can be leaked between the container and host, or between two different containers that might be owned by different entities. Earlier, we discussed how a host operating system can see the processes running within a Windows Server container, but this is not the case with Hyper-V containers. The host operating system is completely unaware of, and unable to tap into, the services running within the Hyper-V containers themselves. These processes are now invisible.

The availability of Hyper-V containers means that even if you have an application that must be strongly isolated, you no longer need to dedicate a full Hyper-V VM to this application. You can now spin up a Hyper-V container, run the application in that container, and have full isolation for the application, while continuing to share resources and provide a better, more scalable experience for that application.

A special note on the topic of Hyper-V containers – since a Hyper-V container is essentially a full virtual machine running on your host server, each one counts as a VM from a licensing perspective. If your container host server is Windows Server 2022 Standard, you are restricted to running two Hyper-V containers, which is probably not going to be very helpful. Windows Server 2022 Datacenter edition allows an unlimited number of VMs to run, including Hyper-V Container VMs.

Docker and Kubernetes

Docker started as an open source project – a toolset, really – that was originally designed to assist with the running of containers on Linux operating systems. Wait a minute, what? The words **Linux** and **open source** have been written once again inside a Microsoft book! What is this world coming to? You see, containers are quickly becoming a big deal, and rightfully so. In Server 2016, Microsoft took some steps to start reinventing the container wheel, with the inclusion of PowerShell cmdlets that could be used to spin up and control containers running on your Windows Server, but the Docker platform has grown at such a fast rate that Microsoft now expects that anyone who wants to run containers on their Windows machines is probably going to do so via the Docker toolset. If you want to utilize or even test containers in your environment, you'll need to get Docker for Windows to get started.

Docker is a container *platform*. This means that it provides the commands and tools needed to download, create, package, distribute, and run containers. Docker for Windows is fully supported to run on both Windows 11 and Windows Server 2022. By installing Docker for Windows, you acquire all of the tools needed to begin using containers to enhance your application's isolation and scalability.

Developers can use Docker to create an environment on their local workstation that mirrors a live server environment, so that they can develop applications within containers and be assured that they will actually run once those applications are moved to the server. Docker is the platform that provides pack, ship, and run capabilities for your developers. Once finished with development, the container package can be handed over to the system administrator, who spins up the container(s) that run the application and deploys it accordingly. The developer doesn't know or care about the container host infrastructure, and the admin doesn't know or care about the development process or compatibility with their servers, because the application's dependencies live within the container.

Linux containers

When running containers on a Windows Server, it makes common sense that your containers would need to be running an instance of the Windows operating system as well, since containers share kernel resources from the host. However, containers in general have been used in the Linux world for much longer than the Microsoft world, and a lot of today's containerized infrastructure is based on Linux operating systems. There are various ways that Microsoft and third parties craft ways to run Linux containers on top of a Windows Server container host. This functionality, of course, includes the isolation of those kernel resources. For example, if your Windows container host server natively runs some Windows Server containers, and then also runs a VM that is then used to host Linux-based containers, this could be one scenario where you run Windows and Linux containers on the same host, even though those systems could never share source code or a kernel.

This topic is ever-evolving, and some of the capabilities are still considered "experimental." If this is a topic that interests you, a good term to start searching for and reading about is **LCOW** (**Linux Containers on Windows**). The following link is a good starting point to begin your investigation of this space: `https://docs.microsoft.com/en-us/virtualization/windowscontainers/deploy-containers/linux-containers`.

Docker Hub

When you work with containers, you build container images that are usable on any server instance running the same host operating system – that is the essence of what containers enable you to do. When you spin up new instances of containers, you just pull new copies of that exact image, which is all-inclusive. This kind of standardized imaging mentality lends well to a shared community of images – a repository, so to speak, of images that people have built that might benefit others. Docker's history is open source, after all. Does such a sharing resource exist, one that you can visit to grab container image files for testing, or even to upload images that you have created and share them with the world? Absolutely! It is called **Docker Hub** and is available at `https://hub.docker.com`.

Visit this site and create a login, and you will immediately have access to thousands of container base images that the community has created and uploaded. This can be a quick way to get a lab up and running with containers, and many of these container images could even be used for production systems, running the applications that the folks here have pre-installed for you inside these container images. Alternatively, you can use Docker Hub to upload and store your own container images:

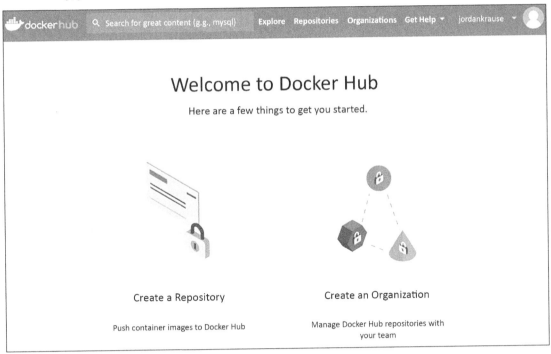

Figure 13.3: Docker Hub

You really should go ahead and create an account for Docker Hub now because if you want to follow along later in the chapter and try out implementing a container with Docker, you'll need a login to do it.

Docker Trusted Registry

If you're anything like me, you think the idea of Docker Hub is a great one: a neat place to store images and even to share them among the community. However, my next inclination is to look at this through an enterprise spyglass, which quickly turns my perspective from *neat* to *unsecured*. In other words, you may not be comfortable placing images in this public repository, or certainly not images that contain anything sensitive to your organization, anyway:

Figure 13.4: Docker Trusted Registry

Here is where **Docker Trusted Registry** may be something to look into. Docker Trusted Registry is a container image repository system, similar to Docker Hub, but it's something that you can contain within your network, behind your firewalls and security systems. This gives you a container-image repository system without the risk of sharing sensitive information with the rest of the world.

Kubernetes

While Docker is our primary interface to build and host containers, allowing us to create platforms within which we can host applications in this new and exciting way, the real magic comes after we are finished with the container's setup. Let's peek into the future a little and assume that you have an application now successfully hosted inside a container. This container can be spun up on a container host server in your environment or even slid over to an Azure container host very easily. This provides easy interaction with the infrastructure needed to seamlessly scale this application up or down, but there is a missing piece to this scalability: **orchestration.**

Kubernetes, often referred to as **K8s**, is a container orchestration solution. This means that Kubernetes orchestrates, or facilitates, how the containers run. It is the tool that enables many containers to run together, in harmony, as if they were one big application. If you intend to use containers to create scaling applications that can spin up new containers whenever additional resources are needed, you will absolutely need to have a container orchestrator, and Kubernetes is currently the best and most popular.

Microsoft recognized this popularity and has taken steps to ensure that Kubernetes is fully supported on Windows Server 2022. In fact, as you know our latest version of Windows Server includes a new class of Windows container called Host Process Containers, which are specifically designed to allow Kubernetes to have better control over these containers. Previously, administering Windows containers involved a lot of logging into the containers directly to manage parts and pieces, but Host Process Containers enable direct management from the Kubernetes administration platform.

The combination of these latest Windows containers and Kubernetes means that you can run hundreds of container nodes on a single server.

As with any software, Kubernetes is not the only name in the game. Docker has its own orchestration platform, called Docker Swarm. While it might make sense that Docker and Docker Swarm would work together better than Docker and any other orchestrator, the numbers don't lie. I heard recently that 82% of companies using scaling applications in the cloud utilize Kubernetes for their container orchestration. Kubernetes even has a specific integration with Azure, which we will outline near the end of this chapter.

As I mentioned earlier, tools such as containers, Docker, and Kubernetes are part of a cloud-first vision. While the use of containers for most companies will start on-site, using their own servers and infrastructure to host containers, this is a technology that is already capable of extending to the cloud. Because the containers themselves are so standardized and fluid – making them easy to expand and move around – sliding them into a cloud environment is easily done.

Working with containers

There are a lot of moving pieces that work together to make containers a reality in your environment, but it's not too difficult to get started. Let's walk through the initial setup of turning Windows Server 2022 into a container-running mega-machine.

Installing the role and feature

The amount of work that you need to accomplish here depends on whether you want to run Windows Server containers, Hyper-V containers, or both. The primary feature that you need to make sure that you install is **Containers**, which can be installed by using either the **Add roles and features** link from inside Server Manager, or by issuing the following PowerShell command:

```
Add-WindowsFeature Containers
```

```
Administrator: Windows PowerShell                                        —  □  ×

Windows PowerShell
Copyright (C) Microsoft Corporation. All rights reserved.

   Install the latest PowerShell for new features and improvements! https://aka.ms/PSWindows

            PS C:\Users\Administrator> Add-WindowsFeature Containers
Success Restart Needed Exit Code        Feature Result
------- -------------- ---------        --------------
True    Yes            SuccessRest...   {Containers}
WARNING: You must restart this server to finish the installation process.


PS C:\Users\Administrator>
```

Figure 13.5: Installing the Containers feature

Additionally, if you intend to run Hyper-V containers, you need to ensure that the underlying Hyper-V components are also installed on your container host server. To do that, install the **Hyper-V role** and accompanying management tools onto this same server.

As indicated following the role and feature installation, make sure to restart your server after these changes.

At this point, you may be wondering, "If my container host server needs to have the Hyper-V role installed, doesn't that mean it must be a physical server? You can't install the Hyper-V role on a virtual machine, right?" *Wrong*. Windows Server 2022 supports something called **nested virtualization,** which was added for containers. You see, requiring physical hardware is becoming a limiting factor for IT departments these days, as almost everything is done from VMs. It makes sense that companies would want to deploy containers, but they may also want their container host servers to be VMs, with multiple containers being run within that VM. Therefore, nested virtualization was required to make this possible. If you run a Windows Server 2019 or 2022 physical hypervisor server and a Windows Server 2019 or 2022 VM inside that server, you will now find that you can successfully install the Hyper-V role right onto that VM. I told you VMs were popular, so much so that they are now being used to run other VMs!

Remember that we can also host and run containers on our Windows 10 and 11 machines! To prep a Windows client for this purpose, simply add the Windows feature called Containers, just like on the server operating system. Keep in mind that the Container feature is only available in the more business-class SKUs of Windows. If you run Windows Pro, Enterprise, or Education you will be able to make use of this feature.

Installing Docker for Windows

Now that our container host server is prepped with the necessary Windows components, we need to grab Docker for Windows from the internet. The Docker interface will provide us with all of the commands that are needed to start building and interacting with our containers.

This is the point where the Docker Hub login becomes important. If you are following along with this chapter to test containers on your own workstation and need to install Docker Desktop for Windows on your Windows 10 or 11 *client*, the easiest way is to visit Docker Hub, log in, and search for the Docker Desktop client software. Here is a link to that software (again, this is the tool you need to use if you install on Windows 10 or 11): `https://hub.docker.com/editions/community/docker-ce-desktop-windows`.

However, since I am sitting on Windows Server 2022, my license for the server also includes licensing for Docker Enterprise, which can be pulled down without having to visit Docker Hub. If I open an elevated PowerShell prompt and run the following two commands, my server will reach out, grab Docker Enterprise, and install it onto my server:

```
Install-Module -Name DockerMsftProvider -Repository PSGallery -Force
Install-Package -Name docker -ProviderName DockerMsftProvider -Force
```

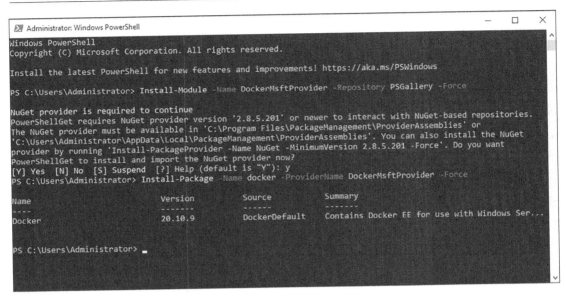

Figure 13.6: Installing Docker Enterprise

After the package installation has finished, Docker is configured on your server as a service, but that service needs to be started with the following command:

```
Start-Service docker
```

Docker commands

Once Docker is installed on your system, whether you are working with a Windows Server 2022 or a Windows 10/11 machine, you now have Docker Engine running on your machine, and it is ready to accept some commands to begin working with containers. If there is a single word to remember when it comes to working with containers, it is **Docker**. That is because every command that you issue to interact with containers will begin with the word *docker*. Let's have a look are some of the common commands that you will be working with.

docker version

Certain container images that you want to run may require particular versions of Docker Engine to be successful. When in doubt about what your current Docker environment is running, you can easily check over version numbers anytime by running docker version.

docker info

While docker version displays version numbers of Docker Engine, docker info steps back and gives some general info and statistics about your Docker container host server. Here you can see a Docker versioning number as well as the current Windows operating system version numbers, along with stats about the server itself such as allocated memory. Probably the most interesting numbers shown in the docker info output are counters for how many containers are on this server, with breakdowns on how many of those containers are running, paused, or stopped.

docker –help

This is sort of like issuing *docker /?*, if that were a real command. The `help` function of Docker generates a list of the possible Docker commands that are available to run. This is a good reference point as you get started.

docker images

After downloading some container images from a repository (we will do this for ourselves in the next section of this chapter), you can use the `docker images` command to view all of the images that are available on your local system.

docker search

Utilizing the `search` function allows you to search the container repositories (such as Docker Hub) for base container images that you might want to utilize in your environment. For example, to search and find images provided from inside Microsoft's Docker Hub repository, issue the following:

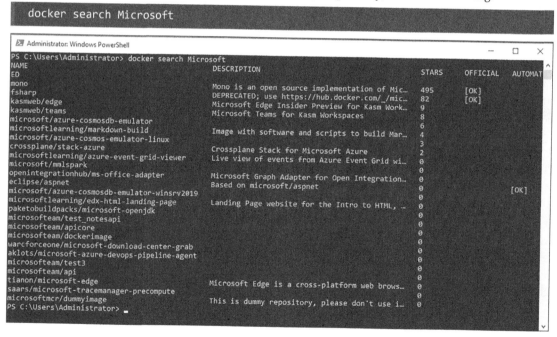

Figure 13.7: Searching the container repository

docker pull

We can use `docker pull` to pull down container images from online repositories. There are multiple repositories from which you can get container images. Most often, you will work with images from Docker Hub or Microsoft's own **Microsoft Container Repository (MCR)**.

Here are some sample `docker pull` commands that show you how to pull container images from Docker Hub, as well as MCR:

```
docker pull Microsoft/nanoserver
docker pull Microsoft/windowsservercore
docker pull mcr.microsoft.com/windows/servercore:ltsc2019
docker pull mcr.microsoft.com/windows/nanoserver:ltsc2022
```

docker run

This is the command to start a new container from a base image. You will find that you can retain multiple container images in your local repository that are all based on the same container image. For example, as you add new things to your containers or update the application inside your containers, you may be building new container images that are now a subset of an existing container image. You may have numerous container images that are all named windowsservercore, for example. In this case, container tags become very important, as they help you to distinguish between different versions of those container images. As an example, here is a command that would start a container based on a windowsservercore image, with which I associated the ltsc2019 tag:

```
docker run -it --rm Microsoft\windowsservercore:ltsc2019
```

In the preceding command, the -it switch creates a shell from which we can interact with a container, which is useful to build and test containers, but you generally wouldn't need that switch to launch production containers that were 100% ready to serve up applications. --rm is a cleanup switch, meaning that once this particular container exits, the container and its filesystem will be automatically deleted.

docker ps -a

You utilize docker ps when you want to view the containers that currently run on your system.

Downloading a container image

The first command we will run on our newly created container host is docker images, which shows us all of the container images that currently reside on our system; here, there are none:

Figure 13.8: No current container images on our system

Of course, there are no container images yet, as we haven't downloaded any. Let's grab a couple so that we can test this out. In addition to base container images that only contain the operating system, Microsoft also provides sample container image files that showcase running .NET applications inside a Nano Server container - that sounds like a fun way to get started with verifying that we can successfully run containers on this new host server.

Once we know the image that we want to download, we can use docker pull to download it onto our server. You can see in the following commands and screenshot that I have downloaded the 2022 version image of Nano Server and verified that it now shows in my docker images command output, and I am also in the process of downloading the 2019 version of Server Core (just for fun). The Nano Server download was finished in a matter of seconds, but the larger Server Core image will take much longer!

```
docker pull mcr.microsoft.com/windows/nanoserver:ltsc2022
docker images
docker pull mcr.microsoft.com/windows/servercore:ltsc2019
```

```
Administrator: Windows PowerShell
PS C:\Users\Administrator> docker pull mcr.microsoft.com/windows/nanoserver:ltsc2022
ltsc2022: Pulling from windows/nanoserver
546fcac75d6a: Pull complete
Digest: sha256:786a24be2bd1945bee9701f95a71d8573ace8641c112dc27206f826bef0229c1
Status: Downloaded newer image for mcr.microsoft.com/windows/nanoserver:ltsc2022
mcr.microsoft.com/windows/nanoserver:ltsc2022
PS C:\Users\Administrator> docker images
REPOSITORY                               TAG        IMAGE ID       CREATED       SIZE
mcr.microsoft.com/windows/nanoserver     ltsc2022   32002da5756a   3 weeks ago   297MB
PS C:\Users\Administrator> docker pull mcr.microsoft.com/windows/servercore:ltsc2019
ltsc2019: Pulling from windows/servercore
8185ee4ed646: Downloading [=======================>                        ]  739.1MB/1.66GB
77b161a779b0: Download complete
```

Figure 13.9: Using docker pull to grab container images from MCR

The preceding commands downloaded a copy of base images, but we want to spin up one of those sample images to see a container in action. Here is a command to download a sample .NET application container image from Microsoft's container repository:

```
docker pull mcr.microsoft.com/dotnet/samples:dotnetapp
```

```
Administrator: Windows PowerShell                                          —   □   ×
PS C:\Users\Administrator> docker pull mcr.microsoft.com/dotnet/samples:dotnetapp
dotnetapp: Pulling from dotnet/samples
546fcac75d6a: Already exists
5565a8943f07: Pull complete
9015675f156c: Pull complete
f18acdf7abeb: Pull complete
241234a98238: Pull complete
6efc49f9a5d3: Pull complete
9fb32d266377: Pull complete
56628e40dee5: Pull complete
2bdeab754e09: Pull complete
Digest: sha256:7ec34625cd4a2a8a0c7e8bd6a1c03e260eb8bc85db0655518e564b84d5293e05
Status: Downloaded newer image for mcr.microsoft.com/dotnet/samples:dotnetapp
mcr.microsoft.com/dotnet/samples:dotnetapp
PS C:\Users\Administrator>
```

Figure 13.10: Downloading the .NET sample container image

After the downloads are finished, running docker images once again shows us the base container images that were downloaded, alongside the sample .NET image:

```
Administrator: Windows PowerShell
PS C:\Users\Administrator> docker images
REPOSITORY                              TAG         IMAGE ID       CREATED       SIZE
mcr.microsoft.com/dotnet/samples        dotnetapp   98ecfca091b0   3 days ago    372MB
mcr.microsoft.com/windows/nanoserver    ltsc2022    32002da5756a   3 weeks ago   297MB
mcr.microsoft.com/windows/servercore    ltsc2019    f44a91b2479e   3 weeks ago   4.42GB
PS C:\Users\Administrator>
```

Figure 13.11: Local container image repository

From these base images, we are now able to launch and run a real container.

Running a container

We are so close to having a container running on our host! Now that we have installed the service, implemented Docker, imported the Docker module into our PowerShell prompt, and downloaded a base container image, we can finally issue a command to launch a container from that image. Let's run the .NET container that we downloaded before, with the following command:

```
docker run --rm mcr.microsoft.com/dotnet/samples:dotnetapp
```

The container starts and runs through its included code, and we see some fun output:

```
Administrator: Windows PowerShell                                              —  □
PS C:\Users\Administrator> docker run --rm mcr.microsoft.com/dotnet/samples:dotnetapp
            42                                                     ,d
            42                          ,d                         42
            42                          42                         42
  ,adPPYb,42   ,adPPYba, MM42MMM 8b,dPPYba,    ,adPPYba, MM42MMM
a8"     `Y42 a8"     "8a 42     42P'   `"8a a8P_____42   42
8b       42 8b       d8 42      42      42 8PP!!!!!!!    42
"8a,   ,d42 "8a,   ,a8" 42,     42      42 "8b,   ,aa   42,
 `"8bbdP"Y8  `"YbbdP"'  "Y428 42        42  `"Ybbd8"'   "Y428

.NET 7.0.3
Microsoft Windows 10.0.20348

UserName: ContainerUser
OSArchitecture: X64
ProcessorCount: 1
TotalAvailableMemoryBytes: 4294496256 (3.00 GiB)
PS C:\Users\Administrator>
```

Figure 13.12: Our first container is up and running!

This container showcases that *all* components necessary for this .NET application to run are included *inside* the container. This container is based on Nano Server, which means it has an incredibly small footprint. In fact, looking back a few pages at the last docker images command that we ran, I can see that this container image is only 372 MB! What a resource saver this is, compared with running this application on a traditional IIS web server.

The main resource for Microsoft documentation on containers is https://aka.ms/windowscontainers. The tools used to interact with containers constantly change, including changes to Docker and Kubernetes. Make sure to check over the Microsoft Docs site to find the latest best practices and approved installation path to prepare your container host servers.

Where is Azure in all this?

This book is focused primarily on functionality provided natively inside the Windows Server operating system, most often utilized on-premise. Our chapter on containers has obviously followed suit. Containers are part of a cloud-first mentality, and there is certainly much to learn on the topic of utilizing Windows containers inside Azure, rather than on classic servers. While this is not our core focus, here is some information regarding ways that containers intersect with Azure.

Azure Container Registry

Earlier in this chapter, we took a look at Docker Hub and pulled some container images from the Microsoft Container Registry. Both of these systems are live and ready to use, but they may be too public-facing for your enterprise's taste. A third option that may be more appropriate when working with containers hosted in Azure is another container registry, useful for the *private* storage of container images, **Azure Container Registry**.

Azure Kubernetes Service (AKS)

I told you that Kubernetes was becoming well-adopted by Microsoft – so much so that there is a new Azure service that is completely interwoven with K8s. If your intentions are to move cloud-ward with your containers, and you're thinking about running those containers inside Azure, AKS can provide you the toolset to manage and scale those containers through its powerful orchestration capabilities. Think about the possibilities here. Store your container images in Azure Container Registry, and then engage AKS to spin up hundreds or even thousands of container instances on Azure VMs at will.

Azure Kubernetes Service for Azure Stack HCI

Azure Stack HCI is all about taking Azure infrastructure and scaling capabilities and bringing them locally into your data center, so that you retain more direct control over those resources. For companies implementing Azure Stack HCI, it is important to know that you can also run AKS within this environment, providing on-premise container solutions that mirror the capabilities of pure Azure.

Summary

Containers are revolutionizing the way that we build and host modern applications. By containerizing apps, we can run many more applications on each physical server, because they are capable of being fully isolated from each other. Additionally, the container mentality allows the development of applications to happen in a much more fluid fashion. App developers can build their applications inside containers running on their own laptops and, once finished, simply hand them over to the infrastructure team to slide that container image onto a production container host server. That host server could be on-premises, or even in the cloud. Orchestration tools such as Kubernetes can then be leveraged to scale that application, increasing or decreasing resource capacity and the number of necessary containers based on load or other factors. The usability of containers in the real world has been expanded greatly by the Docker project. The folks at Docker are clearly the frontrunners in this space, enough that Microsoft has decided to incorporate the use of Docker – an open source project developed for Linux! – straight into Windows Server 2022. We can now utilize both Docker Engine to run containers on our Windows servers, and the Docker client toolset to manage and manipulate containers inside Windows in the same way we work with containers in the Linux world.

Linux containers and Windows Server containers have a lot in common, and function in essentially the same way. Microsoft's ingenious idea to create an additional container scope, the Hyper-V container, brings a solid answer to a lot of common security questions that present themselves when approaching the idea of containers in general. Everyone uses VMs heavily these days; I don't think anybody can disagree with that. Assuming the use of containers evolves into something that is easy to implement and administer, Hyper-V containers could replace many of our existing Hyper-V VMs in the coming years. This will save time, money, and server space.

Speaking of Hyper-V, it has become an integral part of so many of our corporate networks today. In the next chapter, we will learn more about this amazing virtualization technology.

Questions

1. There are three base operating systems that can be used for a Windows Server 2022 container. What are they?
2. Compared to a Windows Server container, what type of container provides even greater levels of isolation?
3. True or false—in Windows Server 2016, you can run both Windows and Linux containers on the same Windows Server host platform.
4. What is the Docker command to see a list of container images on your local system?
5. What is currently the most popular container orchestration software that integrates with Windows Server 2022?
6. True or false—developers can install Docker onto their Windows 10 workstations to start building applications inside containers.
7. What is a common reason that a developer may need to utilize Server Core containers, rather than Nano Server?

Join our community on Discord

Join our community's Discord space for discussions with the author and other readers:

https://packt.link/SecNet

14

Hyper-V

I've always been a country boy. Driving along dirt roads, working on cars, and hunting are all ways that I prefer to fill my free time. Traveling to cities always hits me with a bit of culture shock. All those skyscrapers and tall apartment buildings serve an important purpose though, and serve to fulfill my metaphor: if there isn't enough land to grow outward, you have to build up. The vertical ascension of large cities is similar to what we have seen happening in our datacenters over the past decade. Cities need more and more space for people and businesses, just like we need to house more and more servers every year. Rather than horizontal expansion, with enormous server rooms filled with racks and racks of hardware, we are embracing the skyscraper mentality and virtualizing everything. We build considerably fewer servers but make them incredibly powerful. Then, on top of these super-computers, we can run dozens, if not hundreds, of virtual servers. The technology that provides this hypervisor layer, the ability to run **Virtual Machines (VMs)** in Microsoft-centric shops, is the **Hyper-V** role in Windows Server. This is one of the most critical roles to understand as a server administrator because if your organization is not yet making use of server virtualization, you've been left behind. Virtualization is no longer the way of the future, it is the implied expectation of every datacenter in the world. The following are some topics we are going to explore so that you can become familiar with the virtualization capabilities provided by Microsoft in Windows Server 2022:

- Designing and implementing your Hyper-V Server
- Virtual switches
- Implementing a new virtual server
- Managing a virtual server
- Shielded VMs
- Integrating with Linux
- **Resilient Filesystem (ReFS)** deduplication
- Hyper-V Server...2019?

Designing and implementing your Hyper-V Server

Creating your own Hyper-V Server is usually pretty simple: build a server, install an operating system, install the Hyper-V role, and you're ready to get started. In fact, you can even install the Hyper-V role on a Windows 10 or 11 Pro or Enterprise computer, if you need to run some VMs from your own desktop. While most hardware that is created these days fully supports the idea of being a hypervisor provider, some of you may try installing the Hyper-V role only to end up with the following error message:

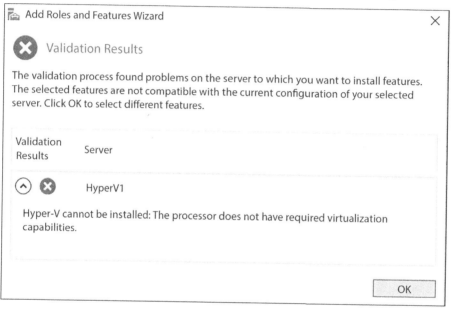

Figure 14.1: Hyper-V compatibility error

Uh oh, that's not good. This means one of two things: either my CPU really doesn't support virtualization, or I simply have some settings turned off inside the BIOS on my server that prevent this from working. There are three considerations you should check on your server to make sure it is ready to run Hyper-V. First, you need to be running an x64-based processor. This is kind of a given since Windows Server 2022 only comes in 64-bit anyway. If you don't have an x64 processor, you're not going to be able to install the operating system in the first place. Second, your CPUs need to be capable of hardware-assisted virtualization. This is typically called either **Intel Virtualization Technology (Intel VT)** or **AMD Virtualization (AMD-V)**. And last but not least, you must have **Data Execution Prevention (DEP)** available and enabled on your system. If you have investigated the hardware itself and it seems to be virtualization-capable, but it's still not working, it is likely that you have DEP currently disabled inside the BIOS of that system. Boot into the BIOS settings and enable DEP along with any other more user-friendly-named settings that might indicate they are currently blocking your ability to run virtual machines.

As long as your processors are happy to run virtual machines, you can turn just about any size of hardware into a hypervisor by installing the Hyper-V role. It is not important to think about *minimum* system requirements because you want your system hardware to be as large as possible in a Hyper-V Server.

The more CPU cores, RAM, and hard drive space you can provide, the more VMs you will be able to run. Even the smallest Hyper-V Servers I have seen in production environments are running hardware such as dual Xeon processors, 96 GB of RAM, and many terabytes of storage space. While 96 GB of RAM may seem like a lot for a single system, if your standard workload server build includes 8 GB of RAM, which is a pretty low number, and you want to run 12 servers on your Hyper-V Server, you are already beyond the capabilities of a Hyper-V Server with only 96 GB of RAM. 8 x 12 is 96, and you haven't left any memory for the host operating system to use! So *the moral of the story?* Go big or go home!

Installing the Hyper-V role

Hyper-V is just another role in Windows Server 2022, but during the installation of that role, you will be asked a few questions and it is important to understand what they are asking so that you can be sure your new Hyper-V Server is built to last and to work in an efficient manner. First of all, you will need to have Windows Server 2022 already installed, and use the **Add roles and features** function in order to install the role called **Hyper-V**:

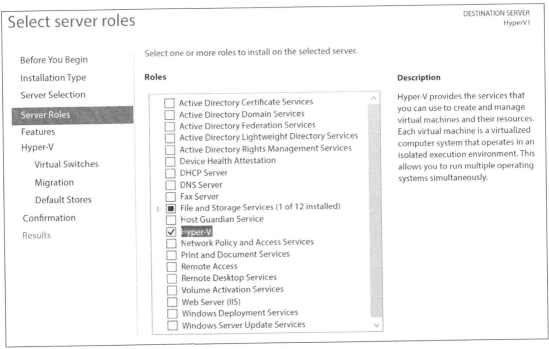

Figure 14.2: Installing the Hyper-V role is quite simple, as long as you meet the prerequisites

As you continue working through the wizard to install the role, you'll come across a screen labeled **Create Virtual Switches**. We will discuss networking in Hyper-V a little bit more in the next section, but what is important here is that you get to define which of your server's physical NICs will be tied into Hyper-V and available for your virtual machines to use. It is a good idea for each Hyper-V Server to have multiple NICs. You want one NIC dedicated to the host itself, which you would not select on this screen. Leave that one alone for the hypervisor's own communications. In addition to that NIC, you will want at least one network card that can bridge the VMs into the corporate network.

This one you would select, as you can see in *Figure 14.3*. If you will be hosting many different VMs on this server, and they need to be connected to different physical networks, you might have to install many different NICs on your Hyper-V Server:

Figure 14.3: Selecting the physical NICs that will be available for VMs to use

After defining NICs, we get to decide whether this Hyper-V Server will handle the live migration of VMs. Live VM migration is the ability to move a VM from one Hyper-V host to another without any interruption of service on that VM. As you can see in *Figure 14.4*, there are a couple of different ways you can set up the server to prepare it for handling live migrations, and take note of the text at the bottom that is telling you to leave this option alone for now if you plan to make this Hyper-V Server part of a cluster. In clustered environments, these settings are handled at a different layer:

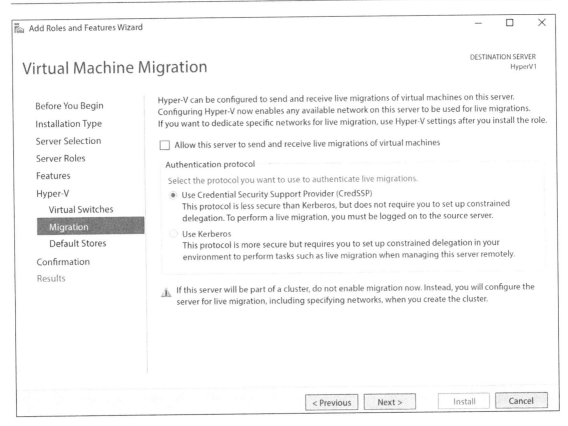

Figure 14.4: Deciding whether you need live migration capabilities

The last screen that I want to point out is the definition of storage locations for your VM data. After creating VMs and digging into what they look like at the hard-disk level (looking at the actual files that are created per VM), you will see that there are two key aspects to a VM: the virtual hard-disk file (VHD or VHDX) and a folder that contains the configuration files for that VM.

As you can see in *Figure 14.5*, the default locations for storing these items seem to be more in line with a piece of software you were installing on a laptop. It always surprises me that these are the default locations specified by Microsoft, as I would assume something as heavy as Hyper-V should have some best practices surrounding storage locations for your VM files and disks, not a shared-user Documents folder. I suppose since Microsoft doesn't know the configuration of your server, it can't make any real guesses as to where you want to store that data, and so it sets the default to be something that would work technically but should probably be changed as a matter of best practice. Many Hyper-V Servers will have dedicated storage, even if only a separate hard disk, on which these files are planned to be stored. Make sure you take a minute on this screen and change the default storage locations of your VM files:

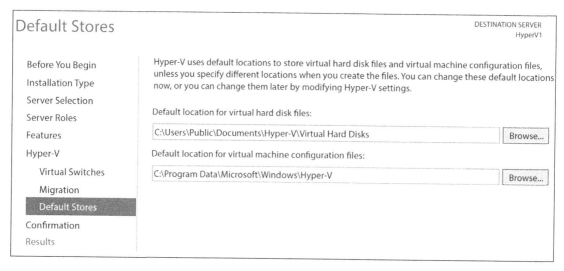

Figure 14.5: Defining default storage locations for VM files

Remember that the version of Windows Server 2022 you are running determines how many VMs you will be able to run on top of this host. Server 2022 Standard limits you to running two VMs, while the Datacenter edition gives you access to launch as many as you can fit on the hardware.

Nested virtualization

Earlier, in *Chapter 13, Containers*, we mentioned nested virtualization, and here the topic comes back into play. Usually, when talking about installing the Hyper-V role on a server, we are talking about installing it onto physical hardware. This hardware becomes your Hyper-V host server, and virtualization prerequisites such as DEP are all related to the hardware itself. There are some circumstances, both related to containers and separately, where you may find yourself wondering, *Do you suppose I could install the Hyper-V role onto...a VM?* The answer is yes! And indeed, this is the very definition of nested virtualization.

In fact, if you remember back to the first screenshot in this chapter where I portrayed an error message encountered when attempting to install the Hyper-V role, that error was because I was attempting to install Hyper-V on a VM. I had simply created a new VM on my physical host, spun up Windows Server 2022 on it, and then tried clicking the box to install Hyper-V on it…but it failed. Why?

New virtual machines are not prepared by default to host other virtual machines. If you've worked within Hyper-V at all before, you probably remember that there are some BIOS-level settings available for each VM and you may be thinking that is where you would visit to enable a VM to be able to do nested virtualization, but the option is not available from inside the Hyper-V management GUI whatsoever. Instead, we must turn to PowerShell on the physical host server in order to enable nested virtualization on our VM.

Launching PowerShell on my Hyper-V physical host, I simply execute the following command to enable my new `HyperV1` VM to be able to do nested virtualization and host additional VMs:

```
Set-VMProcessor -VMName HyperV1 -ExposeVirtualizationExtensions $true
```

Your VM must be powered off for this command to be successful, but following this simple adjustment, your VM will now be prepared to install the Hyper-V role and serve the purposes of nested virtualization in your environment.

AMD processors are now supported

When running nested virtualization by installing the Hyper-V role on a virtual machine, prior to Windows Server 2022, you were limited on the type of physical processor that could support this scenario. New in this release is support for nested virtualization on top of AMD processors.

Virtual switches

Upon completion of the Hyper-V role installation, your first inclination may be to jump right in and start creating VMs, but you should take a minute to make sure that the networking capabilities of your Hyper-V Server are adequate to meet your needs. During the role-installation process, we selected the physical NICs that are to be passed through into Hyper-V, and that screen told us it was going to establish a virtual switch for each of these NICs. But *what does that look like inside the console? And what options do we have for establishing networking between our virtual machines?*

To answer these questions, we need to open up the management interface for Hyper-V. As with any administrative tool of a Windows role, check inside the **Tools** menu of Server Manager, and now that the role has been installed, you will see a new listing for **Hyper-V Manager**. Launch that, and we are now looking at the primary platform from which you will be managing and manipulating every aspect of your Hyper-V environment:

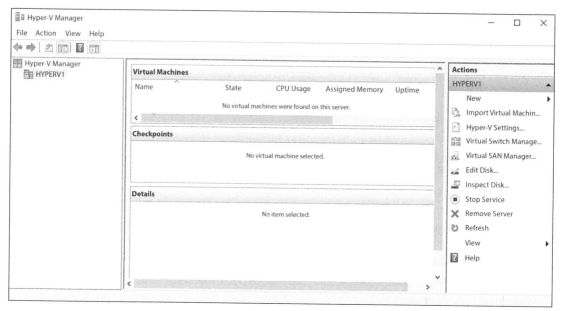

Figure 14.6: First look at Hyper-V Manager

We currently have a lot of blank space in this console because we don't have any VMs running yet. Over on the right side of **Hyper-V Manager,** you can see a link that says **Virtual Switch Manager....** Go ahead and click on that link to be taken into the settings for our virtual switches and networking:

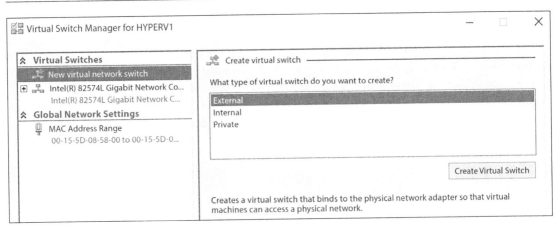

Figure 14.7: Managing virtual switches inside Hyper-V

Toward the left, you see a list of current **Virtual Switches**. On my server, there is only one switch listed there at the moment, which is named after the physical NIC to which it is connected. This is the virtual switch that the role-installation process created for us when we selected the NIC to be included with Hyper-V. If you selected multiple NICs during the role installation, you will have multiple virtual switches available here, each corresponding to a single physical NIC. Every VM you create will have one or more virtual NICs, and you will see shortly that you can choose where each of those virtual NICs gets connected. If there are five different physical networks that your VMs might need to contact, you can use five physical NICs in the Hyper-V Server, plug each one into a different network, and then have five virtual switches here in the console that your VM NICs can be *"plugged"* into.

As you can see in *Figure 14.7*, we have a button named **Create Virtual Switch**, which is self-explanatory. This is where we go to create new switches, but there are three different types of switches that you can create. Let's take just a minute to discuss the differences between them.

External virtual switch

The external virtual switch is the most common type to use for any VMs that need to contact a production network. Each external virtual switch binds to a physical NIC that is installed on the Hyper-V Server. If you click on an external virtual switch, you can see that you have some options for configuring this switch and that you can even change a switch type. In the following screenshot, I have renamed my external virtual switch so that it is easier to identify when I decide to add additional NICs to this server in the future:

Figure 14.8: Renaming an external virtual switch for easy identification

Internal virtual switch

Internal virtual switches are not bound to a physical NIC, so if you create an internal virtual switch and connect a VM to it, that virtual machine will not be able to contact a physical network outside the Hyper-V host server. It's sort of a middleman between the other two types of switches; using an internal virtual switch is useful when you want the VM traffic to remain within the Hyper-V environment but still provide network connectivity between the VMs and the Hyper-V host itself. In other words, VMs connected to an internal virtual switch can talk to each other and talk to the Hyper-V Server, but not beyond.

Private virtual switch

The private virtual switch is just what the name implies: private. VMs plugged into the same private virtual switch can communicate with each other, but not beyond. Even the Hyper-V host server does not have network connectivity to a private virtual switch. Test labs are a great example of a use case for private virtual switches, which we will discuss immediately following this section when we create a new virtual switch of our own.

Creating a new virtual switch

The following is an example I use often. I am running a new Hyper-V Server, which is connected physically to my corporate network, so I can spin up new VMs, connect them to my external virtual switch, and have them communicate directly with the corporate network. This allows me to domain-join them and interact with them like I would any server on my network. Maybe I need to create some VMs that I want to talk with each other, but I do *not* want them to communicate with my production network. A good example of this scenario in the real world is when building a test lab. In fact, I am taking this exact approach for all of the servers that we have used throughout this book. My physical Hyper-V Server is on my production network, yet my entire `Contoso.local` network and all of the VMs running within it are on their own separate network, which is completely segregated from my real network. I did this by creating a new private virtual switch. Remember from the description that when you plug VMs into this kind of switch, they can communicate with other VMs that are plugged into that same virtual switch, but they cannot communicate beyond that switch.

Inside **Virtual Switch Manager**, all I must do is choose the kind of virtual switch that I want to create, **Private** in this case, and click on the **Create Virtual Switch** button. I can then provide a name for my new switch, and I am immediately able to connect VMs to this switch. You can see in *Figure 14.9* that I have created two new private virtual switches: one to plug my test lab VM's internal NICs into and another switch that will act as my test lab's DMZ network:

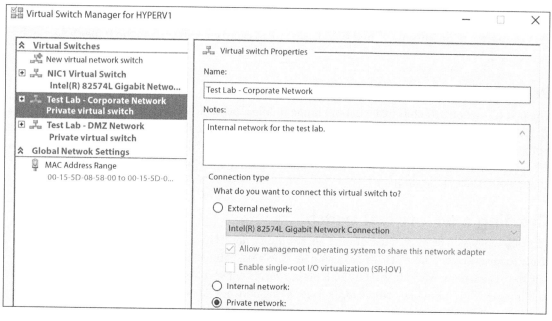

Figure 14.9: Creating new private virtual switches

Receive Segment Coalescing (RSC)

There are not many vast improvements or differences between the way that Hyper-V works in Windows Server 2022 versus its predecessor, 2019, but here we highlight one area of newfound efficiency that relates to our current topic. Virtual switches in Server 2022 are enhanced with RSC, which allows Hyper-V's networking to combine (coalesce) packets together to form larger network segments. Combining network packets causes the CPU to get away with processing fewer overall packets, which improves efficiency in Hyper-V networking, both when interacting with network traffic coming from machines outside the Hyper-V host as well as network interaction between two VMs on the same host.

Implementing a new virtual server

Now we are ready to spin up our first virtual server! Similar to creating new virtual switches, the process for creating a new VM is fairly straightforward, but there are some steps along the way that might need some explanation if you haven't been through this process before. We start with the same management interface from which we do everything in the Hyper-V world. Open up **Hyper-V Manager** and right-click on the name of your Hyper-V Server. Navigate to **New** | **Virtual Machine...** to launch the wizard:

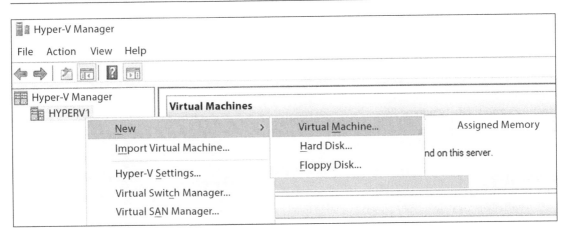

Figure 14.10: Creating a new VM

The first screen where we need to make some decisions is **Specify Name and Location**. Create a name for your new VM, which is easy enough. Then you also have the chance to store your VM in a new location. If you set a good default location for your virtual machines during Hyper-V role installation, chances are that you won't have to modify this field. But in my case, I chose the default options when I installed the role, and so this wizard was going to place my VM somewhere inside C:\ProgramData, and I didn't like the look of that. So I selected the checkbox and chose a location that I like for my VM. You can see that I am using a dedicated disk to store my VMs, which is generally a good practice. Even better practice in a larger network would be to utilize resilient disk space that was accessed through the network, such as a Storage Spaces Direct infrastructure or some kind of SAN:

Figure 14.11: Specifying a storage location for a new VM

Next, you have to decide whether you are creating a **Generation 1** or **Generation** 2 VM. We don't need to discuss this in very much detail, because explanations of the two are clearly stated on the page and in *Figure 14.12*. If your VM is going to be running an older operating system, you should likely go with **Generation 1** to ensure compatibility. Alternatively, if you are planning for a recent operating system to be installed on this new VM, selecting **Generation 2** is probably in your best interests from a new features and security perspective:

Choose the generation of this virtual machine.

◉ Generation 1

    This virtual machine generation supports 32-bit and 64-bit guest operating systems and provides virtual hardware which has been available in all previous versions of Hyper-V.

○ Generation 2

    This virtual machine generation provides support for newer virtualization features, has UEFI-based firmware, and requires a supported 64-bit guest operating system.

⚠ Once a virtual machine has been created, you cannot change its generation.

Figure 14.12: Each VM can be either Generation 1 or Generation 2

Now, define how much memory you want to assign to this particular VM. Keep in mind that this setting is adjustable in the future, so you don't have to plan too hard for this. The amount of RAM you dedicate to this virtual machine will depend on how much RAM you have available in the Hyper-V host system, and how much memory is required to run whatever roles and services you plan to install on this VM. You can specify any amount of memory in this field. For example, if I wanted roughly 2 GB, I could type in 2,000 MB. However, what I find in the field is that most people still stick with the actual amount of MB, because that is what we have always done with hardware. So instead of rounding to 2,000, I am going to set my 2 GB VM to an *actual* 2 GB—or 2,048 MB.

Leaving the box unchecked for dynamic memory means that Hyper-V will dedicate 2,048 MB of its physically available RAM to this specific VM. Whether the VM is using 2,048 MB or 256 MB at any given time, the full 2,048 MB will be dedicated to the VM and will be unusable by the rest of the Hyper-V Server. If you select **Use Dynamic Memory for this virtual machine**, the VM only takes away from the Hyper-V host what it is using at any given moment. If you set it to 2,048 MB, but the VM is sitting idle and only consuming 256 MB, it will only tax Hyper-V with a 256 MB load:

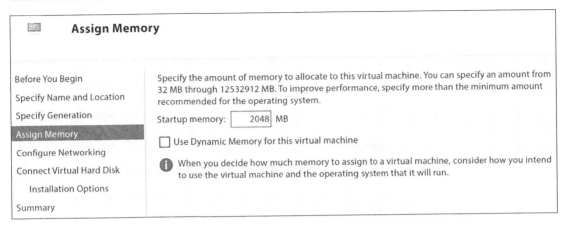

Figure 14.13: Defining memory allocation for the new VM

Configure Networking is the next screen we are presented with, and here we simply choose which virtual switch our VM's NIC gets plugged into. We do have the ability to add additional NICs to this VM later, but for now, we get a standard single NIC during the creation of our new VM, and we simply need to choose where it needs to be connected. For the time being, this new web server I am building will be connected to my Test Lab internal corporate network, so that I can build my web app and test it out before introducing it into a real production network. If I drop down a list of available connections here, you will see that my original external virtual switch, as well as the two new private virtual switches that I created, are available to choose from:

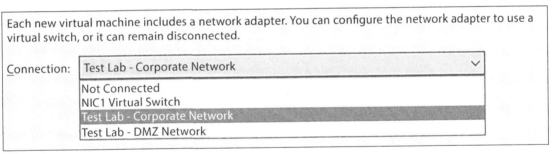

Figure 14.14: "Plug" the new VM into a virtual switch

A few details are also needed so that this new VM can have a hard drive. Most commonly, you will utilize the top option here so that the new VM gets a brand-new hard drive. There are also options for using an existing virtual hard disk if you are booting from an existing file, or attaching a disk later if you aren't yet prepared to make this decision. We are going to allow the wizard to generate a new virtual hard disk, and the default size is 127 GB. I can set this to whatever I want, but it is important to know that it does not consume the full 127 GB of space. The disk size will only be as big as what is being used on the disk, so only a fraction of that 127 GB will be used. I mention this to point out that the number you specify here is more of a *maximum* size, so make sure to plan your disks appropriately, specifying enough size so that you and your applications have the necessary room to grow:

Figure 14.15: Allowing the wizard to create a new virtual hard disk

Our last screen of options in the wizard allows us to define the specifics of the operating system our new VM is going to run on. Or rather, where that operating system will be installed from. We are going to purposefully leave this set to **Install an operating system later** because that is the default option, and it will give us the chance to see what happens when you do not specify any settings on this screen:

You can install an operating system now if you have access to the setup media, or you can install it later.

◉ Install an operating system later

○ Install an operating system from a bootable CD/DVD-ROM

   Media

     ◉ Physical CD/DVD drive: [⌄]

     ○ Image file (.iso):   [   ] [Browse...]

○ Install an operating system from a bootable floppy disk

   Media

     Virtual floppy disk (.vfd): [   ] [Browse...]

○ Install an operating system from a network-based installation server

Figure 14.16: Decisions to be made regarding operating system installation

Starting and connecting to the VM

We have now created a VM, which you can see inside the **Hyper-V Manager** console. Starting the VM is as simple as right-clicking on it and then selecting **Start**. After selecting the option to start the VM, right-click on it again and click on **Connect…** This will open a console window from which you can watch the boot process of your new server:

Figure 14.17: Starting our new virtual machine

Now that our new VM has been started, *what can we expect to see inside the console window?* A boot failure error, of course:

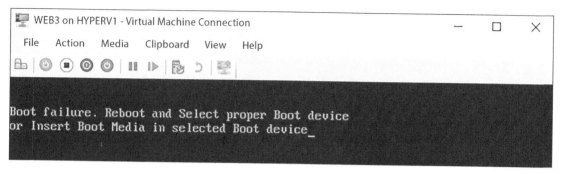

Figure 14.18: The initial start of this VM was not so successful

Installing the operating system

We get a boot failure message because we didn't specify any operating system media during our wizard, and so Hyper-V has created our VM and our new hard disk, but just like when you build a new server out of fresh hardware, you need software to be installed on that hard disk in order for it to do something. Luckily, installing an operating system on a VM is even easier than installing it on a physical server. Heading back into the **Hyper-V Manager** console, right-click on the name of your new VM and go to **Settings...**.

Inside **Settings**, you will see that this VM has a **DVD Drive** automatically listed in **IDE Controller 1**. If you click on **DVD Drive**, you can easily tell it to mount any ISO to that drive. Copy the ISO file of the operating system installer you wish to run to the hard drive of your Hyper-V Server.

I typically place all of my ISOs inside a dedicated folder called ISOs, right alongside my VMs folder, and then **Browse...** to it from this screen. Connecting an ISO to your VM is the same as if you were plugging a physical installation DVD into a physical server:

Figure 14.19: Providing operating system installation media to our new VM

After mounting the media, restart the VM and you will see that our operating system installer kicks off automatically:

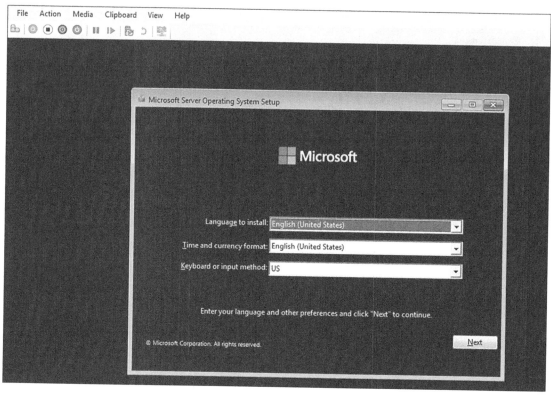

Figure 14.20: The VM is now booting to the installation ISO

Managing a virtual server

We have made use of **Hyper-V Manager** to manage our virtual switches and to create a virtual machine. This tool is all-powerful when it comes to manipulating your VMs, and I find myself accessing it frequently in my daily job. Let's take a look at a few of the other things you can do from inside **Hyper-V Manager,** as well as discuss other methods that can be used to work with the new virtual machines that are being created on your Hyper-V Server.

Hyper-V Manager

As you know, Hyper-V Manager is the primary tool for managing a Hyper-V Server. It is a nice console that gives you a status of your virtual machines and allows you to manage those VMs in a variety of ways. Something we did not cover – because I only have one Hyper-V Server running – is that you can manage multiple Hyper-V Servers from a single **Hyper-V Manager** console. Just like any MMC-style console in the Microsoft world, you can right-click on the words **Hyper-V Manager** near the top-left corner of the screen and select an option that says **Connect to Server....** By using this function, you can pull information from other Hyper-V Servers into this same **Hyper-V Manager** console:

Figure 14.21: Connecting Hyper-V Manager to remote Hyper-V hosts

Furthermore, this enables you to run **Hyper-V Manager** software on a client computer. You can install the Hyper-V role on a Windows 10/11 machine, which will also install this console, and then use that local copy of **Hyper-V Manager** running on your Windows 10/11 desktop to manage your Hyper-V Servers, without needing to log in to those servers directly.

Some of the most useful actions inside **Hyper-V Manager** are listed along the right side of the console in the **Actions** pane – features such as **Virtual Switch Manager** and the ability to create a new VM. Once you have VMs up and running, you will find a lot of useful functions listed inside the context menu that appears when you right-click on a VM, as you can see in *Figure 14.22*:

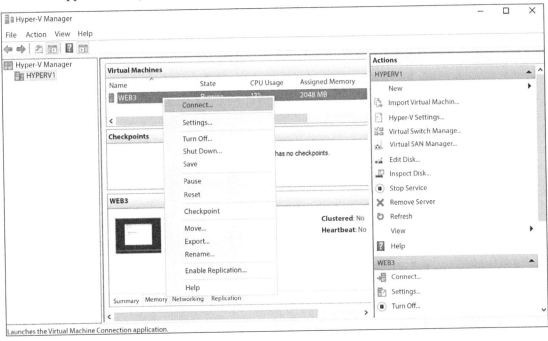

Figure 14.22: Available options in the Actions pane for managing a virtual machine

Some of these are self-explanatory, and some are worth playing around with. We have already used **Connect...** to connect to our VM's console. **Settings...** opens up a ton of possibilities, and we will take a look further inside the **Settings** menu immediately following this section. One of the most common reasons I open this right-click menu is for power functions on my VMs. You can see that you have the ability to **Turn Off...** or **Shut Down...** your VM. Turning it off is like yanking the power cord on a server: it cuts off the power immediately to that server and will cause Windows some grief when doing so. The shutdown function, on the other hand, initiates a clean shutdown, at least when you are using Microsoft operating systems on the VMs. Shutting down a server is no big deal, but the real power here comes from the fact that you can shut down multiple VMs at the same time. For example, if I were running a dozen different VMs for all of my test labs, and I decided that my lab was taking up too many resources and causing problems on my Hyper-V Server, I could select all of my VMs at the same time, right-click on them, then click on **Shut Down...** just once, and it would immediately kick off the shutdown process on all of the VMs that I had selected. Once a VM is shut down or turned off, right-clicking on that VM will give you a **Start** function; you can also select many servers and start them all at once by using this right-click menu.

The Settings menu

Making in-depth modifications to any of your VMs typically means right-clicking on that VM, and then navigating to **Settings...** for that particular VM. Inside **Settings**, you can adjust any aspect of your VM's hardware, which is the most common reason to visit this screen. Immediately upon opening **Settings**, you have the option to **Add Hardware** to your VM. This is the place you would visit to add more hard drive controllers or NICs to your virtual server:

Figure 14.23: Adding new hardware to an existing VM

I don't know if you can tell from the preceding screenshot, but the **Add** button is currently grayed out. This is important. Many functions inside **Settings** can be manipulated on the fly, while the VM is running. Some functions cannot be accomplished unless the VM is turned off. Adding hardware is one of those functions. If you want to add a new hard drive or NIC to your VM, you will need to shut down that server before you can do it.

Next, we should talk about the **Memory** screen. This one is fairly painless, *right?* Simply input the amount of RAM that you want this VM to have available. The reason that I want to point it out is that a major improvement has been made in this functionality since the early days of Hyper-V. Starting with Windows Server 2016 Hyper-V, you can now adjust the amount of RAM that a VM has allocated while it is running! In previous versions of Hyper-V, you were required to shut down the VMs to change their memory allocation, but even though my WEB3 server is currently running and servicing users, I can pop in here and increase RAM at will.

Let's say my 2 GB isn't keeping up with the task load, and I want to increase it to 4 GB. I leave the server running, open **Hyper-V Manager** settings for the VM, and adjust the relevant setting to 4,096 MB:

Figure 14.24: Increasing memory while the VM is running

The amount of memory immediately adjusts, and if I open system properties inside the WEB3 server, I can see that the operating system has updated to reflect the 4 GB of RAM now installed:

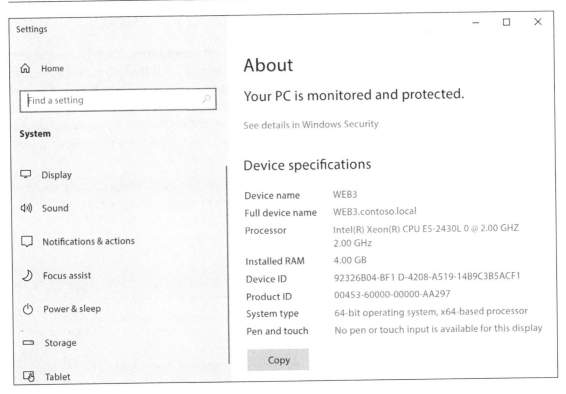

Figure 14.25: WEB3 is immediately increased to 4 GB of memory

Other useful settings screens are the **Processor** and **Network Adapter** sections. Here you define the number of virtual processors currently assigned to the VM and the performance weights associated with these processors. On the **Network Adapter** screen, you can change which virtual switch your virtual NICs are plugged into. I find myself accessing this section often as I move servers from one location to another.

Checkpoints

Another important function inside the **Settings** menu is called **checkpoints**. These were formerly called snapshots, which I think makes a little more sense to most of us. Checkpoints are a function that you can invoke from **Hyper-V Manager** by right-clicking on one or more VMs. It essentially creates a *snapshot in time* of the VM. Another way to look at checkpoints is that they are creating rollback points for your servers. If you create a checkpoint on Tuesday, and on Wednesday somebody makes a configuration change on that server that causes problems, you can restore the checkpoint from Tuesday and bring the VM back to that day's status.

There are a couple of different ways that checkpoints can be run, and the **Settings** menu is where we define those particulars. Simply right-click on any VM, visit the **Settings** screen, and then click on the management task called **Checkpoints**. You can see the options in *Figure 14.26*:

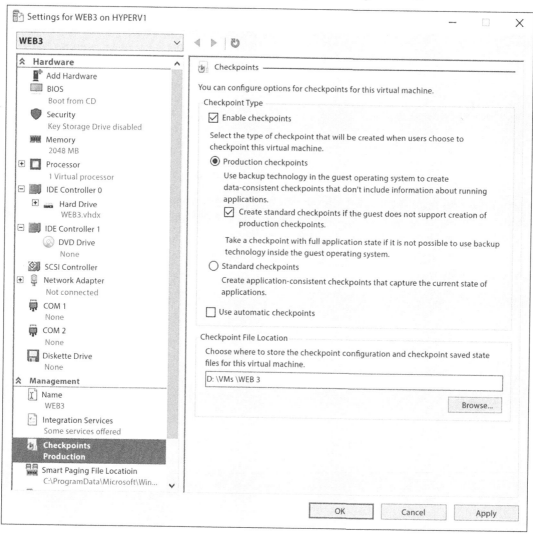

Figure 14.26: Options for configuring checkpoints

These settings are individual for each VM you are running; you could treat checkpoints for WEB1 differently than WEB2, for example. The default way to handle these snapshots in time is called **Production checkpoints**. This is generally the preferred method for creating these quick images of your servers, as it is the cleanest method. When choosing to generate a production checkpoint, Hyper-V invokes Windows backup functions inside the VM's operating system, to create a backup of that server. This would be similar to you logging into that VM and manually launching an operating system backup task. Keep in mind that, when you do this, and therefore when Hyper-V does this for you, it is not a block-by-block identical backup of the VM, but rather a backup file that can then be restored in the future to bring the operating system files back to this point in time. In other words, a production checkpoint brings Windows back to the previous state, but any applications and data that are constantly changing on the server are not captured in the checkpoint, nor restored when the checkpoint is rolled back into place.

Alternatively, the **Standard checkpoints** option does just that. This takes more of a quick-and-dirty capture of the VM, kind of like right-clicking on the VHDX hard drive file and choosing to copy and then paste it somewhere else. Restoring standard checkpoints can be a messier process. Suppose your checkpoint was created while an application on the server was in the middle of an important function, such as a database write. Restoring that checkpoint would bring the server right back to the moment in time that the application was in the middle of that database write. This has the potential to cause issues inside that database.

Once you have decided on which kind of checkpoint is best for your VM, invoking checkpoints is very simple. Back at the main screen in Hyper-V Manager, simply right-click on your VM and select **Checkpoint**. After performing this task, you will see the middle pane of Hyper-V Manager receive some new information in a section you may not have even noticed earlier: **Checkpoints**.

The new checkpoint that we just created is now sitting here, waiting to be restored if the need arises. In the future, right-clicking on this checkpoint and choosing **Apply...** will initiate the restoration process:

Figure 14.27: Viewing and recovering from a previous checkpoint

Configuring auto stop and start

VMware is another very popular hypervisor host platform (competing with Hyper-V in the space), and while this chapter is not in any way a comparison of VMware and Hyper-V, I mention it here to point out a common issue that I encounter in the VMware world. What happens to your virtual machines when the physical host server is shut down, restarted, or even loses power temporarily?

While a sudden loss of power is going to be an interruption to both the physical host and virtual machines no matter what platform you are running, hopefully, you have spent some money on a smart UPS system to keep your host server running during a power outage and it is perhaps even capable of cleanly shutting down that physical host if the power remains offline for an extended period of time.

Assuming a clean shutdown of the physical host occurs, what happens to your VMs? Do they all need to be individually shut down before shutting down the physical host? That may take a long time, yet I see many IT admins do exactly this because they think it is necessary and are worried about messing up the operating systems of their VMs by initiating a shutdown of the host server. Fortunately, you do not have to worry about shutting down VMs in this scenario, and there are options inside Hyper-V Manager to declare what happens with each VM when the host is shutting down.

Inside **Settings** for any VM, scroll down to the bottom option called **Automatic Stop Action**. Here you can see that there are three options available to declare what happens with a VM when the host shuts down. The VM can be cleanly shut down by Hyper-V, the VM can simply be turned off (which may impact Windows on the VM), or Hyper-V can **Save the virtual machine state**. You'll notice the save option is the default for every new VM and is likely the option you want to leave selected.

With this option in place, when your Hyper-V host server shuts down, the VMs are saved (another way to think about it is that they are being paused) so that when they are turned back on they will resume from exactly where they were prior to the host shutdown:

Figure 14.28: Automatic Stop Action settings

Clicking just one option higher on the **Settings** screen for any VM, you will also find **Automatic Start Action** options. As you have likely surmised, these are your options for handling each VM when a Hyper-V host server resumes power after having been powered off. Here you can instruct Hyper-V to leave the VM powered off, to always start this VM when the host starts, or for Hyper-V to decide itself whether or not the VM was running prior to the host shutdown and to start up the VM only if it was previously running. This is the default option for each VM.

Also available on this screen is a **Startup delay** selection. This is useful when you need certain servers (VMs) to boot before others. For example, wanting your domain controller to be online before any domain member servers attempt to boot. You could configure a startup delay of 30 or 60 seconds for any member servers, which would cause them to start after the DC starts:

📠 Automatic Start Action ─────────────────────────────

What do you want this virtual machine to do when the physical computer starts?

◯ Nothing

◉ Automatically start if it was running when the service stopped

◯ Always start this virtual machine automatically

Automatic start delay

Specify a startup delay to reduce resource contention between virtual machines.

Startup delay: [0]   seconds

Figure 14.29: VM auto-start settings

Now you know where options live for configuring auto-stop and auto-start settings on each virtual machine, and it would seem that retaining the default settings and never even visiting these options would produce VM shutdown and startup procedures that fit most environments. Wrapping this topic back to my opening statement about a common problem in VMware, what I find in the wild is that VMware host systems are rarely configured with correct auto-start settings. It is a rare occurrence that host servers go offline. I have seen hosts with uptimes longer than 1,000 days. Someday, however, you will encounter a situation where your host shuts down unexpectedly, and when that happens, do you know with certainty what your hypervisor is going to do with its VMs? Many of the VMware environments I encounter do not have auto start settings configured for VMs, and so when the power goes off and comes back online, servers remain offline until you give them some manual attention.

No matter your hypervisor platform, spend a few minutes reviewing your VM auto stop and auto start procedures to ensure they fall in line with your expectations!

  Check the host BIOS! It's easy enough to check over VM settings to make sure they auto-start following a power outage but do you know whether or not the host server itself is going to auto-power on? This option is typically configured inside the BIOS on your physical server.

Expanding a virtual disk

Hardware changes to virtual machines are quick and easy, due to the nature of VMs and using all virtual resources that can be expanded or condensed with simple clicks of the mouse. Increasing or decreasing CPU cores and RAM resources is very self-explanatory and happens from inside the **VM Settings** menu. One other specific task that is a very normal procedure, but is not quite so straight-forward, is the expansion of a virtual hard disk upon which a VM is running.

You can see in the following screenshot that my WEB3 server has a D: volume, but some yahoo (me) only allocated 5 GB initially, and it's almost full.

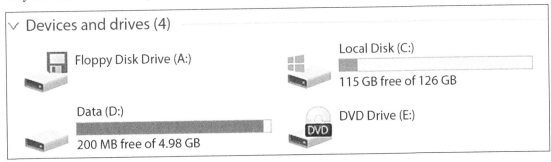

Figure 14.30: My data drive needs more room

On a physical server, this could be complicated, installing a newer and bigger drive and then needing to migrate everything to it. Since this is a VM, could we make things easier by adding a new disk that is larger and then copying everything over, saving us the step of dealing with hardware? Certainly. But there is a much simpler way even than that to deal with disks running out of space. Let's expand the existing data disk! The best part is that this only takes a few minutes.

Open **Hyper-V Manager**, and under **Actions** on the right side of the screen, select **Edit Disk....**

Run through the **Edit Disk** wizard, specifying the **virtual hard disk file** (VHDX file) that you want to manipulate, and on the third screen of the wizard, select the option to **Expand** this disk. Following the **Expand** selection, you will be presented with the current size of the disk and a field where you can populate the new size. I'll go ahead and quadruple the size of this disk from 5 GB to 20 GB:

Figure 14.31: Expanding my data disk on the fly

After finishing that wizard, I revisit WEB3 and, lo and behold... my D: volume is still sitting at 5 GB. What gives? Even though we have now successfully expanded the virtual disk to 20 GB, the D: volume inside Windows has only ever been configured for 5 GB, and the Windows instance inside the VM has no idea what you want to accomplish with this extra free space. Perhaps we intend to expand the D: volume, or we could even use this new space to create a new E: volume should we have the need.

Right-click on the **Start** menu and open **Disk Management**. Inside, you will see the status of disks plugged into the VM, where it is clear the second disk has now been expanded to the larger size:

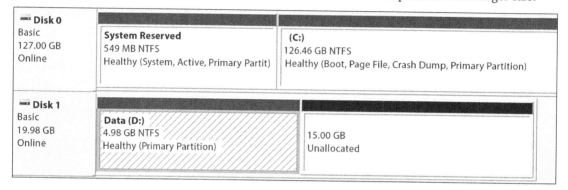

Figure 14.32: Disk 1 has now been expanded

Simply right-clicking on the D: volume and choosing **Extend Volume...** will walk through a very short wizard, after which the D: drive will have been extended to consume the entirety of our newly expanded disk:

Figure 14.33: The data volume is now expanded

Hyper-V console, Remote Desktop Protocol (RDP), or PowerShell

While hardware adjustments to VMs need to be made through Hyper-V Manager, your daily interaction with these VMs running as servers in your environment does not necessarily mean you have to log in to your Hyper-V Server. If you happen to be inside Hyper-V Manager anyway, you can quickly and easily use that **Connect** function to interact with the console of your servers, through the use of the Hyper-V console tool. Accessing your servers this way is beneficial if you need to see something in the BIOS, or otherwise outside of the Windows operating system that is running on that VM, but it's not often that you require this level of console access.

When you have Windows servers running as VMs, it is much more common to interact with these servers in the same way that you would interact with physical servers on your network. While I have been accessing my WEB3 server through the Hyper-V console in this chapter, now that I have Windows Server 2022 installed on WEB3 and I have enabled the RDP capabilities on it, there is no reason why I couldn't just pop open MSTSC and log in to WEB3 that way, straight from my workstation desktop:

Figure 14.34: Using normal support tools to connect to VMs

The same is true for PowerShell or any other traditional way of remotely accessing services on any other server. Since this VM is fully online and has the server operating system installed, I can use PowerShell remoting to manipulate my WEB3 server as well, from another server or from my desktop computer. Once you are finished building out the hardware and installing the operating system on a VM, it's rare that you actually need to use the Hyper-V console to interact with that server. The primary reasons for opening up Hyper-V Manager to reach a VM are to make hardware-level changes on that server, such as adding a hard drive, adjusting RAM, or moving a network connection from one virtual switch to another.

Windows Admin Center (WAC)

We have seen WAC scattered throughout this book and for good reason. WAC is the new super-tool that Microsoft wants server administrators to start using to interact with and manage almost every single one of their servers. VM servers hosted in Hyper-V are no exception; you can make use of the WAC toolset to administer servers running on your Hyper-V hosts and use WAC to manage the host servers themselves.

Shielded VMs

If your day job doesn't include work with Hyper-V, it's possible that you have never heard of shielded VMs. The name does a pretty good job of explaining this technology at a basic level. If a VM is a virtual machine, then a shielded VM must be a virtual machine that is *shielded* or protected in some way, *right?*

A shielded VM is essentially a VM that is encrypted. Rather, the hard drive file itself (the VHDX) is encrypted, using BitLocker. It sounds simple, but there are some decent requirements for making this happen. For the BitLocker encryption to work properly, the VM is injected with a virtual **Trusted Platform Module (TPM)** chip. TPMs are quickly becoming commonplace at a hardware level, but actually using them is still a mysterious black box to many administrators. Shielded VMs can also be locked down so that they can only run on healthy and approved host servers, which is an amazing advantage to the security-conscious among us. This capability is provided by a couple of different attestation options, which we will discuss shortly.

To explain the benefits that shielded VMs bring to the table, we are going to look at an example of what happens when VMs are *not* shielded. Keep in mind that the idea of shielded VMs is quite a bit more important when you think in the context of servers being hosted in the cloud where you don't have any access to the backend, or hosted by some other division inside your company, such as inside a private cloud. Unless you have already taken the time to roll out all shielded VMs in your environment, what I am about to show you is currently possible on *any* of your existing VMs.

You already know that I am running a Hyper-V host server, and on that host, I have a virtual machine called WEB3. Now, let's pretend that I am a cloud-hosting provider and that WEB3 is a web server that belongs to one of my tenants. I have provided my tenant with a private virtual switch for networking so that they can manage the networking of that server, and I don't have access to that VM at the networking level. Also, it is a fact that this WEB3 server is joined to my tenant's domain and network, and I, as the cloud host, have absolutely no access to domain credentials, or any other means that I can utilize to actually log in to that server.

Sounds pretty good so far, *right?* You, as a tenant, certainly wouldn't want your cloud provider to be able to snoop around inside your virtual machines that are being hosted on that cloud. You also wouldn't want any other tenants who might have VMs running on the same cloud host to be able to see your servers in any way. This same mentality holds true in private clouds as well. If you are hosting a private cloud and are allowing various companies or divisions of a company to have segregated VMs running in the same fabric, you will want to ensure those divisions have real security layers between the VMs, and between the VMs and the host.

Now, let's have a little fun and turn villain. I am a rogue cloud-host employee, and I decide that I'm going to do some damage before I walk out the door. It would be easy for me to kill off that WEB3 server completely since I have access to the host administrative console. However, that would probably throw a flag somewhere, and the tenant would just spin up a new web server or restore it from a backup. So, even better than breaking the VM, I'm going to leave it running and then change the content of the website itself. Let's give this company's clients something to talk about!

To manipulate my tenant's website running on WEB3, I don't need any real access to the VM itself because I have direct access to the virtual hard drive file. All I need to do is tap into that virtual hard disk file, modify the website, and I can make the website display whatever information I want.

First, I log in to the Hyper-V Server (remember, this is owned by me since I am the host), and browse to the location of the VHD file that WEB3 is using. This is all on the backend, so I don't need any tenant credentials to get here. Furthermore, nothing is logged with these actions and the tenant will have no way of knowing that I am doing this. I simply right-click on that VHD and select **Mount**:

Figure 14.35: Silently mounting a connection to this virtual hard disk file

Now that the VHD has been mounted to the host server's operating system directly, I can browse that VM's hard drive as if it were one of my own drives. Navigate to the wwwroot folder to find the website files, and change the default page to display whatever you want:

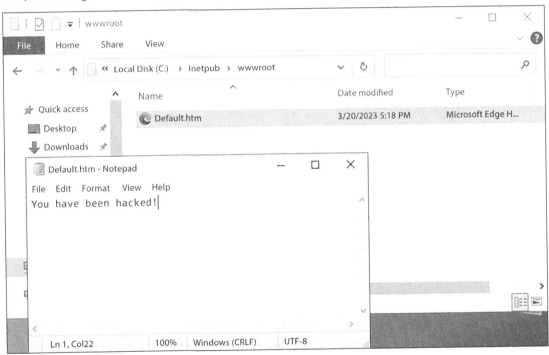

Figure 14.36: Editing content inside a "customer" VM

When I'm finished playing around with the website, I can open up **Disk Management**, right-click on that mounted disk, and select **Detach VHD** to cover my tracks:

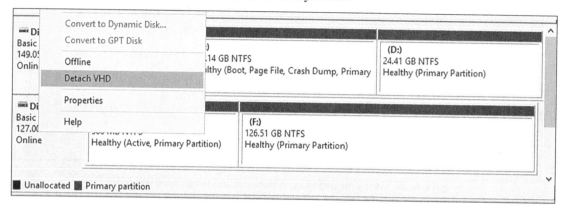

Figure 14.37: Removing the connection to this VHD, my work here is done

And then, just for the fun of it, I copy the entire VHD file onto a USB stick so that I can take it with me and mess around with it more later.

This example cuts to the core of why so many companies are hesitant about server hosting platforms and is precisely why Microsoft began crafting something known as **shielded VMs.**

Encrypting VHDs

The idea behind shielded VMs is quite simple. Microsoft already has a great drive-encryption technology, called BitLocker. Shielded VMs are Hyper-V VMs that have BitLocker drive encryption enabled. When your entire VHD file is protected and encrypted with BitLocker, nobody is going to be able to gain backdoor access to that drive. Attempting to mount the VHD as we just did would result in an error message, and nothing more:

Figure 14.38: Access denied!

Even better is that when you set up your infrastructure to support shielded VMs, you also block Hyper-V console access to the VMs that are shielded. While this in itself isn't as big a deal as drive encryption, it's still important enough to point out. If someone has access to the Hyper-V host server and opens up **Hyper-V Manager**, they will generally have the ability to use the **Connect** function on the tenant VMs in order to view whatever was currently on the console. More than likely, this would leave them staring at a login screen that they, hopefully, would not be able to breach. But if that VM's console had somehow been left in a logged-in state, they would have immediate access to manipulating the VM, even if the drive was encrypted.

So when you create a shielded VM, it not only encrypts the VHD using BitLocker technology but it also blocks all access to the VM's console from Hyper-V Manager.

Does this hardcore blocking have the potential to cause you problems when you are trying to legitimately troubleshoot a VM? What if you need to use the Hyper-V console to figure out why a VM won't boot or something like that? Yes, that is a valid point and one that you need to consider. Shielded VMs are much more secure. So much so that you could, in fact, lock yourself out from being able to troubleshoot issues on that server. As is often the case with everything in the IT world, we are trading usability for security.

Infrastructure requirements for shielded VMs

There are a couple of important pieces in this puzzle that you need to be aware of if you are interested in running shielded VMs.

Guarded hosts

You will need to run one or more guarded host servers to house your shielded VMs. Guarded hosts are essentially Hyper-V Servers on steroids. They will host VMs like any other Hyper-V Server, but they are specially crafted and configured to host these encrypted shielded VMs and to attest their own health as part of this overall security strategy.

Guarded hosts must be running Server 2016, 2019, or 2022 Datacenter, and generally, you want them to boot using UEFI and to contain a TPM 2.0 chip. While TPM 2.0 is not a firm requirement, it is certainly recommended.

These guarded host servers then take the place of your traditional Hyper-V Servers. It is their job to host your shielded VMs.

Host Guardian Service (HGS)

HGS is a service that runs on a server, or more commonly, a cluster of three servers, and handles the attestation of guarded hosts. When a shielded VM attempts to start/boot on a guarded host server, that host must reach over to HGS and attest that it is safe and secure. Only once the host has passed the HGS attestation and health checks will the shielded VM be allowed to start.

HGS is *critical* to making a guarded fabric work. If HGS goes down, *none* of your shielded VMs will be able to start!

There are different requirements for HGS, depending on what attestation mode your guarded hosts are going to utilize. We will learn about those modes in the next section of this chapter. HGS will have to be running Server 2016, 2019, or 2022, and most commonly, you want to use physical servers running in a three-node cluster for this service.

I also want to point out a more recent capability related to HGS that came via Windows Server 2019: **HGS cache.** A previous limitation of Server 2016 shielded VMs was that HGS needed to be contacted every time *any* guarded host wanted to spin up *any* shielded VM. This can become problematic if HGS is unavailable for some temporary reason. New in Server 2019 is the HGS cache for VM keys so that a guarded host is able to start up approved VMs based on keys in the cache, rather than always having to check in with a live HGS.

This can be helpful if HGS is offline (although HGS being completely offline probably means that you have big problems), but the HGS cache has a more valid use case in branch-office scenarios where a guarded host might have a poor network connection to HGS.

Host attestations

Attestation of the guarded hosts is the secret to using shielded VMs. This is the basis of security in wanting to move forward with such a solution in your own environment. The ability of your hosts to attest their health and identity gives you peace of mind in knowing that those hosts are not being modified or manipulated without your knowledge, and it ensures that a malicious host employee cannot copy all of your VM hard drive files onto a USB, bring them home, and boot them up. Those shielded VMs are only ever going to start on the guarded hosts in your environment, nowhere else.

There are two different modes that guarded hosts can use to pass attestation with HGS. Well, actually there are three, but one has already been deprecated. Let's take a minute to detail the different modes that can be used between your guarded hosts and your HGS.

TPM-trusted attestations

This is the best way! TPM chips are physical chips installed on your server's motherboard that contain unique information. Most importantly, this information cannot be modified or hacked from within the Windows operating system. When your guarded host servers are equipped with TPM 2.0 chips, this opens the door to doing some incredibly powerful host attestation. The host utilizes Secure Boot and some code-integrity checks that are stored inside the TPM to verify that it is healthy and has not been modified. HGS then cross-checks the information being submitted from the TPM with the information that it knows about when the guarded host was initially configured, to ensure that the requesting host is really one of your approved guarded hosts and that it has not been tampered with. If you are configuring new Hyper-V Servers, make sure they contain TPM 2.0 chips so that you can utilize these features.

Host key attestations

If TPMs aren't your thing or are beyond your hardware abilities, we can do a simpler host key attestation. The ability of your guarded hosts to generate a host key that can be known and verified by HGS is new as of Windows Server 2019. This uses asymmetric key-pair technology to validate the guarded hosts. Basically, you will either create a new host-key pair or use an existing certificate and then send the public portion of that key or certificate over to HGS. When guarded hosts want to spin up a shielded VM, they reach out to attest with HGS, and that attestation is approved or denied based on this key pair.

This is certainly a faster and easier way to make shielded VMs a reality in your network but is not as secure as a TPM-trusted attestation.

Admin-trusted attestation — deprecated in 2019

If your environment is recent and based on Server 2019 or 2022, don't pay any attention to this one. However, there are folks who are running shielded VMs within a Windows Server 2016 infrastructure, and in that case, there was an additional option for attestation.

Commonly known as admin-trusted attestation, this was a very simple (and not very secure) way for your hosts to attest to HGS that they were approved. Basically, you created an **Active Directory (AD)** security group, added your guarded hosts into that group, and then HGS considered any host that was part of that group to be guarded and approved to run shielded VMs.

The future of shielded VMs

HGS, attestation modes, and shielded VMs are pieces of technology that exist in Windows Server 2022, and Microsoft's documentation has been updated to reflect Server 2022 as included and supported for the use of shielded VMs. However...

Microsoft has also announced that Guarded Fabric and shielded VMs are officially on their list of "Features we're no longer developing." This does not mean they are no longer viable, as they will continue to support the use of shielded VMs, including on Server 2022, but they are ceasing to pour development resources into this on-prem technology.

Integrating with Linux

Many companies utilize Linux in some capacity or another. The use of Linux may actually be poised to make a grander entrance into the Windows Server world now that we have this higher level of integration possible inside Windows Server 2022. There are ways in which your Server 2022 can now be used to interact with Linux VMs:

- **Running in Hyper-V**: VMs hosted on a Hyper-V Server used to be limited to Windows-based operating systems. This is no longer the case. The scope of the Hyper-V virtualization host has now been expanded to accommodate running Linux-based VMs in Hyper-V Manager. There is even good integration with the keyboard and mouse!

- **Linux-shielded VMs**: You now know about running shielded VMs in Hyper-V, and you also know about running Linux-based VMs inside Hyper-V. *Does this mean we can combine those two ideas and run a Linux VM that is also shielded?* Why yes, we certainly can. This capability was introduced in SAC version Windows Server 1709 and also exists in the newest LTSC release of Windows Server 2022.

- **Running in containers**: While most server and Hyper-V administrators won't be chomping at the bit to install Linux on their systems because they simply have no reason to do so, there will definitely be a lot more Linux-y talk coming from anyone on the DevOps side of the IT house. When building scalable, modern applications that are destined for the cloud, we often talk about running these applications inside containers. In the past, hosting containers on a Windows server meant that the container itself had to be running Windows, but no more. You can now host Linux-based containers on top of Windows Server 2022. This allows great flexibility in the application development process and will be an important consideration for the future of containers.

ReFS deduplication

While filesystems and deduplication features are technologies that you may not expect to be discussed when it comes to Hyper-V, the improvements in Server 2019 and 2022 related to ReFS and the deduplication of data carry some huge advantages for Hyper-V Servers. In case these are unfamiliar terms, let's take a minute and define ReFS and deduplication.

ReFS

Anyone who has worked on computers for a while will recognize FAT, FAT32, and NTFS. These are filesystems that can be used when formatting hard drives. The different versions of filesystems translate into different capabilities of how you can utilize that hard drive. For a number of years, NTFS has been the *de facto* standard for all hard disks connected to Windows machines.

That is until Windows Server 2016 came along. We now have a new filesystem option called ReFS. Even if you work in an IT department every day, you may have never heard of ReFS because, so far, it isn't getting used all that much. It is primarily used in servers that are involved with **Storage Spaces Direct (S2D)**. If it's the latest and greatest filesystem from Microsoft, *why isn't it being used as the default option on any new system?* Primarily because ReFS is not a bootable filesystem. That immediately cancels out the capability of systems with a single hard disk to be running ReFS on the whole drive. What that implies is that ReFS is for secondary volumes on servers, perhaps volumes intended to hold large amounts of data.

In those instances where you format a second volume to be ReFS and store data on it, there are some great resiliency and performance advantages to using ReFS instead of NTFS. These advantages were designed to make S2D implementations work better.

Data deduplication

Data deduplication is simply the ability of a computing system to discover multiple bits of data on a drive that are identical and *clean them up*. If there were six copies of the exact same file on a system, deduplication could delete five of them, retaining one for the purposes of all six locations. This idea enables some major space-saving. Data deduplication itself is not new; we had some capabilities introduced way back in Server 2012 regarding this.

Windows Server 2019 is the first platform where it is possible to enable data deduplication on a volume that is formatted via ReFS.

Why is this important to Hyper-V?

Data deduplication can be incredibly advantageous to run on a volume that stores Hyper-V VM hard drive files because, as you can imagine, there will be a ton of information that is duplicated over and over and over again when you are running dozens of VMs. Think about all of those Windows operating system files that will be identical among all of your VMs running on the Hyper-V host. It's pretty obvious why it would be beneficial to enable data deduplication on a volume that stored VHDX files.

ReFS has some big resiliency and performance advantages over NTFS, so it is also obvious that VHDX files would be best served by being stored on a ReFS volume.

Windows Server 2019 and 2022 are the first platforms where you can have your cake and eat it too. We now have the ability to create a ReFS volume for storing virtual machine hard drives and also enable data deduplication on that same volume.

Hyper-V Server...2019?

It's very easy to get excited about virtualization. Build some hardware, install Windows Server 2022, implement the Hyper-V role, and bam! You're ready to start rolling out hundreds and hundreds of VMs in your environment... *right?*

Not necessarily. We haven't talked about licensing yet, and too often our technological prowess is limited by licensing requirements. The same is true with Hyper-V. Every VM that you spin up needs to have its own operating system license, of course. That requirement makes sense. What isn't as obvious, however, is the fact that you can only run a certain number of VMs on your Hyper-V Server, depending on what SKU you use for the host operating system itself.

The biggest *gotcha* is that using Windows Server 2022 Standard edition as your Hyper-V Server will result in the ability to run two VMs. Two! That's it, no more. You will be able to launch a couple of virtual machines and will then be prevented from running anymore. Clearly, the Standard edition SKU isn't designed to be used as a Hyper-V Server.

That leaves you with Windows Server 2022 Datacenter edition. Fortunately, Datacenter allows you to run *unlimited* VMs! This is great news! Except for one thing—Datacenter edition usually costs many thousands of dollars. This is a very limiting factor for deployments of Hyper-V Servers.

All of this talk about licensing and how messy or expensive it can be leads to one point: **Hyper-V Server**. Wait a minute, what are you talking about, Jordan? *Isn't that what this whole chapter has been about? Isn't that just a Windows Server 2022 with the Hyper-V role installed?* No, not at all.

"Hyper-V Server" is its own animal. It has its own installer and a whole different user interface from a traditional server. Installing Hyper-V Server onto a piece of hardware will result in a server that can host an *unlimited* number of Hyper-V VMs, but nothing else. You cannot use this as a general-purpose server to host other roles or services. Hyper-V Server also does not have a graphical user interface.

Hyper-V Server 2019 has one *huge* benefit: it's *FREE*. You are still responsible for licenses on each of the VMs themselves, of course, but to have a free host operating system that can run an unlimited number of VMs, now that is something my wallet can really get behind.

Back the train up. Did I forget to update "2019" in the previous paragraph to say "2022"? Nope. We are talking here about **Hyper-V Server 2019** because, sadly, this is going to be the last version released for this special flavor of Hyper-V Server. Microsoft has been releasing this little-known Hyper-V Server installer alongside Windows Server editions for many years, but starting with Windows Server 2022, they are no longer creating a Hyper-V Server offering. Once again, this has nothing at all to do with installing Windows Server 2022 and then installing the Hyper-V role on top of it, which of course is still fully relevant and what we have been talking about throughout this entire chapter.

This particular section of the chapter, however, is focused on the alternate installation method specifically for "Hyper-V Server 2019," as there is no "Hyper-V Server 2022." This is unfortunate, and Microsoft's recommendation to those seeking the special Hyper-V Server installer is to continue using Hyper-V Server 2019 or to trial run Azure Stack HCI, but that comes at a cost. So we're going to move forward with the former option, as Hyper-V Server 2019 will continue to be viable and supported until the year 2029, and make use of it here today. I expect this is the approach most administrators will take.

If you're following along on these topics within your own lab or network, here is a landing page for downloading a Hyper-V Server 2019 installer:

```
https://www.microsoft.com/en-us/evalcenter/download-hyper-v-server-2019
```

I have burned the ISO installer for Hyper-V Server 2019 onto a DVD (thankfully this one is small enough to actually fit!), and just finished installing it onto my hardware. The installation of the operating system itself was completely familiar: all of the installation screens and options were the same as if I were installing the full version of Windows Server 2019. However, now that the installer has finished and I have booted into the operating system of my Hyper-V Server 2019, everything looks completely different:

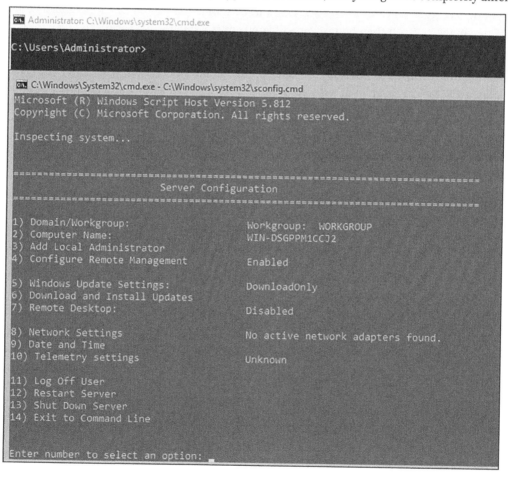

Figure 14.39: Interfacing with Hyper-V Server 2019

We are presented with only a Command Prompt, and inside that prompt, it has auto-launched a configuration utility called **SConfig**. By using the keyboard here, I can do things such as setting the hostname of this server, joining it to a domain, and changing networking settings. Once you have finished using this CLI to set the basic requirements on the server and get it communicating with the network, you really don't need to access the console of this Hyper-V Server again, unless you need to backtrack and revisit this configuration screen to change something. Instead, after configuring Hyper-V Server, you simply utilize **Hyper-V Manager**, or PowerShell, on another server or desktop inside your network, to tap remotely into the management of VMs that are running on this Hyper-V Server.

In *Figure 14.40*, you can see that I have launched **Hyper-V Manager**. I am running this instance of Hyper-V Manager from my Windows 10 machine where I have the Hyper-V role installed. From here, I right-click on **Hyper-V Manager** and choose **Connect to Server...**. I then input the name of my new Hyper-V Server, and the console creates a remote connection. From this remote connection, I can now utilize all functionality inside my Windows 10 Hyper-V Manager as if I were logged straight into the new Hyper-V Server:

Figure 14.40: Remotely connecting to a Hyper-V Server

Similar to the way that most tasks performed on Server Core are handled remotely—through the use of remote consoles or PowerShell—we make all ongoing maintenance and administration of this Hyper-V Server happen from a remote Hyper-V Manager console.

Hyper-V Server gives you the security benefits of a GUI-less interface, combined with the flexibility benefits of hosting an unlimited number of virtual machines, at a price point that nobody can argue with!

Summary

I don't have official numbers, but I will take a risk and say that today there are already more virtual servers running than physical servers to keep our world online. While the battle continues to rage about which hypervisor platform is the best—typically the argument is split between either Hyper-V or VMware—you cannot ignore the fact that virtualization is the way of the future.

Microsoft puts great quantities of time and resources into making sure that Hyper-V always stays ahead of the competition and introduces more and more features with every release so that you can keep your virtualized infrastructure up and running perfectly all the time. *Is the capacity for cloud virtualization even more powerful than on-premise Hyper-V Server?* I would say yes because the infrastructure that is in place at a cloud service provider is going to be the all-powerful Oz compared to what a single company can provide in its own datacenter. *Does this mean you can forget about Hyper-V altogether and just use cloud-provided servers?* Maybe someday, but most aren't ready to take that leap just yet. The need for on-premise servers and services is still immense, and some industries are simply never going to permit their data and applications to be hosted by a third party. In some cases, regulatory compliance reasons will make the decision for you. Understanding the capabilities of Hyper-V and being able to build this infrastructure from the ground up will give you a major advantage when looking for a technology job in a Microsoft-centric organization.

Questions

1. What are the three types of virtual switches inside Hyper-V?

2. If you needed to build a virtual machine that booted using UEFI, which generation of VM would you need to create?

3. True or False—In Windows Server 2022 Hyper-V, you must shut down a VM in order to change its allocated amount of memory (RAM).

4. True or False—The only way to interact with a VM is through the Hyper-V console.

5. What is the name of the technology inside Hyper-V that allows you to take snapshot images of virtual machines that can later be restored?

6. When running shielded VMs in your environment, what is the name of the role that handles the attestation of your Hyper-V host servers?

7. Which is the most comprehensive attestation method for shielded VMs—host key attestation, TPM trusted attestation, or admin trusted attestation?

8. How many virtual machines can run on top of a Windows Server 2022 Standard edition host?

Join our community on Discord

Join our community's Discord space for discussions with the author and other readers:

`https://packt.link/SecNet`

15

Remote Desktop Services

The words "Remote Desktop" usually bring to mind the simple Remote Desktop Connection client that we have utilized for decades to remotely control servers and workstations. Remote Desktop Services is much more powerful and has also been around for many years, but it was originally known as Terminal Services. By crafting a **Remote Desktop Services (RDS)** environment, ideally comprising multiple Windows Server instances, you are taking your first steps into the world of virtualized desktops and centralized computing. An RDS "farm," as it is often lovingly called, provides users with access both inside and outside of the office to a secure virtual session, within which they can run the applications they need and access the data they require in order to do their jobs. Implementing RDS can be a way to provide work-from-home capabilities, even from personal devices, and can allow companies to utilize cheaper, thin-client workstations instead of standard desktops and laptops if their workforce can truly function completely within the RDS environment. This chapter is all about the components that make up RDS and how you can immediately start using it in your own networks.

- Wherefore art thou, role?
- Components of an RDS environment
- Publishing RDS sessions
- RDS licensing
- RDS user profiles
- RemoteApp
- RDS maintenance considerations

Wherefore art thou, role?

What is the first thing you typically need to accomplish on a Windows Server instance to make it do any kind of real work? Oh yeah, install a role. The trouble with this is that our fingers get so used to muscle-memorying their way through the **Add Roles and Features Wizard** screens that you may already be staring at the list of Windows Server roles and getting ready to click on the one called Remote Desktop Services. Stop!

Back up. If you slow down and pay attention when you launch the wizard to install your new role, you will notice that you normally blow right past a screen that asks whether you want to install an RDS component or any other Windows Server component. RDS has an entirely separate section of the **Add Roles and Features Wizard**. The easiest way to deploy RDS is to make use of this second option and continue forward from here.

Figure 15.1: Initial configuration wizard for RDS

Now that you are navigating down the correct role installation road, we have to choose which of the RDS components we would like to install on which server. While possible to place all RDS parts and pieces onto one server, creating a sort of "all-in-one RDS," it is not generally recommended to do so. The next section of this chapter covers descriptions and differences of the RDS components, but it's important to note that RDSH servers should only ever be RDSH servers, while all other RDS roles can exist together on some kind of RDS management or administration server. In our lab environment throughout this chapter, I will be utilizing four RDS-related servers. Three of them will simply be RDSH servers, and the fourth is an RDS-MGMT server that contains all other RDS-related pieces installed on it. Prior to running the **Add Roles and Features Wizard** on my first RDS server, I want to make sure that I have all of my RDS servers spun up, so that this wizard can tap into all four of them to configure the components that I specify.

 If you are adding a node to an existing RDS infrastructure, then there is no need to run this special version of the role installation wizard. We will talk in more depth about this later in the chapter.

Components of an RDS environment

RDS contains many moving parts, and you may get your fingers stuck in them if you aren't clear on what component serves which purpose. Let's take a few pages to describe the different RDS server roles that we are going to be working with.

Remote Desktop Session Host

The most common type of RDS server is called a **Remote Desktop Session Host (RDSH)**. These are the most common because there are usually more RDSH servers than there are servers of any other RDS component type. All user sessions will land on an RDSH server. These are the servers doing the real grunt work: everybody logs in to RDS and they land within virtual sessions that are running on top of RDSH servers. Since every user login consumes resources (CPU, RAM, etc.) and in almost all cases an RDSH server is intended to host multiple user sessions at once, RDSH servers are typically configured to have more resources than other RDS server types.

It is important to note that you usually want an RDSH server to be an RDSH server and nothing else. Do not install RDS Connection Broker, License Manager, Gateway, or anything else on these servers.

Remote Desktop Connection Broker

A good way to think of Remote Desktop Connection Broker is as a built-in load balancer for RDS sessions. New user logins coming into an RDS farm will be distributed across multiple RDSH servers based on weights that are defined within the Remote Desktop Connection Broker properties, and Remote Desktop Connection Broker is also what enables users to disconnect their RDS sessions and be automatically reconnected back to the same session when they reconnect later that day. Remote Desktop Connection Broker makes the decisions about who will land upon which RDSH server.

Remote Desktop License Manager

This one is pretty self-explanatory. Remote Desktop License Manager is the role and toolset that defines RDS licensing. What can get tricky about this topic are the different types of RDS licenses available, which we will discuss later in this chapter.

As you move forward into RDS administration, you are going to quickly realize that almost everything that needs to be configured in the RDS world happens inside Server Manager. This is only partially true of RDS licenses. It is true that you will be defining which server contains the RDS licensing components from within Server Manager, but there is a more specific management tool that is installed in the RDS license server that needs to be used to import RDS **client access licenses (CALs)**.

Remote Desktop Web Access

Remote Desktop Web Access is a web portal that users can log in to from a browser and gain access to their applications or virtual desktops published by RDS. The Web Access component is published by IIS, so you will find this role installed on any RDS server that hosts Remote Desktop Web Access. It is common to combine this with Remote Desktop Gateway, which we will discuss next. If you are going to be working with Remote Desktop environments regularly, you might as well memorize the term "rdweb." This is the last portion of the URL that makes up access to the web access portal. For example, if the DNS name you are using for your RDS environment is gateway.contoso.com, then your Remote Desktop Web Access portal will be:

```
https://gateway.contoso.com/rdweb
```

Remote Desktop Gateway

I almost never find an RDS environment that does not also include a Remote Desktop Gateway instance. Remote Desktop Gateway is the secret ingredient that ties together on-premises and remote employees. Building an RDS farm inside a network and licensing it and allowing the connection broker to take care of distributing user sessions across all of the farm servers is great, but if you are already providing users with a virtual desktop session to do their work, why wouldn't you give them access to also log in to that virtual desktop from outside the office, such as from their homes?

RD Gateway does exactly this. It is designed to listen for incoming connections from the internet on port 443 (although this can be adjusted), so that remote users can utilize a simple RDP icon file on their computers that is designed to flow traffic through the gateway and into the RDS farm that is sitting inside your datacenter.

Alternatively, you can even utilize Remote Desktop Gateway without an RDSH farm to connect users directly to workstations sitting inside the office! In some cases, I find that the only RDS server a company has is a single Remote Desktop Gateway server. The purpose of this server, in these cases, is to take incoming connections from remote workers and securely shuttle their RDP connections into their workstation computers within your company's walls. This enables users to have a work desktop computer that is always in the office, and when working remotely they can launch a Remote Desktop Gateway connection that RDPs them securely into that work desktop, perhaps from a personal laptop (maybe even a Mac!).

RD Gateway is another one of the RDS components that has two different homes for configuration. The primary functionality is configured inside Server Manager, while a separate Remote Desktop Gateway Manager is also installed for deeper levels of configuration.

In a large and robust RDS environment, all of the roles we just discussed would be installed on different servers, with any of them having redundancy capabilities so that you could painlessly survive the failure of a single server. However, most businesses that use RDS do not go so extreme when creating resiliency on these servers, and we will follow the majority with the remaining pages of this chapter as we set up our own RDS environment in a test lab. The configuration steps I follow in these pages will closely reflect the production environments that I most often find in the SMB market.

Publishing RDS sessions

RDS is all about creating a centralized computing environment for users to take advantage of and leaving resource assignment and utilization to the servers, which greatly reduces the need to care about what kind of workstation or laptop somebody is using to connect. Two primary types of connections exist in an RDS environment: publishing full virtual desktops and publishing individual applications, which we will discuss near the end of this chapter.

We are going to build an RDS environment that contains all of the components we outlined earlier, and we are going to use this RDS farm to publish full virtual desktop sessions that users will be able to log in to and work from.

When building a fresh RDS environment, it is helpful to have all of the servers you intend to include already running and initially prepped. These servers should have a final hostname, have reserved or static IP addresses, and already be joined to your domain. For my lab today, I am going to be using the following servers:

- RDS-MGMT – This server will be my Swiss Army knife, doing everything other than hosting user sessions. Upon it we will implement Remote Desktop Gateway, Remote Desktop Connection Broker, Remote Desktop Licensing, and Remote Desktop Web Access.
- RDSH1 – This will be one of my initial session host servers, upon which we will install applications and host user virtual sessions.
- RDSH2 – Another RDSH server: this guy and RDSH 1 will be the initial members of my RDS "farm." User sessions will be load balanced, or brokered, between these two.
- RDSH3 – Later I will add this third node to my farm, so that we can take a real look at what it takes to expand an RDS environment that is already up and running.

Creating an RDS environment

My four servers are already up and running, but at this point I have not installed any roles or RDS components onto them. Here we are going to walk through the steps necessary to build this RDS farm, which can all happen from a single instance of Server Manager. It is important to make sure that all of the servers you intend to manipulate are already added to Server Manager before you start the wizard. You already know how to add multiple servers to the same instance of Server Manager, but if you need a refresher, simply click **Manage** > **Add Servers** and add in all related servers that you are going to modify. This will be important later in the wizard when you need to define these servers to own the different RDS components.

Logging in to RDS-MGMT, I will utilize the **Add Roles and Features** function and make sure to select that second installation type we looked at earlier, **Remote Desktop Services installation**. On the following screen, you will notice an option for **Quick Start**, which is interesting in that there is a shortcut method to create an all-in-one RDS environment on a single server, but this is rarely what a business would want to do in production, and so we will not perform that here either. Instead, continue forward with the option for **Standard deployment**.

Now on the **Deployment Scenario** screen, we are presented with an interesting option. It is easy to intermingle the terms virtual desktop, session, and virtual session. Here we face a fork in the road. The first option for **Virtual machine-based desktop deployment** is not very common; this is a more classic VDI-type environment, where you may have entire virtual machines dedicated to each user. Instead, when talking about RDS, we are almost always talking about publishing virtual desktop sessions to users, where multiple users are going to be logged in to the same RDSH server, sharing hardware resources. This is the direction we want to pursue today and most likely what you will find in your corporate environments. Therefore, go ahead and select **Session-based desktop deployment**.

The wizard now summarizes for us that, based on our selections so far, it is going to be installing for us **Remote Desktop Connection Broker, Remote Desktop Web Access**, and **Remote Desktop Session Host**.

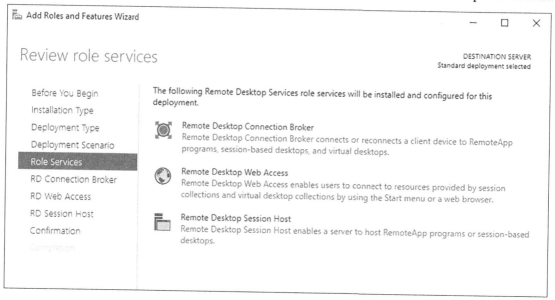

Figure 15.2: Building an RDS session host infrastructure

For each of those three components, our next screens in the wizard are pretty simple. Select the server that you want to host each RDS role, and slide it to the right side of the screen. For example, here I have specified that I would like **RD Connection Broker** to reside on RDS-MGMT.

Figure 15.3: Specifying the RD Connection Broker

Follow suit for defining the home for RD Web Access, which I am also placing on top of RDS-MGMT, and now we visit the last screen asking us to make decisions, what servers are going to be our RD Session Hosts. I do not want RDS-MGMT to host user sessions, because it will be busy doing all other functions, so I am declaring that RDSH1 and RDSH2 are to be my RD Session Host servers. The configuration wizard here is going to reach out to those servers and configure them as needed to be RDSH servers.

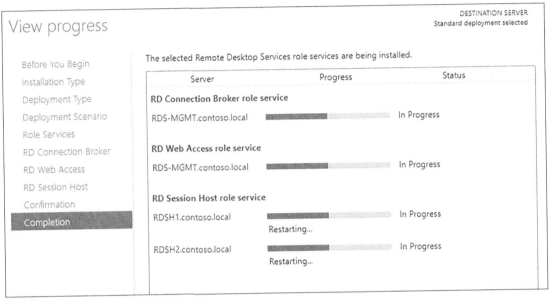

Figure 15.4: Server Manager doing the work for you

Once this configuration wizard is finished installing roles and feature sets onto your RDS environmental servers, you will find that they are prepared to do exactly nothing for you. Our next critical step in the build of this RDS farm is to configure the farm itself, or more accurately, the **RDS collection**.

Your first RDS collection

Through other role installations in Windows Server, you are already familiar with the fact that installing roles does not result in functionality until you invest a little more time and effort and configure those roles. RDS is no different. Now having rolled out the roles, go ahead and open Server Manager and once again, make sure that all of your RDS servers are added into Server Manager, so that it can reach out to any of them to pull or push information as needed. I will be using Server Manager on RDS-MGMT, since I plan for this server to be my primary RDS administration centerpoint.

An RDS collection is generally thought of as a group of RDSH servers that are part of a pool, or "farm," as we keep mentioning. A collection is actually quite a bit more than simply the servers that are included; a collection also includes all configurations and settings that the involved servers are going to adhere to.

Whenever you have Server Manager tapped into servers with RDS components installed, you will find that your primary management functionality of RDS is found by clicking on the words **Remote Desktop Services** listed along the left side of Server Manager. This is your home for the configuration of RDS collections (yes, you can have multiple collections), adding or removing RDSH servers from those collections, and adjusting collection settings; it's also your home for tacking on the additional RDS components that we never got a chance to add during the initial role installation wizard. You'll notice green plus symbols next to **RD Gateway** and **RD Licensing**, which are exactly where you will click to add these two components. In fact, let's do that now.

Figure 15.5: RD Gateway and RD Licensing are not yet installed

Add RD Gateway and RD Licensing

Clicking on the plus symbols next to RD Gateway and RD Licensing will invoke mini-wizards very much like the ones we used a few minutes ago to specify the broker and RDSH servers. Simply select the server that you want to contain each of these roles; I am going to place them both on RDS-MGMT.

You'll have to make a few additional decisions about how the Gateway and Licensing components function. To utilize Remote Desktop Gateway means that you will be accepting traffic that flows in from outside of the network, and those client computers will be reaching out to a DNS name like gateway.contoso.com. To properly protect that traffic, you will of course want to decide on a name, acquire an SSL certificate to protect that name, install the certificate on your Remote Desktop Gateway server, and then specify the name of it here. Since this is a test lab and my server doesn't even have real connectivity to the internet, my wizard recognizes that there is not an SSL certificate installed and is instead asking me to define a name that it can use for generating a self-signed SSL certificate.

Figure 15.6: RD Gateway requires an SSL certificate to protect its traffic

Next is our mini-wizard for adding Remote Desktop Licensing, and this one is as simple as selecting RDS-MGMT as the home for RD Licensing and letting it install. Installing actual RDS CALs into License Manager is entirely different, but we'll talk a little more about that later in the chapter.

Collection configuration

At this point, all RDS components are installed across our three servers. RDS-MGMT is carrying the bulk of the responsibility, and our two RDSH servers are patiently waiting in the wings, ready to receive user sessions sent to them by the gateway and broker.

How do we do that?

The only remaining step to get clients connected to this RDS environment is to officially configure our collection, which again is the collection of settings and servers that will make RDS connections possible. Still inside the Remote Desktop Services section of Server Manager, find the option in the middle pane called **Collections** and click on it. As you can see, there are currently no collections listed, but if you drop down the **TASKS** menu near the top-right corner of your screen, you can select **Create Session Collection** to get things started.

The first step is simply creating a name for your collection: no explanation needed there, but it is important to note that this name will be visible to users when they log in to Remote Desktop Web Access.

Next, we specify which session host servers (RDSH) are going to be part of this collection. As I mentioned earlier, I am going to initially configure my new collection with two nodes, RDSH1 and RDSH2. Moving those two servers into the **Selected** column means that these two servers are going to be able to receive connections for my collection.

Now moving on to the **User Groups** screen, this is where things start to get interesting. By default, you will see your domain's Domain Users group listed here. If you proceed forward with this default setting, in the end, any user who has an Active Directory account in your network will have permission to log in to this RDS collection. Since I want to be a little more selective about who I allow in here, I have removed that group and instead added a new AD security group that I created for exactly this purpose, called **Contoso RDS Users**.

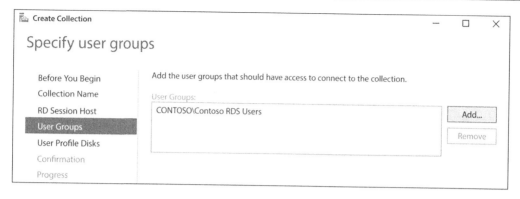

Figure 15.7: Only group members will be allowed to connect

Our next selection screen is called **User Profile Disks.** We will discuss what exactly UPDs are later in the chapter, but a short summary is that every user who logs in to an RDSH receives a Windows profile, just like on any Windows computer, and for the user's profile to remain consistent between both RDSH servers it must be stored in a central location, rather than on RDSH1 and RDSH2 directly. I have created a simple file share on my RDS-MGMT server and am going to use that location for the storage of my User Profile Disks. You'll notice an information box near the bottom of this screen that declares each RDSH server needs to have full control permissions within this share. I have added RDSH1, RDSH2, and RDSH3 (for the future) to have full control NTFS permissions on my new **Profiles** folder and share to meet this requirement.

Figure 15.8: Specifying UPDs and file permissions

That's it! Simply use the **Confirmation** screen to verify everything looks in order, and when you click the **Create** button we will now find our new collection sitting inside Server Manager.

Connecting to it

Contoso RDS (the name of my collection) is now live and able to be connected to. At this point, I could connect to my new collection by using the DNS name of the connection broker server RDS-MGMT. contoso.local. However, I also specified the DNS name gateway.contoso.com in my RD Gateway settings, and that is a cleaner and friendlier name to use for connectivity whether I am inside or outside of the office. To be able to use this same name both inside and outside the network, I need to create a DNS record with that name and point it at my Gateway/Connection Broker server, in my case RDS-MGMT. I have created such a record in my internal DNS and confirmed now that gateway. contoso.com resolves to 10.10.10.45, the IP address of RDS-MGMT.

With DNS squared away, I log in to a client computer, launch a web browser, and receive a login prompt when visiting https://gateway.contoso.com/rdweb.

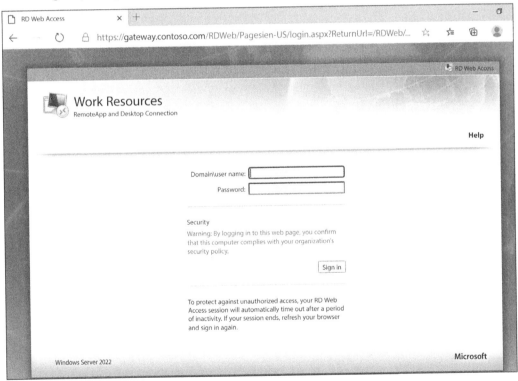

Figure 15.9: RD Web Access is up and running!

 Remember that if you haven't done the work of getting an SSL certificate yet for the DNS name you are trying to use here, you may receive some errors from your web browser. Get your certificate, install it on your Remote Desktop Gateway server, and select it inside **RDS Deployment Properties** to resolve this situation.

Accessing this website proves that Remote Desktop Web Access is up and running, but the first time that I logged in to the portal, I had exactly zero applications inside waiting for me to launch. I'm not going to lie, I was genuinely confused as to why my Contoso RDS connection was not listed in the portal. It took me far too many minutes to realize that when we created this new collection, I had removed the default Domain Users group from having access and instead narrowed it down to only my AD group called Contoso RDS Users. What I never did was add my administrator account to that group, and therefore I was facing an RD Web Access portal, but with nothing inside to click on.

As soon as I added my user account to the Contoso RDS Users group, I logged back in to this **rdweb** page and found my connection to **Contoso RDS** waiting for me. This is good verification that when you publish items through RDS, they are only visible and accessible to those users or groups that you have specified per collection. Double-clicking on this connection downloads an RDP connection file into your web browser's standard downloads location. From here you can launch the connection by clicking on the downloaded RDP file, or you could even visit your downloads folder and then copy out that RDP file for safekeeping. For example, if a user were to save this RDP file on their desktop, future connections to the farm are as easy as double-clicking on that file; they don't even need to log in to the rdweb portal.

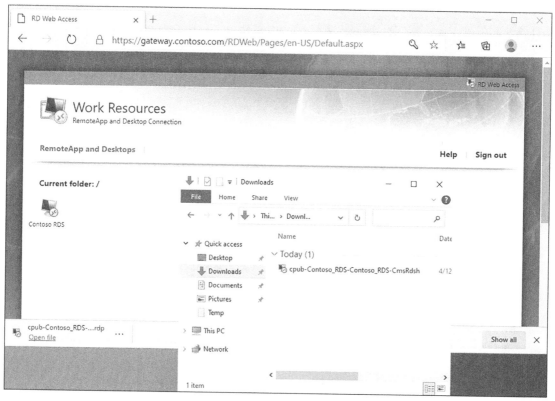

Figure 15.10: RD Web Access now has Contoso RDS available to launch

Whether you launch this RDP connection file from within your web browser, your downloads folder, or by copying the RDP file to another computer and double-clicking it there, you will be asked to sign in to the RDS collection. Once authenticated, you will be logged in to and looking at a virtual desktop session that is completely hosted on one of your RDSH servers. You can see in the following screenshot that my first session has landed on RDSH1.

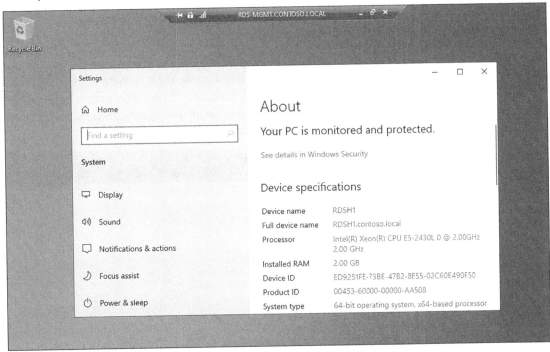

Figure 15.11: Successfully connected to an RDS user session!

 Many companies don't even require their users to log in to the rdweb portal. Instead, if you have already acquired these RDP connection files, you could easily distribute them to everyone's desktop via Group Policy.

We did it! We have successfully built RDS servers, created a collection, and connected to it.

Editing deployment and collection properties

If you have ever worked within an RDS environment before, you probably know that there are various options and settings that can be enabled or disabled, and we did not see many of them in our text so far. Running through the initial configuration wizards will get you an RDS collection up and running, but revisiting configuration screens will provide you access to even more. This functionality is defined inside the **Remote Desktop Services** section of Server Manager, within which we have been working so far, but now that we have a fully published collection we can revisit these screens and find some additional buttons.

Deployment Properties

The higher tier where you may need to view or change settings is **Deployment Properties**. Find these properties by navigating to the **Collections** page inside Server Manager, where you can see information about all of the different RDS collections that are established within your deployment (yes, you can have many collections!). Near the top-right corner of the **COLLECTIONS** screen, there is a small **TASKS** drop-down menu, within which you can choose either **Create Session Collection**, to add another collection to your deployment, or **Edit Deployment Properties**.

Deployment Properties is where you define or change information about your Remote Desktop Gateway, Remote Desktop Licensing server, specific settings about how Remote Desktop Web Access works, and certificates. We will visit the **Certificates** screen when we later discuss RDS maintenance. **Deployment Properties** is the place to visit for settings or configurations that are not specific to an individual RDS collection. Rather, these settings pertain to the entire RDS environment.

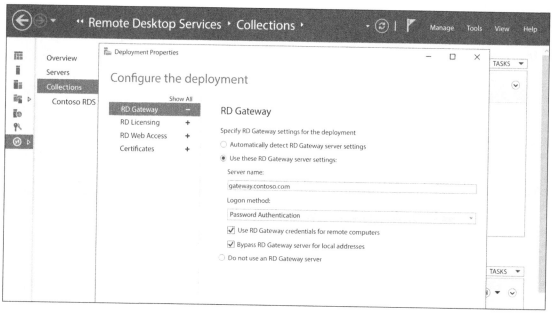

Figure 15.12: RDS Deployment Properties

Collection Properties

In addition to the overarching RDS role properties, you of course have options within each and every RDS collection that can also be tweaked. These are generally the most interesting settings to pore over. Still inside Server Manager, as you add new RDS collections, you will notice that each one is listed separately, under the primary **Collections** section. Selecting any collection will display many pieces of information about that collection, such as which RDSH servers are part of the collection and what user sessions are currently active on this collection. You can see in our next screenshot that my administrator session is still active on RDSH1. Near the top of this screen is a **PROPERTIES** section, with another **TASKS** drop-down menu. This time inside **TASKS**, we have but one item to click – **Edit Properties**.

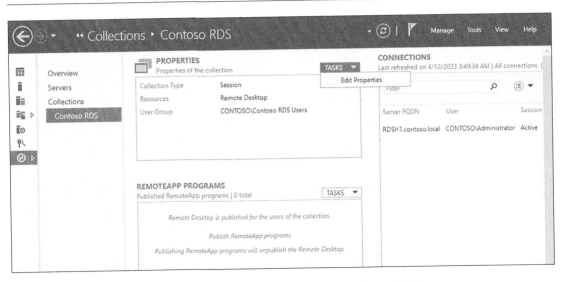

Figure 15.13: Editing properties for an individual RDS collection

Many of the properties here are self-explanatory, things like changing the name of your collection and tweaking general **Security** settings for RDS user connections. **User Groups** is where you can change at any time which users or groups are allowed to access this particular collection. You can even configure detailed **Load Balancing** metrics, which tell the RDS connection broker how to distribute incoming user sessions across your multiple RDSH servers. There are two primary screens that I want to show in more detail, because these are the places where I find many RDS administrators visiting regularly to make changes.

Session

When users connect to an RDS session, their login is running processes and consuming resources from the RDSH server that they are connected to. When users log out of their sessions, they very rarely do an actual "logoff" and therefore release those resources. Instead, most users click the X near the top of their RDP window, which closes their connection but leaves the virtual session hanging open on the server, along with any resources that the session is consuming. This disconnect behavior is purposeful, so that the users can reconnect to RDS later in the day and pick back up where they left off, much like putting a laptop to sleep and waking it up again. However, when you have 25 or 50 or more people who could be logging in to the same RDSH server, that can equate to a lot of resources being consumed unnecessarily, which has a negative impact on those users who are actively logged in to their sessions.

All that to say, it is very common for companies to implement session timeout policies. The **Session** screen is exactly the place to do this. The two most common pieces of information to populate on this screen are as follows. **End a disconnected session** means that any user sessions sitting in a disconnected state will be fully logged off, and therefore will release their resources, after X number of minutes or hours. It is very common to set this between 1 and 4 hours. Secondly, it is common to see **Idle session limit** configured for something like 6 or 8 hours. By combining these two session limits, you mostly guarantee that everybody's RDS session will be automatically disconnected, and then logged off, every night.

This helps to keep resource consumption at an even keel across the RDSH servers, and when users log in the next morning, they simply receive a fresh session and just re-launch their applications from there.

Figure 15.14: RDS session timeout settings

Client Settings

Another common settings screen to visit occasionally is **Client Settings**. When a user connects to an RDS farm, it is possible to pull local resources from their own computer into the RDS session. For example, the workstation's hard drives or printers or even clipboard can be automatically mapped through as connections that are accessible from inside RDS. This way, users can copy text or files between their RDS server session and their local computer, and they can even click **File>Print** inside an RDS session and have the option of printing back to their home printer. These mappings happen within the RDP tunnels, and whether or not those functions are allowed is determined by this **Client Settings** screen. Simply check or uncheck the local resources you want to be accessible from inside user RDS sessions.

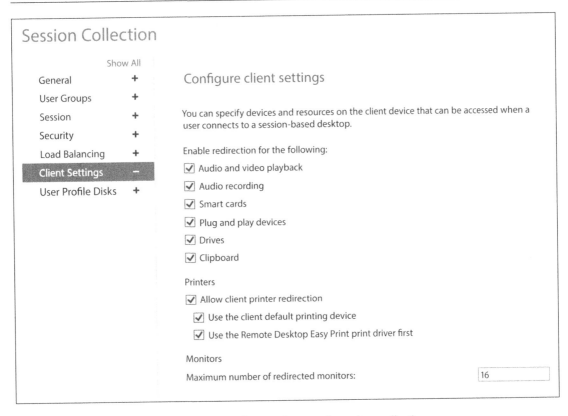

Figure 15.15: RDS client settings, configured per collection

Adding RDSH servers to your collection

During the build of our RDS collection, we identified a server to use as Gateway/Licensing/Web Access/ Connection Broker, and we added two RDSH servers to the collection. Let's pretend this has been up and running for a while but we are now starting to outgrow the original design. We scoped these RDSH servers to handle around 25 users each, but our business has continued to grow and we now have 60 people logging in every day. RDSH1 and RDSH2 are keeping up, but users notice slowness during peak times of the day. The answer to this question is pretty straightforward – we need an RDSH3.

I have built another Windows Server 2022 instance, and the only things I have done with it so far are give it an IP address and a hostname and join it to my domain. In a real-world scenario, I would also need to make sure that all of my installed applications mirrored those of RDSH1 and 2, so that when we introduce RDSH3 into the farm, users are not lacking access to any apps they might need to launch. But in my test lab, I haven't installed applications on any of my RDSH servers, so that is currently not a consideration for me.

Assuming those pieces are accomplished, the next action we need to perform is adding RDSH into this same Server Manager instance from which I am already administering my farm. This step is not obvious – nothing in the console will tell you to do it, but it makes sense once you think about it. How could this copy of Server Manager reach out and manipulate RDSH3 to bring it into the collection if we do not first add RDSH3 as a managed server inside Server Manager? Thankfully you already know how to do this, but as a quick reminder, simply head to **Manage > Add Servers** and add in the name of your new server.

Now that Server Manager knows about RDSH3, I want to head back into the Remote Desktop Services section of Server Manager and visit the primary **Overview** tab. This screen shows me high-level information about my whole RDS deployment, and there are some quick links near the top of this screen. One of those links, option 2, says **Add RD Session Host servers**. Click on this link, specify the new RDSH node, and the wizard gets to work configuring that server to be part of your RDS deployment.

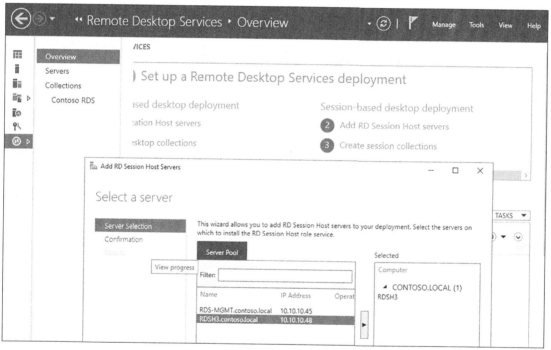

Figure 15.16: Adding RDSH3 to my RDS deployment

But wait, there's more! We are almost to the finish line, but there is one more step to accomplish before user sessions will flow to RDSH3. At this point, Server Manager has reached out to RDSH3 and installed the necessary Remote Desktop components on it, and RDSH3 is now visible inside Server Manager since it is part of our RDS deployment. However, an RDS deployment could contain many different RDS collections, which is the level at which connectivity really happens. So, all we need to do is add RDSH3 to the appropriate RDS collection; in my case, it is my collection called Contoso RDS.

Still inside the **Remote Desktop Services** section of Server Manager, all I have to do is click on my **Contoso RDS** collection and then scroll down to the bottom where there is a section called **HOST SERVERS**. Here you will find another one of those **TASKS** drop-down menus, inside which is an option to **Add RD Session Host Servers**. While this option is called the exact same thing as the wizard we ran just a minute ago to add RDSH3 to our overall deployment, we need to additionally run through this one to now add RDSH3 to this specific collection.

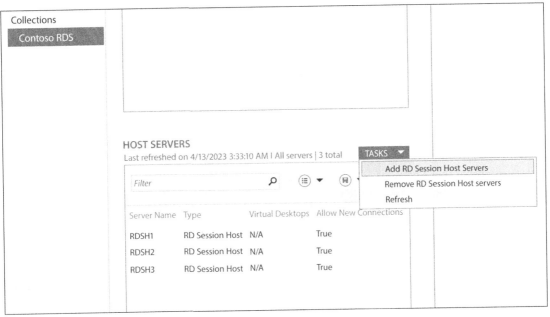

Figure 15.17: RDSH3 is now a farm member and servicing user sessions

Now that RDSH3 is part of our deployment and our collection, it will be included in load balancing for this collection and users' sessions will start to flow to it.

Drain-stop an RDSH for maintenance

Occasionally, you will need to remove an RDSH node from a collection so that you can perform maintenance on it. Perhaps you need to install a new application or update an application, or otherwise investigate and repair something within Windows on that node. It is a very common task to temporarily remove an RDSH server from a collection and add it back again later. These functions are very quick and simple, and if the last screenshot is still burned into your brain, you are already looking at the right place from which to do so.

Inside the **Remote Desktop Services** section of Server Manager, select the name of your collection and scroll down to the bottom of this screen. Here you will see all of the host servers that are part of your collection; these are the RDSH servers currently servicing user connections. Simply right-click on a node and select the only option, **Do not allow new connections**.

Figure 15.18: Temporarily blocking new connections to an RDSH

This will immediately stop new incoming user connections from landing on RDSH3, and you can see in the screenshot that I have already accomplished the same thing on RDSH2, which is indicated by **Allow New Connections = False** for that node.

At this point, all new user sessions to our RDS collection would fall on RDSH1 – that guy is going to be busy! As soon as I am finished with maintenance on RDSH2 and RDSH3, I can simply right-click on them again and select **Allow new connections** to immediately place them back into the farm.

The heading of this section said "drain-stop" – what exactly do I mean by that? When you block an RDSH from receiving new user sessions, it does not change anything with existing sessions. If there were already users logged in to RDSH2 and RDSH3 in my example above, my actions would not have affected them, and they would remain happily connected to those servers. No *new* connections would flow to these servers, so as those users naturally end their sessions or log off for the day, and then log on again next time, they would be redirected to RDSH1 or any other node that is still configured to allow connections. This is important to understand because you cannot expect to block RDSH servers from receiving connections and immediately get to work on those servers. You will have to either forcibly log users out of those nodes, which would be intrusive and disruptive to them, or remove an RDSH from its collection and then wait, possibly until the next business day, to accomplish your maintenance.

Installing applications on an RDSH

The installation of applications is obviously very important in the RDS world: you are providing users with a virtual desktop session from which you expect them to work, and to work, they will need to be able to launch the applications necessary to do their jobs. That means these applications must be installed on every RDSH server upon which a user session might land. In general, every RDSH server that is part of the same collection should have the same applications installed. This also means the same versions of the same applications installed, so you can imagine that application updates and maintenance are a little bit trickier on an RDSH than on a normal workstation.

No users logged in

Whenever installing applications on an RDSH server, it is recommended to make sure all users are logged out of that server (other than yourself, of course). This brings us back to drain-stopping those servers and understanding how to remove nodes from a farm for maintenance purposes. Since the removal of an RDSH from its collection does not mean that it is immediately accessible for performing that maintenance, as it continues to serve existing connections, this also means that many times the installation of new software on an existing RDS collection involves many days' worth of work:

- Day 1 – Drain-stop RDSH1.
- Day 2 – Users are now logged out of RDSH1; install application on RDSH1 and put it back into the farm. Now drain-stop RDSH2.
- Day 3 – Users are now logged out of RDSH2; install application on RDSH2 and put it back into the farm. Now drain-stop RDSH3.
- Day 4 – Users are now logged out of RDSH3; install application on RDSH3 and put it back into the farm.

Whew! That is a lot of days for the installation of a single application. Alternatively, you could likely install the application on all three on the same day, at 3:00am, but…really.

…yes, even for updates

The installation-of-software rules apply whether you are installing a new application that has never been on the RDSH server before, or simply installing an update to that application. If there are any users already logged in to the RDSH server and potentially utilizing the application that you are attempting to update, you could run into problems. Or worse yet, your update installer might finish successfully but perhaps not be able to do everything that it needs to do in the background, which could cause you mysterious problems down the road. Better to be safe than sorry: make sure that when you install applications or application updates onto an RDSH server that you are the only user logged in to it.

Install mode

An RDSH server is a multi-user environment with various user profiles and user registry hives scattered throughout the operating system. When applications get installed onto an RDSH, something needs to ensure that necessary files and regkeys get distributed to the proper locations so that every user account is able to make use of them. Have you ever installed an application that asked you, "Do you want to install this application for only the current user, or for everyone on the system?" On an RDSH server, you would of course select "for everyone on the system" and carry on. Thankfully, most applications are RDS-aware, recognize automatically when you are installing them onto an RDSH server, and take necessary adjustments in the background to ensure the application is installed properly.

But…

Some application installers do not. They have no idea or care in the world where you are installing their app, and if you simply log in to RDSH1 and launch the installer, it *might* work okay for you, but it just as likely may have all kinds of problems in any other user session. You certainly don't want to reinstall the application inside every user session. This is why, **every time that you install any application onto any RDSH server**, you should first put that RDSH into **Install mode**.

Install mode is unique to RDS servers and, if you are going to be working with them, is a command you should memorize right now. It is very simple: before launching your application installer or update installer, open a Command Prompt or PowerShell window and perform the following:

```
change user /install
```

That's it! Your RDS server is now in Install mode, and this causes Windows to understand that any installers need to be nannied a little bit. If the installer is about to put a file or registry key into a place where it might have issues from other user accounts, Windows will re-map those things to more central locations.

When you are finished installing the application, simply place your server back into its standard **Execute mode**:

```
change user /execute
```

If ever you are unsure what mode you are currently running in (it's easy to lose track if you are installing multiple things and rebooting in between), you can easily find out what mode your server is currently running by using:

```
change user /query
```

Figure 15.19: Install mode and Execute mode

Remember Install mode – it helps save you headaches. Also remember that every RDSH server in the same collection should have the exact same applications installed on it to provide your users with a uniform experience every time they log in.

RDS licensing

Every incoming connection that lands on an RDS server must have a valid **client access license (CAL)**. These licenses are available for purchase from any normal avenue through which you purchase your Windows Server licensing, so I cannot tell you the best place to go to get these licenses, only that you need them, and how they work. There are two types of RDS CAL, and we will describe both, but the reality is that almost every RDS farm in the world uses User CALs.

User CALs

User CALs are the normal way to go. As the name implies, every user who is connecting to your RDS farm needs to have a User CAL. These CALs are installed on your Remote Desktop Licensing server, which like inside our test lab might co-exist alongside some other RDS roles, and once licenses are installed the RDSH servers check in with the Remote Desktop License server to ensure there is sufficient licensing to allow the connection to happen.

User CAL limits are not restricted at a technical level. Similar to the way that a lot of Microsoft licensing works, it is essentially an honor system. You could purchase 20 RDS User CALs, or you could purchase 150. Whichever you install on your licensing server, that will green-light RDSH servers to allow users to connect, and from that point there is no monitoring happening in the licensing system to know whether you actually only have 20 people connected or 300.

Also, as with all other Microsoft licensing, you don't want to cheat that system. Your organization may need to be part of an annual true-up where you would have to define and pay for any discrepancies, or you may be large enough you have a Microsoft licensing rep, or you may work with a service provider and they are not going to put their necks on the line by allowing you to cheat the licensing system and purchase fewer CALs than you have users. Make sure you own enough! It is your responsibility . to make sure all users have a valid license.

Device CALs

Device CALs are extremely rare to find in the wild. Again, the name is fairly self-explanatory; in this licensing model, RDS doesn't care at all about how many users are connecting but rather how many unique *computers* are connecting to your RDS farm. Device CALs *are* restricted at a technical level. This type of license would be applicable for a business that has multiple shifts of people who are using the same computers. The general idea is that you would own a Device CAL for every workstation that you own. RDS License Manager keeps track through a temporary certificate of sorts about which computers are connecting, and as long as you have as many CALs as you do computers, you will be fine in this scenario.

The problem is that what I just described is almost never how companies try to use Device CALs. Instead, in the places where I have found them, they are using them simply because they are cheaper, and they are trying to get away with using Device CALs as if they were "Concurrent Connection CALs" – which they are not.

One key benefit to RDS environments is the ease with which you can provide users access to their virtual desktops from a home computer. Are you really going to purchase Device CALs for every home device each of your users might own?

Whenever a computer connects to an RDS farm that uses Device CALs, the license manager knows about it and records it. That CAL is then dedicated to that particular computer for roughly 8 days. If a particular computer does not reconnect after that timeframe, it generally falls off the licensing map, so to speak, until it connects again. In this sense, you might be able to get away with having fewer Device CALs than devices, but you'll always be rolling the dice. There is also a function to manually revoke CALs, and I have literally watched admins approach these CALs in a mindset that they'll just revoke all of their device CALs every day. That is not only ridiculous, but License Manager won't let you do that anyway. You are only allowed to revoke up to 20% of active RDS CALs at any given time. Not 20% each day – 20% of them, period.

The valid use cases for Device CALs are pretty slim. When you are purchasing RDS CALs, it is generally safe to approach that purchase through the assumption that you are going to need User CALs.

Specify the RD License server

You probably don't remember configuring any RDS licensing settings during our farm deployment, and that is because we never did. New RDS environments enter automatically into a 120-day grace period, where user sessions and connections are allowed without having any licensing whatsoever. Once you have acquired your RDS CALs, you will need to accomplish two things to get them working. Specify the RD License server inside **Deployment Properties** and plug the CALs into Remote Desktop License Manager.

Go ahead and edit your overall **Deployment Properties** (not **Collection Properties**) and visit the screen called **RD Licensing**. Here you simply select whether you are using **Per Device** or **Per User** licenses, and make sure that your Remote Desktop License server name is specified. This is all you need to do to tell your entire RDS deployment where the Remote Desktop License server is.

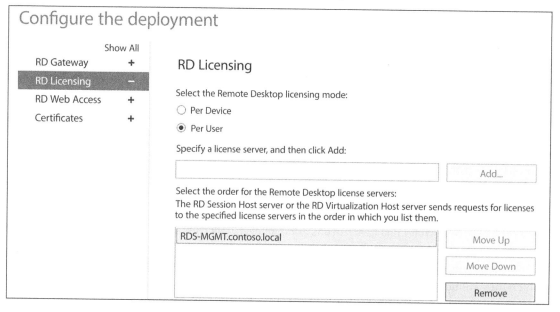

Figure 15.20: Specifying RDS licensing within Deployment Properties

RD Licensing Manager

Strangely, there is no accommodation inside the standard RDS configuration screens to apply or review RDS licensing. For this task, we must visit the older MMC-based console related to this topic. Once a server has been configured via Server Manager as your RD Licensing server, as RDS-MGMT has been in our test lab, you will find a new folder listed inside **Administrative Tools** called **Remote Desktop Services**, and within that folder a management tool called **Remote Desktop Licensing Manager**. Launching Remote Desktop Licensing Manager will bring you to the place where you can add new RDS licensing CALs, view existing ones, or even revoke device CALs if that scenario applies to you.

When building up a fresh RDS environment, you will need to visit this console, right-click on the name of your Remote Desktop licensing server, use the **Activate Server** wizard to paste in the key that you received from Microsoft containing your RDS CALs, and step through the wizard to activate those CALs. This will check in with Microsoft activation servers, and after successful activation, your RDS licensing is ready to roll!

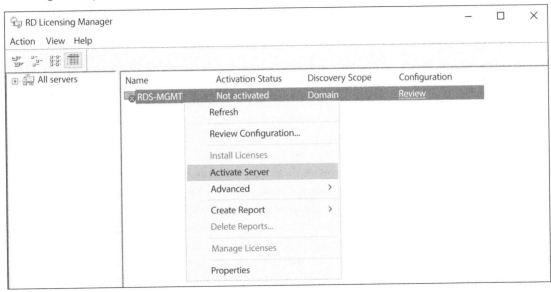

Figure 15.21: Using the older toolset to activate RDS CALs

RDS user profiles

As a generalization, user profiles in the Microsoft Windows world are fairly straightforward. A user account authenticates, usually via Active Directory, and the user is permitted log in to whatever computer or server they are sitting in front of. If this is the first time this user has logged in to this computer, a new Windows user profile is created on that computer. These user profiles, unless you have done some significant tweaking to your operating systems, all reside inside a folder called C:\Users. Additionally, a new section of the registry is created to contain settings specific to this user account.

Local profiles

When RDS began life, it was known as Terminal Server, and this default user profile behavior of the Windows world was exactly what happened on terminal servers whenever a user would log in. This means that each Terminal Server had its own `C:\Users` directory, and that directory could contain hundreds of different user profiles, one for every person who ever logged in to the server. This in itself is not an issue, but it was certainly cumbersome for users when on Monday they would log in to TS1 and set up all of their files, configuration settings, desktop visualization tweaks, and other preferences, and then on Tuesday morning they log in again and wouldn't you know it – they are now logged in to TS2 and all of those tweaks they made yesterday are "gone." They are still on TS1 and the next time the user logs in and happens to land on TS1, they see everything again, but today is not that day, and today they are now re-tweaking everything on TS2.

Allowing a Terminal Server or RDS environment to run local Windows profiles is problematic and effectively dead as an idea. Let me clarify that: it is **effectively** dead as an idea in the RDS world; Windows desktop computers continue to land user data inside `C:\Users` as normal behavior.

Roaming profiles

Clearly some uniformity to user profiles was needed, perhaps empowering users to have a certain collection of settings and for those settings to follow the user around, no matter which RDS server they logged in to. The answer to this question in the 2000s was called roaming profiles. Roaming profiles are just like local profiles, except they are stored in a centralized location. Most likely, roaming profiles are all stored on a network file share, maybe something like `\\FS1\RoamingProfiles`. Microsoft integrated this idea firmly into their ecosystem. When users logged in to a terminal server or RDS server, Active Directory would recognize that this user account had a roaming profile location defined and would also recognize when a user was logging into a normal desktop versus an RDS. In the event that said user was logging in to an RDS, the user's profile would be re-steered toward the user profile on that network share, rather than using a local profile. This was a fantastic idea and was the de facto standard for many years. Roaming profiles were such a big thing that Microsoft modified the Active Directory user configuration screens so that if your company was using roaming profiles, when setting up new user accounts, all you needed to do was specify the location of the profile on this tab and Windows would take care of the rest for you. Now in the year 2023, this profile option still exists.

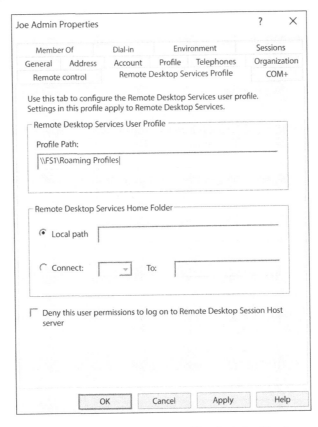

Figure 15.22: Defining roaming profiles via Active Directory

Unfortunately, today if you ask anyone who has worked in IT for more than 15 years what their thoughts are on roaming profiles, be prepared for a gag reflex. Even though it was a great idea, the reality surrounding roaming profiles is that they were quirky. Network speed and latency had a lot to do with it, but it was common that profiles took a very long time to load when users logged in, or would corrupt themselves, sometimes even resulting in the loss of user data. There are certainly ways to make roaming profiles work, but it is no longer a common practice due to the advent of...

User Profile Disks (UPDs)

We now find ourselves looking at the default profile option of today's Remote Desktop Servers. The idea of UPDs is very much like roaming profiles, but rather than a collection of files and folders containing the user profile sitting out there on a network share, the user's profile is contained within its own VHDX file. For anyone who made it through our chapter on Hyper-V, you'll know that this is Microsoft's virtual hard disk file, the same type of file used as a virtual hard drive on a virtual server.

UPDs are stored on a network share, and every user who logs in to your RDS environment gets their own VHDX virtual disk spun up during the login process. Initial login takes a little longer due to the creation of this file, but then the file exists and remains intact so that future logins are faster. While users are logged into an RDSH server, they are primarily referencing their UPD so that files or settings saved within their profile are saved to that virtual disk, but you'll find that C:\Users on the RDSH server is still populated with what look to be classic Windows user profile folders. This is because the RDSH still needs somewhere locally on the server to interact with, and when a UPD-based user account logs in, certain pieces of information are pulled from their VHDX and stored locally on the RDSH server. It's easy to think about these folders inside C:\Users as being temporary profile locations, just remember that the user's primary profile is that VHDX file. This, of course, enables users to be able to tap into any of the RDSH servers in a collection and have the same profile layout, settings, and files no matter where they are logged in.

Telling your RDS environment to use UPDs is very simple. In fact, we have already done it if you are following along with this test lab creation. Create a network share in a central location where all of the RDSH servers can access it, and make sure that NTFS permissions are such that all of the RDSH computer accounts have full control over that shared folder. This is important because the RDSH servers are going to be creating the new VHDX files as new users log in. Then, inside RDS **Collection Properties** (UPDs are configured per collection, not per deployment), visit the **User Profile Disks** screen and simply check the **Enable user profile disks** box. Specify the network share location that you have created for these VHDX files to reside, and then select whether you want all user settings to be stored in this disk or only selected pieces.

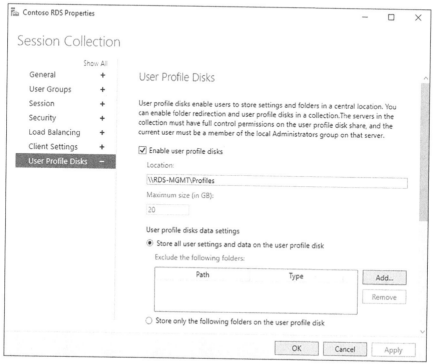

Figure 15.23: Configuring User Profile Disks

User Profile Disks work well and are in use in many RDS deployments across the world today. They do come with some interesting behavior though; as I mentioned, a temporary C:\Users profile is still created for each user as they log in, and for some reason it is very common for RDSH servers configured with UPDs to end up littered with multiple copies of this temp profile. Many times this is the result of something going wrong during user login or logoff. If a temp profile already exists for a user, sometimes during the next login process, rather than re-using that same folder, the RDSH server will decide to create another one. This results in a messy C:\Users folder on the RDSH server, but it generally does not create actual problems for the users, as their data and settings are still ultimately stored inside the VHDX. If you visit C:\Users on your RDSH servers, you may find something similar to the following screenshot. Here I have logged my administrator account in and out of the RDS farm many times, and this has resulted in multiple temporary profiles for the administrator account.

Figure 15.24: Having multiple temp profiles is fairly normal with UPDs

When this happens, cleanup is fairly simple. These temp accounts are not needed, again as the real data is inside the VHDX file. So as long as the user account is not currently logged in to the RDSH server that you are looking into, it is generally safe to simply delete all instances of these temp profiles for that user account. If the user is logged in and actively using one of the temp accounts, then of course you may want to hold off until a time when they are not logged in to that server.

FSLogix

It is most often appropriate to think about RDS user profile options with a "good, better, best" mindset. Roaming profiles are fine, UPDs are better, and FSLogix profiles are as good as it gets. FSLogix used to be its own company, improving centralized profile capabilities as a third-party add-on, until Microsoft acquired them in 2018. RDS profiles that are managed through FSLogix policies are similar in ideology to UPDs, in that profiles are stored in a central location and make use of VHDX files to keep data. One of the primary reasons to utilize FSLogix profiles instead of classic UPDs is for scenarios where you want users to have a good experience with Microsoft Office applications inside an RDS farm. Office applications don't always play well with UPDs, particularly things like Outlook OST files. FSLogix accommodates that and makes login times much faster in these scenarios.

Another big reason to move toward FSLogix profiles is if your business is using OneDrive to sync users' documents/desktop/pictures across all of their devices. This is now a built-in capability of the OneDrive agent and is very useful for maintaining consistency across multiple computers that users may log in to, and for keeping an online backup of their document data. RDS servers are not entirely OneDrive-friendly: users often have to wait for large sync cycles every time they log in to their RDS session, and in many cases OneDrive simply fails to work. This is one area where FSLogix does a much better job than UPDs.

FSLogix has some enhancements to Windows profiles that enable Microsoft Office applications to better interact with RDS servers, and it also includes access control functionality for applications, printers, and a few other items. When you install something like an application or printer on an RDSH server, it is generally true that every user who logs in to the RDSH will have access to it. Application Rule Sets in FSLogix give you the ability to control access to these resources via user rules or group memberships.

The configuration of FSLogix can be fairly simple or pretty complex. I provide this as reasoning as to why we are not walking through the setup of FSLogix profiles together, as it could go in many different directions. In many cases, all you really need to do is import some ADMX/ADML into Active Directory, which provides you with FSLogix configuration settings right inside Group Policy, and configure what you want right there! Once you define FSLogix settings and assign that GPO to your RDSH servers, there is an FSLogix agent to be installed on those same servers, after which your FSLogix profiles are up and running.

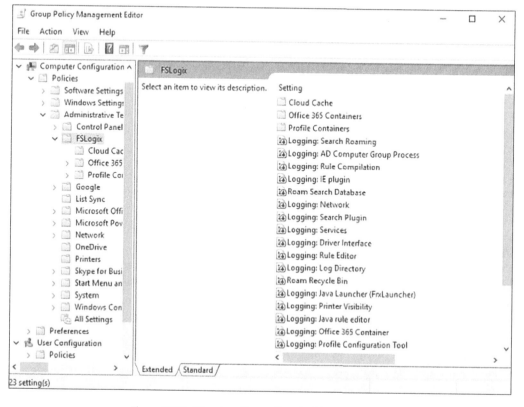

Figure 15.25: FSLogix policy settings inside Group Policy

New versions of FSLogix are being released at a regular cadence, and the documentation is often updated to reflect changes being made, so to kick off your official FSLogix journey, I feel it's best to direct you to the beginning of Microsoft documentation on this subject as the particulars may well change before this book is published:

https://learn.microsoft.com/en-us/fslogix/

Microsoft says, as of this writing, that FSLogix can be used on pretty much any currently supported Microsoft operating system, even specifically calling out Server 2012R2. In my experience, however, FSLogix being used for RDS profile storage does not always work properly with the older versions of operating system. Indeed, I would personally not deploy FSLogix on anything older than Server 2019, based on my own experience.

RemoteApp

You now understand RDS topology and the steps required to publish an RDS collection, upon which virtual sessions can land and users have access to an entire virtual desktop. This, however, is much more access than companies sometimes want to provide, and it can become overly complicated for some use cases. Perhaps you only want to provide access to one or two applications when users connect; they don't need to have access to an entire desktop where they could potentially launch anything installed on the server, or to save files within their profile. Publishing RemoteApp programs through an RDS collection is a way to publish access to a single application or set of applications from within the Remote Desktop Web Access portal.

In fact, the perfect example of a use case for RemoteApps just came across my desk last week. A doctor's office needed to allow their local hospital to have access to one of their on-premises healthcare systems. This doctor's office already has an RDS farm, and we could have simply provided hospital staff with logins and virtual sessions on that RDS farm, but that would have given them access to double-click on any application installed on the RDSH servers, and they preferred to restrict hospital staff to running a single application. The answer? Publish that lone application as a RemoteApp inside a new RDS collection. These are the bare steps to utilizing RemoteApp:

1. Create an RDS deployment; maybe you already have one.
2. Create a new RDS collection to keep these RemoteApps separate from your full virtual sessions. It is possible to host both full desktop sessions and RemoteApps on the same RDS collection and on the same RDSH servers, but Microsoft does not recommend it. Best to keep them separated.
3. It usually makes sense to narrow the scope of this new collection so that only members of a specific group have access. This way you can easily restrict who has access to launch this application.
4. Install the necessary application on your RDSH servers in the collection.
5. Publish a RemoteApp inside your RDS collection properties.

6. Instruct your users to log in to the RDWeb web portal. When they log in, as long as you have made them members of the appropriate group, they will now have an icon to launch this RemoteApp from inside the web portal. This launches an RDP session in the background, but the only information that passes its way to the user's computer is the screen of the individual application that is being clicked on. No virtual desktop is ever shown to the user, only the application.

7. When users are finished with the application, they simply click the X in the top-right corner, and their application closes. To the user, the application behaves as if it was installed on their local computer (even though it never was). In the background, the RDSH servers are actually spinning up an RDP session for the user, and when clicking the X, that session goes into a disconnected state.

Let's publish a quick application or two into an RDS collection so you can see how it really works. I have just finished creating a new collection called **Contoso RemoteApps**. I removed RDSH3 from my existing collection and added it to this new collection. Now, inside **Collection Properties**, I want to visit that section in the middle called **REMOTEAPP PROGRAMS**. Here, simply click the **TASKS** menu or the link right in the middle of this screen that says **Publish RemoteApp Programs**.

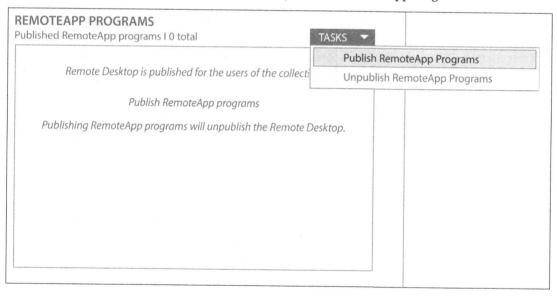

Figure 15.26: Publishing our first RemoteApp

The coolest thing about RemoteApps is how incredibly simple they are to publish. This wizard polls the RDSH servers for a list of installed applications; so as long as you have already installed any apps needing to be published, they will appear in this list. Now you simply decide which apps need to be published inside this collection, select them, and finish out the wizard! I have not installed any custom applications onto RDSH3, but I have a plethora of options for preinstalled apps. For the sake of example, I will publish Calculator and Notepad.

Figure 15.27: Publishing Calculator and Notepad

We are essentially finished. The only thing left to do is log in as a user account and test to make sure that I see and have the ability to launch these applications from the Remote Desktop web portal. Logging in to that portal, you can see in the following screenshot that my two RemoteApp programs are happily waiting for me. You will also notice that I still see my third icon, **Contoso RDS**. This is because the user account that I am testing with is a member of the group to provide me access to this new RDS collection and is still also a member of the group that grants me access to see the other RDS farm that still exists for RDSH1 and RDSH2. I could now click on any of these icons and launch whatever level of access I need in order to do my job.

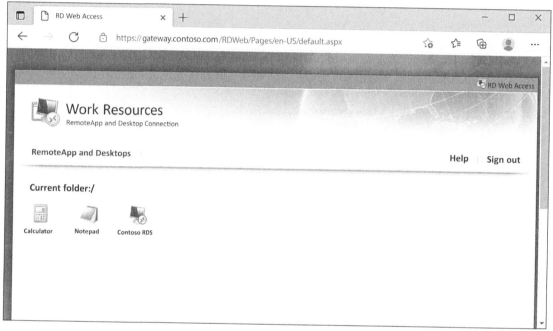

Figure 15.28: We have published RemoteApp programs!

Just like when clicking on the connection to my full Contoso RDS session, clicking on one of these RemoteApps results in my web browser downloading an RDP connection file. This RDP file is preconfigured to launch directly into my new RDS collection and auto-launch whatever RemoteApps that I had clicked on. Users may choose to always visit the RDWeb interface and click on their applications from here, knowing that they will be re-downloading a new copy of that RDP file every single time. They would then have to click on that downloaded file from inside the browser to launch the connection. Or...

If you wanted to copy out the saved RDP connection file from your downloads folder, this file could then be copied to a desktop or even distributed to other users, where they could simply double-click on the RDP connection file to launch their RemoteApp program.

I have tried to show all of this in the following screenshot. You can see the open RDWeb page, the Downloads folder where my RDP connection file was downloaded when I clicked on Notepad, and the open Notepad window. Now, why would you believe me that this instance of Notepad is actually running on RDSH3 and is not simply Notepad installed on my WIN10 machine? If I click **File>Open** inside Notepad, I am clearly browsing the folder structure of RDSH3's hard drive. This Notepad window that I am interacting with is running completely on RDSH3, through a virtual RDS session.

Figure 15.29: Logged into WIN10 at home, but running Notepad on RDSH3

The key benefit of RemoteApps is restriction of access. This is a simple method to provide many users access to many different applications that are installed on the same set of RDS servers, but at the same time ensuring that users only have access to the applications you want them to touch.

RDS maintenance considerations

Maintaining and troubleshooting RDS servers can be an art of its own. They are Windows Server instances, yes, but in many ways you treat them more like workstations, since they are the place where users log in to utilize applications and save documents. However, many different users are logged in to these "workstations" at the same time, which creates complexities we do not normally face on workstations or other types of servers. This final section is a bit of a tips-and-tricks session for some of the common maintenance considerations you will doubtless face during your RDS administration tenure.

Install mode

There is no need to re-hash this; we already covered Install mode in detail earlier in this chapter. But if there is any one thing that I find administrators forgetting to do most often when dealing with RDS servers, it is placing them into Install mode before installing applications, and even more often forgetting to do so before updating existing applications. Don't forget to always use Install mode!

Additionally, make sure all users are logged out of your RDSH server when installing or updating applications. Your admin account should be the only account logged in to the entire server when performing these functions.

Server Manager errors related to RDS

Most RDS configuration happens from within Server Manager, and most often I find administrators turning to the instance of Server Manager on whatever server is your RDS management server. This server probably hosts some or all RDS roles, other than RDSH of course. In my case, that was my RDS-MGMT server that we referenced so many times throughout this chapter. There is no technical reason that you *must* use that central RDS administration server to perform these tasks – Server Manager is intended to be decentralized and capable of administering servers outside of itself, right? A very common issue that I watch administrators struggle through is when trying to launch Server Manager, with the intention of manipulating an RDS configuration setting, from a different RDS server in the deployment. Let's give it a try together and see what happens.

I am logged directly in to RDSH2. This guy's duty in life is to host user sessions, but I have never tried running any RDS administration tools on it. Launching Server Manager, since RDSH2 has a Remote Desktop component installed on it, I of course see the option inside Server Manager for **Remote Desktop Services.** When I click on it, however, things *appear* to be very broken...

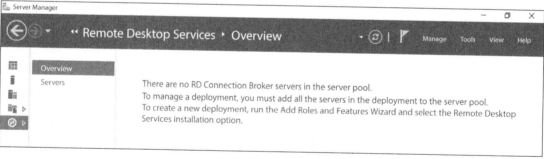

Figure 15.30: Red alert! I think RDS is broken

This is the point where many admins get stuck. They assume that something is really broken, or really misconfigured with RDS, and they escalate whatever ticket they are working on. In some cases, they try rebooting this server over and over, to no avail. The hard reality of this error message is that it is telling you, right into your face, how to fix the issue. Most people just miss it. **"To manage a deployment, you must add all the servers in the deployment to the server pool."** This is Server Manager telling you (I'm paraphrasing here), "Hey admin, if you want to manage RDS from this window, you're gonna have to add all RDS servers into Server Manager, so that I know how to reach them!"

The only thing you need to do is click **Manage** at the top of Server Manager, then **Add Servers**. From here you know what to do, add all RDS-related servers into Server Manager so that it is capable of reaching them, and if you refresh the Remote Desktop screen, it will now light up with all of the information and options you expect.

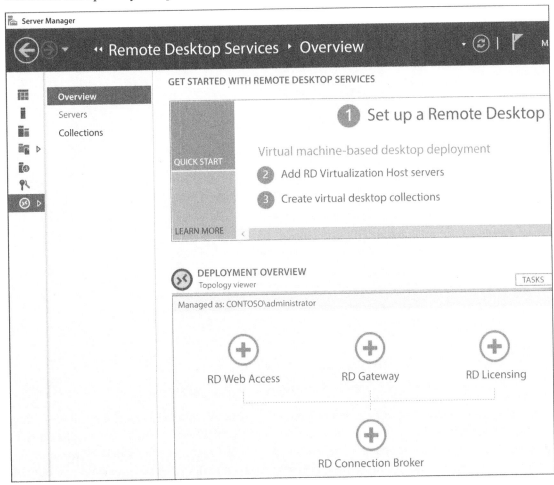

Figure 15.31: Server Manager is happy again

Logging directly in to RDSH servers

Most Windows Server instances are very easy to connect to remotely, by using the Remote Desktop Connection tool and simply creating an RDP connection to log in to them. RDSH servers, when part of an RDS collection, suddenly get finicky about RDP connections coming into them unless those connections are happening via the farm. I'll show you an example. My RDSH1 and RDSH2 servers are just Windows Server 2022 instances, and I was able to RDP successfully into them before I made them RDS servers inside my collection. Now that they are part of the collection, I can obviously connect to them by using my RDS connectivity file that connects me through the farm, just like my users are going to do.

Connecting this way will land me on either RDSH1 or RDSH2, but I do not get to choose which one. If I were to be connecting to one of these servers for maintenance purposes, I would want to be able to easily hop into one or the other at my choosing.

From my WIN10 client machine, I have simply tried to RDP into RDSH2, using the `mstsc.exe` tool. Here is the result:

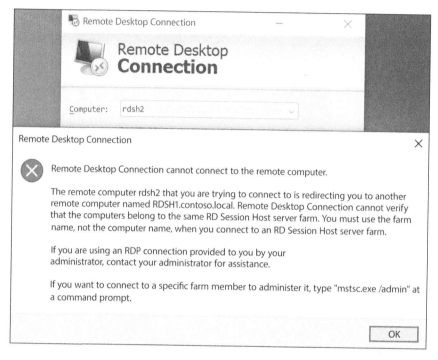

Figure 15.32: I can no longer RDP directly into my RDSH servers

If you have some other form of connectivity tool to connect directly to the console of RDSH2, you could of course utilize that to login directly. Otherwise, if RDSH2 was a virtual machine, like it is in my case, then I could use the Hyper-V console session to log directly in to it as well. However, there is a third option staring us right in the face, buried at the bottom of text in our previous error output:

```
mstsc.exe /admin
```

When you launch `mstsc.exe`, there are a few optional switches that you can call on, which enable special functionality within this tool. These switches enable things like specifying the height and width of the remote desktop session, specifying the use of a saved RDP connection file, or even connecting in a way that you can shadow another user's session. For our purposes today, we simply want to be able to log directly in to RDSH2, and our switch for doing that is called `mstsc.exe /admin`. The `/admin` switch connects you directly to a special session on an RDS, intended for administration of the machine. In our case with RDSH2, it means that it will actually allow us to RDP directly into this server, whereas normal `mstsc.exe` connectivity would not.

SSL certificate replacements

Assuming that you have been following along throughout this chapter, you know that an Remote Desktop Gateway utilizes an SSL certificate, which makes sense because it is permitting connectivity and traffic streams coming inbound to your environment from anywhere in the world. The Remote Desktop Web Access component also makes use of an SSL certificate, because it is a webpage running on port 443 and any user's browser would throw a hissy fit if there was not a valid certificate on that website.

SSL certificates need to be renewed every year in most cases. A common mistake that I watch RDS administrators make is that during SSL renewal for an RD Gateway instance, they head directly into the Remote Desktop Gateway Manager tool. We really haven't even looked at this tool through our chapter on RDS, because it is only used for certain functions and there is no need to touch it in many RDS environments. The replacement of an RD Gateway SSL certificate can be accomplished from inside Remote Desktop Gateway Manager, but it is technically the wrong place to perform this task. Replacing a certificate with a new one via RD Gateway Manager will get the new certificate up and running on your RD Gateway, but only on your RD Gateway. The other components inside RDS that utilize SSL certificates will not be changed or updated, which can then cause you other problems once the old certificate expires.

Avoiding this mistake is an easy matter of changing habits. Rather than grabbing your new certificate and heading directly into Remote Desktop Gateway Manager, visit Server Manager and your overall RDS **Deployment Properties**. There are not a lot of common reasons to visit the overarching **Deployment Properties** on a regular basis, but SSL certificate replacement is one of them. Inside **Deployment Properties**, there is a screen called **Certificates**.

Figure 15.33: Replacing an SSL certificate the right way

This screen is a little confusing, but what it is trying to tell you is that there are actually four different components in RDS that are making use of a certificate. These are the four entities shown in our previous screenshot. Remote Desktop Connection Broker has two, and then Remote Desktop Web Access and Remote Desktop Gateway, as we already discussed.

When replacing a certificate with a fresh one, you want to change it for all four components on this screen. If you were to swap your Remote Desktop Gateway certificate via Remote Desktop Gateway Manager, you would be only 25% complete with your certificate replacement.

The **Create new certificate...** option is interesting, allowing you to generate a self-signed certificate for the task, but is most likely not what you want to accomplish. Instead, acquire your new certificate through whatever means you normally would, and in the end make sure that you have a PFX file that contains both the certificate and the private key. Feel free to go back and visit our chapter on certificates if none of that makes sense. Copy that PFX file to your server where you are administering your RDS deployment, and now utilize the **Select existing certificate...** button to put it into place.

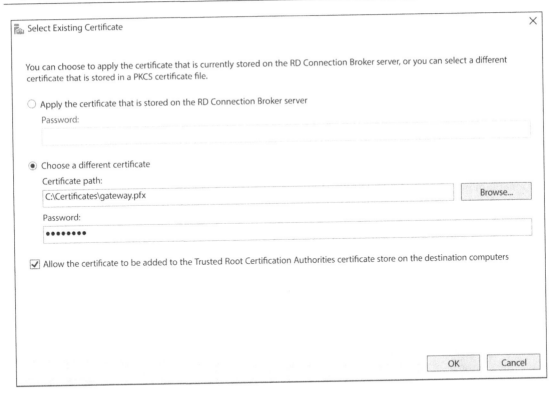

Figure 15.34: Create a PFX file and make use of it here

The critical information to understand is that you have to repeat this process for each of these four RDS components. Select them individually, walk through the **Select existing certificate...** screen for each of them, and in the end, your entire RDS deployment will now be running on the new certificate.

Cloning RDSH servers

When building our test lab RDS farm, I got off easy because I only needed it for testing and screenshot purposes, and so I simply created four new VMs that were running fresh copies of Windows Server 2022 and configured them as needed. When building a production environment RDS farm, it is almost a guarantee that you are going to be additionally installing numerous applications onto your RDSH servers, so that users can launch these applications once connected. Rather than prepping all RDSH servers from scratch and having to deal with running through application installers on each of them, it will be very tempting to in some way image or clone them from each other. Perhaps you create RDSH1 and then install everything you need. This RDSH server is now the perfect example to replicate 3, 4, or 46 more times, and for new RDSH servers, you simply clone the existing one.

If you do this, make sure you sysprep every new one!

We have already covered the topic of sysprep in this book, so I won't re-hash it here. If you clone a server and do not sysprep it, you will certainly cause collisions and issues within your network and Active Directory. Sysprepping a server scrubs key pieces of information from inside Windows, allowing it to run side by side with its clone.

Depending on how your applications behave, you may or may not be able to get away with clone and sysprep. Some applications plug information into files and the registry that utilize the hostname of a server, which will certainly be changing during the clone process. There is no way I can tell you whether or not you will be able to clone RDSH servers in your environment; it would be a matter of trial and error. But if you do, make sure that sysprep is part of that equation. I know some RDS admins who clone servers all the time and love it, and I know some who have had poor enough experiences that they would never even think about doing it. The decision is yours...

Sidder

At some point in your RDS administration journey, you will find yourself staring at the network share location where all of your UPDs reside and scratching your head. You know that every user session creates a new UPD inside this location, as you specified during the RDS deployment wizard. You already know that each UPD is really a VHDX file that is sitting in this location. What we haven't discussed is that these VHDX files are named in a very non-intuitive way. The names of these files are a long GUID, an identifier for the user account to which they are associated. FSLogix profiles do a better job of plugging the username directly into the name of this file so that you can quickly identify which VHDX belongs to which user, but for classic UPDs, you are looking at a lot of nonsense, like this:

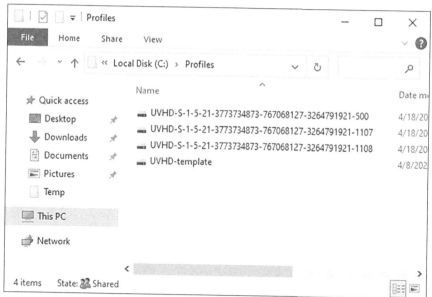

Figure 15.35: A robot must have named these UPDs

Thankfully, there is a free tool available that fills in this knowledge gap! It is called **Sidder**, but since it is not a tool created by Microsoft, I am not going to give you an official download link. It's easily searchable on the internet, but I am disclaiming this one with "use at your own risk."

If you decide to move forward and download Sidder, it is a standalone executable that you can copy to your server where UPDs are stored, and running Sidder displays information to quickly identify which UPD belongs to which user account.

Figure 15.36: Sidder quickly associates usernames with UPDs

GPOs and RDS

GPOs are commonly used to secure or manipulate domain-joined workstations for a company and can be just as easily used to modify RDSH servers. However, it is most likely true that the configurations and settings that you want to push to workstations do not directly apply to your intentions for RDSH servers, and vice versa. It is very common to find all RDSH servers secluded to their own OU inside Active Directory and for that OU to have **Block Inheritance** enabled. It is easy to accidentally break an RDSH server by applying general domain-scope policies to it, so I recommend blocking this inheritance as a general best practice.

What this means, of course, is that any GPOs that you do want to apply to your RDSH servers must be intentionally linked to their particular OU. This is something that is good to keep in mind whenever building a new RDS environment, and also when modifying GPOs in any way, stay conscious of how your changes may or may not impact your RDS farm users.

Summary

Remote Desktop Services has been around for more than 20 years and is still widely used around the world. It has seen many improvements over the years and continues to be a fantastic way to provide a multi-user virtual platform for your workers, where they don't have to worry about what local computer they are using to perform the work, and you don't have to worry about securing whatever that device looks like. You maintain complete control over the centralized RDS compute environment, providing secure access to the resources that employees need.

In fact, RDS is still so commonly used that it has carried over into one of the most common Azure-based resource pools that I find in the SMB market. **Azure Virtual Desktop (AVD)**, formerly known as Windows Virtual Desktop, is a way to provide users with login from anywhere to Azure-based servers that contain virtual user sessions. The capabilities in AVD are extremely similar to RDS on-premises, with the exception that the base operating system for AVD is generally a multi-user Windows 10 platform, rather than straight-up Windows Server 2022. AVD even makes use of FSLogix profiles to keep user information secure and working properly!

Questions

1. What RDS component is responsible for distributing user sessions among multiple servers?
2. Are RDS-related certificates defined in RDS **Collection Properties** or RDS **Deployment Properties**?
3. What is the command you should run to prepare an RDSH server for application installation?
4. What type of RDS CALs are most common?
5. True or False: To prepare a fresh Windows Server instance to become an RDSH member of an existing collection, you must first log in to that server and install the Remote Desktop role.
6. What are the four types of RDS user profiles?
7. How can you launch the Remote Desktop Connection tool in a way that allows you to RDP directly into an RDSH server that is already part of a collection?
8. Bonus question: What animals live on an RDS farm?

Join our community on Discord

Join our community's Discord space for discussions with the author and other readers:

https://packt.link/SecNet

16

Troubleshooting

When dreaming of a position in server or system administration, we often think of designing infrastructure, spinning up new servers, and implementing new technology. The truth can reflect those tasks, but it can just as easily include 3 A.M. wakeup calls to deal with a system being down, poring over event and diagnostic logs, and living on Google and Bing when your acquired knowledge and wisdom just isn't cutting the mustard. Sometimes, hardware breaks. Other times, software freaks out. Certificates expire, internet connections fail, and occasionally, you work on an issue from a certain angle all day only to discover in the end that it was being caused by something entirely different. Working in IT can bring with it great mysteries every single day, which is one of the reasons I love it. This final chapter uncovers some of the tools available in Windows Server 2022 that can assist with troubleshooting, maintenance, and repair:

- Backup and restore
- Task Manager
- Resource Monitor
- Performance Monitor
- Sysinternals tools
- Windows Firewall with Advanced Security
- System Insights
- Remote toolsets
- Event Logs
- MMC and MSC shortcuts

Backup and restore

The need to back up and occasionally restore your servers is, unfortunately, still present in Windows Server 2022. Many dream of a day when servers are 100 percent reliable and stable throughout their lifetimes, unaffected by viruses and rogue software, but today is not that day (that would be a little boring, to be honest).

While there are many third-party tools available on the market that can improve and automate your backup experience when managing many servers, we do have these capabilities baked right into our own Server 2022 operating system, and we should all be familiar with how to utilize them. Maintaining good backups should be priority number one for any business and is the most important troubleshooting component that exists. There are a myriad of reasons why you may fail to repair a server that is having a problem, and sometimes, your only two options are to build from scratch or restore from backup. Ransomware attacks are on the increase, and attackers are targeting companies of all sizes. If you have one bad firewall rule in place, it's only a matter of time before they find their way into your network, and before you know it, every single one of your servers will be encrypted and held for ransom. If you don't have a solid backup system and a restoration plan that spells out exactly how you recover from those backups should the need arise, then you had better have a very deep wallet to pay the ransom because that will be your only option.

For clarity, of course, you should never pay the ransom! If you pay, the hackers who locked down your system in the first place will release your files (if they didn't, they would immediately kick themselves out of the ransom business), but they are also going to build as many backdoors in your network as they possibly can before they do release your data, so that down the road, they can simply reconnect and do it again. Unfortunately, as we have seen recently in the news, failing to keep good backups results in being stuck between a rock and a hard place, where paying the ransom is the only available course of action. Don't let that be *your* story.

Schedule regular backups

Logging in to your servers and launching a manual backup task every day is obviously not feasible for most of our organizations, as the process of running backups would turn into our full-time job. Thankfully, the Windows Server Backup feature gives us the option to create a backup schedule. This way, we can define what we want to back up, where we want to back it up to, and how often this backup should run. Then, we can sit back, relax, and know that our systems are performing this task on their own.

Before we can do anything with backups, we need to install the appropriate feature inside Windows. Using the **Add roles and features** link, go ahead and install the feature called **Windows Server Backup**. Remember that I said *feature* – you won't find Windows Server Backup on the primary **Server Roles** selection screen; you need to move ahead one screen further in the wizard to find **Features**. Once the feature has finished installing, you can launch the **Windows Server Backup** console that is available inside the **Tools** menu of Server Manager. Once inside, click on **Local Backup** in the left-hand side window; you will see some **Actions** appear on the right-hand side of your screen.

As you can see, there is an option listed here called **Backup Once...** that, as the name implies, performs an ad hoc backup job. While this is a nice feature, there is no way that any server administrator is going to log in to all their servers and do this every day. Instead, clicking on the **Backup Schedule...** action will launch a configuration wizard to create a scheduled, recurring backup job:

Figure 16.1: The Windows Server Backup console

The first option you will come across is for deciding what it is that you want to back up. The default option is set to **Full server**, which will take a backup of everything in the operating system. If you want to customize the amount of data that is being backed up, you can choose the **Custom** option and proceed from there. Since I have lots of disk space available to me, I am going to stick with the recommended path of creating full server backups.

Next, we get to the real advantage of using the scheduling concept: choosing how often we run our backup. The most common way is to choose a particular time of day and then let the backup run every day at that allotted time. If you have a server whose data is being updated regularly throughout the day and you want to shorten your window of lost information in the event of needing to perform a restore, you can also specify to back up multiple times per day:

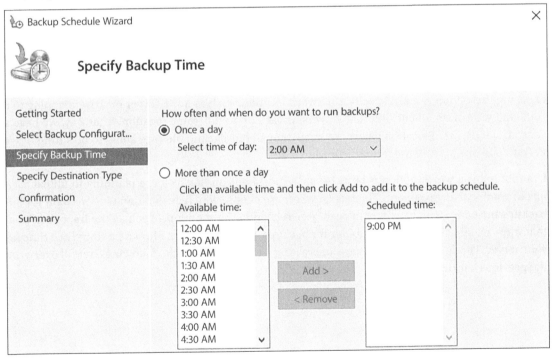

Figure 16.2: Setting a backup schedule

The last screen where we need to make a decision for our scheduled backups is the **Specify Destina-tion Type** screen, where we set the location for our backup files. You can see that there are a couple of different options to store the backup locally on the physical hard disks of the same server where you configure the backups. Storing backup files on a local, dedicated disk or volume can be advantageous because the speed of the backup process will be increased compared to network storage. For servers that you try to back up continually during workdays, this can decrease the resources being used by the backup and increase the number of backups that can be squeezed into a day. Another advantage of using a locally connected disk for backups is that you can create multiple rollback points within your backup schema, keeping multiple days' worth of backup information in case you need to roll back to a particular point in time.

There are also downsides to retaining backups on locally attached storage. One potential showstopper is a ransomware attack. If you have never been part of cleanup efforts following such an attack, you may not realize that ransomware locks down and encrypts all the files it can get its hands on. This almost always means that it encrypts the operating system volume, and any other volume (drive letter) that it can find attached to the system. Additional hard disks and USB drives where you might store backups will almost certainly be pulverized, along with your server, in a ransomware attack.

This brings up another good point – keeping offsite copies of your backups. This is not a chapter about disaster recovery scenarios, but you should absolutely keep copies of your server backups in a second location, whether that be in cloud storage or in another physical building.

I find that most admins prefer to keep all their backup files in a centralized location, and that means choosing the third option on this screen, the one entitled **Back up to a shared network folder**. By choosing this option, we can specify a network location, such as a file server or drive mapping to a NAS, and we can set all our different servers to back up to this same location. That way, we have a central, standardized location where we know that all our backup files are going to be sitting, if we need to pull one out and use it for restoration.

I cannot tell you which option is best, because it depends on how you are planning to utilize back-ups in your own environment. The screen where we choose which destination type we want for our backups includes some good text to read over related to these options, such as the important note that when using a shared network folder for backups, only one backup file can be stored at a time for your server. This is because the process of creating a new backup on the following day will overwrite the previous backup:

Figure 16.3: A warning about backups stored remotely

Once you have chosen a destination for your backups and specified a network share location, if that is the option you have chosen, you are finished in the wizard. Your backup jobs will automatically kick off at the allocated time that you specified during the wizard, and tomorrow, you will see a new backup file for your server. If you are impatient, like me, and want to see the backup job run right now, you can walk through the other **Action** that's available in the **Windows Server Backup** console, called **Backup Once...**, to run a manual backup right away:

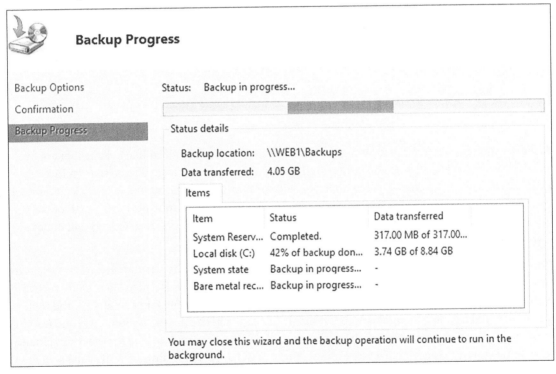

Figure 16.4: My first backup is running

Restoring from Windows

Since you are being diligent and keeping good backups of your servers, the hope is that you will never have to utilize those backup files to restore a server. But, alas, the time *will* come when you have a server that goes sideways, or some data is accidentally deleted, and you must revisit the process of restoring data or an entire server in your infrastructure. If your server is still online and running, the restore process is quite easy to invoke from the same **Windows Server Backup** console. Open the console and choose the **Action** that says **Recover....**

This invokes another wizard that walks us through the recovery process. First, we specify the location of our backup file. If you have a dedicated backup location on the local server, it is pretty simple to find; otherwise, like in my example, where we specified a network location, you should choose **A backup stored on another location**, and then choose **Remote shared folder** to tell it where to find that backup file:

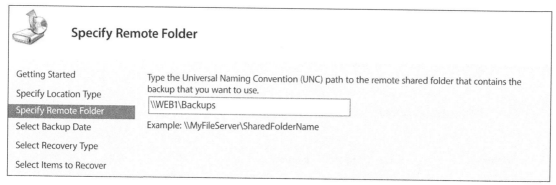

Specify Remote Folder

Getting Started

Specify Location Type

Specify Remote Folder

Select Backup Date

Select Recovery Type

Select Items to Recover

Type the Universal Naming Convention (UNC) path to the remote shared folder that contains the backup that you want to use.

\\WEB1\Backups

Example: \\MyFileServer\SharedFolderName

Figure 16.5: Specifying the location of backup files

Based on your chosen backup location, the wizard will now identify all rollback dates that are available within the backup files. If you have stored your backup files on a local disk so that multiple days' worth of rollback points are available, then you will see numerous dates available to click on. For me, since I chose to store my backups on a network location, that means only one day's worth of backup information is available, and yesterday's date is the only one that I can choose. So, I will choose to restore yesterday's backup and continue working through the wizard.

Now that we have identified the specific backup file that is going to be used for recovery, we get to choose what information from that backup is going to be restored. This is a nice piece of the recovery platform because, often, when we need to restore from backup, it is only for specific files and folders that may have been deleted or corrupted. If that is the case, choose the top option, **Files and folders**. In other cases, you may want to roll the entire server back to a certain date, and for that functionality, you should choose to recover an entire **Volume**. Right now, I am only missing a few files that somehow disappeared between yesterday and today, so I am going to choose the default **Files and folders** option.

The **Select Items to Recover** screen is now presented, which polls the backup file and displays the entire list of files and folders within the backup file. Here, I simply choose which ones I want to restore. This kind of recovery can be critical to your daily management of a file server, where the potential is high for users to accidentally delete information:

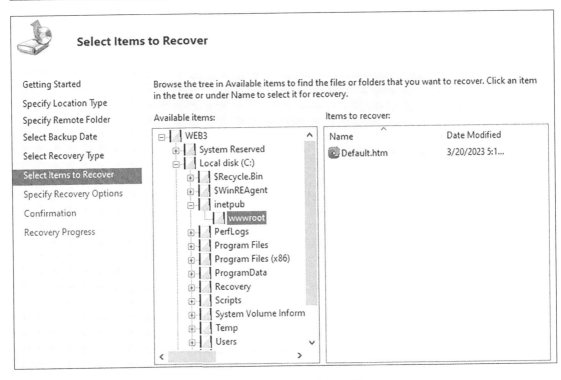

Figure 16.6: Restoring individual files

All that remains is to specify where you want these recovered files to be restored. You can choose for the recovered files to be placed back in their original location, or if you are running this recovery process on a different machine, you can choose to restore the files to a new location that you can grab them from and then place them manually, wherever they now need to reside.

Restoring from the installer disk

Recovery from the console inside Windows is a nice wizard-driven experience, but what if your server has completely crashed? If you cannot get into Windows on your server, you cannot run the Windows Server Backup console to initiate your recovery process. In this case, we can still utilize our backup file that has been created, but we need to use it in combination with a Windows Server 2022 installation disk, from which we can invoke the recovery process.

 It is important to note that this recovery process cannot access locations on the network, and your backup file will have to be stored on a disk attached to your server. You can utilize a USB drive for this purpose during the recovery process, if you did not originally set up your backup job to be stored on an existing locally attached disk.

To make things interesting, I'm going to crash my own server. This is the server that we took a backup of a few minutes ago. I accidentally deleted some very important files in my C:\Windows directory. Whoops! Now, this is all I see when I try to boot my server:

```
Safe Mode
Safe Mode with Networking
Safe Mode with Command Prompt

Enable Boot Logging
Enable low-resolution video
Last Known Good Configuration (advanced)
Debugging Mode
Disable automatic restart on system failure
Disable Driver Signature Enforcement
Disable Early Launch Anti-Malware Driver

Start Windows Normally
```

Figure 16.7: The C:\Windows folder is important – don't delete files from it!

That's not a very friendly screen to see first thing in the morning! Since I seem to be stuck here and unable to boot into Windows, my chances of running the recovery wizard are nil. What to do? Boot to the Windows Server 2022 installer DVD or ISO? That is really my only option, but I want to be careful that I don't simply install Windows afresh, as all of my programs and data could be overwritten in that scenario. Rather, once I get into the Windows Server installer screen, you will notice that there is an option down in the corner to **Repair your computer**. Choose this option to open the recovery options that are available on the installation DVD.

Now you will see the screen adjust to a new blue hue, indicating that we have entered a special portion of the installer disk, from which there are a few options:

Figure 16.8: Recovery options on the Windows Server install disk

Clicking on **Troubleshoot**, you'll find a subset of advanced options that can be used to troubleshoot the operating system from this console outside of the OS itself. If you think you can fix whatever the issue is from **Command Prompt**, choose that option, as shown in *Figure 16.9*, and try to fix it yourself.

For our example, I am pretty sure that I significantly damaged the operating system, so I am going to do a full **System Image Recovery** and click on that button:

Figure 16.9: Running a System Image Recovery from installation media

As long as you have a hard drive connected that contains a Windows Server Backup file, the wizard will launch and pull in the information about the backup. Since I had originally chosen to store my backup file on a network location, I copied the backup files onto a disk and connected it as a second disk to my server. The wizard automatically recognizes that backup file and displays it in the **Select a system image backup** screen:

Figure 16.10: The recovery process recognizes backup files on attached storage

Now, by simply clicking on **Next** a few times to progress through the wizard, my backup image restores on my server:

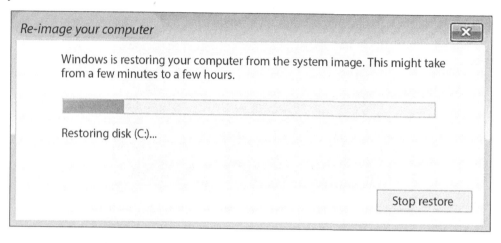

Figure 16.11: Restoring the server via advanced recovery options

Once the restore process has completed, the system reboots and launches itself right back into Windows, where it is fully functional back to the restore point. My test server doesn't have much of anything running on it, so the time that it took to restore was pretty minimal. A production box may take a little longer, but I'd say that 20 minutes from blowing up the server to being fully recovered is a pretty awesome length of time!

Keeping good and recent backup files is critical to your operation's sustainability. I have worked on quite a few systems where the admins took some manual backups after initially configuring their servers but never set up a regular schedule. Even if the data on the server never changes, if you are part of a domain, you never want to rely on old backup files. If a server fails, and you need to recover it, restoring a backup that is only a few days old will generally recover well. But if you restore an image that is six months old, Windows itself will come back online with no problems, and all of your data will exist. However, in that amount of time, your computer account for that server would most certainly have fallen out of sync with the domain, causing authentication errors against the domain controllers. In some cases, you may even have to do goofy things like disjoin and rejoin the server to the domain while following the image restoration to recover communications to the domain. If you keep regular backups to restore from, you won't have to deal with those issues.

Task Manager

If you can remember all the way back to *Chapter 1*, *Getting Started with Windows Server 2022*, you'll know that we already discussed Task Manager. There, we described how to launch it and took a quick look at the different tabs available inside Task Manager. While there is no need to rehash the same information here, it is important to note Task Manager in this chapter regarding troubleshooting, because it is one of the first places you should visit on any server that is portraying performance problems or otherwise strange symptoms.

Task Manager gives you a quick glance at the overall CPU and memory utilization on a server, letting you know how taxed the server is. One of the most common tabs to review on any server is **Processes**, which allows you to sort all the running applications and processes by their CPU or memory consumption, which can quickly identify a problematic application that may be hindering the entire server. Once identified, you can easily right-click on any running process and quickly **End task**, killing that process and freeing up those resources on your server.

When administering RDS servers, you will find yourself often visiting Task Manager to troubleshoot the slowness of one particular session host server. Sometimes, you can identify individual applications that soak up resources in the **Processes** or **Details** tab, while other times, you may want to go even further and review the **Users** tab to see status information about every user who is logged in to that RDSH server. Oftentimes, this is the fastest way to find out how many users are logged in to a particular server, and to quickly identify which user session might be causing grief for the others by consuming an extraordinary amount of server resources:

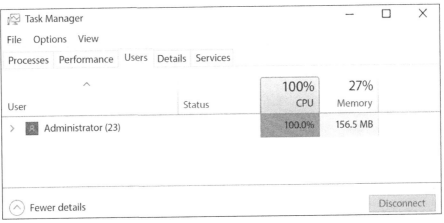

Figure 16.12: The Administrator user is consuming all available CPU

One of the most common reasons I open Task Manager is to visit the **Performance** tab and view system uptime information. While generally more stable than workstation computers, Windows servers do need to be restarted occasionally, and uptime is a good indicator as to whether you should attempt a restart as a first form of troubleshooting. If your server has only been running for two days, you may want to focus your efforts elsewhere and not cause anyone a service interruption by rebooting in the middle of the day. On the other hand, if your server is really crawling and causing slowness, and it has a reported uptime of 120 days, you may want to go ahead and just reboot the thing to see if it resolves the issue.

 Another easy way to view system uptime is by typing **systeminfo** into a Command Prompt or PowerShell window! And taking it one step further, if your server rebooted unexpectedly and you want to find out how long it had been running prior to the restart, visit the **System Event Logs** and search for Event ID 6013. You'll have to calculate seconds into minutes/hours/days, but this event is logged at noon every day, so you always have an ongoing record of system uptime.

In cases where you find Task Manager to be lacking and want to dig a little bit deeper, go ahead and launch the newer **Resource Monitor**. This can be invoked by using the **Start** menu search function, but if you have Task Manager open anyway, visit the **Performance** tab. Way down at the bottom, look for a link called **Open Resource Monitor**.

Resource Monitor

Like Task Manager on steroids, Resource Monitor can take system monitoring and troubleshooting even further. It contains plenty of the same information that we just experienced inside Task Manager but lays things out in a different format. CPU, memory, and disk utilization metrics are present, as well as monitoring of your network interfaces. There are various ways to sort the items that utilize resources, quickly identifying the high hitters for CPU and memory, and there are also right-click functions to end or suspend processes. On the **Overview** tab, as shown in *Figure 16.13*, you'll see that I am able to quickly identify the reason for my high CPU utilization – PowerShell is consuming almost 100% of available CPU resources:

Figure 16.13: Using Resource Monitor to investigate high CPU utilization

Exploring the different tabs inside Resource Monitor will show you more detailed information about CPU, memory, and even disk resource consumption. This is particularly cool because you can see disk storage stats and available disk space right alongside metrics, such as `Disk Queue Length`, which is an important indicator to monitor when hard disk performance may be a bottleneck.

The only tab I haven't mentioned yet is **Network**, which is my favorite place to visit inside Resource Monitor. A fairly common client/server troubleshooting task is to track down what a particular application may be calling for at a network level, and this can be a difficult thing to ascertain. For example, I have installed an application onto a client or server, and this application makes calls to another server to grab information or to interact with it in some way. Let's pretend the application isn't working correctly. First, you do some basic network troubleshooting and verify that the two machines can communicate with each other, by pinging back and forth. This means network traffic is flowing, but the application still won't connect. Your next thought is the firewall – what if the firewall on the receiving server is not allowing the traffic, or perhaps there is even a physical firewall device somewhere in between that is restricting the ports being used by the application? You are unsure of what ports the app may be trying to use, and it's too late in the day to call the software vendor (if one exists).

Resource Monitor to the rescue! Now, if you've been around the block once or twice, you may be thinking, "Couldn't I just install Wireshark and use it to review network traffic leaving my machine?" The answer would be yes, but here we are portraying a similar capability baked right into Windows.

Inside the **Network** tab of Resource Monitor, you can see the list of applications and **Process IDs (PIDs)** that are currently generating network traffic on this computer or server. Keep in mind that Resource Monitor is available inside Windows Server, and it is also available inside Windows 10/11! Launch your application, look for the PID, and check the box next to it. Then, drop down the **TCP Connection** section, and if that application utilizes a TCP traffic stream (or attempts to), as most applications do, you will see right here exactly what server name or IP address the application is calling for, and what ports it is using to attempt a connection. The interesting columns here are **Remote Address** and **Remote Port**:

Figure 16.14: Using Resource Monitor for network troubleshooting

It is easy to see that my Outlook.exe application reaches out to a couple of different IP addresses, using TCP port 443. If this information were from your own application, you could now use this information to verify that the application is calling for the IP or server that you expect, and that the port being used is accessible, listening, and not being blocked on the receiving server or a firewall in between.

Performance Monitor

Another built-in monitoring tool is called Performance Monitor, commonly referred to as **Perfmon**. Almost every component inside Windows Server has predefined performance monitor counters, and Perfmon taps into those counters to display extremely in-depth information about what is happening with those components, but only when you specifically set up reporting to see it. Perfmon does not log anything by default, because to do so would consume plenty of server resources, so this tool is generally only to be used temporarily during troubleshooting or for a specific reason, and then disabled again when you are finished.

The easiest way to launch Perfmon is to **Start | Run** or open a **Command Prompt** or PowerShell, simply type Perfmon, and then press *Enter*. This launches the interface, and by default, you can see that it has plugged in a counter for **% Processor Time**. You can obviously find CPU percentage information in much easier and better-looking places than Perfmon, so this is displayed simply as a sample of data:

Figure 16.15: Performance Monitor default counter

What is very interesting here is that you can quickly see the **Average**, **Minimum**, and **Maximum** data fields. You will find that these fields exist with most counters, and this is some of the most useful information that I have pulled using Perfmon during real-life troubleshooting scenarios.

Right-click anywhere inside that graph and select **Add Counters...**. Here, we can discover the incredible breadth of data counters that are available to monitor with Perfmon:

Figure 16.16: Adding counters to Perfmon

There is no way we can cover everything here, so I'll list out a few examples of counters that are useful in most server performance troubleshooting scenarios:

- Processor > % Processor Time (this is the one added by default)
- Memory > Available MBytes
- Network Interface > Bytes Received/sec
- Network Interface > Bytes Sent/sec (and these can be further defined per-NIC)
- PhysicalDisk > % Disk Time
- PhysicalDisk > Current Disk Queue Length

Many counters are role-specific. Things like Terminal Services > Total Sessions can give you counters on how many users you have logged in to your RDSH hosts. Or you can use Print Queue > Total Jobs Printed when trying to gain an idea of how busy or overworked your print server might be. In a previous job, I often utilized IP-HTTPS, DNS64, and IPsec counters to keep tabs on under-the-hood components within the Microsoft Remote Access technologies.

I have gone ahead and added all the performance-related counters that I specified previously (there are many, many more options available), and the Perfmon data graph has become a mess of multiple colors and overlapping line graphs. While the default graph view is interesting, it's not very easy to follow. Instead, if you drop down the toolbar icon that looks like a little graph, you'll find three options for how to display this data: Line, Histogram bar, and Report. I prefer looking at numbers, but the Report view does not display the average-minimum-maximum, and those are really useful. So, you may find yourself utilizing a combination of all three views on a regular basis:

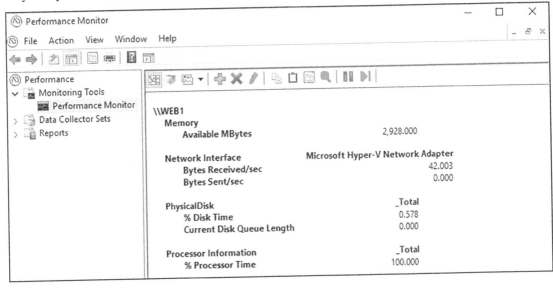

Figure 16.17: Performance metrics in the Report view

This is cool real-time information, but how often do you really dig in and troubleshoot a real-time problem with this much depth? Let's be honest – if you have a server tanking performance during working hours, you are probably going to restart the entire server to get things normalized before using Perfmon for a hardware review. Instead, what I have always found Perfmon to be most useful for is gathering statistics over a certain period of time. A great example is repeated reports of slowness on a particular server. Perhaps an RDSH or Remote Access server where users interact with it every day. Every few days, you receive support tickets indicating that the system was running slowly or wouldn't allow anyone new to log in. By the time that ticket crosses your desk and you hop into the server, whatever the problem was has disappeared, and the server runs happily again.

This is where Perfmon can shine. After defining the performance counters that you are interested in monitoring, you can create your own **Data Collector Set** (which is a collection of counters) and configure it to run on a schedule. Expand **Data Collector Sets**, then right-click on **User Defined** and select **New > Data Collector Set**. Walking through this wizard, you can use some predefined templates to gather common metrics, or you can define your data collector set manually. Pick and choose which performance counters you would like to include and how often the data collector set will log data for each counter (every 15 seconds by default). You can see in *Figure 16.18* that I am working my way through defining a manual list of counters, and I have added some of the classic hardware utilization metrics to my collection list:

Figure 16.18: Adding performance counters to a data collector set

After defining your counters and specifying a location for this data to be saved, the last screen of the wizard provides the option to **Run as**. In many cases, you can leave <**Default**> configured here and your dataset will work just fine, but if any of your counters struggle to gather data, you could alternatively specify a different account here, such as an administrator account. Leave the option selected for **Save and close** and click **Finish**. I want to use this option, rather than one of the others that invokes immediate action, so that we can see where it is inside the Perfmon console that our new data collector set is stored.

Back inside the Perfmon console, looking under the **User Defined** folder, you will see a **New Data Collector Set** that didn't exist previously. This is our new set of counters, ready to be run at any time. This is a nice way to save common sets of performance counters for easy running and reference later, and if you right-click on **New Data Collector Set** and head into **Properties**, you will also find a **Schedule** tab, which allows you to set this data collector up to start on a particular date and time. Then, inside the **Stop Condition** tab, you can define how long you would like these metrics to be gathered. Remember that we set the interval to 15 seconds, so this data collector set will start at the time you specify and will log data from the included counters every 15 seconds for as long as you determine the data collector set should run, with data collection stopping as specified in the **Stop Condition** tab:

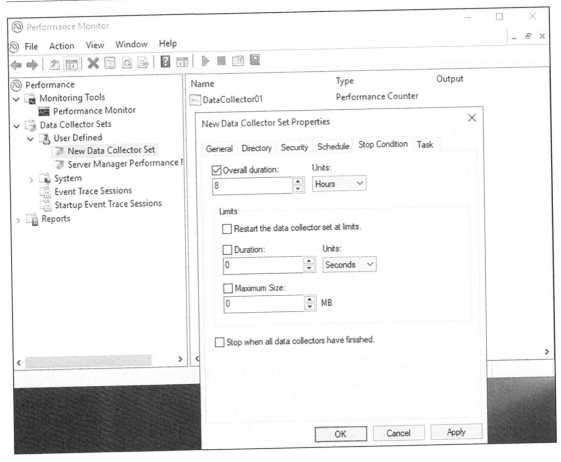

Figure 16.19: Configuring a scheduled runtime for the new data collector set

In the future, if I want to tweak which counters are included in this dataset, I can right-click on **DataCol-lector01**, shown in *Figure 16.19*, and visit **Properties** here to add new counters or remove existing ones.

I have allowed the new data collector set to run for a few minutes and gather some data. Now that I'm finished with the defined runtime, how do I find the data that was generated? Still inside the Perfmon console, look just a little further down the tree for **Reports**. Inside **User Defined** reports, you'll find a folder for your new data collector set. Each time that your collector set runs, it will generate a new file here with a date stamp. Clicking on today's file shows me all the data gathered, and I have the same options available to manipulate the data or change how the graph looks as I did in the live data view:

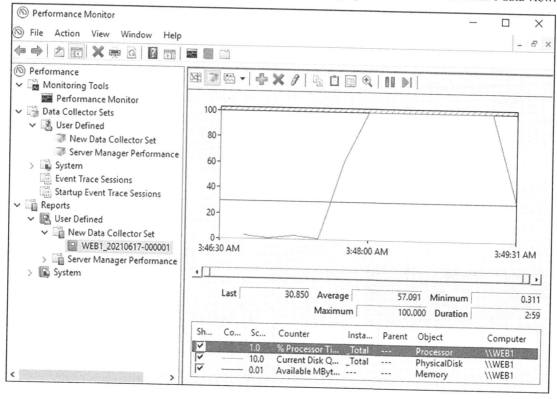

Figure 16.20: Viewing the report following a scheduled data collection run

Scheduled Perfmon datasets can be extremely useful when troubleshooting regularly occurring performance problems on a server. In the example of an RDSH server that we discussed earlier, when tackling reported slowness on that server, you could establish a Perfmon data collector set that takes metrics surrounding hardware utilization. You could include session count metrics to see how many users are logged in at the same time. This Perfmon report could then shed some very interesting and helpful light on the situation; perhaps you simply have too many people connected during the times that hardware is taxed. Or maybe you find that the server slows down at the top of every hour and then use that information to realize that you have backups running at the top of every hour, which leads you in the direction of problem resolution.

Sysinternals tools

Windows Server has many wonderful tools built right into it, but there's always room to improve.

This seems to be exactly what Mark Russinovich was thinking back in the mid-90s, when he and Bryce Cogswell created Winternals and started crafting apps that could do even more advanced actions and data collection within the Microsoft Windows operating systems than was capable with the native toolset. Fast-forward to today, Winternals has been acquired by Microsoft, the conglomeration of tools that were created under that umbrella are now known as the Microsoft Sysinternals tools, and Mark is now CTO of Azure.

These tools are simple, helpful, and effective. Most of them don't even require an installation. Simply download a standalone executable, copy it over to your server, and run it. When finished, you can delete the executable and easily remove any trace of that application from your server. We already looked at one of these tools earlier in the book, TCPView. There are many tools available that serve many different purposes; some of them are even written specifically for Nano Server or Linux machines!

In just a minute we will outline some of these tools for ourselves, but if you're interested in a list of the entire Sysinternals toolset, here is a good link to get started: `https://learn.microsoft.com/en-us/sysinternals/downloads/`

Descriptions of popular tools

Here are some of the Sysinternals tools that I have found most helpful to deal with Windows Server tasks and troubleshooting.

TcpView

We already looked closely at TcpView a few chapters ago; this standalone executable is incredibly useful to monitor all active TCP socket connections on a computer or server. It will show you active connections, and immediately display and highlight new connections being made, or stale connections falling away. This is very useful to troubleshoot application networking.

Disk2vhd

This is a simple tool that makes it incredibly easy to convert a live, running Windows physical server into a VHDX file, making it possible to spin up that VHDX on a Hyper-V server and very quickly convert a physical server into a virtual server. Anybody who has virtualized physical servers before has probably used Disk2vhd, perhaps without realizing it is one of the Sysinternals tools. A major advantage Disk2vhd has over other P2V tools is that you can run it on a server that is online; many of the other tools require you to shut down the server that you are converting.

Autologon

The name really says it all; running this tool and populating the presented fields will cause a computer or server to be configured to automatically bypass the login screen with the provided username and password. While this is not a great idea from a security perspective, some software running on servers insists on the server being logged in for the software to properly operate. In these cases, if that server restarts due to Windows updates or anything else, the server needs to be able to automatically log in during boot, and this tool can accomplish that function. It is possible to also do this directly in the Windows Registry, but the Autologon tool makes it so easy.

Autoruns

There are various different places where applications can be configured to automatically launch during the start of Windows. Sometimes it can be a nuisance to figure out where an app is configured like this if you want to stop that behavior from happening. The Autoruns tool quickly shows you a list of these startup items and a lot of detail about each one.

Diskmon

Shortly, we will take a look at Procmon, which provides a pretty comprehensive look into what goes on under the hood of Microsoft Windows, but if you are tracking down an issue and are interested in looking closely into all disk activity that is happening on your system, Diskmon is particularly useful for that. This can be particularly helpful when figuring out why a certain application or application installer is seizing up or failing; it may be attempting to access or write a file or folder, but doesn't have the permissions to do so.

LogonSessions

Task Manager can be a quick go-to to view different user profiles that are logged in to a server, but the LogonSessions tool provides much more detailed information about every session. With this tool, you can see not only user sessions but also system-level sessions that are authenticated and work behind the scenes. As an example, I just ran LogonSessions on my Windows 10 laptop where I am writing this text, and while I am the only user logged in to the machine, there are 10 active logon sessions. Using the -p switch with this tool displays the entire list of processes that are in use with each session, which can also be really useful!

PsExec

Executing applications or processes on remote systems is possible through remote PowerShell connections or third-party software, but Sysinternals brings a free and powerful option to the table. PsExec can be run on a Windows computer, to launch programs or enact commands on other remote Windows systems. Most software developers worthy of the title now design their server-side applications to run as Windows services, so that they are active and responsive even if the software is not launched on that server. Alas, not all programmers have this skillset, and there are plenty of nuisance applications in the world that require their server to be logged in, and the piece of software to always be running, or it won't be able to serve up any information. PsExec can be utilized to launch such applications from a remote computer, or it can be used to send troubleshooting commands to a remote system that is struggling so much that you may not be able to log in to it.

To give you an idea of how easy it is to run PsExec, here's an example command that I might run on my laptop, to be able to launch an executable on a remote server called WEB1. This example also displays an optional function where you can specify a specific username and password to be used on the remote system:

```
Psexec \\WEB1 "C:\Tools\Application.exe" -u contoso\administrator -p
password123!
```

One very useful switch to keep in your back pocket when working with PsExec is -s. By adding -s to your PsExec command, it will cause your command to run under the SYSTEM account, which can be useful for commands or executions that require unlimited permissions on the recipient computer.

PsKill

If PsExec is used to launch commands or applications, can we assume PsKill is the opposite? Yes, that is exactly what we have at our fingertips with PsKill. This tool can be used to force applications or processes to close on remote systems. Recent versions of Windows also include a built-in command-line tool called TaskKill that can accomplish similar functionality, but it is less powerful and doesn't easily translate into running against remote systems. PsKill is very easy to reach out to remote servers and stop running processes. As a real-world example, just a few weeks ago I was working with a company that has **QuickBooks (QB)** and another finance application integrated together. Both of these components are installed on a server, but users launch QB on their own computers of course, not directly on the server. The third-party component that taps into QB gets fussy if there are any instances of QBW32.exe running on this server, but QB loves to self-launch QBW32.exe for various reasons. This was causing a lot of grief for the customer, and the only solution from the software vendor was to force QBW32.exe to close in order to fix their software. So, we turned to PsKill. If users ever encounter an error in this application, they simply double-click on a batch file that calls PsKill into action. This batch file sits on their local computers, and when they click on it, PsKill reaches over to the QB server and closes any instances of QBW32.exe that are open. It takes mere milliseconds for this to run, and the user is immediately back in action.

While I truly hope this software vendor can figure out a better long-term solution to this problem, for now we have a very fast and effective stopgap solution in place to allow these folks to be successful in their work. Here is the sanitized PsKill command we use to accomplish what I just described:

```
C:\Tools\PsKill.exe \\SERVERNAME -u admin -p <password> QBW32.exe
```

PsShutdown

Many of you have probably used Microsoft's built-in shutdown command to enact a shutdown or reboot from Command Prompt, but generally from the server where you are currently logged in. As with most Sysinternals tools, PsShutdown works similarly to what is already built into Windows but adds a few extra pieces of functionality, including the ability to easily initiate a shutdown or restart against remote systems. There are many special switches that can be used alongside PsShutdown, enabling things like hibernating, locking the computer, displaying a message before shutdown or restart, logging a shutdown reason code in the event logs, plus many more options.

Process Monitor (Procmon)

There are lots and lots of Sysinternals tools, and the purpose here is not to cover all of them but to outline some of the common ones, especially those that I personally find useful. Descriptive text about these tools is helpful, but I'm getting bored with typing, and for these last couple of tools I would rather download and use them than just tell you about them.

Procmon is an evolution and combination of multiple other Sysinternals tools that were always extremely helpful in troubleshooting Windows. Old-school Procmon showed you a bunch of information about running processes on a system. That is great, but doesn't usually tell the full story about what is happening on your computer or server. You could glean a lot more information by combining output from Procmon, Filemon, and Regmon. As their names suggest, Filemon shows detailed information about files being accessed in Windows, and Regmon shows registry information. Filemon and Regmon have now gone by the wayside, as the current flavor of Procmon combines all three of these toolsets into one fantastic troubleshooting interface.

To check this out for yourself, simply download Procmon from the following location, and then launch it: `https://learn.microsoft.com/en-us/sysinternals/downloads/procmon`

Immediately after launching, I am presented with an overwhelming amount of information about what is happening on my Windows system.

Figure 16.21: There is so much data in Procmon!

Procmon displays detailed information about every process on my computer, including every file that is being interfaced and every registry key being accessed, written, removed, or in any way touched. In the previous screenshot you can see that File Explorer has hooks into many places, which makes sense because I have various Word and Excel documents open, as well as multiple instances of File Explorer itself. I also have a lot of OneDrive activity, as my **Document** and **Pictures** folders automatically sync to OneDrive, and this means that an application is always at work in the background.

You'll also notice that there are more than 5 million events shown by Procmon, which is amazingly overwhelming. Since taking the screenshot and typing the previous paragraph, that number has grown to 12 million. Your human brain could never keep up with the activity happening in your operating system, so you will find it most useful to launch Procmon, do whatever it is that you are attempting to do but causing you trouble (such as launch an application or installer), and then pause the collection of Procmon data. This way you have a set of static information that hopefully includes information about what is going wrong with whatever function or application you are working on at that moment. Then this output can be filtered to particular processes or locations, to quickly narrow down the issue.

To throw out another real-world example, I have utilized Procmon multiple times to solve mysteries about why software installation packages failed to run without presenting any error codes. This issue is very frustrating; you know that something is going wrong during installation and it's probably related to some missing prerequisite or permission issue, but where do you even begin to start looking if there is no error presented on screen, and nothing logged in Windows Event Logs?

In this scenario, if you launch Procmon, and then run the problematic installer through until it fails, you can then pause the Procmon output and filter down the data to find the answer you are looking for. Most likely the installer is attempting to access a particular file or registry location that it doesn't have permission to access, or it is simply not finding what it needs, and the installer then bombs. By narrowing down the scope of the Procmon output to the process name of the installer, you can see anything and everything that the installer does as it progresses.

To pause the data collection, simply click the toolbar button called **Capture**. Click it again to restart the data collection. Once paused, use the **Filter** button to narrow in on the data that you want to view. As a test, I launched Procmon, then launched a new instance of Microsoft Edge, and navigated to a couple of websites. If I then pause and filter my Procmon output to only show me information about the msedge.exe process, amazingly Edge performed 344 tasks within about 10 seconds of use. If Edge had been an application that crashed on me and I wanted to investigate why that was happening, I could scroll through this output or sort for **Results** that did not say **SUCCESS**, and there's a good chance that I could figure out what was going wrong by this quick troubleshooting process.

Figure 16.22: Data is filtered down to only msedge.exe

AccessEnum

File permissions on company file servers can be very simple, or incredibly complicated. Some companies handle this very well and determine file access based on top-level folders and shares. For example, you can create a share called *Accounting* and decide that anybody who is part of an Active Directory group called Accounting will have access to the Accounting folder, and everything inside of it. You can also decide that nobody else in the company has access to that entire folder or share. This is easy, and works great.

However, the longer your file server has been up and running, the greater the likelihood that you or a previous administrator has fielded unique situations that encroached on that pure and lovely set of NTFS permissions. Perhaps your CEO, who is not a member of the Accounting group, needed to have access to files inside that Accounting share. He's the CEO, so what are you going to do? Say no? I don't think so, and perhaps that interaction now means that an individual user account has now also been granted access to the entire Accounting share.

No biggie, right? That's not too difficult to keep track of, but what if that same situation happened 50 times over the next year? And others who needed to have access to information only needed access to *some* of the Accounting information, but not all of it. Your Director of HR needed access to some spreadsheets that are inside a subfolder, but they didn't need access to anything else inside Accounting, so you disabled inheritance on the subfolder in order to grant your HR Director access only to the subfolder. Brilliant! You have successfully minimized risk by only giving this person access to the specific things that they need, but you have done so at the expense of the future manageability of that subfolder. Now that inheritance has been disabled, that folder will no longer pay attention to higher-level permission changes that you make. Or perhaps worse, someone may later make additional changes to additional subfolders, and now you have NTFS permission rabbit trails scattered throughout your entire file server.

Any IT administrator who has stepped into an environment that has been running for many years and has been administered by numerous people before them has encountered this scenario. File permissions can be an amazing mess, and you're probably going to be tasked with cleaning it up eventually. I can promise you that the first time a permission change goes wrong and suddenly a shop-floor user has access to sensitive HR documents because your file permissions are all messed up, you will suddenly have a very high-priority project on your plate to figure out who has access to what, and how to fix it.

Enter AccessEnum. While this tool isn't going to magically fix all of your file permission problems, it can help with the first task of that project – quickly determining who has access to what files and folders. Download AccessEnum and launch it on your file server, and you will see all of the files and folders on the system, including information about who has read and write access to them. There is no capability native in Windows that displays information in this format; without AccessEnum you are faced with many mouse clicks to manually gather and lay out this information in your own format. Here you can see what AccessEnum looks like; I have some shared folders on my file server and ran AccessEnum against the D: volume where they all reside. Very quickly I can see that most permissions stack up how I would expect them to, but for some reason, JAdmin has read access to my HR share. Suspicious...

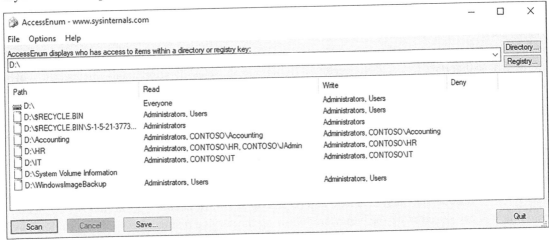

Figure 16.23: Looks like I need to have a conversation with Joe Admin

Windows Firewall with Advanced Security

When thinking about Windows Server troubleshooting, the firewall is probably not one of the first things that comes to mind. However, the Windows Firewall with Advanced Security console can be a very friendly tool to identify and resolve issues that crop up related to networking on our servers. So far in this book, you have already been given instructions on some of the most important things that you can do within WFAS. We discussed the three different firewall profiles and the fact that each individual NIC on a server can be utilizing a different firewall profile. This knowledge really comes into play within a corporate domain environment. When servers run inside your network and can contact a domain controller, their NICs that are connected to that network should always self-assign the Domain firewall profile. This is important because the firewall rules you expect to be in place while that server is inside the network (which is probably at all times) are only in effect when the Domain profile is active. Even if you choose to have the Windows Firewall turned off when inside the network, most companies set up those policies so that ONLY if the Domain profile is active will the firewall be turned off. This implies that if a different profile gets assigned to a NIC, or the Private or Public profile, then the firewall could indeed be turned on and block traffic flow.

If the server is inside the network, why would it ever self-assign the Public or Private profiles? If a domain controller is not available when the server boots, it won't grab the Domain profile. Sometimes it won't grab the Domain profile simply because Windows occasionally goofs when it boots. It is actually a very regular ticket that I see at work where a server is not communicating properly, and after a little bit of discovery, we find that the NIC for that server reports that it uses the Public or Private profile, even though it is on the same LAN as a DC. The three firewall profiles have potentially very different firewall rules and can even turn the firewall on or off, depending on how each profile is configured.

Another scenario is a server with multiple NICs, which increases the chances that one of those NICs may grab the wrong firewall profile upon boot. A common issue I've had to face with deploying DirectAccess in many enterprise environments is that we would almost always be using two NICs, one on the internal network and one inside a DMZ. While deploying the server, we would expect that the internal NIC would use the Domain profile, but the DMZ NIC would use the Public or Private profile, as you *should never* be able to loop back inside the network and contact a DC from inside a DMZ network, right? You would be amazed at the number of times the installation of our DirectAccess server brought to light major security holes that existed in these enterprise-class DMZ networks. It is a very common thing to have that DMZ External NIC receive a Domain profile classification inside the firewall, which definitely means that the NIC was able to successfully contact a domain controller.

The moral of the story with this section is not to rehash the WFAS tool that you have already seen and experienced, but to shed a little more light on how it can be used for troubleshooting purposes. If a server has trouble communicating with something, or something has trouble communicating with that server, take five seconds to pop open WF.MSC and verify that the correct firewall profiles are active. If you have booted a domain-joined server and expect it to run the Domain firewall profile but find that it is not, you can visit SERVICES.MSC and restart the **Network Location Awareness (NLA)** service, and that will usually clear up the behavior. Following the service restart, the Domain profile should then be active on the NIC, assuming, of course, that it can successfully contact a domain controller.

System Insights

We summarized System Insights in *Chapter 1, Getting Started with Windows Server 2022*, but we definitely want to revisit it here in our chapter on troubleshooting. This is because this tool gathers all the right parts and pieces to help us build a comprehensive story about what is going on with our servers, and to help predict critical points at which servers may run out of resources and need to be upgraded or expanded.

System Insights is all about predictive analytics. It is available on any Windows Server 2022 (you just need to enable it) and utilizes performance counters to monitor the system and record data. This data is stored on the local server, which is important because it means you do not have to go through a bunch of work and hoops to implement some kind of centralized database to retain the data, nor perform any cloud work to maintain these metrics. The information collected by System Insights is individual per server and is retained on each server for up to a year.

Once System Insights is up and running, you can tap into the data it collects via PowerShell or **Windows Admin Center (WAC)**. Let's flip the switch to enable System Insights on my WEB1 server and see what it looks like.

All we need to do on WEB1 is install the Windows feature called… you guessed it… **System Insights!** This can be installed using the **Add Roles and Features** wizard in Server Manager, or by running the following PowerShell command:

```
Add-WindowsFeature System-Insights -IncludeManagementTools
```

Bonus feature! You can even install System Insights by pulling up WAC, selecting a server, and then visiting the System Insights tool on the left-hand side of the screen. Here, you will find a simple **Install** button, which will roll System Insights to the server with one click!

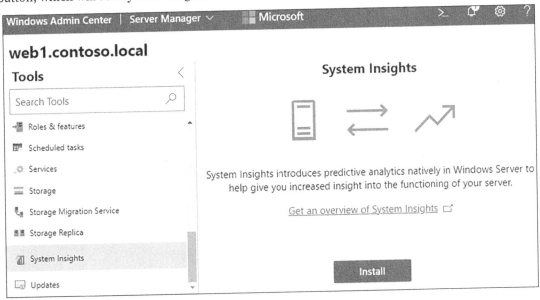

Figure 16.24: Installing System Insights from WAC with a single click

Once the feature is installed, revisit the System Insights screen inside WAC, and you will see four different insight options available. These are the four predictive items that System Insights can help plan and forecast:

- CPU capacity forecasting
- Networking capacity forecasting
- Total storage consumption forecasting
- Volume consumption forecasting

Depending on what stats and hardware you are interested in monitoring, select the appropriate capability and click the **Invoke** button, or select them all just to see what System Insights comes back with. As you can see in *Figure 16.25*, I invoked all four, and currently, they are all reporting green. System Insights has determined that these components of my WEB1 virtual server are in good shape and are forecasted to remain that way:

Figure 16.25: System Insights data displayed inside WAC

Windows Server 2022 brings an enhancement to the storage forecasting capabilities of System Insights. New with this release is a capability to detect disks that behave abnormally, differing from their normal rhythms and patterns.

Remote toolsets

Here is another section where you already have the information you need if you have been working through this book from start to finish, but it never hurts to receive a gentle reminder on taking what you have learned and putting it into practice.

Remote Desktop, Hyper-V console, PowerShell, Sconfig, WAC, **Microsoft Management Console (MMC)** consoles, and Server Manager – these are all different tools, any of which could be used to accomplish similar tasks on your servers. I love training new IT staff on our service desk and working alongside them on tickets, especially in areas where they have limited experience and are hesitant to dive in. Using the Remote Desktop client to RDP into servers is still by far the most common way that administrators log in to their servers to make changes or for any reason, and when you do that all day every day, it is easy to forget about all the other ways that you can interact with those servers. RDP is one of the first things that will quit working when a server is under heavy load or struggling to breathe.

I have watched many an admin attempt to RDP to a server that is having trouble, be unsuccessful at making the RDP connection, and sit for a while at a roadblock, not knowing what to do next. There are so many ways that you can check the status of that server remotely or even reboot it remotely, but these options seem like distant memories when you're on the phone with an angry CEO who just wants their stuff to work *right now*.

Incorporate these remote administration tools into your daily workflow. Some are more efficient than others but continue to utilize them all at various times. That way, when you're in the heat of the moment and facing a difficult situation, muscle memory will take over, and you'll soon become the quickest draw in the West – when tapping into server administration toolsets, anyway.

Event Logs

Any investigatory work on a server is well complemented by Windows Event Logs. Sometimes you catch a server in the act of misbehaving and can utilize all the tools we have discussed so far to figure out, in real time, what is happening and how to remediate it. Other times, you may have experienced a problem – an unexpected restart of a server is a prime example – and even though things are running smoothly again, you are now tasked with answering that enormous question, "What happened?"

The Windows operating system logs a lot of data, all the time. These logs can answer questions when nothing else in the system can, as they provide a historical roadmap of wins and challenges happening within the OS, visible in static text where patterns emerge and details are given.

The tool that is home to Windows Event Logs is called **Event Viewer**. Opening Event Viewer can be accomplished in a few ways. You can seek out Event Viewer in the **Start** search function, but there is also a quick link to open Event Viewer when right-clicking on the **Start** button. A third option is to call EVENTVWR.MSC from **Start** | **Run**, Command Prompt, or PowerShell. When you open this tool, you will see that your most common places to go are inside the folder called **Windows Logs**. Here, you will find **Application, Security,** and **System** event logs. For most log review tasks, these are the three most common sets of logs to visit to seek out information related to diagnosing a problem that occurred:

Figure 16.26: Event Viewer

I find myself spending most of my time inside **Application** and **System** event logs. As you can tell by the names of these logs, application logs will contain information about the applications running on the server, while system logs pertain to the system itself. However, there is definitely some crossover, as "applications" in Windows could also relate to roles, and so you will find some information related to the operating system inside the Application event logs. For security logs, the most common reason that the average server administrator would visit here would be to dig into authentication issues, such as a locked user account. The Security logs are also useful when you're investigating a security breach. Spending any amount of time in the Security logs will quickly overwhelm you because there is a *lot* of information in there, and much of it is ambiguous. Boy, I wish there was a way to filter out some of the noise here...

Filtering event logs

Oh yeah, there *is* a way to filter these logs! I rarely visit event logs *without* filtering in some way, lest I find myself lost in a sea of information for the entire day. While inside any log file, you can right-click on the name of the log (such as **Application** or **System**) and choose **Filter Current Log....** There are many ways that filtering can be accomplished here, but one of the most common is to hide away all informational events. If you find yourself reviewing Windows log files just to peruse information events, you, without a doubt, have too much time on your hands. I'm kidding, of course, but seriously – when you're looking inside event logs, you are likely looking for the cause of a problem. Informational event logs will rarely be helpful in this scenario. Instead, selecting the following checkboxes will rid your Event Viewer view of all informational logs, focusing on all the warnings and errors that are present:

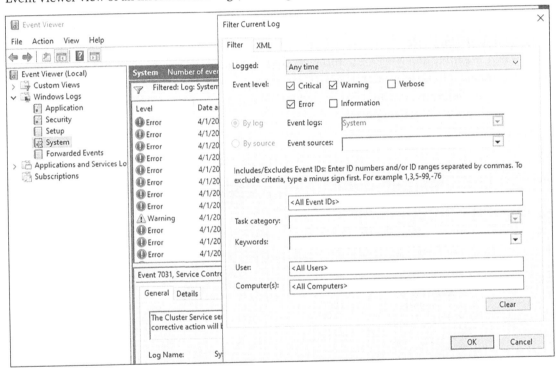

Figure 16.27: Filtering event logs to only display warnings and errors

Once filtered, you can easily scroll through all the errors and warnings listed in this event log and search for clues to help identify whatever issues you are trying to solve. If you identify something interesting, you could note the date and timestamp of that log entry, and then re-include informational events, and search through everything that was being logged during that timeframe. This often helps tell a server's story as it approaches some form of trouble. In many cases, using a combination of Application and System event logs will give you a well-rounded picture of what happened on the system during that time.

Looking at *Figure 16.27*, you can also see a filter option right in the middle to include or exclude Event IDs. Each event type has an identifier number. Once you've latched onto a particular event as being related to a problem that you are troubleshooting, a common question that comes up is, "How often has this issue occurred?" To answer this, you can filter the logs to a particular Event ID simply by typing that ID number into this field. Event Viewer will then show you only instances of that Event ID. You can comma-separate multiple Event IDs to include more information in the log view, while maintaining a view only containing data that you are actually interested in seeing.

An alternative feature that I absolutely love and use all the time is to exclude particular Event IDs. As an example, my System event log is filled with informational events from Service Control Manager, which is just noise that I generally don't care about. I can see that these events have an Event ID number of 7036. In *Figure 16.28*, I have two instances of Event Viewer side by side – one showing the System event log and the other showing the same log but with Event 7036 excluded. This really helps cut the noise and shows me more interesting events that actually pertain to my troubleshooting. In fact, not only was 7036 getting annoying to sift through, but I was seeing a lot of Event ID 81 as well, so I have excluded (hidden) those as well. In *Figure 16.28*, you can also see the method I used to exclude those two Event IDs. Simply use the **Includes/Excludes** field to input particular Event ID numbers, but place a minus (-) in front of each number:

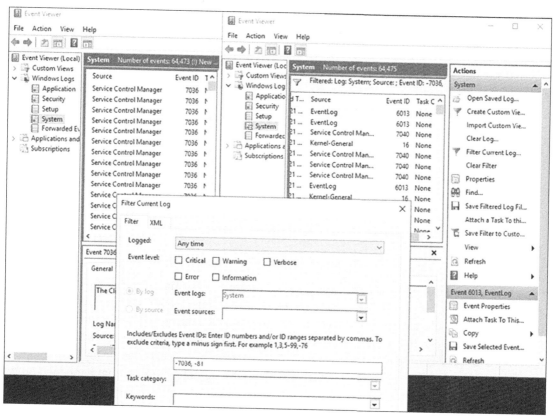

Figure 16.28: Using filters to exclude Event IDs 7036 and 81

When you've finished filtering the logs, to get back to the default view, there is no need to reverse all the filtering settings that you have put into place. Simply right-click on the log file and choose **Clear Filter**. This will immediately set that log file back to showing all events.

You'll notice options in the right-click menu to save log files, save filtered log files, and even to save filters to views for later use. There is a lot of power available inside event log filtering!

Exporting Windows event logs with PowerShell

While using the Event Viewer console is the most common way to review and parse through log files, sometimes, you may wish for a way to easily export all this data and do some other types of manipulation on it, perhaps through Excel spreadsheets or something similar. To make this happen, we would need a way to export the information in these logs into something like a CSV file. Is this possible? You bet!

PowerShell can tap into anything inside Windows, including event logs. PowerShell also has a built-in function to export data into a CSV file, so let's combine those two capabilities and build out some commands that will suck Windows event logs out of Windows, directly into a CSV file. Here are some examples:

```
Get-EventLog -LogName Application | Export-CSV C:\Logs\Application_Logs.csv
```

This command exports the entire contents of the `Application` event logs to a CSV file:

```
Get-EventLog -LogName System -Newest 100 | Export-CSV C:\Logs\System_Logs_
Newest.csv
```

Here, we export the `System` event logs, but you'll notice an extra parameter in there. This time, we only grab the newest 100 events from the log and throw them into a CSV file:

```
Get-EventLog -LogName Security -Newest 50 -ComputerName WEB1 | Export-CSV C:\
Logs\WEB1_Security_Logs.csv
```

As our commands get larger, they do more comprehensive things. This one grabs the latest 50 events from the Security logs but specifies the `WEB1` server. This is a good example to show that you don't even have to be logged in to the server to pull logs from it. Instead, you can run these PowerShell commands from your workstation, against your servers, pulling log information remotely. You could then take this information and apply it to scheduled scripts, perhaps if you wanted to maintain the long-term storage of event log data for particular systems:

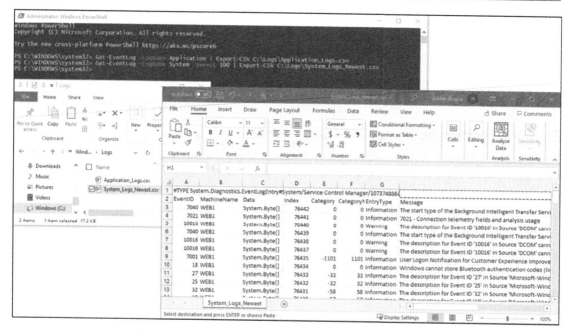

Figure 16.29: Exporting logs to CSV for easy searching and sorting

As you begin working with Windows log files, you will find that Event Viewer does a fantastic job of sorting by log type, and that using Event ID inclusions and exclusions will often find you the information that you are looking for. The one thing that is majorly lacking inside Event Viewer is the ability to easily search for text that exists inside events. When clicking on any event, you can see all the descriptive text that is included inside that log event, but there is no good way to search within that text across all of your event logs. This is where exporting to CSV can be especially handy. Throw those commands in PowerShell to export the log, open the CSV file, and use Excel's search function to find what you are looking for.

Common Event IDs

Exploring event logs on a regular basis will start to form patterns in your brain about what types of events to look for, where to find them, and even which particular Event IDs are commonly searched for in daily troubleshooting and investigations. Here is a quick listing of some Event ID numbers that I keep on a note near my desk, at all times, as I often search for them:

- **4740 (Security log) – User account locked.** This is the first event to search for when investigating a user account lockout issue. Oftentimes, 4740 will show you a "Source computer name," which steers you toward which device in the network is causing the lockout.

- **4625 (Security log) – Account failed to log on.** I often search for 4625 alongside 4740. While 4740 will hopefully tell you which device to review, 4625 will give a reason as to why the account was locked out – for example, if a bad username or password was given.

- **4767 (Security log) – User account unlocked.** Corresponding logs related to user account lockouts. Check these to find unlock events.

- **6013 (System log) – System uptime.** Every day at noon, every Windows computer and server logs this event. It shows, in seconds, the amount of uptime that the system has been running for. This can be useful to take a historical look at how long a server has been running. For example, you may need to determine how long a server had run prior to an unexpected restart, as this information could be critical to figuring out why a machine locked up or crashed.

- **6008 (System log) – Unexpected shutdown.** Many times, when a server unexpectedly restarts, it's not too concerning. All computers do that occasionally. If, however, you are investigating a server because it has unexpectedly restarted numerous times, you'll want to start searching for patterns about what is happening surrounding each of those unexpected restarts. Event 6008 is the event that is logged, and it will show you the exact timestamp of the unexpected shutdown event. Filtering for 6008 will give you a quick way to see all the instances of the unexpected shutdown. You can then document and dig into the logs surrounding each of those timestamps to gain further information.

While this is simply a short list of common events I search for, I'm sure that, depending on your role in IT, you will add many more Event IDs to your own "Common Event ID" lists.

MMC and MSC shortcuts

You have probably noticed that many of the management consoles that we utilize to configure components inside Windows Server 2022 bear a striking resemblance to each other. What happens under the hood with a number of these consoles is that you are shown a snap-in function, a specific set of tools that are snapped into a generic console tool called the MMC. In fact, rather than opening all these management functions from inside Server Manager, for many of them, you could simply type MMC by navigating to **Start | Run** or Command Prompt and invoking the generic MMC console. From here, you can click on the **File** menu and choose **Add or Remove Snap-ins:**

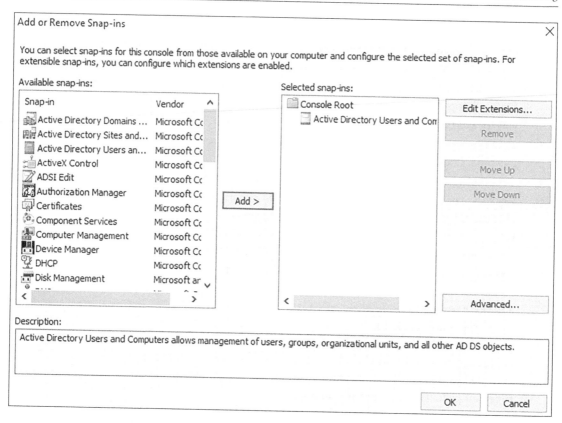

Figure 16.30: Using MMC to snap in management consoles

Choose the management snap-in that you would like to work in, and add it to the console. There are a large number of management functions that can be accessed through the standard MMC console, and even some functions where MMC is the preferred, or perhaps the only, method for interacting with certain components of Windows – for example, when we utilized MMC to review certificates installed on the local computer back in *Chapter 6, Certificates.*

Another interesting way to open many of the management consoles is by using their direct **MSC** tool name. An MSC file is simply a saved configuration of an MMC console session. There are many MSC shortcuts stored in Windows Server 2022 out of the box. If a given management console can be launched by an MSC, all you need to do is type in the name of the MSC by navigating to either **Start | Run**, Command Prompt, or a PowerShell window, and it will immediately launch into that particular management console without needing to snap anything in, and without any need to open Server Manager whatsoever. Since I tend to prefer using a keyboard over a mouse, I always have a PowerShell window or Command Prompt window open on each system I'm working with, and I can very quickly use that window to open any of my MSC administrative consoles. Let's show one example, so that you know exactly how to use this functionality, and then I will provide a list of the common MSCs that I find useful on a day-to-day basis.

Open an elevated PowerShell window, type WF.MSC, and press *Enter*:

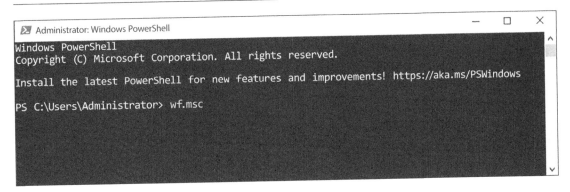

Figure 16.31: Launching a management console via the MSC shortcut

The **Windows Defender Firewall with Advanced Security** window will open and is ready to accept input from you. We didn't have to poke through **Control Panel** or open the regular **Windows Firewall** and then click on the **Advanced Settings** link, which are the common ways to get into this console by using a mouse. By knowing our MSC shortcut name, we were able to take a direct route to open the full WFAS console, which is where I often go to check particular firewall rules or statuses:

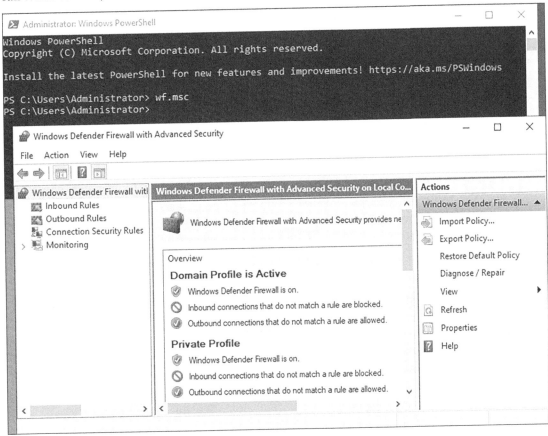

Figure 16.32: The fastest way to access Windows Defender Firewall is via WF.MSC

Now that you've seen how an MSC command works, and again, there are many different places where you can type in the name of an MSC and invoke it, I want to leave you with a list of common MSC consoles that you can use to quickly gain access to many administrative consoles on your servers:

- `DSA.MSC`: Active Directory Users and Computers
- `DSSITE.MSC`: Active Directory Sites and Services
- `DNSMGMT.MSC`: DNS Manager
- `GPEDIT.MSC`: Local Group Policy Editor
- `GPMC.MSC`: Group Policy Management Console
- `CERTSRV.MSC`: Certification Authority Management
- `CERTTMPL.MSC`: Certificate Template Management
- `CERTLM.MSC`: Local Computer Certificates Store
- `CERTMGR.MSC`: Current User Certificates Store
- `COMPMGMT.MSC`: Computer Management
- `DEVMGMT.MSC`: Device Manager
- `DHCPMGMT.MSC`: DHCP Manager
- `DISKMGMT.MSC`: Disk Management
- `EVENTVWR.MSC`: Event Viewer
- `PERFMON.MSC`: Performance Monitor
- `SECPOL.MSC`: Local Security Policy Console
- `FSMGMT.MSC`: Shared Folders
- `WF.MSC`: Windows Defender Firewall with Advanced Security (WFAS)
- `shell:startup`: While not an MSC, this is a shortcut that opens the logged-in user's `Start Menu\Programs\Startup` folder. This is a useful location to visit when looking for a program running on startup that you can't find elsewhere, or when you want to cause an application to start every time this user logs in to the computer.
- `shell:common startup`: Similar to `shell:startup`, but this launches into the `Public User's Startup` folder. Shortcuts added here will auto-launch whenever *any* user logs in to the system.

Summary

Designing and building brand-new servers rarely presents challenges, and if they are encountered, those issues are typically low priority, since the new server won't yet affect a production workforce. Troubleshooting existing servers, on the other hand, can be very stressful and requires quick, on-the-fly recollection of tools and command sets available inside the operating system that can be used to identify issues and resolutions. I hope this chapter has given you the ammunition needed to feel more confident in those situations, and to become the "go-to" person in your IT department when it comes to diagnosing server problems and digging deep into problems that arise.

This brings us to the end of our story on Windows Server 2022. Many of the topics we discussed could fill entire books, and I hope that the ideas provided in this volume are enough to prompt you to dig further into the technologies that you plan to work with.

Microsoft technology reigns supreme in most data centers across the globe. The new and updated features inside Windows Server 2022 will ensure that this trend continues long into the future.

Questions

1. What is the MSC shortcut to open Active Directory Users and Computers?
2. True or False – You should always store server backups on the same server that you are backing up for performance reasons.
3. Which Windows monitoring tool can be used to graph CPU utilization over a 24-hour period?
4. True or False – System Insights stores all data on a centralized RADIUS server.
5. Which Sysinternals tool can be used to terminate a process running on a remote system?
6. What is the MSC shortcut to open Windows Defender Firewall with Advanced Security?
7. Which PowerShell cmdlet can be used to gather Windows log files?
8. Which Event ID can be used to calculate system uptime?

Join our community on Discord

Join our community's Discord space for discussions with the author and other readers:

https://packt.link/SecNet

Appendix: Answers to the End-of-Chapter Questions

Chapter 1: Getting Started with Windows Server 2022

1. In Windows Server 2022, how can you launch an elevated PowerShell prompt with two mouse clicks?

   Answer: Right-click on the Start button and select **Windows PowerShell** (**Admin**) from the Quick Admin Tasks menu.

2. What is the keyboard combination to open the Quick Admin Tasks menu?

   Answer: *WinKey + X*

3. What is the name of Microsoft's cloud service offering?

   Answer: Microsoft Azure

4. Which Windows Server release model has disappeared with the advent of Windows Server 2022?

   Answer: SAC

5. How many virtual machines can run on top of a Windows Server 2022 Standard host, with default licensing?

   Answer: 2

6. What installation option for Windows Server 2022 does not have a graphical user interface?

   Answer: Server Core

7. Which is the correct verbiage for the latest release of Windows Server 2022, Long-Term Servicing Branch (LTSB) or Long-Term Servicing Channel (LTSC)?

   Answer: LTSC

8. What is the correct tool from which to change configurations on Windows Server 2022, Windows Settings or Control Panel?

   Answer: Both, although Windows Settings is the preferred method for most configuration options.

Chapter 2: Installing and Managing Windows Server 2022

1. What is the name of the new web-based, centralized server management tool from Microsoft (fun fact, this toolset was formerly known as **Project Honolulu**)?

   Answer: Windows Admin Center (WAC)

2. True or False—Windows Server 2022 needs to be installed onto rack-mount server hardware.

   Answer: False. Windows Server 2022 can be installed onto physical hardware or as a virtual machine instance.

3. True or False—By choosing the default installation option for Windows Server 2022, you will end up with a user interface that looks quite like Windows 10.

   Answer: False. The default installation option for Server 2022 will land you with a Server Core instance with no graphical interface.

4. What is the PowerShell cmdlet that displays currently installed roles and features in Windows Server 2022?

   Answer: `Get-WindowsFeature | Where Installed`

5. True or False—Server Manager can be used to manage many different servers at the same time.

   Answer: True

6. What is the name of the toolset that can be installed onto a Windows 10 computer in order to run Server Manager on that client workstation?

   Answer: Remote Server Administration Tools (RSAT)

7. Which built-in tool is used to prepare the Windows operating systems for imaging or replication?

   Answer: Sysprep

Chapter 3: Active Directory

1. Inside Active Directory, a container (folder) that holds computer and user accounts is called a(n)...

   Answer: Organizational Unit (OU)

2. What is the term for creating a computer account inside Active Directory prior to that computer being joined to your domain?

   Answer: Prestaging the account

3. Which management tool is used to specify that certain physical locations in your network are bound to particular IP subnets?

   Answer: Active Directory Sites and Services

4. What is the name of a special domain controller that cannot accept new information, only synchronize from an existing domain controller?

   Answer: Read-Only Domain Controller (RODC)

5. What tool is needed to create a fine-grained password policy?

   Answer: Active Directory Administrative Center

6. What must be configured inside DNS prior to establishing a forest trust?

   Answer: Conditional forwarder

7. What is the command-line command that shows you all FSMO role holders at once?

   Answer: `netdom query fsmo`

8. True or False—It is faster to manually remove a domain controller from the domain than it is to follow the Server Manager role removal wizard.

   Answer: True! It is quite a bit faster to simply delete the DC object and then clean up the mess. However, Microsoft's recommendation for a clean DC removal is always to run the role removal via either Server Manager or PowerShell.

Chapter 4: DNS and DHCP

1. What kind of DNS record directs email flow?

   Answer: MX record

2. Which type of DNS record resolves a name to an IPv6 address?

   Answer: AAAA record

3. Which DNS zone type resolves IP addresses backward into hostnames?

   Answer: Reverse Lookup Zone

4. What DHCP option is often used for VoIP phone provisioning?

   Answer: Option 66

5. Which mode of DHCP failover is often used between branch offices and a primary site?

   Answer: Hot standby mode

6. What is the standard recommendation and default setting for Maximum Client Lead Time when configuring load-balanced DHCP failover?

   Answer: One hour

7. Which Windows Server roles can IPAM tap into?

   Answer: Active Directory, DNS, DHCP, and NPS! We didn't talk about NPS in this chapter because we have not yet covered any NPS material, but it is a fourth role that can report data into IPAM.

Chapter 5: Group Policy

1. Are screensaver settings computer or user configuration?

   Answer: User configuration

2. Do domain-level or OU-level links process first?

   Answer: Domain-level links process before OU-level links, meaning that OU-level links will overwrite domain-level links when in conflict.

3. What is the special GPO setting that forces user settings to apply to any user on a given computer?

   Answer: Group Policy loopback processing

4. What type of GPO filtering do you configure inside the GPO itself, such as with a mapped network drives policy?

   Answer: Item-level targeting

5. True or false—It is possible for a user to override a Group Policy preference.

   Answer: True

6. What is the default timer between Group Policy background refresh cycles?

   Answer: 90 minutes

7. What kind of GPO filtering could be utilized to assign settings only to laptop computers?

   Answer: WMI filtering

8. If you find a USB stick on the ground labeled "CEO financials," what should you do with it?

   Answer: Burn it. As in literally set it on fire.

Chapter 6: Certificates

1. What is the name of the role inside Windows Server 2022 that allows you to issue certificates from your server?

   Answer: Certification Authority

2. What kind of CA server is typically installed first in a domain environment?

    Answer: Enterprise root CA

3. Should you install the certification authority role onto a domain controller?

    Answer: No, this is not a recommended scenario.

4. After creating a new certificate template, what next step needs to be taken before you can issue certificates to your computers or users from that new template?

    Answer: The new certificate template must be published.

5. What is the general name of the GPO setting that forces certificates to be issued without manual intervention by an administrator?

    Answer: Certificate Auto-enrollment

6. An SSL certificate will only be able to validate traffic properly if it shares _____ key information with the web server.

    Answer: Private

7. What is the primary piece of information that a public certification authority needs in order to issue you a new SSL certificate (hint: you generate this from your web server)?

    Answer: Certificate Signing Request (CSR)

8. What kind of file contains both a certificate and a private key?

    Answer: PFX file

Chapter 7: Networking with Windows Server 2022

1. How many bits in length is an IPv6 address?

    Answer: 128 bits

2. Re-write the following IPv6 address in condensed form: `2001:ABCD:0001:0002:0000:0000:0000:0001`

    Answer: `2001:ABCD:1:2::1`

3. What is the name of the command that is similar to tracert but displays the local NIC that traffic is flowing out of?

    Answer: `PATHPING`

4. True or False—On a server with multiple NICs, you should input a default gateway address onto each of those NICs.

    Answer: False. Doing so will cause routing issues. You should only ever have one default gateway address on a system, no matter how many NICs it has.

5. What is the PowerShell cmdlet that can be used to create new routes on a Windows Server?

    Answer: New-NetRoute

6. Which Windows Server operating systems can be used with Azure Network Adapter in order to connect them directly to Azure virtual networks?

    Answer: Windows Server 2022, 2019, 2016, and 2012 R2

7. Which connectivity method between a local data center and Azure provides the fastest, most robust, and most reliable connection?

    Answer: Azure ExpressRoute

Chapter 8: Remote Access

1. What does AOVPN stand for?

    Answer: Always-on VPN

2. What are the two primary protocols used for connecting AOVPN clients?

    Answer: IKEv2 and SSTP

3. In which version of Windows 10 was AOVPN released?

    Answer: Windows 10 1607

4. In what special instance would an AOVPN client be required to be joined to your domain?

    Answer: When you want to utilize the AOVPN device tunnel

5. Does DirectAccess require your corporate internal network to be running IPv6?

    Answer: No, your internal network can be completely IPv4.

6. What is the name of the internal website that DirectAccess clients check in with to determine when they are inside the corporate network?

    Answer: Network Location Server (NLS)

7. What ports are used by Teredo and IP-HTTPS?

    Answer: Teredo uses UDP 3544, while IP-HTTPS uses TCP 443.

8. How do you provision DirectAccess configuration settings to the client machines?

    Answer: With Group Policy

9. What role does a Web Application Proxy server hold in a federation environment?

    Answer: WAP can be implemented as an AD FS proxy.

Chapter 9: Hardening and Security

1. What is the name of the antimalware product built into Windows Server 2022?

   Answer: Microsoft Defender Antivirus

2. When a domain-joined computer is sitting inside the corporate LAN, which Microsoft Defender Firewall profile should be active?

   Answer: The Domain Profile

3. Other than the Domain Profile, what are the other two possible firewall profiles inside Microsoft Defender Firewall?

   Answer: Public and private

4. When creating a firewall rule to allow IPv4 ping replies, what protocol type must you specify inside your inbound rule?

   Answer: ICMPv4

5. What is the easiest way to push standardized Microsoft Defender Firewall rules to your entire workforce?

   Answer: Group Policy

6. A virtual machine whose virtual hard disk file is encrypted is called a...?

   Answer: Shielded VM

7. What is the name of the Microsoft technology that parses domain controller information in order to identify pass-the-hash and pass-the-ticket attacks?

   Answer: Advanced Threat Analytics

8. Which inbound RDP port number is considered safe to open on your external firewall?

   Answer: Trick question—none! Please never do this!

9. What third-party tool can you use to disable TLS 1.0 on Windows Server?

   Answer: IIS Crypto

Chapter 10: Server Core

1. True or False—Server Core is the default installation option for Windows Server 2022.

   Answer: True

2. True or False—You can utilize PowerShell to change a Server 2022 from Server Core mode to Desktop Experience mode.

   Answer: False. Switching back and forth is not possible in Windows Server 2022.

3. Bonus point: What is the last version of Windows Server that allowed for on-the-fly changing of a server back and forth between Server Core and Desktop Experience?

   Answer: Server 2012 R2

4. When sitting in front of the console of a freshly booted Windows Server 2022 Server Core instance, what application do you see on the screen?

   Answer: The Sconfig utility

5. When sitting in front of the console of a freshly booted Windows Server 2019 Server Core instance, what application do you see on the screen?

   Answer: Command Prompt

6. What cmdlet can be used to view the current networking configuration on a Server Core?

   Answer: `Get-NetIPConfiguration`

7. Which PowerShell cmdlet can be used to configure the hostname of a Server Core?

   Answer: `Rename-Computer`

8. Name some of the management tools that can be used to remotely interface with a Server Core.

   Answer: PowerShell, Server Manager, RSAT, and Windows Admin Center

9. What is the name of the utility built into Server Core that can be launched from the console to provide quick task links for configuring IP addresses, hostnames, and domain membership?

   Answer: `Sconfig.exe`

10. What movie reference did I make at the beginning of this chapter?

    Answer: Honey, I Shrunk the Kids

Chapter 11: PowerShell

1. What is the fastest way to get from Command Prompt into PowerShell?

   Answer: Simply type the word `powershell` and press *Enter*.

2. What is the cmdlet that will display all available PowerShell cmdlets?

   Answer: `Get-Command`

3. What PowerShell cmdlet can be used to connect your PowerShell prompt to a remote computer?

   Answer: `Enter-PSSession`

4. What file extension does a PowerShell scripting file have?

   Answer: `.PS1`

5. To which setting is the Default Execution Policy configured on a fresh Windows Server 2022 instance?

    Answer: `RemoteSigned`

6. What key on your keyboard can be used to auto-populate the remainder of a cmdlet or filename when working in a PowerShell prompt?

    Answer: Tab

7. Which service must be running on a system before it can be connected to by a remote PowerShell connection?

    Answer: The WinRM service

8. Why do you think Windows Terminal is not installed in Windows Server 2022 by default?

    Answer: Windows Server 2022 is built on Windows 10 code, not Windows 11.

Chapter 12: Redundancy in Windows Server 2022

1. Which technology is more appropriate for making web server traffic redundant – Network Load Balancing or failover clustering?

    Answer: Network Load Balancing

2. Is website traffic generally stateful or stateless?

    Answer: Stateless

3. In Network Load Balancing, what do the acronyms DIP and VIP stand for?

    Answer: Dedicated IP address and Virtual IP address

4. What are the three NLB modes?

    Answer: Unicast, Multicast, and Multicast IGMP

5. In Windows Server 2022, is Network Load Balancing a role or a feature?

    Answer: NLB is a feature.

6. What roles are most often used with failover clustering?

    Answer: Hyper-V and file services

7. What type of small device can now be used as a cluster quorum witness (this is brand new as of Server 2019)?

    Answer: A USB memory stick

8. True or False—Storage Spaces Direct requires the use of SSD hard drives.

    Answer: False. You may use any type of hard drive with S2D.

9. What is the difference between Storage Spaces and Storage Spaces Direct?

Answer: Storage Spaces combines hard drives on a single server to create a larger storage pool to be used by that server. Storage Spaces Direct combines hard disk space across multiple servers for increased performance, growth, and resiliency.

Chapter 13: Containers

1. There are three base operating systems that can be used for a Windows Server 2022 container. What are they?

Answer: Nano Server, Server Core, Windows Server

2. Compared to a Windows Server container, what type of container provides even greater levels of isolation?

Answer: Hyper-V container

3. True or False—In Windows Server 2016, you could run both Windows and Linux containers on the same Windows Server host platform.

Answer: False. The ability to run Windows and Linux containers is new as of Windows Server 2019.

4. What is the Docker command to see a list of container images on your local system?

Answer: docker images

5. What is currently the most popular container orchestration software that integrates with Windows Server 2022?

Answer: Kubernetes

6. True or False—Developers can install Docker onto their Windows 10 workstations to start building applications inside containers.

Answer: True

7. What is a common reason that a developer may need to utilize Server Core containers, rather than Nano Server?

Answer: Application compatibility and dependencies

Chapter 14: Hyper-V

1. What are the three types of virtual switches inside Hyper-V?

Answer: External, internal, and private

2. If you needed to build a virtual machine that booted using UEFI, which generation of VM would you need to create?

Answer: Generation 2

3. True or False—In Windows Server 2022 Hyper-V, you must shut down a VM in order to change it's allocated amount of memory (RAM).

    Answer: False. You can adjust a VM's RAM count on the fly.

4. True or False—The only way to interact with a VM is through the Hyper-V console.

    Answer: False. Once your VM's operating system is installed, you can interact with it through any other traditional administration methods, such as RDP.

5. What is the name of the technology inside Hyper-V that allows you to take snapshot images of virtual machines that can later be restored?

    Answer: Checkpoints

6. When running shielded VMs in your environment, what is the name of the role that handles the attestation of your Hyper-V host servers?

    Answer: Host Guardian Service

7. Which is the most comprehensive attestation method for shielded VMs—host key attestation, TPM trusted attestation, or admin trusted attestation?

    Answer: TPM trusted attestation

8. How many virtual machines can run on top of a Windows Server 2022 Standard edition host?

    Answer: Two

Chapter 15: Remote Desktop Services

1. What RDS component is responsible for distributing user sessions among multiple servers?

    Answer: Remote Desktop Connection Broker

2. Are RDS-related certificates defined in RDS collection properties or RDS deployment properties?

    Answer: Certificates are defined at the RDS deployment tier.

3. What is the command you should run to prepare an RDSH server for application installation?

    Answer: `change user /install`

4. What type of RDS Client Access Licenses (CALs) are most common?

    Answer: Remote Desktop Per-User CALs

5. True or False—To prepare a fresh Windows Server to become an RDSH member of an existing collection, you must first log in to that server and install the Remote Desktop role.

    Answer: False. Server Manager from an existing server can easily reach into this new instance and configure everything that it needs.

6. What are the four types of RDS user profiles?

   Answer: Local profiles, roaming profiles, User Profile Disks (UPDs), and FSLogix profiles

7. How can you launch the Remote Desktop Connection tool in a way that allows you to RDP directly into an RDSH server that is already part of a collection?

   Answer: `mstsc.exe /admin`

8. Bonus question: What animals live on an RDS farm?

   Answer: Cows, they're always moooving from one session host to another.

   Wow, tossing a dad joke into a technical book: #LifeGoals.

Chapter 16: Troubleshooting

1. What is the MSC shortcut for opening Active Directory Users and Computers?

   Answer: `DSA.MSC`

2. True or False—You should always store server backups on the same server that you are backing up for performance reasons.

   Answer: This is a trick question that is sort of true, sort of false. While it is true that backups will be most performant when kept on locally attached storage, you should store backups in a separate location in case the server completely dies or is taken by ransomware.

3. Which Windows monitoring tool can be used to graph CPU utilization over a 24-hour period?

   Answer: Performance Monitor

4. True or False—System Insights stores all data on a centralized RADIUS server.

   Answer: False. System Insights stores data on the local server where it is installed.

5. Which Sysinternals tool can be used to terminate a process running on a remote system?

   Answer: PsKill

6. What is the MSC shortcut for opening Windows Defender Firewall with Advanced Security?

   Answer: `WF.MSC`

7. Which PowerShell cmdlet can be used to gather Windows log files?

   Answer: `Get-EventLog`

8. Which event ID can be used to calculate system uptime?

   Answer: 6013

packt.com

Subscribe to our online digital library for full access to over 7,000 books and videos, as well as industry leading tools to help you plan your personal development and advance your career. For more information, please visit our website.

Why subscribe?

- Spend less time learning and more time coding with practical eBooks and Videos from over 4,000 industry professionals
- Improve your learning with Skill Plans built especially for you
- Get a free eBook or video every month
- Fully searchable for easy access to vital information
- Copy and paste, print, and bookmark content

At www.packt.com, you can also read a collection of free technical articles, sign up for a range of free newsletters, and receive exclusive discounts and offers on Packt books and eBooks.

Other Books You May Enjoy

If you enjoyed this book, you may be interested in these other books by Packt:

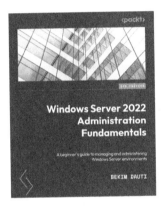

Windows Server 2022 Administration Fundamentals

Bekim Dauti

ISBN: 9781803232157

- Grasp the fundamentals of Windows Server 2022
- Understand how to deploy Windows Server 2022
- Discover Windows Server post-installation tasks
- Add roles to your Windows Server environment
- Apply Windows Server 2022 GPOs to your network
- Delve into virtualization and Hyper-V concepts
- Tune, maintain, update, and troubleshoot Windows Server 2022
- Get familiar with Microsoft's role-based certifications

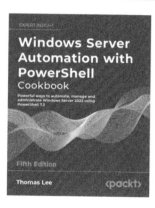

Windows Server Automation with PowerShell Cookbook, Fifth Edition

Thomas Lee

ISBN: 9781804614235

- Perform key admin tasks on Windows Server
- Keep your organization secure with JEA, group policies, logs, and Windows Defender
- Use .NET Framework for administrative scripting
- Manage data and storage on Windows, including disks, volumes, and filesystems
- Report system performance using built-in cmdlets and WMI to obtain single measurements
- Apply the right tools and modules to troubleshoot and debug Windows Server
- Create, manage, and back up a second VM using the subnetwork in Azure
- Learn how to set up a VPN in Azure with PowerShell

Packt is searching for authors like you

If you're interested in becoming an author for Packt, please visit authors.packtpub.com and apply today. We have worked with thousands of developers and tech professionals, just like you, to help them share their insight with the global tech community. You can make a general application, apply for a specific hot topic that we are recruiting an author for, or submit your own idea.

Share your thoughts

Now you've finished *Mastering Windows Server 2022, Fourth Edition*, we'd love to hear your thoughts! Scan the QR code below to go straight to the Amazon review page for this book and share your feedback or leave a review on the site that you purchased it from.

https://packt.link/r/1837634505

Your review is important to us and the tech community and will help us make sure we're delivering excellent quality content.

Index

Download a free PDF copy of this book

Thanks for purchasing this book!

Do you like to read on the go but are unable to carry your print books everywhere?

Is your eBook purchase not compatible with the device of your choice?

Don't worry, now with every Packt book you get a DRM-free PDF version of that book at no cost.

Read anywhere, any place, on any device. Search, copy, and paste code from your favorite technical books directly into your application.

The perks don't stop there, you can get exclusive access to discounts, newsletters, and great free content in your inbox daily

Follow these simple steps to get the benefits:

1. Scan the QR code or visit the link below

https://packt.link/free-ebook/9781837634507

2. Submit your proof of purchase
3. That's it! We'll send your free PDF and other benefits to your email directly

Made in the USA
Middletown, DE
13 September 2024

60894558R00402